£3·00

AJ Legal Handbook

AJ Legal Handbook
This handbook is based on a series of articles which first appeared in the *Architects' Journal* during 1971 and 1972 and which have been extensively revised and updated.

AJ Legal Handbook

Edited by
Evelyn Freeth
and **Peter Davey**

The Architectural Press
London

ISBN 0 85139 365 9 (Cloth edition)

ISBN 0 85139 366 7 (Paperback edition)

First published in book form 1973
Second edition 1978

© The Architectural Press Ltd 1973, 1978

Printed litho in Great Britain
by W & J Mackay Ltd, Chatham

Consultant editor

EVELYN FREETH—Previously Principal of the Royal West of England Academy School of Architecture, and Reader in Architecture in the University of Bristol; formerly an architect with extensive knowledge of the law. Currently specialising in building contract and matters relating to professional aspects in the construction industry. In this edition Evelyn Freeth has contributed Legal Studies 1 and 18 and updated Legal Studies 6, 8, 11 and 15.

Contributors

GEORGE BURNET—Writer to the Signet; secretary of the Scottish Building Contracts Committee; Legal adviser to the Royal Incorporation of Architects in Scotland: Legal Study 5 and the Scottish supplements to Legal Studies 8 and 11

PETER FRANKLIN—Professional and technology officer, Building Control Group, Scottish Development Department; author of *Building Regulations (Scotland) Checklists and Index:* Legal Study 14

J. F. GARNER—Professor of public law at Nottingham University; author of *Public Control of Land, Administration Law, Control of Pollution Encyclopaedia, Law of Sewers and Drains:* Legal Study 9

SIR DESMOND HEAP—Consultant, formerly Comptroller and City Solicitor to the Corporation of London; author of *An Outline of Planning Law,* and other works; general editor of *Encyclopaedia of Planning Law and Practice;* member of the editorial board for *Journal of Planning and Environmental Law:* Legal Study 12

DONALD KEATING, QC—Barrister, member of Lincoln's Inn; author of *The Law of Building Contracts:* Legal Study 4

DONALD MACFADYEN—Advocate: Legal Study 2

RODERICK MALES—Director of Professional Training, School of Architecture, University of Manchester; Practice Consultant: Legal Study 17

VINCENT POWELL-SMITH—Lecturer in law at University of Aston Department of Building; author of *The Building Regulations Explained and Illustrated:* Legal Study 13

ANGUS STEWART—Advocate: updated Legal Studies 7 and 10

GEORGE YOUNG—Administrator, Yorke Rosenberg Mardall; member of RIBA working group on RIBA *Handbook of Architectural Practice and Management:* Legal Study 3

Consultant editors to the first edition were

GEORGE BURNET

PETER DAVEY Architect and journalist on the staff of *The Architects' Journal*

EVELYN FREETH

GEORGE STRINGER Solicitor, formerly legal adviser to the RIBA and Secretary to the Joint Contracts Tribunal

Contributors to the first edition whose work has been updated here were

WILLIAM GILL—Barrister and architect; author of *The Law of Arbitration, Evidence and Procedure in Arbitration;* editor of *Rimmer's Law Relating to the Architect* and Emden and Gill's *Building Contracts Practice;* editor for English Arbitration Law in *International and EEC Year Book on Arbitration 1976/7* (Legal Study 8)

ANDREW GROTRIAN—Advocate (Legal Studies 7 and 10)

DAVID KEATE—Architect associate of Building Design Partnership; formerly secretary of RIBA Professional Conduct Committee (Legal Study 15)

WILLIAM NIMMO-SMITH—Advocate (joint author of Legal Study 2)

GEORGE STRINGER—(Legal Studies 7 and 10)

Contents

Key to law report abbreviations

AC	Appeal Cases
All ER	All England Law Reports
All ER Rep	All England Law Reports Reprint
BLR	Building Law Reports
CA	Court of Appeal
CH	Chancery Reports
C & P	Carrington & Payne (1823–41)
EQ	Equity
ER	English Reports
Exch	Exchequer Reports
Giff	Gifford
HL	House of Lords
KB or QB	King's Bench or Queen's Bench
LJCP	Law Journal Common Pleas
LJKB	Law Journal King's Bench
LR	Law Reports
LT	Law Times
QBD	Queen's Bench Division
SC	Session Cases
SJ	Solicitor's Journal
SLT	Scots Law Times
Taunt	Taunton Reports
TLR	Times Law Reports
WLR	Weekly Law Reports

AJ Legal Handbook

Section 1
Introduction to the law

Blessings of Brittain (*sic*) or a Flight of Lawyers—'*A Darksome cloud of locusts swarming down*'—Milton

Legal study 1

Introduction to English law

This study is intended to introduce English law and its relevance to the architect. It outlines some basic legal concepts before discussing the law of contract, agency, torts and property; these are the basic areas of most concern to architects. Later studies in the series will discuss these topics in detail. An appendix briefly summarises the history of English law

1 The importance of law

Ignorantia juris non excusat
1.01 The well worn maxim that ignorance of the law is no excuse applies with equal force to everyone including architects. Everyone who offers a service to others and claims expertise to do what he offers has a responsibility to society in general and to his clients in particular to know the law.

Architects and the law
1.02 Architects and other professional people are under a special obligation to have a sound working knowledge of the law in every aspect of the services they give. The responsibility is a heavy one. In matters such as building law and regulations, planning legislation and building contracts, clients seem to expect near infallibility. Architects should always be capable of advising what action should be taken, when and in what circumstances, but readers must realise that architects must never assume the role of barristers or solicitors in offering advice in purely legal matters. At most they should do no more than express their considered opinions, which should be reinforced by knowledge and enlightened judgement. All architects should tell their clients to seek their own legal advice on matters that exceed the knowledge an architect can reasonably be expected to have.

The legal system—rules of society
1.03 People living in all types of community have one thing in common: mutually agreed rules of conduct appropriate to their way of life, with explicit consequences for failure to observe the rules. This is what law is about. The more varied the activities and the more complex the social structure, the greater is the need for everyone to be aware of the part he or she must play in formulating and observing the rules. In highly developed communities these rules have grown into a complex body of law. In England and Wales the law is continually developing and being modified as personal rights and social responsibilities are re-interpreted.

The English system of law
1.04 There is no single code of English law such as exists in many countries, though there is an increasing tendency towards codification, and the statute books already contain codes covering many areas of law. Roman law, on which most of the continental codes were based, failed to make a lasting impression in England; Roman laws, like their architecture, disappeared with the legions. Roman influence has survived to a much greater degree in Scotland where, by the Act of Union of 1707, a largely independent system has

been preserved. This accounts for many differences between English and Scottish law (see Scottish sections of this handbook, particularly LEGAL STUDY 2).

THE LAWYER *1790*

2 The legal system

2.01 English law may be conveniently divided into two main parts—unwritten and written—there are several branches of these.

Common law
2.02 Common law—the unwritten law—includes the early customary laws assembled and formulated by judges, with modifications of the old law of equity (para 7.09). Common law therefore means all other than enacted law (para 2.06) and rules derived solely from custom and precedent are rules of common law. It is the unwritten law of the land because there is no official codification of it.

Judicial precedent
2.03 The basis of all legal argument and decision in the English courts is founded upon the application of rules

announced in earlier decisions and is called *Stare decisis* (let the decision stand). From this has evolved the doctrine of judicial precedent, now a fundamental characteristic of common law.

2.04 Two factors contributed to the important position that the doctrine of judicial precedent holds today: the Judicature Acts (para 7.12) and the creation of the Council of Law Reporting which is responsible for issuing authoritative reports which are scrutinised and revised by judges and which contain a summary of arguments by counsel and of the judgements given. It is essential for the operation of a system of law based on previous cases that well authenticated records of arguments and decisions be available to all courts and everyone required to advise on the law. There has never been an official publication dealing with law reports; a guide to the most common reports is given in the introduction of this handbook.

Authority of a judgement
2.05 Legally, the most important part of a judgement is that where the judge explains the principles on which he has based his decision. A judgement is an authoritative lecture on a branch of the law; it includes a *ratio decidendi* (the statement of facts or grounds for the decision) and one or more *obiter dicta* (things said by the way, often not directly relevant to the matters at issue). It is the *ratio decidendi* which creates precedents for the future. Such precedents are binding on every court with jurisdiction inferior to the court which gave the decision; even courts of equal or superior jurisdiction seldom fail to follow an earlier decision. Until recently both the Court of Appeal and the House of Lords regarded themselves as bound by their own decisions; both have now to some extent freed themselves from this limitation.

Legislation
2.06 Legislation—the written or enacted law—comprises the statutes, acts and edicts of the soveriegn and his advisers. Although historically enacted law is more recent than common law because Parliament has only been in existence since the 13th century, legislation by Acts of Parliament takes precedence over all other sources of law and is absolutely binding on all courts while it remains on the statute books. If an Act of Parliament conflicts with a common law rule, it is presumed that Parliament was aware of the fact and that there was a deliberate intention that it should do so.

2.07 All legislation must derive its authority directly or indirectly from Parliament; the only exception being that in cases of national emergency the Crown can still legislate by Royal Proclamation. In its statutes, Parliament usually lays down general principles, and in most legislation Parliament delegates authority for carrying out the provisions of statutes to non-parliamentary bodies. Subordinate legislation is required which may take the form of Orders in Council (made by the government of the day—in theory by the sovereign in Council), regulations, statutory instruments or orders made by government departments, and the by-laws of statutory undertakings and local authorities.

2.08 The courts are required to interpret Acts in accord with the wording employed. They may not question or even discuss the validity of the enactment. Rules have been established to help them interpret ambiguities: there is a presumption that Parliament in legislative matters does not make mistakes, but in general this principle does not apply to statutory instruments unless the governing Act says anything to the

contrary. The courts may decide whether rules or orders are made within the powers delegated to the authorised body ordered to make them, or whether they are *ultra vires* (outside the body's power). By-laws must not only be *intra vires* but also reasonable.

Branches
2.09 Of the branches of the law, those with the greatest general effect are civil law and criminal law; others are ecclesiastical (canon), military and naval, and administrative laws. These latter derive more than most from Roman law.

Civil law
2.10 Civil law is related to the rights, duties and obligations of individual members of the community to each other, and it embraces all the law to do with family, property, contract, commerce, partnerships, insurance, copyright, and the Law of Torts (para 5). The latter governs all actionable wrongs against persons and property—actions for damages, such as defamation, trespass, nuisance, negligence and a wide variety of other matters.

Criminal law
2.11 Criminal law deals with wrongful acts harmful to the community and punishable by the State. Except when wrongful action may fall within the scope of both civil and criminal wrong, architects are usually concerned with civil law.

Architects and the courts
2.12 Architects involved in civil cases in England are likely to find themselves in the High Court where actions are tried before puisne judges (or in a County Court before a County Court Judge if damages are claimed for less than £1 000).* Appeals from the High Court go to the Court of Appeal and if further appeal is allowed, to the House of Lords (see para 7.13 for notes on relationships of the courts).

2.13 The procedure for initiating an action in the High Court is as follows: first the plaintiff's solicitor issues and serves a writ on the defendant; the writ sets out the nature of the action and the defendant must reply. Then, the plaintiff describes his case in a statement of claim, or first pleading. The defendant must reply within a fortnight with a second pleading setting out his objections to the plaintiff's case. These are laid before a Master (usually a senior barrister) who decides whether the case can proceed or whether further pleadings are required for clarification.

2.14 Discovery of documents, the next stage, starts when the Master is satisfied: both sides must reveal the papers they intend to use. After a fortnight, the summons for directions is issued when the Master makes arrangements for the trial, which takes place when it can be fitted in to the time table of the Court.

3 The law of contract

3.01 'Agreement' signifies concurrence between two or more persons about opinions held or actions to be done or forborne. A 'contract' is simply an agreement between individuals which can be enforced in law; if it is breached, the

---

* This figure refers to cases in contract and tort (but excluding libel and slander), but the figure may be unlimited by agreement. Jurisdiction in actions relating to land (section 48) was raised to a rateable value of £1 000 by the Administration of Justice Act 1973. For Equity matters (eg trusts, mortgages, dissolution of partnerships etc) the upper limit is £5 000. Under the County Court Fees Order 1959 (last amended 1971) in sections 39–42 limits may be raised by agreement.

law gives remedy. Most people enter into contracts many times a day, though we may not always recognise them as legally binding; one is created with every purchase made in a shop or with every journey made by bus or train. Whether it involves only small amounts or vast undertakings the law regarding a contract is the same. Apart from building contracts to which architects are not parties but which depend almost entirely upon them for satisfactory fulfilment, they have other more direct contractual obligations: contracts for services to clients (employers): partnership agreements and contracts of employment between employees and employers (see LEGAL STUDY 3).

Types of contract

3.02 As the law requires that certain agreements must be in writing and in the form of a deed,* contracts must be considered under two main classes: first, speciality contracts, ie those made by deed, as required for conveyances of land, leases of property for periods of more than three years, and articles or deeds of partnership (see LEGAL STUDY 3). The second class consists of simple contracts (those that need not be under seal) which may be made informally: they may be oral or even implied by conduct (though they can be in writing). Problems may arise in cases where there is no written evidence of contract owing to possible difficulties of establishing proof on precisely what had been agreed on.

Essentials of a valid contract

3.03 All that is required of most contracts in both classes to make them valid and legally enforceable is that they comply with certain relatively simple and clearly defined rules. These are as follows:

1 *Agreement* Parties to the contract must agree at the outset that there shall not merely be a moral but a legal obligation to fulfil what they are promising to undertake and there must be evidence that agreement exists.

2 *Certainty* There must be certainty about the terms of the agreement. Since the contract is created as the result of an 'offer' made by one party and 'acceptance' by the other, he who makes the offer and he who accepts it are presumed to be of one mind. In these circumstances the law will not interfere and once a contract document is signed, both parties are bound to accept it as a whole.

3 *Consideration* There must be some 'consideration' involved to bind the parties. The law of contract was originally developed to meet the needs of commerce, and this is reflected in the rule that only an agreement which has an element of bargain will be enforced by the Courts. English law is peculiar in that it will not enforce gratuitous contracts such as a promise to make some gift in the future. So there must be an agreement by which each party gives something to the other in return for the benefit he is receiving. This 'something' is known as consideration. Consideration then simply means that something must be paid, or exchanged, for the contract to be binding and enforceable in law. It can be money or a service or some other benefit. Whatever it is, the consideration must be definite and certain.

4 *Capacity to contract* The parties to the contract must have proper capacity to enter into legal relations. This condition offers protection to infants (in law younger than 18), the mentally disordered, and persons under the influence of drink or drugs against committing themselves to binding agreements. For example, for infants (under the Infants

Relief Act 1874) certain types of contract are void; in other cases some exceptions are made for contracts to meet necessities.

5 *Consent* Consent to the agreement must be genuine and freely given. That is, it must not be obtained by fraud, misrepresentation of fact, or under duress.

6 *Legality of object* The object must not be for any purpose which contravenes the law (such as agreements to commit crimes or torts—para 5).

7 *Object* The object of the contract must be possible.

3.04 All the above must be present for a fully enforceable contract. The absence of one might lead the contract to be one of the following:

1 Void—without any legal effect.

2 Voidable—it may cease to be effective at the instance of one of the parties; for example it can be voided if it can be shown to have been induced by fraud.

3 Unenforceable—a valid contract in the main, but lacking evidence or presentation in the form required by law.

Discharge

3.05 Discharge (ending) of contracts may arise:

1 By agreement—a mutual decision by both parties to bring their contractual relationship to an end.

2 By performance—each party having duly fulfilled his obligations under the contract.

3 By breach—either because one party fails to perform his part of the agreement or repudiates his liability; such behaviour would entitle the injured party to an action for damages or in some circumstances to treat the contract as discharged.

4 By frustration—when performance of the agreement proves to have been impossible from its inception and is, therefore, a void contract.

5 By operation of law—in practice when a contract is entered into for a specified period of time the contract is discharged at the end of that period.

6 By lapse of time—unless there are provisions in the contract itself, lapse of time does not generally discharge the contract, though it may render it unenforceable in law. The Limitation Act 1939 provides for limitation of court action for enforcing contracts. Simple contracts are barred from actions after a period of six years from the time when an action could have been brought (ie from the time when a contentious point was discovered); twelve years is the period for speciality contracts (para 3.02). But see important decisions, made in 1976 and 1977, considered in para 5.14.

Conditions and warranties

3.06 In the Sale of Goods Act 1893, which is concerned with contracts for exchange of goods for money, two expressions are used which occur frequently in other aspects of contract: conditions and warranties. The difference is that a condition is regarded as going to the root of the contract; a breach of a condition gives the right to repudiate the contract. A warranty is regarded only as supplementary (collateral) to the main purposes of the contract and breach only entitles to a claim for damages. Whether a particular stipulation is a condition or a warranty is a question of construction in each contract. In either case it can only be effective if it is part of the contract; 'mere representation' prior to the making of the contract are neither conditions or warranties, and their breach will result in neither damages nor the right to repudiate the contract.

Implied terms

3.07 An important recent addition to the legislation for

---

* Deed—a written or printed document effecting a legal agreement. Execution of deeds (eg sealing and delivery) must also include signatures, and in the case of a corporation the affixing of the seal of the corporation. Delivery is held to be performed by the person who executes the deed placing his finger on the seal, and saying 'I deliver this as my act and deed'.

contract, amending and reinforcing the Sale of Goods Act 1893, is the Supply of Goods (Implied Terms) Act 1973. The conditions implied in the Sale of Goods Act are mainly concerned with the quality of goods; as for instance that goods being bought for any particular purpose must be reasonably fit for that purpose, ie that they are of merchantable quality. This term is defined by section 62(1) of the Principal Act, and again in section 7(2) of the Supply of Goods (Implied Terms) Act 1973. It is a definition of great interest to people working in the construction industry. See also section 53 for implied undertakings as to quality and fitness; and section 4 for exclusion of implied terms and conditions; amending the provisions of section 14 and section 55 of the Principal Act respectively.

3.08 It is well to remember that it is not only the implied terms relating to the sale of goods that are met with in the construction industry. The Standard Forms of Contract themselves bristle with them and are frequently coming before the courts for interpretation. The House of Lords in one of the most important cases in modern times dealt with the points made in the previous paragraph as follows: 'A person contracting to do work and supply materials warrants that the materials which he uses will be of good quality and reasonably fit for the purpose for which he is using them, unless the circumstances of the contract are such as to exclude any such warranty' (*Young and Marten v McManus Childs* (1968) 2 All ER 1169).

3.09 More recently, and of rather special interest to architects and designers generally, there was the important decision reached in the case of *Greaves (Construction) Ltd v Baynham Meikle* (1974–75). This case was concerned with design liabilities and, apart from its general implications, raised important points which arise particularly in 'package deal' situations. It was concerned with the design and erection of a storage warehouse where within a few months after completion the first floor was damaged by the vibration caused by trucks carrying heavy oil drums. The damage was alleged to be due to inadequate design. The designer had been warned that heavy loads would be involved and also about the danger of vibration and should have taken these matters into account. It was held that there had not only been a breach of duty by the designer but also a breach of an implied term that the design should be fit for the purposes intended, ie the storage and traffic of loaded trucks. (See also para 5.08 *et seq* on negligence and duty of care).

Misrepresentation
3.10 The Misrepresentation Act 1967 amends the law relating to innocent misrepresentation as do sections 11 and 35 of the Sale of Goods Act 1893, with which it must be read.

3.11 Misrepresentation in relation to the Law of Contract is '. . . an untrue statement of fact made by one party either before or at the time of entering into the contract with the intention that the other party will act upon it'. A misrepresentation may be either innocent or fraudulent. Innocent misrepresentation is made in the belief that the statement is true, without intention to deceive. Fraudulent misrepresentation is 'made knowingly, or without belief in its truth, or recklessly careless whether it be true or false' (Lord Herschell in *Derry v Peek* (1889) All ER Rep 1).

3.12 In cases of fraud, the plaintiff may:
1 Sue for damages for the tort of deceit.
2 Repudiate the contract, or have it rescinded by the court (with or without claiming damages).

The Learned A——S or a legal Construction of Rogues and Vagrants

3 Affirm the contract and still, if he wishes, claim damages for deceit.

3.13 Before the Misrepresentation Act 1967, an injured party could only rescind the contract: he had no case against a supposedly innocent misrepresentation even though he may have suffered loss thereby. The new Act (section 2) gives the right for anyone suffering loss as a result of misrepresentation to sue for damages, whether or not the misrepresentation was made fraudulently. The onus is on the person making the misrepresentation to prove that he had reasonable grounds to believe and did believe up to the time the contract was made that the facts he represented were true.

3.14 Sections 4(1) and (2) of the Misrepresentation Act refer respectively to section 11(1) and section 35 of the Sale of Goods Act 1893, making important amendments to clauses about acceptance of goods. Before the Misrepresentation Act a buyer lost his right to repudiate goods for a breach of condition once ownership had passed to the buyer. Now, goods may be rejected by the buyer even though the ownership has passed to him.

Trade Descriptions Act 1968
3.15 This act is closely associated with the Sale of Goods Act, but distinct from it. The Sale of Goods Act puts obligations on the seller with regard to the general description and quality of goods. It gives rights to the buyer to insist that those goods supplied to him compare in all respects with what he ordered; if not, money must be refunded. The Trade Descriptions Act imposes much stricter rules about the accuracy of the description both of goods and services. Its purposes and provisions are intended to extend far beyond everyday transactions in shops. The Trade Descriptions Act deals only with selling goods and not with selling buildings or land but the Misrepresentation Act deals with the latter. As an example of the Acts' application, the Trade Descriptions Act does not cover an estate agent's literature, but the Misrepresentation Act does and there would be a civil claim if a house were bought on the faith of a misrepresentation—and an infringement of the Misrepresentation Act is a criminal offence. Powers for enforcement of the law are vested in the local weights and measures authority and in the Board of Trade.

3.16 For so vast and important a subject, this discussion of contract law is much restricted. In general an architect's knowledge of contract is confined to a fairly expert understanding of the standard forms of building contract (see LEGAL STUDIES 4 and 5). Too often he overlooks the fact that he is part of the world of commerce for which the law of contract has been developed. It is increasingly desirable that architects extend their interest and reading more widely in this field. Whenever an architect recommends or selects materials and components (whether chosen as a result of trade catalogue description, or samples, persuasive 'sales talk' or any other means) and when he commissions specific works, he must remind himself that legislation such as the Sale of Goods Act 1893, the Misrepresentation Act 1967, Trade Descriptions Act 1968 and others have special relevance for him (see para 3.07).

4 The law of agency

Definition
4.01 The term 'agency' implies the relationship which comes into being when one party (the agent) is employed by another (the principal) to enter into contractual obligations with a third party on the principal's behalf; that is to undertake acts for the principal.

4.02 The law of agency is uncodified, but forms part of the law of contract. As such, the conditions already outlined in para 3.03 as being necessary for creation of a legal contract are equally applicable to the contractual relationship of agency. This section is concerned with the general liabilities of agents and, in particular with the architect's position as agent.

Types of agency
4.03 The extent of authority in each case is governed by the type of agency. Agents may be:
1 Universal, having unrestricted authority to act on a principal's behalf under power of attorney.
2 General, where the agent is appointed to act in transactions in a particular sphere eg as estate managers.
3 Special, where agent and principal contract for one particular commission (as is usual with architects).

Agent's duty and liability
4.04 An agent's duty is simply to apply reasonable skill and diligence to all he has been employed to do; in so doing he must see that he does not put himself in a position where his own interests might be in conflict with his duty. The degree of liability depends largely upon the type of agency. In general the principal is liable for all conduct of his agent falling within the scope and purpose for which the agency is created. Therefore, every act the agent performs on behalf of his principal must be within the scope of his authority and is binding in law on the principal (but see para 5.04 for torts).

4.05 When the relationship exists on the basis of a definite contract for services, as it does between employer and employee, the employer is liable for the conduct of his employees for acts committed in the course of employment. Conversely, for any act in excess of what is authorised and which adversely affects him in any way the principal must accept the consequences and obtain redress (if this is necessary and possible), from his employee. The maxim applicable here is *Qui facit per alium facit per se* (he who acts through another is deemed to act in person).

4.06 The contractual relationship between employer and agent differs from that of a normal contract of employment under which the employer (master) is in the position of being able to direct the manner in which the employee (servant) carries out his duties. In the absence of any specific agreement to the contrary an agent in the ordinary sense of the term is free to perform his duties in his own way. Neverthe-

PROOF of SEDUCTION.

less, in the conduct of business affairs on behalf of his employer, particularly in all correspondence with persons invited to tender for contracts and on similar matters, the architect must safeguard himself by disclosing the name of the client on whose authority he is acting as agent. In cases of unusual or unorthodox action he should obtain his principal's approval.

Memorandum of agreement—architect and employer
4.07 In the past it was not uncommon for architects to enter into an agency situation far too casually—often by the mere interchange of cordial letters accompanied by copies of the RIBA conditions of engagement and scale of fees. In a modern business context this method is no longer to be recommended, no matter how pleasant appears to be the personal relationship of the parties concerned. The accepted method today is to exchange a formal memorandum, either specially drawn up by a solicitor, or on the form prepared by the RIBA described as 'for general use between a building owner and an architect or firm of architects'. This memorandum of agreement is clear in its terms and carefully related to the RIBA conditions of engagement, a copy of which is required to be annexed (clause 1 of the memorandum (see also LEGAL STUDY 17 at 2.01)).

Architect's authority as agent
4.08 An architect's authority is strictly limited by the terms of his employment. He exercises his authority for the general direction and supervision of the building contract as agent to his employer in the first place, and in this capacity his duty is clearly to protect his client's interests in all his dealings with all parties. In this, his responsibility is well defined by the law of agency, subject to any provisions in the conditions of his own employment which may be expressed in the memorandum of agreement with his employer. He also stands between the two parties to the building contract—his own employer (the building owner) and the contractor—deriving authority from the contract conditions (clause 2). For the architect this clause is of utmost importance, since he must always bear in mind that the building contract is between the employer and the building contractor, and he has no power to vary, waive, or dispense with any conditions or part of the agreement, except in so far as the contract gives him express discretion and power to do so (see LEGAL STUDY 4).

4.09 The architect's duties as agent do not arise while he is employed as a designer, they begin when he is instructed to invite tenders on behalf of the building employer and continue during the progress of the job until final completion and settlement. Throughout the whole period of execution and settlement of the works he must carefully balance his loyalties fairly, taking account of the interests of both building employer and contractor, in his exercise of the general control of the job (see LEGAL STUDY 15). In addition to understanding his own responsibilities and authority as agent, an architect must fully appreciate those of every member of the building team, including clerk of works and site foreman (the agents of employer and contractor respectively) and all others with whom he comes in contact if he is to exercise proper control of the works.

5 The law of torts

5.01 The law of torts has a complicated and highly technical history originating in the common law; it is a branch of civil law which has many facets and a huge volume of accumulated case law of considerable interest through which it has evolved. The word 'tort' is French, and its use in English law poses many difficulties of definition even to lawyers. The law of torts has special reference to civil wrongs incurred by individuals for which the law provides a remedy in damages. There are, seemingly, as many civil wrongs as there may be crimes. A short list, including battery and assault (to persons and land), defamation (libel and slander), nuisance, and negligence, gives some indication of the range of the subject. Nuisance, negligence, defamation, dangerous property liabilities, and breaches of statutory duties are all of special importance to property owners and their professional advisers.

Characteristics of torts
5.02 The essential character of a tort may be briefly stated as 'a civil wrong not arising out of contract: a wrong done to an individual and in respect of which only the individual wronged can obtain redress'. It is a fundamental concept of the law of torts that 'you owe a duty to *all* persons you can reasonably foresee would be directly or closely affected by your actions, for it is assumed that you ought reasonably to have them in mind when you commit your acts. This is in contrast with the law of contract, in which a duty is owed only to the person with whom you make agreement' (Lord Atkin in *Donoghue v Stevenson* (para 5.12)).

5.03 Two points must be noted: first a tort *may* arise from circumstances which are a breach of contract and second, the same conduct is capable of violating more than one set of rules at the same time. In the latter circumstances a tort may be both a civil wrong for which the individual may sue for damages, and a criminal offence for which the State will prosecute. For instance, the act of driving a car dangerously, without due care and failing to foresee the consequences, could result in personal injury to an individual and be, at the same time, a breach of criminal law. In such cases the interest of the State takes precedence over that of the individual; nevertheless both State and individual have cause for legal action.

Vicarious liability
5.04 A person is clearly liable for his own torts; he may also be vicariously liable for the wrongful act of another. This situation arises more often from the master/servant relationship than that of employer/independent contractor. The former is a 'contract of service', the latter 'for services'. The two have differing consequences: most importantly the employer is usually vicariously liable (*in tort*) under a contract of service but not (with some exceptions) under a contract for services (but see para 5.06). The difference between the two relationships is that the independent contractor in the case of

'for services' contract undertakes to perform some service or work, but has discretion as to the way he does it, and the employer is thus excluded from directing how it should be done.

5.05 This distinction depends on the measure of control which the employer is entitled to exercise over the acts of the employee. Care must be taken to distinguish between service and services, between independent contractor and employee, and between agent and employee. The RIBA memorandum of agreement is specifically 'for services'. In the same way a builder who does work for what is often loosely termed an 'employer' is, in fact, not an employee but an independent contractor.

5.06 Generally the employer is not liable for the torts of an independent contractor, though he is if he authorises or ratifies the tort, or intereferes and assumes control, because by so doing the master/servant relationship arises. An employee (servant) on the other hand is always liable for his own torts and his employer is also liable jointly and severally if the tort is committed in the course of the employment. For example, failure by an employee to do his work properly, resulting in injury to others, renders the employer liable. LEGAL STUDY 3 gives further details of the relationship between employer and employee.

Strict liability
5.07 The rule in *Rylands v Fletcher* (1868) (LR 3HL 330) (one of the most famous tort cases) defines certain liabilities more closely. It refers to what are called torts of strict liability, that is where a man may be liable for damages in circumstances where proof of negligence and wrongful intention is not necessary. This rule places a duty on the occupier of land to take care that things on the land do not escape and cause damage. The case arose from circumstances where the defendant had employed independent contractors to construct a reservoir on his land, in the process of which some disused mine-shafts were breached, quite unknown to the defendant and his contractor, and which connected with the plaintiff's own mine workings at a lower level. When the completed reservoir was filled, water escaped and flooded the plaintiff's mines. It was found that the defendant had not been negligent, nevertheless he was held liable. The rule— one of strict liability—was given in the judgment by Lord Blackburn as follows, and admirably sums up this form of liability: 'A person who for his own purposes brings on his lands and collects and keeps there anything likely to do mischief if it escapes, must keep it at his peril, and, if he does not do so, is *prima facie* answerable for all the damage which is the natural consequence of its escape.'

Negligence and duty of care
5.08 Negligence involves a breach of duty to exercise reasonable care or skill. It may result from carelessness, and often does, but the law takes no cognisance of carelessness in the abstract. A man is not regarded as liable to everybody who is damaged as a result of his carelessness, only where there is a duty to take care and where failure in that duty has caused damage. Negligence has been defined as 'the omission to do something which a reasonable man, guided upon by those considerations which ordinarily regulate the conduct of human affairs, would do, or do something which a prudent and reasonable man would not do' (Alderson, B., in *Blyth v Birmingham Waterworks Co* (1856), 11 Exch 781 at p784). Subject to qualifications such as the rule in *Rylands v Fletcher* (para 5.07) to prove negligence, it must be shown that the wrongdoer owed a legal duty of care to the injured

party and that damage actually resulted from a wrongful action.

Architect's duty of care

5.09 An architect's duty to his client arises in contract, but to third persons it is defined in tort. To his client he has a contractual duty to use care and skill—as measured by professional standards of other architects. A breach of that duty is, therefore, a breach of contract for which, if the client has suffered loss, he may bring an action for damages.

5.10 In tort, in addition to the normal and general duty of care he shares with all men, his obligations are extended by virtue of his special situation and skills as a professional expert. The courts have often had to consider this. The test to be applied is—what is reasonable in the circumstances of the case, having regard to the particular profession, or occupation? Case law relies upon the pronouncements of Lord Tindall in *Lanphier v Phipos* (1831) 8 c & p 475. 'Every person who enters into a learned profession undertakes to bring to the exercise of it a reasonable degree of care and skill. He does not undertake, if he is an attorney, that at all events you shall gain your case, nor does a surgeon undertake that he will perform a cure; nor does he undertake to use the highest possible skill. There may be persons who have higher education and greater advantages than he has, but he undertakes to bring a fair, reasonable and competent degree of skill. . . . The question whether the architect . . . has used a reasonable and proper amount of care and skill is one of fact, and it appears to rest on the consideration whether other persons exercising the same profession, and being men of experience and skill therein, would or would not have acted in the same way as the architect in question.'

5.11 Many acts of negligence in the architectural profession have been committed by salaried staff, and attempts at denial of liability serve little purpose since employers are vicariously liable (para 5.04).

5.12 The tort of negligence was greatly clarified by judgment in the case known to all lawyers as 'the snail in the bottle case'—*Donoghue v Stevenson* (1932) AC 562. The gist of it was that a friend of the plaintiff (a woman named Donoghue) bought her a bottle of ginger beer manufactured by the defendant Stevenson. The bottle allegedly contained a decomposed snail; as the result of consuming the beverage Donoghue was said to have suffered from gastro-enteritis and shock. This case established that the manufacturer owed a duty of care to all persons who consumed his products. It is one of the most important of all cases in the law of torts and out of it came definitions by Lord Atkin which have since served as a general guide to determining to whom a duty of care is owed: 'You must take reasonable care to avoid acts or omissions which you can reasonably foresee would be likely to injure your neighbour. Who then is my neighbour? The answer seems to be—persons who are so closely and directly affected by my act that I ought reasonably to have them in contemplation as being so affected when I am directing my mind to the acts or omissions which are called in question'.

Statutory duty of care

5.13 Where Acts of Parliament delegate powers to councils and other bodies there is also an implicit liability. Except when a statute itself provides its own remedy the breach of a duty imposed by statute resulting in injury to an individual constitutes a tort actionable for damages. The recent case of *Dutton v Bognor Regis* UDC (1971) 2 All ER 1003, has important

implications particularly for local government officials whose legal liability has thereby been widened. The original High Court case revolved mainly around the duty of care owed by a local council in the exercise of its statutory powers to someone who suffered financial loss, in this instance as the result of a building inspector's negligence in approving unsatisfactory foundations. The relevant part of the decision, which has subsequently been confirmed by the Court of Appeal, being that it was held that the purpose of building by-laws, including the inspection of the site in course of erection, is the protection of the public. If the local authority exercises its statutory powers to the injury of the public the injured person may be entitled to sue. An example of statutory obligations which concern architects in practice are those imposed under the Offices, Shops and Railway Premises Act 1963 and the Health and Safety at Work etc Act 1974.

Liability and Limitations Act 1939

5.14 The interest and significance of the case of *Dutton v Bognor Regis* UDC referred to in the foregoing paragraph has been revived by the more recent case of *Sparham-Souter and Another v Town and Country Developments (Essex) Ltd and Benfleet Urban District Council (Times* Law Report, 10 February 1976). *Dutton v Bognor Regis* had marked a significant advance in the law as to defective premises. But the decision, made before the Defective Premises Act 1973 came into force on 1 January 1974, had been on the basis that the 'cause of action' ran from the time when the house was 'completed', whereas under the decision in *Sparham-Souter* it ran from the time the purchaser knew, or ought to have known, of the defects. The effect, therefore, as summed up in *The Times* Law Report, is that 'a person who buys a house which develops defects and causes him loss or damage may bring an action at common law against a local authority, alleging negligence in inspection and certification, many years after the alleged negligent acts; for the owner's cause of action does not accrue under the Limitation Act 1939 until he is in a position to discover the defects'. *Dutton* was important because, for the first time, council surveyors were made liable for negligent inspection. *Sparham-Souter* is important because it greatly extends their liability and, by implication, that of architects and builders. In reporting the case, the AJ (18 February 1976), commented that, 'at the moment, the law has only been changed in respect of local authorities' surveyors. But the judgement is likely to be used as a precedent in any new case of architect's negligence. Those most likely to be affected are retired partners or partners of firms that have closed down. If *Sparham-Souter* is regarded as a precedent in cases which involve such people, they could be sued many years after their connection with their firm or indeed architecture had ceased'. Following hard upon the heels of *Sparham–Souter* has since come the decision of the House of Lords (May 1977) in the case of *Anns v London Borough of Merton*. The story is the familiar one where structural defects were the consequence of inadequate foundations and the responsibilities of local authorities was again in question. At the time of building the authority was the Mitcham Borough Council whose duties and liabilities were subsequently taken over by the new London Borough of Merton. The outcome of the Lords Appeal was briefly that local authorities are liable to householders for defects in their homes which council inspectors fail to spot when carrying out their duties to inspect foundations etc. The decision establishes it as a duty of the authority to consider whether or not they should inspect foundations and if they so determine, to exercise reasonable care to secure that the builder does not cover in work which does not comply with the Building Regulations. That duty is owed to all owners/occupiers (except the builder himself if he is also the owner). The particular owner/occupier at the time when the state of the building becomes such that there is present an imminent danger to the health or safety of persons occupying it will become entitled to maintain an action against the local authority; and that the period of limitation commences not when the building is just completed but at the time when the cause of action has accrued.

Negligent statements

5.15 The case of *Clay v A. J. Crump & Sons Ltd* (1963) (3 All ER 687) outlines the law of negligent statements. An architect had stated that a wall on a demolition job was safe, but the wall collapsed and the architect was held liable for his negligent statement. A more recent example emphasises the importance of a duty of care, which in no way depends on any client/architect relationship or on payment of professional fees and, therefore, calls for even more than usual caution in giving casual advice. The House of Lords decided in *Hedley Byrne & Co Ltd v Heller & Partners Ltd* (1964) (AC 465), that where a person made a statement to someone who it was known would be relying upon his special skill and ability, the adviser had a special duty of care in respect of the advice given. Therefore unless some qualification is made to the effect that no responsibility is accepted for the statement, the person making a negligent statement would be held liable for what he says.

Nuisance and trespass

5.16 Nuisance and trespass are two aspects of the law of torts deserving careful study by architects. Nuisance may be classed as public or private. Public nuisance is not a tort but a criminal offence and the responsibility of the State. Private nuisances are usually interference by noise, smells, smoke or other means with the enjoyment of an individual's land or property (see also LEGAL STUDY 6 para 3.01).

5.17 Trespass may take the form of temporary or permanent entry upon land owned by another, or it may be committed by placing or throwing objects upon such land. The frequently displayed 'Trespassers will be prosecuted' notice is unfounded—prosecution implies crime, and trespass is not a crime but a tort, for which a civil action only may be brought unless it is accompanied by some offence of malicious damage, like the breaking down of fences, which would bring it within the scope of the Criminal Damage Act 1971.

5.18 Trespass denotes any direct unlawful interference with the owner's (or his lawful tenant's) possessions or enjoyment of his land, and is actionable as such, irrespective of what the trespasser's intentions were and without proof of damage being necessary. Direct entry of any kind in the air space over land or premises, or digging beneath, constitutes trespass. Exceptions are that the Civil Aviation Act 1949 permits aircraft to fly over at a reasonable height, and mining rights are sometimes owned by others and can be exploited by them.

5.19 As far as architects and building contractors are concerned even the slightest infringements are actionable, however innocent the intentions; for example it is trespass for a surveying assistant to set foot on adjoining property without authority or, in the case of building operations, to allow any soil disturbance, or anything to overhang or fall or be thrown over the land. Land and property owners are generally suspicious of 'surveyors' and irritated by nearby 'works', so the greatest care must be exercised to see that irritation does not reach flash point and lead to legal action. A property owner's 'common duty of care' does not apply to trespassers, but only to lawful visitors whose presence is condoned by the owner or tenant of the premises. This excuses him of vicarious liability for injury sustained by trespassers (see para 5.04).

6 The law of property

6.01 Property law is dealt with extensively in LEGAL STUDIES 6 and 7 which should be consulted for details. This section is intended only to provide a brief introduction to some of the concepts. Some notes on the early history of property law are given in the appendix (para 7.02 *et seq*).

6.02 Until 1925, three separate laws applied to holding land —all included useless technicalities inherited from feudal times: freeholds, leaseholds (a special law for personal property) and copyholds (a form of 'unfree tenure' in which tenants held land at the will of the lord in a manner not far removed from slavery). In 1925 copyhold was abolished and seven reforming Acts, known generally as the Real Property Acts of 1925, were passed, including the Law of Property Act 1925, and the Land Registration Act 1925. All had the object of simplifying the land laws. In the process of simplification an attempt was made to make land transfer by conveyancing easier, and the number of legal 'estates' was reduced to two: freehold and leasehold; and the number of legal 'interests' (para 6.06) which could exist over land to five (Law of Property Act 1925, section 1 (1)).

Estates of freehold

6.03 The two legal estates created by the 1925 reforms are:
1 An estate in fee simple absolute in possession.
2 A term of years absolute.
A tenant in fee simple is for all practical purposes the absolute owner of his property. His is a freehold property. The word 'fee' indicates an estate of inheritance—in other words an interest in the land which does not come to an end with his

death but is capable of being inherited by another. 'Simple' means without restriction to any particular class or sex of person, for instance, eldest sons or male descendants. 'Absolute' means that the owner has unconditional enjoyment of it without fear of any change taking place as the result of a remarriage or similar happening. 'In possession' means that the holder of the estate must be in actual possession of the land or receive all its rents and profits.

6.04 Absolute title has a special significance under the provisions of the Land Registration Act 1925 (section 5) since it determines that the registered proprietor of lands with an 'absolute title' has a *State guaranteed* title that no other person has a better right to the land.

Estates of less than freehold
6.05 'A term of years absolute' denotes a leasehold, which may be granted for a specified number of years (eg 999 years) or for as little as a week. The ordinary weekly tenancy of a house is capable of being a legal 'estate'. 'Absolute' in this case means that the holding is unconditional and, provided the terms of the lease have been complied with, cannot be terminated either by landlord or tenant (lessor or lessee) except by mutual agreement. A leasehold tenancy involves the Law of Contract (para 3) and agreement by deed (para 3.02) with conditions, covenants and so on.

Legal interests in land
6.06 The other important achievement of the 1925 legislation was to reduce the number of legal interests in land which are 'capable of subsisting or of being conveyed or created at law' to five (Law of Property Act 1925 (section 1, paragraph (2a)). Briefly they are:
1 Easements.
2 Rent charges in possession.
3 Charges by way of legal mortgage.
4 Land tax and tithe rent charges etc.
5 Rights of entry.
'All other estates, interests and charges in or over land effect as equitable interests' (section 3)—see para 7.09 *et seq* for notes on Equity.

6.07 Of all the legal interests in land the laws affecting easements have special importance for architects. These are covered in detail in LEGAL STUDY 6.

7 Appendix: Legal history

Origins of English law
7.01 The roots of English law lie deep in the foundations of English history. The seeds of custom and rules planted in Anglo-Saxon and earlier times have developed and grown gradually into a modern system of law. The Normans interfered little with common practices they found, and almost imperceptibly integrated them with their own mode of life. William I did not regard himself as a conqueror, but claimed to have come by invitation as the lawful successor of Edward the Confessor—whose laws he promised to re-establish and enforce.

Feudal system and land law
7.02 The Domesday Book (1086), assembled mainly by itinerant judges for taxation purposes, provided William I with a comprehensive social and economic survey of his newly acquired lands. The feudal system in England was more universally applied than it was on the Continent—a result perhaps of the thoroughness of the Domesday survey. Consequently, in England feudal law was not solely a law

for tne knights and bishops of the realm, nor of some parts of the country alone: it affected every person and every holding of land. It became part of the common law of England.

7.03 To the knowledge acquired from Domesday, the Normans applied their administrative skills; they established within the framework of the feudal system new rules for ownership of land, new obligations of loyalty to the administration under the Crown, and reorganised arrangements for control of the people and for hearing and judgment of their disputes. These were the true origins of our modern legal system.

7.04 Ultimate ownership of land in England is still, in theory, in the Crown. The lord as 'landowner' merely held an 'estate' or 'interest' in the land, directly or indirectly, as tenant from the king. A person holding an estate of the Crown could, in turn, grant it to another person, but the ownership still remained in the Crown. The tenant's 'interest' may have been of long or short duration and as varied as the kinds of services that might be given in return for the 'estate'. In other words many different estates and interests in land existed. Tenure and estate are distinct. 'Tenure' refers to the relation of the landlord to his overlord, at its highest level to the King. 'Estate' refers to the duration of his interest in the land, and has nothing whatever to do with the common use of the word.

Possession not ownership
7.05 English law as a result has never used the concept of ownership of land but instead has concentrated on the fact of 'possession', mainly because ownership can refer to so many things and is ill-fitted to anything so permanent and immovable as a piece of land. A man's title to land in England is based on his being able to prove that he has a better right to possession of it than anyone else who claims it.

Real and personal property
7.06 Law makes a distinction between 'real' and 'personal' property. The former are interests in land other than leasehold interests; the latter includes leasehold interests and applies to movable property (personal property and chattels). A leasehold interest in land is classed as 'personal' rather than 'real' property because in early times it was not possible to recover a leasehold interest by 'real' actions for the return of the thing (*res*). In common law a dispossessed owner of freehold land could bring an action for recovery of possession and an order would be made for the return to him of his land. For the recovery of personal (tangible or movable) articles his remedy was limited to a personal action in which the defendant had the option of either returning the property or paying its value.

Beginnings of common law
7.07 Foundations of both the common law and the courts of justice were laid by Henry II (1154–1189). In his reign the 'King's justice' began to be administered not only in the King's Court—the *Curia Regis*—where the soveriegn usually sat in person and which accompanied him on his travels about the country, but also by justices given commissions of assize directing them to administer the royal justice systematically in local courts throughout the whole kingdom. In these courts it was their duty to hear civil actions which previously had been referred to the central administration at Westminster. It was the judges of assize who created the common law. On completion of their circuits and their return to Westminster they discussed their experiences and judgments given in the light of local customs and systems of

law. Thus a single system common to all was evolved; judge-made in the sense that it was brought together and stated authoritatively by judges, but it grew from the people in that it was drawn directly from their ancient customs and practices.

7.08 Under the able guidance of Edward I (1272–1307) many reforms were made, notably in procedures and mainly in the interest of the subject as against the royal officials, and the law began to take its charactcristic shape. Three great common law courts became established at Westminster:
1 The King's Bench, broadly for cases in which the Crown had interest.
2 Common pleas, for cases between subject and subject.
3 Exchequer, for those having a fiscal or financial aspect.
However, as administered in these courts, the common law was limited in its ability to meet every case. This led to the establishment of the principles of Equity.

Equity
7.09 In the Middle Ages the common law courts failed to give redress in certain types of cases where redress was needed, either because the remedy the common law provided (ie damages) was unsuitable or because the law was defective in that no remedy existed. For instance, the common law did not recognise trusts and at that time there was no way of compelling a trustee to carry out his obligations. Therefore disappointed and disgruntled litigants exercised their rights of appeal to the King—the 'fountain of all justice'. In due course, the King, through his Chancellor (keeper of his conscience, because he was also a bishop and his confessor), set up a special Court of Chancery to deal with them.

Rules of equity
7.10 During the early history of the Court of Chancery, equity had no binding rules. A Chancellor approached his task in a different manner to the common law judges; he gave judgment when he was satisfied in his own mind that a wrong had been done and he would order that the wrong be made good. Thus the defendant could clear his own conscience at the same time. The remedy for refusal was invariably to be imprisoned until he came to see the error of his ways and agree with the court's ruling. It was not long before a set of general rules emerged in the Chancery Courts which hardened into law and became a regular part of the law of the land. There is, however, another and even more fundamental aspect of equity. Though it developed in the Court of Chancery as a body of law with defined rules, its ideal from earliest times was the simple belief in moral justice, fairness, and equality of treatment for all, based on the idea of natural justice as opposed to the strict letter of the law. Equity in that sense has remained to this day a basic principle of English justice.

Common law and equity in the nineteenth century
7.11 Up to the end of the fifteenth century the Chancellor had generally been a bishop, but after the Reformation the position came to be held by professional lawyers undcr whom the rules of equity became almost as rigid as those of common law; and the existence of separate courts administering the two different sets of rules led to serious delays and conflicts. By the end of the eighteenth century the courts and their procedures had reached an almost unbelievable state of confusion, mainly due to lack of co-ordination of the highly technical processes and overlapping jurisdiction. Charles Dickens describes without much exaggeration something of the troubles of a litigant in Chancery in the case of '*Jarndyce v Jarndyce*' (*Bleak House*).

Judicature Acts 1873–1875
7.12 Nineteenth century England was dominated by a spirit of reform, which extended from slavery to local government. The law and the courts did not escape reform, and the climax came with the passing of the Judicature Acts of 1873 (and much additional and amending legislation in the years that followed) whereby the whole court system was thoroughly reorganised and simplified, by the establishment of a single Supreme Court. The Act also brought to an end the separation of common law and equity; they were not amalgamated and their rules remained the same, but henceforth the rules of both systems were to be applied by all courts. If they were in conflict, equity was to prevail.

The Supreme Court 1875–1971
7.13 The main object of the Judicature Act 1873 was an attempt to solve the problems of delay and procedural confusion in the existing court system by setting up a Supreme Court. This consisted of two main parts:
1 The High Court of Justice, with three Divisions, all courts of Common Law and Equity. As a matter of convenience cases concerned primarily with Common Law questions being heard in the Queen's Bench Division; those dealing with Equitable problems in the Chancery Division; and the Probate, Divorce and Admiralty Division with the three classes indicated by its title.
2 The Court of Appeal—hearing appeals from decisions of the High Court and most appeals from County Courts.

Modern reforms
7.14 In 1970, mainly as the result of recommendations by a Royal Commission on Assizes and Quarter Sessions under the Chairmanship of Lord Beeching, Parliament made further reforms between the Chancery Division, the Queen's Bench Division, Commercial Court, Admiralty Court, and the newly formed Family Division. The latter for dealing with guardianship, adoption, divorce and other matrimonial matters.

Courts Act 1971
7.15 The Courts Act 1971 then followed, with effect from January 1972 and the object of separating civil from criminal proceedings throughout the country and of promoting speedier trials. The Act established the Crown Court in all cities and main towns for hcaring criminal cases in continuous session, leaving the High Court to deal with civil actions. The County Courts, Magistrates' Courts and the Coroners' Courts remain unaffected by the new changes; but the Act abolished all Courts of Assize and Quarter Session and various

Lawyers going the Circuit

other long-established courts of special jurisdiction, such as the Liverpool Court of Passage and the Tolzey and Pie Poudre Courts of Bristol and others whose usefulness had long been in decline.

References

OSBORN, P. G. A concise law dictionary. London, 1964, Sweet & Maxwell

WALKER, R. J. and WALKER, M. G. The English legal system. 3rd Edition, London, 1972, Butterworth

NEWTON, CLIVE R. General principles of law. London, 1972, Sweet & Maxwell (Concise College Texts)

SIMS, R. S. and SCOTT, D. M. M. 'A' level English law. 4th Edition, London, 1974, Butterworth

KEATING, D. The law and practice of building contracts. London, 1969, Sweet & Maxwell. (New edition in preparation)

MUNKMAN, JOHN Employer's liability at common law. 8th Edition, London, 1975, Butterworth

PARRIS, JOHN Building law reports. London, 1976, George Godwin

Legal study 2

Introduction to Scots law

This study outlines basic concepts and procedures of Scottish law before discussing differences between Scottish and English law in branches particularly relevant to architects. It should be read in conjunction with LEGAL STUDY 1

1 Law and Scotland

1.01 To many Scots, their legal system is an institution which expresses their individuality as a nation and is at least the equal of the more widespread English system of law. Despite the union of the Scottish and English legislative bodies in 1707 into the Parliament of Great Britain, the Treaty of Union preserved Scottish law and courts. As a result, Scottish law is still in many respects entirely different from English, particularly in branches which have a territorial nature such as the law of landholding and criminal law. But since 1707 much legislation has been enacted for the whole of the UK, and appeals have been permitted from the Scottish civil courts to the House of Lords (which until 1866 contained no Law Lords from Scotland). As a result, much English law has been superimposed, sometimes unhappily, on what had previously been an entirely Scottish system.

2 Sources

2.01 Many of the Acts of the Scottish Parliament prior to 1707 are still in force, applying only to Scotland. Legislation is still one of the principal sources of Scottish law. Considerations applicable to it are the same as for English law (see LEGAL STUDY 1 para 2.06). Some legislation is not applicable to Scotland, while some is applicable there alone. In the latter case the procedure for its enactment may be slightly different.

2.02 The two other principal sources of modern Scottish law are to be found in judicial decisions (see LEGAL STUDY 1 para 2.03) and the works of 'institutional' writers (para 2.09). Together making up the common law, they form a body of law which has grown up over almost as long a period as English law and has been changed and added to by statute.

LAST SITTING of the OLD COURT of SESSION 11 of JULY 1808

300

Contract

4.02 In Scottish law the element of consideration essential to the formation of a binding contract in England is unnecessary (LEGAL STUDY 1 para 3). A contract is an agreement between parties which is intended to have legal effect. It is therefore perfectly possible to have a gratuitous contract, ie one in which all obligations rest on one side.

4.03 Sealed contracts (LEGAL STUDY 1 para 3.02) have no place in Scottish law, but certain contracts must be in writing to be properly constituted; the most important examples of these are contracts relating to heritable property (ie land and buildings), and leases and contracts of employment for more than one year.

Jus quaesitum tertio

4.04 In Scottish law, parties to a contract may confer an enforceable right on a third party who takes no part in the formation of the contract. Provided appropriate circumstances obtain, a right known as a *jus quaesitum tertio* can be conferred on the third party, which enables him to enforce provisions in his favour agreed upon by the contracting parties. This is particularly important in relation to enforcement of building conditions. Where several feuars (vassals, para 2.03) hold land from the same superior, building conditions imposed in the feu contract may, in appropriate circumstances, be enforceable by one feuar against another; for example, alterations of particular kinds may be prevented (see LEGAL STUDY 7).

Partnership

4.05 In contrast to the English position (LEGAL STUDY 3) a Scottish partnership is not in law simply a collection of individuals. The firm has a legal personality—ie an existence of its own—separate from the persons who compose it, and it can, for example, sue for debts owed to it in its own name. The separate existence of the firm does not however prevent the personal liability of partners from being unlimited. Partnership law is dealt with in detail in LEGAL STUDY 3.

Delict

4.06 The law of delict is the part of the law which deals with righting of legal wrongs, in the civil, as opposed to criminal, sense. Broadly it is the Scottish equivalent of the English law of torts (LEGAL STUDY 1 para 5). The background and details of the Scottish law of delict and the English law of torts are different in too many respects to mention here. But they cover broadly the same ground, with the Scottish law concentrating more on general theory and less on specific wrongs than corresponding English law. Most actions based on delict arise out of negligence.

Property

4.07 Property law is perhaps the field in which Scottish and English law diverge most widely, particularly in relation to the law of land ownership. Differences are so great and fundamental that consideration of them is deferred to LEGAL STUDY 7. LEGAL STUDY 1 para 6 gives some basic concepts of English property law.

References

WALKER, D. M. The Scottish legal system. 2nd Edition, Edinburgh, 1963, W. Green & Son

COULL, J. W. and MERRY, E. W. Principles and practice of Scots law. London, 1971, Butterworth

MARSHALL, ENID A., General principles of Scots law. 2nd Edition, Edinburgh, 1975, W. Green & Son (Concise College Texts)

WALKER, D. M. Principles of Scottish private law. 2nd Edition, 2 Vols, London, 1975, Oxford University Press

WALKER, D. M. The law of delict in Scotland. 2 Vols, Edinburgh, 1966, W. Green & Son

Acknowledgements

Illustrations in LEGAL STUDIES 1 and 2 are by courtesy of the Trustees of the British Museum or are taken from John Kay's *Original Portraits* (Edinburgh 1837).

AJ Legal Handbook

Section 2
The office and the law

Legal study 3

The office and the law

This study describes the problems and advantages of common forms of association for architects with special emphasis on partnership. Also discussed are the rights and responsibilities of employers and employees. Of particular interest are the sections which deal with statutory responsibility for welfare safety and the insurance requirements imposed for the benefit of office staff and premises.
The attention of Scottish readers is drawn to para 7 in which differences between English and Scots law are discussed

1 Running an architectural business

1.01 The manager of an architectural business, as opposed to the manager of an architectural project, faces a wide variety of legal problems of which probably the two most important and universal arise from formal modes of organisation which he adopts and from his status as employer in a labour intensive operation. First he is concerned with relationships between the owners of the business, second with the owners and people with whom they contract, and third with relationships between employer and employee.

1.02 Apart from working as self-employed principals, there are two basic forms of organisation which architects may adopt to run their architectural practices: partnership (para 2) and unlimited liability companies. Architects may also form and own limited companies (LEGAL STUDY 15 para 2.14) but under the present professional codes the role of such companies must be limited to certain non-professional activities, such as ownership or leasing of office premises, ownership of office equipment, furniture and cars, and employment of non-professional staff. The latter restriction is curious because provided the contract between the client and architect is with a partnership or unlimited company, liability for negligence by the employees of the limited company remains with the partners or shareholders of the unlimited company (see LEGAL STUDY 1 para 5.04). Practice through limited liability companies is also to be permitted for certain overseas work (para 3.11 and LEGAL STUDY 15 para 2.16).

2 Partnership

2.01 Partnership is the most common form of association found between architects in the UK, partly because of the requirements of the professional codes and partly because, for the sake of business, it is usually the most appropriate; architects go into partnership because they want the benefits of mutual support and combined resources. Partnership is a form of contract (see LEGAL STUDY 1 para 3.01) and so the existence of a partnership can sometimes be inferred in law from the behaviour of the parties even if no deed of partnership exists.

The choice of the right person is fundamental and highly personal. It is also circumscribed by both the ARCUK and RIBA Codes of Professional Conduct. The RIBA Code says: 'a member shall not have or take as partner or co-director in his firm any person who is disqualified for registration by reason of the fact that his name has been removed from the

register under section 7 of the Architects [Registration] Act 1931; any person disqualified for membership of the RIBA by reason of expulsion under bylaw 5.1; any person disqualified for membership of another professional institution by reason of expulsion under the relevant disciplinary regulations (unless the RIBA otherwise allows); any person who is an undischarged bankrupt; or any person who engages in any of the occupations proscribed under rule 2.1 even though that person engages in any such occupation in a firm or company separate from the architectural firm.'*

The ARCUK Code's corresponding prohibitions are all contained within the RIBA's Code (see LEGAL STUDY 15). In addition to these professional prohibitions is it now contrary to the law, when choosing one's partners, to discriminate on the grounds of sex or marital status.†

No one should consider entering any partnership without first studying very carefully all the provisions of the Partnership Act 1890, which is short, more straightforward and more easily understood than most legislation. It is divided into four main parts:
a Definition and nature of partnership;
b Relations of partners to firms dealing with them;
c Relations of partners to one another;
d Dissolution and its consequences.

Definition

2.02 The essentials for recognition of a partnership are contained in the Partnership Act of 1890 which states that partnership is a 'relation which subsists between persons carrying on a business in common with a view to profit'. The practice of architecture is a business, varying from firms with 200 associates and branches in Liberia, to one man recently registered who picks up what work he can and does it in his spare time at home. A single act, such as designing a house for an aunt, does not make a business, but if there is a series of acts, a business exists. If two or more architects carry on such a business in common and their intention is to make a profit—even though they fail lamentably—they are in partnership. The requirement of acting in common is important. Barristers for example are in business with a view to profit, but their occupation of chambers is merely a sharing of facilities—they do not practise in common.

Sharing facilities

2.03 If two or more architects do not intend to practise in partnership, but merely share facilities, they must take great

---

* RIBA Code Principle 2.7
† Sex Discrimination Act 1975

care to avoid the possibility of third persons with whom any of them have dealings being led to assume that they practise together as partners. Normally shared ownership of property and sharing of net profits is *prima facie* evidence of existence of a partnership. This may be particularly important to architectural practices, since profit sharing is quite a common means of remunerating staff, and it is important to draft any contract of employment including such a provision very carefully from both the employer's and the employee's points of view.

Importance of clarity

2.04 Considerable importance may be attached to the existence of a partnership. For example, if two men work together occasionally over several years and then a case of negligence arises, both can be sued if a partnership exists. If there is no partnership, however, one man may be out of trouble. It can be vital to a client or supplier of a practice to establish whether he is dealing with a partnership or one man. Architects are recommended on all possible occasions to make this point clear, particularly when they work as group practices and consortia (see para 3.14).

2.05 Even though there are ways of determining whether a partnership exists and the 1890 Act sets out terms which apply if partners have nothing written down, it is much more satisfactory if intending partners agree that they are going into business together and set out the terms of their relationship in a deed of partnership (see LEGAL STUDY 1 para 3.02). The deed should cover the points set out in checklist 1.

Name of practice
2.06 Having decided the terms of agreement, the partners must decide what to call the firm. Four things are critical:
1 If the name they choose is other than the names of all current partners, it must be registered under the Registration of Business Names Act 1916 with the Registrar of Companies who issues forms for the purpose.
2 Nothing in the name should imply that it is a limited company.
3 If the name includes the word 'architect' or 'architects' it is advisable to check with ARCUK.
4 The use in the firm's name of the name of a retired, former or deceased partner is permissible provided there is no intent to mislead. Caution is necessary to avoid the implication that such a person is still involved in the practice.

Rights and liabilities of partners
2.07 The rights of partners as to shares of capital, control of management and shares of profit should be governed by the deed of partnership, because in the absence of such evidence, under the Partnership Act 1890 all would be entitled to equal shares. Similarly with regard to liabilities, the Act lays down provisions for protection of third persons dealing with a partnership, but there is nothing to prevent the partnership agreement providing for cross-indemnities*.

2.08 In England a partnership is a collection of individuals, not a corporate body; in addition to all his normal individual liabilities, each partner has added responsibilities as a member of a partnership. He is the agent (see LEGAL STUDY 1 para 4.01) of all other partners when he acts in the usual way of business, and such acts are binding on them all. For example, taking on work for the firm or accepting settlements of debts, even on a job of another partner, may be usual acts, buying

drawing boards might be usual, but buying an aeroplane might not (see para 7.02 for position in Scots law).

Torts and crimes
2.09 Every partner who makes any admission or representation or action in the course of carrying on in the usual way of the firm's business binds the firm and his fellow partners; unless it is outside his authority to act for the firm in that particular matter, and the person with whom he is dealing knows that he has no authority or does not believe him to be a partner (s.5 Partnership Act 1890). Similarly any torts, for example acts of professional negligence (see LEGAL STUDY 1 para 5.08) and negligent statements where it may be construed that the partner was speaking as a member of the firm, are regarded as committed by all in the partnership.

2.10 If a partnership is sued, a partner may be proceeded against jointly, or jointly and severally (checklist 2). If a partnership is sued jointly one or more partners may be sued at the same time; when judgment is given, even if it is not satisfied, no further action can be taken against any of the other partners. If an action is brought against a firm jointly and severally, the partners may be sued singly or together. When judgement is given against one, further action may be brought against the others one by one or together until the full amount is paid. If only some of the partners are sued, they may apply to the courts to have their other partners joined with them as co-defendants.

2.11 Partners are not liable for the criminal actions of other partners, unless they contributed to them or have knowledge of them. But the RIBA has always considered a man liable for breaches of the Code of Professional Conduct by his fellow partners (see LEGAL STUDY 15 pare 1.07).

Incoming and retiring partners
2.12 Incoming partners are not liable for the firm's acts committed before they became partners. A retiring partner remains responsible for debts incurred before his retirement, but he may be discharged from his liability by agreement between himself, the other partners and their creditors.
Partnership firms must be alive to the fact that changes in the membership of the firm may have tax effects upon it, eg when an existing partnership admits a new partner and when a partner retires or dies.
The effect of a change in partnership is that tax assessments are made on the basis of a cessation and reassessment unless an election is made for the preceding year basis to continue (s.15 of Income and Corporation Taxes Act 1970—an Act which consolidates tax legislation generally). Such an election has to be made within two years of the change and signed by all partners (s.17 Finance Act 1971). Financial matters of this nature are, however, too specialised for full discussion here and should always be referred to the firm's accountants (see also para 3.03).

2.13 Under the Statute of Limitations liability runs from the date of any cause of action for twelve years for contracts under seal but for six years for contracts under hand. Until 1976 it was commonly thought that the date of the cause of action was the date on which the negligent act was committed: this was usually interpreted as running from the date of the Final Certificate. But in February 1976 the Court of Appeal held that the date of the cause of action is effectively the date of the discovery of the damage*. Although the case did not

---

* Cross indemnity: In cases where partners deal only with their own jobs, they may arrange to indemnify each other if a case of negligence arises.

* Sparham-Souter and Another v Town and Country Developments (Essex) Ltd and Benfleet Urban District Council. At the time of writing there is still a possibility of an appeal to the House of Lords.

specifically concern an architect it seems most likely to be cited as a precedent should a similar case arise in future.

The effects of this case are most likely to be on former partners or partners of firms now defunct who will have to consider whether they should maintain indemnity insurance in their own names for the remainder of their lives. Retired partners would be well advised to check that their continuing previous firm is specifically extending insurance to protect them. (See also LEGAL STUDY 1, para 5.14.)

Dissolution

2.14 A partnership comes to an end:
1 At the end of a fixed term if it has been so set up.
2 At the end of a single specific commission, if it was set up for the commission alone.
3 On the death or bankruptcy of any partner.
4 If any partner gives notice (technically a partnership ends on the death or retirement of a partner, and a new partnership is formed when an incoming partner enters; in practice, partnership agreements may make provision for continuity in such circumstances).

2.15 A partner cannot be expelled by a majority unless his agreement says so, but if a partner wishes to end the firm but is prevented by his fellows, he may apply to the court for a dissolution on one of the grounds shown in checklist 3.

Types of partner

2.16 The law is not concerned with distinctions between senior and junior partners. It is up to the partners to decide how to share profits, but their liabilities are unlimited unless special provision is made.

2.17 In May 1974 the RIBA issued a Practice Note which requires that in an architect's practice all those persons who are held out to be partners shall be described as such without further distinction. In particular the term 'salaried partner' is to be avoided. All persons described as partners must share in the decision-making of the business and to do so effectively must have access to appropriate information. They are also fully responsible for the professional conduct of their practice and for keeping themselves and their partners properly informed of partnership matters.

2.18 Although all partners must accept such responsibility and require such information, by the Partnership Act 1890, some (but not all) partners may have their liability limited by agreement with the other members of the partnership. The other partners agree to indemnify such partners for liability above a certain figure. Such partners may draw a smaller share of the profits than the others and they rely for income mainly on a guaranteed remuneration. This device is often used to encourage talented members of staff to remain with a firm and share in its management while ensuring that they do not have to outlay capital to join the partnership.

2.19 Under the Limited Partnership Act 1907 the liability of some but not all partners may be limited. Although limited partnership is not referred to specifically in the RIBA Practice Note of 1974 it seems likely that practice in this form would contravene the intention of the Note. (See also para 7 for application of Scots law.)

Associates

2.20 It is common in architects' firms to recognise the status and contribution of senior staff by calling them 'associates'. The device is often used to retain important staff members while preventing them having any real responsibility or appreciable share of the profits. The title 'associate' is not referred to in the Partnership Acts; it has no meaning in law and if it is not intended that associates be partners and share in the liabilities of the partnership, it is extremely unwise to use the term 'associate partner', and would also probably contravene professional codes. If people were misled into thinking associates are partners, associates might find themselves liable as though they were partners, having all the liabilities without much profit. A man or woman should be either partner or associate, and the distinction should be clear. (See also para 2.17 and LEGAL STUDY 15.)

3 Other forms of association

3.01 Under the current professional code, the practice of architecture (accepting commissions from clients, carrying out work whether personally or through employed staff, and drawing fees) must be carried on without limitation of the architect's liability to his client other than, by prior written agreement, the exclusion of liability for loss of use, loss of profits or other consequential loss. The client must feel confident that his architect will assume full responsibility in executing his commission and will not be tempted into rashness and possible negligent conduct by the protection of limited liability. If a client suffers damage because of his architect's professional negligence, he must have access to everything his architect owns until his loss has been compensated (ARCUK and RIBA Codes 2.4.1. of Notes to Principles and Rules and LEGAL STUDIES 15, 16 and 17).

3.02 It follows that the only forms under which architecture may be practised (except by individual practitioners) are partnership (para 2) or incorporation as an unlimited liability company (para 3.08) and an architect's professional staff may be employed only by one of these three. Choice of partnership or company is made on financial (taxation) grounds.

Financial status of companies

3.03 Partnerships are collections of individuals who are liable to income tax and surtax on their profits whether they are drawn out or left in the firm. Companies are legal entities liable to corporation tax on profits distributed to shareholders. Thus the decision whether to form a company is determined primarily by financial considerations. Income tax and surtax rates should be compared with the corporation tax rate, taking into account the earning power of the firm and the partner's personal situations.

Partnerships, as indeed are all architects in practice, are liable to comply with all the requirements of the Value Added Tax as from 1 April 1973. An architect's 'professional services', whether in his design or supervisory work, are not exempt from this taxation and the percentage appropriate must be added to his charges to his clients.

3.04 For a company to store reserves of undistributed, untaxed profits for the future is not so easy as may be imagined. Companies of the kind likely to be operated by architects, in which only a few people have financial interest, may be judged by the Inland Revenue not to have distributed a reasonable proportion of their profits, and a surtax direction may be made under which retained profits are treated as if they had been distributed to the shareholders. Thus the manoeuvrability of a company may be no greater than that which is legitimately available to a partnership.

General requirements of companies

3.05 The activities of companies are governed principally by

the Companies Acts of 1948 and 1967. These are largely concerned with protection of shareholders by ensuring that they
have access to company information and they have guarantees
on how the company paperwork should be organised. It is
essential to go through the provisions to preserve the legal
position of a company.

3.06 ARCUK, though not at the moment the RIBA, has clear
rules on the way in which an architect may use companies,
known as 'service companies'.
1 A service company may not carry on the practice of
architects and subject to paragraph 8 below may not employ
architects or other professional staff.
2 An architect must continue to carry on his practice in the
normal way, personally entering into contracts with his
clients.
3 An architect must not divest himself of any of his professional responsibilities, or attempt to transfer any of them
to the company.
4 The operation of the company must not bring architects
into conflict with any of the principles of the Code.
5 A service company may own the office premises, office
furniture and equipment, giving the architect shares in the
company to the value of the purchase price of these assets
and leasing back to him the premises and supply of services
(including secretarial staff but not professional staff) at an
agreed rental.
6 The control and shares of the service company must be
vested in the professional partners and in no circumstances
may anyone in a proscribed occupation hold a share.
7 The service company may not act for any enterprise other
than a firm of which the architect is a principal.
8 Those architectural practices who have or wish to have
unlimited service companies employing architects and other
professional staff are required to notify the Registrar and to
forward to her a copy of the Memorandum and Articles of
Association showing, in particular, the objects of the company
and the names of the directors and shareholders, and each
individual case will be considered on its merits.
Any Company which is not acting in accordance with the
above rules must be regarded as a limited liability company,
and subject to Principle 2 of the Code of Professional
Conduct.*
It seems that a 'service company', being the owner of the
architect's office premises and equipment, may not for
example lease any part of those premises to, say, a quantity
surveyor or do dye-line printing for a neighbouring consultant.

Directors
3.07 The restrictions on persons who may be partners in an
architect's practice (para 2.01) apply also to directors of
companies set up by architects to provide services to their
practice.

Unlimited liability companies
3.08 The status of a member (shareholder) of an unlimited
company is broadly the same as that of a partner in a partnership; he is liable to an unlimited extent for debts of the
company. It is slightly easier for him to resign, for the
company does not end with the retirement of one member
if the others agree to the transfer of his shares (compare
para 2.14).

* ARCUK Annual Report 1975–6

3.09 An unlimited company may have up to 50 members.
Company business is transacted by its directors; not all
shareholders have to be directors, and vice-versa, but all
shareholders are liable for acts of the company.

3.10 If a firm is to be conducted entirely through an unlimited liability company, initial skill is necessary in drafting
the memorandum and articles of association to ensure that
they conform with the professional codes. Also, they must
enable those who would otherwise be the principals of a
partnership to have control over the disposal of the holdings
of retiring or deceased colleagues.

Limited liability companies
3.11 Although carrying on the practice of architecture in the
form of a limited liability company is totally contrary to the
professional codes (ARCUK Rule 2.4), architects may operate
a limited company as a service company subject to the
ARCUK rules, quoted above (para 3.06). Such a company
may carry on any activities not fundamental to architects'
professional operations; and it may have limited liability for
these. The company may own freehold property or leases,
cars, furniture and other equipment, and may perform
subsidiary functions such as printing, model making and
general administration. The liabilities of such a company in
contract and in tort are limited to the face value of the
members' shareholdings, but the usual reason for setting up
such companies is for financial benefit (para 3.03).

3.12 The liabilities so limited are separate from professional
liability. If a company car is involved in an accident as a
result of which the company is found liable for damages
which, even after insurance, exceed its assets, the shareholders would be personally liable for no more than the face
value of their shares. But if an architect, operating a service
company, incurs a liability to his client, the fact that some of
his assets are held by the company does not protect them.
He may have to realise the full, not face, value of his shares
in the company to meet his liabilities. (See also LEGAL
STUDY 15, para 2.14, 2.15).

Limited liability and overseas work
3.13 An architect is permitted to carry on practice through
the medium of a limited liability company in such foreign
countries as permit their own architect nationals to practice
in that way. Under a Practice Note published in September
1976 (LEGAL STUDY 15, para 2.16 *et seq*) the RIBA permits
architects to establish limited liability companies in the UK
to carry out work in those countries where such protection is
permitted provided that the control of the company is vested
in professional persons and provided also that the company
may only work on projects to be constructed outside the UK.
The Practice Note is precise and firm and should be consulted by any practice considering setting up such a company.

Group practices and consortia
3.14 Firms may come together to work in several forms of
association, whether for a single project or on a more permanent basis. This section is not concerned with the operational and management factors for and behind the choice of
form, only with the legal issues. Further guidance is given
in the RIBA *Handbook of architectural practice and management*
(1973 edition) and in the *Guide to group practice and consortia*
(RIBA 1965). The creation of any association needs to be
carefully checked with the professional indemnity insurers
of each party.

Loose groups
3.15 Associations in which firms or individuals group to pool knowledge and experience. Such a group does not need to be registered but some short constitution is desirable which clearly distinguishes it from a partnership (see para 2.04). In Company Law a more formal 'Memorandum and Articles of Association' is necessary and is of far greater significance because it must set out the most important provisions of the company's constitution, including the activities which the company may carry on and is accordingly of special concern to persons who deal with it.

Group practices
3.16 Individual private firms may be grouped for their mutual benefit and to give better service while each retains some independence:
1 Association of individual firms. The degree of association may vary considerably from simply sharing office accommodation, and facilities and expenses, or extending to a fully comprehensive system of mutual help. Beyond agreeing a division of overhead expenses they retain the profits of the individual firms and their normal responsibility to their respective clients. It may be permissible for the facilities shared to be organised as a 'service company' (para 3.06), but any proposal to do so should be checked with ARCUK.
2 Co-ordinated groups. For large jobs or extensive development projects it is not unusual for the work to be undertaken by several architectural firms with one of them appointed to co-ordinate the activities of the others. The co-ordinating firm is solely liable to the client but the individual firms are nevertheless liable to the co-ordinating firm for torts committed in their areas of activity.
3 Single project partnerships and group partnerships may be entered into on terms which are entirely a matter for individual agreement between the parties and are similar in law to any ordinary partnership.

Consortia
3.17 In law consortia are little different from group practices. The term normally implies the association of firms of different professional skills acting as one for carrying out projects jointly yet retaining their separate identities, and each with their own responsibility to the building owner. A consortium may be formed for the duration of a single contract or on a more regular and permanent basis.

Difficulties
3.18 Clearly any association of practices, whether permanent or temporary, must be very carefully planned. If firms are to merge completely, assets should be carefully assessed (including work in progress) and specific agreement is necessary on debts including liabilities relating to previous contracts. These could be significant if a pre-merger job became the subject of a claim for professional negligence.

Agreements
3.19 If the constituent firms are to preserve their identities and to continue to practice in their own right as well as on common projects, the form of agreement becomes more critical and more complex. A new firm (group or consortium partnership or company) should be created to contract with clients for common projects. The agreement which sets up the new firm must resolve how far member firms' assets are brought in, to what extent member firms are liable for liabilities of the group, and the degree of independence retained by each member to carry on its own activities. The RIBA's guide gives draft articles of association for various types of *grouping* but a solicitor should always be consulted.

4 Architects as employers and employees

4.01 Legal relationships between employer and employee are largely defined in common law (see LEGAL STUDY 1 paras 2.02 and 5.04) but increasingly such relationships are defined in statutes. The relationship of employer and employed (master and servant) is according to common law a voluntary relationship into which the parties may enter on terms laid down by themselves with limitations imposed by the general law of contract (LEGAL STUDY 1 para 3.01) and by a series of statutes which have since the '60s progressively defined the rights and duties of both employer and employee.

Vicarious liability
4.02 An employer is liable for contracts entered into by an employee on behalf of his firm, provided the employee acts or is seen to be acting as authorised agent of the firm. Employers are also liable for torts (but not crimes) committed by an employee in the course of his employment (see LEGAL STUDY 1 para 5.04). Even so, employees are responsible for exercising proper care in performing their duties.

Choice of employees
4.03 Vicarious liability makes judgement in choice of employees very important because bargaining between employer and prospective employee need not be characterised by special good faith (*uberrimae fidei*—which must obtain between partners) so employees are not bound to disclose their past (but they must not misrepresent it). It is curious, and perhaps unfortunate, that the rule of *caveat emptor* (let the buyer beware) still applies in this relationship. In practice the relationship requires mutual confidence if it is to succeed. An employer is not completely free to change his own staff. His choice is restricted by the Race Relations Act 1968 (see 4.04), the Sex Discrimination Act 1975 (para 4.11) and regulations imposing restrictions on employing people from abroad. His freedom to terminate the contract of any of his staff is constrained in other directions.

Race Relations Act
4.04 Under the Race Relations Act 1968, firms may not refuse to employ or deliberately omit to employ on grounds of race, colour, national or ethnic origin an applicant for available work for which he is qualified.

Contracts of employment
4.05 Given an offer of a job, acceptance and consideration (see LEGAL STUDY 1 para 3.03), a contract of employment comes into being between prospective employer and employee. It is important that when an offer is made, care is taken to see that both parties understand what is intended: apart from the bad effect on human relations, undesirable legal consequences may follow.

Verbal contracts
4.06 A verbal offer should be clear and concise; it should be made at the end of an interview. Vague possibilities should not be allowed to retain hazy importance. Such an offer should desirably include the salary to be paid, the period of notice and, if the work to be done is specific, identification of the task. If the job is dependent on some special factor—eg satisfactory references, registration as an architect or the employer's being appointed to a certain project—such qualifications of the offer should be made clear.

Written contracts
4.07 Though a verbal contract can be valid, it is sensible to follow a verbal offer as soon as possible by written confirma-

tion of the terms, and employees should write accepting or seeking further clarification if necessary. By committing everything to paper, confusion can be avoided later.

Breaking contracts before work starts
4.08 Should either side find the contract impossible or undesirable to fulfil before employment starts, the other party may expect to recover damages in the courts. The most an employee can expect to recover is the salary due for his period of notice. Even employees who have transferred their homes may have no additional redress. The risk was theirs and was one which they would have been prudent to defer until they were settled in new employment.

4.09 If an employee withdraws before starting work, in most cases, the employer is in a weaker position. Except for very senior posts or those which require specific skills or trades there is little he can do. There is little practical value in holding an unwilling man to working out his notice and the law is inclined to favour him as the weaker party. A senior man who fails to turn up can seriously damage a firm's ability to carry out a project on time, but since he could at any point have given his period of notice, damages may well be limited.

Conditions of service
4.10 An employer is not required to give his employees a written contract and he is largely free, within the constraints of the market to negotiate with his staff what conditions shall apply to them, for example the amount of holiday or their pension rights. But there are certain areas where the law does intervene.

Sex discrimination
4.11 Discrimination in Great Britain in employment on grounds of sex or marital status is now proscribed. Generally speaking, in choosing a new employee or deciding to fire an existing one, an employer must not let the facts of that person's sex or marital status influence him. Moreover, the terms offered for the same or broadly similar work at a single establishment and the opportunities for training and the use of facilities must not discriminate against women.
Exceptions are permitted where sex is a genuine occupational qualification primarily on the grounds of physiology or decency. The situation most likely for architects is a job in the UK which also requires duties to be performed in a country whose laws and customs are such that a woman could not effectively carry out the task.
Advertisements for job vacancies now need careful drafting to avoid their suggesting any discrimination.
Those who feel themselves discriminated against may complain to an industrial tribunal which, if it supports the complaint, may order the payment of compensation and may also recommend action to remove the discrimination. The Equal Opportunities Commission may serve a notice on an employer not to commit further unlawful acts.

Equal pay
4.12 Under the Equal Pay Act 1970, which came into force at the end of 1975, women are entitled, broadly speaking, to treatment equal to men in pay and other conditions of employment when they are employed on work of the same or broadly similar nature.

Pay and prices
4.13 In an increasingly stringent economic climate and in the attempt to overcome inflation successive governments have sought ways of controlling pay and prices. At the time of writing (1977), a series of measures, some exhortatory,

some with full statutory powers, have imposed restrictions on the employer's freedom to improve pay and benefit conditions for individuals or groups of employees. Because of the short life of these measures, it is not possible to predict what the requirements will be in the future but in the past they have affected architects and employers who, accordingly are strongly advised to watch the lay and technical press for announcements of new measures.

Prices
4.14 Architects' prices are the fees they charge to their clients. During the period of price restraint, it has been agreed by the professional bodies that the minimum fees prescribed by the RIBA Conditions of Engagement should be maxima (see LEGAL STUDY 17). To try to ensure that businesses do not make unreasonable profits during periods of price and pay restraint, there are requirements for firms of certain levels of sales or fee turnover to keep records and for larger firms to submit periodic returns of income, expenditure and profit to the Prices Commission. Firms, such as architects, which supply professional services are covered by the regulations. The Commission has power to instruct a firm to reduce its prices if its profits have risen above a certain historic level (reference level). It is not clear how architects may reduce their prices, ie fees, when the maintenance of those fees is an obligation under their professional codes for breach of which they may, under another statute, be struck off their professional register.

Notice
4.15 Minimum periods have been established by the Contracts of Employment Act 1972 and the Employment Protection Act 1972 (see paras 4.25 *et seq* and checklist 4).

Maternity
4.16 An employee may not be dismissed because of her pregnancy or any reason connected with it. If the pregnancy prevents her doing her normal job, she must be offered a suitable alternative if possible. If she stays at work until the eleventh week before the baby is due and has worked for her employer for at least two years, she will be entitled to maternity payment for the first six weeks of her absence. She will be entitled to resume her old job or a suitable alternative if she wishes to return to work not more than twenty-nine weeks after the birth provided that she told her employer that she wished to do so before she stopped work. An employee engaged to take the place of an absent pregnant employee should be told when taken on that the job is temporary and why. An employer may claim a full rebate of any proper maternity payment from the Maternity Fund.

Overseas workers
4.17 A person who is not a citizen of the EEC and who wishes to secure employment in the UK must normally have a work permit, although there are exceptions for certain categories of Commonwealth citizen. The permit can only be obtained by the employer who must satisfy the Department of Employment that he has made efforts to engage a suitable UK worker. Once the employee has entered the country on a permit, he may, provided he stays in the same type of employment, change his employer but each successive new employer will in turn have to apply for a permit. After four years in approved employment, a non-UK citizen may apply for the removal of any time limit associated with his permit. Rules for overseas citizens studying in the UK will generally allow them to take up periods of employment necessary for and associated with their studies.

Further information and forms for applying for permits may be obtained from employment offices or from the Overseas Labour Section of the Department of Employment.

Industrial relations
4.18 After much political debate, the Industrial Relations Act of 1971 was replaced by the Trade Union and Labour Relations Act of 1974. Major changes of principle dealt with the status of unions, their membership and the right to join or stay out of a union. These issues are too complex to deal with here but we may expect that architects, who already in the public service are acquainted with unions, will find themselves increasingly involved with them. After a short and very troubled life the National Industrial Relations Court has disappeared. Industrial Tribunals remain and are the place in which complaints from employees are eventually resolved. To try to prevent matters getting to that pitch the Advisory, Conciliation and Arbitration Service (ACAS) has been more formally established. As its name implies, it offers advice on industrial relations, provides a conciliation service and can arrange for arbitration.

4.19 The procedures for the recognition of unions are revised and an obligation is placed on employers to give certain kinds of information about the firm's affairs to recognised unions. The employee's right to belong to an independent trade union without interference from his employer is protected.

4.20 Amongst its other duties, the ACAS may publish codes of industrial relations practice. The original Code published under the 1971 Act is still in being and although it does not have the force of law, its observance will be taken into account 'if relevant' by a Tribunal in cases of alleged unfair employment practices.
Its main principles are:
that collective bargaining be freely conducted on behalf of employees and employers on the general interest of the country;
that there should be orderly procedures for the settlement of disputes;
that employees and employers should be able to associate freely in their own organisations which should be effective to regulate relations between them;
that employees should be free and secure, protected from unfair treatment at the hands of employers or anyone else.

4.21 Under the Code, both employers and employees are recognised as having responsibilities and the latter are reminded that theirs extend to their fellow employees, to the public and to their profession if they have one. The Code sets out employment policies, principles of communication and consultation, collective bargaining, employee representation, grievance and dispute procedures and disciplinary procedures.

4.22 It cannot be assumed that because a firm is a moderate-sized professional partnership and not a huge industrial combine, good relations will develop and persist without effort. The Code is valuable reading for all practices.

Statement of main terms of employment
4.23 Although a written contract is not necessary, the Contracts of Employment Act 1972 requires that certain principal terms of the engagement be stated in writing. With the exceptions noted in checklist 4, employers must provide all employees who work for sixteen hours or more a week with a written statement not later than thirteen weeks after the beginning of the employment which must include the items given in checklist 4. The statement may refer the employee to a document which contains all the required information and which is posted or available in a place where the employee has reasonable opportunities for reading it in the course of his employment. It is to be expected that the usual procedure for architects to adopt would be to complete a form of contract as between employer and employee. Suitable forms are published by law stationers for this purpose. The RIBA has had it in mind to publish a form particularly appropriate for salaried architects but this has not yet appeared.
If a contract is used instead of the written statement it must include all the required information, as well as the note on disciplinary rules and grievance procedure even though this is not strictly a contract matter.

4.24 The Employment Protection Act has imposed or is about to impose certain other obligations on employers which even though not written into the contract must be met:
1 If an employer becomes insolvent owing arrears of salary to his employees, they may recover these, subject to certain maxima.
2 An employee who is laid off or put on short time because his employer cannot provide him with work is entitled to a guaranteed payment for a limited period.
3 An employee suspended on statutory medical grounds is entitled to payment for the period of suspension up to a maximum of twenty-six weeks. These grounds are specific industrial hazards which are unlikely in the normal event to affect an architect.
4 An employee is entitled to time off for certain trade union activities and for public duties such as being a JP or a local councillor.
5 All employees, subject to the normal time qualifications, must be given for each pay period a pay statement itemising principally: gross pay, the amounts and purpose of each fixed and variable deduction, and net pay.

Termination and dismissal
4.25 When a person's employment comes to an end, the minimum period of notice to which they are entitled is laid down by the Contracts of Employment Act as amended by the Employment Protection Act 1975 (see checklist 4). This period of notice is not necessarily the same as the period of payment. It is open to the employer and employee to agree longer periods of notice than the statutory minima and to record these in the contract. Notice, even the statutory period, may be dispensed with in grave circumstances, or if both parties waive their rights.

Summary dismissal
4.26 For a grave offence the employer may dismiss an employee on the spot and without notice. Deliberately setting fire to the office or dipping into the cash box is a possible example.

Other dismissal
4.27 Apart from such offences an employer must give the appropriate notice. An employee is then entitled to ask for a written statement of the reason for his dismissal. The employer has to show that the reason was: (*a*) redundancy; (*b*) the employee's conduct; (*c*) his inability or lack of qualifications to do the job for which he was employed; (*d*) statutory unfitness; or some other substantial reason. If the employer cannot give one of these reasons or if the employee considers the reason untrue or inadequate, then he may complain to a tribunal that he has been unfairly dismissed. An employer will be prudent, if he is considering

dismissing someone, to give him a written warning first and a chance to amend his ways. Otherwise he may be on the uncomfortable and possibly costly road to defending a claim in front of a tribunal, as a result of which he may be required to re-engage or re-instate the employee or, failing that, to make payments which could run into thousands of pounds.

Fixed-term contracts
4.28 If a contract is for a fixed term of two years or more, the employee is still entitled to renewal at the end of the term, provided the job still exists, unless he has agreed in writing with his employer to waive his right.

Redundancy
4.29 Jobs may end without breach of contract and without either side wishing it. Work may simply have run out either for the firm as a whole or for the particular skill of an employee. This is popularly known as redundancy, although since 1965 when the Redundancy Payments Act came into force, redundancy has a specific meaning.

4.30 An employer has always been able to cushion such blows by giving an extended period of notice with or without some form of payment, not as compensation due for loss but as a moral gesture. Now precise rules are established by statute which define redundancy, its amount and those who are entitled to receive payments. There are further rules which establish the procedure for handling redundancies.

4.31 Broadly, employees under 65 (60 for women) who work more than 21 hours a week* and have worked continuously for the same employer for more than two years after age 18 are entitled to a lump-sum compensation known as redundancy payment if they are dismissed because their employer's need for their sort of work at their normal place of employment has lessened or disappeared or if the employer has gone out of business. If the employer offers other suitable work in his business and the employee refuses, he may not be entitled to payment. The amount of payment is determined by length of service, age and salary of the employee and is normally tax-free. Disputes about settlement are settled by industrial tribunals. Redundancy payments are for the benefit of employed persons: they are not payable to self-employed persons, to 'free-lance' agency workers or, obviously, to partners. If an employee, while under notice of redundancy, is made an offer to continue work with his employer on his previous terms, he will not be entitled to a redundancy payment unless he has good grounds for not accepting the offer. If he is made an offer to continue work on different terms or at a different place, he is allowed a trial period to see if it will work out. If in that period he decides that the job is not suitable he may refuse it and still be entitled to a redundancy payment. Entitlement to payment is not affected if the redundant employee, with the approval of his employer, leaves before the contractual period of the notice has expired.

Working overseas
4.32 Employees who normally work in the UK will not find their entitlement affected if they are temporarily working abroad when they receive notice. Employees whose contracts are for work normally outside the UK will not be entitled to redundancy payment unless they are in the UK at their employer's requirement when they receive notice.
Periods of work overseas with the same employer for which social security contributions are not payable, ie usually after the first twelve months continuous service abroad, are not

* This may be reduced shortly to 16 hours a week

reckonable as weeks of service for the calculation of a redundancy payment but will not break the continuity of the employee's service.

Redundancy and fixed-term contracts
4.33 Even if a contract of employment is for a fixed term, employees may be entitled to redundancy payments if they are dismissed either during the course of their contract or at the end of it, if the other conditions of redundancy are satisfied. If the employer does not intend to re-engage at the end of the term, the contract must include a specific provision that there will be no entitlement to redundancy payment. Such a provision does not affect the employee's rights to a redundancy payment if the contract has to be ended before the end of the term.

Employers' rebates
4.34 An employer who properly makes a redundancy payment is entitled to claim a rebate from the redundancy fund of half the payment made.

Handling redundancy
4.35 If an employer recognises an independent trade union for a certain type of work, he is obliged to consult it about his proposals for redundancy in that field whether or not the persons affected are members of the union and whatever their length of service. He will have to give the union specified information about the situation and will have to reply to representations made by it.

An employer also has to give advance warning to the Department of Employment about significant redundancies. The periods laid down are the same as those for consultation with a union: 10–99 redundancies at one place of work over a period of 30 days or less, 60 days advance warning; 100 or more redundancies over a period of 90 days or less, 90 days advance warning.

Other conditions
4.36 Although not required by law, it is wise to make clear in the contract the situation on certain other conditions.

Confidential information
4.37 In the course of employment, employees gain information about their employer's business the disclosure of which could be damaging to the employer. Common law generally assumes that employees may not disclose such information either during the course of employment or subsequently. However, there are difficulties in leaving this to implication in the contract and it is preferable to include a specific provision to prevent such information being disclosed.

4.38 No such conditions may be implied to prevent an ex-employee setting up in practice. Any conditions written into the contract to prevent this must be explicit and carefully drafted as, if they are unreasonable, they may be set aside by the courts. Reasonable conditions might prevent an architect dealing with clients of his previous employer or they could restrict his activities in time and place.

Employment and Codes of Conduct
4.39 The 1976 Codes of Professional Conduct include at Rule 2.5 an architect's code of employment. It is prudent to cover some of these matters, at least 2.5.5, in regard to spare-time practice, in the contract of engagement. The Practice Note published in the RIBA *Journal* of June 1963 is still relevant as is its advice that without specific restriction against spare-time practice in a person's contract such

practice is impliedly permitted (see LEGAL STUDY 15, RIBA Notes—Principle 2).

References

4.40 Employers are frequently asked to provide references for past and present employees. If this system is to have any meaning, an employer must be able to be honest and fair without fear. Even if a reference is derogatory, a referee is not liable for defamation provided that what he says is true and his motive in writing it was exercise of his duty to society. But if his motive was improper, malicious for instance, then he could be liable and could be sued for libel. An employer often makes great efforts to help his staff when giving references; he must be careful for if he exaggerates a man's abilities and acts recklessly, he may well find himself liable for deceit to the person seeking the reference; references are subject to the Misrepresentation Act (see LEGAL STUDY 1 para 3.10).

5 Premises and persons

5.01 Employers have a statutory obligation to provide employees with safe and decent working conditions. For office workers these are set out in the Offices, Shops and Railway Premises Act 1963, and regulations made under it.

5.02 Under the Act, architects' offices and the activities normally associated with them count as office premises. Some activities such as model making (if they are carried on in distinct parts of the premises and to sufficient extent) might be within the scope of the Factories Acts; factory inspectors should be consulted.

Application to act

5.03 Office premises are outside the Act if they are occupied only by self-employed people, or if only the employees are immediate relatives of the occupier, or if all employees work less than 21 hours on the premises. Thus an architect in practice by himself with a part-time typist coming in a couple of hours a day is not affected, but if he employs a full-time assistant, even if he works at home, the part of his house used as an office is governed by the Act. If the premises are only used temporarily (for less than six weeks) they are not affected. Premises which fall within the scope of the Act must be registered in the prescribed way; for private practice this is normally through the local authority.

5.04 Architects in public offices or in industry are not normally responsible for registering their offices; if they are, they must usually register through local factory inspectors.

5.05 To ensure that the Act is respected, inspectors appointed by the enforcing authority have the power to enter premises to which the Act applies. They may inspect them, question anyone or ask to see relevant certificates or notices. They should have evidence of their authority and it is good practice to ask to see this before taking anyone round. After an inspection, a report should be issued explaining what must be done to comply with the Act. Non-compliance can result in a fine but there is provision for appeal through the courts.

5.06 The Act and regulations made under it cover a wide variety of conditions which cannot be dealt with here in detail. They include the amount of space to be provided for each person on the premises, cleanliness, heating, ventilation and lighting, provision of washing and sanitary facilities and of drinking water, facilities for storing outdoor clothing, seating, floor safety, stairs and machinery and the provision

of first aid equipment; in offices of more than 150 persons, a person trained in first aid is required.

Accidents

5.07 Employers are required to notify the enforcing authority of accidents on the premises which cause the death, or the disablement for more than three days, of a person employed to work on the premises. A record must be kept of all accidents as they occur. In any case this is useful as a check against the possibility of persons making claims for accidents which did not happen on office premises (see also para 5.09).

Employee's right to information

5.08 Because the Act is primarily for the benefit of employees and because some employees are forgetful or unscrupulous, the occupier is obliged to give his employees information about the Act either by posting up an abstract in a sufficiently prominent place or by giving them an explanatory booklet.

Division of responsibility

5.09 One of the potentially confusing aspects of the Act is the division of responsibility between owner and occupier, particularly in multi-occupied buildings. The employer, if not the occupier (eg a window cleaner's boss), is responsible for notifying the occupier of accidents to his employees and for notifying his own employees of the provisions of the Act.

Single occupation
5.10 An employer who occupies a whole building is responsible for ensuring that all provisions of the Act are met.

Multi-occupation
5.11 When a building is in multi-occupation responsibility is divided:
The owner is responsible for cleaning, lighting and safety of the common parts, washing and sanitary facilities, fire alarms and signposting and keeping free from obstruction all exits and means of escape in the building as a whole. Occupiers are responsible for all other provisions of the Act within the parts of the building that they occupy.

Occupier's liability

5.12 An occupier has a duty of care to all lawful entrants on his premises. He must take all reasonable practical steps to make his premises safe for his visitors and to protect all hazards or give sufficient warning of them although visiting workpeople such as window-cleaners are responsible for their own safe working methods. If it is foreseeable that persons unlikely to be able to read warnings (eg children, the blind) may seek to get into hazardous areas, the protection must be adequate to keep them out.
If a landlord has tenants to whom he has a repairing obligation, and this can obviously include architects who sub-let part of their office, it is he, the landlord, who has a responsibility to anyone who could be affected by his failure to keep the premises properly maintained.
It is also wise to bear in mind that responsibility for injury or damage arising from defects caused by improper maintenance, or indeed construction, is not avoided by the disposal of the premises to another party. This clearly concerns architects both as designers and as owners or occupiers of premises.
Since 1963 the office employer, including the architect, has had statutory responsibilities to provide a minimally satisfactory working environment for his employees (the Offices, Shops and Railway Premises Act). In line with an intensive phase of employee-centred legislation, the accent was shifted from premises to people with the Health and Safety

at Work Act 1974. This act has many implications for architects as professional designers of buildings: here we are only concerned with the architect as employer, employee and occupier of premises.

Health and Safety at Work Act 1974

5.13 This act is directed not at occupiers of premises but at people who work, employers, employees, self-employed persons, their responsibilities to each other and to third parties who may be affected by the work process or its results.

The employer now must maintain safe systems of work and keep his plant and premises in safe condition; he must give adequate instruction, training and supervision for the purposes of safety to those who work for him. Unless he employs fewer than five people he must prepare a written statement of his business's safety policies, organisation and arrangements and make it known to his employees; in step with the trend to greater consultation at work, he may be required to set up means whereby his safety measures may be explained and discussed.

The policy statement may be a simple letter reminding employees of the Act and the responsibilities of employers and employees under it, and naming the persons to whom safety duties are delegated. A safety programme will be a more detailed document which should include, inter alia, reminders on keeping stairways and corridors clear of obstruction, the marking and guarding of temporary hazards, use of machinery, fire procedures, accidents, first aid.

The employee in his turn has a duty to exercise reasonable care to himself and his fellow employees and to co-operate with his employer in carrying out statutory requirements.

Enforcement

5.14 To ensure that the law is respected, inspectors appointed by the enforcing authority have the power to enter premises to which the Act applies. They may inspect them, question anyone or ask to see relevant certificates or notices. They should have evidence of their authority and it is good practice to ask to see this before taking anyone round. After an inspection, a report should be issued explaining what must be done to comply with the Act. Non-compliance can result in a fine but there is provision for appeal through the courts.

5.15 Under the Health and Safety at Work Act, inspectors have the power to make 'improvement' notices under which the offending practice must cease or the deficiency must be remedied within a certain period. More fearsomely, they also have a power to issue a 'stop' notice under which the practice must cease or the premises not be used until their requirements have been met. A further indication of the gravity with which these new offences are now regarded is that, whereas previously if a person suffered as a result of an employer's or occupier's action, he could recover his damage under civil law, such an offence under this Act is now a crime. The offender may be liable to a fine even though no one has suffered damage. It is helpful to remember that, although insurance may be taken out against the possibility of damages being awarded against you, you may not use insurance to protect yourself against the results, for example fines, of your criminal acts.

Fire certificates

5.16 The Fire Precautions Act 1971 took over the fire provisions of the Offices, Shops and Railway Premises Act 1963 in January 1977. A fire certificate must be obtained from the enforcing authority. For private practices this is normally the local fire authority and for public bodies, the factory inspectorate. For a certificate to be granted, requirements on means of escape, keeping them clear and properly signposted, firefighting equipment, fire alarm systems and arrangements for fire drills have to be satisfied. A fire certificate is not required for small firms in their own premises. One is required for an office where more than 20 people are employed at one time, where more than 10 people are employed other than on the ground floor or where, in a multi-occupied building, either of these numbers is exceeded in total. (See LEGAL STUDY 13 for construction regulations requirements.)

5.17 If after a certificate has been issued, alterations are made to the premises which may significantly affect the requirements of that certificate, the issuing authority should be advised. The authority has continuing powers of inspection to see whether the premises are being kept in the original standard and whether changes have been made which render those standards inadequate.

6 Insurance

6.01 A practice protects itself by insurance against financial risks. Some of these are ordinary risks such as fire, some are eventualities which a firm is not obliged to cover, but which, as a good employer, it may wish to provide for, such as prolonged sickness of a member of staff. But there are cases when a firm is obliged in law to cover damage caused to other persons. Insurances which cover all these risks, except professional indemnity (see LEGAL STUDIES 15 and 16), are outlined below.

Public liability

6.02 An owner or lessee of premises, or someone carrying on a business in premises, may be legally liable for personal injury or damage to property of third parties caused by his negligence or that of his staff (see para 4.02 and LEGAL STUDY 1 para 5.04).

6.03 Since several people may be involved in a single incident, and the level of damages may be very high, it is important for cover to be:
1 Appropriate to status—owner, lessee or occupier.
2 Extended to cover principals' and employees' actions, not only on the premises, but anywhere while on business.
3 Extended to cover abroad if principals or employees are liable to be abroad on business.

Employer's liability

6.04 An employer is legally liable for personal injury caused to an employee in the course of his employment by the employer's negligence or that of another member of staff. It is important to provide cover:
1 For injuries during employment whether occasioned on or off the employer's premises.
2 For injuries overseas if employees are liable to be abroad on business.

Employer's Liability Act 1969

The Employer's Liability (Compulsory Insurance) Act 1969, and the Statutory Instrument (1971 No 1117) making General Regulations which came into operation on 1st January 1972, requires that every employer who carries on business in Great Britain shall maintain insurance under approved policies with authorised insurers against liability for bodily injury or disease sustained by employees and arising out of and in the course of their employment in that business. The size of the business is immaterial: a single clerical or technical assistant qualifies whether full-time or only part-time. The Act also provides for employees not ordinarily resident but who may be temporarily in Great Britain in the course of employment for a continuous period of not less than 14 days in the same way as it applies to all employees normally resident. The Act does not apply to Northern Ireland. The maximum penalty for non-compliance is a fine of up to £200 for any day on which the Employer is not insured. As from the 1st January 1973, under Sections 6 and 7 of the General Regulations 1971, there are further obligations upon the Employer to display copies of the Insurance Certificate at the place or places of business for the information of his employees.

Motor vehicles
6.05 There are two points to note about car insurance:
1 Carrying third party cover is a legal requirement. Cover may be invalidated if a car is used for purposes not covered by the policy. Thus it is important to establish that cars owned and operated by a firm are covered for business use and for carrying normal professional impedimenta and that cars owned by employers and used by them in their duties are covered for occasional business use.
2 If staff use their own cars on the firm's business, their cover must be adequate, particularly in respect of cover for fellow employees. Their policies should also be checked to ensure that they include a third party indemnity in favour of the employer, otherwise if a chain results from an incident while the car is used on the firm's business, insurers may repudiate liability.

7 Differences between English and Scots law partnerships

7.01 The Partnership Act 1890, with the Registration of Business Names Acts 1916 and the Limited Partnership Act 1907, all of which are referred to earlier, apply equally to Scottish partnerships. There is, however, an important difference between English and Scottish law regarding the meaning of the word 'firm'.

7.02 As explained in para 2.08, in England a partnership is a collection of individuals and not a corporate body, but in Scotland a partnership is a legal persona, distinct in its own right from the partners of which it is composed. In the event of bankruptcy, therefore, the creditors of individual partners do not have a claim on the estate of the firm, although the creditors of the firm qualify for dividends from the estate of individual partners. In England, however, the firm's creditors have a claim only on the firm's estate and the partners' creditors on their private estates, each to the exclusion of the other.

7.03 The difference between the Laws of Scotland and England result in the following features in Scotland:
1 A partnership itself owns the funds of the partnership and the partners are not joint owners of partnership funds (though the tax position of a Scottish partnership is exactly the same as for an English one—para 3.03).
2 A firm is the principal debtor in debts owed by the partnership, although the debts must in the first place be constituted against the firm.
3 A partner may sue or be sued by a firm and a firm may be either a debtor or creditor to any of its partners.
4 A firm can be sequestrated* without any of the partners themselves being sequestrated.

*Sequestration: appropriation of income of a property (or firm) to satisfy claims against the owners.

5 When a partner retires or when a partner joins the firm, the existing partnership comes to an end and a new one is created unless the partnership agreement itself provides to the contrary. The result is that a new partner is not liable for the debts of the firm incurred before his admission and a retiring partner is on the other hand liable for the debts of the firm up to the date of his retirement (see para 2.13).

Associates
7.04 Mention is made in para 2.20 of the practice of creating 'associates' from senior staff. At present this is more common in England than Scotland and is almost unknown in Scotland outside architectural firms. While the additional status thus afforded to the persons concerned may be desirable, great care should be taken to define the powers of associates and to avoid any possibility of the public being misled into thinking they are partners.

Other branches of law
7.05 Paras 4 and 5 deal with the rights and responsibilities of the architect as employer and employee and discuss the effect of the Offices, Shops and Railway Premises Act 1963 and the Health and Safety at Work Act 1974. The remarks apply equally to architects practising in Scotland, to which statutes mentioned also apply.

Checklist 1: Items to be considered when drawing up deed of partnership

Note: The terms of a partnership agreement, like any other contract, may be widely varied by mutual consent of the parties. Where no provision is made those of The Partnership Act 1890 will apply. The figures in brackets (   ) refer to relevant clauses in that Act.

Name of parties to the Deed (partners)

Name of firm (4(1)).	(a) If not in names of all partners, must be as 'registered' under s.1 of the Registration of Business Names Act 1916. (b) Nothing to suggest that it is a Limited Company. (See para 2.06).
Places of Business	
Commencement and Duration	Date Agreement is to start and whether to continue for a fixed term of years or for a single project. Provisions for continuation (27).
Provision of Capital	Amount. Proportion to be contributed by each partner. Distinctions between what is: (a) not partnership capital—a premium. and (b) capital which is partnership property—contribution to working capital. Capital should be expressed in money terms. Any special agreement for interest on capital (24(3)) and (4). Valuation and repayments on death etc: (42 & 43). Rules for settlement for accounts after dissolution (44).
Property	What (if any) partners bring to the firm (including contracts) (20–22 & 24). What (a) belongs to firm as a whole (b) as co-owners but not partnership property (c) individual ownership for use in the partnership business (24).
Mutual rights and duties	If these are to be differentiated then specify them, eg times spent on holidays, work brought into firm etc.
Miscellaneous earnings	For example, lectures, journalistic work, various honoraria . . . whether to be paid into firm.
Profits and losses	Basis for division among partners; if not equally then specify (24(1)). Any reservations, eg about guaranteed minimum share of profits in any individual case.
Banking and Accountants	Arrangements for signing cheques, presentation of audited accounts etc (28).
Employment of 'locum tenens'	Authority for, circumstances and terms.
Constitution of firm	Provisions for changes (36).
Retirement at will	Age, fixed term or partnership for life, notice of retirement etc. Arrangements for consultants and for payments during retirement.
Dissolution	Any special circumstances. (See para 2.14 and checklist 3).
Restrictions on practice	Any covenant in respect of restraint of practising in competition (must be reasonable to interests of parties and public). Areas of operation.
Insurances	Various, including liability of surviving partners for dead partners' share in firm.
Arbitration	Method, number of arbitrators etc.

Checklist 2: Liability for civil cases under Partnership Act

Debts and obligations of firm	Jointly in absence of agreement to the contrary (5–13 inclusive).
Torts, including negligence	Jointly and severally.
Contracts	Jointly and severally—if partners have expressly agreed to be so liable. Note: a deceased partner's estate may be severally liable to the prior payments of his private debts.

Checklist 3: Grounds for dissolution of partnership

A. By agreement of parties

(a) Agreement per deed	End of fixed term or of single project.
(b) By expiration, or notice (32)	If for undefined time—any partner giving notice of intention (32 (c)).
(c) Illness	Special provisions in Deed (to avoid need to apply to Courts (35)). Note: Expulsion. No majority of partners can expel unless express agreement in Deed (25). There can be no implied consent to expel.

B. By operation of law and courts

Death and bankruptcy	Subject to express agreement partnership is dissolved as regards *all* by death or bankruptcy of *any* partner (33).
Illegality	Any event making it illegal to carry on business of firm.

If partner insane

If partner incapable of carrying on his part of Agreement

If partner guilty of conduct prejudicial to the interests of the firm

If partner wilfully and persistently breaches the Agreement or if his conduct is such that the others can no longer carry on business with him

If firm can only carry on at a loss

If, in the opinion of the Courts, it is just and equitable that the firm should be dissolved

Checklist 4: Information to be given to employees under Contracts of Employment Act 1972

1 *Information to be given in written statement*

Names of both parties, employer and employee

Date on which employment began

Title or description of job

Scale or rate of pay and method of calculation

Intervals at which payment is made

Hours of work

Holidays, holiday pay and accrual

Conditions of absence due to sickness or injury

Sick pay provisions

Pension rights if any

Period of notice. Minimum periods are:
    Employer to employee
        Continuous employment of 4 weeks or more: one week
        Continuous employment of 2 years or more: two weeks
        For each additional complete year, add one week's notice
            to a maximum of 12 weeks
    Employee to employer
        Continuous employment of 4 weeks or more: one week

Disciplinary rules and grievance procedure

Model written statements are given in the Guide to the Act. It is intended that after April 1968, the statement will also have to record whether or not a contracting-out certificate is in force for the particular employment. This relates to the new social security pension provisions and employers' own schemes.

Notice of changes in terms of employment

Section 5 of the Contracts of Employment Act requires that if after the date to which the statement relating to the employee's particulars of terms of employment there is a change of the terms the employer shall, not more than one month after the change, inform the employee of the nature of that change in a further written statement.

2 *Persons covered by the Act*

All persons working 16 hours a week for one employer or for 8 hours a week if they have worked for the same employer for five years or more.

3 *Persons excluded from the provisions of the Act*

The categories most likely to concern architects are:

Persons who normally work abroad

Fixed-term contracts

Employments not expected to last for more than 12 weeks

Husband or wife of the employer

References

RIBA Guide to group practice and consortia

DRAKE, C. D. Labour law. 2nd Edition. London, 1973, Sweet & Maxwell

STEWART-PEARSON, N., ed. Legal problems of employment. London, 1976, The Industrial Society

PORTER, R. Guide to employment conditions. London, 1976, George Godwin

PATERSON, P. and ARMSTRONG, M. An employer's guide to equal pay. London, 1972 (Supplement 1975), Kogan Page

ROBERTSON, B. J. and M. D., An employer's guide to the Employment Protection Act 1975. London, 1975, Kogan Page

ARSCOTT, P. and ARMSTRONG, M. An employer's guide to health and safety management. London, 1976, Kogan Page. Offices, shops and Railway Premises Act 1963. A general guide. 2nd edition. 1971, HMSO

EQUAL OPPORTUNITIES COMMISSION. Equal pay opportunities: (a) A guide for employers, (b) A guide for employees. London

DEPARTMENT OF THE ENVIRONMENT Industrial relations code of practice. 1972 (reprinted 1976), HMSO

DEPARTMENT OF EMPLOYMENT Contracts of Employment Act 1972: A guide to the Act incorporating changes made by the Employment Protection Act 1975. 1976

DEPARTMENT OF EMPLOYMENT The Employment Protection Act 1975. A series of guides

DEPARTMENT OF EMPLOYMENT Redundancy Payments. 10th revision. 1976, HMSO

DEPARTMENT OF EMPLOYMENT The Employment Protection Act 1975. Provisions for handling redundancy. 1976, HMSO

DEPARTMENT OF EMPLOYMENT Overseas workers. Employment of overseas workers in Great Britain. Leaflet OW, 1976

Acknowledgements

Illustrations are by courtesy of the RIBA and the Mary Evans Picture Library.

AJ Legal Handbook

Section 3
Building contracts

Legal study 4

The standard form of contract

This study discusses the standard form of contract and comments on important clauses, describing some of the more difficult problems which arise when the contract is used. Scottish readers should read LEGAL STUDY 5 *in conjunction with this article*

1 Meaning of terms

1.01 The 'Standard Form of Building Contract', usually abbreviated hereafter to 'the standard form', refers to the latest edition of the document formerly known as 'the RIBA Form'. In 1909, the form was agreed between the RIBA and the precursor of the NFBTE. In 1931, the Joint Contracts Tribunal, then consisting of the RIBA and NFBTE was set up to publish, and when necessary amend, the contract. Since then, the RICS, the major local authority associations, the Scottish Building Contracts Committee, the two principal organisations representing specialist sub-contractors and the Association of Consulting Engineers have been invited to join the Tribunal. Two members of the CBI attend meetings of the Tribunal but as observers only.
Since 1931, the Tribunal has published new editions of the contract in 1939, 1950, 1957 and 1963 and at even more frequent intervals amended and revised versions. The version referred to is the 1963 edition (July 1977 Revision). It is a long and elaborate document and is to be distinguished from the shorter form issued for small building works and from the special 'fixed-fee' version. Neither the shorter form nor the fixed fee version is discussed (but see Supplement to this study).

1.02 There are six variants of the standard form as follows:
1 Form for use by local authorities where quantities form part of the contract.
2 As variant 1 where quantities do not form part of the contract.
3 Form for private use where quantities form part of the contract.
4 As variant 3 where quantities do not form part of the contract.
5 Form for use by local authorities for contract with approximate quantities.
6 Form for private use with approximate quantities.

2 Nature of the standard form

2.01 Each of the variants creates a lump sum contract, similar in essence to an agreement, say, to reglaze a window for £5. But under the standard form the lump sum is subject to adjustment in many carefully defined circumstances and there are elaborate and detailed conditions regulating the rights of the employer and the contractor. Despite its length the document does not deal with certain important matters, for example, standards of workmanship or materials and responsibility for nominated subcontractors; it then becomes necessary to gather the rights of the parties from the general law and certain decided cases.

2.02 Because the standard form takes effect by agreement and not by statute it can be amended in any way the parties choose; but care should be taken when attempting any amendment lest unintended ambiguities and inconsistencies are introduced. Further, any amendment to be effective must be in or referred to in the document itself and not merely in the contract bills (or specification in the without quantities variants). In the case of *Gleesons v Hillingdon* (1970) the conditions were not amended and in the appendix completion was stated to be 24 months after possession. The contract bills provided for completion in stages from 12 to 24 months. It was held that, having regard to clause 12(1), the bills must be ignored so that liquidated damages were not recoverable before 24 months. (See also para 16.05.)

2.03 The six variants of the form do not differ in principle, but the description of the contract work is very exact where quantities form part of the contract (variants 1 and 3), and may be less exact where they do not (variants 2 and 4). Variants 5 and 6 are 'remeasurement contracts', first issued by the Joint Contracts Tribunal in October 1975 (see para 16.04). The forms for the use of local authorities do not differ in substance from the forms for private use but contain provisions necessary to accord with local government law and practice.

3 Nature of the commentary

3.01 The object of the commentary is to provide an introduction to the form and a discussion of some of the more important problems which arise with its use. A copy of each clause of variant 1 is printed above the relevant section of the commentary. The principal differences between the variants are indicated in the commentary. In general in the without quantities variant 'specification' should be read for 'contract bills'. Reference to clauses are to the conditions of contract unless the text indicates that the articles of agreement are referred to. A very brief statement of the subject matter of long clauses is often given but there is no summary or paraphrase as such. The commentary is in part derived from passages in the author's book *Building Contracts* (fourth edition) to which further reference can be made, particularly for the law of contract generally.

4 The articles of agreement

4.01 This part of the form names the parties, architect, quantity surveyor, records certain matters in the recitals (beginning 'WHEREAS') and in clauses 1 and 2 of the articles sets out in summary form the agreement between the parties.

more to the advantage of the employer than the contractor for the contract to be under seal.

5 Clause 1: Contractor's obligations

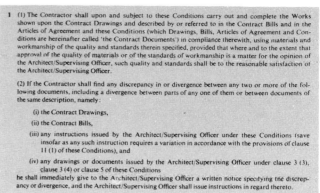

1 (1) The Contractor shall upon and subject to these Conditions carry out and complete the Works shown upon the Contract Drawings and described by or referred to in the Contract Bills and in the Articles of Agreement and these Conditions (which Drawings, Bills, Articles of Agreement and Conditions are hereinafter called 'the Contract Documents') in compliance therewith, using materials and workmanship of the quality and standards therein specified, provided that where and to the extent that approval of the quality of materials or of the standards of workmanship is a matter for the opinion of the Architect/Supervising Officer, such quality and standards shall be to the reasonable satisfaction of the Architect/Supervising Officer.

(2) If the Contractor shall find any discrepancy in or divergence between any two or more of the following documents, including a divergence between parts of any one of them or between documents of the same description, namely:

    (i) the Contract Drawings,

    (ii) the Contract Bills,

    (iii) any instructions issued by the Architect/Supervising Officer under these Conditions (save insofar as any such instruction requires a variation in accordance with the provisions of clause 11 (1) of these Conditions), and

    (iv) any drawings or documents issued by the Architect/Supervising Officer under clause 3 (3), clause 3 (4) or clause 5 of these Conditions

he shall immediately give to the Architect/Supervising Officer a written notice specifying the discrepancy or divergence, and the Architect/Supervising Officer shall issue instructions in regard thereto.

5.01 The contractor has to carry out and complete the contract works but he is both entitled to the benefit of the conditions and subject to the obligations which they impose upon him.

The position of the architect
5.02 He is the employer's agent with authority to exercise those powers which the contract gives him (see further para 15.05). As such agent he is entitled to and has a duty to protect the employer's interests. But because of the grave disadvantages suffered by the contractor if the architect fails to certify properly or otherwise exercise in a proper manner duties given to him by the contract, the courts have for long recognised that the intention of the contract is to place the architect to some extent in an independent position. He has to act fairly and professionally. This does not mean that he has a duty or right to dispense palm tree justice to the parties. He must at all times seek to perform as exactly as possible his duties under the contract. Thus, for example, it is wrong to permit a contractor to carry out work to a standard lower than that required by the contract because the architect discovers that the contractor has tendered low; it is also wrong to insist on a standard of work higher than the contract standard because the employer demands it. Architects are reminded that quite apart from what the courts have explained as their role under the building contract, Rule 1.4 of the RIBA Code of Professional Conduct requires all members and students of the RIBA to act impartially in all matters of dispute between the building owner and the contractor and to interpret the conditions of the building contract with entire fairness as between the parties. (See LEGAL STUDY 15 para 2.07.) This duty to act fairly is often extremely difficult for a client to appreciate. If necessary it must be pointed out to him that the House of Lords have recently affirmed that this is the basis upon which contractors tender for a contract when the standard form is to be used.

5.03 It is sometimes thought that the architect must not consult with the employer on matters within the sphere of his independent duty. This is not so. He is entitled to consult with the employer, and if the employer makes representations as to such matters as the standard of work he should consider them. But when the architect comes to make his decision then he should make up his own mind, doing his best to decide what the parties must have intended according to the contract documents and circumstances obtaining at the time of entering into the contract. He should then certify or give his decision accordingly whether or not he thinks it will

---

Articles of Agreement

made the...day of...19

BETWEEN

of (or whose registered office is situate at)

(hereinafter called 'the Employer') of the one part and

of (or whose registered office is situate at)

(hereinafter called 'the Contractor') of the other part. WHEREAS the Employer is desirous of*

(hereinafter called 'the Works') at

and has caused Drawings and Bills of Quantities showing and describing the work to be done to be prepared by or under the direction of

of...

....his Architect

*State nature of intended Works.

AND WHEREAS the Contractor has supplied the Employer with a fully priced copy of the said Bills of Quantities (which copy is hereinafter referred to as 'the Contract Bills') AND WHEREAS the said Drawings numbered...to...inclusive (hereinafter referred to as 'the Contract Drawings') and the Contract Bills have been signed by or on behalf of the parties hereto:

NOW IT IS HEREBY AGREED AS FOLLOWS:

1 For the consideration hereinafter mentioned the Contractor will upon and subject to the Conditions annexed hereto carry out and complete the Works shown upon the Contract Drawings and described by or referred to in the Contract Bills and in the said Conditions.

2 The Employer will pay to the Contractor the sum of...

(£   ) (hereinafter referred to as 'the Contract Sum') or such other sum as shall become payable hereunder at the times and in the manner specified in the said Conditions.

††3 [A] The term 'the Architect' in the said Conditions shall mean the said...of...

in the event of his death or ceasing to be the Architect for the purpose of this Contract, such, other person as the Employer shall nominate for that purpose, *not being a person to whom the Contractor shall object for reasons considered to be sufficient by an arbitrator appointed in accordance with clause 35 of the said Conditions.* ††Provided always that no person subsequently appointed to be the Architect under this Contract shall be entitled to disregard or overrule any certificate or opinion or decision or approval or instruction given or expressed by the Architect for the time being.

††3 [B] The term 'the Supervising Officer' in the said Conditions shall mean the said...of...or,

in the event of his death or ceasing to be the Supervising Officer for the purpose of this Contract, such other person as the Employer shall nominate for that purpose, *not being a person to whom the Contractor shall object for reasons considered to be sufficient by an arbitrator appointed in accordance with clause 35 of the said Conditions.* ††Provided always that no person consequently appointed to be the Supervising Officer under this Contract shall be entitled to disregard or overrule any certificate or opinion or decision or approval or instruction given or expressed by the Supervising Officer for the time being.

*4 The term 'the Quantity Surveyor' in the said Conditions shall mean...of...

or, in the event of his death or ceasing to be the Quantity Surveyor for the purpose of this Contract, such other person as the Employer shall nominate for that purpose, *not being a person to whom the Contractor shall object for reasons considered to be sufficient by an arbitrator appointed in accordance with clause 35 of the said Conditions.*††

††Footnote.—Article 3 [A] is applicable where the person concerned is entitled to the use of the name 'Architect' under and in accordance with the Architects (Registration) Acts, 1931 to 1938. Article 3 [B] is applicable in all other cases. Therefore complete whichever is appropriate and delete the alternative. Where Article 3 [A] is completed the expression 'Supervising Officer' shall be deemed to have been deleted throughout the Conditions annexed hereto. Where Article 3 [B] is completed the expression 'Architect' shall be deemed to have been deleted throughout the said Conditions.

*Footnote.—In cases where the Works are to be carried out under the direction of officials of the Local Authority, insert the names of such officials as are to perform the respective functions of the 'Architect/Supervising Officer' and the 'Quantity Surveyor' under this Contract.

††Footnote.—Strike out words in italics in cases where 'the Architect' 'the Supervising Officer' or 'the Quantity Surveyor' is an official of the Local Authority.

Contracts under seal
4.02 In ordinary circumstances the contract need not be under seal. If it is under seal the parties remain liable for 12 years from the date of any cause of action accruing, instead of the usual six years. In practice it is probably likely to be

please the employer. It is in this way that the architect must act in an independent manner.

The architect's reasonable satisfaction

5.04 The current clause 1 (1) was introduced in July 1976. Previously the works generally had to be to the architect's reasonable satisfaction. In a sense this continues in that the architect before certifying under clause 30 must be satisfied that the works accord with the contract and he should not apply unreasonable tests in considering whether he is satisfied. But the term 'to the reasonable satisfaction of the architect' has now a special meaning as applying only to that class of materials or workmanship referred to in clauses 1 (1) and 30 (7) (a) (i) where the architect's decision as expressed in his final certificate is (subject to certain qualifications) conclusive. Whether or not materials or workmanship come within this class requires consideration of the contract documents in particular of the contract bills. As examples consider: 'finish to the architect's approval', and 'to the standards of BSS No. . . .' (with no reference to the architect). The first example comes, it is suggested within clause 30 (7) (a) (i), the second does not.

Arbitration

5.05 See clause 35. Subject to certain special provisions (clause 30 (7) is the most important) either party can challenge the architect's decisions by going to arbitration, but it must be remembered that arbitration is usually neither speedy nor cheap unless both parties co-operate to make it so.

Method of work

5.06 It is not the architect's function to direct the contractor as to the way he shall carry out the works; but the contractor must carry out works included in the bills and these some-sometimes include temporary works, eg formwork or other falsework.

Liability for design

5.07 The contractor must carry out the works shown upon the contract drawings and described by or referred to in the contract bills. He is not responsible if such works prove to be unsuitable for the purpose which the employer or the architect had in mind, but the contractor may have certain duties relating to design. The contract bills may include such duties; compliance with the Building Regulations (see clause 4) often involves some design considerations, and further, it is probably the contractor's implied duty to bring to the architect's attention obvious errors in the architect's design of which the contractor has actual knowledge. In any event he has an express duty to give notice to the architect of any discrepancy or divergence which he finds (see clause 1 (2) and, for statutory requirements, clause 4 (1) (b)).

6 Clause 2: Architect's instructions

> **2** (1) The Contractor shall (subject to sub-clauses (2) and (3) of this Condition) forthwith comply with all instructions issued to him by the Architect/Supervising Officer in regard to any matter in respect of which the Architect/Supervising Officer is expressly empowered by these Conditions to issue instructions. If within seven days after receipt of a written notice from the Architect/Supervising Officer requiring compliance with an instruction the Contractor does not comply therewith, then the Employer may employ and pay other persons to execute any work whatsoever which may be necessary to give effect to such instruction and all cost incurred in connection with such employment shall be recoverable from the Contractor by the Employer as a debt or may be deducted by him from any monies due or to become due to the Contractor under this Contract.
>
> (2) Upon receipt of what purports to be an instruction issued to him by the Architect/Supervising Officer the Contractor may request the Architect/Supervising Officer to specify in writing the provision of these Conditions which empowers the issue of the said instruction. The Architect/Supervising Officer shall forthwith comply with any such request, and if the Contractor shall thereafter comply with the said instruction (neither party before such compliance having given to the other a written request to concur in the appointment of an arbitrator under clause 35 of these Conditions in order that it may be decided whether the provision specified by the Architect/Supervising Officer empowers the issue of the said instruction), then the issue of the same shall be deemed for all the purposes of this Contract to have been empowered by the provision of these Conditions specified by the Architect/Supervising Officer in answer to the Contractor's request.
>
> (3) All instructions issued by the Architect/Supervising Officer shall be issued in writing. Any instruction issued orally shall be of no immediate effect, but shall be confirmed in writing by the Contractor

> to the Architect/Supervising Officer within seven days, and if not dissented from in writing by the Architect/Supervising Officer to the Contractor within seven days from receipt of the Contractor's confirmation shall take effect as from the expiration of the latter said seven days.
> Provided always:
> (a) That if the Architect/Supervising Officer within seven days of giving such an oral instruction shall himself confirm the same in writing, then the Contractor shall not be obliged to confirm as aforesaid, and the said instruction shall take effect as from the date of the Architect's/Supervising Officer's confirmation, and
> (b) That if neither the Contractor nor the Architect/Supervising Officer shall confirm such an oral instruction in the manner and at the time aforesaid but the Contractor shall nevertheless comply with the same, then the Architect/Supervising Officer may confirm the same in writing at any time prior to the issue of the Final Certificate, and the said instruction shall thereupon be deemed to have taken effect on the date on which it was issued.

6.01 The contractor must comply with architect's instructions. Failure to comply gives rise to the right under this clause to have work carried out by others and in some circumstances can result in the employer having the right to determine the contractor's employment (see clause 25 (1) (c)).

Power to issue instructions

6.02 The architect can only issue instructions where a clause gives him express power. The clauses are 1 (2) (discrepancies); 4 (1) (by-laws etc); 5 (errors in setting out); 6 (3) (opening up and testing); 6 (4) (removal of work or materials); 6 (5) (dismissal of employee); 11 (1) (variations); 11 (3) (prime cost and provisional sums); 15 (2), 15 (3) (defects); 20[c] (c) (ii) (damage by fire); 21 (2) (postponement of work); 27 (nominated subcontractors); 28 (nominated suppliers); 32 (3), 33 (1) (war); 34 (antiquities). Subclause 2 provides a special procedure for determining whether a purported instruction is within the architect's powers (but as to arbitration see para 5.05).

Form of instructions
6.03 The contract contemplates that instructions will be in writing but the contractor cannot ignore oral instructions and clause 2 (3) makes elaborate provisions, which should be studied, for oral instructions.

Site meeting minutes

6.04 Sometimes the architect and contractor expressly agree that such minutes are to operate as the confirmation of oral instructions contemplated by clause 2 (3). If there was no express agreement as to the status of the minutes it must be decided in each case whether it was intended that they should act as confirmation under clause 2 (3).

7 Clause 3: Contract documents

> **3** (1) The Contract Drawings and the Contract Bills shall remain in the custody of the Architect/Supervising Officer or of the Quantity Surveyor so as to be available at all reasonable times for the inspection of the Employer or of the Contractor.
>
> (2) Immediately after the execution of this Contract the Architect/Supervising Officer without charge to the Contractor shall furnish him (unless he shall have been previously furnished) with—
> (a) One copy certified on behalf of the Employer of the Articles of Agreement and of these Conditions,
> (b) two copies of the Contract Drawings, and
> (c) two copies of the unpriced Bills of Quantities, and (if requested by the Contractor) one copy of the Contract Bills.
>
> (3) So soon as is possible after the execution of this Contract the Architect/Supervising Officer without charge to the Contractor shall furnish him (unless he shall have been previously furnished) with two copies of the descriptive schedules or other like document necessary for use in carrying out the Works.
> Provided that nothing contained in the said descriptive schedules or other documents shall impose any obligation beyond those imposed by the Contract Documents.
>
> (4) As and when from time to time may be necessary the Architect/Supervising Officer without charge to the Contractor shall furnish him with two copies of such drawings or details as are reasonably necessary either to explain and amplify this Contract Drawings or to enable the Contractor to carry out and complete the Works in accordance with these Conditions.
>
> (5) The Contractor shall keep one copy of the Contract Drawings, one copy of the unpriced Bills of Quantities, one copy of the descriptive schedule or other like documents referred to in sub-clause (3) of this Condition, and one copy of the drawings and details referred to in sub-clause (4) of this Condition upon the Works so as to be available to the Architect/Supervising Officer or his representative at all reasonable times.
>
> (6) Upon final payment under clause 30 (6) of these Conditions the Contractor shall if so requested by the Architect/Supervising Officer forthwith return to the Architect/Supervising Officer all drawings, details, descriptive schedules and other documents of a like nature which bear his name.
>
> (7) None of the documents hereinbefore mentioned shall be used by the Contractor for any purpose other than this Contract, and neither the Employer, the Architect/Supervising Officer nor the Quantity Surveyor shall divulge or use except for the purposes of this Contract any of the prices in the Contract Bills.
>
> (8) Any certificate to be issued by the Architect/Supervising Officer under these Conditions shall subject to clause 27 (d) hereof, be issued to the Employer, and immediately upon the issue of any certificate the Architect/Supervising Officer shall send a duplicate copy thereof to the Contractor.

7.01 This clause should be read with the articles of agreement, clause 1 (1) (definitions), clause 1 (2) (notification of discrepancies), clause 5 (accurately dimensioned drawings for setting out) and clauses 6 (1) and 12 (1) (effect of the contract bills).

Definition of contract documents
7.02 See clause 1 (1). They are: contract drawings, contract bills, articles of agreement and the conditions. Other documents such as a contractor's covering letter with his tender are not contract documents unless the parties have expressly so agreed.

Duty to provide drawings and details
7.03 The architect must provide them 'as and when from time to time may be necessary' (clause 3 (4)). This, it is thought, means at such times as may be necessary to enable the contractor to comply with his duties as to progress required by clause 21. For the contractor's claim in respect of alleged delays in the provision of drawings and details see para 28.02 *et seq.*

Issue of certificates
7.04 They are to be issued to the employer with a copy to the contractor. When using the private variant they are to be issued to the contractor and, strictly, no copy need be sent to the employer, although as a matter of good practice a copy should be sent.

8 Clause 4: Statutory obligations, notices, fees and charges

> 4 (1) (a) The Contractor shall comply with, and give all notices required by, any Act of Parliament, any instrument rule or order made under any Act of Parliament, or any regulation or byelaw of any local authority or of any statutory undertaker which has any jurisdiction with regard to the Works or with whose systems the same are or will be connected (all requirements to be so complied with being referred to in these Conditions as 'the statutory requirements').
>
> (b) If the Contractor shall find any divergence between the statutory requirements and all or any of the documents referred to in clause 1 (2) of these Conditions or any variation instruction issued in accordance with clause 11 (1) of these Conditions, he shall immediately give to the Architect/Supervising Officer a written notice specifying the divergence.
>
> (c) If the Contractor gives notice under paragraph (b) of this sub-clause or if the Architect/Supervising Officer shall otherwise discover or receive notice of a divergence between the statutory requirements and all or any of the documents referred to in clause 1 (2) of these Conditions or any variation instruction issued in accordance with clause 11 (1) of these Conditions, the Architect/Supervising Officer shall within 7 days of the discovery or receipt of a notice issue instructions in relation to the divergence. If and insofar as the instructions require the Works to be varied, they shall be deemed to be Architect's/Supervising Officer's instructions issued in accordance with clause 11 (1) of these Conditions.
>
> (d) (i) If in any emergency compliance with paragraph (a) of this sub-clause requires the Contractor to supply materials or execute work before receiving instructions under paragraph (c) of this sub-clause the Contractor shall supply such limited materials and execute such limited work as are reasonably necessary to secure immediate compliance with the statutory requirements.
>
> (ii) The Contractor shall forthwith inform the Architect/Supervising Officer of the emergency and of the steps that he is taking under this paragraph of this Condition.
>
> (iii) Work executed and materials supplied by the Contractor under sub-paragraph (i) of this paragraph shall be deemed to have been executed and supplied pursuant to an Architect's/Supervising Officer's instruction in accordance with clause 11 (1) of these Conditions provided that the emergency arose because of a divergence between the statutory requirements and all or any of the documents referred to in clause 1 (2) of these Conditions or any variation instruction issued in accordance with clause 11 (1) of these Conditions, and the Contractor has complied with sub-paragraph (ii).
>
> (e) Provided that the Contractor complies with paragraph (b) of this sub-clause, the Contractor shall not be liable to the Employer under this Contract if the Works do not comply with the statutory requirements where and to the extent that such non-compliance of the Works results from the Contractor having carried out work in accordance with the documents referred to in clause 1 (2) of these Conditions or any variation instruction issued in accordance with clause 11 (1) of these Conditions.
>
> (2) The Contractor shall pay and indemnify the Employer against liability in respect of any fees or charges (including any rates or taxes) legally demandable under any Act of Parliament, any instrument, rule or order made under any Act of Parliament, or any regulation or byelaw of any local authority or of any statutory undertaker in respect of the Works. Provided that the amount of any such fees or charges (including any rates or taxes other than value added tax) shall be added to the Contract Sum unless they
>
> (a) arise in respect of work executed or materials or goods supplied by a local authority or statutory undertaker for which a prime cost sum is included in the Contract Bills or for which a prime cost sum has arisen as a result of Architect's/Supervising Officer's instructions given under clause 11 (3) of these Conditions, or
>
> (b) are priced or stated by way of a provisional sum in the Contract Bill.
>
> (3) None of the provisions of clause 27 (nominated sub-contractors) nor of clause 28 (nominated suppliers) of these Conditions shall apply where prime cost sums are included in the Contract Bills or arise as a result of an instruction by the Architect/Supervising Officer in regard to the expenditure of provisional sums in respect of any fees or charges for work executed or materials or goods supplied by a local authority or statutory undertaker solely in pursuance of its statutory obligations. Such fees or charges shall be dealt with under the provisions of sub-clause (2) of this Condition and any amount properly paid by the Contractor to any local authority or statutory undertaker shall be added to the amount that would otherwise be stated as due in the next interim certificate.

8.01 This clause which was considerably amended and enlarged in the July 1976 revisions to the JCT Forms imposes

heavy obligations. The contractor has both to comply with and give statutory notices and also comply with relevant statutory requirements including the Building Regulations 1972 which, outside London, now replace the local by-laws formerly in operation. Breach of these duties (in addition to giving rise to the possibility of criminal proceedings) makes the contractor liable in damages to the employer. The architect may also be liable to the employer and, in some circumstances, to the contractor—see *Townsend (Builders) Ltd v Cinema News etc Ltd* (1959) 1 WLR 119. Note the contractor's duty to give notice of a variation required by compliance with building regulations and the like.

8.02 Clause 4 (1) (e), part of the 1976 revision, protects a contractor who either gives the requisite notice to the architect or who has not found any divergence from statutory requirements.

8.03 Clause 4 (3) was introduced in the July 1975 revision. It deals with such matters as connections to street mains by gas boards or the provisions of crossovers by local authorities. Delay by a statutory undertaker is a ground for extension of time (clause 23 (1)) but not for payment of loss on expense under clause 24 (1).

9 Clause 5: Levels of setting out of the works

> 5 The Architect/Supervising Officer shall determine any levels which may be required for the execution of the Works, and shall furnish to the Contractor by way of accurately dimensioned drawings such information as shall enable the Contractor to set out the Works at ground level. Unless the Architect/Supervising Officer shall otherwise instruct, in which case the Contract Sum shall be adjusted accordingly, the Contractor shall be responsible for and shall entirely at his own cost amend any errors arising from his own inaccurate setting out.

9.01 The words '*unless the architect ... shall otherwise direct ...*' seem to give the architect power to order the employer to pay for the contractor's error. If, which is not certain, they have this meaning it is thought that such power should only be exercised in special circumstances.

10 Clause 6: Materials, goods and workmanship to conform to description, testing and inspection

> 6 (1) All materials, goods and workmanship shall so far as procurable be of the respective kinds and standards described in the Contract Bills.
>
> (2) The Contractor shall upon the request of the Architect/Supervising Officer furnish him with vouchers to prove that the materials and goods comply with sub-clause (1) of this Condition.
>
> (3) The Architect/Supervising Officer may issue instructions requiring the Contractor to open up for inspection any work covered up or to arrange for or carry out any test of any materials or goods (whether or not already incorporated in the Works) or of any executed work, and the cost of such opening up or testing (together with the cost of making good in consequence thereof) shall be added to the Contract Sum unless provided for in the Contract Bills or unless the inspection or test shows that the work, materials or goods are not in accordance with this Contract.
>
> (4) The Architect/Supervising Officer may issue instructions in regard to the removal from the site of any work, materials or goods which are not in accordance with this Contract.
>
> (5) The Architect/Supervising Officer may (but not unreasonably or vexatiously) issue instructions requiring the dismissal from the Works of any person employed thereon.

10.01 This clause defines the kinds and standards of materials, and workmanship which the contract requires and gives the architect certain important powers. So far as the contract bills do not describe standards, the contractor must carry out the work in accordance with the standards implied by law. These are that he must do the work with all proper skill and care (or as it is sometimes expressed—in a good and workmanlike manner) and supply materials: 1 reasonably fit for the purpose for which they will be used, and 2 of good quality.

Exclusion of the usual implied obligations
10.02 The implied obligations just set out can be excluded if the circumstances show that the parties did not intend them to apply. Thus:

1 There is no obligation as to fitness for a particular purpose if that purpose was not made known to the contractor at the time of making the contract.

2 There is no obligation as to fitness for purpose of materials where there was no reliance upon the skill and judgment of the contractor in the choice of those materials. Thus, say an architect, without reliance on the contractor, specifies for use on a roof 'Somerset 13 tiles', then the contractor is not liable if Somerset 13 tiles of good quality are not fit for use on that roof. The contractor is, however, subject to what is said in para 10.03, liable if the tiles fail because, for example, they laminate owing to some latent defect of quality, even though the defect could not have been detected by the exercise of proper skill and care on his part (*Young and Marten Ltd v McManus Childs Ltd* (1968) 2 All ER 1169).

3 There is no obligation as to latent defects of quality of materials where the circumstances showed that the parties did not intend the contractor to accept such obligation. Thus it seems (although the point is not clear) that, in the example just cited, the contractor would not have been liable for the latent defects in the tiles if the employer (or the architect on his behalf) had required the contractor to purchase them from a supplier who, to the knowledge of the parties, would only supply them upon terms which substantially limited the contractor's remedies against the supplier in respect of such defects (see *Young and Marten* and *Gloucestershire County Council v Richardson* (1969) 2 All ER 1181). Such requirement would have shown an intention that the contractor was not to be liable.

4 In the case of a nominated supplier whose contract of sale restricts, limits or excludes the liability of the nominated supplier to the contractor, and the architect has specifically approved such restriction, limitation or exclusion, the employers' rights against the contractor are restricted, limited or excluded to the same extent—see clause 28, sub-clause (d) and para 32.04.

Position of employer
10.03 If there is no breach of an express term, and the implied terms as to fitness or quality are excluded, the employer normally has no remedy against the contractor or subcontractor or supplier. This is a situation which should be avoided if possible. If the contractor will not accept liability one way of protecting the employer is to obtain a warranty direct from the supplier or subcontractor concerned. For nominated subcontractors there is available from the RIBA a 'Form of Agreement between an Employer and a sub-contractor nominated under the standard form of Building Contract 1963 Edition'. For nominated suppliers there is available from the RIBA a form of warranty.

Effect of price on standards
10.04 The question whether the price is low or high should be ignored when considering the requisite standard unless the parties have expressly or by implication agreed that price is to be considered. Thus it seems that the architect can accept a lower standard than usual where the parties have agreed at the time of contract that the price is low and that the contractor is to 'build down to a price'.

Effect of proposed use of works on standards
10.05 Where the use is known to the contractor at the time of contract it can, probably, be taken into account in considering the requisite standard where the bills are silent. But it is better to have express agreement on possible matters of dispute, eg as to tolerances and how far they are cumulative.

Clause 6 (3): Testing
10.06 The architect is not bound to order tests under this clause before saying that he is not reasonably satisfied. If he orders tests and the work, materials or goods are found to be satisfactory the contractor has rights to an extension of time (clause 23 (i)), payment of loss and expense (clause 24 (1) (b)) and the cost of the tests. But it is thought that where tests of parts of a class of work, eg piling, show that the whole must be rejected the contractor is not entitled to payment for tests in respect of those parts, eg individual piles, which pass the test nor to the other rights set out above.

Clause 6 (4): Removal
10.07 There is no provision for re-execution, because, upon the removal of the unsatisfactory work, materials or goods the contractor's duty to complete remains and no further instruction is required. For the architect's remedies for non-compliance with an instruction see clauses 2 (1), 25 (1) (c) and 30 (2). Defects which appear after practical completion are dealt with under clause 15.

Without quantities variant
10.08 References in clause 6 to the contract bills should be read as references to the specification.

11 Clause 7: Royalties and patent rights

> 7 All royalties or other sums payable in respect of the supply and use in carrying out the Works as described by or referred to in the Contract Bills of any patented articles, processes or inventions shall be deemed to have been included in the Contract Sum, and the Contractor shall indemnify the Employer from and against all claims, proceedings, damages, costs and expenses which may be brought or made against the Employer or to which he may be put by reason of the Contractor infringing or being held to have infringed any patent rights in relation to any such articles, processes and inventions.
>
> Provided that where in compliance with Architect's/Supervising Officer's instructions the Contractor shall supply and use in carrying out the Works any patented articles, processes or inventions, the Contractor shall not be liable in respect of any infringement or alleged infringement of any patent rights in relation to any such articles, processes and inventions and all royalties damages or other monies which the Contractor may be liable to pay to the persons entitled to such patent rights shall be added to the Contract Sum.

12 Clause 8: Foreman-in-charge

> 8 The Contractor shall constantly keep upon the Works a competent foreman-in-charge and any instructions given to him by the Architect/Supervising Officer shall be deemed to have been issued to the Contractor.

12.01 The foreman-in-charge is the contractor's agent to receive instructions. To avoid confusion he should be named.

13 Clause 9: Access for architects to the works

> 9 The Architect/Supervising Officer and his representatives shall at all reasonable times have access to the Works and to the workshops or other places of the Contractor where work is being prepared for the Contract, and when work is to be so prepared in workshops or other places of a sub-contractor (whether or not a nominated sub-contractor as defined in clause 27 of these Conditions) the Contractor shall by a term in the sub-contract so far as possible secure a similar right of access to those workshops or places for the Architect/Supervising Officer and his representatives and shall do all things reasonably necessary to make such right effective.

14 Clause 10: Clerk of works

> 10 The Employer shall be entitled to appoint a clerk of works whose duty shall be to act solely as inspector on behalf of the Employer under the directions of the Architect/Supervising Officer and the Contractor shall afford every reasonable facility for the performance of that duty. If any directions are given to the Contractor or to his foreman upon the Works by the clerk of works the same shall be of no effect unless given in regard to a matter in respect of which the Architect/Supervising Officer is expressly empowered by these Conditions to issue instructions and unless confirmed in writing by the Architect/Supervising Officer within two working days of their being given. If any such directions are so given and confirmed then as from the date of confirmation they shall be deemed to be Architect's/Supervising Officer's instructions.

14.01 The clerk of works is to act 'solely as inspector'. He is not the architect's agent to give instructions and it is a source of confusion and dispute if he purports to do so. The clause provides for the position if the clerk of works gives 'directions'. They are to be of no effect unless converted into architect's instructions by the architect within two days. Such directions can lead to uncertainty on the part of the contractor. It is suggested that the clerk of works be discouraged from giving directions in ordinary circumstances. If directions are given it at least reduces the possible problems if they are in writing and the architect immediately confirms, amends or rejects them.

Work done before confirmation of direction
14.02 The architect can, if it is a variation, subsequently sanction it in writing under clause 11 (1). This may be particularly appropriate where the contractor has carried out extra work in an emergency upon the direction of the clerk of works.

Resident architect
14.03 A person so entitled is sometimes appointed to the site of a large contract. His position should be sharply distinguished from that of the clerk of works and should be defined in a communication to the contractor stating clearly how far, if at all, he is not to have all the powers to issue architect's instructions given by the terms of the contract.

15 Clause 11: Variations, provisional and prime cost sums

> 11 (1) The Architect/Supervising Officer may issue instructions requiring a variation and he may sanction in writing any variation made by the Contractor otherwise than pursuant to an instruction of the Architect/Supervising Officer. No variation required by the Architect/Supervising Officer or subsequently sanctioned by him shall vitiate this Contract.
>
> (2) The term 'variation' as used in these Conditions means the alteration or modification of the design, quality or quantity of the Works as shown upon the Contract Drawings and described by or referred to in the Contract Bills, and includes the addition, omission or substitution of any work, the alteration of the kind or standard of any of the materials or goods to be used in the Works, and the removal from the site of any work materials or goods executed or brought thereon by the Contractor for the purposes of the Works other than work materials or goods which are not in accordance with this Contract.
>
> (3) The Architect/Supervising Officer shall issue instructions in regard to the expenditure of prime cost* and provisional sums included in the Contract Bills and of prime cost sums which arise as a result of instructions issued in regard to the expenditure of provisional sums.
>
> (4) All variations required by the Architect/Supervising Officer or subsequently sanctioned by him in writing and all work executed by the Contractor for which provisional sums are included in the Contract Bills (other than work for which a tender made under clause 27 (g) of these Conditions has been accepted) shall be measured and valued by the Quantity Surveyor who shall give to the Contractor an opportunity of being present at the time of such measurement and of taking such notes and measurements as the Contractor may require. The valuation of variations and of work executed by the Contractor for which a provisional sum is included in the Contract Bills (other than work for which a tender has been accepted as aforesaid) unless otherwise agreed shall be made in accordance with the following rules:—
>
> > (a) The prices in the Contract Bills shall determine the valuation of work of similar character executed under similar conditions as work priced therein;
> >
> > (b) The said prices, where work is not of similar character or executed under similar conditions as aforesaid, shall be the basis of prices for the same so far as may be reasonable, failing which a fair valuation thereof shall be made;
> >
> > (c) Where work cannot properly be measured and valued the Contractor shall unless otherwise agreed be allowed:
> >
> > > (i) the prime cost of such work calculated in accordance with the 'Definition of Prime Cost of Daywork carried out under a Building Contract' issued by the Royal Institution of Chartered Surveyors and the National Federation of Building Trades Employers and current at the date of tender as defined in clause 31D (6) (a) of these Conditions (or as defined in the Formula Rules where clause 31F of these Conditions applies) together with percentage additions to each section of the prime cost at the rates set out by the Contractor in the Contract Bills; or
> > >
> > > (ii) where the work is within the province of any specialist trade and the said Institution and the appropriate body representing the employers in that trade have agreed and issued a definition of prime cost of daywork, the prime cost of such work calculated in accordance with that definition and current at the date of tender as defined in clause 31D (6) (a) of these Conditions (or as defined in the Formula Rules where clause 31F of these Conditions applies) together with percentage additions on the prime cost at the rates set out by the Contractor in the Contract Bills.
> > >
> > > Provided that in any case vouchers specifying the time daily spent upon the work (and if required by the Architect/Supervising Officer the workmen's names) and the materials employed shall be delivered for verification to the Architect/Supervising Officer or his authorised representative not later than the end of the week following that in which the work has been executed;
> >
> > (d) The prices in the Contract Bills shall determine the valuation of items omitted; provided that if omissions substantially vary the conditions under which any remaining items of work are carried out the prices for such remaining items shall be valued under rule (b) of this sub-clause.
>
> (5) Effect shall be given to the measurement and valuation of variations under sub-clause (4) of this Condition in Interim Certificates and by adjustment of the Contract Sum; and effect shall be given to the measurement and valuation of work for which a provisional sum is included in the Contract Bills under the said sub-clause in Interim Certificates and by adjustment of the Contract Sum in accordance with clause 30 (5) (c) of these Conditions.
>
> (6) If upon written application being made to him by the Contractor, the Architect/Supervising Officer is of the opinion that a variation or the execution by the Contractor of work for which a provisional sum is included in the Contract Bills (other than work for which a tender made under clause 27 (g) of these Conditions has been accepted) has involved the Contractor in direct loss and/or expense for which he would not be reimbursed by payment in respect of a valuation made in accordance with the rules contained in sub-clause (4) of this Condition and if the said application is made within a reasonable time of the loss or expense having been incurred, then the Architect/Supervising Officer shall either himself ascertain or shall instruct the Quantity Surveyor to ascertain the amount of such loss or expense. Any amount from time to time so ascertained shall be added to the Contract Sum, and if an Interim Certificate is issued after the date of ascertainment any such amount shall be added to the amount which would otherwise be stated as due in such Certificate.
>
> *Footnote.—The term 'prime cost' may be indicated by the abbreviation 'P.C.' in any document relating to this Contract (including the Contract Bills), and wherever the abbreviation is used it shall be deemed to mean 'prime cost'.

15.01 This clause provides for: the ordering or sanctioning of variations (clause 11 (1)); the meaning of variations (clause

11 (2)); instructions in regard to prime cost and provisional sums (clause 11 (3)); the valuation of variations and provisional sum work (clause 11 (4)); giving effect to such valuation (clause 11 (5)); claims for loss or expenses additional to such valuation (clause 11 (6)).

15.02 The words '. . . *he may sanction in writing* . . .' (clause 11 (1)) give the architect discretion to sanction a variation where there has not been any instruction. There is no express guidance as to the exercise of the discretion and it is suggested that it should only be exercised when in all the circumstances it is reasonable to do so.

Definition of variation
15.03 Clause 11 (2) must be referred to if any dispute arises as to whether work is or is not a variation. The opinion of the architect on this as on other matters is (subject to clause 30 (7)) subject to review by the arbitrator. If there is a dispute and the contractor, for example, contends that work shown on a drawing is a variation but the architect does not agree, it is a convenient course to record that the work is done without prejudice to the contractor's contentions. If agreement cannot subsequently be arrived at the point can be determined by the arbitrator. In the without quantities variant the specification replaces the contract bills in the definition of a variation. With either variant, merely permitting the contractor to depart from a specified or agreed method of construction does not ordinarily amount to a variation although the particular circumstances must always be considered.

'Deemed' variation under clause 11 (2)
15.04 This can arise when, for example, it is found that the quantity of work necessary to comply with drawing exceeds the bill item. The contractor is entitled to payment under clause 11 although there was no prior instruction or subsequent sanctioning in writing; but note his duty under clause 1 (2) to give notice of any discrepancy he finds. Breach of this duty makes him liable, it is submitted, to any loss thereby suffered, eg because it deprived the architect of the opportunity to require a variation minimising the financial results of the discrepancy.

Limitation on architect's powers
15.05 Despite the apparent width of the architect's power to order variations it is generally thought that he cannot order variations of such extent or nature as to change the nature of the works as originally contemplated. Further, the architect's powers are limited to those given by the conditions. He can neither vary the conditions nor release the contractor from the obligation to perform the contract. He cannot, without the contractor's agreement, require work the subject matter of a prime cost sum (see clause 27) to be carried out by the contractor, and probably cannot omit work in order to have it carried out by another contractor or nominated subcontractor. He cannot, it is thought, order variations after practical completion. He can vary work to be carried out by nominated subcontractors.

Prime cost and provisional sums
15.06 'Provisional sum' is used in the sense of expenditure the amount of which is unknown when the contract is entered into. 'Prime cost sums' are estimates of the sums which will appear in the subcontracts to be entered into between the contractor and nominated subcontractors or nominated suppliers (see further clauses 27 and 28).

Measurement and valuation of variations
15.07 This is governed by clause 11 (4). The measurement and valuation is by the quantity surveyor and the rules for the valuation appear in subclauses (a) to (d) 'unless otherwise

agreed'. The contract does not say who can make the agreement but it is desirable that it should be between the architect and a responsible agent of the contractor, and it is useful, as a matter of evidence, for it to be in writing. If a contractor quotes a price for a variation it should be clearly agreed whether or not it includes any 'claim' he might make under clause 11 (6) or otherwise (see further para 28.02 below). It is not clear how far, if at all, the contract authorises the architect to agree a price materially higher than that payable under the ordinary rules; if the architect thinks the proposed price is higher he should (quite apart from any duty he may owe the employer under clause 1.14 of the RIBA *Conditions of engagement*, if applicable) seek the employer's consent before making the agreement.

The quantity surveyor
15.08 Subject to any special agreement as referred to above, he values in accordance with the rules and ordinarily the architect issues his certificate in accordance with the valuation. But the architect is not bound to follow the quantity surveyor's valuation. He may take the view that the quantity surveyor is wrong in principle, eg as to whether clause 11 (4) (a) or clause 11 (4) (b) applies, or he may be of the opinion that a deduction must be made in respect of work which does not accord with the contract (see clause 30 (2) and para 34.04).

Pricing errors in contract bills
15.09 Unless there is a case for rectification of the contract (see para 17.02) both parties are bound by these errors in carrying out the original contract work. It is sometimes said that such errors should be taken into account in pricing variations. It is thought that, unless there is a special express agreement, as for example, where the parties have followed *Code of procedure for selective tendering*, no adjustments should be made arising out of such errors (see further clause 13).

Clause 11 (4) (b)
15.10 The rule of valuation '. . . *work not of a similar character or executed under similar conditions . . .*' is in practice probably the most difficult of application. It is necessary first to decide whether it applies and then, if it does, how to apply it. It seems that one must look at the position as at the time of acceptance of the tender and consider the character of the work then priced and the conditions under which the parties must have contemplated it would be carried out. If the character of the varied work or the conditions under which it was carried out differ then clause 11 (4) (b) applies. It is thought that the following may be examples of its application: material changes in quantities; winter working instead of summer working; wet instead of dry; high instead of low; confined working space instead of ample working space. If it is decided that the rule applies the next question is its effect. This varies according to the circumstances. Bill rates are to be the basis of prices 'so far as may be reasonable, failing which a fair valuation . . . shall be made'. So the range is from no or very little change in bill rates to a 'fair valuation' which probably means the same thing as 'a reasonable sum'. Note that in some circumstances clause 11 (4) (b) may give grounds for paying less than bill rates. It is sometimes difficult to distinguish between a ground for extra payment under clause 11 (4) (b) and a claim for loss and expense under clause 11 (6). Prudent contractors put their claim in the alternative. See also discussion of claims in para 28.02.

Without quantities variant—the schedule of rates
15.11 In the without quantities variant the schedule of rates is the starting document for the valuation of variations. It is a 'schedule of the rates upon which the contractor's estimate was based' (clause 3 (3)), and must therefore be in existence at the time of making the contract. The contract states that it need only be provided *after* the contract is entered into (clause 3 (3)), but as it is so important for the pricing of variations the architect may well consider it prudent to insist upon its production and perusal before the contract is entered into.

Clause 11 (4) (c): Daywork vouchers
15.12 It appears that if the contractor does not comply strictly with the proviso as to delivery of vouchers the architect can refuse payment at daywork rates. To avoid an argument by the contractor that there has been a waiver of the requirements of the proviso the architect should insist on weekly provision of vouchers. They should be verified promptly.

Clause 11 (6): Claims for loss and expense
15.13 Delay in completion or interruption in the regular progress of the works caused by variations is a common ground for an application under clause 11 (6). There are often also grounds for an extension of time under clause 23 (e) but the difference in subject matter of the two clauses should be kept distinct. Clause 11 (6) provides grounds for extra payment; clause 23 (e) provides relief from liability to pay liquidated damages, and circumstances can arise when only one of the clauses applies. The contractor's written communication to the architect should show clearly whether it is an application under clause 11 (6) notice under clause 23, or both. If the contractor claims payment for delay due to lateness in receiving instructions this should be the subject of a claim under clause 24 (1) (a) or at common law (see para 28.02).

Requirement of written application
15.14 Without this there is no right to payment under this clause. It must be given 'within a reasonable time of the loss or expense having been incurred', but as to this see para 15.16.

The nature of 'direct loss or expense'
15.15 This is not explained or defined, but where variations cause delay it will often include an extension of those items in the contract bills, the price of which is affected by time and which have had to be expended for a longer period than that contemplated by the bills. The inquiry into such charges is likely to be more difficult where the without quantities form is used but the principle is similar. The following are, it is thought, within the meaning of the term: increases in head office and supervision charges and uneconomic working of labour and, where the variation has prevented the contractor taking on other work, such *net* profit as was reasonably foreseeable by the employer as likely to result from the variation. There is no generally accepted method of establishing the heads of claim just mentioned and it is thought that if the architect is satisfied that they have been incurred he must do his best to ascertain their amount upon information, which may be less exact than that appropriate for, say, a simple extension of preliminary items. Nothing is due under 11 (6) which is recoverable under 11 (4).

The ascertainment of loss or expense
15.16 The architect can, it is submitted, require the contractor to furnish him with reasonable information to enable him to ascertain the loss and expense. When ascertained it should be included in an interim certificate, but it cannot be ascertained until the contractor has been involved in such loss and expense. Thus where preliminary items have not yet been expended an extension of such items cannot be justified. By the same reasoning it appears that notice under the clause is in time if given within a reasonable time of the exhaustion of the relevant bill item.

Provisional ascertainment

15.17 The clause does not provide expressly for a provisional ascertainment and this may give rise to a difficulty. The architect at an early stage may be satisfied that some loss and expense has been incurred but is not able to ascertain it with a reasonable degree of certainty until much later, perhaps even until the final certificate stage. Probably he has an implied power to make a provisional ascertainment, but the position is not clear. A course he can take is to agree with the contractor to make a provisional ascertainment for inclusion in an interim certificate subject to revision up or down in or before the final certificate.

16 Clause 12: Contract bills

> 12   (1) The quality and quantity of the work included in the Contract Sum shall be deemed to be that which is set out in the Contract Bills which Bills unless otherwise expressly stated in respect of any specified item or items shall be deemed to have been prepared in accordance with the principles of the Standard Method of Measurement of Building Works 5th edition Imperial, revised March 1964/5th edition Metric* by the Royal Institution of Chartered Surveyors and the National Federation of Building Trades Employers, but save as aforesaid nothing contained in the Contract Bills shall override, modify, or affect in any way whatsoever the application or interpretation of that which is contained in these Conditions.
>
> (2) Any error in description or in quantity in or omission of items from the Contract Bills shall not vitiate this Contract but shall be corrected and deemed to be a variation required by the Architect/ Supervising Officer.
>
> *Footnote.—Delete whichever edition is inapplicable*

16.01 This is one of the key clauses to the form. It defines exactly the work included in the contract sum as being work of 'the quality and quantity . . . which is set out in the contract bills'. It is the basis for the adjustment of the contract sum according to the actual quantities and quality of work carried out by the contractor in accordance with the contract. For 'deemed' variations and discrepancies see clause 12 (2), the notes below to clause 12 and para 15.04.

The standard method of measurement

16.02 Unless otherwise expressly stated in respect of any specified item or items the contract bills are deemed to have been prepared in accordance with the principles of the standard method of measurement. If they have not been so prepared there is an error which must be corrected and the correction is deemed to be a variation required by the architect. For example, if there is no provision in the contract bills for excavation in rock but in carrying out the work it becomes clear that such excavation is necessary then, it seems, the bills must be read as if they included an item for excavation in rock (see the *Standard method of measurement* section on excavation and earthwork D6 (e)), and the contractor will become entitled to extra payment.

Remeasurement

16.03 Unless expressly or impliedly agreed, there is no general right to remeasurement. An implied agreement can arise when items or bills are—marked 'provisional'. In some cases there may be a dispute as to the existence of an error in the bills, which dispute can only be resolved upon a remeasurement. It is thought that either party may, if it is reasonable in the circumstances, require remeasurement of a disputed item or items.

Approximate quantities contract

16.04 In 1975 the JCT issued a form for use with approximate quantities. It should be used where the works have not been designed in sufficient detail to enable bills complying with the *Standard method of measurement* to be prepared. It is a remeasurement contract. If it is used *Practice note 20* should be obtained and studied.

Conflict between bills and conditions

16.05 The words beginning '. . . *but save as aforesaid* . . .' show that in any such conflict the conditions prevail—see the case of *Gleesons v Hillingdon* (1970) referred to in para 2.02.

Special conditions as to time, insurance and the like written into the contract bills are of no effect unless either the conditions of contract are expressly amended or the articles of agreement are endorsed with, for example, some words stating that special conditions appearing on certain pages of the contract bills form part of the contract, notwithstanding anything appearing in clause 12 or elsewhere in the conditions of contract. Where it is desired to place an obligation on the contractor to complete in sections, the sectional completion supplement should be used (see para 20.02).

Without quantities variant

16.06 The quality and quantity of the work included in the contract sum is that 'shown upon the contract drawings or described in the specification'. This can result in a profound difference in the definition of the works for which the contract sum is payable. In the with quantities variant the works are described with the high degree of exactness required by the *Standard method of measurement*. But there is no standard method for the preparation of contract drawings or specifications. They may be prepared in great detail so that they describe the work for which the contract sum is payable in exact terms, or they may be lacking in detail and describe such work in wide terms. The latter class of contract drawings and specification invites dispute as to whether work is contract work or extra work. In the variants without quantities there is greater opportunity than in the with quantities variants for it to be said on behalf of the employer that, although an item in dispute is not expressly shown or described in the contract documents, it is not extra work because it is necessary ancillary work impliedly included in the work for which the original contract sum is payable.

Clause 12 (2): Errors

16.07 In the with quantities variant errors can arise from discrepancies between contract drawings and contract bills, from mathematical errors of measurement and from noncompliance with the *Standard method of measurement* (see para 16.02). In the without quantities variant it is more difficult to give effect to clause 12 (2) because of the problem of defining an 'error'.

17 Clause 13: Contract sum

> 13   The Contract Sum shall not be adjusted or altered in any way whatsoever otherwise than in accordance with the express provisions of these Conditions, and subject to clause 12 (2) of these Conditions any error whether of arithmetic or not in the computation of the Contract Sum shall be deemed to have been accepted by the parties hereto.
>
> 13A (1)   (a) In this Condition and in the supplemental agreement pursuant hereto and annexed to these Conditions (hereinafter called the 'VAT Agreement') 'tax' means the value added tax introduced by the Finance Act 1972 which is under the care and management of the Commissioners of Customs and Excise (hereinafter and in the VAT Agreement called 'the Commissioners').
>
> (b) The Employer and Contractor shall on the same date as executing the Articles of Agreement execute the VAT Agreement.
>
> (2) Any reference in these Conditions to 'Contract Sum' shall be regarded as such Sum exclusive of any tax and recovery by the Contractor from the Employer of tax properly chargeable by the Commissioners on the Contractor under or by virtue of the Finance Act 1972 or any amendment thereof on the supply of goods and services under this Contract shall be under the provisions of this Condition and of the VAT Agreement.
>
> (3) To the extent that after the date of tender as defined in Clause 31D (6) (a) of these Conditions the supply of goods and services to the Employer becomes exempt from the tax there shall be paid to the Contractor an amount equal to the loss of credit (input tax) on the supply to the Contractor of goods and services which contribute exclusively to the Works.

17.01 Unless there is a case for rectification the parties are bound by any errors incorporated into the contract sum. For the question whether pricing errors affects the pricing of variations see para 15.09. For the correction of errors in items (not prices) in the contract bills see clause 12 (2).

The equitable remedy of rectification

17.02 In certain circumstances an order can be obtained from the court that the contract be read as rectified to correct an error. Reference should be made to a legal textbook but the broad principle is that rectification can be obtained only if it is clearly proved that the parties were in agreement but by an error wrote their agreement down wrongly.

18 Clause 14: Materials and goods unfixed or off site

> 14 (1) Unfixed materials and goods delivered to, placed on or adjacent to the Works and intended therefor shall not be removed except for use upon the Works unless the Architect/Supervising Officer has consented in writing to such removal which consent shall not be unreasonably withheld. Where the value of any such materials or goods has in accordance with clause 30 (2) of these Conditions been included in any Interim Certificate under which the Contractor has received payment, such materials and goods shall become the property of the Employer, but subject to clause 20 [B] or clause 20 [C] of these Conditions (if applicable), the Contractor shall remain responsible for loss or damage to the same.
>
> (2) Where the value of any materials or goods has in accordance with clause 30 (2A) of these Conditions been included in any Interim Certificate under which the Contractor has received payment, such materials and goods shall become the property of the Employer, and thereafter the Contractor shall not, except for use upon the Works, remove or cause or permit the same to be moved or removed from the premises where they are, but the Contractor shall nevertheless be responsible for any loss thereof or damage thereto and for the cost of storage, handling and insurance of the same until such time as they are delivered to and placed on or adjacent to the Works whereupon the provisions of sub-clause (1) of this clause (except the words 'where the value' to the words 'the Employer but') shall apply thereto.

18.01 This clause should be read with clause 30 (2) and (2A) (certification for payment). The position as to materials and goods intended for the works is as follows:
1 As soon as brought to or adjacent to the works they must not be removed without the architect's consent (clause 14 (1)).
2 When paid for, the property passes to the employer (clause 14 (1)).
3 When built into the works, the property passes to the owner of the land by operation of law whether paid for or not. Materials and goods off site need only be included in a certificate at the architect's discretion (see clause 30 (2A)); if so included the property passes to the employer (clause 14 (2)). The employer has no interest in or right to retain the contractor's plant and equipment unless and until the contractor's employment has been determined under clause 25.

19 Clause 15: Practical completion and defects liability

> 15 (1) When in the opinion of the Architect/Supervising Officer the Works are practically completed, he shall forthwith issue a certificate to that effect and Practical Completion of the Works shall be deemed for all the purposes of this Contract to have taken place on the day named in such certificate.
>
> (2) Any defects, shrinkages or other faults which shall appear within the Defects Liability Period stated in the appendix to these Conditions and which are due to materials or workmanship not in accordance with this Contract or to frost occurring before Practical Completion of the Works, shall be specified by the Architect/Supervising Officer in a Schedule of Defects which he shall deliver to the Contractor not later than 14 days after the expiration of the said Defects Liability Period, and within a reasonable time after receipt of such Schedule the defects, shrinkages and other faults therein specified shall be made good by the Contractor and (unless the Architect/Supervising Officer shall otherwise instruct, in which case the Contract Sum shall be adjusted accordingly) entirely at his own cost.
>
> (3) Notwithstanding sub-clause (2) of this Condition the Architect/Supervising Officer may whenever he considers it necessary so to do, issue instructions requiring any defect, shrinkage or other fault which shall appear within the Defects Liability Period named in the Appendix to these Conditions and which is due to materials or workmanship not in accordance with this Contract or to frost occurring before Practical Completion of the Works, to be made good, and the Contractor shall within a reasonable time after receipt of such instructions comply with the same and (unless the Architect/Supervising Officer shall otherwise instruct, in which case the Contract Sum shall be adjusted accordingly) entirely at his own cost. Provided that no such instructions shall be issued after delivery of a Schedule of Defects or after 14 days from the expiration of the said Defects Liability Period.
>
> (4) When in the opinion of the Architect/Supervising Officer any defects, shrinkages or other faults which he may have required to be made good under sub-clauses (2) and (3) of this Condition shall have been made good he shall issue a certificate to that effect, and completion of making good defects shall be deemed for all the purposes of this Contract to have taken place on the day named in such certificate.
>
> (5) In no case shall the Contractor be required to make good at his own cost any damage by frost which may appear after Practical Completion of the Works, unless the Architect/Supervising Officer shall certify that such damage is due to injury which took place before Practical Completion of the Works.

19.01 This clause provides for: a certificate of practical completion (clause 15 (1)); the delivery of a schedule of defects, usually at the end of, but in any event not later than 14 days after the expiration of the defects liability period (clause 15 (2)); the issue from time to time of instructions to make good particular defects which appear in the defects liability period (clause 15 (3)); a certificate of completion of making good defects (clause 15(4)); damage by frost (clause 15 (5)). The clause should be read with clause 1 (architect's

satisfaction), clause 6 (standard of work) and para 34.10 for the way in which it fits into the final contract procedure.

Meaning of practical completion
19.02 It is not defined in the contract but it has been said (by Lord Dilhorne, *Westminster CC v Jarvis Ltd* (1970) 1 All ER 943, 948) that it does not mean the stage when the work 'was almost but not entirely finished' but 'the completion of all the construction work that has to be done'. Such completion is subject to defects which may thereafter appear and may be dealt with under clause 15 (*ibid* at p949). Lord Justice Salmon at the Court of Appeal stage of *Jarvis Ltd v Westminster CC* said:
'I take these words to mean completion for all practical purposes ie for the purpose of allowing the council to take possession of the works and use them as intended. If completion in clause 21 means completion down to the last detail, however trivial and unimportant, then clause 22 would be a penalty clause and as such unenforceable.'
Neither explanation is binding as to the meaning of the words for the purpose of considering whether the contractor has reached the stage of practical completion and the legal position is not clear. It is suggested that the architect can issue his certificate despite minor defects if (1) he is reasonably satisfied that the works accord with the contract, (2) there is adequate retention, (3) the employer will not suffer loss due to disturbance or otherwise, (4) he obtains a written acknowledgement of the existence of the defect and an undertaking to put it right from the contractor. If the defects are other than trivial the views of the employer should first be obtained.

Form of certificate
19.03 This is not prescribed by the contract but it should be clear and definite. The RIBA issues forms.

Effect of certificate of practical completion
19.04 It fixes the commencement of the defects liability period (clauses 15 (2), (3), 16 and Appendix) and of the period of final measurement (clause 30 (5) (a) and Appendix). It gives rise to the right to the release of the first half of the retention percentage (clause 30 (4) (b)); it is the time for the release of the obligation to insure under clause 20 [A] where clause 20 [A] applies; it is the end of the contractor's liability for damage to the works (see below para 23.03) arising as an incident of his obligation to complete.

Meaning of defects
19.05 For the contractor's obligations as to standards of workmanship, materials and goods see clauses 1, 6. The following are not defects for which the contractor is liable: the failure of the architect's design; the unsuitability for their purpose of goods or materials of good quality and exactly as described in the contract bills or as required by an instruction of, or sanctioned in writing by, the architect (see clauses 1, 2, 6 (i), 11 and 12).

Effect of site inspections
19.06 It is in general no excuse for a contractor to say that the architect or the clerk of works ought to have observed bad work on site inspections. For the position after the final certificate has been issued see clause 30 (7) (b).

Frost damage
19.07 The contractor is responsible for frost damage appearing within the defects liability period provided the architect certifies that the damage is due to injury which took place before practical completion.

Instructions under clause 15 (3): Making good defects

19.08 This clause enables the architect in a proper case to issue instructions before the schedule under clause 15 (2), but he should only do so when 'he considers it necessary so to do'. One of the matters to be taken into account in considering whether it is necessary to issue such instruction is probably whether it is reasonable to leave the defect unremedied until after issue of the schedule.

19.09 The meaning of the words '. . . *and (unless the architect shall otherwise instruct . . .) entirely at his own cost . . .*' is not certain. If, as seems likely, they give the architect power to instruct that the employer shall pay for the remedying of defects such power should, it is suggested, only be exercised in special circumstances.

Architect's remedies

19.10 For breach of an instruction to make good defects a notice under clause 2 (1) can be given and if it is not complied with, others can be employed to do the work necessary and the cost deducted from the retention percentage. Further, until defects have been made good the architect need not, and should not (subject to para 19.11), issue his certificate under clause 15 (4), so that the second half of the retention percentage is not released (clause 30 (4) (c)), and the issue of the final certificate, with the protection it usually affords the contractor (see clause 30 (7)), may be delayed. It is not clear whether the power of determination under clause 25 (1) (c) can be exercised after practical completion but the remedies just set out ought to be sufficient to make it unnecessary to attempt to rely on clause 25.

Irremediable breach

19.11 The architect may include a defect in an instruction or the schedule, but then find on representation by the contractor that it cannot be remedied except at a cost which is unreasonable in comparison with the loss to the employer and the nature of the defect. In such circumstances he has, it is thought, a discretion to issue his certificate under clause 15 (4) and to make a reduction in the amount certified for payment in respect of the works not properly carried out, being the amount by which the works are reduced in value by reason of the unremedied defect (see clause 30 (2), 30 (4) (c), 30 (6)), but where approval of the quality of any material or the standards of any workmanship is a matter for his opinion, he should not issue a final certificate (see clauses 1 (1), 30 (7) and paras 5.04 and 34.14).

Defects appearing after expiry of defects liability period

19.12 If defects appear after the issue of the certificate under clause 15 (4) the architect can no longer issue instructions under clause 15, but the appearance of the defect is the disclosure of a breach of contract by the contractor. The employer is entitled to damages, and the architect should adjust any further certificate to reflect the effect upon the value of the works. In accordance with common law rules as to mitigation of damages the contractor, if it is reasonable to do so, should be given the opportunity of rectifying the defects. An unqualified final certificate should not be issued if the defects are unremedied (see clause 30 (7) and para 34.14). For circumstances in which a final certificate should not be issued, see para 19.11.

20 Clause 16: Partial possession by employer

16 If at any time or times before Practical Completion of the Works the Employer with the consent of the Contractor shall take possession of any part or parts of the same (any such part being hereinafter in this clause referred to as 'the relevant part') then notwithstanding anything expressed or implied elsewhere in this Contract:—

(a) Within seven days from the date on which the Employer shall have taken possession of the relevant part the Architect/Supervising Officer shall issue a certificate stating his estimate of the approximate total value of the said part, and for all the purposes of this Condition (but for no other) the value so stated shall be deemed to be the total value of the said part.

(b) For the purposes of sub-paragraph (ii) of paragraph (f) of this Condition and of sub-clauses (2) (3) and (5) of clause 15 of these Conditions, Practical Completion of the relevant part shall be deemed to have occurred and the Defects Liability Period in respect of the relevant part shall be deemed to have commenced on the date on which the Employer shall have taken possession thereof.

(c) When in the opinion of the Architect/Supervising Officer any defects, shrinkages or other faults in the relevant part which he may have required to be made good under sub-clause (2) or sub-clause (3) of clause 15 of these Conditions shall have been made good he shall issue a certificate to that effect.

(d) The Contractor shall reduce the value insured under clause 20 [A] of these Conditions (if applicable) by the full value of the relevant part, and the said relevant part shall as from the date on which the Employer shall have taken possession thereof be at the sole risk of the Employer as regards any of the contingencies referred to in the said clause.

(e) In lieu of any sum to be paid or allowed by the Contractor under clause 22 of these Conditions in respect of any period during which the Works may remain incomplete occurring after the date on which the Employer shall have taken possession of the relevant part there shall be paid or allowed such sum as bears the same ratio to the sum which would be paid or allowed apart from the provisions of this Condition as does the Contract Sum less the total value of the said relevant part to the Contract Sum.

(f) (i) Within fourteen days of the date on which the Employer shall have taken possession of the relevant part there shall be paid to the Contractor from the sums then retained under clause 30 (3) of these Conditions a percentage (which percentage shall be equal to half the Retention Percentage) of the total value (subject to paragraph (iii) of this sub-clause) of the relevant part.

(ii) On the expiration of the Defects Liability Period named in the Appendix to these Conditions in respect of the relevant part or on the issue of the Certificate of Completion of Making Good Defects in respect of the relevant part, whichever is the later, there shall be paid to the Contractor from the sums then retained under clause 30 (3) of these Conditions a percentage (which percentage shall be equal to half the Retention Percentage) of the total value (subject to paragraph (iii) of this sub-clause) of the relevant part.

(iii) Where the total value of the relevant part includes works in respect of which a final payment to a nominated sub-contractor has been made under the provisions of clause 27(e) of these Conditions, the said total value for the purposes of paragraphs (i) and (ii) of this sub-clause shall be deemed to be reduced by the value of the said sub-contractor's work carried out in the relevant part.

20.01 This provides for the situation where, before the works are completed, the employer, with the consent of the contractor, takes possession of part or parts, and provides for the application to each part of provisions as to practical completion, defects, insurance, and retention percentage analogous to those which apply to the whole and for a proportionate reduction of any liquidated damages payable. If possession is given in sections the architect must apply this clause and has no power, without the consent of the parties, to issue a certificate of practical completion for an average date of completion.

Duty to complete in sections

20.02 This clause does not impose such a duty. If it is required obtain and use the JCT Sectional Completion Supplement, *Practice note 21*.

Use but not possession

20.03 Neither the standard form nor the JCT Sectional Completion Supplement provides for the situation where the employer requires use of part of the premises, say for storage, but not possession. Amendment is necessary particularly as to risk and insurance (for problems which arose in one case see *English Industrial Estates v Wimpey* (1973) (Lloyd's Rep 118).

21 Clause 17: Assignment of sub-letting

17 The Contractor shall not without the written consent of the Employer assign this Contract, and shall not without the written consent of the Architect/Supervising Officer (which consent shall not be unreasonably withheld to the prejudice of the Contractor) sub-let any portion of the Works.

Provided that it shall be a condition in any sub-letting which may occur that the employment of the sub-contractor under the sub-contract shall determine immediately upon the determination (for any reason) of the Contractor's employment under this Contract.

21.01 The contractor cannot without the employer's written consent assign the contract in the sense of getting others to perform his duties. Further it seems that the contractor is required to obtain the employer's consent to assign money due under the contract. In the private variant the employer is prohibited from assigning the contract without the consent of the contractor.

21.02 The words '. . . *sub-let* . . .' mean that the contractor without the architect's consent must not subcontract parts of his duties. Subcontractors in respect of whom the architect has given his consent are often and conveniently termed 'approved subcontractors'.

Breach of clause 17
21.03 It is a ground for determination by the employer, see clause 25 (1) (d).

'Specified' subcontractors
21.04 This is a term sometimes applied to subcontractors who are specified in the bills but who are not intended to be nominated and subject to clauses 27 and 28. There is no provision in the standard form for 'specified' subcontractors and such provision in the bills can cause legal difficulties, in particular in reducing the contractor's ordinary liability for subcontractors.

22 Clause 17A: Fair wages

> 17A (1) (a) The Contractor shall pay rates of wages and observe hours and conditions of labour not less favourable than those established for the trade or industry in the district where the work is carried out by machinery of negotiation or arbitration to which the parties are organisations of employers and trade unions representative respectively of substantial proportions of the employers and workers engaged in the trade or industry in the district.
>
> (b) In the absence of any rates of wages, hours or conditions of labour so established the Contractor shall pay rates of wages and observe hours and conditions of labour which are not less favourable than the general level of wages, hours and conditions observed by other employers whose general circumstances in the trade or industry in which the Contractor is engaged are similar.
>
> (2) The Contractor shall in respect of all persons employed by him (whether in carrying out this Contract or otherwise) in every factory, workshop or other place occupied or used by him for the carrying out of this Contract (including the Works) comply with the general conditions required by this Condition. The Contractor hereby warrants that to the best of his knowledge and belief he has complied with the general conditions required by this Condition for at least three months prior to the date of his tender for this Contract.
>
> (3) In the event of any question arising as to whether the requirements of this Condition are being observed, the question shall, if not otherwise disposed of, and notwithstanding anything in clause 35 of these Conditions (the provisions of which shall not apply to this Condition), be referred through the Minister of Labour or his successor for the time being to an independent Tribunal for decision.
>
> (4) The Contractor shall recognise the freedom of his workpeople to be members of Trade Unions.
>
> (5) The Contractor shall at all times during the continuance of this Contract display, for the information of his workpeople, in every factory, workshop or place occupied or used by him for the carrying out of this Contract (including the Works) a copy of this Condition. Where rates of wages, hours or conditions of work have been established either by negotiation or arbitration as described in paragraph (a) of sub-clause (1) of this Condition or by any agreement commonly recognised by employers and workers in the district a copy of the award agreement or other document specifying or recording such rates hours or conditions shall also be exhibited by the Contractor or made available by him for inspection in any such place as aforesaid.
>
> (6) The Contractor shall be responsible for the observance of this Condition by sub-contractors employed in the carrying out of this Contract, and shall if required notify the Employer of the names and addresses of all such sub-contractors.
>
> (7) The Contractor shall keep proper wages books and time sheets showing the wages paid to and the time worked by the workpeople in his employ in and about the carrying out of this Contract, and such wages books and time sheets shall be produced whenever required for the inspection of any officer authorised by the Employer.
>
> (8) If the Employer shall have reasonable ground for believing that the requirements of any of the preceding sub-clauses of this Condition are not being observed, he or the Architect/Supervising Officer on his behalf shall be entitled to require proof of the rates of wages paid and hours and conditions observed by the Contractor and sub-contractors in carrying out the Works.

22.01 This clause does not appear in the private variant.

23 Clause 18: Injury to persons and property and employer's indemnity

> 18 (1) The Contractor shall be liable for, and shall indemnify the Employer against, any liability, loss, claim or proceedings whatsoever arising under any statute or at common law in respect of personal injury to or the death of any person whomsoever arising out of or in the course of or caused by the carrying out of the Works, unless due to any act or neglect of the Employer or of any person for whom the Employer is responsible.
>
> (2) Except for such loss or damage as is at the risk of the Employer under clause 20 [B] or clause 20 [C] of these Conditions (if applicable) the Contractor shall be liable for, and shall indemnify the Employer against, any expense, liability, loss, claim or proceedings in respect of any injury or damage whatsoever to any property real or personal in so far as such injury or damage arises out of or in the course of or by reason of the carrying out of the Works, and provided always that the same is due to any negligence, omission or default of the Contractor, his servants or agents or of any sub-contractor his servants or agents.

Contractor's liability under clause 18 (1) in respect of personal injuries
23.01 It is very wide.

Contractor's liability under clause 18 (2) in respect of property
23.02 This is very wide, although the employer must prove default. Subject to the exceptions if clause 20 [B] or 20 [C] applies, the contractor is liable under this clause for: claims by third parties whose property is damaged; claims by the employer in respect of his property and, it seems, damage to the works.

23.03 In addition to his liability under clause 18 (2) the contractor must as an incident of his duty to complete (see clause 1 (1)) make good any damage to the works, such as that due to vandalism or theft, occurring before practical completion and not caused by the employer's negligence or default nor within the risks accepted by the employer where clause 20 (B) or 20 (C) is used. The contractor's plant equipment and unfixed goods and materials are at his risk. Goods and materials when certified for remain at his risk.

Employer and contractor liable to third party
23.04 In AMF *International Ltd v Magnet Bowling Ltd* (1968) 1 WLR 1028 both employer and contractor were held liable to a third party for damage to the third party's property; it was held that the employer could not recover under the indemnity in clause 18 (2) because the indemnity did not apply where, as was the case, the third party's loss arose partly as a result of the employer's negligence. But the employer succeeded in recovering from the contractor the sum he had to pay the third party because the damage arose from the contractor's failure to comply with items in the bills requiring the diversion of storm water and the protection of the works.

24 Clause 19: Insurance against injury to persons and property. Clause 19A: Excepted risks—nuclear perils etc Clause 20: Insurance of the works against fire etc

> 19 (1) (a) Without prejudice to his liability to indemnify the Employer under clause 18 of these Conditions the Contractor shall maintain and shall cause any sub-contractor to maintain such insurances as are necessary to cover the liability of the Contractor or, as the case may be, of such sub-contractor in respect of personal injury or death arising out of or in the course of or caused by the carrying out of the Works not due to any act or neglect of the Employer or of any person for whom the Employer is responsible and in respect of injury or damage to property, real or personal, arising out of or in the course of or by reason of the carrying out of the Works and caused by any negligence, omission or default of the Contractor, his servants or agents or, as the case may be, of such sub-contractor, his servants or agents. The insurance in respect of claims for personal injury to, or the death of, any person under a contract of service or apprenticeship with the Contractor or the sub-contractor as the case may be, and arising out of and in the course of such person's employment, shall comply with the Employer's Liability (Compulsory Insurance) Act 1969 and any statutory orders made thereunder or any amendment or re-enactment thereof. For all other claims to which this sub-clause applies the insurance cover shall be the sum stated in the Appendix to these Conditions (or such greater sum as the Contractor may choose) for any one occurrence or series of occurrences arising out of one event.
>
> (b) As and when he is reasonably required so to do by the Employer the Contractor shall produce and shall cause any sub-contractor to produce for inspection by the Employer documentary evidence that the insurances required by this sub-clause are properly maintained, but on any occasion the Employer may (but not unreasonably or vexatiously) require to have produced for his inspection the policy or policies and receipts in question.
>
> (c) Should the Contractor or any sub-contractor make default in insuring or in continuing or in causing to insure as provided in this sub-clause the Employer may himself insure against any risk with respect to which the default shall have occurred and may deduct a sum or sums equivalent to the amount paid or payable in respect of premiums from any monies due or to become due to the Contractor.
>
> (2) (a) The Contractor shall maintain in the joint names of the Employer and the Contractor insurances for such amounts of indemnity as may be specified by way of provisional sum items in the Contract Bills in respect of any expense, liability, loss, claim, or proceedings which the Employer may incur or sustain by reason of damage to any property other than the Works caused by collapse, subsidence, vibration, weakening or removal of support or lowering of ground water arising out of or in the course of or by reason of the carrying out of the Works excepting damage
>
> (i) caused by the negligence, omission or default of the Contractor, his servants or agents or of any sub-contractor his servants or agents;
>
> (ii) attributable to errors or omissions in the designing of the Works;
>
> (iii) which can reasonably be foreseen to be inevitable having regard to the nature of the work to be executed or the manner of its execution;
>
> (iv) which is at the risk of the Employer under clause 20 [B] or clause 20 [C] of these Conditions (if applicable);
>
> (v) arising from a nuclear risk or a war risk;
>
> (b) Any such insurance as is referred to in the immediately preceding paragraph shall be placed with insurers to be approved by the Employer, and the Contractor shall deposit with him the policy or policies and the receipts in respect of premiums paid.
>
> (c) Should the Contractor make default in insuring or in continuing to insure as provided in this sub-clause the Employer may himself insure against any risk with respect to which the default shall have occurred and the amounts paid or payable by the Employer in respect of premiums shall not be set against the relevant provisional sum in the settlement of accounts under clause 30 (5) (c) of these Conditions.

19A Notwithstanding the provisions of clauses 18 (2) or 19 of these Conditions, the Contractor shall not be liable either to indemnify the Employer or to insure against any damage, loss or injury caused to the Works, the site, or any property, by the effect of ionising radiations or contamination by radioactivity from any nuclear fuel or from any nuclear waste from the combustion of nuclear fuel, radioactive toxic explosive or other hazardous properties of any explosive nuclear assembly or nuclear component thereof, pressure waves caused by aircraft or other aerial devices travelling at sonic or supersonic speeds.

20 *[A] (1) The Contractor shall in the joint names of the Employer and Contractor insure against loss and damage by** fire, lightning, explosion, storm, tempest, flood, bursting or overflowing of water tanks, apparatus or pipes, earthquake, aircraft and other aerial devices or articles dropped therefrom, riot and civil commotion (excluding any loss or damage caused by ionising radiations or contamination by radioactivity from any nuclear fuel or from any nuclear waste from the combustion of nuclear fuel, radioactive toxic explosive or other hazardous properties of any explosive nuclear assembly or nuclear component thereof, pressure waves caused by aircraft or other aerial devices travelling at sonic or supersonic speeds) for the full value thereof (plus the percentage (if any) named in the Appendix to these Conditions to cover professional fees) all work executed and all unfixed materials and goods, delivered to, placed on or adjacent to the Works and intended therefor but excluding temporary buildings, plant, tools and equipment owned or hired by the Contractor or any sub-contractor, and shall keep such work, material and goods so insured until Practical Completion of the Works. Such insurance shall be with insurers approved by the Employer and the Contractor shall deposit with him the policy or policies and the receipts in respect of premiums paid; and should the Contractor make default in insuring or continuing to insure as aforesaid the Employer may himself insure against any risk in respect of which the default shall have occurred and deduct a sum equivalent to the amount paid by him in respect of premiums from any monies due or to become due to the Contractor. Provided always that if the Contractor shall independently of his obligations under this Contract maintain a policy of insurance which covers (*inter alia*) the said work, materials and goods against the aforesaid contingencies to the full value thereof (plus the aforesaid percentage (if any)), then the maintenance by the Contractor of such policy shall, if the Employer's interest in that policy of insurance is endorsed thereon, be a discharge of the Contractor's obligation to insure in the joint names of the Employer and Contractor; if and so long as the Contractor is able to produce for inspection as and when he is reasonably required so to do by the Employer documentary evidence that the said policy is properly endorsed and maintained then the Contractor shall be discharged from his obligation to deposit a policy or policies and receipts with the Employer but on any occasion the Employer may (but not unreasonably or vexatiously) require to have produced for his inspection the policy and receipts in question.

(2) Upon acceptance of any claim under the insurances aforesaid the Contractor with due diligence shall restore work damaged replace or repair any unfixed materials or goods which have been destroyed or injured remove and dispose of any debris and proceed with the carrying out and completion of the Works. All monies received from such insurances (less only the aforesaid percentage (if any)) shall be paid to the Contractor by instalments under certificates of the Architect/Supervising Officer issued at the Period of Interim Certificates named in the Appendix to these Conditions. The Contractor shall not be entitled to any payment in respect of the restoration of work damaged, the replacement and repair of any unfixed materials or goods, and the removal and disposal of debris other than the monies received under the said insurances.

*[B]. All work executed and all unfixed materials and goods, delivered to, placed on or adjacent to the Works and intended therefor (except temporary buildings, plant, tools and equipment owned or hired by the Contractor or any sub-contractor) shall be at the sole risk of the Employer as regards loss or damage by fire, lightning, explosion, storm, tempest, flood, bursting or overflowing of water tanks, apparatus or pipes, earthquake, aircraft and other aerial devices or articles dropped therefrom riot and civil commotion (excluding any loss or damage caused by ionising radiations or contamination by radioactivity from any nuclear fuel or from any nuclear waste from the combustion of nuclear fuel, radioactive toxic explosive or other hazardous properties of any explosive nuclear assembly or nuclear component thereof, pressure waves caused by aircraft or other aerial devices travelling at sonic or supersonic speeds). If any loss or damage affecting the Works or any part thereof or any such unfixed materials or goods is occasioned by any one or more of the said contingencies then, upon discovering the said loss or damage the Contractor shall forthwith give notice in writing both to the Architect/Supervising Officer and the Employer of the extent, nature and location thereof and

(a) The occurrence of such loss or damage shall be disregarded in computing any amounts payable to the Contractor under or by virtue of this Contract.

(b) The Contractor with due diligence shall restore work damaged, replace or repair any unfixed materials or goods which have been destroyed or injured, remove, and dispose of any debris and proceed with the carrying out and completion of the Works. The restoration of work damaged, the replacement and repair of unfixed materials and goods and the removal and disposal of debris shall be deemed to be a variation required by the Architect/Supervising Officer.

*[C]. The existing structures together with the contents thereof owned by him or for which he is responsible and the Works and all unfixed materials and goods, delivered to, placed on or adjacent to the Works and intended therefor (except temporary buildings, plant, tools and equipment owned or hired by the Contractor or any sub-contractor) shall be at the sole risk of the Employer as regards loss or damage by fire, lightning, explosion, storm, tempest, flood, bursting or overflowing of water tanks, apparatus or pipes, earthquake, aircraft and other aerial devices or articles dropped therefrom, riot and civil commotion (excluding any loss or damage caused by ionising radiations or contamination by radioactivity from any nuclear fuel or from any nuclear waste from the combustion of nuclear fuel, radioactive toxic explosive or other hazardous properties of any explosive nuclear assembly or nuclear component thereof, pressure waves caused by aircraft or other aerial devices travelling at sonic or supersonic speeds), and the Employer shall maintain adequate insurance against those risks.** If any loss or damage affecting the Works or any part thereof or any such unfixed materials or goods is occasioned by any one or more of the said contingencies then, upon discovering the said loss or damage the Contractor shall forthwith give notice in writing both to the Architect/Supervising Officer and to the Employer of the extent, nature and location thereof and

(a) The occurrence of such loss or damage shall be disregarded in computing any amounts payable to the Contractor under or by virtue of this Contract.

(b) (i) If it is just and equitable so to do the employment of the Contractor under this Contract may within 28 days of the occurrence of such loss or damage be determined at the option of either party by notice by registered post or recorded delivery from either party to the other. Within 7 days of receiving such a notice (but not thereafter) either party may give to the other a written request to concur in the appointment of an arbitrator under clause 35 of these Conditions in order that it may be determined whether such determination will be just and equitable.

(ii) Upon the giving or receiving by the Employer of such a notice of determination or, where a reference to arbitration is made as aforesaid, upon the arbitrator upholding the notice of determination, the provisions of sub-clause (2) (except sub-paragraph (vi) of paragraph (b)) of clause 26 of these Conditions shall apply.

(c) If no notice of determination is served as aforesaid, or, where a reference to arbitration is made as aforesaid, if the arbitrator decides against the notice of determination, then

(i) the Contractor with due diligence shall reinstate or make good such loss or damage, and proceed with the carrying out and completion of the Works;

(ii) the Architect/Supervising Officer may issue instructions requiring the Contractor to remove and dispose of any debris; and

(iii) the reinstatement and making good of such loss or damage and (when required) the removal and disposal of debris shall be deemed to be a variation required by the Architect/Supervising Officer.

***Footnote.**—*Clause 20 [A] is applicable to the erection of a new building if the Contractor is required to insure against loss or damage by fire, etc.; clause 20 [B] is applicable to the erection of a new building if the Employer is to bear the risk in respect of loss or damage by fire, etc.; and clause 20 [C] is applicable to alterations of or extensions to an existing building; therefore strike out clauses [B] and [C] or clauses [A] and [C] or clauses [A] and [B] as the case may require.*

****Footnote.**—*In some cases it may not be possible for insurance to be taken out against certain of the risks mentioned in this clause. This matter should be arranged between the parties at the tender stage and the clause amended accordingly.*

24.01 Clauses 19, 19A and 20 should be considered together. They should be referred to for their exact words, but a general introduction follows. Clause 19 provides for the contractor to insure: in all cases against his liability for personal injuries and to property (clause 19 (1) (a)); as may be specified by way of provisional sum items, in the joint names of the employer and himself, against liability or loss to the employer due to damage to property caused otherwise than by the contractor's negligence and certain other exceptions (clause 19 (2) (a)). Clause 20 has three alternatives. Under clause 20 (A) the contractor must in the joint names of himself and the employer insure the works against fire and other named contingencies. Under clause 20 (B) or clause 20 (C) the works are at the risk of the employer as regards such contingencies. Each version of clause 20 has provision for restoration and rebuilding subject to the determination of the contractor's employment in certain circumstances.

Clause 19 (2) (a): Insurance

24.02 The need for such insurance must be considered according to the circumstances of each case. It is particularly important when working in cities where neighbouring properties may be damaged by the carrying out of the works. The architect must give instructions for the placing of the insurance (see clause 11 (3)) to be paid for out of the provisional sum. The exceptions are such that it may be prudent in some cases for the employer to arrange further insurance outside that contemplated by the standard form.

Clause 20 (A): Insurance

24.03 This is the usual clause for insurance of the works. The risks to be covered do not include damage by theft or vandalism, but the contractor is liable for such damage (see para 23.02). Many contractors cover such risks by a so-called 'all risks' policy.

Clause 20 (B): Fire etc—employer's risk

24.04 The use of this alternative clause has been criticised on the grounds that by transferring to the employer such a wide range of risks of damage to the works, it gives the contractor no inducement to take reasonable care of the works. It seems that the employer is liable even where the fire or other contingency was caused by the contractor's own negligence.

Clause 20 (*B*): *Insurance*

24.05 In the private variant the employer must insure and produce the policy for inspection by the contractor.

Clause 20 (C): Alterations

24.06 This alternative is recommended for use where alterations or extensions are to be made. The risks of damage both to the existing structures and to the works are borne by the employer. The special provisions for determination are in place of the right of the contractor to determine arising under clause 26 (1) (c) (ii).

25 Clause 21: Possession, completion and postponement

21 (1) On the Date for Possession stated in the Appendix to these Conditions possession of the site shall be given to the Contractor who shall thereupon begin the Works and regularly and diligently proceed with the same, and who shall complete the same on or before the Date for Completion stated in the said Appendix subject nevertheless to the provisions for extension of time contained in clauses 23 and 33 (1) (c) of these Conditions.

(2) The Architect/Supervising Officer may issue instructions in regard to the postponement of any work to be executed under the provisions of this Contract.

25.01 This clause should be read with clause 22 (liquidated damages) and 23 (extension of time).

25.02 If '. . . *possession of the site* . . .' cannot be given on the date for possession the architect should issue instructions for postponement of the works under clause 21 (2) and can grant an extension of time under clause 23 (e). Failure to take these steps may invalidate the provisions for payment of liquidated damages. If the postponement is to be longer than the period referred to in clause 26 (1) (c) he should, after consulting the employer, try to make a special agreement with the contractor to avoid the danger of a determination.

25.03 The words '. . . *complete the same* . . .' mean completion to the stage of practical completion (for meaning see para 19.02).

Clause 21 (2): Postponement
25.04 Note the contractor's right to extension of time (clause 23 (e)), to loss and expense under clause 24 (1) (e) and, if the whole of the works are suspended for the period of delay stated in the appendix, to determination (clause 25 (1) (c) (iv)).

26 Clause 22: Damages for non-completion

> **22** If the Contractor fails to complete the Works by the Date for Completion stated in the Appendix to these Conditions or within any extended time fixed under clause 23 or clause 33 (1) (c) of these Conditions and the Architect/Supervising Officer certifies in writing that in his opinion the same ought reasonably to have been completed, then the Contractor shall pay or allow to the Employer a sum calculated at the rate stated in the said Appendix as Liquidated and Ascertained Damages for the period during which the Works shall so remain or have remained incomplete, and the Employer may deduct such sum from any monies due or to become due to the Contractor under this Contract.

26.01 This clause gives the employer the right to deduct or claim liquidated damages if the contractor fails to achieve practical completion by the date for completion extended as may be necessary under clause 23 and the architect has given his certificate under this clause. The certificate is, it seems, required in order to ensure that the architect has properly considered any notices of delay under clause 23 and has granted all extensions of time to which the contractor is entitled. The clause only seems to contemplate one certificate but probably in certain circumstances more than one can be given, eg when the completion date is past and a certificate has been issued but subsequently a cause of delay arises entitling the contractor to an extension of time.

Liquidated damages
26.02 If there is no provision for liquidated damages, ascertainment of damage suffered for non-completion can involve the parties in long and costly proceedings. Where the parties have made and agreed upon a genuine pre-estimate of damages such proceedings are avoided. The rate agreed, termed here 'liquidated and ascertained damages', will be given effect to by the courts, without inquiry into the actual loss suffered. Thus, for example, a contractor cannot resist payment merely by showing that the works when completed stood empty, neither can the employer claim more than the agreed rate by showing that it was much less than the rents he has lost. The agreed rate cannot be set aside merely because 'the consequences of the breach are such as to make precise pre-estimation almost an impossibility. On the contrary that is just the situation when it is probable that pre-estimated damage was the true bargain between the parties' (*Dunlop v New Garage Co* (1915) AC 79, 86). The contractor can, however, have the agreed rate set aside and make the employer prove, and be limited to, his actual loss if the rate was a penalty. This means not merely that it exceeded the actual loss but that the rate was so high that it could not have been a genuine pre-estimate.

Deduction of liquidated damages
26.03 The architect certifies for payment in full under clause 30 and the employer can deduct liquidated damages. In practice, although not required by the contract and not

binding upon the parties, it is a convenient course for the architect when giving his certificate under clause 22 to set out his calculation of the employer's right to liquidated damages and send a copy to each party.

27 Clause 23: Extension of time

> **23** Upon it becoming reasonably apparent that the progress of the Works is delayed, the Contractor shall forthwith give written notice of the cause of the delay to the Architect/Supervising Officer, and if in the opinion of the Architect/Supervising Officer the completion of the Works is likely to be or has been delayed beyond the Date for Completion stated in the Appendix to these Conditions or beyond any extended time previously fixed under either this clause or clause 33 (1) (c) of these Conditions.
>
> (a) by *force majeure*, or
>
> (b) by reason of any exceptionally inclement weather, or
>
> (c) by reason of loss or damage occasioned by any one or more of the contingencies referred to in clause 20 [A], [B] or [C] of these Conditions, or
>
> (d) by reason of civil commotion, local combination of workmen, strike or lockout affecting any of the trades employed upon the Works or any of the trades engaged in the preparation manufacture or transportation of any of the goods or materials required for the Works, or
>
> (e) by reason of Architect's/Supervising Officer's instructions issued under clauses 1 (2), 11 (1) or 21 (2) of these Conditions, or
>
> (f) by reason of the Contractor not having received in due time necessary instructions, drawings, details or levels from the Architect/Supervising Officer for which he specifically applied in writing on a date which having regard to the Date for Completion stated in the Appendix to these Conditions or to any extension of time then fixed under this clause or clause 33 (1) (c) of these Conditions was neither unreasonably distant from nor unreasonably close to the date on which it was necessary for him to receive the same, or
>
> (g) by delay on the part of nominated sub-contractors or nominated suppliers which the Contractor has taken all practicable steps to avoid or reduce, or
>
> (h) by delay on the part of artists tradesmen or others engaged by the Employer in executing work not forming part of this Contract, or
>
> (i) by reason of the opening up for inspection of any work covered up or of the testing of any of the work materials or goods in accordance with clause 6 (3) of these Conditions (including making good in consequence of such opening up or testing), unless the inspection or test showed that the work materials or goods were not in accordance with this Contract, or
>
> *(j) (i) by the Contractor's inability for reasons beyond his control and which he could not reasonably have foreseen at the date of this Contract to secure such labour as is essential to the proper carrying out of the Works, or
>
> (ii) by the Contractor's inability for reasons beyond his control and which he could not reasonably have foreseen at the date of this Contract to secure such goods and/or materials as are essential to the proper carrying out of the Works, or
>
> (k) by reason of compliance with the provisions of clause 34 of these Conditions or with Architect's/Supervising Officer's instructions issued thereunder, or
>
> (l) by a local authority or statutory undertaker in carrying out work in pursuance of its statutory obligations in relation to the Works, or in failing to carry out such work,
>
> then the Architect/Supervising Officer shall so soon as he is able to estimate the length of the delay beyond the date or time aforesaid make in writing a fair and reasonable extension of time for completion of the Works. Provided always that the Contractor shall use constantly his best endeavours to prevent delay and shall do all that may reasonably be required to the satisfaction of the Architect/Supervising Officer to proceed with the Works.
>
> *Footnote.—Strike out either or both of the sub-clauses (j) (i) or (j) (ii) if not to apply.

27.01 This clause imposes a duty upon the architect of considering notices of certain specified causes of delay by the contractor and, where the facts justify such a course, granting extensions of time. His decisions under this and clause 22 are subject to arbitration, even it seems, after the final certificate has been given (see para 34.15).

Notice of cause of delay
27.02 Notice is sufficient. There does not have to be an application for extension of time as such. But it is submitted that before the architect performs his duty of considering the delay and granting any appropriate extension he is entitled to such information from the contractor as he may reasonably require for this purpose. In particular this is important if clause 31F (the 'formula' fluctuations clause) applies; see clause 31F (7) (b) (ii) and para 35.11.

Notice late or not given
27.03 Probably (although the point is not clear) the architect need not grant an extension if a notice is never served. If the notice is late he probably must grant an extension but for no greater period than if it had been given in time taking into account any steps to avoid or reduce delay which the architect could have taken by some instruction or reasonable requirement (see proviso to clause 23). See further para 27.09.

Applications for loss and expense under clause 11 (6) and 24 (1)
27.04 An extension of time relieves the contractor from liability for liquidated damages but gives him no right to extra payment. The causes of delay in clauses 23 (e), (f), (h),

(i) and (k) are however part of the grounds for recovery of loss and expense under clauses 11 (6), 24 (1) and 34. The contractor must make it clear whether notice of a cause of delay is also an application under one of these clauses.

27.05 The words '. . . *the completion of the works* . . .' mean that notice must be given upon the progress of the works being delayed but an extension is to be made only if the completion of the works is likely to be or has been delayed. Thus, for example, a delay in the progress of the works at an early stage may, by the performance by the contractor of his duty to use his best endeavours to prevent delay, be reduced or eliminated by the time of completion. It is thought that the contractor's performance of such duty or his compliance with the architect's reasonable requirements (see clause 23) includes, where necessary, the alteration of his programme without any instruction under clause 21 (2). If the architect gives such instruction the contractor may be able to claim loss and expense under clause 24 (1) (e).

Clause 23 (a)
27.06 The meaning of the term '. . . *force majeure* . . .' is difficult to state exactly, but very broadly the words extend to special circumstances quite outside the control of the contractor and not dealt with elsewhere in the contract. Interference by government and the effect of epidemics are examples of events which are probably within the sub-clause.

Clause 23 (b)
27.07 To be '. . . *exceptionally inclement weather* . . .' ordinary seasonal bad weather is not sufficient.

Clause 23 (c)
27.08 The '. . . *contingencies referred to in clause* 20 (*A*), (*B*) *or* (*C*) . . .' are very wide and their underlying causes may, in some instances, be due to acts of negligence on the part of the contractor.

Clause 23 (f)
27.09 The phrase '. . . *neither unreasonably distant from* . . .' refers to drawings etc. If these were in fact late but the contractor has failed to make a specific application at the time required, the architect should not refuse to consider whether to make an extension but can, it is thought, take into account the effect, if any, of such failure when considering the amount of any extension (see para 27.03). The failure by the architect to grant an extension on the grounds of delay in issue of instructions or drawings or other causes within the control of the employer or his agents ordinarily invalidates the entire liquidated damages provisions.

Clause 23 (g)
27.10 If there is an extension of time on grounds of '. . . *delay on the part of nominated subcontractors or nominated suppliers* . . .' this deprives the employer of remedy for delay in completion of the works, and neither the contractor nor the nominated supplier or subcontractor has to pay the liquidated damages for the extension. In addition, the extension must be granted whatever the cause of the delay, including the making good of his own bad work by a nominated subcontractor before completion of his sub-contract work (*Westminster City Council v Jarvis Ltd* (1970) 1 All ER 943). But where defects are discovered in the sub-contract works after the nominated subcontractor has purported to complete the works and the works have been accepted by the architect and contractor, there is no right for an extension, even where accepted with some suspicion (*ibid*). The employer's interests in respect of loss caused by delay on the part of nominated

subcontractors and nominated suppliers can be protected by obtaining warranties of timely completion from them. The RIBA issue for this purpose a form of agreement between an employer and a subcontractor nominated under the standard form of Building Contract 1963 edition and a form of warranty to be given by nominated suppliers. For nominated sub-contractors and nominated suppliers generally, see clauses 27, 28, and para 31.03.

Clause 23 (j)
27.11 The sub-clauses '. . . *which he could not reasonably have foreseen* . . .' are optional in the sense that the parties are expressly invited to consider deleting them or one of them. If the sub-clauses are used the words quoted limit their effect.

27.12 The phrase '. . . *the architect shall so soon as he is able to estimate the length of the delay* . . .' refers to the delay in the completion of the works. Although it is better that the architect should make his extension before completion if possible, it seems that he is entitled to make it after completion, if that is as soon as he is able to estimate the length of the delay. See also clause 31F (7) (b) (ii) and para 35.11.

27.13 The words '. . . *a fair and reasonable extension of time* . . .' acknowledge that the period of extension sometimes has to be arrived at as a matter of judgment considering many factors, which may include:
1 The exact terms and application to the facts of the sub-clause in question.
2 The amount of the immediate delay in the progress of the works.
3 The effect of any causes of delay which are not within clause 23.
4 The effect of concurrent causes of delay whether within clause 23 or not and whether one of them is a critical or overriding cause of delay and, if so, for what period.
5 The extent to which the contractor has complied with the proviso to clause 23.

28 Clause 24: Loss and expense caused by disturbance of regular progress of the works

24 (1) If upon written application being made to him by the Contractor the Architect/Supervising Officer is of the opinion that the Contractor has been involved in direct loss and/or expense for which he would not be reimbursed by a payment made under any other provision in this Contract by reason of the regular progress of the Works or of any part thereof having been materially affected by:

    (a) The Contractor not having received in due time necessary instructions, drawings, details or levels from the Architect/Supervising Officer for which he specifically applied in writing on a date which having regard to the Date for Completion stated in the Appendix to these Conditions or to any extension of time then fixed under clause 23 or clause 33 (1) (c) of these Conditions was neither unreasonably distant from nor unreasonably close to the date on which it was necessary for him to receive the same; or

    (b) The opening up for inspection of any work covered up or the testing of any of the work materials or goods in accordance with clause 6 (3) of these Conditions (including making good in consequence of such opening up or testing), unless the inspection or test showed that the work, materials or goods were not in accordance with this Contract; or

    (c) Any discrepancy in or divergence between the Contract Drawings and/or the Contract Bills; or

    (d) Delay on the part of artists tradesmen or others engaged by the Employer in executing work not forming part of this Contract; or

    (e) Architect's/Supervising Officer's instructions issued in regard to the postponement of any work to be executed under the provisions of this Contract;

and if the written application is made within a reasonable time of it becoming apparent that the progress of the Works or of any part thereof has been affected as aforesaid, then the Architect/Supervising Officer shall either himself ascertain or shall instruct the Quantity Surveyor to ascertain the amount of such loss and/or expense. Any amount from time to time so ascertained shall be added to the Contract Sum, and if an Interim Certificate is issued after the date of ascertainment any such amount shall be added to the amount which would otherwise be stated as due in such Certificate.

(2) The provisions of this Condition are without prejudice to any other rights and remedies which the Contractor may possess.

Nature of clause 24
28.01 This is sometimes thought of as the only clause under which claims can be made, but as appears below this is not correct. Clause 24 (1) provides a right for the contractor in certain carefully defined circumstances to obtain payment to be added to the contract sum and certified for payment, in

respect of some of the more common causes of disturbance of the progress of the works. Clause 24 (2) preserves any other rights and remedies which the contractor may possess; in practice this usually means claims for damages.

Claims generally

28.02 The term 'claim' has no exact meaning, but for present purposes it may be considered as any claim for payment by the contractor in respect of the original contract work arising other than under clause 30 (2). Any such claim falls under one of the following categories:

1 A right to payment arising under a clause of the contract.
2 A claim for damages ordinarily for breach of contract.
3 A claim under neither 1 nor 2.

If a claim comes within 1 the architect follows whatever procedure the contract prescribes according to the clause relied on by the contractor. The architect need not consult the employer, although he may do so if he thinks it desirable (see para 5.03). If the claim falls within 2 the architect should consult the employer and should not include any sum in a certificate in respect of such a claim without the employer's agreement, for the contract gives him no power to certify in respect of claim for damages. If the claim falls within 3 the contractor has no right to payment. The architect cannot certify save on the employer's direction and any payment will be made *ex gratia*.

Claims under the contract (category 1)

28.03 They can arise under clauses 4 (2) (statutory requirements), 11 (variations), 12 (2) (deemed variations), 15 (defects), 20 (insurance), 24 (1) (disturbance), 31 (fluctuations), 32 and 33 (war), 34 (antiquities). There is no general provision which requires the contractor to specify the clause upon which he relies, although a duty to do so may be implied. In any event the contractor must comply with the requirement of any particular clause upon which he relies, and, it is thought, provide the architect with reasonable information which shows that the right to certification and payment has arisen.

Claims for damages (category 2)

28.04 Such claims are not extinguished merely because there are contractual rights covering similar grounds (clause 24 (2)). This sometimes gives rise to difficult problems, particularly with regard to claims in respect of alleged delay in the issue of instructions and drawings. When considering whether a claim is established under clause 24 (1) (a) the architect must be satisfied that the requirements as to specific application in writing for such instructions, and written application for loss and expense have been complied with. But if the contractor can show that he was in fact delayed and suffered loss through the lack of drawings or details at such times as were necessary for him to receive them it seems that he can claim damages for breach of clause 3 (4) even if he has not made the applications necessary to establish a claim under clause 24 (1) (a). Further, if instructions were not given at reasonable times, then again, despite the absence of written applications, there is *prima facie* a breach of the term implied at common law that instructions will be given at reasonable times. In each case the contractor may establish a right to damages although the amount recoverable may be reduced by any failure on his part to take reasonable steps to reduce his loss by applying for drawings or instructions.

Claims other than for damages or under the contract (category 3)

28.05 Such claims give rise to no right in law to any payment. There is no right for a contractor to be paid for unanticipated losses merely because they were due to causes outside his control; neither is it a ground for extra payment 'that the basis of the contract has gone'—unless it has gone because of the employer's default in which case the claim falls into category (2). In certain circumstances the contractor may be able to show that he is excused from further performance because the contract has become frustrated within the meaning of that term as explained by the courts. Frustration rarely arises. It usually requires a fundamental change of circumstances or an event of a catastrophic or fundamental nature which results in a complete stoppage of work.

Comparison with clause 11 (6)

28.06 See paras 15.15 to 15.17 for a discussion of 'direct loss and expense'. There may be a difference in the requirements as to notice under the two clauses. Under clause 24 written application must be made within a reasonable time of it becoming apparent that the regular progress of the works or of any part has been materially affected. Under clause 11 (6) it seems that notice may in some circumstances be given later (see para 15.16).

Regular progress of the works

28.07 An agreed programme of works is some, but not conclusive, evidence of what '. . . *regular progress of the works . . .*' should be.

28.08 For clarification of the phrase '. . . *and if the written application . . .*' see para 27.04 for notices under clause 23.

29 Clause 25: Determination by employer

25 (1) Without prejudice to any other rights or remedies which the Employer may possess, if the Contractor shall make default in any one or more of the following respects, that is to say:—

(a) If he without reasonable cause wholly suspends the carrying out of the Works before completion thereof, or

(b) If he fails to proceed regularly and diligently with the Works, or

(c) If he refuses or persistently neglects to comply with a written notice from the Architect/Supervising Officer requiring him to remove defective work or improper materials or goods and by such refusal or neglect the Works are materially affected, or

(d) If he fails to comply with the provisions of either clause 17 or clause 17A of these Conditions, then the Architect/Supervising Officer may give to him a notice by registered post or recorded delivery specifying the default, and if the Contractor either shall continue such default for fourteen days after receipt of such notice or shall at any time thereafter repeat such default (whether previously repeated or not), then the Employer may within ten days after such continuance or repetition by notice by registered post or recorded delivery forthwith determine the employment of the Contractor under this Contract, provided that such notice shall not be given unreasonably or vexatiously.

(2) In the event of the Contractor becoming bankrupt or making a composition or arrangement with his creditors or having a winding up order made or (except for purposes of reconstruction) a resolution for voluntary winding up passed or a provisional liquidator receiver or manager of his business or undertaking duly appointed, or possession taken, by or on behalf of the holders of any debentures secured by a floating charge, of any property comprised in or subject to the floating charge, the employment of the Contractor under this Contract shall be forthwith automatically determined but the said employment may be reinstated and continued if the Employer and the Contractor his trustee in bankruptcy liquidator provisional liquidator receiver or manager as the case may be shall so agree.

(3) The Employer shall be entitled to determine the employment of the Contractor under this or any other contract, if the Contractor shall have offered or given or agreed to give to any person any gift or consideration of any kind as an inducement or reward for doing or forbearing to do or for having done or forborne to do any action in relation to the obtaining or execution of this or any other contract with the Employer, or for showing or forbearing to show favour or disfavour to any person in relation to this or any other contract with the Employer, or if the like acts shall have been done by any person employed by the Contractor or acting on his behalf (whether with or without the knowledge of the Contractor), or if in relation to this or any other contract with the Employer the Contractor or any person employed by him or acting on his behalf shall have committed any offence under the Prevention of Corruption Acts, 1889 to 1916, or shall have given any fee or reward the receipt of which is an offence under sub-section (2) of section 117 of the Local Government Act 1972 or any re-enactment thereof.

(4) In the event of the employment of the Contractor under this Contract being determined as aforesaid and so long as it has not been reinstated and continued, the following shall be the respective rights and duties of the Employer and Contractor:

(a) The Employer may employ and pay other persons to carry on and complete the Works and he or they may enter upon the Works and use all temporary buildings, plant, tools, equipment, goods and materials intended for, delivered to and placed on or adjacent to the Works, and may purchase all materials and goods necessary for the carrying out and completion of the Works.

(b) The Contractor shall (except where the determination occurs by reason of the bankruptcy of the Contractor or of him having a winding up order made or (except for the purposes of reconstruction) a resolution for voluntary winding up passed), if so required by the Employer or Architect/Supervising Officer within fourteen days of the date of determination, assign to the Employer without payment the benefit of any agreement for the supply of materials or goods and/or for the execution of any work for the purposes of this Contract but on the terms that a supplier or sub-contractor shall be entitled to make any reasonable objection to any further assignment thereof by the Employer. In any case the Employer may pay any supplier or sub-contractor for any materials or goods delivered or works executed for the purposes of this Contract (whether before or after the date of determination) in so far as the price thereof has not already been paid by the Contractor. The Employer's rights under this paragraph are in addition to his rights to pay nominated sub-contractors as provided in clause 27 (c) of these Conditions and payments made under this paragraph may be deducted from any sum due or to become due to the Contractor.

(c) The Contractor shall as and when required in writing by the Architect/Supervising Officer so to do (but not before) remove from the Works any temporary buildings, plant, tools, equipment, goods and materials belonging to or hired by him. If within a reasonable time after any such requirement has been made the Contractor has not complied therewith, then the Employer may (but without being responsible for any loss or damage) remove and sell any such property of the Contractor, holding the proceeds less all costs incurred to the credit of the Contractor.

(d) The Contractor shall allow or pay to the Employer in the manner hereinafter appearing the amount of any direct loss and/or damage caused to the Employer by the determination. Until after completion of the Works under paragraph (a) of this sub-clause the Employer shall not be bound by any provision of this Contract to make any further payment to the Contractor, but upon such completion and the verification within a reasonable time of the accounts therefor the Architect/Supervising Officer shall certify the amount of expenses properly incurred by the Employer and the amount of any direct loss and/or damage caused to the Employer by the determination and, if such amounts when added to the monies paid to the Contractor before the date of determination exceed the total amount which would have been payable on due completion in accordance with this Contract, the difference shall be a debt payable to the Employer by the Contractor; and if the said amounts when added to the said monies be less than the said total amount, the difference shall be a debt payable by the Employer to the Contractor.

29.01 This clause provides for: determination of the contractor's employment by the employer for certain specified defaults (clause 25 (1)); automatic determination upon bankruptcy, liquidation and other events symptomatic of insolvency (clause 25 (2)): determination for corruption (clause 25 (1)—not in the private version); the effect of determination (clause 25 (4)). Certain of the defaults specified in clause 25 (1) are such that, if committed by the contractor, the employer is at common law entitled to treat the contract as at an end forthwith even if he does not rely on this clause. But whether it is proposed to proceed under this clause or at common law, very careful consideration should be given to the facts and procedure and in most cases legal advice obtained. The reason is that if the contractor is wrongfully turned off the site the employer will have to bear the costs of completion by another contractor and have to pay damages or a reasonable sum to the contractor. Further, if the contractor disputes the validity of the determination it is not clear whether an interim injunction requiring him to leave the site can be obtained.

29.02 The words '. . . *such notice shall not be given unreasonably or vexatiously* . . .' govern any determination under clause 25 (1). What is unreasonable or vexatious depends upon all the relevant circumstances of any particular case and ultimately, if the determination is disputed, upon the view taken by the arbitrator.

Procedure
29.03 It must be followed carefully. Two notices are required in each case plus upon a determination under clause 25 (1) (c) an additional prior notice from the architect.

Delay in progress by contractor
29.04 Failure to comply with an agreed programme may be some, but certainly is not conclusive, evidence of failure to proceed regularly and diligently. Thus the failure to comply with the programme may be due to the employer's default, or a cause of delay appearing in clause 23, or it may be that the contractor is proceeding at a rate and in a manner which satisfies his obligation to proceed regularly and diligently even though it differs from the programme. In any event it must always be considered whether the determination is unreasonable or vexatious.

Clause 25 (2): Bankruptcy and the like
29.05 Determination is automatic but in practice if the employer wishes to take advantage of the clause it is advisable to tell the contractor, trustee in bankruptcy etc that he relies on the clause. Difficult legal questions are particularly liable to arise upon bankruptcy and the liquidation of an insolvent company.

Clause 25 (4): Consequences of determination
29.06 The sub-clause must be studied for its effect.
1 Sub-clause (b) '. . . *use all temporary buildings plant* . . .'. This does not bind persons not party to the contract, eg owners of cranes, scaffolding and other equipment who have hired it to the contractor.

2 Sub-clause (b) '. . . *assign to the employer* . . .'. See also clauses 17, proviso; 27 (a) (x); 28 (b) (v). The value of this right to an assignment seems to be small. Probably new sub-contracts or direct contracts will have to be negotiated. For direct payment see para 31.11.
3 Sub-clause (d) '. . . *any direct loss and/or damage* . . .'. This is very wide.
4 Sub-clause (d) '. . . *shall not be bound* . . .'. The employer need pay nothing more until completion.

30 Clause 26: Determination by contractor

26 (1) Without prejudice to any other rights and remedies which the Contractor may possess, if

(a) The Employer does not pay to the Contractor the amount due on any certificate (otherwise than as a result of the operation of Clause 1(2)(b) of the supplemental agreement annexed to these Conditions (the VAT Agreement)) within 14 days from the issue of that certificate and continues such default for seven days after receipt by registered post or recorded delivery of a notice from the Contractor stating that notice of determination under this Condition will be served if payment is not made within seven days from receipt thereof; or

(b) The Employer interferes with or obstructs the issue of any certificate due under this Contract; or

(c) The carrying out of the whole or substantially the whole of the uncompleted Works (other than the execution of work required under clause 15 of these Conditions) is suspended for a continuous period of the length named in the Appendix to these Conditions by reason of:

(i) by *force majeure*, or

(ii) loss or damage (unless caused by the negligence of the Contractor, his servants or agents or of any sub-contractor, his servants or agents) occasioned by any one or more of the contingencies referred to in clause 20 [A] or clause 20 [B] of these Conditions (if applicable), or

(iii) civil commotion, or

(iv) Architect's/Supervising Officer's instructions issued under clauses 1 (2), 11 (1) or 21 (2) of these Conditions unless caused by reason of some negligence or default of the Contractor, or

(v) the Contractor not having received in due time necessary instructions, drawings, details or levels from the Architect/Supervising Officer for which he specifically applied in writing on a date which having regard to the Date of Completion stated in the Appendix to these Conditions or to any extension of time then fixed under clause 23 or clause 33 (1) (c) of these Conditions was neither unreasonably distant from nor unreasonably close to the date on which it was necessary for him to receive the same, or

(vi) delay on the part of artists tradesmen or others engaged by the Employer in executing work not forming part of this Contract, or

(vii) the opening up for inspection of any work covered up or of the testing of any of the work materials or goods in accordance with clause 6 (3) of these Conditions (including making good in consequence of such opening up or testing), unless the inspection or test showed that the work materials or goods were not in accordance with this Contract, then the Contractor may thereupon by notice by registered post or recorded delivery to the Employer or Architect/Supervising Officer forthwith determine the employment of the Contractor under this Contract; provided that such notice shall not be given unreasonably or vexatiously.

(2) Upon such determination, then without prejudice to the accrued rights or remedies of either party or to any liability of the classes mentioned in clause 18 of these Conditions which may accrue either before the Contractor or any sub-contractors shall have removed his temporary buildings, plant, tools, equipment, goods or materials or by reason of his or their so removing the same, the respective rights and liabilities of the Contractor and the Employer shall be as follows, that is to say:—

(a) The Contractor shall with all reasonable dispatch and in such manner and with such precautions as will prevent injury, death or damage of the classes in respect of which before the date of determination he was liable to indemnify the Employer under clause 18 of these Conditions remove from the site all his temporary buildings, plant, tools, equipment, goods and materials and shall give facilities for his sub-contractors to do the same, but subject always to the provision of sub-paragraph (iv) of paragraph (b) of this sub-clause.

(b) After taking into account amounts previously paid under this Contract the Contractors shall be paid by the Employer:—

(i) The total value of work completed at the date of determination.

(ii) The total value of work begun and executed but not completed at the date of determination, the value being ascertained in accordance with clause 11 (4) of these Conditions as if such work were a variation required by the Architect/Supervising Officer.

(iii) Any sum ascertained in respect of direct loss and/or expense under clauses 11 (6), 24 and 34 (3) of these Conditions (whether ascertained before or after the date of determination).

(iv) The cost of materials or goods properly ordered for the Works for which the Contractor shall have paid or for which the Contractor is legally bound to pay, and on such payment by the Employer any materials or goods so paid for shall become the property of the Employer.

(v) The reasonable cost of removal under paragraph (a) of this sub-clause.

(vi) Any direct loss and/or damage caused to the Contractor by the determination.

Provided that in addition to all other remedies the Contractor upon such determination may take possession of and shall have a lien upon all unfixed goods and materials which may have become the property of the Employer under clause 14 of these Conditions until payment of all monies due to the Contractor from the Employer.

30.01 This clause is to be compared with clause 25. It gives the contractor the right to determine his employment, leave the site and recover the equivalent of damages, including loss of profit upon the happening of certain events some of which are the employer's fault or within his control and others which are misfortunes for which the employer has no responsibility. Clause 26 (1) (a) provides for non-payment of a certificate; clause 26 (1) (b) deals with interference with or obstruction by the employer in the issue of any certificates; clause 26 (1) (c) deals with suspension of work. The events described in clauses 26 (1) (a) and (b) may, according to the circumstances, be such as to entitle the contractor at common law to treat the contract as at an end even if he does not rely on the clauses.

Clause 26 (1) (a): Deduction from certificates

30.02 The employer may make deductions under clause 2 (1), 19 (1) (c), 20 (A) (1), 22, 27 (c). These rights of deduction are not expressly referred to in clause 26 (1) (a) but it is thought that a purported determination under this sub-clause would not be valid or would ordinarily be held to be unreasonable or vexatious (see proviso to clause) if based solely upon a deduction which the employer was entitled to make.

Clause 26 (1) (b)

30.03 The phrase '*interferes with or obstructs the issue of any certificate* . . .' includes preventing the architect performing his duties, or directing the architect as to the amount for which he is to give his certificate or as to the decision which he should arrive at on some matters within the sphere of his independent duty (see para 5.02).

Clause 26 (1) (c)

30.04 If work '. . . *is suspended for a continuous period* . . .'. See the Appendix which suggests periods of three months in respect of fire, flood etc where clause 20 (A) or 20 (B) is applicable, and one month for the other causes within the sub-clause. It should be considered whether these periods are sufficient having regard to the consequences for the employer if the contractor determines. For example in a job where there is complex engineering one month might be inadequate.

Loss on damage caused by contractor's negligence

30.05 The words in clause 26 (1) (c) (ii) were introduced by the 1973 amendment and prevent him relying on his own negligence to obtain the benefits of the sub-clause. Even with earlier versions of the form such negligence could be brought to the attention of the arbitrator to support an argument that determination was unreasonable.

Instructions caused by negligence or default of the contractor

30.06 The words in clause 26 (1) (c) (iv) beginning '*unless caused*' were introduced by the 1973 amendment. See the last note, but it seems that the contractor can still determine for a suspension caused by a nominated subcontractor or nominated supplier.

30.07 For discussion of the term '. . . *shall not be given unreasonably or vexatiously* . . .' see para 29.02.

Clause 26 (2) Proviso

30.08 This gives the contractor a lien until everything has been paid under the sub-clause and may be very important in its effect. It may not be effective where the employer is insolvent.

31 Clause 27: Nominated sub-contractors

27 The following provisions of this Condition shall apply where prime cost sums are included in the Contract Bills, or arise as a result of Architect's/Supervising Officer's instructions given in regard to the expenditure of provisional sums, in respect of persons to be nominated by the Architect/Supervising Officer to supply and fix materials or goods or to execute work.

(a) Such sums shall be deemed to include 2½ per cent. cash discount and shall be expended in favour of such persons as the Architect/Supervising Officer shall instruct, and all specialists or others who are nominated by the Architect/Supervising Officer are hereby declared to be sub-contractors employed by the Contractor and are referred to in these Conditions as 'nominated sub-contractors'. Provided that the Architect/Supervising Officer shall not nominate any person as a sub-contractor against whom the Contractor shall make reasonable objection, or (save where the Architect/Supervising Officer and Contractor shall otherwise agree) who will not enter into a sub-contract which provides (*inter alia*):—

(i) That the nominated sub-contractor shall so carry out and complete the sub-contract Works as to enable the Contractor to discharge his obligations under clause 1 (1) of these Conditions so far as they relate and apply to the sub-contract Works or to any portion of the same and in conformity with all the reasonable directions and requirements of the Contractor.

(ii) That the nominated sub-contractor shall observe, perform and comply with all the provisions of this Contract on the part of the Contractor to be observed, performed and complied with (other than clause 20 [A] of these Conditions, if applicable) so far as they relate and apply to the sub-contract Works or to any portion of the same.

(iii) That the nominated sub-contractor shall indemnify the Contractor against the same liabilities in respect of the sub-contract Works as those for which the Contractor is liable to indemnify the Employer under this Contract.

(iv) That the nominated sub-contractor shall indemnify the Contractor against claims in respect of any negligence, omission or default of such sub-contractor, his servants or agents or any misuse by him or them of any scaffolding or other plant, and shall insure himself against any such claims and produce the policy or policies and receipts in respect of premiums paid as and when required by either the Employer or the Contractor.

(v) That the sub-contract Works shall be completed within the period or (where they are to be completed in sections) periods therein specified, that the Contractor shall not without the written consent of the Architect/Supervising Officer grant any extension of time for the completion of the sub-contract Works or any section thereof, and that the Contractor shall inform the Architect/Supervising Officer of any representations made by the nominated sub-contractor as to the cause of any delay in the progress or completion of the sub-contract Works or of any section thereof.

(vi) That if the nominated sub-contractor shall fail to complete the sub-contract Works or (where the sub-contract Works are to be completed in sections) any section thereof within the period therein specified or within any extended time granted by the Contractor with the written consent of the Architect/Supervising Officer and the Architect/Supervising Officer certifies in writing to the Contractor that the same ought reasonably so to have been completed, the nominated sub-contractor shall pay or allow to the Contractor either a sum calculated at the rate therein agreed as liquidated and ascertained damages for the period during which the said Works or any section thereof, as the case may be, shall so remain or have remained incomplete or (where no such rate is therein agreed) a sum equivalent to any loss or damage suffered or incurred by the Contractor and caused by the failure of the nominated sub-contractor as aforesaid.

(vii) That payment in respect of any work, materials or goods comprised in the sub-contract shall be made within 14 days after receipt by the Contractor of the duplicate copy of the Architect's/Supervising Officer's certificate under clause 30 of these Conditions which states as due an amount calculated by including the total value of such work, materials or goods, and shall when due be subject to the retention by the Contractor of the sums mentioned in sub-paragraph (viii) of paragraph (a) of this Condition, and to a discount for cash of 2½ per cent. if made within the said period of 14 days.

(viii) That the Contractor shall retain from the sum directed by the Architect/Supervising Officer as having been included in the calculation of the amount due in any certificate issued under clause 30 of these Conditions in respect of the total value of work, materials or goods executed or supplied by the nominated sub-contractor a percentage (which percentage shall be equal to the percentage currently being retained by the Employer under clause 30 of these Conditions) of such value; and that the Contractor's interest in any sums so retained (by whomsoever held) shall be fiduciary as trustee for the nominated sub-contractor (but without obligation to invest); and that the nominated sub-contractor's beneficial interest in such sums shall be subject only to the right of the Contractor to have recourse thereto from time to time for payment of any amount which he is entitled under the sub-contract to deduct from any sum due or to become due to the nominated sub-contractor; and that if and when such sums or any part thereof are released to the nominated sub-contractor they shall be paid in full less only a discount for cash of 2½ per cent. if paid within 14 days of the date fixed for their release in the sub-contract.

(ix) That the Architect/Supervising Officer and his representatives shall have a right of access to the workshops and other places of the nominated sub-contractor as mentioned in clause 9 of these Conditions.

(x) That the employment of the nominated sub-contractor under the sub-contract shall determine immediately upon the determination (for any reason) of the Contractor's employment under this Contract.

(b) The Architect/Supervising Officer shall direct the Contractor as to the total value of the work, materials or goods executed or supplied by a nominated sub-contractor included in the calculation of the amount stated as due in any certificate issued under clause 30 of these Conditions and shall forthwith inform the nominated sub-contractor in writing of the amount of the said total value. The sum representing such total value shall be paid by the Contractor to the nominated sub-contractor within 14 days of receiving from the Architect/Supervising Officer the duplicate copy of the certificate less only (i) any retention money which the Contractor may be entitled to deduct under the terms of the sub-contract (ii) any sum to which the Contractor may be entitled in respect of delay in the completion of the sub-contract Works or any section thereof, and (iii) a discount for cash of 2½ per cent.

(c) Before issuing any certificate under clause 30 of these Conditions the Architect/Supervising Officer may request the Contractor to furnish to him reasonable proof that all amounts included in the calculation of the amount stated as due on previous certificates in respect of the total value of work, materials or goods executed or supplied by any nominated sub-contractor have been duly discharged, and if the Contractor fails to comply with any such request the Architect/Supervising Officer shall issue a certificate to that effect and thereupon the Employer may himself pay such amounts to any nominated sub-contractor concerned (to which amounts the Employer may add an amount for any value added tax which would have been properly due to the nominated sub-contractor) and deduct the same from any sums due or to become due to the Contractor.

(d) (i) The Contractor shall not grant to any nominated sub-contractor any extension of the period within which the sub-contract Works or (where the sub-contract Works are to be completed in sections) any section thereof is to be completed without the written consent of the Architect/Supervising Officer. Provided always that the Contractor shall inform the Architect/Supervising Officer of any representation made by the nominated sub-contractor as to the cause of any delay in the progress or completion of the sub-contract Works or of any section thereof, and that the consent of the Architect/Supervising Officer shall not be unreasonably withheld.

(ii) If any nominated sub-contractor fails to complete the sub-contract Works or (where the sub-contract Works are to be completed in sections) any section thereof within the period specified in the sub-contract or within any extended time granted by the Contractor with the written consent of the Architect/Supervising Officer, then if the same ought reasonably so to have been completed the Architect/Supervising Officer shall certify in writing accordingly; any such certificate shall be issued to the Contractor and immediately upon issue the Architect/Supervising Officer shall send a duplicate copy thereof to the nominated sub-contractor.

(e) If the Architect/Supervising Officer desires to secure final payment to any nominated sub-contractor before final payment is due to the Contractor, and if such sub-contractor has satisfactorily indemnified the Contractor against any latent defects, then the Architect/Supervising Officer may in an Interim Certificate include an amount to cover the said final payment, and thereupon the Contractor shall pay to such nominated sub-contractor the amount so certified less only a discount for cash of 2½ per cent. Upon such final payment the Contractor shall, save for latent defects, be discharged from all liability for the work materials or goods executed or supplied by such sub-contractor under the sub-contract to which the payment relates.

(f) Neither the existence nor the exercise of the foregoing powers nor anything else contained in these Conditions shall render the Employer in any way liable to any nominated sub-contractor.

(g) (i) Where the Contractor in the ordinary course of his business directly carries out works for which prime cost sums are included in the Contract Bills and where items of such works are set out in the Appendix to these Conditions and the Architect/Supervising Officer is prepared to receive tenders from the Contractor for such items, then the Contractor shall be permitted to tender for the same or any of them but without prejudice to the Employer's right to reject the lowest or any tender. If the Contractor's tender is accepted, he shall not sub-let the work without the consent of the Architect/Supervising Officer.

Provided that where a prime cost sum arises under Architect's/Supervising Officer's instructions issued under clause 11 (3) of these Conditions it shall be deemed for the

31.01 This clause should be read with clause 11 (3) (expenditure of prime cost and provisional sums), clause 28 (nominated suppliers) and clause 30 (5) (c) (settlement of accounts). Clause 27 provides for the nomination of sub-contractors and the provisions of the sub-contract which should be used (clause 27 (a)); payment of nominated sub-contractors (clause 27 (b)); direct payment to nominated sub-contractors (clause 27 (c)); extension of time to nominated sub-contractors (clause 27 (d)); final payment to nominated sub-contractors (clause 27 (e)); absence of liability of employer to nominated sub-contractors (clause 27 (f)); contractor's tender for prime cost items (clause 27 (g)).

Contractor's liability for nominated sub-contractors

31.02 The general principle is that a contractor who performs his obligations through a sub-contractor is as responsible for that sub-contractor's default as if it were his own even though consent has been given to the sub-letting. This is the starting point for the position here. Thus the contractor in ordinary circumstances is liable for defects in the materials and workmanship of a nominated sub-contractor and all the usual remedies are available to the architect, eg under clauses 6 and 2 (1), 15, 25 and 30 (2) (see para 34.04 below). But the terms of the contract and the circumstance of nomination lead to a substantial reduction from that liability which the contractor has in respect of approved (under clause 17) sub-contractors. Thus:

1 *Delay on the part of a nominated sub-contractor*—see clause 23 (g) and para 27.10 above.

2 *Repudiation by a nominated sub-contractor.* If a nominated sub-contractor repudiates his sub-contract or commits a fundamental breach, eg shows that it is quite incapable of performance, the architect must nominate a new sub-contractor and any increased costs of completing by the new sub-contractor fall upon the employer (*NW Metropolitan Hospital Board v T. A. Bickerton & Sons Ltd* (1970) 1 All ER 1039).

3 *Design.* If a nominated sub-contractor carries out design it may be a difficult question in any particular case to say how far, if at all, the contractor is liable for any failure of such design.

4 *Delay in giving information.* It is often necessary to obtain information from nominated sub-contractors or proposed nominated sub-contractors as to the details of their work before they carry it out, to enable adequate instructions, details and drawings to be given to the contractor. Failure to give such information may delay the progress of the works. If the failure arises before nomination it will ordinarily give the contractor rights under clauses 23 (f) and 24 (1) (a) or to claim damages for lack of drawings or instructions (see para 28.04). If the failure arises after nomination it depends upon the circumstances whether or not it gives the contractor such rights.

5 *Guarantee of performance.* Such a guarantee is sometimes required. If given by the nominated sub-contractor to the contractor alone it is very doubtful whether the employer has any rights in respect of the guarantee.

Protection of the employer

31.03 If no steps are taken to protect the employer he will have no redress in law against the contractor or nominated sub-contractor in respect of the matters just set out where the contractor is not liable. Methods of protecting the employer include:

1 Only nominate if it is really necessary.

2 Write the full terms of the proposed sub-contract, including any performance specification or guarantees, into the Contract Bills. This may be of assistance but there are legal difficulties. In so far as the Contract Bills seek to impose duties on the contractor outside those imposed by the Conditions, the Bills may be ineffective; see clause 12 (1) and para 16.05.

3 Obtain warranties of performance direct from the nominated sub-contractor in consideration of nomination. The RIBA issues a Form of Agreement between an Employer and a nominated sub-contractor intended to deal with problems 1, 3, 4 and 5 above and which might afford some protection in respect of problem 2. It may be that a price increase will be demanded if either of the courses 2 or 3 suggested in this paragraph is sought to be followed. If this happens the employer should be told and asked whether he prefers to accept the risks.

Delay in nominating

31.04 This can give rise to claims for extension of time under clause 23 (f), for loss and expense under clause 24 (1) (a) and probably to damages at common law (see para 28.04). Further it seems that such claims can arise out of delay caused by the nomination, without the contractor's previous agreement, of a proposed sub-contractor who is not willing to enter into the form of sub-contract contemplated by sub-clause (a).

No pc or provisional sum

31.05 There is no power of nomination in respect of an item which is not a pc sum or provisional sum. Neither, it seems, is there any right to nominate a sub-contractor who is to design (although this is frequently done and contractors waive the objection they might take).

31.06 The words '. . . *shall be deemed to include* 2½ *per cent discount* . . .' mean that the contractor cannot recover such discount from the employer unless the architect nominates a person who will not give it and the architect and contractor agree that the discount will be paid by the employer.

31.07 The words '*provided that the architect* . . .' mean that the architect must not nominate a person who is not prepared to enter into a sub-contract in the form contemplated by sub-clause (a). The standard form (FASS form) of sub-contract is such a sub-contract.

31.08 The words '. . . *shall make reasonable objection* . . .' mean that the contractor can make reasonable objection to the proposed nominated sub-contractor but not, it seems, to the nature of the sub-contract works.

Sub-clause (a) (vii)

31.09 It is in the employer's interest that there should be a provision to this effect in the sub-contract, for it gives the architect a sanction against improper work by the nominated sub-contractor. If the architect, as he is entitled to do (clause 30 (2), 27 (b)), refuses to include a sum in his certificate in respect of the bad work the nominated sub-contractor cannot sue the contractor because the sum is not included in the certificate.

Sub-clause (b)

31.10 This sets out the procedure for certifying in respect of nominated sub-contractor's work. The procedure must be followed to enable the nominated sub-contractor to be paid. No deduction should be made by the architect in respect of any claim for delay or otherwise which the contractor may have against the nominated sub-contractor.

Sub-clause (c): Direct payment

31.11 This right of direct payment arises only in respect of sums already certified but not paid by the contractor and can be validly made after the insolvency of the contractor where the employment of the contractor has been reinstated and continued (see clause 25 (2)). A right of direct payment to any sub-contractor or supplier nominated or not also arises under clause 25 (4) (b) upon determination of the contractor's employment, but if the contractor has become insolvent the right under clause 25 should only be exercised after taking legal advice. Direct payment cannot be made save under one of these two clauses. There is no legal duty upon the employer to make direct payment unless he has entered into the Form of Agreement between an Employer and a nominated sub-contractor, in which case he owes a duty as between himself and the nominated sub-contractor to make direct payment under this clause in certain circumstances.

Sub-clause (d): Extension of time

31.12 The architect has to consider the grounds for extension under the sub-contract. If the standard form is used they are those appearing in clause 23 save (g). The architect's certificate under sub-clause (d) (ii) is necessary to enable the contractor to enforce his claim against the sub-contractor for delay in completion under clause 8 of the standard form of sub-contract.

Sub-clause (e): Final payment

31.13 The contractor is entitled to be 'satisfactorily indemnified' by the sub-contractor before losing the security afforded by the retention money.

Sub-clause (g): Contractor's tender

31.14 The effect of the proviso to sub-clause (g) (i) is that where the architect wishes to nominate a sub-contractor to carry out work the subject of a provisional sum (see clause 11 (3)) he must allow the contractor the benefit of clause 27 (g) (i).

32 Clause 28: Nominated suppliers

> 28 The following provisions of this Condition shall apply where prime cost sums are included in the Contract Bills, or arise as a result of Architect's/Supervising Officer's instructions given in regard to the expenditure of provisional sums, in respect of any materials or goods to be fixed by the Contractor.
>
> (a) Such sums shall be deemed to include 5 per cent. cash discount and the term prime cost when included or arising as aforesaid shall be understood to mean the net cost to be defrayed as a prime cost after deducting any trade or other discount (except the said discount of 5 per cent.), and shall include any tax or duty not otherwise recoverable under this contract by whomsoever payable which is payable under or by virtue of any Act of Parliament on the import, purchase, sale, appropriation, processing, alteration, adapting for sale or use of the materials or goods to be supplied, and the cost of packing carriage and delivery. Provided that, where in the opinion of the Architect/Supervising Officer the Contractor has incurred expense for special packing or special carriage, such special expense shall be allowed as part of the sums actually paid by the Contractor.
>
> (b) Such sums shall be expended in favour of such persons as the Architect/Supervising Officer shall instruct, and all specialists, merchants, tradesmen or others who are nominated by the Architect/Supervising Officer to supply materials or goods are hereby declared to be suppliers to the Contractor and are referred to in these Conditions as 'nominated suppliers'. Provided that the Architect/Supervising Officer shall not (save where the Architect/Supervising Officer and the Contractor shall otherwise agree) nominate as a supplier a person who will not enter into a contract of sale which provides (*inter alia*):—
>
> (i) That the materials or goods to be supplied shall be to the reasonable satisfaction of the Architect/Supervising Officer.
>
> (ii) That the nominated supplier shall make good by replacement or otherwise any defects in the materials or goods supplied which appear within such period as is therein mentioned and shall bear any expenses reasonably incurred by the Contractor as a direct consequence of such defects, provided that:—
>
> (1) where the materials or goods have been used or fixed such defects are not such that examination by the Contractor ought to have revealed them before using or fixing;
>
> (2) such defects are due solely to defective workmanship or material in the goods supplied and shall not have been caused by improper storage by the Contractor or by misuse or by any act of neglect of either the Contractor or the Architect/Supervising Officer or the Employer or by any person or persons for whom they may be responsible.
>
> (iii) That delivery of the materials or goods supplied shall be commenced and completed at such times as the Contractor may reasonably direct.

> (iv) That the nominated supplier shall allow the Contractor a discount for cash of 5 per cent. if the Contractor makes payment in full within 30 days of the end of the month during which delivery is made.
>
> (v) That the nominated supplier shall not be obliged to make any delivery of materials or goods (except any which may have been paid for in full less only the discount for cash) after the determination (for any reason) of the Contractor's employment under this Contract.
>
> (c) All payments by the Contractor for materials or goods supplied by a nominated supplier shall be in full, and shall be paid within 30 days of the end of the month during which delivery is made less only a discount for cash of 5 per cent. if so paid.
>
> (d) Where the said contract of sale between the Contractor and the nominated supplier in any way restricts, limits or excludes the liability of the nominated supplier to the Contractor in respect of materials or goods supplied or to be supplied, and the Architect/Supervising Officer has specifically approved in writing the said restrictions, limitations or exclusions, the liability of the Contractor to the Employer in respect of the said materials or goods shall be restricted, limited or excluded to the same extent. The Contractor shall not be obliged to enter into a contract with, nor expend prime cost sums in favour of, the nominated supplier until the Architect/Supervising Officer has specifically approved in writing the said restrictions, limitations or exclusions.

32.01 This clause should be read with clause 11 (3) (expenditure of prime cost and provisional sums), clause 27 (nominated sub-contractors) and clause 30 (5) (c) (settlement of accounts). Clause 28 deals with nominated suppliers and provides for: price (clause 28 (a)); terms of the contract which should be used with a nominated supplier (clause 28 (b)); payment to nominated suppliers (clause 28 (c)); approved limitation of contractor's liability (clause 28 (d)).

Contractor's liability for goods supplied by nominated supplier

32.02 Nomination in itself ordinarily shows that there has been no reliance on the contractor's skill and judgment, so that the contractor is not liable if the goods of a nominated supplier, of good quality, are unfit for their intended purpose (see paras 10.01, 10.02 above). The contractor's liability in respect of the default of the nominated supplier is the same as that for nominated sub-contractors set out in para 31.02 making the necessary allowances for the difference that a supplier does not fix. It follows that the methods available to protect the employer discussed in para 31.03 should be considered. A direct warranty from the nominated supplier may be just as important as in the case of a nominated sub-contractor. This is because suppliers very often use exclusion or limitation clauses of the kind discussed in para 10.02 (3). If approved in writing by the architect such exclusion or limitation operates for the benefit of the contractor. The contractor is always in ordinary circumstances responsible for patent defects ie defects which he ought by the exercise of proper skill, as an experienced contractor to have observed.

Other comparisons with nominated sub-contractors

32.03 The position is (after making the necessary allowance for the fact that the contractor is to fix) similar to that set out in paras 31.04 to 31.08, but there is no right for the contractor to make reasonable objection to a nomination; there is no equivalent to clauses 27 (c), (d) or (g); there is no equivalent to clauses 27 (b) and (e) because the contractor's duty to pay is not dependent upon prior certification.

Sub-clause (d): Application for approval of exclusion clause

32.04 Early nomination of sub-contractors and suppliers is desirable for many reasons. This is one of them as regards suppliers. If application is made the architect must consider it carefully and ordinarily consult with the client. Approval may substantially reduce the client's rights under the contract. Refusal, if the nomination was late, may cause delay and give the contractor grounds for a claim.

33 Clause 29: Artists and tradesmen

> 29 The Contractor shall permit the execution of work not forming part of this Contract by artists, tradesmen or others engaged by the Employer. Every such person shall for the purposes of clause 18 of these Conditions be deemed to be a person for whom the Employer is responsible and not to be a sub-contractor.

33.01 For delay caused by artists, tradesmen and others see clauses 23 (h), 24 (1) (d) and 26 (1) (c) (vi).

34 Clause 30: Certificates and payments

30 (1) Interim valuations shall be made whenever the Architect/Supervising Officer considers them to be necessary for the purpose of ascertaining the amount to be stated as due in an Interim Certificate. The Architect/Supervising Officer shall from time to time as provided in this sub-clause issue Interim Certificates stating the amount due to the Contractor from the Employer, and the Contractor shall be entitled to payment therefor within 14 days from the issue of that Certificate. Before the issue of the Certificate of Practical Completion, Interim Certificates shall be issued at the Period of Interim Certificates specified in the Appendix to these Conditions. After the issue of the Certificate of Practical Completion, Interim Certificates shall be issued as and when further amounts are due to the Contractor from the Employer provided always that the Architect/Supervising Officer shall not be required to issue an Interim Certificate within one calendar month of having issued a previous Interim Certificate.

(2) The amount stated as due in an Interim Certificate shall, subject to any agreement between the parties as to stage payments, be the total value of the work properly executed and of the materials and goods delivered to or adjacent to the Works for use thereon up to and including a date not more than seven days before the date of the said certificate less any amount which may be retained by the Employer (as provided in sub-clause (3) of this Condition) and less any instalments previously paid under this Condition. Provided that such certificate shall only include the value of the said materials and goods as and from such times as they are reasonably, properly and not prematurely brought to or placed adjacent to the Works and then only if adequately protected against weather or other casualties.

(2A) The amount stated as due in an Interim Certificate may in the discretion of the Architect/Supervising Officer include the value of any materials or goods before delivery thereof to or adjacent to the Works provided that:

(a) Such materials or goods are intended for inclusion in the Works;

(b) Nothing remains to be done to such materials or goods to complete the same up to the point of their incorporation in the Works;

(c) Such materials or goods have been and are set apart at the premises where they have been manufactured or assembled or are stored, and have been clearly and visibly marked, individually or in sets, either by letters or figures or by reference to a pre-determined code, so as to identify:

(i) Where they are stored on premises of the Contractor, the Employer, and in any other case, the person to whose order they are held; and

(ii) Their destination as being the Works;

(d) Where such materials or goods were ordered from a supplier by the Contractor or a sub-contractor, the contract for their supply is in writing and expressly provides that the property therein shall pass unconditionally to the Contractor or the sub-contractor (as the case may be) not later than the happening of the events set out in paragraphs (b) and (c) of this sub-clause;

(e) Where such materials or goods were ordered from a supplier by a sub-contractor, the relevant sub-contract is in writing and expressly provides that on the property in such materials or goods passing to the sub-contractor the same shall immediately thereon pass to the Contractor;

(f) Where such materials or goods were manufactured or assembled by a sub-contractor, the sub-contract is in writing and expressly provides that the property in such materials or goods shall pass unconditionally to the Contractor not later than the happening of the events set out in paragraphs (b) and (c) of this sub-clause;

(g) The materials or goods are in accordance with this Contract;

(h) The Contractor furnishes to the Architect/Supervising Officer reasonable proof that the property in such materials or goods is in him and that the appropriate conditions set out in paragraphs (a) to (g) of this sub-clause have been complied with;

(i) The Contractor furnishes the Architect/Supervising Officer with reasonable proof that such materials or goods are insured against loss or damage for their full value under a policy of insurance protecting the interests of the Employer and the Contractor in respect of the contingencies referred to in clause 20 of these Conditions, during the period commencing with the transfer of property in such materials or goods to the Contractor until they are delivered to, or adjacent to, the Works.

(3) (a) In respect of any Interim Certificate issued before the issue of the Certificate of Practical Completion the Employer may, subject to paragraph (c) of this sub-clause, retain a percentage (in these Conditions called "the Retention Percentage") of the total value of the work, materials and goods referred to in sub-clauses (2) and (2A) of this Condition.* The Retention Percentage shall be 5 per cent. unless a lower rate shall be agreed between the parties and specified in the Appendix to these Conditions as the Retention Percentage.

(b) If any Interim Certificate is issued after the issue of the Certificate of Practical Completion but before the issue of the Certificate for the residue of the amounts then so retained referred to in sub-clause (4) (c) of this Condition the Employer in respect of the said Interim Certificate may, subject to paragraph (c) of this sub-clause, retain a percentage (which percentage shall be equal to half the Retention Percentage) of the total value of the work, materials and goods referred to in sub-clauses (2) and (2A) of this Condition.

(c) The amount which the Employer may retain by virtue of paragraphs (a) and/or (b) of this sub-clause shall be reduced by the amounts of any releases of retention made to the Contractor in pursuance of clause 16 (f) and/or clause 27 (e) of these Conditions.

(4) The amounts retained by virtue of sub-clause (3) of this Condition shall be subject to the following rules:—

(a) The Employer's interest in any amounts so retained shall be fiduciary as trustee for the Contractor (but without obligation to invest), and the Contractor's beneficial interest therein shall be subject only to the right of the Employer to have recourse thereto from time to time for payment of any amount which he is entitled under the provisions of this Contract to deduct from any sum due or to become due to the Contractor.

(b) On the issue of the Certificate of Practical Completion the Architect/Supervising Officer shall issue a certificate for one moiety of the total amounts then so retained and the Contractor shall be entitled to payment of the said moiety within 14 days from the issue of that certificate.

(c) On the expiration of the Defects Liability Period named in the Appendix to these Conditions, or on the issue of the Certificate of Completion of Making Good Defects, whichever is the later, the Architect/Supervising Officer shall issue a Certificate for the residue of the amounts then so retained and the Contractor shall be entitled to payment of the said residue within 14 days from the issue of that certificate.

(5) (a) The measurement and valuation of the Works shall be completed within the Period of Final Measurement and Valuation stated in the Appendix to these Conditions, and the Contractor shall be supplied with a copy of the priced Bills of Variation not later than the end of the said Period and before the issue of the Final Certificate under sub-clause (6) of this Condition.

(b) Either before or within a reasonable time after Practical Completion of the Works the Contractor shall send to the Architect/Supervising Officer all documents necessary for the purposes of the computations required by these Conditions including all documents relating to the accounts of nominated sub-contractors and nominated suppliers.

(c) In the settlement of accounts the amounts paid or payable under the appropriate contracts by the Contractor to nominated sub-contractors or nominated suppliers (including the discounts for cash mentioned in clauses 27 and 28 of these Conditions), the amounts paid or payable by virtue of clause 4 (2) of these Conditions in respect of fees or charges, the amounts paid or payable in respect of any insurances maintained in compliance with clause 19 (2) of these Conditions, the tender sum (or such other sum as is appropriate in accordance with the terms of the tender) for any work for which a tender made under clause 27 (g) of these Conditions is accepted and the value of any work executed by the Contractor for which a provisional sum is included in the Contract Bills shall be set against the relevant prime cost or provisional sum mentioned in the Contract Bills or arising under Architect's/Supervising Officer's instructions issued under clause 11 (3) of these Conditions as the case may be, and the balance, after allowing in all cases *pro rata* for the Contractor's profit at the rates shown in the Contract Bills, shall be added to or deducted from the Contract Sum. Any amount or value to be so set against the relevant prime cost or provisional sum shall be exclusive of value added tax. Provided that no deduction shall be made in respect of any damages paid or allowed to the Contractor by any sub-contractor or supplier.

(6) So soon as is practicable but before the expiration of the period the length of which is stated in the Appendix to these Conditions from the end of the Defects Liability Period also stated in the said Appendix or from completion of making good defects under clause 15 of these Conditions or from receipt by the Architect/Supervising Officer of the documents referred to in paragraph (b) of sub-clause (5) of this Condition, whichever is the latest, the Architect/Supervising Officer shall issue the Final Certificate. The Final Certificate shall state:—

(a) The sum of the amounts already paid to the Contractor under Interim Certificates and Certificates issued under sub-clauses (4) (b) and (4) (c) of this Condition, and

(b) The Contract Sum adjusted as necessary in accordance with the terms of these Conditions, and the difference (if any) between the two sums shall be expressed in the said certificate as a balance due to the Contractor from the Employer or to the Employer from the Contractor as the case may be, and subject to any deductions authorised by these Conditions, the said balance shall as from the fourteenth day after the issue of the said certificate be a debt payable as the case may be by the Employer to the Contractor or by the Contractor to the Employer.

(7) (a) Except as provided in paragraphs (b) and (c) of this sub-clause (and save in respect of fraud), the Final Certificate shall have effect in any proceedings arising out of or in connection with this Contract (whether by arbitration under clause 35 of these Conditions or otherwise) as

(i) conclusive evidence that where the quality of materials or the standards of workmanship are to be to the reasonable satisfaction of the Architect/Supervising Officer the same are to such satisfaction, and

(ii) conclusive evidence that any necessary effect has been given to all the terms of this Contract which require an adjustment to be made of the Contract Sum save where there has been any accidental inclusion or exclusion of any work, materials, goods or figure in any computation or any arithmetical error in any computation, in which event the Final Certificate shall have effect as conclusive evidence as to all other computations.

(b) If any arbitration or other proceedings have been commenced by either party before the Final Certificate has been issued the Final Certificate shall have effect as conclusive evidence as provided in paragraph (a) of this sub-clause after either

(i) such proceedings have been concluded, whereupon the Final Certificate shall be subject to the terms of any award or judgment in or settlement of such proceedings, or

(ii) a period of twelve months during which neither party has taken any further step in such proceedings, whereupon the Final Certificate shall be subject to any terms agreed in partial settlement,

whichever shall be the earlier.

(c) If any arbitration or other proceedings have been commenced by either party within 14 days after the Final Certificate has been issued, the Final Certificate shall have effect as conclusive evidence as provided in paragraph (a) of this sub-clause save only in respect of all matters to which those proceedings relate.

(8) Save as aforesaid no certificate of the Architect/Supervising Officer shall of itself be conclusive evidence that any works materials or goods to which it relates are in accordance with this Contract.

30B (1) In this Condition 'the Act' means the Finance (No. 2) Act 1975; 'the Regulations' means the Income Tax (Sub-Contractors in the Construction Industry) Regulations 1975 S.I. No. 1960; " 'contractor' " means a person who is a contractor for the purposes of the Act and the Regulations; 'evidence' means such evidence as is required by the Regulations to be produced to a 'contractor' for the verification of a 'sub-contractor's' tax certificate; 'statutory deduction' means the deduction referred to in section 69(4) of the Act or such other deduction as may be in force at the relevant time; " 'sub-contractor' " means a person who is a sub-contractor for the purposes of the Act and the Regulations; 'tax certificate' is a certificate issuable under section 70 of the Act.

(2) (a) At the date of tender as defined in clause 31D (6) (a) of these Conditions (or as defined in the Formula Rules where clause 31F of these Conditions applies) the Employer was a 'contractor'/was not a 'contractor'* for the purposes of the Act and the Regulations. Sub-clauses (3) to (9) of this Condition shall not apply if, in this paragraph, the Employer is stated not to be a 'contractor'.

(b) If in paragraph (a) hereof the words "was a 'contractor' " are deleted nevertheless if, at any time up to the issue and payment of the Final Certificate, the Employer becomes such a 'contractor', the Employer shall so inform the Contractor and the provisions of this Condition shall immediately thereupon become operative.

(3) (a) Not later than 21 days before the first payment under this Contract is due to the Contractor or after sub-clause (2) (b) of this Condition has become operative the Contractor shall:

either

(i) provide the Employer with the evidence that the Contractor is entitled to be paid without the statutory deduction;

or

(ii) inform the Employer in writing, and send a duplicate copy to the Architect/Supervising Officer, that he is not entitled to be paid without the statutory deduction.

(b) If the Employer is not satisfied with the validity of the evidence submitted in accordance with paragraph (a) (i) hereof, he shall within 14 days of the Contractor submitting such evidence notify the Contractor in writing that he intends to make the statutory deduction from payments due under this Contract to the Contractor who is 'a sub-contractor' and give his reasons for that decision. The Employer shall at the same time comply with sub-clause (6) (a) of this Condition.

(4) (a) Where sub-clause (3) (a) (ii) applies, the Contractor shall immediately inform the Employer if he obtains a tax certificate and thereupon sub-clause (3) (a) (i) shall apply.

(b) If the period for which the tax certificate has been issued to the Contractor expires before the final payment is made to the Contractor under this Contract the Contractor shall, not later than 28 days before the date of expiry:

either

(i) provide the Employer with evidence that the Contractor from the said date of expiry is entitled to be paid for a further period without the statutory deduction in which case the provisions of sub-clause (3) (b) hereof shall apply if the Employer is not satisfied with the evidence;

or

(ii) inform the Employer in writing that he will not be entitled to be paid without the statutory deduction after the said date of expiry.

(c) The Contractor shall immediately inform the Employer in writing if his current tax certificate is cancelled and give the date of such cancellation.

(5) The Employer shall, as a 'contractor' in accordance with the Regulations, send promptly to the Inland Revenue any voucher which, in compliance with the Contractor's obligations as a 'sub-contractor' under the Regulations, the Contractor gives to the Employer.

(6) (a) If at any time the Employer is of the opinion (whether because of the information given under sub-clause (3) (a) (ii) of this Condition or of the expiry or cancellation of the Contractor's tax certificate or otherwise) that he will be required by the Act to make a statutory deduction from any payment due to be made the Employer shall immediately so notify the Contractor in writing and require the Contractor to state not later than 7 days before each future payment becomes due (or within 10 days of such notification if that is later) the amount to be included in such payment which represents the direct cost to the Contractor and any other person of materials used or to be used in carrying out the Works.

*Footnote.— *Where the Employer at tender stage estimates the Contract Sum to be £250,000 or over the Retention Percentage should be not more than 3 per cent.*

*Footnote.—*Strike out as applicable.*

(b) Where the Contractor complies with paragraph (a) of this sub-clause he shall indemnify the Employer against loss or expense caused to the Employer by any incorrect statement of the amount of direct cost referred to in that paragraph.

(c) Where the Contractor does not comply with paragraph (a) of this sub-clause the Employer shall be entitled to make a fair estimate of the amount of direct cost referred to in that paragraph.

(7) Where any error or omission has occurred in calculating or making the statutory deduction the Employer shall correct that error or omission by repayment to, or by deduction from payments to, the Contractor as the case may be subject only to any statutory obligation on the Employer not to make such correction.

(8) If compliance with this Condition involves the Employer or the Contractor in not complying with any other of these Conditions, then the provisions of this Condition shall prevail.

(9) The provisions of clause 35 of these Conditions (arbitration) shall apply to any dispute or difference between the Employer or the Architect/Supervising Officer on his behalf and the Contractor as to the operation of this Condition except where the Act or the Regulations or any other Act of Parliament or statutory instrument rule or order made under an Act of Parliament provide for some other method of resolving such dispute or difference.

34.01 This clause provides for: issue of interim certificates (clause 30 (1)); amount of interim certificates (clause 30 (2)); certification of materials or goods before delivery to the works (clause 30 (2A)); right to the retention percentage (clause 30 (3)); nature of the retention percentage (clause 30 (4) (a)); first moiety of the retention percentage (clause 30 (4) (b)); residue of the retention percentage (clause 30 (4) (c)); period of final measurement and valuation (clause 30 (5) (a)); documents necessary for the final account (clause 30 (5) (b)); settlement of accounts in respect of prime cost and provisional sums and the like (clause 30 (5) (c)); issue of and contents of the final certificate (clause 30 (6)); effect of final certificate (clause 30 (7)); effect of certificates (clause 30 (8)); statutory tax deduction scheme (clause 30B). (Clause 30A, counter-inflation, is not ordinarily made part of the form.)

Architects' independent duty
34.02 For the extent and nature of the architect's duty to certify in an independent manner see paras 5.02 and 5.03.

Clause 30 (2)
34.03 The words '... the total value ...' mean that the amount certified should take into account adjustments for variations (clause 11 (5)), loss and expense ascertained under clauses 11 (6), 24 (1) and 34 (2) and price fluctuations (clause 31) but not, it is submitted, sums which the employer is entitled to deduct under clauses 2 (1), 19 (3), 20 (A) (1), 22 and 27 (c). See also para 26.03.

34.04 It is submitted that '... properly executed ...' means that the architect can take into account whether the work is in accordance with the contract, and if part of it is not, issue his certificate for a less sum than the value of the work if properly executed. It is important that he considers the value of the works carefully because the contractor can readily obtain immediate summary judgment for the amount of the certificate, and the employer will not usually find it easy to satisfy the court that he has an arguable defence to the sum claimed.

34.05 For the passing of ownership of property in materials and goods '... delivered to or adjacent to the works ...' see clause 14 and para 18.01.

Clause 30 (2A): Certification in respect of off-site goods
34.06 This clause and clause 14 (2) were incorporated in revisions published from April 1966. The architect is given a discretion to certify for payment in respect of goods and materials not on the site. If goods and materials are not on the site the employer has less protection in the event of the contractor's insolvency and certain other circumstances than if they are on the site. The detailed provisions of this clause exist in order to reduce the risks involved in certifying for off-site goods and materials and should be carefully followed. It is suggested that instead of the code allowed by clause 30

(2A) (c) it is better to use plain language such as 'SOLD, the property of .... (the employer) for use at .... (the works)'. The requirements as to insurance in clause 30 (2A) (i) were introduced in the 1975 amendment and are important for the protection of the client's interests.

Certification under clause 30 (2A) in respect of goods of sub-contractor or supplier
34.07 A request for such certification must come through the contractor. He may object. The material and goods remain at his risk (clause 14 (2)). If they are lost or damaged or by fraud or negligence disposed of by a sub-contractor or supplier, the contractor is, as between himself and the employer, liable to replace them at his own cost.

Clause 30 (3)
34.08 With reference to the words 'the employer may ... retain ...', retention may be applied to the value of the work, materials and goods adjusted by the valuation of variations under clause 11 (4), but not to loss or expense ascertained under clauses 11 (6), 24 (1) and 34 (2) nor to fluctuations where clause 31D applies.

Clause 30 (4) (a)
34.09 The intention in the words '... fiduciary as trustee ...' is, it is thought, that upon the employer's bankruptcy or liquidation as an insolvent company, as the case may be, the trustee in bankruptcy or liquidator holds the balance, if any, of the retention percentage as trustee for the contractor, ie it must be paid over to the contractor. But there are often legal difficulties in the operation of the clause.

Clause 30 (4) (b)
34.10 For the certificate referred to in the words 'on the issue of the certificate of practical completion' see clause 15. From the stage of practical completion until final certificate there is a detailed but clear procedure to be carried out, which may be conveniently summarised as follows:
1 Certificate of practical completion (clause 15 (1)), and at the same time:
2 Certificate for first moiety (half) of retention percentage (clause 30 (4) (b)).
3 Period of final measurement and valuation runs from certificate of practical completion and if none is stated is six months; contractor must be supplied with priced bills of variations within period and before the issue of the final certificate (clause 30 (5) (a), Appendix).
4 Before or within reasonable time after practical completion, contractor must send all documents necessary for the final account (clause 30 (5) (b)).
5 Defects liability period begins and if none stated is six months from certificate of practical completion (clause 15 (2) appendix).
(i) Schedule of defects to be delivered not later than fourteen days after expiration of defects liability period (clause 15 (2)).
(ii) Particular defects may be required to be made good before such schedule or such fourteen days, whichever is the earlier (clause 15 (3)).
(iii) Certificate of completion of making good defects when in opinion of the architect they have been made good (clause 15 (4)).
6 Certificate for residue of retention percentage on expiration of defects liability period or certificate of completion of making good defects whichever is the later (clause 30 (4) (c)). Note: it is contemplated that the contractor at this stage will have been paid substantially in full, and the period thereafter is for final adjustment of accounts one way or the other.

Further certificates for payment may be issued if amounts are due to the contractor (clause 30 (2)).

7 Final certificate as soon as is practicable but before the expiration of a period which, if none is stated, is three months from the latest of: end of defects liability period; completion of making good defects under clause 15; receipt of necessary documents from contractor (clause 30 (6)).

8 There is a 14-day period from the issue of the final certificate for either party to challenge the final certificate by arbitration or other proceedings, for the effect of which see clause 30 (7) (c). Before the 1975 amendment only the contractor could challenge the final certificate during this period.

Clause 30 (6) Final certificate

34.11 With reference to '... *expiration of the period ... stated in the appendix ...*', if none is stated it is three months. In the private variant there is no provision for inserting a different period and clause 30 (6) provides three months.

34.12 The words '*the contract sum adjusted as necessary ...*' refer to clauses 4 (2), 6 (3), 7, 11 (5), 11 (6), 12 (2), 13 (A), 15 (2), 20 (A) (2), (20) (B), 20 (C), 24 (1), 30 (5) (c), 31 (D) (4) or 31(F), 32, 33, 34 (2).

34.13 The words '... *or to the employer ...*' mean that the final certificate can be in favour of the employer for the return of moneys overpaid in earlier certificates. It is not necessary to hold back payment from earlier certificates merely to keep something in reserve.

Conclusive effect of final certificate
34.14 The final certificate is not merely the last certificate—it is, if properly issued in accordance with the contract, a document of considerable legal importance. Subject to certain qualifications it is conclusive evidence that, where the quality of materials or the standards of workmanship are to be to the reasonable satisfaction of the architect, they are to such satisfaction (see also para 5.04), and that any necessary effect has been given to all the terms of the contract which require an adjustment to be made of the contract sum. For the exact effect of the qualifications refer to clause 30 (7) but in summary they are:

1 Where proceedings have been commenced by either party before the issue of the final certificate the conclusiveness of the certificate becomes limited as set out in clause 30 (7) (b).

2 Where proceedings have been commenced by either party within 14 days of its issue the final certificate is then conclusive save only in respect of all matters to which the proceedings relate.

3 Fraud (clause 30 (7) (a)).

4 Mathematical error (clause 30 (7) (a) (ii)).

Matters not within the final certificate
34.15 It is submitted that questions of extension of time under clause 23 and the architect's certificate under clause 22 are not within the range of matters upon which the final certificate is conclusive. Further, the certificate cannot deal with any claim for damages made by the contractor (see para 28.04), nor with claims for consequential losses (see above) by the employer.

Emergency amendment
34.16 In connection with counter-inflation legislation then in force the JCT in December 1975 issued Emergency Amendment No 1/1975: Additional Clause 30A, all of which should be obtained and referred to if the employer, which

will be a body in the public sector, suggests that the contract is such as to require the use of the amendment. It is not intended to incorporate the amendment in future revisions of the standard form; and it does not therefore appear in the July 1977 revision.

35 Clause 31: Fluctuations

*31A The Contract Sum shall be deemed to have been calculated in the manner set out below and shall be subject to adjustment in the events specified hereunder:—

(a) (i) The prices (including the cost of employer's liability insurance and of third party insurance) contained in the Contract Bills are based upon the rates of wages and the other emoluments and expenses (including holiday credits) which will be payable by the Contractor to or in respect of workpeople engaged upon or in connection with the Works in accordance with the rules or decisions of the National Joint Council for the Building Industry and the terms of the Building and Civil Engineering Annual and Public Holidays Agreements which will be applicable to the Works and which have been promulgated at the date of tender, or in the case of workpeople so engaged whose rates of wages and other emoluments and expenses (including holiday credits) are governed by the rules or decisions or agreements of some body other than the National Joint Council for the Building Industry, in accordance with the rules or decisions or agreements of such other body which will be applicable and which have been promulgated as aforesaid.

(ii) If any of the said rates of wages or other emoluments and expenses (including holiday credits) are increased or decreased by reason of any alteration in the said rules, decisions or agreements promulgated after the date of tender, then the net amount of the increase or decrease in wages and other emoluments and expenses (including holiday credits) together with the net amount of any consequential increase or decrease in the cost of employer's liability insurance, of third party insurance, and of any contribution, levy or tax payable by a person in his capacity as an employer shall, as the case may be, be paid to or allowed by the Contractor.

(b) (i) The prices contained in the Contract Bills are based upon the types and rates of contribution, levy and tax payable by a person in his capacity as an employer and which at the date of tender are payable by the Contractor. A type and a rate so payable are in the next sub-paragraph referred to as a 'tender type' and a 'tender rate'.

(ii) If any of the tender rates other than a rate of levy payable by virtue of the Industrial Training Act, 1964, is increased or decreased, or if a tender type ceases to be payable, or if a new type of contribution, levy or tax which is payable by a person in his capacity as an employer becomes payable after the date of tender, then in any such case the net amount of the difference between what the Contractor actually pays or will pay in respect of workpeople whilst they are engaged upon or in connection with the Works or because of his employment of such workpeople upon or in connection with the Works, and what he would have paid had the alteration, cessation or new type of contribution levy or tax not become effective, shall, as the case may be, be paid to or allowed by the Contractor.

(iii) The prices contained in the Contract Bills are based upon the types and rates of refund of contributions, levies and taxes payable by a person in his capacity as an employer and upon the types and rates of premium receivable by a person in his capacity as an employer being in each case types and rates which at the date of tender are receivable by the Contractor. Such a type and such a rate are, in the next sub-paragraph, referred to as a 'tender type' and a 'tender rate'.

(iv) If any of the tender rates is increased or decreased or if a tender type ceases to be payable or if a new type of refund of any contribution levy or tax payable by a person in his capacity as an employer becomes receivable or if a new type of premium receivable by a person in his capacity as an employer becomes receivable after the date of tender, then in any such case the net amount of the difference between what the Contractor actually receives or will receive in respect of workpeople whilst they are engaged upon or in connection with the Works or because of his employment of such workpeople upon or in connection with the Works, and what he would have received had the alteration, cessation or new type of refund or premium not become effective, shall, as the case may be, be allowed by or paid to the Contractor.

(v) The references in the two preceding sub-paragraphs to premiums shall be construed as meaning all payments howsoever they are described which are made under or by virtue of an Act of Parliament to a person in his capacity as an employer and which affect the cost to an employer of having persons in his employment.

(vi) Where the Contractor elects to contribute to a recognised occupational pension scheme instead of participating in the Reserve Pension Scheme established under the Social Security Act 1973 the Contractor shall for the purpose of recovery or allowance under this clause be deemed to pay employer's contributions to the Reserve Pension Scheme.

(vii) The references in sub-paragraph (i) to (iv) and (vi) of this paragraph to contributions, levies and taxes shall be construed as meaning all impositions payable by a person in his capacity as an employer howsoever they are described and whoever the recipient which are imposed under or by virtue of an Act of Parliament and which affect the cost to an employer of having persons in his employment.

(c) (i) The prices contained in the Contract Bills are based upon the market prices of the materials and goods specified in the list attached thereto which were current at the date of tender. Such prices are hereinafter referred to as 'basic prices', and the prices stated by the Contractor on the said list shall be deemed to be the basic prices of the specified materials and goods.

(ii) If after the date of tender the market price of any of the materials or goods specified as aforesaid increases or decreases, then the net amount of the difference between the basic price thereof and the market price payable by the Contractor and current when the materials or goods are bought shall, as the case may be, be paid to or allowed by the Contractor.

(iii) The references in the two preceding sub-paragraphs to 'market prices' shall be construed as including any duty or tax (other than any value added tax which is treated, or is capable of being treated, as input tax (as referred to in the Finance Act 1972) by the Contractor) by whomsoever payable which is payable under or by virtue of any Act of Parliament on the import, purchase, sale, appropriation, processing or use of the materials or goods specified as aforesaid.

*31B The Contract Sum shall be deemed to have been calculated in the manner set out below and shall be subject to adjustment in the events specified hereunder:—

(a) (i) The prices contained in the Contract Bills are based upon the types and rates of contribution, levy and tax payable by a person in his capacity as an employer and which at the date of tender are payable by the Contractor. A type and a rate so payable are in the next sub-paragraph referred to as a 'tender type' and a 'tender rate'.

(ii) If any of the tender rates payable by virtue of the Industrial Training Act 1964, is increased or decreased, or if a tender type ceases to be payable, or if a new type of contribution, levy or tax which is payable by a person in his capacity as an employer becomes payable after the date of tender, then in any such case the net amount of the difference between what the Contractor actually pays or will pay in respect of workpeople whilst they are engaged upon or in connection with the Works or because of his employment of such workpeople upon or in connection with the Works, and what he would have paid had the alteration, cessation or new type of contribution, levy or tax not become effective, shall, as the case may be, be paid to or allowed by the Contractor.

*Footnote.—Parts A, C, D, and E should be used where the parties have agreed to allow the labour and materials cost and tax fluctuations to which Part A refers. Alternatively Part F should be used where the parties have agreed that the contract price shall be adjusted by the NEDO Formula Method under the Formula Rules.
Parts B, C, D and E should be used where neither Part A nor Part F is used.

(iii) The prices contained in the Contract Bills are based upon the types and rates of refund of contributions, levies and taxes payable by a person in his capacity as an employer and upon the types and rates of premium receivable by a person in his capacity as an employer being in each case types and rates which at the date of tender are receivable by the Contractor. Such a type and such a rate are in the next sub-paragraph referred to as a 'tender type' and a 'tender rate'.

(iv) If any of the tender rates is increased or decreased or if a tender type ceases to be payable or if a new type of refund of any contribution levy or tax payable by a person in his capacity as an employer becomes receivable or if a new type of premium receivable by a person in his capacity as an employer becomes receivable after the date of tender, then in any such case the net amount of the difference between what the Contractor actually receives or will receive in respect of workpeople whilst they are engaged upon or in connection with the Works or because of his employment of such workpeople upon or in connection with the Works, and what he would have received had the alteration, cessation or new type of refund or premium not become effective, shall, as the case may be, be allowed by or paid to the Contractor.

(v) The references in the two preceding sub-paragraphs to premiums shall be construed as meaning all payments howsoever they are described which are made under or by virtue of an Act of Parliament to a person in his capacity as an employer and which affect the cost to an employer of having persons in his employment.

(vi) Where the Contractor elects to contribute to a recognised occupational pension scheme instead of participating in the Reserve Pension Scheme established under the Social Security Act 1973 the Contractor shall for the purpose of recovery or allowance under this clause be deemed to pay employer's contributions to the Reserve Pension Scheme.

(vii) The references in sub-paragraphs (i) to (iv) and (vi) of this paragraph to contributions, levies and taxes shall be construed as meaning all impositions payable by a person in his capacity as an employer howsoever they are described and whoever the recipient which are imposed under or by virtue of an Act of Parliament and which affect the cost to an employer of having persons in his employment.

(b) (i) The prices contained in the Contract Bills are based upon the types and rates of duty if any and tax if any (other than any value added tax which is treated, or is capable of being treated, as input tax (as referred to in the Finance Act 1972) by the Contractor) by whomsoever payable which at the date of tender are payable on the import, purchase, sale, appropriation, processing or use of the materials and goods specified in the list attached thereto under or by virtue of any Act of Parliament. A type and a rate so payable are in the next sub-paragraph referred to as a 'tender type' and a 'tender rate'.

(ii) If in relation to any materials or goods specified as aforesaid a tender rate is increased or decreased, or a tender type ceases to be payable or a new type of duty or tax (other than any value added tax which is treated, or is capable of being treated, as input tax (as referred to in the Finance Act 1972) by the Contractor) becomes payable on the import, purchase, sale, appropriation, processing or use of those materials or goods, then in any such case the net amount of the difference between what the Contractor actually pays in respect of those materials or goods, and what he would have paid in respect of them had the alteration, cessation or imposition not occurred, shall, as the case may be, be paid to or allowed by the Contractor. In this sub-paragraph the expression 'a new type of duty or tax' includes an additional duty or tax and a duty or tax imposed in regard to specified materials or goods in respect of which no duty or tax whatever was previously payable (other than any value added tax which is treated, or is capable of being treated, as input tax (as referred to in the Finance Act 1972) by the Contractor).

31C (1) If the Contractor shall decide subject to clause 17 of these Conditions to sublet any portion of the Works he shall incorporate in the sub-contract provisions to the like effect as the provisions of clauses 31 A, 31 D and 31 E/clauses 31B, 31D and 31E (as applicable) which are applicable for the purposes of this Contract.

(2) If the price payable under such a sub-contract as aforesaid is decreased below or increased above the price in such sub-contract by reason of the operation of the said incorporated provisions, then the net amount of such decrease or increase shall, as the case may be, be allowed by or paid to the Contractor under this Contract.

31D (1) The Contractor shall give a written notice to the Architect/Supervising Officer of the occurrence of any of the events referred to in such of the following provisions as are applicable for the purposes on this Contract:

(a) Clause 31 A(a)(ii);
(b) Clause 31 A(b)(ii);
(c) Clause 31 A(b)(iv);
(d) Clause 31 A(c)(ii);
(e) Clause 31 B(a)(ii);
(f) Clause 31 B(a)(iv);
(g) Clause 31 B(b)(ii);
(h) Clause 31 C(2).

(2) Any notice required to be given by the preceding sub-clause shall be given within a reasonable time after the occurrence of that to which the notice relates, and the giving of a written notice in that time shall be a condition precedent to any payment being made to the Contractor in respect of the event in question.

(3) The Quantity Surveyor and the Contractor may agree what shall be deemed for all the purposes of this Contract to be the net amount payable to or allowable by the Contractor in respect of the occurrence of any event such as is referred to in any of the provisions listed in sub-clause (1) of this Condition.

(4) Any amount which from time to time becomes payable to or allowable by the Contractor by virtue of clause 31 A or clause 31 B or clause 31 C of these Conditions shall, as the case may be, be added to or subtracted from:

(a) The Contract Sum; and

(b) Any amounts payable to the Contractor and which are calculated in accordance with either sub-paragraph (i) or sub-paragraph (ii) of paragraph (b) of sub-clause 2 of clause 26 of these Conditions; and

(c) The amount which would otherwise be stated as due in the next Interim Certificate.

Provided:

(i) No addition to or subtraction from the amount which would otherwise be stated as due in an Interim Certificate shall be made by virtue of this sub-clause unless on or before the date as at which the total value of work, materials and goods is ascertained for the purposes of that Certificate the Contractor shall have actually paid or received the sum which is payable by or to him in consequence of the event in respect of which the payment or allowance arises.

(ii) No addition to or subtraction from the Contract Sum made by virtue of this sub-clause shall alter in any way the amount of profit of the Contractor included in that Sum.

(5) Clause 31 A, clause 31 B and clause 31 C shall not apply in respect of:

(a) Work for which the Contractor is allowed daywork rates under clause 11 (4) (c) of these Conditions.

(b) Work executed or materials or goods supplied by any nominated sub-contractor or nominated supplier (fluctuations in relation to nominated sub-contractors and nominated suppliers shall be dealt with under any provision in relation thereto which may be included in the appropriate sub-contract or contract of sale), or

(c) Work executed by the Contractor for which a tender made under clause 27 (g) of these Conditions has been accepted.

(d) Changes in the rate of value added tax charged on the supply of goods or services by the Contractor to the Employer under this Contract.

(6) In Clause 31 A and clause 31 B of these Conditions:

(a) The expression 'the date of tender' means the date 10 days before the date fixed for the receipt of tenders by the Employer; and

(b) The expression 'materials' and 'goods' include timber used in formwork but do not include other consumable stores, plant and machinery.

(c) The expression 'workpeople' means persons whose rates of wages and other emoluments (including holiday credits) are governed by the rules or decisions or agreements of the National Joint Council for the Building Industry or some other like body for trades associated with the building industry.

31E There shall be added to the amount paid to or allowed by the Contractor under:

(a) Clause 31 A(a)(ii);
(b) Clause 31 A(b)(ii);
(c) Clause 31 A(b)(iv);
(d) Clause 31 A(c)(ii);
(e) Clause 31 B(a)(ii);
(f) Clause 31 B(a)(iv);
(g) Clause 31 B(b)(ii);

the percentage stated in the Appendix to these Conditions.

***31F** (1) (a) (i) The Contract Sum shall be adjusted in accordance with the provisions of this clause and the Formula Rules current at the Date of Tender issued for use with this clause by the Joint Contracts Tribunal for the Standard Form of Building Contract hereinafter called 'the Formula Rules'.

(ii) Any adjustment under this clause shall be to sums exclusive of value added tax and nothing in this clause shall affect in any way the operation of clause 13A (value added tax) and the VAT Agreement executed pursuant to sub-clause (1) (b) of clause 13A of these Conditions.

(b) The Definitions in rule 3 of the Formula Rules shall apply to this clause.

(c) The adjustment referred to in this sub-clause shall be effected (after taking into account any Non-Adjustable Element) in all certificates for payment (other than those under clause 16 (f) and clause 30 (4) of these Conditions (release of retention)) issued under the provisions of these Conditions.

(d) If any correction of amounts of adjustment under this clause included in previous certificates is required following any operation of rule 5 of the Formula Rules such correction shall be given effect in the next certificate for payment to be issued.

(2) (a) (i) Interim valuations shall be made before the issue of each Interim Certificate and accordingly the words 'whenever the Architect/Supervising Officer considers them to be necessary' shall be deemed to have been deleted in clause 30 (1) of these Conditions.

(ii) The words 'Before the issue of the Certificate of Practical Completion, Interim Certificates shall be issued at the Period of Interim Certificates specified in the Appendix to these Conditions. After the issue of the Certificate of Practical Completion' in clause 30 (1) of these Conditions shall be deemed to have been deleted and the following words substituted: 'Interim Certificates shall be issued at the Period of Interim Certificates specified in the Appendix to these Conditions including any Period during which the Certificate of Practical Completion is issued. After the end of the Period of Interim Certificates in which the Certificate of Practical Completion is issued,'.

(b) The Retention Percentage referred to in clause 30 (3) (a) of these Conditions shall apply to any adjustment of the Contract Sum under this clause and accordingly

(i) the words 'together with the net total of the adjustments to the Contract Sum to be effected under clause 31F in the said Interim Certificate and effected in any previous Interim Certificates' shall be deemed to have been added to clause 30 (2) of these Conditions after the words 'seven days before the date of the said certificate'; and

(ii) the words 'together with the net total of the adjustments' shall be deemed to have been added to clause 30 (3) (a) of these Conditions after the words 'total value of the work, materials and goods'; and

(iii) the words 'together with the net total of the adjustments' shall be deemed to have been added to clause 30 (3) (b) of these Conditions after the words 'total value of the work, materials and goods'.

(c) A reference to arbitration on a dispute or difference under clause 23 of these Conditions may be opened before Practical Completion or alleged Practical Completion of the Works or termination or alleged termination of the Contractor's employment under this Contract or abandonment of the Works and accordingly the words 'under clause 23 or' shall be deemed to have been added to clause 35 (2) of these Conditions after the words 'on any dispute or difference'.

(d) The words '(or as defined in the Formula Rules where clause 31F of these Conditions applies)' shall be deemed to have been added after the words 'of these Conditions' in clause 13A (3) of these Conditions.

(3) For any article to which rule 4 (ii) of the Formula Rules applies the Contractor shall insert in a list attached to the Contract Bills the market price of the article in sterling (that is the price delivered to the site) current at the Date of Tender. If after that Date the market price of the article inserted in the aforesaid list increases or decreases then the net amount of the difference between the cost of purchasing at the market price inserted in the aforesaid list and the market price payable by the Contractor and current when the article is bought shall, as the case may be, be paid to or allowed by the Contractor. The reference to 'market price' in this sub-clause shall be construed as including any duty or tax (other than any value added tax which is treated, or is capable of being treated, as input tax (as defined in the Finance Act 1972) by the Contractor) by whomsoever payable under or by virtue of any Act of Parliament on the import, purchase, sale, appropriation or use of the article specified as aforesaid.

(4) (a) Where the supply and fixing of any goods or the execution of any work is to be carried out by a sub-contractor nominated by the Architect/Supervising Officer the sub-contract between the Contractor and the nominated sub-contractor shall provide if required for adjustment to be made of the sub-contract sum for cost fluctuations by reference to whichever of the following has been tendered upon by the sub-contractor and approved in writing by the Architect/Supervising Officer prior to the issue of the nomination instruction:

(i) in the case of electrical installations, heating and ventilating and air conditioning installations, lift installations, structural steelwork installations and in the case of catering equipment installations, the relevant specialist formula (see the Formula Rules, rule 50, rule 54, rule 58, rule 63 and rule 69);

(ii) where none of the specialist formulae applies, the Formula in Part I of Section 2 of the Formula Rules and one or more of the Work Categories set out in appendix A to the Formula Rules;

(iii) where neither sub-paragraph (i) nor sub-paragraph (ii) applies, some other method.

(b) If the Contractor shall decide, subject to clause 17 of these Conditions, to sub-let any portion of the Works, he shall, unless the Contractor and sub-contractor otherwise agree, incorporate in the sub-contract provisions for formula adjustment of the sub-contract sum namely:

(i) in the case of electrical installations, heating and ventilating and air conditioning installations, lift installations, structural steelwork installations and in the case of catering equipment installations, the relevant specialist formula;

(ii) where none of the specialist formulae applies, the Formula in Part I of Section 2 of the Formula Rules and one or more of the Work Categories set out in appendix A to the Formula Rules appropriate to such sub-contract works.

(5) The Quantity Surveyor and the Contractor may agree any alteration to the methods and procedures for ascertaining the amount of formula adjustment to be made under this clause and the amounts ascertained after the operation of such agreement shall be deemed for all the purposes of this Contract to be the amount of formula adjustment payable to or allowable by the Contractor in respect of the provisions of this clause. Provided always:

(i) that no alteration to the methods and procedures shall be agreed as aforesaid unless it is reasonably expected that the amount of formula adjustment so ascertained will be the same or approximately the same as that ascertained in accordance with Part I or Part II of Sections 2 of the Formula Rules whichever Part is stated to be applicable in the Contract Bills; and

(ii) that any agreement under this sub-clause shall not have any effect on the determination of any adjustment payable by the Contractor to any sub-contractor to whom sub-clause (4) refers.

(6) (a) If at any time prior to the issue of the Final Certificate under clause 30 (6) of these Conditions formula adjustment is not possible because of delay in, or cessation of, the publication of the Monthly Bulletins, adjustment of the Contract Sum shall be made in each Interim Certificate during such period of delay on a fair and reasonable basis.

(b) If publication of the Monthly Bulletins is recommenced at any time prior to the issue of the Final Certificate under clause 30 (6) of these Conditions the provisions of this clause and the Formula Rules shall operate for each Valuation Period as if no delay or cessation as aforesaid had occurred and the adjustment under this clause and the Formula Rules shall be substituted for any adjustment under paragraph (a) hereof.

(c) During any period of delay or cessation as aforesaid the Contractor and Employer shall operate such parts of this clause and the Formula Rules as will enable the amount of formula adjustment due to be readily calculated upon recommencement of publication of the Monthly Bulletins.

***Footnote:** *Part F is used where the parties have agreed that fluctuations should be dealt with by adjustment of the Contract Sum under the Price Adjustment Formulae for Building Contracts. Parts A—E should be deleted where Part F applies.*

(7) (a) (i) If the Contractor fails to complete the Works by the Date for Completion stated in the appendix to these Conditions or within any extended time fixed under clause 23 or clause 33 (1) (c) of these Conditions formula adjustment of the Contract Sum under this clause shall (but subject to sub-clause (c) (i) hereof) be effected in all interim certificates issued after the aforesaid Date for Completion (or any extension thereof) by reference to the Index Numbers applicable to the Valuation Period in which the aforesaid Date for Completion (or any extension thereof) falls.

(ii) If for any reason the adjustment included in the amount certified in any Interim Certificate which is or has been issued after the aforesaid Date for Completion (or any extension thereof) is not in accordance with sub-paragraph (i) hereof, such adjustment shall be corrected to comply with the aforesaid sub-paragraph.

(b) Paragraph (a) of this sub-clause shall not operate unless:

(i) the printed text of clause 23 of these Conditions is unamended and sub-clause (j) (i) and sub-clause (j) (ii) of that clause have not been deleted in the Contract Conditions executed by the Employer and the Contractor, and

(ii) the Architect/Supervising Officer has, in respect of every written notification by the Contractor under clause 23 of these Conditions, made in writing such extensions of time, if any, for completion of the Works as he considers to be in accordance with that clause; provided always that the Contractor has given the Architect/Supervising Officer such information as the Architect/Supervising Officer may reasonably require for this purpose.

(c) Where the condition in paragraph (b) (i) hereof is fulfilled:

(i) any formula adjustment of the sub-contract sum in respect of any supply and fixing of goods, or the execution of any work, by a sub-contractor nominated by the Architect/Supervising Officer (hereinafter called 'the sub-contract works') shall not be affected by any operation of paragraph (a) of this sub-clause;

(ii) subject to sub-paragraph (iii) hereof any formula adjustment of the sub-contract sum for such sub-contract works shall be effected in all Interim Certificates which include a direction within the terms of clause 27 (b) of these Conditions by reference to the Index Numbers applicable to the Valuation Period (or in the case of lift installations and structural steelwork installations the Index Numbers applicable at the relevant dates for adjustment) to which any Interim Certificate including the aforesaid direction relates;

(iii) if a nominated sub-contractor shall fail to complete the sub-contract works within the period specified in the sub-contract or within any extended time granted by the Contractor with the written consent of the Architect/Supervising Officer and the Architect/Supervising Officer has issued the certificate (with a duplicate copy to the nominated sub-contractor) referred to in clause 27 (d) (ii) of these Conditions, formula adjustment of the sub-contract sum shall (if the sub-contract so provides) be effected in all Interim Certificates which include a direction within the terms of clause 27 (b) of these Conditions and which are issued after the date in the aforesaid certificate (that is the day on which the sub-contract works ought for the purposes of clause 27 (d) (ii) of these Conditions to have been completed) issued under clause 27 (d) (ii), by reference to Index Numbers applicable to the Valuation Period in which that date falls.

35.01 There need be no price fluctuations clause at all in which case the price remains fixed whatever changes there may be in wages, prices of materials and relevant impositions arising from Government legislation. But the contract contemplates that at the very least clause 31B will be used together with the ancillary clauses, 31C to E. If clause 31B is the only operative clause its effect is very limited. It is directed to certain alterations in costs arising from statutory changes only. It provides for alterations in statutory contributions, levies and taxes payable by, or refunds or premiums receivable by, a person in his capacity as employer, and for alterations in statutory duties or taxes affecting materials or goods specified in a list attached to the contract bills. If clause 31A is also used, fluctuations extend to alterations in wages, emoluments and expenses and in market prices in materials and goods specified in a list attached to the contract bills.

Bonus schemes
35.02 In a case where clause 31A applied it has been held that the increase in cost in operating a bonus scheme, based upon wage rates, where that scheme was voluntarily entered into by the contractors, is not an increase recoverable under the clause (*Sindall v N.W. Thames Regional Hospital Authority* (1976) currently on appeal to the House of Lords).

The additional percentage
35.03 31A does not apply to increases in head office and administrative costs, neither does it apply to consumable stores, plant and machinery other than timber used in formwork (see clause 31D (6) (b)). Presumably for these and other reasons which show that clause 31A does not provide a contractor with an indemnity against increased costs there was introduced in 1973 clause 31E which expressly provides for the contractor to insert in the appendix an additional percentage to be added to the amount paid in respect of fluctuations.

Formula adjustment: clause 31F
35.04 This method of calculating fluctuations was introduced in July 1973 and is alternative to 31B with or without 31A. Notes appear below in para 35.10 and 35.11.

Sub-contractors
35.05 The contractor must incorporate the relevant fluctuations clause in sub-contracts with approved (see clause 17) sub-contractors (clause 31C (1)). Clauses 31A, 31B do not apply to nominated suppliers (clause 31D (5) (b)) or work executed by the contractor for which a tender made under clause 27 (g) was accepted (clause 31D (5) (c)). The current edition of the standard form of sub-contract incorporates fluctuations clauses which correspond with clauses 31A, B, C and D.

Daywork
35.06 Clauses 31A, B and C do not apply to work for which the contractor is allowed daywork rates under clause 11 (4) (c) (ii).

Notice essential
35.07 Notice within a reasonable time of the relevant event is a condition precedent to any payment to the contractor in respect of that event (clause 31D, (1) (2)).

Promulgation of wage awards
35.08 Where clause 31A is relied on the contractor cannot claim an increase in respect of a wage award which becomes effective during the course of carrying out the works but which has been promulgated at the date of tender (clause 31 (A), (a) (i)). 'Date of tender' means the date 10 days before the date fixed for the receipt of tenders by the employer.

Contractor's delay in completion
35.09 The contractor is entitled to any benefit arising under clauses 31A and 31B, where they apply, even though he has overrun time without grounds for extension.

Formula adjustment: the clause 31F alternative
35.10 This is an alternative to clauses 31A to E. It provides for fluctuations in costs to be dealt with by the application of formulae prepared by Government-sponsored bodies and published as monthly bulletins. The JCT issued the new clause together with a set of specially prepared rules termed the 'Formula Rules' which by incorporation become part of the contract where the clause is used. They further issued practice note 18. For the detailed application of the clause it is necessary to obtain the Formula Rules and desirable to obtain the practice note. To give effect to the clause many amendments have to be made to the contract but it does not have to be physically altered; the necessary effect is achieved by clause 31F (2). Clause 31F does not apply to nominated sub-contractors.

Note: A second series of the SFBC Formula Rules was published in April 1977, Editor.

Contractor's delay in completion where 31F applicable
35.11 *Prima facie* clause 31F does not continue to apply after the date for completion, extended as may be necessary. The effect is that the contractor does not have the benefit of price increases where the delay is his own fault. But this non-continuance of the application of the clause is subject to clause 23 remaining unamended with sub-clauses (j) (i) and (ii) not having been deleted and further subject to the architect, in respect of every written notification by the contractor under clause 23 having made in writing such extensions of time, if any, for completion of the works as he considers to be in accordance with that clause and always provided that the contractor has given the architect such information as he might reasonably require. So although clause 31F does not amend clause 23 the effect is to put upon an architect who has received proper information from the

contractor a duty of considering extensions of time very promptly.

36 Clause 32: Outbreak of hostilities

*32 (1) If during the currency of this Contract there shall be an outbreak of hostilities (whether war is declared or not) in which the United Kingdom shall be involved on a scale involving the general mobilisation of the armed forces of the Crown, then either the Employer or the Contractor may at any time by notice by registered post or recorded delivery to the other, forthwith determine the employment of the Contractor under this Contract:

Provided that such a notice shall not be given

    (a) Before the expiration of 28 days from the date on which the order is given for general mobilisation as aforesaid, or

    (b) After Practical Completion of the Works unless the Works or any part thereof shall have sustained war damage as defined in clause 33 (4) of these Conditions.

(2) The Architect/Supervising Officer may within 14 days after a notice under this Condition shall have been given or received by the Employer issue instructions to the Contractor requiring the execution of such protective work as shall be specified therein and/or the continuation of the Works up to points of stoppage to be specified therein, and the Contractor shall comply with such instructions as if the notice of determination had not been given.

Provided that if the Contractor shall for reasons beyond his control be prevented from completing the work to which the said instructions relate within three months from the date on which the instructions were issued, he may abandon such work.

(3) Upon the expiration of 14 days from the date on which a notice of determination shall have been given or received by the Employer under this Condition or where works are required by the Architect/Supervising Officer under the preceding sub-clause upon completion or abandonment as the case may be of any such works, the provisions of sub-clause (2) (except sub-paragraph (vi) of paragraph (b)) of clause 26 of these Conditions shall apply, and the Contractor shall also be paid by the Employer the value of any work executed pursuant to instructions given under sub-clause (2) of this clause, the value being ascertained in accordance with clause 11 (4) of these Conditions as if such work were a variation required by the Architect/Supervising Officer.

Footnote.—The parties hereto in the event of the outbreak of hostilities may at any time by agreement between them make such further or other arrangements as they may think fit to meet the circumstances.

37 Clause 33: War damage

33 (1) In the event of the Works or any part thereof or any unfixed materials or goods intended for, delivered to and placed on or adjacent to the Works sustaining war damage then notwithstanding anything expressed or implied elsewhere in this Contract:

    (a) The occurrence of such war damage shall be disregarded in computing any amounts payable to the Contractor under or by virtue of this Contract.

    (b) The Architect/Supervising Officer may issue instructions requiring the Contractor to remove and/or dispose of any debris and/or damaged work and/or to execute such protective work as shall be specified.

    (c) The Contractor shall reinstate or make good such war damage and shall proceed with the carrying out and completion of the Works, and the Architect/Supervising Officer shall grant the Contractor a fair and reasonable extension of time for completion of the Works.

    (d) The removal and disposal of debris or damaged work, the execution of protective works and the reinstatement and making good of such war damage shall be deemed to be a variation required by the Architect/Supervising Officer.

(2) If at any time after the occurrence of war damage as aforesaid either party serves notice of determination under clause 32 of these Conditions, the expression 'protective work' as used in the said clause shall in such case be deemed to include any matters in respect of which the Architect/Supervising Officer can issue instructions under paragraph (b) of sub-clause (1) of this Condition and any instructions issued under the said paragraph prior to the date on which notice of determination is given or received by the Employer and which shall not then have been completely complied with shall be deemed to have been given under clause 32 (2) of these Conditions.

(3) The Employer shall be entitled to any compensation which may at any time become payable out of monies provided by Parliament in respect of war damage sustained by the Works or any part thereof or any unfixed materials or goods intended for the Works which shall at any time have become the property of the Employer.

(4) The expression 'war damage' as used in this Condition means war damage as defined by section 2 of the War Damage Act, 1943, or any amendment thereof.

37.01 Clauses 32 and 33 regulate the position in circumstances which might otherwise bring the contract to an end by the operation of the doctrine of frustration of contracts.

38 Clause 34: Antiquities

34 (1) All fossils, antiquities and other objects of interest or value which may be found on the site or in excavating the same during the progress of the Works shall become the property of the Employer, and upon discovery of such an object the Contractor shall forthwith:

    (a) Use his best endeavours not to disturb the object and shall cease work if and insofar as the continuance of work would endanger the object or prevent or impede its excavation or its removal;

    (b) Take all steps which may be necessary to preserve the object in the exact position and condition in which it was found; and

    (c) Inform the Architect/Supervising Officer or the Clerk of Works of the discovery and precise location of the object.

(2) The Architect/Supervising Officer shall issue instructions in regard to what is to be done concerning an object reported by the Contractor under the preceding sub-clause, and (without prejudice to the generality of his power) such instructions may require the Contractor to permit the examination, excavation or removal of the object by a third party. Any such third party shall for the purposes of clause 18 of these Conditions be deemed to be a person for whom the Employer is responsible and not to be a sub-contractor.

(3) If in the opinion of the Architect/Supervising Officer compliance with the provisions of sub-clause (1) of this Condition or with an instruction issued under sub-clause (2) of this Condition has involved the contractor in direct loss and/or expense for which he would not be reimbursed by a payment made under any other provision in this Contract then the Architect/Supervising Officer shall either himself ascertain or shall instruct the Quantity Surveyor to ascertain the amount of such loss and/or expense. Any amount from time to time so ascertained shall be added to the Contract Sum, and if an Interim Certificate is issued after the date of ascertainment any such amount shall be added to the amount which would otherwise be stated as due in such a Certificate.

38.01 For meaning of the words '. . . *direct loss and expense* . . .' see discussion of clauses 11 (6) and 24 (1).

39 Clause 35: Arbitration

*35 (1) Provided always that in case any dispute or difference shall arise between the Employer or the Architect/Supervising Officer on his behalf and the Contractor, either during the progress or after the completion or abandonment of the Works, as to the construction of this Contract or as to any matter or thing of whatsoever nature arising thereunder or in connection therewith (including any matter or thing left by this Contract to the discretion of the Architect/Supervising Officer or the withholding by the Architect/Supervising Officer of any certificate to which the Contractor may claim to be entitled or the measurement and valuation mentioned in clause 30 (5) (a) of these Conditions or the rights and liabilities of the parties under clauses 25, 26, 32 or 33 of these Conditions), then such dispute or difference shall be and is hereby referred to the arbitration and final decision of a person to be agreed between the parties, or, failing agreement within 14 days after either party has given to the other a written request to concur in the appointment of an Arbitrator, a person to be appointed on the request of either party by the President or a Vice-President for the time being of the Royal Institute of British Architects.

(2) Such reference, except on article 3 or article 4 of the Articles of Agreement, or on the questions whether or not the issue of an instruction is empowered by these Conditions, whether or not a certificate has been improperly withheld or is not in accordance with these Conditions, or on any dispute or difference under clauses 32 and 33 of these Conditions, shall not be opened until after Practical Completion or alleged Practical Completion of the Works or termination or alleged termination of the Contractor's employment under this Contract or abandonment of the Works, unless with the written consent of the Employer or the Architect/Supervising Officer on his behalf and the Contractor.

(3) Subject to the provisions of clauses 2 (2), 30 (7) and 31 D (3) of these Conditions the Arbitrator shall, without prejudice to the generality of his powers, have power to direct such measurements and/or valuations as may in his opinion be desirable in order to determine the rights of the parties and to ascertain and award any sum which ought to have been the subject of or included in any certificate and to open up, review and revise any certificate, opinion, decision, requirement or notice and to determine all matters in dispute which shall be submitted to him in the same manner as if no such certificate, opinion, decision, requirement or notice had been given.

(4) The award of such Arbitrator shall be final and binding on the parties.

**(5) Whatever the nationality, residence or domicile of the Employer, the Contractor, any sub-contractor or supplier or the Arbitrator, and wherever the Works, or any part thereof, are situated, the law of England shall be the proper law of this Contract and in particular (but not so as to derogate from the generality of the foregoing) the provisions of the Arbitration Act, 1950 (notwithstanding anything in section 34 thereof) shall apply to any arbitration under this Contract wherever the same, or any part of it, shall be conducted.

Footnote.—The provisions of this Condition do not apply to any dispute that may arise between the Employer and the Contractor as referred to in Clause 3 of the Supplemental Agreement annexed to these Conditions (the VAT Agreement).

**Footnote.—Where the parties do not wish the proper law of the contract to be the law of England and/or do not wish the provisions of the Arbitration Act, 1950 to apply to any arbitration under the contract held under the procedural law of Scotland (or other country) appropriate amendments to this sub-clause should be made.*

Arbitrator's jurisdiction

39.01 Subject to the exceptions effected by clauses 2 (2), 30 (7) and 31D (3), the arbitrator's jurisdiction is very wide and extends, for example, to the review of all decisions of the architect. The exception which is of greatest importance in practice is that brought about by clause 30 (7) discussed above at para 34.14. The employer, as well as the contractor can challenge the architect's decisions and ask the arbitrator to alter or set them aside.

Arbitration after completion

39.02 This is the ordinary rule (clause 35 (2)) but the exceptions are wide in their effect particularly as regards certificates. LEGAL STUDY 8 gives further details of arbitration practice and procedure.

40 Supplemental Agreement: VAT

40.01 VAT is a tax chargeable on the supply of goods and services unless they are zero-rated or a person supplies exempt goods or services. Very broadly the position is that the contractor does not have to charge the employer with tax in most cases where the work is not that of repair or maintenance because most building works are zero-rated. Any sub-contractor has to charge the next contractor above him and so up the line to the main contractor but each person in turn who has to pay the tax can recover it, ultimately, if necessary, from the Customs and Excise. In certain circumstances some tax may be payable by the employer. If it is, this supplemental agreement regulates the position. It provides for the contractor making a provisional assessment upon each interim certificate and for a final statement and for the employer to have the right, upon indemnifying the contractor as to costs, to cause him to challenge the amount of tax claimed. Thus VAT is dealt with exclusively by this supplemental agreement and is a matter for the contractor and the employer to deal with. The contract sum under the main body of the contract is exclusive of VAT. The architect therefore ignores it in his valuations and other matters arising under the contract. For this reason, with a view to saving space, the supplemental agreement has not been printed. If problems arise relating to VAT the supplemental agreement must be obtained and studied together with *Practice note 17* issued by the JCT and prepared after consultation with the Commissioners of Customs and Excise.

References

KEATING, D. Building contracts. London, 1969, Sweet & Maxwell. For a detailed and highly critical study of the form, see I. N. DUNCAN WALLACE, Building and civil engineering standard forms, London, 1969 (with supplements, 1970, 1971) Sweet & Maxwell

RIBA
Conditions of engagement. 1971, as amended 1975 and 1976.
Code of procedure for selective tendering. 1977 (National Joint Consultative Committee)
ROYAL INSTITUTION OF CHARTERED SURVEYORS. Standard method of measurement of building works. 5th Edition (metric) 1970
RIBA Standard form of agreement between employer and subcontractor, 1973
FEDERATION OF ASSOCIATIONS OF SPECIALISTS AND SUB-CONTRACTORS. Form of subcontract to be used where subcontractor is nominated under RIBA form of contract, 1976
RIBA Form of warranty to be given by a nominated supplier, 1970

Acknowledgements

The contract is reproduced by courtesy of the RIBA.
The print at the beginning of this section is reproduced by courtesy of Chelsea Public Library.

Appendix

Appendix

	Clause
Defects Liability Period [if none other stated is 6 months from the day named in the Certificate of Practical Completion of the Works].	15, 16 and 30
Insurance cover for any one occurrence or series of occurrences arising out of one event.	19 (1) (a) £
Percentage to cover Professional fees.*	20 [A]
Date for Possession.	21
Date for Completion.	21
Liquidated and Ascertained Damages.	22 at the rate of £ per
**Period of delay: (i) by reason of loss or damage caused by any one of the contingencies referred to in clause 20 [A] or clause 20 [B] (if applicable). (ii) for any other reason.	26
Prime cost sums for which the Contractor desires to tender.	27 (g)
Period of Interim Certificates [if none stated is one month].	30 (1)
Retention Percentage (if less than five per cent.).†	30 (3)
Period of Final Measurement and Valuation [if none stated is 6 months from the day named in the Certificate of Practical Completion of the Works].	30 (5)
Period for issue of Final Certificate [if none stated is 3 months].††	30 (6)
Percentage addition.	31E
Formula Rules	31 F (1) (a) (i)
Rule 3	Base Month 19
Rule 3	Non-Adjustable Element % (not to exceed 10%)
Rules 10 and 30 (i)	***Part I/Part II of Section 2 of the Formula Rules is to apply

*Footnote.—Where the professional persons concerned with the Works are all employees of a Local Authority no percentage should be inserted, but care should be taken to include in the sum assured the cost to the Employer of their services.

**Footnote.—It is suggested that the periods should be (i) three months and (ii) one month. It is essential that periods be inserted since otherwise no period of delay would be prescribed.

***Footnote.—Strike out according to which method of formula adjustment (Part I—Work Category Method or Part II—Work Group Method) has been notified in the Bills of Quantities issued to tenderers.

†Footnote.—The Percentage will be five per cent unless a lower rate is specified here.

††Footnote.—The period inserted must not exceed 6 months.

Supplement to Legal Study 4

This section briefly describes some other forms of contract that the architect may encounter, and adds short notes on basic tendering procedures in general use today

4. S.1 *Other standard forms*
The purpose of this Supplement is to draw attention which could lead to further study of the forms themselves to the various standard forms of building and civil engineering contracts, other than the 'Standard Form' discussed in detail in Legal Study 4 and the Scottish supplement referred to in Legal Study 5.
The ever-changing and expanding pattern of building and civil engineering works today frequently involves the architect, either directly or in association with professional colleagues in related fields, in what were traditionally regarded as civil engineering projects and which are usually outside his own experience. Nowhere is evidence of this more pronounced than in arrangements within the construction industry as a whole for competitive contracting and subcontracting of work. Architects can no longer afford to remain ill-informed about these arrangements.
Many of the standard forms, including those in civil engineering and government use have similarities and almost as many contrasting variations. The recommendations of the Banwell Committee's Report in 1964* pointed to the need for some common form of contract for building construction in the building and civil engineering industries; or at least, as a first step, one for building and one for engineering. Some of the forms now in use are briefly commented upon in what follows. At the same time it must be remembered that there is a wide range of construction in which the building client deals not with professional advisers but directly with the contractors—as in private-house building, work on improvement grants, and general repair and maintenance work—in all of which adequate protection in contract form is highly desirable for all parties.

4. S.2 *Fixed Fee Form of Prime Cost Contract* (JCT)
This type of contract was first devised and published in 1946 for works on repair of war damaged property, but its use was understandably limited, so after considerable amendment in 1967 by the Joint Contracts Tribunal, the present form was revised in October 1976 in order to bring a number of clauses in line with amendments made to the other JCT Standard Forms. The basis of the contract is that in return for carrying out the work shown on the drawings and description in the specification the contractor is paid the prime cost of that work, plus a fixed fee of an amount agreed between the parties before the contract is signed and duly recorded in the Second Schedule to the Contract form.
In theory this contract might be used for any type of work and any size of job, provided the exact nature and scope of the work is reasonably certain and can be specified so that a fair estimate of the prime cost can be made before the contract is entered into. In order to arrive at the amount of fee, therefore, it is necessary to agree an estimate of what the prime cost of the works will be. As the Form is unrelated to any bills of quantities the preparation of any estimate depends upon specification and limited drawings. The amount of the estimate is entered in the Third Schedule under three headings, namely: 1. Builder's general work, 2. nominated sub-contractors' work and 3. materials and goods to be supplied by nominated suppliers. What the Contract does not provide for is any adjustment of the fixed fee. If the ascer-

* See Reference list to this Supplement

tained prime cost varies from the original estimate neither the contractor nor the employer can claim any revision of the fee. The possibility of the need to vary the work in any way that might appreciably affect the original estimate of the prime cost is anticipated in clause 3 (1) which states that . . . 'The architect may issue to the contractor such instructions as he thinks fit. Provided always that the architect shall not by virtue of this sub-clause be enabled to issue an instruction requiring any alteration in the nature or the scope of the works'. A footnote to the clause makes it quite clear that . . . *the parties may however agree to such an alteration but their agreement MUST be embodied in a separate or supplemental contract*. In practice such an agreement is quite simply made, recording the particulars of the instruction, the revision of the estimated prime cost resulting therefrom and such adjustment to the fixed fee as might be agreed. This is a form of agreement calling for quite a degree of good faith between the parties. Consequently it is best, and for this reason most commonly used, when negotiated with a single contractor. But if an element of competition is desired an estimate of the prime cost can be prepared by the quantity surveyor from specification and drawings on which selected contractors can be invited to tender in competition by quoting the fixed fee they would require.

The Fixed Fee Form of Prime Cost Contract where particulars and scope of the contract can be clearly defined at the outset has considerable advantages to both contractor and employer. To the former the assurance of certainty and it guarantees his cost; and to the latter a welcome speed up of pre-contract procedures, particularly when the contractor is agreed beforehand. At the same time it does not rule out the element of competition by seeking alternative tenders for the fee. Its successful working depends upon the choice of a reliable and responsible contractor and diligent and 'reasonable' architectural supervision.

JCT Practice Note No. 16 (May 1969) on the use of the Fixed Fee Form of Prime Cost Contract is still valid and should be consulted. It helps to clarify some of the difficulties on which questions have been referred to the Council, notably in respect of clauses 3 and 7 (1).

4. S.3 The 'ICE Form'—for Civil Engineering Work

A standard form prepared and issued by the Institution of Civil Engineers jointly with the Association of Consulting Engineers and the Federation of Civil Engineering Contractors—with the full title *General Conditions of Contract and Form of Tender, Agreement and Bond for use in connection with Civil Engineering Construction*. Differences between this contract and the RIBA Standard Forms are too numerous and too complicated to be dealt with satisfactorily in notes as brief as these must necessarily be; though many of them will be immediately evident. The contract is not intended—or indeed suitable—for essentially building work. It is issued in one version only to be used for public and private sectors alike. The Form of Tender and Agreement are equivalent to the RIBA Articles of Agreement and Appendix and follow a similar pattern, while the Bond—although optional within the contract—is a feature absent from the RIBA forms.

The use of the various contract documents deemed to form part of the Agreement in the ICE Form makes interesting comparison with those of the RIBA Forms and might tend to confuse those more familiar with the latter. In the ICE Form these documents are listed as: (a) The Tender, (b) Drawings, (c) General Conditions, (d) Specification, (e) Bills of Quantities and (f) The Schedule of Rates and Prices (if any). The importance of the Specification—which plays a relatively minor role in the RIBA Bills of Quantities contract—should

be specially noted, also the different role of the Bills of Quantities themselves. The ICE Form of Contract cannot be strictly termed a Bills of Quantities Contract because the quantities are assumed as being approximate (estimated) only. The engineering practice is for the 'actual and correct quantities' to be remeasured by the engineer—Classes 55 and 56. In this and in other ways there are marked differences which closely concern the authority of the architect and the engineer in regards to their respective duties and responsibilities in the control of the contracts. (See also LEGAL STUDY 8 on settlement of disputes, para 5.06.)

A revised edition of the ICE Form—the 5th—was issued in June 1973. The changes then made were relatively moderate, and confined in the main to redrafting to improve the general clarity of the document, while bringing it up to date to meet changes found necessary since the last edition was published in 1955. A Form of Sub-Contract, designed for use in conjunction with the ICE General Conditions of Contract (as amended 30th March 1973 to conform with the Fifth Edition of the ICE Conditions) is available from the Federation of Civil Engineering Contractors.

4. S.4 GC/Wks/1 Form—for Government Contracts

This form, prepared by government departments for their own purposes, is primarily for use with Bills of Quantities and Schedules Contracts. The form in current use—GC/Wks/1, 1st Edition November 1973—is a much revised version of what was formerly known as CCC/Wks/1. A second shorter form (GC/Wks/2, Edition 1, dated April 1974) lays down similar General Conditions of Government Contracts for minor works. The document is in fact not a contract form but, as its full title implies . . . *General Conditions of Government Contracts for Building and Civil Engineering Works*. Clause 1 (1) defines that 'the Contract means the document forming the tender and acceptance thereof'. In short, all documents including the Conditions, Specification, Bills of Quantities and drawings are taken together as complementary to one another and deemed to form one contract. There are no formal articles of agreement as with the JCT and ICE Forms, but the Tender is submitted with a special form which with acceptance establishes the contract. Nor are there separate forms for use with or without quantities. The GC/Wks/1 Form is strictly for use by Government Departments (although the Ministry of Transport in fact uses the ICE Form) and is not suitable for adaptation to other uses, eg public bodies or the private sector of the industry. Local authorities will, of course, normally use the appropriate variant of the RIBA Standard Forms. (See also LEGAL STUDY 8 para 5.07.)

4. S.5 Agreements for Minor Building Works (JCT)

The Joint Contracts Tribunal has sanctioned the following alternative agreements and conditions for use with minor building and maintenance work:

1 A Form of Agreement (yellow in colour) for use where a specification or specification and drawings have been prepared; when the work is to be carried out for an agreed lump sum and where an Architect or Supervising Officer has been appointed on behalf of the Employer. The form is not appropriate for works for which bills of quantities have been prepared or for which a schedule of rates is required for valuing variations; it is also unsuitable for prime cost work, and is specifically endorsed 'not for use in Scotland'. It is really a 'better than nothing contract', the use of which will normally be restricted to minor works, eg house extensions or a very small building capable of illustration and description on drawings and/or specification where the preparation of quantities could not have been expected, yet in which certain

necessary and reasonable safeguards as to general standards of control, insurances, dates for completion etc, are desirable.

2 An alternative version (white)—published in December 1974, revised 1975—for use where similar conditions as to the lump sum figure and supervision prevail, but where a grant or grants under Part VII of the Housing Act 1974 will be made. This version includes Forms of Authority for Payment of Renovation Grant, and notes (which do not form part of the Agreement) on VAT, clause 14.

3 An Agreement (pink) similar to 2 above—but for use where no architect or supervising officer has been appointed on behalf of the employer. This variant was first issued in December 1970, revised in 1975 and issued under the sanction of the Joint Contracts Tribunal.

4. S.6 *FAS Short Form of Contract*

The Faculty of Architects and Surveyors publishes a short form of contract similar to the JCT Minor Works contract and in editions for private and local authority use, intended for small jobs, alterations and additions and other works for which no quantities are taken off. This form comprises Articles of Agreement and a Schedule of Conditions and covering in almost irreducible brevity the usual provisions to be found in the larger standard forms yet sufficiently flexible for additions and variation to meet any special needs or wishes of the contracting parties. It requires only the incorporation of a specification, and possibly drawings if deemed necessary.

4. S.7 *Standard Form of Nominated Sub-contract*

(NFBTE/FASS Sub-contract), (The 'Green Form')
Issued with the approval of the National Federation of Building Trades Employers, the Federation of Associations of Specialists and Sub-Contractors, and the Committee of Associations of Specialist Engineering Contractors, this form, as its full title indicates, is for use when the Sub-Contractor is nominated under the JCT form of main contract. This form has accordingly been drafted with the Standard Form of Tender for a Nominated Sub-Contractor, and other documents relevant to the employment of sub-contractors, in mind. It should therefore be studied closely in relation to those documents. The current issue (1963) was revised in July 1975. A similar form (Blue) is issued for use where the sub-contractor is *not* nominated by the architect.

4. S.8 *Placing of Contracts*

Since the decision of the Government in 1957 to accept the recommendation of the Banwell Committee and to revert to the practice of firm price tendering, and to advise local authorities and nationalised industries to act similarly, the practice has had the general approval of the whole of the construction industry, which has agreed to follow the National Joint Consultative Council's Code of Procedure (current edition 1972). As a consequence the use of open competition as a means of placing building contracts is on a decline. On the other hand there has been a marked increase in the method of awarding contracts as an outcome of negotiation with a limited number—often only one contractor, who is invited to negotiate a tender figure for the work. 'Design and Construct' contracts are also in wide use, though not wholly approved by the clients' professional advisers for reasons partly their own and partly because they believe (often quite erroneously) that the method may not in the long run be in the building employer's interest, particularly in matters related to design and cost control of the project. Its advantages lie where the experience of the contractor, working on highly specialised types of construction and building techniques, can be brought into the project at its inception.

4. S.9 *Tendering Procedures*

Types of contract It is convenient to consider the various kinds of contract available for building and civil engineering works from the basis of what is offered by the contractor for carrying out the works required, and the manner in which he receives his remuneration. On this basis there are three main types:

1 *Fixed price* The price, not necessarily a firm one, is agreed before the job starts.

(a) *Lump sum* In its simplest form this is a contract where the fixed price is a lump sum and where no quantities have been prepared. The builder is responsible for carrying out all the work shown on drawings and described in a specification for the fixed price—a sum determined by him on whatever basis he thinks fit. This is the usual form for a small job carried out by the local builder without help of an architect. It may or may not be a firm price contract, ie one which does not allow for adjustments in prices of materials and labour.

(b) *Bills of quantities* This is based on fully detailed bills to every item of which the builder has affixed his price. The aggregate of the quantities so priced, which would include allowances for his overheads and profits, constitutes the contract sum. The individual items provide a schedule for the valuation of any variation which might occur during the progress of the works.

2 *Reimbursement* This is usually applied when the extent of the works to be undertaken is not fully known before the contract is let and the final total price cannot be estimated accurately; therefore re-measurement must be made at a later date. This type includes:

(a) *Schedule* The sum fixed is the aggregate value of items of the work the builder has actually executed, determined by rates given in a 'Schedule of Rates'. It will be seen that this type has similarities in practice to that described above where the priced items in a bill of quantities may be used to determine rates for re-measurement purposes.

(b) *Approximate quantities* The JCT Standard Form, issued in October 1975, was designed for this purpose. The work is carried out by the contractor in the normal way and under 'conditions' similar to those of the other standard forms; it is then measured and priced at rates established in the bill. The form is used when the client has been unable to determine all his requirements in advance, or for similar reasons. It is said to have the advantages of providing a competitive basis at the time of submission of the tender and gives a fair indication of the ultimate cost at the time of letting the contract.

3 *Cost-reimbursement* The title 'cost reimbursement contract' embraces all those under which the contractors are employed to carry out the work on the basis that the cost, whatever it may be, is paid by the employer, and the contractor is remunerated for his services by the payment of a fee. The different methods of fixing the fee to be paid are fundamental matters which go to the root of this type of contract and fall into three categories.

(a) *Costs plus percentage on cost* The Simon Report criticised this, commonly known as 'cost plus contract', as being a most unsatisfactory form of contract on the grounds that the more profligate the contractor was in the employment of labour and the purchases of materials, the more profit he would earn. It argued that there was no financial incentive to organise the work efficiently, purchase the materials economically or direct labour with skill but, on the contrary, there was gain to the contractor if these steps were *not* taken.

(b) *Cost plus fixed fee* In this type the contractor is reimbursed his whole cost of carrying out the work but his own profit remuneration will be a fee which does not vary unless additional work is done beyond that contemplated when the contract is entered into. The fee may be fixed arbitrarily as a

lump sum but usually, and preferably, bears some relationship to an estimate of the cost of the works.

(c) *Cost, plus fluctuating fee based on estimate* This form
varies from the cost plus fixed fee contract in that the fee
fluctuates according to the relationship between the estimate
and the actual cost of the work. The contractor should receive
a proportion of the saving of cost below estimate or contribute
to part of the excess cost over estimate, and the normal fee
should be increased or decreased by a percentage according to
whether there is or is not a saving on the estimate. The
Simon Report considered this as the best type of cost-
reimbursement contract, in that it offered incentive for strict
economy and proper supervision of labour and purchase of
materials and that in order to earn the maximum profit the
contractor should be as alert and anxious to run the job
successfully as under any other form of contract.

4. S.10 *Reports and References*
The comments in this supplement are of necessity condensed.
They derive much from the very important Reports (Simon,
Banwell, McEwen Younger, and Wood) quoted in the
Reference list below and which are worth consulting at first
hand. (All are obtainable from HMSO.) Each of these Reports
served as a starting point for its successor and many of the
recommendations made have been implemented in whole or
part over the years. There is still, however, little sign of the
establishment of a satisfactory contract for general use both
for building and engineering projects, as recommended in
the Banwell Committee's Report in 1964. Nevertheless it
may be reasonable to suppose that this was partly the intention of the Department of the Environment's consultative

document circulated in 1972, entitled *Proposals for a building
bill;* and to hope that future regulations, perhaps under
powers given by the Health and Safety at Work Act 1974,
may one day help to bring this about.

References

Tendering procedures and contractual arrangements. Survey
by McCanlis, E. W. Research & Information Group.
London, 1967, RICS
Management of building contracts. London, 1970, NJCC
Code of Practice for Selective Tendering 1972. London,
1973, NJCC
RIBA Handbook of architectural practice and management.
Revised single volume Edition, 1973
Which builder? Tendering and contractual arrangements.
London, 1975, Aqua Group, Granada Publishing

Reports
Simon Report 1944. The placing and management of building
contracts
Banwell 1964. The placing and management of contracts for
building and civil engineering works
McEwen Younger 1964. Organisation and practices for
building and civil engineering (refers to procedure in
Scotland)
Wood 1975. The public client and the construction industries.
EDC Committee for Building 1967. Action on the Banwell
report
EDC Committee for Civil Engineering 1968. Contracting in
civil engineering after Banwell

Legal study 5

Scottish contracts

This study outlines the use of common forms of Scottish building contract and describes the nature and use of the Scottish Supplement to the JCT Form. In a final section, problems of interpreting certain clauses of the JCT Form in Scotland are discussed.
This study should be read in conjunction with LEGAL STUDY 4

1 Regulations and General Conditions of Contract 1954

1.01 In the last ten years since the Standard Form of Building Contract published by the Joint Contracts Tribunal was introduced into Scotland a diminishing amount of work has been carried on under the traditional Scottish Regulations and General Conditions of Contract published in 1954 which until 1966 were the standard conditions used in Scotland for building contracts. Until local government re-organisation in 1975 a fair number of Scottish local authorities still used these 'Scottish conditions' but the new regional and district authorities are now all using the Standard Form and only a small number of mainly private contracts chiefly in the rural areas of Scotland are carried out under the Scottish conditions. It is not the purpose of this article to discuss these conditions in detail, but it should be noted that they differ in a number of important respects from the Standard Form: first they are written primarily for separate trades contracts; secondly they have in mind that the Scottish Mode of Measurement will be employed; thirdly unlike the Standard Form where there is in effect a partnership between the contractor and the architect the Scottish conditions envisage a situation where the architect is very much in command and the contractor is obliged to do what the architect requires of him without reference to the actual conditions themselves. Further it is not necessary for the architect's instructions to be given in writing. The contractor is entirely responsible for setting out the work and is required to amend at his own cost any errors arising from inaccurate setting out. Retention money deducted by the employer remains his property until paid over to the contractor.

1.02 The Scottish conditions are unsatisfactory today because they were intended for use with building methods and customs which have now largely been superseded, and because they leave undefined a number of important matters which are covered by the Standard Form; furthermore since their publication in 1954 they have not been brought up to date in any way and latterly were always accompanied by a large number of amendments and additional clauses inserted by the employer. They are now out of print and unobtainable and no longer as was suggested in the 1st Edition of this Handbook is it thought that they would represent 'a custom of the trade' in Scotland where the Standard Form to all intents and purposes has been widely adopted.

2 Use of the JCT standard form in Scotland

2.01 In 1964, following the publication of the Banwell and McEwen Younger reports on the building industry, the Ministry of Public Building and Works in Scotland invited the Royal Incorporation of Architects in Scotland to form a

committee charged with introducing the JCT conditions of contract to Scotland, so fulfilling recommendations of both reports that it would be in the interests of the industry if the same conditions of contract obtained on both sides of the border. The RIAS accepted this invitation and a committee was formed with similar representation to that of the Joint Contracts Tribunal; the committee quickly decided to limit alterations to the JCT conditions to changes required because of differences in Scots law or building practice.

Scottish supplement
2.02 These changes are contained in a document entitled *Building contract and Scottish supplement to the* JCT *conditions of contract*. This is the document to use in Scotland to create a contract between employers and contractors: it corresponds to the articles of agreement used in England. The JCT form itself is not used to make the contract and it is not necessary to purchase a copy for each contract. One important change from previous practice is obvious: the parties are required to sign a formal contract, whereas in the past virtually all building contracts in Scotland had been let simply by an exchange of letters between the contractor and the architect acting as agent for the employer. Although there was available if required a formal contract designed for use with the Regulations and General Conditions of Contract, this had long since fallen into disuse.

2.03 It is still perfectly possible in Scotland to enter into a contract by an exchange of letters, though it is strongly recommended, particularly in contracts of any size, that parties should sign the formal Scottish contract. The additional time and trouble which this takes is probably well worthwhile. Nowadays a large building project involves major financial expenditure for the client and he must take a number of important decisions. He must realise as quickly as possible that a change of mind during the progress of the building is inevitably going to be expensive. The sooner he realises the importance of the obligations he is taking on the better, and possibly the easiest way of bringing these home to him is to ask him to sign a formal contract.

2.04 The JCT conditions of contract contain a number of alternative clauses and they have attached an appendix which must be completed at the time of signing the contract: this fixes for example the rate of liquidated damages, the dates of and intervals between certificates and the completion date. All these and other non-standard information could be included in an exchange of letters, but the letter would have to be very carefully drawn and it is easier to sign a printed contract and at the same time be assured that all essential information has been included. Many local authorities in Scotland still continue to let their building contracts by an exchange of letters presumably because they have always done so and habits die slowly, but curiously enough they all refer to the Scottish supplement and usually its provisions are spelt out in the preliminary sections of the bills of quantity. Granted that the formality of a building contract may frighten some smaller contractors and recognising that there may be difficulties in getting the signatures of councillors to formal documents (which could surely be overcome) it does seem that some local authorities are needlessly complicating matters, and for reasons which are made clear in para 3 it could well be to a contractor's advantage to insist on the execution of a formal building contract especially when private contracts are being arranged.

Scots law and arbitration

2.05 Possibly the most important reason for signing a formal contract is to ensure, where work is being carried out in Scotland, that Scots law applies to any arbitration and is the proper law of the contract. The July 1977 revision of the Standard Form (as the RIBA conditions are now commonly known) contains a clause ensuring that English law applies not only to arbitrations, but also becomes the proper law of the contract. Because of the terms of clause 12 of the JCT conditions (see LEGAL STUDY 4 para 16), this would automatically have precedence over any statement in the contract bills that Scots law applies and it is not therefore enough to include a reference to Scots law as the proper law of the contract in the contract bills. Such a statement must be contained in the document creating the contract between the employer and the contractor and the appropriate clause is found in the formal Scottish building contract.

2.06 Even though an exchange of letters is legally all that is required to create the contract, by the time all the above points have been covered in a letter it will be as long as, if not longer than, the formal printed contract.

3 The building contract

3.01 While the building contract itself is quite straightforward, one or two minor clauses should be commented upon. References in this LEGAL STUDY are to the JCT Standard Forms of Building Contract, and to the Scottish Supplement issued by the Scottish Building Contracts Committee—in both cases to the July 1977 Revisions.

3.02 Clause (Second) of the building contract refers in section (c) to Appendix No. III in which are set out the provisions for payment of VAT. This is similar to the supplemental agreement at the end of the English form with only minor differences in wording which do not affect the rights and duties of the employer and contractor. Articles 3 and 4 of the articles of agreement used in England are combined in Clause (Third) of the building contract, which deals with the appointment of a new architect/supervising officer and quantity surveyor should this be necessary.

3.03 The other clause is the one at the end 'And both parties consent to registration hereof for preservation and execution. . . .' This gives the parties to the contract a useful additional course of action outside any course open to them in terms of the contract conditions. Furthermore it is a course open only to parties contracting under Scots law.

3.04 The clause provides that once the building contract has been registered in the Books of Council and Session (which is an official register located in Register House, Waterloo Place, Edinburgh) and an extract obtained, the extract can be handed to a Sheriff Officer or Messenger-at-Arms and used as an equivalent to a court decree on which diligence (ie proceedings for recovery of money) for the sum due to the contractor or to the employer as the case may be, can proceed.

BUILDING CONTRACT

BETWEEN

(hereinafter referred to as "the Employer")

AND

(hereinafter referred to as "the Contractor")

WHEREAS the Employer is desirous of

(hereinafter referred to as "the Works") and the Contractor has offered to carry out and complete the Works for the sum of £

(hereinafter and in the Appendices hereto referred to as "the Contract Sum") which offer has been or is hereby accepted by the Employer THEREFORE the Employer and the Contractor have agreed and hereby agree as follows: — (First) The Contractor shall carry out the Works in accordance with the Drawings numbered

one of these to be deleted according to the type of Contract.

and the [*] Bills of Quantities/Specification annexed and signed as relative hereto, (Second) the Works shall be completed in accordance with, and the rights and duties of the Employer and the Contractor shall be regulated by (A) the Schedule of Conditions of The Standard Form of Building Contract [*] Local Authorities/Private Edition [*] with/without Quantities (1963 Edition) (July 1977 Revision) issued by The Joint Contracts Tribunal which is held to be incorporated in and forms part of this Contract, as amended and modified by the provisions contained in the Scottish Supplement forming Appendix No. I hereto, (B) the Abstract of the said Schedule of Conditions forming Appendix No. II hereto, and (C) the provisions for payment of VAT forming Appendix No. III hereto, (Third) the term [*] "the Architect"/"Supervising Officer" used in the said Schedule of Conditions shall mean

delete as required.

and the term "the Quantity Surveyor" shall mean

and in the event of the said Architect/Supervising Officer or Quantity Surveyor ceasing to be employed for the purpose of the Contract the Employer shall nominate another person or persons to the vacant appointment (provided that the Architect/Supervising Officer* or the Quantity Surveyor* shall not be a person or persons to whom the Contractor shall object for reasons considered to be sufficient by an Arbiter appointed in accordance with Clause 35 of the said Schedule of Conditions (as amended hereafter)): provided further that no person or persons subsequently appointed to be the Architect/Supervising Officer under this Contract shall be entitled to disregard or over-rule any certificate or opinion or decision or approval or instruction given or expressed by the Architect/Supervising Officer as the case may be for the time being, and (Fourth) this Contract shall be regarded as a Scottish Contract and shall be construed and the rights of parties and all matters arising hereunder determined in all respects according to the Law of Scotland: And both parties consent to registration hereof for preservation and execution: IN WITNESS WHEREOF these presents are executed at

delete if Employee of a Local Authority.

on the
day of   19   before these witnesses subscribing.

....................witness
....................address
....................occupation
....................witness
....................address
....................occupation   ....Employer
....................witness
....................address
....................occupation
....................witness
....................address
....................occupation   ....Contractor
....................witness
....................address
....................occupation

N.B. This document is set out as for execution by individuals or firms: Where Limited Companies or Local Authorities are involved amendment will be necessary and the appropriate officials should be consulted.

Both parties sign here and on pages 7, 8 and 11 as indicated.

SCOTTISH BUILDING CONTRACT COMMITTEE

Memorandum issued by the Committee

(on which are represented the Royal Incorporation of Architects in Scotland, the Scottish Branch of the Royal Institution of Chartered Surveyors, the Scottish National Federation of Building Trades' Employers, the Convention of Scottish Local Authorities, the Federation of Specialists and Sub Contractors (Scottish Board) the Committee of Associations of Specialist Engineering Contractors (Scottish Branch) and the Association of Consulting Engineers (Scottish Group)).

ON THE

Building Contract and Scottish Supplement July 1977 to the Standard Form of Building Contract issued by the Joint Contracts Tribunal (July 1977 Revision)

I.—BUILDING CONTRACT.

In Scotland it is not essential to sign a formal document to conclude a binding contract and in the past many building contracts have been let on an informal exchange of letters. None the less the Committee feel it is highly desirable that all contracts in future should be concluded by the parties thereto signing the Building Contract, which is the appropriate Scottish legal document substituted for the English form of Articles of Agreement.

The Committee wish to emphasise that if a Contract is let by an exchange of letters in which the terms of the Standard Form of Building Contract only (i.e. without mentioning the Scottish Supplement) are incorporated by reference, the parties will almost certainly find that English Law is the appropriate Law of the Contract. The simple and sure way of ensuring that Scots Law will apply, is to sign the Building Contract. The Committee also wish to remind parties to a Contract of the importance of completing the Abstract of Schedule of Conditions (Appendix II) prior to the signing of the Building Contract.

NOTES.

1. Insert the name and address of the Employer and the Contractor in the heading.
2. A short description of the Works should be inserted in lines 1/3.
3. Insert the Contract Sum in line 5, in words and figures.
4. The Architect's and the Quantity Surveyor's name should be inserted in Clause (Third).

Attention is drawn to the fact that where the work is carried out under the control of a Local Authority official who is not a registered architect and therefore not entitled to the definition "Architect" the expression "Supervising Officer" is to be substituted therefor, as provided in the Local Authority Editions.

5. The parties to a Contract are advised to take legal advice on the method of signing the Contract and completion of the attestation clause but if this is impossible the following points should be observed.

    (a) It is not necessary to sign each page of the Building Contract and Scottish Supplement. Both parties need now sign only at the foot of pages 2, 7, 8 and 11, before two witnesses, who sign only on page 2, to the left of the signatory's signature, adding the word "Witness" after their signatures and their addresses and occupations under their signatures.

    (b) A limited company should execute the Contract in accordance with its Articles with the addition of its company seal.

6. The Building Contract is not liable to stamp duty unless the clause "And both parties consent to registration hereof for preservation and execution" is retained, when the stamp duty is 50p. The parties should take legal advice on whether or not the clause should be retained.

II.—SCOTTISH SUPPLEMENT.

a) APPENDIX I.

    (i) V, XII. Two of the three alternatives must be deleted.

    (ii) I, II, VI, IX, X, XII. Delete as required.

    (iii) XV. This section should be deleted if the Contract is not being let on a separate trades basis.

b) APPENDIX II.

This Appendix *must* be completed prior to the signing of the Building Contract, and signed by the Employer and the Contractor.

c) APPENDIX III.

No amendments are required to this Appendix but it must be signed by the Employer and the Contractor.

The necessary procedure can be summarised briefly as follows:

1 As soon as both parties have signed the building contract it should be sent to the Inland Revenue Office in Edinburgh and stamped with an official 50p stamp.

2 Thereafter, or later if more convenient, the contract should be registered in the Books of Council and Session and an extract obtained.

3.05 The building contract registered as described above is then ready to use but three requirements must be fulfilled:

1 The parties concerned must be clearly identifiable—in the case of the building contract there is no doubt on this score, as the parties concerned are the employer and the contractor.

2 The sum of money payable must be clearly identifiable—again in the case of the building contract where there is a sum of money due to a Contractor, the sum concerned would be the amount brought out, for example, in architect's certificates.

3 The date from which the sum is owed must be capable of being fixed—the date would be 14 days from the presentation (or issue) of an architect's certificate. While this facility is available to parties contracting under Scots law it is fair to say that the writer has no knowledge of its ever being put into effect in a building contract. The reasons for this are purely a matter for conjecture, but in these days of economic stringencies it is perhaps surprising that no contractor has seen fit to make use of it when an employer has delayed in paying a certificate.

3.06 Since the passing of the Conveyancing and Feudal Reform Act 1970 it is only necessary for the building contract and Scottish supplement to be signed at the end of the formal contract itself and at the end of each of the three appendices. Since the abolition of the stamp duty on agreements, building contracts are not liable to stamp duty at all, unless as mentioned above in para 3.03, the clause 'And both parties consent to registration hereof for preservation and execution' is retained when the stamp duty is 50p.

3.07 The process of executing a document 'under seal' (LEGAL STUDY 1 para 3.02 and LEGAL STUDY 4 para 4.02) is not known in Scotland, and therefore the reference to the period for which the parties remain liable referred to in LEGAL STUDY 4 para 4.02 does not apply to Scotland. The period within which an action must be raised in Scotland is now governed by the Prescriptions and Limitations (Scotland) Act 1973 and in general is five years from the date within which the pursuer found he had a cause of action with an overall period of twenty years still applying.

4 The Scottish supplement—Appendix 1

Section 1: Interpretation of terms

APPENDIX No. I   **SCOTTISH SUPPLEMENT**

(to be read in conjunction with the Schedule of Conditions of The Standard Form of Building Contract)

I.—INTERPRETATION OF TERMS.

The following words and expressions where occurring in the foregoing Building Contract and the said Schedule of Conditions shall have the meaning shown in the right hand column hereunder, unless the context otherwise requires.

1.	Articles of Agreement	The foregoing Building Contract.
2.	Arbitrator	Arbiter.
3.	Section 117 Local Government Act 1972	Section 68 Local Government (Scotland) Act 1973.
4.	Real or personal	Heritable or moveable.
5.	Contract Drawings	The drawings enumerated in the Contract and on which the Contract is based and from which the [*] Bills of Quantities/Specifications have been prepared.
6.	Execution of the Contract (Clause 3)	Formal adoption and signing of the Building Contract.
7.	Appendix to these Conditions	Appendix No. II of this Document.

* delete as required.

4.01 Section 1 contains definitions and interpretations of words occurring in the conditions of contract. These are all self-explanatory although it is probably worth mentioning the reason for the first, the Standard Method of Measurement. Until the introduction of the JCT conditions into Scotland, all contracts employed the Scottish mode of measurement issued with the approval and authority of the Joint Standing Committee of Architects, Surveyors and Building Contractors in Scotland. The JCT conditions stipulate that bills be drawn in accordance with the Standard Method of Measurement, which in 1964 was unknown to the industry in Scotland, and it was therefore felt necessary that not only should the use of the Standard Method of Measurement be authorised, but that the way should be left open for return to the Scottish mode if the standard method proved unsatisfactory.

Section II: Contract bills, Clause 12 (with quantities)

II.—CONTRACT BILLS. CLAUSE 12 (With Quantities).

* delete as required.

[*] The Standard Method of Measurement of Building Works 5th Edition Imperial, revised 1964 shall apply.

[*] The Standard Method of Measurement of Building Works 5th Edition Metric shall apply.

4.02 Section II allows users of the contract to opt for either the metric or imperial edition of the Standard Method of Measurement, as provided for in clause 12 of the JCT conditions.

Section III: Value Added Tax, clause 13A

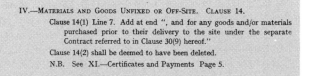

III.—VALUE ADDED TAX CLAUSE 13A.
Clause 13A (1) (a): Lines 1/2 Delete "the Supplemental Agreement pursuant hereto and annexed to these Conditions (hereinafter called the "VAT Agreement")" and substitute "Appendix No. III."
Line 4 Delete "the VAT Agreement" and substitute "Appendix No. III."
Clause 13A (1) (b) shall be deemed to have been deleted.
Clause 13A (2) Delete "the VAT Agreement" and substitute "Appendix No. III."

4.03 This section contains minor amendments to the supplemental agreement necessitated by the way in which the provisions for the payment of VAT are incorporated in the Scottish supplement but as mentioned above do not affect the rights and duties of either the employer or the contractor.

Section IV: Materials and goods unfixed or off-site, clause 14

IV.—MATERIALS AND GOODS UNFIXED OR OFF-SITE. CLAUSE 14.
Clause 14(1) Line 7. Add at end ", and for any goods and/or materials purchased prior to their delivery to the site under the separate Contract referred to in Clause 30(9) hereof."
Clause 14(2) shall be deemed to have been deleted.
N.B. See XI.—Certificates and Payments Page 5.

4.04 This clause makes two amendments to clause 14 of the Standard Form, by an addition to 14 (1) and clause 14 (2) being deemed to have been deleted. (See also Section XI, Certificates and payments and para 4.21 *et seq.*)

Section V: Insurance of works against fire, etc, clause 20

V.—INSURANCE OF WORKS AGAINST FIRE, ETC. CLAUSE 20.
* delete as required.   [*] Clause 20[A] shall apply
[*] Clause 20[B] shall apply
[*] Clause 20[C] shall apply
N.B.—Clause 20[A] is applicable to the erection of a **new building** if the **Contractor** is required to insure against loss or damage by fire, etc. Clause 20[B] is applicable to the erection of a **new building** if the **Employer** is to bear the risk in respect of loss or damage by fire, etc. Clause 20[C] is applicable to alterations or extensions to an **existing building**.

4.05 Section V allows users of the contract to opt for one or other of three insurance alternative clauses 20 (A), 20 B, or 20 C, of the JCT conditions.

Section VI: Extension of time, clause 23

VI.—EXTENSION OF TIME. CLAUSE 23.
* delete as required.   [*] Clause 23(j)(i) shall/shall not apply.
[*] Clause 23(j)(ii) shall/shall not apply.

4.06 Clause 23 (j) is divided into two sub-clauses in the July 1976 revision of the Standard Form and this section of the contract allows users of the contract to opt for one or other of the alternatives available.

Section VII: Determination by employer, clause 25

VII.—DETERMINATION BY EMPLOYER. CLAUSE 25.
Clause 25(2) shall be deemed to have been deleted and the following substituted therefor:—
Clause 25(2)(a) In the event of a provisional liquidator being appointed to control the affairs of the Contractor the Employer may terminate the employment of the Contractor under this Contract by giving him seven days written notice (sent by registered post or recorded delivery) of such termination.
(b) In the event of the Contractor becoming bankrupt or making a composition or arrangement with his creditors or having his estate sequestrated or being rendered notour bankrupt or entering into a trust deed for his creditors or having a winding up order made

or (except for the purposes of reconstruction) a resolution for voluntary winding up passed or a receiver or manager of his business or undertaking duly appointed, or possession taken, by or on behalf of the holders of any debenture secured by a floating charge, the employment of the Contractor under this Contract shall be forthwith automatically determined.
(c) In the event of the employment of the Contractor being determined under sub-clause (a) or (b) hereof, it may be reinstated and continued if the Employer and the Contractor, his trustee in bankruptcy, provisional liquidator, liquidator, receiver or manager as the case may be shall so agree.
Clause 25(3) (c) Private Editions/25(4) (c) Local Authority Editions.
Delete "and sell any such property of the Contractor" and substitute "and sell any such property so far as belonging to the Contractor."

4.07 Clause 25 (2) of the Standard Form contains a provision that the appointment of a provisional liquidator to manage the affairs of the contractor gives the employer grounds to determine his employment automatically. Although in England the appointment of a provisional liquidator is understood to be relatively rare, in Scotland the majority of company liquidations start off with the appointment by the court of such an official, who may well after his investigation find the company to be solvent with the result that he petitions for his discharge. It was therefore felt sensible to include the provision in the Scottish supplement which gives the employer the option to terminate the contractor's employment on the appointment of a provisional liquidator by giving him seven days written notice, instead of having automatic termination as in England, and this is contained in clause 25 (2) (a).

4.08 Section VII also contains an amendment to clause 25 (3) (c) or 25 (4) (c) (when Local Authority contracts are concerned) where, in order to meet the requirements of Scots law, there have been added the words '*so far as belonging to the Contractor*'. This also makes it clear that the employer is only entitled, in the event of the bankruptcy of the main contractor, to sell property (ie temporary plant, buildings, tools, equipment, goods and materials) which belong to the contractor.

Section VIII: Determination by contractor, clause 26

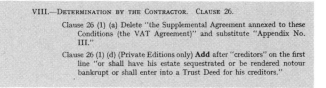

VIII.—DETERMINATION BY THE CONTRACTOR. CLAUSE 26.
Clause 26 (1) (a) Delete "the Supplemental Agreement annexed to these Conditions (the VAT Agreement)" and substitute "Appendix No. III."
Clause 26 (1) (d) (Private Editions only) **Add** after "creditors" on the first line "or shall have his estate sequestrated or be rendered notour bankrupt or shall enter into a Trust Deed for his creditors."

4.09 Section VIII makes a minor amendment to clause 26 (1) (a) which is self-explanatory and also amends clause 26 (1) (d) (private editions only) adding the words '*or shall have his estate sequestrated or be rendered notour bankrupt or shall enter into a Trust Deed for his creditors*'; this is to bring into the clause the traditional phraseology used in Scottish bankruptcies.

Section IX: Nominated sub-contractors, clause 27

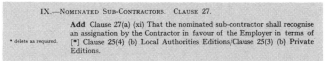

IX.—NOMINATED SUB-CONTRACTORS. CLAUSE 27.
Add Clause 27(a) (xi) That the nominated sub-contractor shall recognise an assignation by the Contractor in favour of the Employer in terms of
* delete as required.   [*] Clause 25(4) (b) Local Authorities Editions/Clause 25(3) (b) Private Editions.

4.10 Section IX adds an additional clause xi to clause 27 (a), requiring a nominated sub-contractor to recognise an assignation by the contractor in favour of the employer under clause 25 (4) (b) (or clause 25 (3) (b) where the private edition is being used). This clause has been added to clarify the situation and to conform with the requirements of Scots law.

Section X: Nominated suppliers, clause 28

X.—NOMINATED SUPPLIERS. CLAUSE 28.

* delete as required **Add** Clause 28(b) (vi) That the nominated supplier shall recognise an assignation by the Contractor in favour of the Employer in terms of [*]Clause 25(4) (b) Local Authorities Editions/Clause 25(3) (b) Private Editions.

4.11 Section X adds an additional clause vi to clause 28 (b), requiring a nominated supplier to recognise an assignation by the contractor in favour of the employer under clause 25 (4) (b) or clause 25 (3) (b) where the private edition is being used. This clause has been added to clarify the situation and to conform with the requirements of Scots law.

Section XI: Certificates and payments, clause 30

XI. CERTIFICATES AND PAYMENTS CLAUSE 30.

Clause 30 (2A) shall be deemed to have been deleted.

Add Clause 30(7)(a)(iii) Nothing in the immediately preceding sub-clause shall prevent the Employer from deducting or adding liquidate and ascertained damages in accordance with Clause 22 hereof from any sum due by him to the Contractor or by the Contractor to the Employer as the case may be under the Final Certificate.

Add Clause 30(9) If the Architect/Supervising Officer is of the opinion that it is expedient to do so the Employer may enter into a separate contract for the purchase from the Contractor or any Sub-Contractor of any goods and/or materials prior to their delivery to the site which the Contractor is under obligation to supply in terms of this Contract, and upon such contract being entered into the purchase of the said goods and/or materials shall be excluded altogether from this Contract and the Contract Sum shall be adjusted accordingly: provided that when the Employer enters into a separate contract with any Sub-Contractor (1) he shall do so only with the consent of the Contractor, which consent shall not be unreasonably withheld, and (2) payment by the Employer to the Sub-Contractor for any of the said goods and/or materials shall in no way affect any cash discount or other emolument to which the Contractor may be entitled and which shall be paid by the Employer to the Contractor.

4.12 In the Scottish supplement, clause 30 (2A) shall be deemed to have been deleted. Additional clauses added are clauses 30 (7) (a) (iii) and clause 30 (9). See also para 4.22.

Section XII: Statutory tax deduction scheme, clause 30B

XII.—STATUTORY TAX DEDUCTION SCHEME. CLAUSE 30B.

Clause 30B(2)(a)

* Delete as required. [*] At the date of tender the Employer was "a contractor" for the purposes of the Act.
[*] At the date of tender the Employer was not "a contractor" for the purposes of the Act.

4.13 This is a new section made necessary to meet the provisions of the Finance (No 2) Act 1975 and Regulations issued thereunder (Income Tax (Sub-Contractors in the Construction Industry) Regulations 1975, S.I. 1960).

Section XIII: Fluctuations, clause 31

XIII.—FLUCTUATIONS. CLAUSE 31.

* delete as required. [*] Clause 31A, C, D & E shall apply.
[*] Clause 31B, C, D & E shall apply.
[*] Clause 31F shall apply subject to the following amendments:

Sub-Clause (1) (a) (ii) Delete "the VAT agreement executed pursuant to Sub-Clause (1) (b) of Clause 13A of these Conditions." and substitute "the provisions of Appendix No. III."

Sub-Clause (7) (a) (i) Delete "in the Appendix to these conditions" and substitute "in Appendix No. II".

N.B.—Clause 31F should be used where the parties have agreed to use the NEDO Price Adjustment Formulae for Building Contracts in which case Parts A, B, C, D & E should be deleted. When the formulae are not being used, Parts A, C, D & E should be used when the parties have agreed to allow full fluctuations and Parts B, C, D & E in all other cases: in either case Clause 31F should be deleted.

4.14 This section provides for selection of either of the traditional methods of calculating fluctuations (including the percentage addition now allowed under clause 31 (E)) or alternatively for the formula method introduced under clause 31 (F) in 1974. It should be noted that one or other of the three alternatives must be adopted and on no account should the whole of clause 31 be deleted in its entirety.

Section XIV: Arbitration, clause 35

XIV.—ARBITRATION. CLAUSE 35.

Clause 35(1) Delete "the President or a Vice-President for the time being of the Royal Institute of British Architects" and substitute "the Sheriff of any Sheriffdom in which the Works or any part thereof are situated."

Clause 35(2) Delete "except on article 3 or article 4 of the Articles of Agreement" and substitute "except on clause (Third) of the foregoing Building Contract."

Clause 35(4) shall be deemed to have been deleted and the following substituted therefor:—

Clause 35(4) The Arbiter shall have power to award compensation or damages and expenses to or against any of the parties to the arbitration.

Clause 35(5) shall be deemed to have been deleted and the following substituted therefor:—

Clause 35(5) The law of Scotland shall apply to all arbitrations under these presents and the award of the Arbiter shall be final and binding on the parties, subject always to the provisions of Clause 3 of the Administration of Justice (Scotland) Act 1972.

Add Clause 35(6) The Arbiter shall be entitled to remuneration and reimbursement of his outlays.

Add Clause 35(7) No action shall lie and no proceedings under this clause shall be instituted against the Employer unless such action is raised or such proceedings are instituted within five years after the date of the receipt by the Contractor of the priced Bills of Variation. Proceedings shall be deemed to be instituted when an application is made to the Employer for arbitration in terms of this clause.

4.15 Section XII makes several amendments to clause 35 of the RIBA conditions dealing with arbitration (see LEGAL STUDY 4 para 39 and LEGAL STUDY 8).

4.16 The first amendment deletes the reference to the president or the vice-president of the RIBA in clause 35 (1) and substitutes the sheriff of any Sheriffdom (LEGAL STUDY 2 para 3.03) '*in which the works or any part thereof are situated*'. It has long been the custom in Scotland in the event of the parties failing to agree on an arbiter, to refer the appointment to the sheriff and it was decided that this should continue.

4.17 Clause 35 (5) which has been added in the Scottish supplement contains an important amendment providing the parties to an arbitration in a building contract in Scotland with a right of appeal to the Court of Session or even to the House of Lords on a question of law only. With the possible exception of some arbitrations held under statute it has long been an established feature of Scottish arbitrations that there was no appeal against the arbiter's decision unless he had misconducted himself in some serious way so as to bring about an obvious miscarriage of justice. However, as parties to an arbitration in a building contract under English law had, by virtue of the English Arbitration Act, a right of appeal to the Court of Appeal, it was felt appropriate to provide a similar right in Scotland, but since this was first introduced in 1965, Scots law has been changed by virtue of the Administration of Justice (Scotland) Act 1972, which entitles parties by statute to appeal to the Court of Session on questions of law only. Section 3 of that Act is in the following terms:

(1) Subject to express provision to the contrary in an agreement to refer to arbitration, the arbiter or oversman may, on the application of a party to the arbitration, and shall, if the Court of Session on such an application so directs, at any stage in the arbitration state a case for the opinion of that Court on any question of law arising in the arbitration.

(2) This section shall not apply to an arbitration under any enactment which confers a power to appeal to or state a case for the opinion of a court or tribunal in relation to that arbitration.

(3) This section shall not apply to any form of arbitration relating to a trade dispute within the meaning of the Industrial Courts Act 1919 or relating to an industrial dispute within the meaning of the Industrial Relations Act 1971; to

any other arbitration arising from a collective agreement within the meaning of the said Act of 1971; or to proceedings before the Industrial Arbitration Board described in section 124 of that Act.

(4) This section shall not apply in relation to an agreement to refer to arbitration made before the commencement of this Act.'

Although the writer does not know of any arbitration in which one of the parties has appealed in terms of clause 35 (5), it is understood that in a recent big arbitration in Scotland an appeal has been intimated in terms of clause 3 of the above act and is thus making legal history.

4.18 Two other small amendments to the arbitration clause have been made because of peculiarities in Scots law. The first gives the arbiter power to award compensation or damages to or against any of the parties to an arbitration and the second specifically states that an arbiter will be entitled to be paid for his services; without this specific power, an arbiter in Scotland would not be entitled to charge a fee for his services (see LEGAL STUDY 8).

4.19 Clause 35 (7) added in the Scottish supplement imposes a time bar of three years from the date of receipt by the contractor of the priced bills of variation for raising an action against the employer by the contractor and this repeats a provision contained in the former 1954 Scottish Regulations and General Conditions of Contract. A recent decision in the Court of Session has thrown doubts on the validity of this clause which at the time of going to press is under active reconsideration.

Section XV: Contracts let on a separate trades basis

XV.—[*] CONTRACTS LET ON A SEPARATE TRADES BASIS.

* to be deleted where not applicable.

Clause 15(1) "Practical Completion of the Works" in this clause shall be deemed to refer to completion of the whole works subject to Clause 16 of the said Schedule of Conditions.

Clause 21(1) and (2) shall be deemed to have been deleted and the following substituted therefor:—

Clause 21(1) On the date for possession stated in Appendix II possession of the site shall be given to the contractors. The Contractor shall carry out his work at the times and in the manner necessary for the expeditious completion of the Works and as set forth in the contract documents.

Clause 21(2) (a) The Contractor shall be bound to co-operate for the due completion of the whole works with contractors and others directly engaged by the Employer who may be employed on the work for the due completion of the Works. Any differences of opinion regarding such co-operation or the spaces on the site to be allocated to the various contractors for their plant, tools or materials shall be determined by the [*] Architect/Supervising Officer.

* delete as required.

Clause 21(2) (b) If the Contractor shall make default in the due performance of the preceding sub-section the [*] Architect/Supervising Officer may give written notice to the Contractor as provided for under Clause 2(1) of the said Schedule of Conditions and the Employer may take such action as is provided for therein.

Clause 21(2) (c) The defaulting contractor shall relieve the Employer of any claim made by another contractor, or others directly engaged by the Employer under Clause 24(1) (d) of the said Schedule of Conditions.

Clauses 22 and 23. These clauses shall be deemed to apply to each individual contractor so far as relating to the section of the Works for which he is responsible.

Clauses 23(h) and 24(1) (d) Delete "artists, tradesmen or others" and substitute "another contractor, artist or others."

Add Clause 30(5) (d) If the [*] Architect/Supervising Officer desires to secure final payment to a contractor before the final certificate is due, the [*] Architect/Supervising Officer may authorise such payment in the form of an interim certificate.

....................................Employer   ....Contractor

4.20 The final section of the Scottish supplement contains amendments necessary to the Standard Form if it is to be used in a separate trades contract. It should be emphasised however that as the Standard Form was framed with an all-trades contract in mind it is not basically suitable for separate trades contracts, which until comparatively recent times was the traditional way of letting building contracts in Scotland. A decreasing amount of work is being carried out under separate trades contracts in each year, but in certain rural parts of the country, contracts are still let in this way largely because none of the local contractors are geared to take on the responsibilities of a main contractor.

4.21 The amendments contained in section XIV provide for co-operation between contractors and settling of disputes between them by the architect and stipulate that if a particular contractor defaults in performance of his work, then the employer may evoke the terms of clause 2 (1) (LEGAL STUDY 4 para 5.05) and after due notice, employ others to do the work at the defaulting contractor's expense.

Sections IV and XI: Payment for off-site goods, clauses 14 and 30*

IV.—MATERIALS AND GOODS UNFIXED OR OFF-SITE. CLAUSE 14.

Clause 14(1) Line 7. Add at end ", and for any goods and/or materials purchased prior to their delivery to the site under the separate Contract referred to in Clause 30(9) hereof."

Clause 14(2) shall be deemed to have been deleted.

N.B. See XI.—Certificates and Payments Page 5.

XI.—CERTIFICATES AND PAYMENTS. CLAUSE 30.

Clause 30 (2A) shall be deemed to have been deleted.

Add Clause 30(7)(a)(iii) Nothing in the immediately preceding sub-clause shall prevent the Employer from deducting or adding liquidate and ascertained damages in accordance with Clause 22 hereof from any sum due by him to the Contractor or by the Contractor to the Employer as the case may be under the Final Certificate.

Add Clause 30(9) If the Architect/Supervising Officer is of the opinion that it is expedient to do so the Employer may enter into a separate contract for the purchase from the Contractor or any Sub-Contractor of any goods and/or materials prior to their delivery to the site which the Contractor is under obligation to supply in terms of this Contract, and upon such contract being entered into the purchase of the said goods and/or materials shall be excluded altogether from this Contract and the Contract Sum shall be adjusted accordingly: provided that when the Employer enters into a separate contract with any Sub-Contractor (1) he shall do so only with the consent of the Contractor, which consent shall not be unreasonably withheld, and (2) payment by the Employer to the Sub-Contractor for any of the said goods and/or materials shall in no way affect any cash discount or other emolument to which the Contractor may be entitled and which shall be paid by the Employer to the Contractor.

4.22 These sections are discussed again here because they both deal with the same subject, payment for off-site goods and materials, provided for by clauses 14 (2) and 30 (2A) of the standard form. Under English law it is understood that provided the stringent provisions of clause 30 (2A) are followed the right of property in off-site goods and materials is satisfactorily transferred from the main contractor to the employer. This is not the position under Scots law because except in a contract of sale or purchase (which a building contract is not) the right of property in an article does not necessarily pass from A to B simply because A had paid B for it.

4.23 The problem was solved in Scotland by taking the specific off-site goods and materials out of the building contract and transferring them into a contract of sale. Two special documents are available in Scotland to effect this, namely a contract of sale between an employer and a main contractor and a second one between a main contractor and a sub-contractor. These two contracts are the means by which transactions dealing with off-site goods and materials are taken out of the building contract with the consequent result that the contract sum in the building contract is reduced by the amount paid for them and the architect issues a variation order to this effect.

* See also paras **4.04** and **4.10**

4.24 There are a number of important points to notice in connection with both contracts of sale:

1 The conditions listed in the instructions attached to the contract must be carefully complied with, particularly those regarding the contract between the main contractor and the sub-contractor or supplier. These instructions are in fact identical to what is contained in clause 30 (2A) of the standard form.

2 The architect must, as has been said above, reduce the contract sum by means of a variation order, the reduction being equivalent to the total cost of the materials and goods being purchased. The purchase price is paid for in two instalments, 95% normally at the time of the purchase and 5% normally at the end of the defects liability period, and it is essential that a receipt for the price is obtained from the contractor or the sub-contractor as the case may be.

3 The goods and materials concerned must be fully described in the contract.

4 A separate contract is required for each purchase separated by a period of time, although several items can be included in each contract.

4.25 The risk an employer runs in paying a contractor or sub-contractor for goods and materials before they have been delivered to the site arises in the event of the bankruptcy of either the contractor or the sub-contractor. If for example a main contractor went bankrupt unless the right of property had been successfully transferred to the employer the liquidator could successfully resist any attempt by the employer to claim these goods as his own, even though the employer had paid for them.

4.26 The Scottish Supplement therefore provides that clause 14 (2) should be deleted and adds clause 30 (9) which gives the architect the power to recommend the employer to enter into a separate contract with the contractor or a sub-contractor for the purchase of certain goods and materials prior to their delivery to the site, although there is no obligation on the employer to do so if he does not wish to. Subsequently it was discovered that there was a loophole in the insurance provisions contained in clause 14 (1) and an addition has been added to this clause in the Scottish Supplement under which the main contractor's responsibility for the insurance of off-site goods and materials is made clear.

4.27 The July 1977 revision of the Standard Form gives the employer a similar optional right to pay a nominated sub-contractor for off-site goods and/or materials belonging to him, but this right could not immediately be available in Scotland for reasons similar to those quoted above. However these have now been overcome by means of a second contract of sale between the employer and sub-contractor with the consent of the main contractor. A clause dealing with the use of this contract is included in the 1977 revision of the Scottish Supplement

5 The Scottish supplement—Appendix II

5.01 Appendix II is similar to the appendix annexed to the Standard Form except that it allows for sectional completion under clause 21 by providing for different dates for possession and for completion of the various sections. It is understood, however, that with the publication of the Sectional Completion Contract (which has also been adopted in Scotland) this will be altered in the next revision of the Scottish Supplement. It should be noted that Appendix II must be completed prior to the signing of the building contract by the two parties.

APPENDIX No. II — **ABSTRACT OF SCHEDULE OF CONDITIONS**

	Defects Liability Period (if none other stated is 6 months from the day named in the Certificate of Practical Completion of the Works).	Clauses 15, 16 and 30
	Insurance cover for any one occurrence or series of occurrences arising out of one event.	Clause 19 (1) (a) £
*1 where the professional persons concerned with the Works are all employees of a Local Authority no percentage should be inserted but care should be taken to include in the sum assured the cost of professional services.	Percentage to cover Professional fees [*1].	Clause 20[A] %
	Date for Possession (Clause 21).	
	Date for Completion (Clause 21).	
	Liquidate and Ascertained Damages.	Clause 22 at the rate of £ per
*2 It is suggested that the periods should be (i) three months, and (ii) one month. It is essential that periods be inserted since otherwise no period of delay would be prescribed.	Period of delay [*2]. (i) by reason of loss or damage caused by any one of the contingencies referred to in Clause 20[A] or Clause 20[B] (if applicable). (ii) for any other reason.	Clause 26
	Prime cost sums for which the Contractor desires to tender.	Clause 27(g)
	Period of Interim Certificates (if none stated is 1 month).	Clause 30(1)
*3 the percentage will be 5% unless a lower rate is specified here.	Retention Percentage (if less than 5%) [*3].	Clause 30(3) %
	Period of Final Measurement and Valuation (if none stated is 6 months from the day named in the Certificate of Practical Completion of the Works).	Clause 30(5)
*4 the period inserted must not exceed 6 months.	Period for Issue of Final Certificate (if none stated is 3 months) [*4].	Clause 30(6) (Local Authority Contract only)
	Percentage addition.	Clause 31E %
	Formula Rules Clause 31F (1) (a) (i)	Rule 3 Base Month 19
*5 Not to exceed 10%.		Rule 3 Non adjustable element % (Local Authority Contract only)[*5]
*6 Delete as required.		Rules 10 & 30 (i) Part I/Part II of Section 2 of the Formula Rules is to apply [*6].

......Employer ......Contractor

6 The Scottish supplement—Appendix III

6.01 As already pointed out, this Appendix is equivalent to the supplemental agreement included at the end of the Standard Form and sets out the necessary provisions for payment of Value Added Tax. These provisions are incorporated by way of an appendix and not as a supplemental agreement because this is administratively simpler (the Appendix does not need to be witnessed or executed under seal or even stamped) and because this is the traditional way in Scotland of dealing with additional matters to a contract.

7 JCT form: Scottish problems

7.01 The following comments on certain paragraphs in LEGAL STUDY 4 should be noted when work is being carried out in Scotland.

Definition of contract documents (para 7.02)

7.02 A certain amount of confusion has arisen in Scotland over use of the word 'specification' in clause 3 of the RIBA conditions, probably because in a with-quantities form, the specification (with a small s) is not a contract document, but in the without quantities form, the Specification (with a capital S) is a contract document. In the with-quantities form the architect's requirements to the contractor are to be found in the preamble to the bills and the specification contains his general instructions which do not have the same status. In that case, the preamble contains information which in Scotland would otherwise have been found in the specification.

Statutory obligations (para 8.01)

7.03 Scotland has its own building regulations which are sanctioned by the Building (Scotland) Act, 1959 (see LEGAL STUDY 14).

Conflict between bills and conditions (para 16.04)

7.04 Because of the terms of clause 12, to ensure that parties to a contract in Scotland are contracting under Scottish law, it is essential to ensure that a clause stating that Scottish law is to apply to the contract is included in the contract documents; it is not enough to state in the contract bills that Scots law applies (see also para 2.05).

Rectification (para 17.02)

7.05 Scots law provides the same remedies as those described in this paragraph. The most common error of this type (known in Scotland as 'error in expression') arises after the contract has been signed by both parties and it is discovered that owing to some accidental mistake, the contract does not represent the parties' agreement.

Determination by employer (para 29)

7.06 In England, there appears to be considerable doubt about the validity of the provisions of clause 25 when detailing the employer's rights in the event of the bankruptcy of the main contractor. Some of these doubts are shared in Scotland, but the best legal opinions obtainable suggest that clause 25 (2) is perfectly valid against a liquidator of a bankrupt contractor trading as a limited company, as also is the power given in clause 25 (3) (b) to an employer to pay direct any suppliers or sub-contractors for materials or goods delivered or works executed. This is true whether the supplier or sub-contractor concerned is nominated or not. But note that as far as is known, such opinions have not been tested by the Scottish courts; therefore the matter cannot be beyond doubt until a decision of the Court of Session is available.

References

ROYAL INSTITUTION OF CHARTERED SURVEYORS. Standard method of measurement of building works. 1968, 5th Edition (metric) 1970

Building Standards (Scotland) (Consolidation) Regulations. 1970. HMSO

Building Standards (Scotland) Amendment Regulations. 1973. HMSO

Acknowledgements

The Scottish supplement is reproduced by courtesy of the Scottish Building Contract Committee.

AJ Legal Handbook

Section 4
The law of property and land

Legal study 6

English land law

This study outlines land and property law as it affects architects. Of particular interest is the discussion of easements, including rights of light and air and party walls in common law. Also covered are conveyancing, restrictive covenants, trespass, and some aspects of landlord and tenant law including architects' duties for surveys and problems concerning architects' own office premises. Scottish readers should read LEGAL STUDY 7 *which covers roughly the same area of Scots law.* LEGAL STUDY 9, *English statutory authorities, and* LEGAL STUDY 12, *Planning law, give further details of some aspects of land law*

1 Introduction

1.01 The purpose of this study is not to enable architects to become their own home conveyancers, nor does it attempt to cover all the subject of real property (LEGAL STUDY 1 para 7.06) and conveyancing. And, although the history of the subject is of great importance to lawyers and is touched upon where necessary, the study deals almost entirely with the law as it is in 1977. Architects are not expected to be commercial conveyancers, but as they work in offices and design buildings to be erected on other people's land, they should be aware of such aspects of land law as will affect them personally as occupiers of property and possibly restrict their designs of buildings for clients. It is the client's solicitor's task to advise on title to land and possible restrictions on its use, but it is hoped that this article will assist architects by discussing some of the problems upon which they are entitled to seek reassurance from the client or his solicitor.

History
1.02 Land law was originally based on the feudal system of tenure (LEGAL STUDY 1 para 7.02), all land being held in some form from the sovereign. As land always was, and perhaps property still is, the most secure form of investment, land law developed more rapidly than other branches of the law. Development was, however, towards complexity. Cromwell referred to the then state of real property law as 'a tortuous and ungodly jumble'. Despite modest statutory reforms in the 19th century, little was done to simplify the law until 1925 when F. E. Smith became Lord Chancellor and fulfilled a student ambition by persuading Parliament to pass seven major Acts which form the basis of modern real property and conveyancing law (LEGAL STUDY 1 para 6.01). The 1925 legislation can be said to have been pure law reform, or lawyers' law. Since then, much social legislation has been enacted, particularly concerning landlord and tenant and planning, placing restrictions on what the Englishman may do with his castle; but very few amendments have been necessary to land law itself.

2 Conveyancing

2.01 The title 'land law' has been chosen as the old distinctions between real property and personal property (LEGAL STUDY 1 para 7.06) have largely disappeared. Land law is 'static' and lays down the rights and obligations attendant upon the ownership of land; conveyancing is the art of creating and transferring those rights and liabilities. Although land law and conveyancing are mutually dependent, the art of deducing title and transferring it to others need not concern an architect, but it is useful to understand the distinction between the two methods of transferring land (registered and unregistered conveyancing—see below) and public records of title and restrictions.

2.02 Until 1925 the only method of conveyancing required solicitors to investigate every transaction concerning not only the land itself but also the many persons who might be entitled to an interest either in the land or in its income and proceeds of sale, to ensure that the proposed vendor had an unencumbered right to dispose of it. Title had to be deduced for a period of 40 years before the proposed sale, and there was the danger that some document evidencing transactions creating equitable interests in the land would be missing and the purchaser would not obtain clear title. In the large areas of England and Wales where land is not yet subject to compulsory registration of title, it is still necessary to deduce title in this way, but since the Law of Property Act 1969 only for a period of 15 years. Conveyancing in these areas still requires the signing of deeds, and advantage has rarely been taken of voluntary registration available since 1925.

Registration
2.03 Registration of title was introduced by the Land Registration Act 1925 and substitutes State guaranteed titles for the laborious system described above. After a title is investigated in the old way by the Land Registry, it is entered on the register, and all subsequent dealings are similarly registered, so that a perusal of the register informs any pro-

posed purchaser of the vendor's powers to sell the land. The register is, however, private and the consent of the vendor is required before the entries can be inspected. Simple substitution of the purchaser's name for that of the vendor transfers title. In recent years there has been a great acceleration in the extension of registration, and it is intended that the whole country shall be subject to compulsory registration by 1980.

Land charges

2.04 One of the great dangers of unregistered conveyancing was that a purchaser in good faith might find his title defeated, and similarly the owner of an undisclosed equitable interest in the land might lose his interest in favour of a purchaser. By the Land Charges Act, public registers were created, kept by the Central Land Charges Department of the Land Registry and the local registries maintained by the clerks of county councils, boroughs and district councils.

Central register

2.05 Entry of a charge constitutes notice of an interest registered as against a purchase, and in simple terms a failure to register an interest makes it void against a purchaser. The Land Registration Act lays down a number of interests which are registerable, but the architect need note only the estate contract (ie an agreement to sell the land to another person), restrictive covenants (para 5.01) and equitable easements (para 4.01). The demerit of the Central Land Charges Register is that charges are against the name of the person who was the owner of the land at the time the charge was made, and it is therefore necessary to know the names of all the persons who have owned the land since 1925.

Local registers

2.06 Local land charges registries are more important for architects in that the matters to be registered, usually by the local authority, include the following: planning consents, restrictions and conditions, compulsory purchase orders, building and improvement lines under the Highways Act 1959 and the Planning Acts (see LEGAL STUDY 12), charges for making up roads, improvements to houses, intended major road works and public health restrictions—eg smokeless zones (see LEGAL STUDY 9). The advantage of local land charges registers is that matters are registered against the land or property, not the name of the person who happened at the time to be the owner.

2.07 On payment of a search fee, anyone may inspect the central and local land registers, either by post or in person. Architects should, however, note that, except in county boroughs, they should search in both the county council and the district council registers (LEGAL STUDY 9 clarifies local authority structure).

3 Trespass and boundaries

3.01 Trespass to land consists of any unauthorised intrusion by one person onto the land of another (LEGAL STUDY 1 para 5.17). Besides unauthorised entry to property it includes, for example, driving a nail into another's wall, growing a creeper up it or even propping scaffolding or a ladder against it.

3.02 It is trespass to enter another's land below the surface or to invade the air space above it, for example with the eaves of a building (though there are exceptions to this rule—see LEGAL STUDY 1 para 5.18). As recently as 1970, a deferred injunction was granted against a firm of building contractors, the jib of whose tower crane necessarily extended over the plaintiff's premises. But the court took a practical view of the difficulties of construction on confined sites and it made the injunction operable only on the date when it was anticipated that construction would be completed (*Woollerton and Wilson Ltd v Richard Costain Ltd* (1970) 1 All ER 483).

3.03 Trespass does not necessarily involve damage to property or land. If building operations are likely to necessitate the contractor going onto adjoining land or erecting temporary scaffolding and the like on it, the client should be advised to negotiate a temporary licence* for the duration of the contract period.

3.04 Even a slight projection of eaves over adjoining land is a technical trespass and if such an arrangement is contemplated, the building owner should be advised to negotiate a licence or better an express easement (para 4.01) of 'eaves drop'.

Boundaries

3.05 Exact boundaries are fixed by provable acts of adjoining owners, by orders of certain authorities or by presumption.

Provable acts

3.06 Provable acts of owners include not only the straightforward case of definition in title deeds by words or reference to attached plans or existing building, but also title obtained by 12 years' undisturbed possession.

Orders

3.07 Establishment of boundaries by orders of authorities is now almost entirely historical. Under the Enclosure Acts, the Tithes Acts and certain Agriculture Acts, awards were made, defining boundaries precisely. Particularly in rural areas such an award may help in determining a boundary obliterated by time. The boundaries defined under the Ordnance Survey Acts are only general in so far as private boundaries are concerned. In areas of registered land (para 2.03) there is power for boundaries to be defined precisely, in default of agreement, by the Land Registrar. When this step has been taken, the plan on the register is definitive. The general plan on the register is not.

Presumption

3.08 In the absence of clear definition on title deeds or by order and so on, certain presumptions apply but it should be noted that they are presumptions only, and can be rebutted.

Rivers and streams

3.09 If a watercourse is tidal (and quite small streams may be) the soil of the bed of the river or stream belongs to the Crown, or the Duchies of Cornwall or Lancaster, where appropriate. As a general rule, the boundary between the bed of a tidal stream and adjoining land is the line of medium high water mark. Although this sounds a little remote from reality, the writer has had experience of considerable development being held up when it was discovered that a stream which flowed across the sites drained into the River Mersey at a point some 15 miles away and was tidal. In the end it was necessary to purchase from the Duchy of Lancaster a strip of land ½ mile long and varying between 3ft and 18in wide. In the case of non-tidal rivers and streams it is assumed that adjoining owners own land to the middle of the bed.

Highways

3.10 The boundary between lands separated by a highway is, as a general rule, the middle line of the highway—whether

---

* A licence is a consent given for a terminable period. It must be given for a consideration (LEGAL STUDY 1 para 3.03) even if only for 5p a year.

public or private. The same presumption does not apply to railways, and now that tracks are being taken up all over the country it is necessary to purchase the bed from British Rail.

Hedges and ditches
3.11 The presumption here is that the hedge stands on the earth excavated from the ditch, that the earth would be on the land of the person making the ditch and that *prima facie*, therefore, where two fields are separated by a hedge and ditch, both belong to the owner of the field in which the ditch does *not* lie. Where fields are divided by a hedge only, or a hedge with a ditch on both sides, no presumption as to ownership arises.

Fences
3.12 In rural areas, fences are primarily a protection against intrusion and no presumption arises as to their marking or boundary. In built-up areas, fences have been used for making boundaries for many years and the presumption is that the fence is built on the land of the person erecting it. The existence of supporting posts on one side and not the other raises the presumption that the boundary line is the blank face of the planks on the other side.

Trees
3.13 An owner of land may without notice lop off as much of the branches of an adjoining owner's trees as overhang his property. An action will lie if the roots of an adjoining owner's trees project and cause damage, and although this presumption has never been tested by the courts, it would seem that the owner suffering damage can cut intruding roots just as he can cut branches.

Walls
3.14 For party walls see para 4.14. Walls that divide for example two gardens are assumed in the absence of other evidence to be similar to party walls.

4 Easements

4.01 Easements are rights which one owner of land may acquire over the land of another. They should be distinguished from: profits, ie rights to take something off another's land eg to cut grass or peat, to fish or shoot; natural rights, eg rights of support of land (not buildings); public rights, eg rights of way over highways; restrictive covenants and licences.

4.02 The essentials of an easement are:
1 There must be a dominant and servient tenement*. The two properties need necessarily adjoin each other.
2 The easement must benefit the dominant tenement ie the dominant tenement must have a right which the servient tenement must suffer.
3 The two tenements must not both be owned and occupied by the same person.
4 The easement claimed must be capable of forming the subject matter of a grant. Although the list of easements is reasonably limited to rights of way, rights of light, rights of support, it is capable of extension. For example in 1955 the right to use a neighbour's lavatory was held to be an easement and in 1956 the right to use paths through a park not for the purpose of getting from A to B but for taking walks was held to be one. The alleged right must, however, be reasonably capable of being defined, and therefore there cannot be an easement for a general flow of air, for an undisturbed view or for privacy.

* Tenement—a plot of land held by an owner (leaseholder or freeholder).

Acquisition of easements
4.03 Easements may be acquired in three basic ways, as follows.

Expressly
4.04 Easements acquired expressly are formed by deed (LEGAL STUDY 1 para 3.02) conferring the right upon the dominant tenement owner and thereafter upon his successors in title. Similarly a right can be reserved off land which is to form the servient tenement.

Impliedly
4.05 Probably the only easement which will be implied in favour of a person selling land is an easement of necessity, eg where a sale of land will leave a vendor without any access to the plot he has retained, or on the sale of part of a divided house by the owner of the other part, there will usually be an implied easement of support. Easements are more readily implied in favour of purchasers than vendors. By the Law of Property Act 1925 every 'conveyance' of land (which includes a lease) automatically passes to the purchaser all 'liberties, privileges, easements, rights and advantages whatsoever appertaining to or reputed to appertain to the land'.

Prescription
4.06 Long user* *nec vi, nec clam, nec precario*—without force, secrecy or permission—can give rights to easements. An easement by prescription can only be claimed by one freehold owner against another and, with certain exceptions, user must be shown to have been continuous. Only two methods of acquiring easements by prescription are considered here: at common law and under the Prescription Act 1832. At common law an easement could be acquired by prescription only if it could be proved to have been used from time immemorial (ie from 1189). In fact, user for 20 years before the claim was made would normally be accepted, but a claim could always be defeated by showing eg that a right of light claimed for a building could not have existed since 1189 if the building had been constructed in 1500.

4.07 The Prescription Act 1832 laid down periods in general and for rights of light in particular (the latter are discussed in para 3.12).

4.08 The 1832 Act provides that uninterrupted user for 20 years before some action by the dominant owner for confirmation of a right of easement or by the servient owner for a declaration that a right does not exist means that the claim cannot be defeated merely by showing that it cannot have existed since 1189. The Act further provides that user without interruption for 40 years before action confirms an absolute and indefeasible easement. In both cases user must be of right ie *nec vi, nec clam, nec precario*. 'Interruption' is important because if an owner wishes to establish an easement by prescription, he must not acquiesce to interruption of his right for one year by the owner of the property on which he wishes to establish the easement. Acquiescence to interruption does not necessarily imply agreement; the owner who wishes to establish the easement may simply not notice an interruption (though it must not be secret ie *cum clam*). Any period during which the owner of the land on which the easement is claimed could not give consent to establishing an easement (eg because he was an infant or a lunatic) must be added to the 20-year period. Any period in excess of three years

* User is the legal term for enjoyment of use.

during which the servient tenement is leased must be added
to the 40-year period.

Extinguishment of easements
4.09 Apart from an express release by deed, the most important method of extinguishing an easement is by the dominant
and servient tenements coming into the same ownership and
possession.

Types of easement
Rights of way
4.10 A right of way, whether acquired expressly or by prescription, may be limited as to both frequency and type of use,
eg a right obtained for passage by horse and cart in the 19th
century will not extend to passage for many caravans if the
dominant tenement has become a caravan site.

Rights of support
4.11 Although the natural right of support for land by other
land has been distinguished from an easement (para 4.01)
it is possible for one building to acquire an easement of support against another after a period of 20 years. The only
remedy against this would be for the owner of the supporting
building to seek a declaration during the 20 years that the
supported building has no right to support. It should be
noted that where two detached buildings adjoin on separate
plots an easement cannot be acquired requiring a person who
removes his abutting wall to weatherproof the exposed flank
wall of the remaining building (but if the wall is a party wall
other rules apply (see para 4.14)).

Rights of light
4.12 To a considerable extent the law relating to rights of
light has been rendered of secondary importance by daylighting regulations under planning legislation (LEGAL STUDY
12) but a knowledge of the law is still required. There is no
right to light generally, but only in respect of some definite
opening, such as a window or skylight. The owner of the
dominant tenement has a right only to such amount of light
as is necessary for 'ordinary purposes'. Many years user of
an exceptional amount of light does not prevent an adjoining
owner from building so as to reduce light; this was held in a
case where an architect claimed that he had enjoyed and
needed more light for his office than for ordinary office purposes.
The decision whether or not enough light is left for ordinary
purposes must, therefore, depend on personal obesrvation,
and all the scientific methods now available for measuring
light and the so-called 45° rule from the centre of a window
can do no more than help the judge make up his mind. It
should also be noted that if light could be obtained from an
existing but blocked skylight, then this must be counted as
an available alternative source.

4.13 Under the Prescription Act 1832 as amended by the
Right of Light Act 1959, it was provided that an absolute
right of light could be obtained only after 20 years uninterrupted user. Because of the possibility of prescriptive rights
being acquired over bomb damaged sites, the 1959 Act
provided a temporary extension of the period to 27 years for
actions alleging infringement beginning before that date. The
1959 Act also provided for registration as a local land charge
(para 2.06) of a theoretical wall of stated dimensions in such
a position as would prevent an adjoining owner from claiming
a prescriptive right of light because the owner of the servient
tenement did not erect a permanent structure to the registered dimensions. This useful provision avoids the cumber-
ous procedure by which screens and hoardings had to be

erected by the person seeking to prevent a right of light being
acquired over his land; in any case such hoardings would now
be subject to planning control (LEGAL STUDY 12).

Party walls in common law
4.14 Party walls outside London and Bristol are subject to
rights at common law (for the situation in London and Bristol
see LEGAL STUDY 13). There is no exact definition of party
walls in common law, but they might be described as walls
which are divided down the long axis on plan into two strips,
each strip belonging to the owner of the land on which it
stands; each half is the subject to an easement of support in
favour of the other half. Thus an owner has rights to such
support as is necessary to maintain his structure, but there
are no restrictions as to what he may do with his half of the
wall provided he does not weaken it. If one owner removes
his building, he is obliged to waterproof the exposed party
wall. See LEGAL STUDY 13 for the complicated procedures
necessary when changes to party walls are contemplated in
London.

4.15 Extensions can bear only on the half of the wall belonging to the owner of the building being extended, unless the
consent of the adjoining owner is obtained; this cannot be
enforced as it can in London (LEGAL STUDY 13).

5 Restrictive covenants

5.01 To some extent restrictive covenants, which are negative and intended to prevent the person who gives the covenant and his successors in title from doing something on their
land, have been superseded by planning control, but not
entirely so. The complicated history and rules concerning
who may claim the benefit and who must accept the burden
are avoided here, but briefly, a restrictive covenant is obtained
by agreement, more usually by reservation at the time of sale,
and prevents the convenantor and his successors in title from,
for example, building more than one house of a certain value
on the servient tenement or, in the case of estate sales by beer
barons in the 19th century using land or a building for manufacture or sale of 'ale porter, beer, wines, spiritous liquor'.
Any private covenants running with the land are additional
to planning conditions which may be imposed and they must
also be satisfied.

5.02 Restrictive covenants have been particularly important
in development of estates whereby a developer ensures in his
sales or leases that each purchaser or lessee covenants not
only with the original owner but with all other purchasers
before or after to maintain his property or not to add to it,
or to maintain estate roads and open spaces and so on (see
LEGAL STUDY 9 for other road maintenance duties). If such
covenants are included in leases, they are immediately
apparent to a subsequent assignee of both registered and
unregistered land by inspection of the title, but where they
are imposed on a freehold sale, additional protection is
provided by the requirement that they be registered in the
Central Land Registry (para 2.05). Architects should request
that their clients obtain confirmation that there are no restrictive covenants applying to a site that would impede
design.

Discharge of restrictive covenants
5.03 Many restrictive covenants imposed in former years are
no longer of real benefit to the owners of adjoining lands and
may indeed be anti-social or in conflict with reasonable redevelopment proposals. Power is given to the Lands Tribunal
by section 84 of the Law of Property Act 1925 as amended

by section 28 of the Law of Property Act 1969 for the discharge or modification of any covenant if the tribunal is satisfied that, *inter alia*, changes in the neighbourhood make the covenant obsolete or that the restriction does not now secure practical advantages of substantial value to the person entitled to its benefit or it is contrary to public policy (ie planning policy). Compensation may be awarded in lieu of the covenant.

6 Landlord and tenant covenants

6.01 The vast majority of leases with which architects are concerned on behalf of their clients, particularly of trade and business premises, are the subject of formal agreements defining precisely the respective rights and obligations of the parties. Whether the architect's client is a tenant who wishes to rebuild, alter or repair premises, or a landlord who requires evidence to recover damages from a tenant who has failed to observe a covenant for repair, regard must be had first to the express terms of the lease, and the client's solicitor should be asked to advise on the meaning and extent of the terms. The following general remarks, except where otherwise stated, introduce the law only in so far as the lease has not stated to the contrary.

Doctrine of waste
6.02 'Waste' consists of an act or omission which causes or is likely to cause a lasting alteration to the nature of the land and premises to the prejudice of the person who has the reversion (ie the landlord). Voluntary waste is some positive act such as pulling down or altering buildings. Permissive waste implies an omission whereby premises are allowed to fall into disrepair and decay. Waste can also include ameliorating waste: some change which improves the value of the reversion. A landlord is able to obtain an injunction to prevent all three kinds of waste but damages only in respect of voluntary or permissive waste. The measure of damages recoverable by the landlord is the amount of depreciation in the selling value of his reversion.

Fixtures
6.03 Landlord's fixtures are those that the tenant may not remove and include not only fixtures attached at the beginning of the term of the lease or fixed by the landlord during the term but also those fixed by the tenant but which he is not allowed to remove. Tenant's fixtures are quite simply those he is allowed to remove. Two general rules should be noted:
1 If the object and purpose of the fixture was permanent improvement of the land or building it is a landlord's fixture.
2 Neither the method of fixing nor the amount of damage to either fixture or the premises by its removal do more than throw light on the likely purpose of the fixing.

6.04 There are many cases on this subject and they do not really show any logical pattern—eg a temporary army hut bolted to its foundations was not a fixture but a removable corrugated iron hut was: a wooden barn and a windmill which rested upon their foundations by weight alone were not landlord's fixtures, but large chambers and towers for the preparation of sulphuric acid, similarly resting upon their foundations, were held to be landlord's fixtures. One important general rule is, however, that in the absence of agreement to the contrary an article that would otherwise appear to be a landlord's fixture may nevertheless be removed by the tenant if he had fixed it for trade or ornamental purposes. Again in the absence of agreement to the contrary, tenants must remove their fixtures before the end of tenancy.

Alterations and improvements
6.05 *Prima facie* any alteration is either voluntary waste which reduces the value of the premises, or ameliorating waste, which enhances such value. Even an express condition not to make any alterations without consent is subject to the statutory proviso that such consent may not be unreasonably withheld, provided that the alteration will be an improvement (Landlord and Tenant Act 1927). Whether or not a proposed alteration is an improvement is a question of fact to be considered from the tenant's point of view. It should be noted that it is the tenant's responsibility to prove that the landlord's consent is being unreasonably withheld, that the landlord may object on aesthetic, artistic and even sentimental grounds and that although the Act forbids the taking of any premium as a condition of giving consent, the landlord may reasonably require the tenant to pay the landlord's legal and other expenses (including architects' and surveyors' fees) plus a reasonable amount for any diminution in the value not only of the leased premises but also of any adjoining premises of the landlord.

Repairing covenants
Surveys
6.06 Architects are frequently asked to prepare a schedule of dilapidations at the beginning of a tenancy, during the course of or at the end of the lease. The importance of initial schedules is that in the absence of any covenant to do works as a condition of the grant of the lease, any repairing covenant must be construed with reference to the original condition of the premises. Different phrases may be used but generally the tenant's obligation is to 'repair, keep in repair and deliver the premises in repair at the end of the term'. Repair may include the replacement or renewal of parts but not renewal of the whole or substantially the whole of the premises.

6.07 'Good and tenantable repair' is a term used almost exclusively in leases of houses and flats and in such cases (unless the amount of the rent brings the premises within the restrictions of the Housing Acts with the statutory implication that the premises were and will be kept fit for human habitation) the covenant could include an obligation to put the premises into repair as well as keep them in repair. Otherwise this phrase means 'such repair as having regard to the age, character and locality of the premises would make it reasonably fit for occupation by another reasonably minded tenant of the same class'.

6.08 It is the tenant's responsibility to prove that a bad state of repair is within the exception of 'fair wear and tear'. In general terms the phrase means that the tenant is not responsible for damage resulting from exposure to the natural elements or reasonable use. Although not liable for direct damage the tenant could be liable for consequential damages —eg he might not be liable for repair of tiles slipping from a roof after a storm, but he would be liable for damage to the interior of the premises from flooding resulting from his failure to take steps to prevent rain entering.

Enforcement of repairing covenants
6.09 Under the Leasehold Property (Repairs) Act 1938 as extended by the Landlord and Tenant Act 1954, a landlord cannot forfeit the lease or even begin an action for damages in respect of a tenant's failure to observe a repairing covenant unless he has first served on the tenant a notice under section 146 of the Law of Property Act 1925 clearly specifying the breach. If the tenant serves a counter-notice within 28 days the landlord cannot take any action without the consent of the court. Architects are frequently asked to produce a

schedule of defects to accompany such a notice (see also para 6.12).

Consents
6.10 It is emphasised that what has been stated is always subject to the express wording of the lease and also to the many statutory provisions for the protection of tenants of certain types of premises, particularly houses. Architects should remember that a client's tenancy may come at the end of a long line of underleases, and the consents of superior landlords may be required for any work which the client has requested.

Mortgages
6.11 It is not proposed to discuss this subject in detail, but architects should remember that alteration to premises will alter the value of the mortgagee's security. For this reason most mortgages contain covenants requiring the mortgagee's consent to works. As with leases, there may be several mortgagees having different priorities of charge on the premises, and the architect should ask the client whether or not the property is mortgaged, and if it is request him to obtain any necessary consents.

Architect's responsibilities for surveys
Dilapidations
6.12 If asked to prepare a schedule of dilapidations, an architect should first find out from his client's solicitor the terms of the lease, so that he is clear as to which portions of the building come within the repairing covenant. These are the only portions he need examine. As tenant's fixtures are removable by the tenant, only dilapidations to landlord's fixtures need usually be catalogued, but because of the difficulties of assessing ownership of fixtures, it is often wise to examine dilapidations on anything that is at all doubtful.

6.13 Estimates of cost of making good dilapidations are often required. Unless an architect has much experience of this kind of work, it is advisable to involve a quantity surveyor. When lessor and lessee cannot agree about the extent of damages or the extent of responsibility for making them good, their dispute may have to be resolved in the courts. In such cases the schedule of dilapidations becomes evidence and it is therefore important that it is very clearly drawn. When making a survey for a schedule the possibility that matters might come to court should be borne in mind.

Surveys of property to be purchased
6.14 Architects are often asked to inspect property for clients who intend to purchase or lease. An examination of the property is required, bearing in mind the proposed use and taking into account all defects and dilapidations. Useful guides to technical points to be noted in such a survey are given in *Architectural practice and procedure* and in *Guide to domestic building surveys.*

6.15 It is important to note that if defects are not observed, the architect may be held to be negligent. For example, where a surveyor failed to detect woodworm when making a survey of a house and his client was involved in loss, the surveyor was held to be negligent and damages were assessed as the difference between the market value and the actual value of the house. (*Stewart v Brechin* (HA) *& Co* (1959) SC 306). In another case, an architect was asked to make a survey and failed to discover several defects. He said that he was merely asked to prepare plans of the building to enable the plaintiff to carry out improvements and alterations, though he admitted that he was asked to carry out an inspection of the drains. The plaintiff was awarded damages equal to the loss of value caused by the undetected defects (*Moss v Heckingbottom* (1958) 172 EG 207).

Hidden defects
6.16 It is often wise, particularly when investigating old property, to open up and inspect hidden portions of the building. If this is not done, the limitations of the investigation should be clearly pointed out to the client, and he should be asked to take a decision as to whether the expense of opening up is worth while. He must of course be informed of the probability or otherwise of eg rot. If rot is discovered and it was not mentioned in the survey and the architect did not recommend opening up to check, he is almost certainly negligent.

7 Business tenancies—architects' offices

7.01 This review of business tenancies can be in outline only, and it is written from the point of view of architects as tenants of office premises. Two preliminary matters which recent cases involving architect tenants have shown to be of importance concern landlord's rights of forfeiture and rights of assignment.
1 An architect should be careful if a lease offered includes an absolute right of forfeiture in the event of bankruptcy, as he will find that he cannot raise finance from either a building society or a bank on the security of such a lease.
2 Care should be taken to check the wording of covenants empowering assignment or subletting, not only in the immediate lease offered (where the landlord may have only a right of reasonable objection) but also in any superior lease (where the superior landlord may have reserved an absolute right of refusal without reasonable cause). Consent may be obtained from the immediate landlord but refused by the superior landlord.

Protection of business tenants
7.02 Part II of the Landlord and Tenant Act 1954 as amended by part I of the Law of Property Act 1969 provides a substantial measure of protection to occupiers of business premises by providing in effect that the tenant may continue in occupancy indefinitely, unless the landlord satisfies the court that a new tenancy ought not to be granted for certain defined statutory reasons (para 7.03). If the tenant receives notice of determination (not less than six nor more than 12 months' notice) expiring not earlier than the existing tenancy would otherwise have ended, he may within two months of receipt serve a counter notice on the landlord that he is unwilling to leave and then apply to the court for a new tenancy.

7.03 There are seven reasons which might prevent the grant of a new tenancy, the first three of which, if proved, prevent the grant absolutely, the latter four being left to the discretion of the court.
1 If, on termination of the existing tenancy, the landlord intends to demolish or reconstruct the premises and could not reasonably do so without possession of the whole. (Since the 1969 Act, this does not prevent a new tenancy of the whole or part of the premises if the landlord will be able to do the work without seriously 'interfering' with the tenant's business.)
2 If the landlord proves that he intends to occupy the premises for his own business or as a residence. (Since 1969 the landlord may successfully resist if he intends the premises to be occupied by a company in which he has a controlling interest.)

3 If the landlord proves the premises are part of a larger holding for which he could obtain a substantially larger rent than for the individual parts.

4 If the tenant fails to keep the premises in repair.

5 If there are persistent delays in paying rent.

6 If there are breaches of covenant.

7 If the landlord is willing to provide suitable alternative accommodation on reasonable terms.

Compensation

7.04 If the court cannot grant a new tenancy for any of the first three reasons above, the tenant will be entitled to compensation of the rateable value or twice the rateable value where the tenant and his predecessors in the same business have occupied for 14 years or more.

New tenancy

7.05 The length of a new tenancy (but not exceeding 14 years), the rent and any other terms are fixed by the court.

References

TURNER, HAMILTON H. Architectural practice and procedure. 6th Edition, London, 1974, Batsford

BOWYER, J. T. Guide to domestic building surveys. (2nd Edition, London), 1972, Architectural Press

Acknowledgements

Prints in this section are from the Mary Evans Picture Library.

Legal study 7

Law of property in Scotland

This study should be read with LEGAL STUDY 6 *which covers the same areas of English law and with* LEGAL STUDIES 10 *and 12 for further details of some aspects of land law and planning*

1 Introduction

1.01 The term 'property' is used in Scots law to denote both a right and the subject of a right. The right can be described as the right of using and disposing of a thing as one's own. This may be subject to many different statutory, contractual or other restrictions. Property as the subject of the right is classified either as heritable or moveable. Heritable property is property which by its nature is immoveable, for example land or buildings, while moveable property consists of things such as furniture or motor cars, which by their nature can be moved.

Heritable and moveable property

1.02 Moveable property may become heritable through attachment to heritable property. Building materials are moveable until they are incorporated in the building, when they become part of the heritage. Articles such as light fittings, a central heating system or machinery, which are installed in a building, become part of the heritable property if they are sufficiently attached to or connected with the building. The question whether or not moveable property has become heritable in this way, ie has become a 'fixture', depends on the whole circumstances and has given rise to a large body of case law. The important point in deciding this is generally the degree of attachment to the heritage (whether for example the thing in question can be removed without damage to itself or the heritage). Things may also be heritable because they are essential accessories of the heritage, as for example the keys of a house, or unattached articles essential for the operation of fixed machinery. Articles such as pictures or fitted carpets are not regarded as fixtures, since they are only lightly attached. Fitted cupboards, and gas or electric fires which are built in, would be.

1.03 In certain circumstances heritable property may become movable. Examples are minerals removed from the land, or standing timber which is felled.

1.04 Whether property is heritable or moveable may be of considerable importance in, among others, questions of valuation for rating and in interpretation of contracts for the sale of heritage, where it is necessary to know what is included in the sale. Houses, for example, are often sold 'complete with fixtures and fittings'. Felled timber or harvested crops would not in the absence of express provision in the contract be included in a sale of land.

Corporeal and incorporeal

1.05 Heritable and moveable property are both further classified as corporeal or incorporeal property, the former being tangible, the latter consisting of intangible rights. Examples of incorporeal property are servitude rights (para 3.07) such as rights of wayleave for pipes, or certain security rights in heritage, which are heritable, and patent or copyright rights (LEGAL STUDY 11) which are moveable.

2 Corporeal heritable property and feudal law

2.01 A valid title to land is obtained by having a title recorded in the Register of Sasines. Provided the title so recorded appears to be good, it is unquestionable provided that it is followed by possession for a period of 10 years. Thus if A grants B a title to land and B records the title, enters the land and stays there unchallenged for the requisite period, his title cannot then be challenged on some extraneous ground, for example that A has no right to the land in the first place, or that he gave B more than he was entitled to himself (for the English position see LEGAL STUDY 6 para 2.01 *et seq*).

2.02 Basically the Scots law of land tenure is feudal law, modified and now greatly attenuated by a number of statutes. All rights to land derive from the Crown. Originally the Crown made grants of land to its subjects in return for military or other services. In this relationship the Crown was the feudal superior and the subject the vassal. The Crown's vassal could in turn make grants of land to other persons, in which case he would stand in the position of superior *vis-a-vis* the persons to whom he made grants, who would be his vassals.

Feuing

2.03 The position today derives from this. A very large proportion of land in Scotland is held on feu, although there are also many cases where the proprietor in effect owns the whole right to the land. The Crown is still in theory the paramount superior of all land, although this has little practical importance. The rights to certain types of property, such as the foreshore, are still largely vested in the Crown, however.

2.04 Today the vassal who holds property on feu pays a feu duty rather than rendering services for his land. This can be substantial but frequently it is purely nominal. Provided he pays his feu duty his successors (whether they succeed on his death or through a purchase of his interest) hold the land in perpetuity though if he fails in his obligations his superior may be entitled to eject him from the feu. The vassal may sell his interest in the land, or part of it, or feu the whole or parts to other persons, himself retaining an interest as mid-superior. If he sells or feus parts he may still be liable to his superior for the whole feu duty. But he may make an arrangement with him to allocate the feu duty so that each part of the land is liable for a proportion only. If he does not do so, each part and each proprietor is liable for the whole. Under the Conveyancing and Feudal Reform (Scotland) Act, 1970, he can now compel the superior to come to such an arrangement.

2.05 The Land Tenure Reform (Scotland) Act 1974, although it has not abolished feu duties outright, has done much to pave the way for their eventual disappearance by 1 banning the creation of new feu duties, 2 making it compulsory to redeem existing feu duties when properties are sold (the purchaser makes a lump sum payment which is fixed according to a statutory formula) and by 3 allowing vassals to insist on redemption, in return for a lump sum payment, at other times. The act also introduces elaborate provisions to prevent superiors from frustrating the purpose of the reform by exacting other kinds of periodic payment, for example by creating long leases for dwelling houses. It may happen that several houses, for example in one tenement, together make up a single feu burdened by a single feu duty which has not been formally allocated among the individual flats. In such a case the provisions for redemption do not apply. But as has already been mentioned, the 1970 act allows any single proprietor to insist on allocation; and once the feu duty has been allocated, the provisions of the 1974 act will apply.

Restrictions on ownership by vassals
2.06 Although in many respects the vassal is in the position of absolute owner of the land, his right of ownership may be subject to many conditions and restrictions contained in his title. The superior may, for example, regulate the number and type of buildings the vassal may erect, and the use to which the property may be put. He may require the vassal to erect buildings of a certain type within a certain time, to keep any buildings in good repair, insure them with an approved company and rebuild them within a certain time in the event of their destruction. He may also require the vassal to contribute to the cost of building or maintaining roads serving the feu. These are examples of conditions which, if properly framed in a feudal title, can be enforced by the superior against all vassals in perpetuity. Before starting to design, architects should suggest to their clients that the feudal title of the property should be examined to check for conditions. The client's solicitor will do this.

Pre-emption
2.07 The superior may also insert a clause of pre-emption, stipulating that if the vassal wishes to sell he must first offer the property to the superior, either at a fixed price or, more commonly, at a price which he has been offered and for which he would sell if the superior does not exercise his right. Such a right is now exercisable on the occasion of the first sale only and must be exercised within 21 days of the vassal's offer to the superior.

2.08 Not any and every condition is enforceable by the superior, however. The superior must have an interest to enforce the condition, which in fact is fairly readily assumed, and the condition must be precise in its terms so that the

vassal will be able to ascertain, through reading the condition, what is required of him. There is a presumption that the vassal is free to do as he wishes with his property, and when a condition is being interpreted he will always receive the benefit of the doubt if there is any ambiguity.

Jus quaesitum tertio
2.09 Some feuing conditions are enforceable by persons other than the superior; this right is called *jus quaesitum tertio* (LEGAL STUDY 2 para 4.04). If, for example, a superior feus out lots of land on which buildings are to be erected according to a uniform plan, one feuar may in certain circumstances object to another feuar breaching the feuing conditions. The breach must affect him directly in some way, for instance by damaging his amenity. If it is stated in the title that certain things may be done only with the permission of the superior, however, other vassals may not object to these things if the superior's permission is obtained. Otherwise the fact that a superior acquiesces in a breach of the conditions is of no consequence in a question between vassals.

Altering and discharging conditions
2.10 A superior may alter or discharge feuing conditions, though, if other vassals have a right to object to a breach, their consent must be obtained. In return for waiving conditions, the superior may demand a lump payment or, indeed, any other consideration he thinks he can obtain but not, since the 1974 act, any increase in feu duty or other periodic payment or the imposition of such a payment. This system led to a situation in which desirable alterations or developments could be held up by a superior intent on getting the best price he can for waiving conditions which the work would infringe. This has finally led to statutory reform in the shape of the Conveyancing and Feudal Reform (Scotland) Act, 1970. Under sections 1 and 2 of the act the Lands Tribunal has power to vary or discharge any 'land obligation', (including feuing conditions and rights such as servitudes) which for a variety of reasons has become unreasonable, or unduly burdensome compared with any benefit it might bring, or the existence of which impedes some reasonable use of the land. This includes powers formerly held by a sheriff (LEGAL STUDY 2 para 2.04) under the Housing (Scotland) Act 1966 to allow the division of a single dwelling-house into two or more dwellings in breach of the feuing conditions, and the sheriff's power has thus ended. The Lands Tribunal has power to order payment of compensation and to add or substitute different provisions. It is of course still open to the parties to come to a private arrangement and there may be situations in which such an arrangement is more convenient than an application to the Tribunal.

Leases
2.11 A proprietor may lease his property to another, the basis of the contract being that the tenant has the right to occupy and make use of the property in return for payment of rent. There are numerous statutory provisions regulating leases of various kinds, mainly by restricting rents or providing some degree of security of tenure for the tenant. It is not proposed to deal with this subject in the present article in any detail.

Business tenancies
2.12 It should be noted, however, that the statutory provisions relating to security of tenure in business tenancies which apply in England (LEGAL STUDY 6 para 7.01 *et seq*), do not extend to Scotland. Thus the architect in Scotland who rents his office premises relies wholly on his contract with

his landlord for security of tenure, there being no corresponding Scottish legislation.

Surveys

2.13 The responsibilities of Scottish architects with regard to surveys are the same as for English architects (LEGAL STUDY 6 para 6.12 *et seq*).

3 Other restrictions of corporeal heritable property

3.01 Apart from any restrictions in his title, numerous other restrictions, both statutory and otherwise, may affect the proprietor of heritable property.

Statutory restrictions

3.02 It is not proposed to enter into the statutory restrictions in detail, but obvious examples of these are the Town and Country Planning Acts and the numerous statutes and regulations governing compulsory purchase (LEGAL STUDY 12). In addition various bodies have power to enter land or premises compulsorily (LEGAL STUDY 10). The Burgh Police (Scotland) Acts and the Public Health (Scotland) Acts prohibit the carrying on of a large number of activities, defined as statutory nuisances, on various kinds of property. A proprietor is also subject to building regulations administered by the appropriate local authority in respect of any building operations he may wish to carry out (LEGAL STUDY 14).

3.03 In addition the occupier of premises is obliged under the Occupiers' Liability (Scotland) Act 1960 to take reasonable care to see that persons entering the premises (which include land and other types of property) do not suffer injury owing to the state of the premises. His failure to do so may result in his being liable in negligence.

Common structures

3.04 In his use of his property the proprietor may also have to take into account the interests of his neighbours in a variety of ways. Where there is a common gable or dividing wall between two properties, either proprietor may object to the other carrying out operations which may be injurious to it, since it is common property. Where the property is a flatted or tenement building in which each house is owned separately, each proprietor has a common interest in the property outwith his own, so far as necessary for his support and shelter. Thus although the external walls of each property belong to individual proprietors, they may not interfere with them in such a way as to endanger the other properties. Similarly each proprietor is sole owner of his floors and ceilings, down to the mid-point of the joists, but must not interfere with them in such a way as to weaken his neighbour's floor or ceiling. The roof of a tenement property belongs to the owner of the top storey, but all proprietors in the building have a common interest in seeing that it is properly maintained and they may compel the owner to keep it in repair and to refrain from damaging it. Common stairs and passages are the common property of all to whose premises they form an access, and all are obliged to maintain them. If alterations to common property or the roof are contemplated it is often (though not always) necessary to obtain the consent of all proprietors. Clients should be advised to consult their solicitors who can check the feudal titles and, if necessary, attempt to obtain consents.

3.05 These rules apply to all tenement property in Scotland, unless, as frequently happens, there is express provision to the contrary in the titles (see para 2.06 *et seq*), in which case the provisions in the titles prevail over the common law rules. A check on the feudal titles by the client's solicitor should reveal feuing conditions which may affect design.

Natural rights

3.06 A proprietor may also have to take account of servitude rights and natural rights of his neighbours or others. Natural rights arise independently of any separate contract or title, through ownership of the land. They include right of support of land. Thus a proprietor may not quarry up to the boundary of his land if this would lead to subsidence of his neighbour's land. He is not entitled to interfere with a stream flowing through his land in such a way as to change its natural flow as it comes to his neighbour's land, since all the riparian proprietors have a common interest in the stream and may object if they are deprived of its natural flow. He may not carry on operations on his property which constitute a 'nuisance', ie which interfere with his neighbour's right to the comfortable enjoyment of his property. What is or is not a nuisance at common law depends on the nature of the neighbourhood, but it may consist of excessive noise or foul smells. If a nuisance has existed without challenge for a period of 20 years or more, however, it cannot be objected to.

Servitudes

3.07 A servitude, in contrast to a natural right, is founded on agreement, whether express or implied. A servitude may be positive or negative; a positive servitude entitles the person who has right to the servitude to do certain things, such as obtaining access to his property over his neighbour's; a negative servitude entitles one proprietor to insist that another refrains from certain acts, for example erecting buildings over a certain height. Property may be subject to many different kinds of servitude, including servitudes of support, stillicide (which entitles the proprietor of property to let rainwater from his own house fall on his neighbour's ground) and of light, affecting mainly urban property, and servitudes of way or access, pasturage and the drawing or conducting of water, affecting land.

Express or implied servitudes

3.08 Servitudes may be constituted either by express agreement, which may be followed by recording in the Register of Sasines so that the servitude appears in the title, or by implied agreement. For example where A sells part of his land to B and the only means of access is over A's land, there is an implied agreement that B has a servitude right of access over A's land. Positive servitudes may also be constituted by uninterrupted use for a period of 20 years, and may lapse if not exercised for that period. Negative servitudes lapse only if a breach is allowed to continue for 20 years without interruption.

Defeating acquisition of implied servitudes

3.09 Servitudes roughly correspond to easements in England. Methods of preventing easements being obtained by prescription (ie long use) are discussed in LEGAL STUDY 6 (paras 4.08 and 4.13) but these are not applicable in Scotland to servitudes. However, many of the matters which are subjects of servitudes, including support, stillicide and light, are within the provisions of the Scottish Building Regulations (LEGAL STUDY 14) which are much more comprehensive and detailed than the English ones. In most cases, the regulations prevent new buildings being designed so that their proprietors acquire onerous servitudes by implication over their neighbours' properties.

Rights of way

3.10 Land may be subject to a public right of way, which is a right for members of the public to pass by a definite route over land, from one public place to another. Such a right is almost invariably constituted by use for a period of 20 years, and lapses if not used for that period.

3.11 The Prescription and Limitation (Scotland) Act 1973 now gives in one statute the various periods of occupation or use required to set up rights over land, from ownership to rights of way, and conversely the periods of non-use which will defeat claims, for example, of servitude.

4 Incorporeal heritable property

4.01 This type of property consists, broadly speaking, of rights over heritage. Servitudes are one example, and rights to leases and feu duties are others. Security rights over land are another, as for example the right of a building society over property on the security of which it has granted a mortgage (LEGAL STUDY 6 para 6.11).

5 Corporeal moveable property

5.01 Ownership of moveable property does not depend, as does that of heritage, on possession of a documentary title. The possessor of an article is presumed to be the owner in the absence of proof to the contrary. A person is the legal possessor of an article even if he has placed it in the hands of some other person who is his agent or servant, or whom he places in the position of custodier of the property for some reason. Thus a person taking a car to a garage for repair puts the garage in the position of custodier and does not in the eyes of the law lose possession of his car. Accordingly he continues to be the presumed owner. Similarly if an article is on hire, the legal possessor is the person who hires it out and not the person to whom it is hired.

6 Incorporeal moveable property

6.01 This type of property consists of rights which are not, generally speaking, directly connected with heritage. Shares in a limited company and a partner's interest in his firm (LEGAL STUDY 3) are both moveable, even though the company or firm may own heritage. Other examples are rights to debts or rights under contracts. Trade names and trade marks are further legal examples, as are rights to designs and copyright (LEGAL STUDY 11).

AJ Legal
Handbook

Section 5
Arbitration

Legal study 8

Arbitration

This study describes the nature of arbitration, arbitration procedure and making awards. It also discusses problems of being an expert professional witness at arbitrations. This is how most architects are involved in arbitration. The final section discussing differences between English and Scots arbitration law is essential reading for anyone involved in an arbitration in Scotland

1 Nature of arbitration

1.01 The settlement of disputes by reference to arbitration, originally governed by the rules of common law, was a practice adopted by merchants and traders many years before it first received Parliamentary recognition under the Arbitration Act of 1697. Common law arbitrations of this kind are today regulated by the Arbitration Act 1950 which provides a general code for all written arbitration agreements between disputing or potentially disputing parties. Of more recent origin is the introduction of statutory legislation in a very wide variety of fields with special provisions which often exclude wholly or in part those of the 1950 Act and substitute their own codes of procedure and practice.

1.02 Arbitrations, to use the term in its broadest sense, include not only those of the kind with which architects are most familiar, and which arise under the standard building contracts, but also the various forms of land tribunals, and industrial tribunals which have become so common a feature of the present time. Except in the quasi-judicial role he plays in the administration of every building contract, not every architect has either the interest or the capacity to arbitrate on the disputes of others. However, he may never know when he is likely to be called upon to do so; or whether he should be involved, on behalf of his clients, in such a dispute. It is more likely that he may be concerned directly as an expert witness in public or private hearings, or on planning inquiries and similar tribunals where the rules of evidence and procedure differ only marginally from an arbitration hearing. All these possibilities are anticipated in the RIBA Conditions of Engagement (S.4.80) as follows: 'For qualifying to give evidence, settling proofs, conferences with solicitors and counsel, attendance in Court or at arbitration or town planning inquiries, or before other tribunals, for services in connection with litigation, and for arbitration . . .' One and all of these serve to emphasise the importance of being prepared beforehand with a reasonably wide knowledge of the law and practice of arbitration.

What is arbitration

1.03 Arbitration has been defined as 'a method of settling disputes and differences between two or more parties by which such disputes are referred to one or more persons nominated for the purpose. These disputes are determined after a hearing in a quasi-judicial manner, either instead of having recourse to an action at law or, by order of the Court, after such an action has been commenced.' The features to note in this definition are:
1 There must be a real dispute, and not a mere difference of opinion.

2 There must be an agreement between the parties to refer the dispute to one or more specially nominated persons for hearing and settlement.
3 It must be the intention that the parties settle their differences in this way other than in the Courts of Law.
It might appear that this last point would infer an intention to override the authority of the Courts, and so be contrary to the rule of English Law that nothing may be done to oust their jurisdiction, or to interfere with justice and public policy. Accordingly, arbitration clauses must be so worded as to ensure that this authority is maintained; for instance, any provision that parties may not have recourse at all to a Court of Law is void. (The Arbitration Act 1950, S.4(1) does not prevent a person bringing a Court action but it gives his opponent an opportunity to commence arbitration proceedings in the first instance.)

Reference of arbitration

1.04 A 'reference' to arbitration may originate in one of the following ways:
1 By agreement between the parties—voluntarily.
2 By requirements of a Statute—legal mandate.
3 By order of the Court—compulsorily.

1.05 A voluntary agreement will be made by the mutual consent of the parties to refer disputes when they arise, or in anticipation of the possibility of dispute at a future time. Agreements of this nature, as with any other form of contract are open to variation and determination by the parties themselves (see LEGAL STUDY 1 para 3). They may be made orally and informally, but as the Arbitration Act excludes all but written agreements, oral agreements are unenforceable by the Courts, and enjoy none of the advantages and safeguards of the Arbitration Act. They must consequently rely upon the rules of common law, and not upon the provisions of a statute, with the initial handicap that they lack evidence of precise terms. In practice, therefore, it is usual for the parties either to subscribe to a separate agreement concerning the mode of settling any differences—actual or possible, or to arrange for the inclusion of an arbitration clause in their main contract, as is done in the RIBA Standard Form of Building Contract. Either method ensures the statutory support of the Arbitration Act 1950 with its code governing procedures, and the powers and duties of nominated arbitrators.

1.06 By requirements of Statutes. Provision for settlement of disputes by arbitration, or indeed by any other means, may be made by Statute or Statutory Instruments. Some Statutes often accept, with or without exceptions or variation, the general application of the Arbitration Act 1950. Others totally exclude the operation of the Act by special provisions in the Statute itself, as, for instance, does the Agricultural Holdings Act 1948. In circumstances where a dispute is referred to arbitration under a Statute which embodies a special procedure, the general rule is that the arbitration clauses in the Statute may override the Arbitration Act, but only to the extent that there is any inconsistency between them (Arbitration Act 1950. Section 31 (1)).

1.07 By Order of Court. Under powers derived from the Judicature (Consolidation) Act 1925, where an action is pending or is at any stage in the High Court, a judge may refer it to an Official Referee for Inquiry (See Order 36 A, R.S.C. 1962). More recently the County Courts Act, 1959, empowers a judge with the consent of the parties to refer any proceedings to arbitration. Anyone with the slightest doubts about the judicial nature of an arbitration hearing, or the arbitrator's authority, should be reassured by the numerous references in the Arbitration Act 1950 to the supervisory powers of the Courts in cases of difficulty, if any need arises for legal advice and guidance on rules of law and where there is any adverse conduct of the arbitration proceedings.

Enforcement of Arbitration Agreement
1.08 Refusal to settle a dispute by arbitration, where there exists an agreement by free consent of the parties to do so, is a breach of contract for which the remedies of the civil law may, and should, be invoked by either party to that contract. The decision to take action rests with the individual who considers himself aggrieved.

Arbitration, conciliation and valuation
1.09 It is necessary to distinguish arbitration from conciliation and valuation. Arbitration is always a judicial process which must have regard to the fundamental rules laid down by the Courts, particularly those relating to evidence. In arbitration there must first be a dispute. The parties have agreed that the arbitrator shall determine all matters of fact and law referred to him and are bound by the final decision made in his award. Should the parties not comply with his decision, it may be enforced in the same manner as a judgement of the Court, ie refusal to conform becomes contempt of court.

Conciliation
1.10 In conciliation, the role of the conciliator is simply to bring the parties together in an endeavour to promote the settlement of a complaint or dispute without the necessity of reference to a court or tribunal. Unlike the arbitrator, he makes no decision on his own but merely assists the parties themselves to agree, and has no statutory powers of enforcement. Recently, by the provisions of the Industrial Relations Act, 1971, the Secretary of State for Employment has been empowered to appoint Conciliation Officers (Section 146). These officers have been given statutory powers to effect the conciliation of parties in industrial disputes. These powers do not apply to simple contracts where the dispute does not involve industrial action.

Valuation
1.11 The difference between arbitration and valuation rests upon the distinction between the quasi-judicial nature of the former in the consideration of the facts presented and, in the case of valuation where the person appointed to make a decision does so as the result of his own skill and experience, usually without hearing any evidence. A valuation arises from an agreement by two parties to be bound by the decision

of a third party with the object of *preventing a dispute* arising. On the other hand an arbitration depends entirely upon the *existence of a dispute* which must be settled by this form of judicial inquiry. The basic effect of the distinction is that the Arbitration Act 1950 does not apply to valuation. An arbitrator's award may be enforced by the Courts, and he himself may not be sued for negligence; whereas the valuer has no such statutory protection, and could be liable in an action for negligence.

When is arbitration available?
1.12 It is not always easy to decide whether a 'dispute or difference' has arisen between the parties. The terms of the contract, the arbitration clause or any written submission must be carefully examined, as not every dispute is necessarily subject to a reference to arbitration. Clause 35 of the RIBA form is particularly comprehensive, but architects should note that under clause 30 (7) the final certificate is conclusive evidence 'in any proceedings ... (whether by arbitration under clause 35 of these conditions or otherwise) that the works have been properly carried out and completed'. Arbitration under the RIBA form is invoked only by one party serving on the other a 'notice of dispute', so architect/arbitrators should rarely be troubled by questions as to whether a dispute or difference has arisen.

1.13 Certain matters are not suitable for arbitration even under clause 35. Where a party to a contract refuses to complete, the proper remedy is for the plaintiff to sue for damages in the courts, or to ask the courts for specific performance (an order to the defaulting party requiring him to fulfil his part of the contract which is rarely granted in building contract cases). Similarly, failure to pay a certificate is a matter for action in the courts.

Parties to arbitration
1.14 Only the parties to a contract containing an arbitration clause are normally allowed to go to arbitration. Certainly no other person can be compelled to submit to an arbitration but there is no reason why third or more parties cannot submit to arbitration if everyone agrees. A major disadvantage of the present building contract arbitration clause is that it may be necessary to mount a series of eliminating arbitrations and actions in the courts before for example a building owner can recover his losses from all persons who have contributed to his damage. Under the RIBA form, for example, an arbitration might be begun between employer and contractor when the contractor might prove that fault lies with the architect or with a nominated sub-contractor. It is then necessary for the employer to start an action against the architect to recover his losses in so far as the arbitrator has found in the contractor's favour.

Capacity of arbitrators
1.15 Although the parties to a contract are free to choose their own arbitrator, where there is a written agreement section 6 of the Arbitration Act 1950 applies, and such agreement, in the absence of contrary intentions, is deemed to include reference to a sole arbitrator. The principal categories of people who may not act as arbitrators are bankrupts, minors, persons of unsound mind and those who are deaf, dumb or blind, persons convicted of perjury, any person who has an interest in, or a bias against the parties, or any part of the proceedings.

1.16 It is often difficult to decide what is or is not included in the last category. If the parties appointing the arbitrator are both fully aware of the arbitrator's interest, and they still appoint him, the courts will not intervene in the appointment. There are several leading cases and the reader is referred to them in text books on the subject.

Jurisdiction of arbitrators

1.17 Every architect appointed as an arbitrator should ensure that he is competent to adjudicate the facts in dispute, and in this sense 'competent' means that such matters are within his jurisdiciton. An arbitration, being a private tribunal, is not open to members of the public as is a court of law, and the arbitrator must see that all procedure, evidence, and everything relating to the hearing before him is carried out correctly.

Arbitration and architects

1.18 It is not possible to make any accurate assessment of how many arbitrations are held, mainly because a good feature of arbitration is the privacy under which it takes place. However, it may be observed that the arbitration work which goes on is much greater than is realised, and also that it is on the increase. It is equally clear that architects are frequently in demand for this type of work, especially where the reference involves a standard form of building contract where their expert knowledge and experience is an obvious advantage. Expertise is seldom enough. The successful arbitrator rests his authority not so much on his technical knowledge as on his judicial capacity to control the proceedings before him, to deal fairly, and to exclude from his mind all considerations which affect the case except those derived from the evidence. The RIBA have published an invaluable booklet *The architect as arbitrator* which is of equal interest to all arbitrators, summarising most of the main points. The Appendices print in full the Arbitration Act 1950, and three Forms of Application for Appointment of an arbitrator.

Disputes between architects and clients

1.19 Rather special problems arise when architects and their clients are in dispute, possibly over fees and other matters. Provisions for disputes and arbitration are made under Sections 7.4 and 7.5 of the RIBA Conditions of Engagement (see LEGAL STUDY 17 para 13.01).

Partnership disputes

1.20 Cases occur on the construction of the articles of a partnership. The law of partnership is an intricate subject (LEGAL STUDY 3 para 2), and the architect-arbitrator is not advised to deal with such cases without legal assistance. Most articles of partnership contain an arbitration clause, for it would be injurious for everyone to know that partners are at odds; and partners usually prefer to place their disputes before a private tribunal rather than before the public courts.

2 Procedure

Appointment of arbitrators

2.01 In arbitration agreements which generally concern architects, there is either an express clause for the parties to appoint an arbitrator, or the method of his appointment may be prescribed in the agreement. This mode of appointment is similar to the procedure laid down in clause 35 of the RIBA contract. Where there is no provision at all in the agreement on the number and appointment of arbitrators, the parties are bound by section 6 of the Arbitration Act 1950. If the parties cannot agree on the appointment of a single arbitrator under section 6, the court will make the appointment on the application of one of the parties (section 10 of the Act).

2.02 In most cases, therefore, architects are appointed as sole arbitrators. The arbitration agreement should also make provision for events such as the death, incapacity, refusal to act, or incapability to act of the appointed arbitrator. The parties who appoint the original arbitrator should also nominate his successor, or apply to the RIBA president to fill the vacancy. In the event of a complete deadlock the court may be asked to make a fresh appointment. An arbitrator should not be appointed verbally. The procedure adopted by the RIBA when the president is asked by the parties to an arbitration agreement (or under the provisions of clause 35) to appoint an arbitrator is as follows. The RIBA asks the parties to supply brief details of the dispute and to complete an application form. This form contains an undertaking which protects the proposed arbitrator, because it asks for a guarantee of payment of his fees, or for the security to be provided for them. The guarantee in the RIBA form does not, of course, cover a defaulting party who refuses to pay any fees at all. But in any action brought in the courts the RIBA application form would be strong evidence against a defaulting party. When the parties have completed the RIBA application form (it is always preferable that both parties to the contract should sign but not always possible) it is returned to the RIBA and either a senior member or the legal officer suggests the names of three competent architects to the president. If he approves these, they are approached in the suggested order. The first nominee to accept is formally appointed and sent the application form which also contains his appointment and space for him to sign acceptance.
Sometimes the parties may request an arbitrator with special qualifications, and the RIBA maintains lists of solicitors, barristers, quantity surveyors, engineers and accountants who are appointed in such circumstances. They can also be appointed when it appears to the president that a person with such qualifications would be most appropriate having regard to the nature of the dispute disclosed by the applicants.

Preparing for arbitration

2.03 As soon as an architect has accepted his nomination as an arbitrator (ie as soon as he signs the acceptance form sent him by the RIBA), the procedure of arbitration is set into action. Prudent arbitrators write to the parties at once to confirm their appointment. They should, at the same time, state the scale of fees they intend to charge, for this may have a decisive effect on whether or not the parties wish to proceed further (para 3.14).

2.04 Where the arbitrator has accepted appointment otherwise than from the RIBA president, one or other of the parties should deposit the arbitration agreement with the arbitrator, or state the main causes of the dispute in outline as is generally done on the RIBA application form. An arbitrator (unless legally qualified) should not at the outset give his opinion on points of law to the parties, nor should he ask the parties to produce documents (other than the outline of material facts in dispute) to attempt to construe their contents before the hearing.

2.05 The next stage is for the arbitrator to make a full and searching study of the terms of the agreement, and to achieve a clear conception of the intention of the parties, and the matter, or matters, in dispute. Only disputes which arise out of a particular contract or contracts can be included in the reference.

2.06 The arbitrator should be careful not to exceed his authority when he studies the arbitration agreement, for it was held in *Walford Baker & Co v Macfie & Sons* (1915) 84 LJKB 2221, that any consideration of a contract other than the contract referred to the arbitrator by the parties constituted legal misconduct. If the matters in the dispute, or the arbitration itself, have arisen under an Act of Parliament, that Act governs everything, including the duties and powers of the arbitrator. An example of an arbitration dispute within the provisions of a statute which concerns architects is a dispute between owners of adjoining buildings sited in the metropolis which is governed by the provisions of the London Building Acts. It was recently decided in *Crawford v Prowting* (1972) 2.*W.L.R.*749 that in the absence of a specific order by an arbitrator, there is no duty on a claimant to proceed with his claim expeditiously.

The hearing

2.07 Although the arbitrator has absolute power to decide how a case should be heard, the procedure usually followed, including rules of evidence (para 4.08) and examination of witnesses (para 2.08), is the same as that used in civil actions in the courts. The parties may however decide by prior agreement that the arbitrator should not be bound by such rules.

2.08 Where there is difficulty in deciding which party is the claimant, the one who has to prove his case is entitled to be heard first. Procedure is generally as follows:
1 The claimant opens his case, either alone or by counsel. If there is a counterclaim, he opens his defence to it at the same time.
2 The claimant or his counsel calls and examines his own witnesses who may be cross-examined* by the respondent, or his counsel. If a witness is cross-examined, the claimant may re-examine him but only upon matters raised in cross-examination.
3 The respondent opens his case, either alone, or by counsel.
4 The respondent or his counsel calls and examines his own witnesses, who are in turn cross-examined by the claimant, or by his counsel. If a witness is cross-examined the respondent or his counsel may re-examine him but only upon matters raised in cross-examination.
5 The respondent, or his counsel, sums up his case to the arbitrator.
6 The claimant, or his counsel, replies to the summing up. Thus the party who has the right to begin, also has the last word.

Legal representation

2.09 If one of the parties is represented by counsel or solicitor and his opponent is not, it is best that the unrepresented party ask the arbitrator for an adjournment so that his own legal adviser may be appointed. If the arbitrator refuses such a request, his subsequent award might be set aside on the ground of unfairness (*Whatley v Morland* (1833) 2 Dowl 249).

2.10 Under no circumstances should an arbitrator hear or receive evidence from one of the parties behind the back of the other party. If he does get a letter from one party, he should immediately inform his opponent, otherwise his award may be set aside (*Harvey v Shelton* (1844) 7 Beav 455).

Viewing property
2.11 An arbitrator is not bound to view property which is the subject of a dispute, but may do so at his own discretion.

Arbitrators should be prepared to do so, but both parties should be present, for taking view of property is real evidence —ie first evidence and not hearsay (*Munday v Black* (1861) 30 LJCP 193).

Other rules of conduct

2.12 Over and above the necessity to follow the rules of evidence there are certain other rules of conduct which the arbitrator must observe:
1 To act fairly to both parties and observe the ordinary rules of natural justice. For example the arbitrator must never hear one party in the absence of the other.
2 To decide on matters in dispute and no more.
3 To comply strictly with the terms of the submission or agreement.
4 To decide the issue according to the legal rights of the parties.
5 Not to delegate arbitral duties (unless the parties agree) to a stranger for the legal maxim *Delagatus non protest delegare* prevails in all arbitrations. An arbitrator may, however, consult persons of skill and knowledge and reports from experts. He may also seek advice on drawing up his award, on the conduct of the reference and on general principles of law, but not upon the actual questions of law in the case (unless he is also a lawyer, when he may put a point of law to a learned friend).

3 The award

Basic rules for an award

3.01 There are 10 basic rules which are essential for an award to be valid, irrespective of the provisions of the Arbitration Act 1950:
1 The award should comply with the conditions of the arbitration agreement.
2 Unless the parties wish otherwise, the award should be in writing.
3 The arbitrator's decision must be certain, and not ambiguous. For example, the parties' performance of the award must be certain: the amount of money to be paid must be specified; specific explanation must be given on the performance of directions; the time of performance of the award must be set out. An award is uncertain if it is not in the form as required by section 26 of the Act (*Marguilies Brothers Ltd v Dafnis Thomaides & Co* (UK) *Ltd* 1958, 1 WLR 398).
4 The award must not be ambiguous in any of its parts.
5 The award must be within the scope of the arbitration agreement. For example, if an arbitrator has been asked to define boundaries of land, he need not investigate questions of title (*Doe d Lord Carlisle v Bailiff of Morpeth* (1810) 3 Taunt 378).
6 The award must contain all matters referred to in the agreement, but must not go outside it (*Duke of Beaufort and Swansea Harbour Trustees* (1860), 29 LJCP (2d) 582). For example, when there is a claim for several sums, and the arbitrator awards one lump sum, this is valid, unless the agreement deems otherwise. In a leading case, an arbitrator was asked to decide on certain defects in a building, and what was required to restore it, and to settle claims for extras on such restoration. The arbitrator awarded a fixed sum to settle all matters, and did not give any reason for the cause of the defects. It was held that his award was bad, because all matters in the dispute had not been decided (*re Rider and Fisher* 1837).
7 The award must finally settle the dispute between the parties. It must deal with all matters referred to the arbitrator by the parties as set out in the agreement. The award will be bad should the arbitrator delegate his judicial authority to a

---

* Cross-examination is interrogation of one party's witnesses by the other party or his counsel.

counsel who may be briefed to appear at the hearing; and it may be used by counsel not only in the examination of his own witness, but also in the cross-examination of an expert witness who appears for his opponent. Accordingly, proof of evidence should be set out so that learned counsel can bring forward the principal matters in issue without any difficulty for the parties at the hearing. For much the same reasons, the expert witness should have direct discussion with learned counsel on technical points; although such a meeting is generally arranged through the solicitor who briefs counsel.

4.07 It may be feasible and, if so, convenient for copies of the proof of evidence to be distributed and, subject always to the arbitrator's approval, be read by the witness at the hearing. Alternatively they may be used as notes from which counsel will direct his questions to the witnesses and which they will answer accordingly. Documentary evidence is based upon well-known rules of procedure. It opens with a statement of the witness's name, address and qualifications, with reference to any special matters which suggest why he should be suitably qualified to represent his side. Thereafter, it proceeds to give an interpretation of the subject matter with any facts relevant to his witness, eg a day or time when he visited the site or property. Nothing descredits a witness and his testimony more easily than an admission that he has not seen the site! The expert witness should try to impress on the arbitrators his own process of reasoning and persuade the tribunal to listen to his own words before he leads up to his answer. His 'proof' of evidence must be clear, concise and precise; he must avoid technical detail of any kind except where it is absolutely essential. In its drafting, he must always bear in mind that he will be subjected to searching examination and cross-examination on its contents, and particularly on the professional opinions he has put forward in his evidence.

Rules of evidence

4.08 In every Court of Law the rules of evidence, ie procedures in examination, re-examination, and cross-examination, are well known and must always be applied. In principle, these procedures and rules apply in nearly every form of legal tribunal including arbitration hearings (unless the parties to the 'reference' have otherwise agreed). They must be observed in arbitration hearings as in other legal tribunals whether at a public or private hearing—or at the discretion exercised by the person in charge of the proceedings. In consequence it is possible for the rules of evidence to be less formal and complicated in arbitration than in the public courts. Thus, subject to the accepted rules as to what questions may or may not be asked, and as to what documents may be produced, the admissibility of any question is for the decision of a judge in a court of record and therefore for an arbitrator at an arbitration hearing.

4.09 The Law of Evidence is too complicated for consideration at any length in this chapter. All that can be attempted is to outline the general principles and to emphasise that no professional person or layman should contemplate the task of accepting the post of an arbitrator unless he knows fairly well the rules of evidence. His conduct of the proceedings and validity of his ultimate award may depend upon it. Full details are to be found in William H. Gill's 'The Law of Arbitration'. This work was originally published in 1965 under the title 'Evidence and Procedure in Arbitration'.*

* The Evidence Act 1938, the Civil Evidence Act 1968 and the Civil Evidence Act 1972, all apply to arbitrations and their procedure.

4.10 There are two main categories of evidence; primary and secondary. Primary evidence denotes the best evidence available as being that of persons who have directly observed facts or heard statements, and it includes original documents. Where the best evidence is not procurable, secondary evidence will be allowed, eg certified copies of statements or documents, etc. Evidence may be rejected which cannot be adequately proved. The principle in regard to acceptance of secondary evidence generally is to allow it only if the original document is in possession of an opponent, or a stranger to the case, because it has been lost, damaged, or cannot be brought to the hearing because it is physically impossible to do so.

Hearsay evidence

4.11 At common law hearsay evidence was not admissible. However, under the Civil Evidence Act 1968 both oral and documentary hearsay statements are generally admissible in civil proceedings subject to certain procedural safeguards.

Leading questions

4.12 Every party, or his counsel, when he examines his own witnesses (ie examination-in-chief) must be careful to avoid putting a leading question; that is to say questions which by their form suggest the answer desired. In practice, there is little for the arbitrator to query because if leading questions are constantly asked counsel for the other side will soon rise to put in an objection! Only in cross-examination are leading questions allowed; and there are, in fact, certain exceptions to the rule that they must not be put in examination-in-chief or in re-examination, namely:
1 On introductory matters such as the name, occupation and address of the witness.
2 On matters not in dispute.
3 To identify persons or things, and
4 To assist the memory of the witness.
Note that in re-examination questions must usually be confined to matters raised in cross-examination, though the arbitrator may consent to fresh issues being raised by either party if the other is agreeable; but he must be careful that in doing so he does not in any way extend the terms of his 'reference'. In the courts questions may not be asked which introduce wholly new matter. In cross-examination the rules on leading questions are somewhat relaxed and may be freely asked as long as they do not wilfully mislead by mis-statement or false assumption. Vexatious questions must not be asked or any that are irrelevant to the case. Questions as to opinion and belief are not generally admissible.

Giving evidence

4.13 Another important point for witnesses to note is that it is very helpful to have a brief conference with counsel or solicitor prior to the hearing, to have a clear understanding of the difference between examination-in-chief and cross-examination, for in the former the advocate will not ask the witness any leading questions.

4.14 In giving evidence at the hearing, the most vital matter for the expert witness is not to say too much, for it is often more prudent to say less, and confine answers to 'yes' or 'no'. Witnesses should pay close attention to the advocate, for many witnesses give rambling answers as a result of inattention to the advocate's questions. In the case of double-barrelled questions, witnesses should attempt to break them down themselves, and answer them separately: 'To the first part of your question my answer is . . . and to the second part of your question my answer is . . .'.

4.15 The witness should keep his sentences, and his statements, as brief as possible. Even in a heated moment of argument, such as when the advocate is offensive, the witness should remain calm, and give a concise answer. The arbitrator has to see that irrelevant questions are not put to witnesses in arbitration cases.

5 Arbitrations under standard building contracts

The RIBA form
5.01 The arbitration clause (no 35) of the RIBA Standard Form of Contract constitutes a written agreement within the terms of the Arbitration Act 1950, with provisions for reference to a sole arbitrator. A number of its aspects are exceptional to the general rules in the interests of the special needs of the very complex building contract, particularly in respect of arrangements for the immediate settlement of certain matters during the progress of the works as a safeguard against delay. Important features are that any question arising from the contract may be the subject matter of a 'reference'; and no matters are excluded because under the provisions of the contract they are solely at the discretion of the architect; and in no case is a decision of the architect necessary before going to arbitration.

Alternatives to arbitration
5.02 As it stands there is nothing in the agreement to prevent the parties from trying to settle their differences without going to arbitration; this is where the conciliatory efforts of the architect can, and so often do, play an important part. Nor is there anything therein to prevent either party referring their dispute to the courts; an alternative which might indeed be more straightforward when the main and possibly the only issue is simply a question of law. Nevertheless the courts are quite consistent in their view that, if there is an agreement to refer disputes to arbitration, then the parties must settle them that way.

5.03 Clause 35 (1) provides in a general way for any disputes likely to arise between employer (or his architect on his behalf) and the contractor about the interpretation of the contract or anything arising out of it, either (1) during the progress, or (2) after completion, or (3) on abandonment of the works. It should be noted here that 'completion' and 'abandonment' has reference to the *works* and is not expressed to have reference to the *contract*. If a contract is abandoned or determined all its provisions go, including those as to arbitration. It is provided for by clauses 25 and 26, however, that the employment of the contractor may be determined and not the whole of the contract. In such circumstances the arbitration clause is still applicable.

Instant arbitration
5.04 It is the general intention, in order to avoid any adverse effects upon the progress of the works, that arbitration should not take place until after practical completion. Clause 35 (2) refers to certain specific types of dispute, eg questions whether or not the issue of an instruction by the architect is empowered by the conditions, or whether a certificate has been improperly withheld; in addition to the more obvious problems which arise in the event of the death or resignation of the architect or quantity surveyor. All these are important reasons for an immediate settlement in order that the contract may proceed without undue interruption and for which Clause 35 makes special arrangements under the heading of 'instant arbitration'. (See also LEGAL STUDIES 4 and 5 and LEGAL STUDY 8 on Scottish arbitrations.)

5.05 The general pattern of the agreements used for engineering and Government contracts have many similarities to the RIBA clause 35, and the provisions of the Arbitration Act 1950 apply to each; in consequence the arbitration processes already discussed are the same. For present purposes the important differences between the agreements may be quite briefly stated.

The Institute of Civil Engineers form
5.06 Clause 66 of the Institute of Civil Engineers General Conditions of Contract* form is entitled 'Settlement of Disputes' and as it opens with its more significant variation the first two sentences are worth quoting in full. 'If any dispute or difference of any kind whatsoever shall arise between the Employer or the Engineer and the Contractor in connection with or arising out of the Contract or the carrying out of the Works (whether during the progress of the Works or after their completion and whether before or after the determination abandonment or breach of the Contract) it shall be referred to and settled by the Engineer who shall state his decision in writing and give notice of the same to the Employer and the Contractor. Such decision in respect of every matter so referred shall be final and binding upon the Employer and the Contractor until the completion of the work and shall forthwith be given effect to by the Contractor who shall proceed with the Works with all due diligence whether notice of dissatisfaction is given by him or by the Employer as hereinafter provided or not. . . .'
By RIBA standards the rules for appointment of an arbitrator appear to be designed to discourage rather than encourage any attempt at arbitration. References to a mutually agreed arbitrator may be made if the engineer fails to give his decision . . . 'for a period of three calendar months after being requested to do so, or after either the Employer or the Contractor be dissatisfied with such decisions, etc. . . .' As if to emphasise still further the key position which the engineer holds the final paragraph in Clause 66 (1) (b) states 'that no decision given by the Engineer in accordance with the foregoing provisions shall disqualify him from being called as a witness and giving evidence before an arbitrator on any matter whatsoever relevant to the dispute or difference so referred to the arbitrator as aforesaid.'

Government Contracts form GC/Wks/1†
5.07 Clause 61 of the Government form is short. It purports to provide for arbitration in 'All disputes, differences or questions between the parties to the Contract in respect to any matter arising out of or relating to Condition 51 or as to which the decision or report of the Authority or of any other person is by the Contract expressed to be final and conclusive . . . etc.' The essential difference between this and the RIBA form lies in the scope of the arbitration, which under the RIBA clause 35 is unlimited, whereas the clause 61 of the GC/Wks/1 form specifically excludes a large number of outlawed matters and thereby imposes definite restrictions on the arbitrator's terms of reference in that he may not arbitrate on matters regarding the Authority (as specified in each Contract in the Abstract of Particulars), the Superintending Officer, or the Minister responsible—all of whom have powers of final decision. When arbitration *is* available, unless the parties otherwise agree, the reference shall not take place until after the completion, alleged completion, or abandonment of the works or determination of the contract.

Arbitration in Scotland
5.08 The process of arbitration in Scotland is dealt with

* Fifth Edition (June 1973)
† First Edition (September 1977)

fully in paragraphs 7 below, with particular reference to the 'Scottish Supplement to the RIBA' Schedule of Conditions of Building Contract.

The new GC/Wks/1 Form for Government Contracts, by the addition of clause 61 (4), makes provision—previously lacking—for the application of Scottish Law.

The ICE contract also does so in section 67, as follows: 'If the Works are situated in Scotland the contract shall in all respects be construed and operate as a Scottish Contract and shall be interpreted in accordance with Scots Law (see LEGAL STUDY 2).

6 Summary of advantages and disadvantages of arbitration

6.01 An arbitration often has considerable advantages over an action at law, especially when the dispute involves issues of fact, particularly if these are technical. An arbitration can however be unduly lengthy if the arbitrator, though qualified technically to deal with the issues of fact, finds that there are also complicated questions of law involved. With the consent of the parties, and at their cost, a legal adviser can be engaged to sit with the arbitrator and advise him on legal points, but the decisions even on law must be the arbitrator's and not his adviser's.

6.02 The principal advantages usually claimed for arbitration are:

1 Where a dispute involves technical matters in the main, or when specialist experience of a particular profession or business is involved, an arbitrator with expert knowledge can deal with the questions more expeditiously. Obviously it could take a great deal of time to explain even the most common technical terms to a lay judge but on the other hand an arbitrator will often find that counsel at an arbitration insist on leading the evidence as if the arbitrator had no technical qualifications even if he is an architect. In such circumstances as much time can be wasted as in the courts, but the arbitrator must be careful not to interfere too much with the advocate's presentation of his case.

2 Technical disputes can be dealt with more speedily in arbitration than in the courts. Again this is not always true. While it is not necessary to wait in the queue for a hearing, the speed of the preliminaries is dictated by the enthusiasm of the parties and a reluctant party can delay for a considerable time.

3 The day and place of the hearing can be fixed to suit the convenience of the parties, witnesses, counsel and arbitrator.

4 Proceedings are private and less formal than in the courts.

5 An express provision may be made in the arbitration agreement that the arbitrator may view property in dispute, whereas in the courts this matter is entirely at the discretion of the judge.

6 It is frequently claimed that arbitration is cheaper than litigation but this is rarely likely to be true. The arbitrator has to be paid, the judge does not; the room has to be hired, the court does not. Solicitors, counsel and witnesses cost the same. Arbitrations can also be very lengthy; at the time of writing this article two arbitrations under building and civil engineering contracts have been running for 90 and 110 days respectively.

7 Although arbitration is thought to be definite and final as regards facts, appeals are frequent and if the arbitrator states his award in the form of a Special Case there will have to be hearing before the court. If the matter had been before the court in the first instance the judge could have dealt simultaneously with questions of fact and questions of law. Perhaps

the major disadvantage of arbitration is that already introduced in para 1.14—the inability to call as co-defendants other persons or companies who may have really caused the loss.

6.03 Architects involved in arbitrations as parties, expert witnesses or arbitrators are faced with no easy task. The increasing complexity of the commercial world must lead to an increasing number of arbitrations. The law of arbitration is a very important branch of English law, and it is to be hoped that more architects, and others in similar professions, will devote much more attention to this subject than in the past.

7 Arbitrations in Scotland

7.01 Generally the parties to a contract in Scotland are always entitled, but not compelled, to refer their disputes to the courts for a decision. In cases where they decide to have their disputes solved outside the courts, they are referred to the decision of an arbiter under a process known as arbitration. In modern practice, many commercial contracts contain an arbitration clause, and almost invariably a building contract contains one.

7.02 The process of arbitration in England is clearly defined by the English Arbitration Act, but that Act does not apply to Scotland, apart from clause 4 (2). Because of the protocol set out in the first schedule to the Act, this clause entitles a party to an arbitration to apply to the court to sist (stop) proceedings if the other party starts legal proceedings in court against him during the process of the arbitration. The court is bound to do this unless the judge feels that the arbitration cannot proceed or there is no dispute.

7.03 Until the passing of the Administration of Justice (Scotland) Act 1972 the only statute dealing with arbitrations in Scotland was the Arbitration (Scotland) Act 1894 which consists of seven sections dealing only with the appointment of an arbiter and an oversman in differing circumstances. Section 3 of the 1972 Act, however, in effect gives statutory authority to clause 35 (5) of the Scottish supplement and is in the following terms:

'1 Subject to express provision to the contrary in an agreement to refer to arbitration, the arbiter or oversman may, on the application of a party to the arbitration, and shall, if the Court of Session on such an application so directs, at any stage in the arbitration state a case for the opinion of that Court on any question of law arising in the arbitration.

2 This section shall not apply to an arbitration under any enactment which confers a power to appeal to or state a case for the opinion of a court or tribunal in relation to that arbitration.

3 This section shall not apply to any form of arbitration relating to a trade dispute within the meaning of the Industrial Courts Act 1919 or relating to an industrial dispute within the meaning of the Industrial Relations Act 1971; to any other arbitration arising from a collective agreement within the meaning of the said Act of 1971; or to proceedings before the Industrial Arbitration Board described in section 124 of that Act.

4 This section shall not apply in relation to an agreement to refer to arbitration made before the commencement of this Act.'

Recently there has been a considerable growth in statutory arbitrations under specific Acts of Parliament such as the Workmen's Compensation Acts and the Agricultural Holdings (Scotland) Acts, but this article is concerned only with commercial arbitrations in general and building contract relations in particular to which these statutes do not apply. Such law as exists on commercial arbitrations in Scotland is therefore based on case law and what might loosely be described as 'use and wont'.

Arbitrations under Scottish supplement

7.04 The Scottish supplement adopts the arbitration clause (clause 35) of the Standard Form, but makes a number of important amendments as discussed below (LEGAL STUDY 5 para 2.05).

7.05 The reference in clause 35 (1) of the Standard Form to the president or vice-president of the RIBA where the parties have failed to agree on the appointment of an arbiter is deleted, and the Scottish supplement states that in the case of failure to agree 'the Sheriff of any Sheriffdom in which the works of any part thereof are situated' shall be petitioned to make the appointment. Prior to local government reorganisation in Scotland such petitions were invariably presented to a judge known as the Sheriff-Substitute, but this appointment no longer exists and the responsible judge is now known as the Sheriff. In the case of works covering a large area of ground in one or more Sheriffdoms any Sheriff having jurisdiction can be petitioned.

7.06 The Scottish supplement adds a new clause 35 (4) in the following terms—'The arbiter shall have power to award compensation or damages and expenses to or against any of the parties to the arbitration.' This additional clause is required because in Scots law, although an arbiter probably has implied power to award expenses, he does not, unless expressly given the power to do so, have the right to find either party liable in damages (*Mackay v Leven Commissioners* (1893) 2 LR 1093).

Clause 35 (5)

7.07 Clause 35 (5) has been added in the Scottish supplement in the following terms: 'The law of Scotland shall apply to all arbitrations under these presents and the award of the Arbiter shall be final and binding on the parties provided that at any stage of the arbitration the Arbiter may, and if so requested by either of the parties, shall prepare a statement of facts in a Special Case for the opinion and judgment of the Court of Session on any question or questions of law arising in the arbitration, and both parties to the arbitration shall be bound to concur in presenting to the Court a Special Case in the terms prepared by the Arbiter and in which the statement of facts prepared by him is agreed to by the parties, with such contentions as the parties or either of them may desire to add thereto for the opinion and judgment of the Court; and the Arbiter and the parties to the arbitration shall be bound by the answer or answers returned by the Court of Session, or if the case is appealed to the House of Lords, by the House, to the question or questions of law stated in the case.'
But its importance has been greatly reduced by the passing of the Administration of Justice (Scotland) Act referred to in para 7.03.

7.08 However, when first introduced it provided a new concept for commercial arbitrations in Scotland where it was a well-established part of the law of Scotland that the award of an arbiter was binding in fact and law on the parties and could not be reviewed by the court on its merits however unjust it might seem to be. The chance of an honest error by an arbiter was one of the risks taken by the parties when agreeing to refer their dispute to his decision, and was thus a basic difference between the law in Scotland and England,

in which country the Arbitration Act provided for an appeal to the Court of Appeal on a question of law. Until the passing of the 1972 Act no appeal was possible in Scotland without clause 35 (5) which was introduced to the Scottish supplement so that parties to an arbitration in a building contract could as far as possible be on exactly the same terms as their opposite numbers in England. In spite of the clause the writer is not aware of any arbitration in Scotland since its introduction where one of the parties has taken advantage of its provisions, but it is understood that the arbiter's decision in a recent large building arbitration in Scotland is to be the subject of an appeal to the Court of Session under the provisions of section 3 of the 1972 Act.

Clause 35 (6)

7.09 The Scottish supplement also adds clause 35 (6) in the following terms: 'The arbiter shall be entitled to remuneration and reimbursement of his outlays.'

7.10 This clause is necessary because, at common law in Scotland, an arbiter had no right to remuneration for his services unless he has stipulated his fee before accepting office. At one time this rule was absolute, but it has been modified somewhat by the decision in the case of *McIntyre Brothers v Smith* (1930) SC 129, where is was stated: 'In accordance with general practice, the rule must now be assumed that a professional man undertaking the duties of an arbiter is entitled in the absence of any agreement to the contrary, to be remunerated for his services as arbiter in the same way as he is entitled to receive remuneration for his services in any other professional employment.' In the majority of building arbitrations, where the arbiter is a professional person, his right to a fee is safeguarded by this decision, but this is only a modification of the common law, and a specific right to payment of a fee is desirable, particularly where the arbiter could be a non-professional person.

Clause 35 (7)

7.11 The Scottish supplement adds clause 35 (7) which is in the following terms: 'No action shall lie and no proceedings under this Clause shall be instituted against the Employer unless such action is raised or such proceedings are instituted within three years after the date of the receipt by the Contractor of the priced Bills of Variation. Proceedings shall be deemed to be instituted when an application is made to the Employer for Arbitration in terms of this Clause.'

7.12 When first introduced this clause provided that the three year period was to run from the date of receipt by the contractor of the final measurement, but the present wording was adopted when investigation showed that there was considerable difference of opinion in the industry in Scotland as to precisely what did constitute the final measurement, with the consequent problems of fixing the date for commencement of the three year period. It was thought that the date of receipt of the 'priced bills of variation' could be precisely established but in practice similar difficulties have made themselves obvious and this clause is now under active reconsideration, particularly following the Court of Session case of *John Laing Construction Limited v Livingston Development Corporation* 1975 in which the judge refused a plea of time bar put forward by the Corporation. Furthermore the passing of the Prescriptions and Limitations (Scotland) Act 1973 throws further doubts on the need for a clause of this nature at all.

Importance of using Scottish supplement

7.13 Reference should be made at this point to an important House of Lords case: *James Miller & Partners Ltd v Whitworth Street Estates (Manchester) Ltd* decided in 1970. Briefly the facts of this case were as follows. The contractors were a Scottish company with a registered office in Scotland; the employers were an English company who owned premises in Dumbarton and the contract was under the Standard Form of building contract, with an arbitration clause in terms of clause 35, before the publication of amendments to the clause included in the Scottish Supplement. The employers asked the arbiter, a Scottish architect, to state a case for the decision of the English high court in accordance with the Arbitration Act, but he refused to do so on the gound that it was a Scottish arbitration. The House of Lords decided that the arbitration was to be governed by the Law of Scotland, so that the arbiter could not be required to state a case for the opinion of the English high court (para 3.09).

7.14 As a result of this decision the Joint Contracts Tribunal added clause 35 (5) to the Standard Form with the intention of providing that English law would apply to arbitrations wherever they may take place and should be the proper law of the contract as a whole. However, if the Scottish supplement is employed in any contract the law of Scotland will apply to all arbitrations and will also be the proper law of that particular building contract.

Selection of arbiter

7.15 In Scotland, as an arbiter is in effect a private judge selected by the parties themselves, virtually anybody can be appointed and there are few personal disqualifications that cannot be waived by the parties. It has even been decided that a minor can act as an arbiter. If an arbiter shows himself committed to a certain point of view before taking up the reference he is disqualified, and similarly if he accepts office with a promise to one party that he will do his best for him. In some building contracts, there is an arbitration clause in which the architect himself is appointed as arbiter on all disputes arising under the contract. One would think in such a case that the architect could not approach the question with the completely open mind of an outside person, and moreover although he himself does not have a direct financial interest, he is incidentally involved in the financial outcome. But it has been held repeatedly by the courts in Scotland that employment by one of the parties to the arbitration is no bar to an arbiter acting.

7.16 As noted above (para 7.03) the Arbitration (Scotland) Act deals with the appointment of an arbiter. Prior to the Act, a submission to an un-named arbiter was not competent in Scotland, though this has been completely altered by section 1 of the Act, which permits reference to un-named people or holders of a specific office. Where the parties have failed to agree on the nomination of a single arbiter, section II of the Act provides that the arbiter may be appointed by the court on the application of either party to the arbitration. Section III provides that where two arbiters are envisaged and one of the parties refuses to nominate one, the court may make the appointment. The fourth section of the Act gives two arbiters the power to appoint an oversman which, prior to the Act, had not been allowed, and the fifth states that the terms of the Act shall apply to all references before or after the passing of the Act.

7.17 The remaining two sections of the Act state that applications to the court under the Act can either be to the sheriff court or to the court of session and that the Act shall apply only to Scotland.

Appointment of clerk

7.18 It is not necessary to have a clerk and many arbitrations are conducted perfectly satisfactorily without one; but in any arbitration where the procedure is in the least formal, it is common for an arbiter to appoint a clerk who is responsible for organising the arbitration and all its documentation. Although not necessarily so, the clerk is usually a solicitor and in addition to his duties as clerk to the submission, he frequently advises the arbiter on legal points of procedure which occur during the process of the arbitration; he is not in any way responsible for decisions which the arbiter makes on the strength of his advice, however. The clerk is responsible for keeping arbitration papers, and all communications from the arbiter to the parties should be channelled through the clerk who is also responsible for making the decisions of the arbiter known to the parties. If the arbiter proposes to appoint a clerk, it is usual for him to do so simultaneously with his acceptance of the office of arbiter.

Submissions

7.19 In Scotland, a reference to an arbiter is begun by a document known as a submission. This is the contract by which the parties to the arbitration confer jurisdiction on the arbiter. The length of time during which they wish to submit themselves to his jurisdiction is a matter for the parties to determine by the terms of the contract. A clause in the submission frequently gives an arbiter power to decide a dispute between two specified dates, and where the endurance of the arbitration is left blank the period is a year and a day from the date of the submission.

Form

7.20 There is no technical style for a submission, so long as the words used make the dispute clear to the arbiter; a special submission is one which refers a single specified dispute to the decision of the arbiter, and a general submission is one where all disputes arising between two parties are referred to the decision of an arbiter (although this does not cover disputes which were not in existence at the date of the submission). It is important to note that the death of one of the parties, or of the arbiter himself, ends the arbitration; similarly, if the contract is terminated for any reason, so also is the arbitration.

Procedure and hearing in an arbitration

7.21 Having had the submission, in all but the most informal types of arbitration, it is usual for an arbiter to accept the office by minute annexed to the submission. If an oversman (para 7.16) is required, this is the appropriate stage for his nomination.

7.22 While an arbiter is master of the procedure of his own arbitration, he must conform to the requirements of the parties as laid down in the submission. He is however entitled to take all steps to inform himself about the matter upon which he has been called upon to decide. He is therefore bound to make sure that he is properly informed as to the precise nature of the question, and that he investigates such facts as he considers relevant to the issue. He must hear both sides to the dispute as may be necessary to enable him to decide the case unbiasedly. He must not grant to one side what he refuses to the other.

7.23 In the ordinary course, in a formal submission, the clerk is responsible for the preparation of what is known as an interlocutor sheet (an interlocutor is the name given to the orders or instructions issued by the arbiter in the course of the hearing). The first interlocutor is an order from the arbiter requiring the pursuers (or claimants) to lodge their claim within a specified number of days and thereafter giving the respondents (or defenders) a further period of time within which to lodge their answers to the claim. Having lodged their original claim and answers, the parties almost always wish to adjust their pleadings, and an arbiter normally issues a further interlocutor giving the parties a specified time to do this. This process can be repeated at the arbiter's discretion until the parties have finalised their pleadings, when the arbiter makes an interlocutor closing the record, as it is known.

7.24 The closing of the record marks the end of the period within which the parties are entitled to adjust their pleadings. The closed record is the name given to the document which contains the adjusted claim of the pursuer and the adjusted answer of the defender. It is to be contrasted with the open record, which contains the claim and answers as originally lodged before adjustment. Prior to the formal hearing, the arbiter may, if he so wishes, decide to visit the object of the parties' dispute.

Hearing
7.25 A hearing is then convened at a place and time to be selected by the arbiter, bearing in mind the convenience of the parties. At the hearing, and at any stage of the arbitration, the parties may be represented by counsel, and the normal rules of evidence are followed during the hearing. The arbiter normally takes advice from his clerk (if the latter is a lawyer), on what may or may not be admitted in evidence if there is any dispute on this point. At the conclusion of the hearing, the arbiter may issue a verbal decision, but often he indicates to the parties that he wishes to defer his decision until he has had time to consider the evidence laid before him (known as 'avizandum'), when he issues his decision as proposed findings.

Proposed findings
7.26 In a Scottish arbitration an arbiter usually issues proposed findings in the first instance and gives the parties time to lodge representations against these. If representations are received, a further hearing is held by the arbiter to consider them but after this, or if there are no representations lodged within the time specified, the arbiter issues his final interlocutor containing his findings. In the final interlocutor he may if he has been asked to do so, deal with the question of expenses and damages, but if he has not been asked to award damages, he should not make any reference to this in the interlocutor. In the final interlocutor the Arbiter should state that, as the terms of his remit have now been exhausted, the arbitration has been concluded.

Challenge of the award
7.27 Until clause 35 (5) of the Scottish supplement was introduced and more recently until the 1973 Act was enacted there was no appeal in Scotland against an arbiter's decision unless the arbiter had during the process of the arbitration misconducted himself in such a way as to make the award obviously biased, ie if he had accepted a bribe from one or other of the parties, or if the award dealt with a subject which was not the matter of the submission to the arbiter, but arbiters are now becoming used to the fact that on questions of law they may be appealed either under contract or under statute to the Court of Session or subsequently to the House of Lords. Whether or not this will make potential arbiters reluctant to accept appointment remains to be seen.

7.28 There is an important difference between clause 35 (5) and the provisions of the Administration of Justice (Scotland) Act 1973. Under the former the arbiter is entitled to state a case to the Court of Session on a question of law should he wish to do so, and if requested by either of the parties he must do so. Under the Act again he may do so if he wishes to, but he is not obliged to do so simply because he is asked to state a case by one of the parties; if in the face of a request he refuses to do so the complaining party must then petition the courts and only if the courts instruct him to do so is the arbiter obliged to present a special case. It is also important to note that under both provisions it is only on a question of law that the arbiter can be appealed; on questions of fact his decision is binding. It may at first glance seem obvious whether a question is one of fact or law, but in practice it can be very difficult to differentiate between the two, and if there is a difference of opinion between the parties as to whether an appeal is required or not an arbiter can easily find himself in a very difficult situation.

7.29 Any arbiter who either at the request of the parties or on the instructions of the Court of Session finds himself with having to prepare a special case should immediately take legal advice on how this is to be done, either from his clerk, if he has appointed one and he is legally qualified, or from some other source. A 'special case' is the name given to the legal process employed and its preparation is a technical matter which would normally be out with the skills of a lay arbiter. Briefly in it the arbiter sets out in it the facts which he has found proven from the evidence submitted to him by the parties, and then lists the questions of law on which he requires the court's ruling. Normally the case would be debated in court by counsel for the two parties, and while the arbiter would wish to be present in court while the debate is taking place it is highly unlikely that he would be required to take part.

7.30 Once the Court of Session has given its decision on the questions set out in the special case (subject to an over-riding right of appeal to the House of Lords) these decisions are binding on the parties and can be incorporated by the arbiter in his final interlocutor. If one of the parties to an arbitration refuses to comply with the terms of the award (whether or not this follows on the decision of the Court of Session after a special case) the other party can take action in the courts to have it enforced.

References

GILL, WILLIAM H. Barrister at law. Evidence and procedure in arbitration. 2nd Edition, London, 1973, Sweet & Maxwell — The law of arbitration. London, 1975
PARRIS, JOHN Barrister at law. The law and practice of arbitration. London, 1974
WALTON, ANTONY QC Russell on arbitration. 18th Edition, 1970
RIBA Handbook The architect as arbitrator. Reprinted 1972.
ICE Arbitration Procedure. 1973

The illustration at the start of this section is reproduced by courtesy of the Trustees of the British Museum, the one at the end from John Kay (*op cit*).

AJ Legal Handbook

Section 6
Statutory authorities and consents

Legal study 9

English statutory authorities

This study first explains English local authority structure before describing clients' rights to mains services from statutory undertakers (including local authorities). Particularly important is its guide to local authority officers' powers and his discussion of the complicated law relating to sewers.
He also covers private streets, housing associations and grants and licences for special premises. Scottish readers should consult LEGAL STUDY 10 *as well as this article*

1 Introductory

1.01 Local government in England and Wales, outside London, was completely reorganised on 1 April 1974, when the Local Government Act 1972 came into force. The pattern of local authorities is now simpler than it was before 1974, but Greater London* (reorganised in 1965 by the London Government Act 1963) is differently administered, and there are also less important differences between England and Wales. These three parts of the country should therefore now be considered separately.

1.02 In *London,* functions are divided between the Greater London Council (covering the whole area, with a total population of some 10m), 32 London boroughs and the City of London. The GLC is responsible for the preparation of the development plan and traffic circulation, but development control, building control (LEGAL STUDY 13) refuse collection (but not disposal, which is the responsibility of the GLC), clean air and rating are the concern of the London boroughs and the City. Housing is principally the concern of the boroughs but may also be provided by the GLC.

1.03 In *England* outside the GLC area, the country is divided between 6 metropolitan areas (West Midlands, Merseyside, Greater Manchester, West Yorkshire, South Yorkshire and Tyne and Wear) and 38 'ordinary' counties. In the metropolitan areas there is a metropolitan county for each area, and a varying number of metropolitan districts, each with a council, within each county. Outside those areas there are 38 counties, each with a county council and a number of districts (approximately 390 in total) each again with a council. In addition rural parishes which existed before 1974 have been allowed to continue. Further, some of the pre-1974 district councils have been re-formed with parish council status. As an additional complication district councils have been allowed to apply for a charter giving themselves the status of a borough, although this is solely a ceremonial matter. Some parishes have been allowed to call themselves 'towns' and have appointed 'town mayors', again with no real legal significance.

1.04 In *Wales* there are no metropolitan areas. There are 8 counties, each divided into districts with councils at each level. Also each district is divided into a number of 'communities' which have the functions of the English parishes.

1.05 County councils are responsible everywhere for the

preparation of development plans and have certain limited functions in connection with development control. They are also responsible for fire services, main and district highways, refuse disposal and a few other functions. Outside the metropolitan areas county councils are also responsible for education and welfare services, which in the metropolitan areas are the responsibility of the district councils. All district councils are responsible for housing, refuse collection, drainage, clean air and public health generally (but *not* sewerage and water supply), detailed development control, parks and open spaces and building controls, etc. A district council may also (by arrangement with the county council) undertake the maintenance of urban roads (other than trunk roads), bridleways and footpaths within its district. The parishes (communities in Wales) have very few substantial functions, but may provide and maintain recreation grounds, bus shelters and roadside seats.

1.06 Since April 1974, the provision and maintenance of sewers and sewerage disposal, together with water supply and distribution and the prevention of river pollution, has been the responsibility of special authorities, the 10 regional water authorities (9 in England, 1 in Wales). These authorities are appointed by the Secretary of State with some members nominated by the local authorities within their areas, and administration of many important sections in the Public Health Acts was transferred to them from local authorities by the Water Act 1973 (which came into effect on 1 April 1974).

General characteristics of local authorities
1.07 The essential characteristic of every local authority under this complicated system is that it is governed by a council elected on a wide franchise at four year intervals. In districts, one-third of the councillors retire on 3 out of 4 years every year; but a non-metropolitan district may resolve that all their members shall retire together. In counties all members retire together every fourth year. There are now no aldermen elected by the councillors.

1.08 Local authorities are legal persons, capable of suing and being sued in the courts, entrusted by Parliament with a range of functions over a precisely limited geographical area. Each local authority is subject to the doctrine of *ultra vires;* ie it can perform only those functions conferred on it by Parliament, and only in such a manner as Parliament may have laid down. On the other hand, within the powers defined by Parliament, each local authority is its own master. In the two-tier or three-tier system there is no question of an appeal from the lower rank authorities (the district or the parish) to the higher rank (the county council) or from the parish to the district. If the individual authority has acted within its

* An extensive area including the whole of the former county of Middlesex and the boroughs of Croydon and East and West Ham

statutory powers, its decision is final, except in cases precisely laid down by Parliament, where (as in many planning situations) there may be a right of appeal to a minister of the central Government (LEGAL STUDY 12). If, however, a local authority has overstepped the limits of its legal powers, a private citizen who has been aggrieved in consequence may apply to the courts for an order requiring the errant local authority to keep within its powers. Thus, a ratepayer at Fulham successfully obtained an order against the borough council, requiring the council to stop spending ratepayers' money on the provision of a service for washing clothes for members of the public, when the council had statutory powers to provide a service for washing only the bodies of members of the public (*Attorney-General v Fulham BC* (1921) 1 CH 440).

Officers

1.09 All local authorities are alike in that they employ officers and workmen to carry out their instructions, while the elected members assembled in council make decisions as to what is to be done. Officers of the authority—chief executive, solicitor, treasurer, surveyor, architect, planning officer, and many others—play a large part in the decision-making process: they advise the council on the courses of action open to them, and also on the consequences of taking such actions. When a decision has been taken, it is then the duty of appropriate officers of the council to implement it: to notify persons concerned and to take any executive decisions or other action necessary to give effect to the main decision. It is sometimes said that the officers give advice and take action, while the council decides all matters of policy; although basically true (for statutes almost invariably confer the power to exercise discretion on the authority itself) this does not clarify what happens in practice. 'Policy' is incapable of precise definition, for what is policy to some local authorities and in some circumstances may be regarded as routine administration by other authorities or in different circumstances. Thus, every local authority approves its development plan in the final form. Some small local authorities like to settle the details of each improvement or standard grant approved under the Housing Act 1974 (para 4.02), though most authorities would be content to leave details in such matters to their officers, trusting them to bring before the council (or a committee) particulars of any difficult case.

Committees

1.10 In practice, all local authorities conduct their affairs by the committee system. Committees, consisting of named councillors, are usually considerably smaller in membership than the council as a whole* and are entrusted with specified functions of the council. Thus, every county council has a planning committee and a finance committee and most district councils will have a parks committee and a housing committee, although details vary from authority to authority. Since reorganisation, committees have tended to be wider in scope, and policy or 'general resources' committees are common. Every matter requiring a council decision within the terms of reference of a particular committee is first brought before the committee. The committee then considers the matter and either recommends a certain decision to the council or may itself make the decision. Whether the committee decides on behalf of the council depends on whether the council has delegated to the committee power to take the decision on its behalf, either in that particular matter, or in

matters of that kind or falling within a particular class. Section 101 of the Local Government Act 1972 confers on all local authorities power to arrange for any of its functions (except levying a rate or raising a loan) to be discharged by a committee, a sub-committee or an officer.

1.11 Proceedings in committee are often, but not necessarily, held in private and tend to be informal. Officers attend, and volunteer advice and often take part in the discussion, although any decision is taken on the vote or assent of the councillors present. Council meetings and meetings of specified committees such as the education committee are more formal; the press and members of the public are entitled to be present unless they have been excluded by special resolution of the council (Public Bodies (Admission to Meetings) Act 1960 as amended by s.100 of the Local Government Act 1972) and proceedings are conducted in accordance with the council's standing orders. Officers do not speak at a council meeting unless their advice is expressly requested, and as much business consists of receipt of reports from committees, discussion tends to be confined to more controversial topics. Because of the presence of the press and public, party politics tend to be more obvious at council meetings; often in committee, members from opposing political parties will agree, and members of a single party may disagree with one another. In recent years however, there has been a tendency for authorities to be more closely organised on party political lines. When this occurs, 'group' meetings may be held preceding the committee meetings. Thus on important matters, decisions at committee meetings tend to be 'rubber stamps' of decisions already taken at the group meeting of the political party in power on the council.

1.12 The law requires that councils must meet at least four times a year. Most councils arrange committee meetings in a cycle, monthly or perhaps every six weeks, so that each committee will normally meet at least once between council meetings. The system whereby committees are given delegated powers (as is now customary) provides for a reasonably expeditious dispatch of business, but there may be long delays where the council meets less often than once a month and there is no adequate provision for delegation to committees and/or to officers.

Officers' powers

1.13 All discretionary powers are in the first instance conferred on a local authority. Therefore when an officer of a council who was asked for information as to the planning position in respect of a particular piece of land, carelessly gave the wrong information, saying that planning permission was not required, it was held by the courts that the council were not bound by this statement. It could not be taken as the decision of the council, as the officer had no power to act on their behalf (*Southend-on-Sea Corporation v Hodgson (Wickford) Ltd* (1961) 2 All ER 46). Similarly, when a public health inspector served a notice on the owner of property requiring certain work to be undertaken, it was declared that the notice was void and of no effect, because the statute required that the local authority should themselves decide to serve such a notice, and under the then existing law they could not delegate such a duty to one of their officers (*Firth v Staines* (1897) 2 QB 70). As a consequence of local government reorganisation there are many more large authorities than there were before 1974. They are also frequently differently organised. In place of the town or county clerk, the principal officer is often known as the 'Chief Executive', and often he has no departmental responsibilities. He may be assisted by a small management team of chief officers such as the Director

---

* There are no general rules, but a council of say 48 members may place about 12 councillors on each of its committees. Recently there has been a tendency to streamline committee organisation, leaving more routine matters to the discretion of officers.

of Technical Services, the Director of Welfare Services, etc, each having broad responsibilities and a number of departments subordinate to him. The committee structure also may be different from the pre-1974 system, being organised rather on a functional basis than one paralleled to departments.

A local authority does not stand outside the common law in respect of acts of negligence by its officers and employees. The decision in the case of *Anns v London Borough of Merton* (1977) 2 All ER 492, in the House of Lords has strongly emphasised the extent of the legal liability of local authorities for the actions of their officers. (See LEGAL STUDY 1 paras 5.13 and 5.14.)

Finding the right officer
1.14 Architects in the course of their professional business are obliged to have dealings with numerous local authority officials. Table 1 shows the purposes for which a permission, licence or certificate may have to be obtained from the local authority, giving the officer initially responsible (see LEGAL STUDIES 12 and 13). First, however, it is essential to ascertain the authority in whose area the site lies.

Table 1 Responsibilities of local authority officers

Subject matter	Officer	Local authority
Planning	planning officer or surveyor	DC
Building regulations	building inspector or surveyor	DC
Development in a private street	surveyor	CC
Surface water sewerage	engineer	WA*
Sewer connections	do	WA*
Blocked sewers	do	WA*
Housing grants; housing generally	environmental health officer or (sometimes) surveyor	DC
Height of chimneys or other clean air matters	environmental health officer	DC
Petroleum licensing; most other licensing	petroleum inspector (often public health inspector or surveyor)	CC
Music and dancing licences	local magistrate's clerk	
Liquor licences	do	—

Key: CC, county council; DC, district council; WA, regional water authority

Notes
*The water authority will often have made arrangements for the DC to carry out sewerage functions on their behalf (Water Act 1973, sections 14 and 15)
London In Greater London, in all cases (except for music and dancing and liquor licences) the responsible authority is the London borough council
Planning In planning the authority given above should be contacted in the first instance, although the county council (or the Greater London Council) may ultimately make the decision
Roads In the counties highway functions are commonly administered by district or divisional surveyors, responsible to the county surveyor but stationed locally often at district council offices. In the case of trunk and special roads (motorways) the highway authority is the Secretary of State for the Environment but the local county surveyor acts as his agent at local level.

2 Connections to services—statutory undertakers

2.01 When starting to design a building for a client, any architect is obliged at an early stage to consider the availability of mains services and the rights of his client as landowner regarding the various statutory undertakers: sewer and highway authorities, water, gas, and electricity supply undertakings, and possibly the water authority if it is proposed to use a water course as a means of disposing of effluent from the building. The legal provisions regulating these matters are discussed below.

Sewers
2.02 Sewers are conduits (artificial or natural) used for conveying effluent (ie waste liquids—clear water, surface water from covered surfaces, land or buildings, foul water or trade effluent) from two or more buildings not within the same curtilage*. A conduit which takes effluent from one building only or a number of buildings all within the same curtilage is in law a 'drain'. This distinction is important, as a landowner never has any legal right to let his effluent flow into a drain belonging to another person (even if that other person is a local authority) unless he has acquired such a right by at least 20 years' use or as the result of an agreement with the other person (LEGAL STUDY 6 para 4.06). The same rule applies to a private sewer; but if the conduit to which he proposes to drain his effluent is a *public* sewer, he will have certain valuable rights to use it. All public sewers are vested in (owned by) the water authorities, and a sewer is a public sewer if it existed as a sewer (regardless of who constructed it) before 1 October 1937, if it was constructed by a local authority after 1 October 1937 and before 1 April 1974 or by the water authority since that date† and was not designed to serve *only* property belonging to the authority (eg a council housing estate); or if it has been adopted as a public sewer since 1 October 1937.

Rights to connection
2.03 If there is within any distance a public sewer capable of serving his property, any landowner has by section 34 of the Public Health Act 1936 a right to cause his own drains or private sewer to communicate with it and to discharge foul and surface water from his premises to it. Connecting sewers or drains from the premises to the public sewer must be constructed at the expense of the landowner concerned. Sometimes—but not often—the water authority may itself construct 'laterals', or connecting drains leading from the main sewer to the boundary of the street to which house drains may be connected.

2.04 There are a few exceptions from this general rule:
1 No substance likely to injure the sewer or to interfere with the free flow of its contents, no chemical refuse or steam or any petroleum spirit or calcium carbide, may be caused to flow into a public sewer (Public Health Act 1936 section 27).
2 The general rule does not apply to trade effluents.
3 The general rule does not permit a communication directly with a storm-water overflow sewer (section 34 (1) (c) of the Act).
4 Where separate public sewers are provided for foul and for surface water, foul water may not be discharged into a sewer provided for surface water, and surface water may not,

---

* Curtilage: in non-technical terms, the natural boundaries of a particular building; thus the curtilage of an ordinary dwelling-house would include the garage, the garden and its appurtenances, and any outbuildings

† Under the Water Act 1973 all public sewers formerly vested in the local county borough or district council vested in the water authority on 1 April 1974

without the consent of the water authority, be discharged into a sewer provided for foul water (section 34 (1) (b) of the Act). It is particularly important that an architect should know whether the authority's sewerage network is designed on the separate system, as he may in turn have to provide a separate drainage for the building he is designing (see *AJ services handbook*, section 4). If it is desired to cross the boundary of a local or water authority in order to drain into a public sewer, it is no longer necessary to obtain the 'foreign' authority's consent.

Procedure

2.05 A person wishing to connect his sewer or drain to a public sewer must give the water authority* written notice of his proposal, and the authority may within 21 days of notice refuse to permit him to make the communication if the mode of construction or condition of the drain or sewer is such that the making of the communication would be prejudicial to their sewerage system (section 34 (3) of the Act) but they may not so refuse for any other reason. Further, within 14 days of the proposals so served on the authority, they may give notice that they intend to make the communication to the public sewer (section 36 (1) of the Act). The private landowner is then obliged to permit the authority to do the work of making the house drains or sewer connect with the public sewer, and he has to bear the water authority's reasonable expenses so incurred. This may include a reasonable sum extra on the actual cost by way of establishment expenses: section 36 of the Local Government Act 1974 (but *only* if the expenses have been incurred by the *local* authority). When making the communication, the authority (or the private owner if he is allowed to do the work himself) has power as necessary to break open any street (sections 36 (4) and 279 of the 1936 Public Health Act read with the Public Utilities Street Works Act 1950).

2.06 Any dispute with the authority under these provisions may be settled by way of an appeal to the local magistrates, or in some cases by a reference to arbitration. The landowner has a right to this redress if, for example, he is refused permission to make a communication with a public sewer.

Approval

2.07 The arrangements proposed to be made for the 'satisfactory provision' for drainage of a building must be approved by the local authority at the time when the building plans are considered under the Building Regulations (Public Health Act 1936 section 37 and LEGAL STUDY 13). Disposal of the effluent may be to a public sewer, or to a cesspool or private septic tank, and in case of surface water to a highway drain or a watercourse or to the sea. In this instance note that the powers remain with the district council and have not been transferred to the water authority.

2.08 It remains to deal with discharges to highway drains, and to watercourses and to the sea, and with the special case of trade effluent. If it is desired to drain to a septic tank or similar receptacle on another person's land, this is a matter for private negotiation for an express easement (LEGAL STUDY 6 para 4.04) with such other landowner.

2.09 If there is no existing main sewer into which the property could be drained, the owner or occupier (usually with the owners etc of other premises) may requisition the water

authority to provide a public sewer, under section 16 of the Water Act 1973. They must then satisfy conditions specified by the authority, the most important of which is likely to be that those requisitioning the sewer shall undertake to meet any 'relevant deficit' of the water authority in consequence of constructing the sewer. But this section applies only to sewers to be used for domestic purposes.

Highway drains
2.10 A landowner has no legal right to cause his drains (or sewers) to be connected with a highway drain, and this applies equally to surface water drains taking effluent from roads and paved surfaces on a private housing estate. Such drains may, in accordance with the statutory provisions outlined above, be connected with a public sewer, but if it is desired to connect with a drain or sewer provided for the drainage of a highway and vested in the highway authority, the consent of the highway authority must first be obtained: the highway authority will normally be the county council and will be a different body from the sewer authority (the water authority). A public sewer may be used to take surface water from a highway, but that does not affect its status as a public sewer, nor does the fact that house drains may in the past have been connected (probably unlawfully) with a highway drain convert such highway drain into a public sewer (*Rickarby v New Forest RDC* (1910) 26 TLR 586). It is only to public sewers that drains or sewers may be connected by right.

Rivers
2.11 If it is desired to discharge effluent into a watercourse, the consent of the water authority* must be obtained for making of a new or altered discharge of trade or sewage effluent under section 34 of the Control of Pollution Act 1974.† Such consent may not be unreasonably withheld, and any question as to whether such consent has been unreasonably withheld in a particular case would be determined by reference to the Secretary of the Environment (section 39 of the 1974 Act). Consents may be granted subject to conditions and any conditions so imposed must be entered in a register maintained by the river authority. To discharge effluent into a watercourse without prior consent of the water authority or in a manner contrary to any conditions imposed in a consent (1974 Act sections 31 and 32) is a criminal offence. Similarly, discharge to a pond or stream not with the jurisdiction of a water authority normally results in a statutory nuisance, which may then be made the subject of proceedings before the local magistrates by the local authority (Public Health Act 1936 sections 92 to 100 and section 259).

The sea
2.12 A private landowner has at common law no legal right to discharge his sewage or other polluting matter to the sea; indeed, as the Crown originally owned the foreshore between high and low tides, he might not have any legal right to take his drain or sewer as far as the water. However, even if such a right can be acquired, and at the present day the Crown's rights have in many cases been sold or leased to local authorities or private landowners, it seems that the discharge of

---

* There are now ten regional water authorities (including the Welsh National Water Development Authority (covering the whole of England and Wales. Their functions include sewage disposal and sewerage, river pollution prevention, and water conservation and distribution. The district council may not act as their agent in such a case.

† This part of this Act is not yet in force, but similar controls exist under the Rivers Prevention of Pollution Acts 1951 and 1961 (to be replaced by the 1974 Act).

---

* In practice the district council will often act as agent for the water authority in the exercise of these functions, under arrangements entered into under section 15 of the Water Act 1973

sewage by means of a pipe into the sea is subject to the same control of the water authority (Control of Pollution Act 1974; see definition of 'controlled waters' in section 56 thereof). There must also be no nuisance caused as a consequence, and no breach of a local by-law made by a sea fisheries committee prohibiting the discharge of matter detrimental to sea fish or sea fishing (Sea Fisheries Regulation Act 1888 section 2). If effluent discharging into the sea does cause a nuisance, any person harmed thereby can take proceedings for an injunction and/or damages, as in *Foster v Warblington UDC* (1906) 1 KB 648, where guests at a banquet were poisoned from oysters taken from a bed which had been affected by sewage.

Trade effluents
2.13 In the case of a proposed discharge of 'trade effluent', the special controls of the Public Health (Drainage of Trade Premises) Act 1937, as amended by the Public Health Act 1961 and the Control of Pollution Act 1974, apply. 'Trade effluent' is defined in the Act of 1937 as meaning 'any liquid, either with or without particles of matter in suspension therein, which is wholly or in part produced in the course of any trade or industry carried on at trade premises, and, in relation to any trade premises, means any such liquid as aforesaid which is so produced in the course of any trade or industry carried on at those premises, but does not include domestic sewage' (1937 Act section 14 (1)).
Liquid produced 'solely in the course of laundering articles' is not normally trade effluent within this definition, being excluded expressly by section 4 (4) of the Act, but the Secretary of State for the Environment may by order direct that this exemption shall not apply to laundry premises specified in the order. 'Trade premises' are not defined in the Act, but the term means any premises used or intended to be used for carrying on any trade or industry; under section 63 of the 1961 Act it is clear that effluent from premises used for agricultural or horticultural purposes, or for scientific research or experiment are to be treated as trade premises for these purposes.

2.14 Where it is intended to discharge trade effluent as defined above into a public sewer, consent has first to be obtained from the water authority.* This is done by the owner or occupier of the premises serving on the authority a 'trade effluent notice'. This must specify (in writing) the nature or composition of the proposed effluent, the maximum quantity to be discharged in any one day, and the highest proposed rate of discharge of the effluent. This notice (for which there is no standard form) is then treated by the authority as an application for their consent to the proposed discharge. No effluent may then be discharged for a period of two months (or such less time as may be agreed by the authority). A decision, when given by the authority, may be a refusal to permit the discharge or a consent thereto, and in the latter case a consent may be given subject to conditions as to a number of matters 'including a payment by the occupier of the trade premises of charges for the reception and disposal of the effluent', as specified in section 59 of the Public Health Act 1961. These conditions may be varied (not more frequently than once every two years) by direction given by the water authority. The owner or occupier of trade premises has a right of appeal to the Secretary of State for the Environment against a refusal of consent to a discharge, against the conditions imposed in such a consent, or against a direction subsequently given varying the conditions (1937 Act section 3, 1961 Act section 66), and such a direction

* The district council may act as their agent

may now be given varying the conditions relating to any discharge (even one made before the passing of the 1937 Act; 1974 Act sections 43 and 44).

2.15 In practice, however, it is frequently desirable for an industrialist's professional advisers to discuss disposal of trade effluent with the officers of the water authority, with a view to an agreement being entered into between the owner of the premises and the authority under section 7 of the 1937 Act. This will avoid the need to serve a trade effluent notice, and better terms can often be obtained by negotiation than by the more formal procedure of the trade effluent notice. The contents of any such agreement becomes public property, as a copy has to be kept at the water authority's offices and made available for inspection and copying by any person (1937 Act section 7 (3)).

Water supply
2.16 The water supply authority will be the water authority but where before 1974 supply was made by a statutory water company this will remain in existence but act on behalf of the water authority (Water Act 1973 section 12). Each water supply undertaking may have its own private Acts of Parliament regulating its affairs, but the third schedule to the Water Act 1945 now applies to most undertakings, and in what follows this is assumed to be the case; but readers dealing in practice with a particular water undertaking should ascertain whether there are any local statutory variations.
Rights to connection (domestic uses)
2.17 If the owner or occupier of premises within the area served by a water supply undertaking wishes to have a supply for *domestic purposes*, he must give at least 14 days' notice to the undertakers and lay a supply pipe (ie a pipe leading from the 'communication pipe' to his premises) at his own expense; if the supply pipe passes through any property belonging to another owner, his consent must be obtained in the form of an express easement or a licence (LEGAL STUDY 6 paras 3.03 and 4.01). The 'communication pipe' (ie that part of the pipe serving the premises which leads from the main to the boundary of the street in which the main is laid or to the stopcock) must then be laid by the undertakers, and they must connect the supply pipe with the communication pipe (Water Act 1945, third schedule, paras 40 and 41), and thereupon provide a supply of water (*ibid* para 30). However, the owner will not be entitled to a supply from a trunk main if his fittings do not comply with the undertakers' by-laws. The undertakers will also have an excuse for not providing a supply if such failure is due to 'frost, drought, inevitable accident and other unavoidable cause, or the execution of necessary works'. Moreover, in most circumstances the undertakers may require the provision of a separate service pipe for each house or other building supplied (*ibid* para 42). Any breaking up of streets must be effected by the undertakers and not by the owner requiring the supply (*ibid* part VI).

2.18 This assumes of course that the water main in the nearest street is within a reasonable distance from the house or other premises to be served. Where the main is not readily available, the owner of the premises may persuade other owners in the district to serve a requisition on the undertakers requiring them to extend their mains. If enough owners and occupiers of premises in the area requiring a domestic supply sign a requisition and the aggregate amount of water rates payable annually would be not less than one-eighth of the expense of extending the main, and each owner and occupier agrees to take a supply for at least three years, then (in the absence of any 'unavoidable accident or other unavoidable cause'), the undertakers are obliged to extend their mains within a period of three months (Water Act 1945, third schedule, para 29).

Non-domestic premises
2.19 Owners or occupiers of premises requiring a supply of water for industrial or other (non-domestic) purposes (as in the case of sewers) must come to terms for a supply with the undertakers; they have no legal rights to insist on a supply.

Gas supply
2.20 The responsible authority for gas supply is the British Gas Corporation operating under the Gas Act 1972.

2.21 If the owner or occupier of premises requires a supply of gas for any purpose (not necessarily domestic), he must serve a notice on the Corporation at one of their local offices specifying the premises, and the day on which it is desired the service shall begin—and a reasonable time must be given (Gas Act 1972, schedule 4, para 2). The owner or occupier has to pay the cost of any pipe that may be laid upon the property of the owner or in the possession of the occupier, and for so much of any pipe as may be laid for a greater distribution distance than 30ft (9.144 m*) from any of the Corporation's pipes. The Corporation must comply with such a request, but only if the premises are within 25yd (22.860m) of any of their mains not being a main used for a separate supply for industrial purposes or for conveying gas in bulk.

2.22 Once premises have been so connected to a gas main, the Corporation must give a supply of gas (on the usual charges), unless the failure was due to circumstances not within their control. The Corporation is not obliged to give a supply of gas for any purpose other than lighting or domestic use in any case where the capacity of the main is insufficient for the purpose, unless a special agreement has been entered into (Gas Act 1972, schedule 4, para 3). No distinction is drawn in other respects between gas supplied for domestic purposes and gas supplied for other purposes.

Electricity supply
2.23 The responsible authorities for the supply of electricity are the 12 electricity boards operating under the Electricity Act 1947.

2.24 If the owner or occupier of premises within the area of an electricity board requires a supply of electricity for any purpose (not necessarily domestic), he must serve a notice on the board specifying the premises in respect of which the supply is required, and the maximum power that will be required (Electric Lighting (Clauses) Act 1899, schedule, para 27 (2) as applied by the Electricity Act 1947). The Board must then provide a supply, subject to the following conditions:
1 The premises are within 50yd (45.720 m) from a distributing main maintained for general supply to private consumers (*ibid* para 27 (1)).
2 The owner or occupier concerned must bear the cost of an electric line that is laid on the property of the owner or in the possession of the occupier, and also of so much of any electric line more than 60ft (18.288 m) from any distributing main of the board.
3 The electric lines, fitting and apparatus on the premises

---

* The Act says 30ft exactly. All conversions in this article are therefore to the nearest millimetre.

must, to the reasonable satisfaction of the board, be in good order and condition and not calculated to affect injuriously the use of energy by the board or other persons (*ibid* para 27(5)). Any differences as to the application of these provisions must be referred to arbitration (para 27 (6)).
4 The owner or occupier may also be required to enter into an agreement with the board to take a supply for a period of at least two years at the usual charge, but so that the annual payment shall not be less than 20 per cent on the outlay by the board of providing any electric lines required.

Telephones
2.25 The Post Office (now a public corporation under the Post Office Act 1969) has no special duties relating to the supply of telephone services; the owner or occupier of premises must negotiate for a supply on the Post Office's own terms, and normally all the equipment remains the property of the Post Office and is maintained by them.

Construction of mains
2.26 All public undertakings have inherent powers to negotiate on terms with private landowners for the grant of easements or 'wayleaves' (LEGAL STUDY 6 para 4.01 *et seq*) to enable them to place mains, cables, wires, apparatus and so on over or under privately owned land. They also have powers to break open public streets for the purpose of constructing mains. Water authorities acting as sewerage authorities (Public Health Act 1936 sections 15 and 16), water supply authorities (*ibid* applied by section 119 of the Act, and the Water Act 1945), the Gas Corporation (Gas Act 1972, schedule 4, para 1, and section 39 thereof), electricity boards (Electricity Act 1919 section 22—the consent of the local authority may be required to the placing of an overhead line) and the Post Office (Telegraph Act 1863 section 6 as applied by the Post Office Act 1969) all have statutory powers enabling them to place such mains and apparatus in private land, without the consent of the landowner or occupier concerned, on payment of proper compensation. Private persons have no such compulsory rights, although rights may be compulsorily acquired for an oil or other pipeline under the Pipelines Act 1962.

2.27 All statutory undertakers can also be authorised, without the consent of the landowner, to place their mains, apparatus and so on on 'controlled land' (land forming part of a street or highway maintainable or prospectively maintainable at public expense—para 3.01 *et seq*) or in land between the boundary of such a highway and any improvement line prescribed for the street (Public Utilities Street Works Act 1950).

3 Private streets

3.01 It is not within the scope of this study to describe the whole law governing the making up of a private street by county councils at the expense of the frontagers to such a street, but the special rules that regulate the construction of a building in a 'private street' can be outlined.

Definition
3.02 A private street may or may not be a highway (ie any way, footpath, bridlepath or carriageway over which members of the public have rights to pass and repass), but the word 'private' means, not that it is necessarily closed to the public (although it may be), but that the street has not been adopted by a highway authority, and therefore it is not maintainable by them on behalf of the public. It must also be a 'street', an expression which has not been precisely defined, but which

includes a cul-de-sac, lane or passage (Highways Act 1959 section 295 (1)). This does not mean, however, that every country road is a street; in a leading case, it was said by Pollock, Master of the Rolls, that 'it appears to me that what one has to find before one can determine that the highway in question is a street, is that the highway has become a street in the ordinary acceptation of that word, because by reason of the number of houses, their continuity and their proximity to one another, what would be a road or highway has been converted into a street' (*Attorney General v Laird* (1925) 1 CH 318 at p 329).

Advance payments code
3.03 As a general principle, before a new building may be erected in a new street as explained above, the developer must either pay to the local authority or secure to their satisfaction (by means of a bond or mortgage etc) a sum equivalent to the estimated cost, apportioned to the extent of the frontage of the proposed building to the private street, of carrying out street works to such an extent that the street would be adopted by the highway authority (the advance payments code—Highways Act 1959 section 192 *et seq*). 'Street works' means sewering, levelling, paving, metalling, flagging, channelling, making good and lighting. The standards required are not specified in the legislation, but clearly they must not be unreasonably stringent. In general, the standard prevailing for similar streets in the authority's district is required.

Section 40 of Highways Act 1959
3.04 However, the necessity to pay or give security in advance of the building work being started can be avoided if an agreement has been entered into with the local authority under section 40 of the Highways Act 1959, pursuant to an exception from the general principle contained in section 192 (3) (a) of the Act.

3.05 Under section 40, the local authority may enter into an agreement with the developer of land on either or both sides of a private street; the authority can agree to adopt the street as a highway maintainable at public expense when all the street works have been carried out to their satisfaction, and the developer agrees to carry them out within a stated time. If the works are not so carried out, the local authority can still use their statutory powers to carry out the works (or to complete them), at the expense of the frontagers; it is therefore customary for the developer to enter into a bond for his performance with a bank or insurance company.

3.06 Such an agreement takes the street, or the part of the street to which the agreement relates, outside the operation of the above general principle. The developer can then sell building plots or completed houses 'free of road charges' to purchasers. Though the street may not have been made up at the time of purchase, the purchaser is protected, as the developer has agreed to make up the street; if he fails to carry out his promise, the local authority will be able to sue on the bond and recover sufficient* to pay for street works expenses without having to charge them to the frontagers. If the authority should proceed against the frontagers, they in turn normally have a remedy against the developer and on the bond, but this may depend on the terms of their purchase.

3.07 The architect is not necessarily professionally concerned in such matters, but it is suggested that it is his duty to be aware of the potential expense to his client of building in an unmade private street, and he should advise his client to consult his solicitor in any difficult case, or where the exact legal position is not clear.

4 Grants

4.01 Below are considered circumstances in which a building owner is able to obtain a grant from the local authority (in this case, the district council) for some alteration or extension of his dwelling. All statutory provisions considered here concern dwelling-houses (or flats and so on), but it may be possible in development areas to obtain grants for industrial development.

Grants under the Housing Act 1974
4.02 There are now three basic kinds of grant under this statute: an *improvement grant* for provision of new dwellings by conversion of existing houses and other buildings, an *intermediate grant* for bringing existing dwellings up to a standard of amenity and a *repairs* grant, available only in a housing action area or a general improvement area. A *special* grant also may be obtained for houses in multiple occupation. Similar grants were payable under earlier Housing Acts, but these are now replaced by the 1974 Act.

Improvement grants
4.03 An improvement grant is discretionary; it cannot be claimed from the local authority (the district council) as of right. A claim may be made by any person who is the owner in fee simple (LEGAL STUDY 1 para 6.03) or of a leasehold interest (of which at least five years remain unexpired) for financial assistance from the local authority for improvement† of an existing dwelling, or for the conversion of a house or other building into two or more dwellings, or the conversion of an 'other' building into a single dwelling. In each case the dwelling so improved or provided by conversion must, when the work has been completed, measure up to the minister's *standard* (DOE Circular 160/74). This means that the dwelling must:
1 Be substantially free from damp.
2 Have adequate natural lighting and ventilation in each habitable room.
3 Have adequate and safe provision throughout for artificial lighting, and have sufficient electric socket outlets for the safe and proper functioning of domestic appliances.
4 Be provided with adequate drainage facilities.
5 Be in a stable structural condition.
6 Have satisfactory internal arrangement.
7 Have satisfactory facilities for preparing and cooking food.
8 Be provided with adequate facilities for heating.
9 Have proper facilities for the storage of fuel (where necessary) and for the storage of refuse.
10 Conform with the specifications applicable to the thermal insulation of roof spaces laid down in Part F of the Building Regulations in force at the date of the grant approval.
In addition the Act itself provides (section 61) that the dwelling must provide satisfactory housing accommodation for at least 30 years (unless the local authority agree to a shorter period), it must be provided with all the standard amenities (see para 4.09) and it must be in good repair (ignoring internal decorative repair).

---

* Provided the bond was for a sufficient amount; inflation may cause problems here.

† An expression which is defined (Housing Act 1974, section 84) to include alteration and enlargement and such works of repair or replacement as are needed for the purpose of enabling the dwelling to attain the relevant standard as to the amenities available.

4.04 Further, it is provided in section 62 that no application for an improvement grant (and a similar provision applies to intermediate grants) may be entertained if the rateable value of the dwelling before *improvement* exceeds £400 in Greater London or £250 elsewhere. If the works proposed are for a conversion the maximum rateable values are £600 in Greater London or £350 elsewhere (S.I. 1974 No. 526).

4.05 Satisfactory accommodation to this standard must be provided as the result of the improvement. In a particular case the local authority may waive any of the requirements of the *standard*, if it appears to them to be impracticable for the dwelling to conform with the standard at reasonable expense.

4.06 Normally the grant should be applied for (on the approved form) and a decision on it obtained before the improvement work starts but the local authority may consider an application even after work has begun if they are satisfied 'that there were good reasons for beginning the works before the application was approved' (1974 Act section 57 (s)).

Amount

4.07 The exact amount of the grant is at the local authority's discretion but they may pay not more than a prescribed limit (1974 Act section 64 (1)). This prescribed limit is calculated by reference to the following factors:
1 First the 'estimated expense' must be calculated; this means the proper actual expenditure required for the execution of the works, including professional fees, but not including the applicant's own time etc on a 'do-it-yourself' job. Not more than 50 per cent of this expenditure may be incurred on repairs or replacements.
2 Second, the estimated expense may not exceed the 'eligible expense'. Unless special conditions* apply, this will normally be £5 000 for each dwelling improved or provided.
3 The actual grant will then be an 'appropriate percentage' of the estimated expense or the eligible expense (whichever is the *less*). This percentage is 50 per cent in most cases, but it is 60 per cent if the premises are in an area declared by the local authority to be a general improvement area and 75 per cent if the premises are within a housing action area (see 1974 Act sections 63 and 64).

4.08 The grant will not normally be paid until the work has been completed, but it may be paid by instalments as the work proceeds (1974 Act section 82). There are now elaborate provisions requiring the deposit of certificates of owner occupation or availability for letting before an application can be approved, and also conditions applicable to the use of a building, or to the rent at which it may be let, wherever a grant has been made.

Intermediate grants

4.09 Intermediate grants (formerly known as standard grants) are in many ways similar to improvement grants, but they can be demanded as of right; if the statutory provisions are met, the local authority cannot refuse to pay a grant (1974 Act section 65). They are claimed in the same manner as improvement grants, but they apply only to specified improvements made to a dwelling existing *before* 3 October 1961. These works are the provision of one or more of the following standard amenities, in so far as the dwelling in question does not have them. The maximum grant for each

---

* This may be increased by the Secretary of State in a particular case. Also if the house converted was of three or more storeys the figure will be £5 800 not £5 000. The figures quoted above were announced in the House of Commons on 19 July 1977.

amenity is shown below but the actual amount of the grant payable is calculated by reference to the actual expense, limited to an 'eligible expense' of the cost of the various items specified below, *plus* not more than £800 for repairs and replacements. The grant is then the appropriate percentage of that total eligible expense (see para 4.07).
1 Fixed bath or shower £180
2 Hot and cold water supply at a fixed bath or shower £230
3 Wash-hand basin £70
4 Hot and cold water supply at a wash-hand basin £120
5 Sink £180
6 Hot and cold water supply at a sink £150
7 Water closet £270
In some cases a grant may be made for the provision of some of the amenities, and special rules apply to provision for registered disabled persons.

4.10 When an intermediate grant is claimed, the authority must be satisfied that when the work has been carried out the dwelling will not be unfit for human habitation, but will be in good repair having regard to its age, character and locality (but disregarding internal decorative repair), that the standard amenities have been provided and that it is likely to remain fit and available as a dwelling for a period of at least 15 years (1974 Act section 66). Similar conditions to the improvement grants apply also to intermediate grants.

Special grants

4.11 Special housing grants, limited to the estimated expense but computed on the intermediate grant scales, are paid for provision of the standard amenities for houses in multiple occupation (1974 Act sections 69 and 70) ie any house which 'is occupied by persons who do not form a single household' (Housing Act 1969 section 58 (1)).

Repairs grants

4.12 These grants may be claimed only in respect of dwellings within a housing action area or a general improvement area. The decision to make a grant towards *repairs* is at the discretion of the local authority, but in exercising their discretion, they must have regard to the question whether the applicant would suffer undue hardship if he had to finance the work without the assistance of a grant (1974 Act section 71). The amount of the grant will be the appropriate percentage (para 4.07) of the eligible expense, which latter figure may not exceed £1 500.
In addition in a housing action area the local authority may at their discretion give assistance (by grant or the provision of materials) for the carrying out of *environmental works* (1974 Act section 45).

Development areas

4.13 Under the Housing Act 1971, grants payable under the Housing Act 1969 (replaced by the 1974 Act) could have been increased in development and intermediate areas. This will no longer apply however, as the 1971 Act also has in effect been replaced by the 1974 Act.

Agriculture

4.14 Under the Hill Farming and Livestock Rearing Acts 1946 and 1959, a grant may be obtained from the Minister of Agriculture, Fisheries and Food towards the cost of improving a dwelling as part of a scheme prepared with 'a view to the rehabilitation of livestock rearing land'.

Conversion of closets

4.15 A grant not exceeding half the cost may be claimed towards the expenditure incurred by the owner of a dwelling in converting an earth or pail closet to a wc, either pursuant to a notice served by the authority, or where it is proposed to undertake the work voluntarily. In the latter case the grant is payable at the local authority's discretion (Public Health Act 1936 section 47).

Clean air

4.16 Where a private dwelling (an expression which includes part of a house) is situated within a smoke control area, a grant may be claimed from the local authority amounting to 70 per cent of the expenditure reasonably incurred in adapting any fireplace or fireplaces in the dwelling to enable them to burn only 'authorised fuels' such as gas, electricity, coke or specially prepared solid fuels (Clean Air Act 1956 section 12). A similar grant may be obtainable for certain religious buildings (*ibid* section 15).

Historic buildings

4.17 In the case of a building of special historic or architectural interest, whether or not it is 'listed' as such (under section 54 of the Town and Country Planning Act 1971), a grant towards the cost of repair, restoration or maintenance may be obtained from the local authority under the Local Authorities (Historic Buildings) Act 1962, but such grants are entirely discretionary and no amounts are specified in the legislation. Grants under the Housing Act (above) also may be payable in such cases.

Airport noise

4.18 Under the Civil Aviation Act 1971 section 29A (as amended), a grant may be obtained from the manager of the aerodrome (normally the British Airports Authority) for a building 'near' an aerodrome towards the cost of insulating it, or any part of it, against noise attributable to the use of the aerodrome. The details of such grants are specified in schemes approved by the Secretary of State for Aviation, and further particulars are obtainable from the Secretary of State or the Authority*.

Water supply

4.19 Where a local authority has required a house to be connected to a piped water supply and the expense is likely to exceed £60, the owner would be best advised not to carry out the work himself as the authority would then be empowered to do the work itself in default. It would be able to recover from the owner no more than £60 towards its expenses (Public Health Act 1936 section 138 as amended by section 30 of the Water Act 1945 and section 78 of the Public Health Act 1961). The local authority also has discretionary powers to make a grant towards all or any part of the expenses incurred in the provision of a separate service pipe for the supply of water for any house which has a piped supply from a main, but which does not have a separate service pipe (Housing Act 1964 section 96).

5 Housing associations and societies

5.01 A housing association may be formed on a charitable basis for provision of houses for those in need, or for special groups of persons, such as elderly or handicapped, in a specified area. Such an association may also be constituted by an industrial firm for housing its employees, or by a group of persons proposing to build its own homes by voluntary (or part voluntary) and co-operative labour. Frequently such associations are strictly housing societies† having acquired

corporate personality by registration with the Registrar of Friendly Societies. However, a housing association (which may be incorporated as a company under the Companies Acts, or by other means), which complies with the provisions of the Housing Acts (see definition in section 189 of the Housing Act 1957) and, in particular, does not trade for profit, is entitled to be considered for certain benefits under the Housing Acts.

Benefits

5.02 First, the association may be able to obtain 'assistance' from the local housing authority in whose area they propose to build. This may mean making arrangements so that the association can improve existing council-owned houses, or acquisition of land by the local authority, which can then be sold or leased to the association for building houses; or, with the consent of the Secretary of State for the Environment, the authority may make grants or loans on mortgage (at favourable rates of interest—usually 0.25 per cent above the ruling rate charged to local authorities by the Public Works Loan Board) to the association to enable them to build houses. Registered housing associations may also be able to obtain grants from the Secretary of State towards housing projects, under part III of the Housing Act 1974.

5.03 When the local authority has agreed to make arrangements of one of these kinds, houses provided as a result will attract annual subsidies from the central government; these are payable to the local authority in the first instance, but the authority must pass on an equivalent amount to the housing association.

Housing Corporation loans

5.04 These provisions depend on the good will of the local authority; a housing association cannot insist on being given assistance. As an alternative, an association may be able to get help by way of loans for obtaining land and general advice from the Housing Corporation, a public body set up under the Housing Act 1964.

5.05 A loan of money to an association from the Housing Corporation has an additional advantage in that the mortgage given by the association to secure such a loan may be deferred to a mortgage granted by a building society, thereby enabling the association to obtain better terms from the building society (Housing Act 1964 section 8). However, houses provided by an association with the co-operation in one form or another of the Housing Corporation do not attract government subsidies.

5.06 A housing association registered under the Industrial and Provident Societies Act 1964 may make 'special arrangements' for provision of houses direct with the Secretary of State*; the Secretary of State may then make an advance of money, and any houses provided under such an arrangement and kept available for letting will attract an annual Exchequer subsidy.

Setting up a housing association

5.07 In practice people proposing to form a housing society would be well advised to obtain advice from the Housing Corporation (Sloane Square House, London, SW1 W8NT), and those proposing to set up an association should get in touch with the National Federation of Housing Societies (86 Strand, London WC2R OEG).

---

* The only aerodromes to which this provision applies at present are Heathrow, Gatwick, Stansted and Prestwick

† The term 'housing association' is the wider one including a housing society which is a special kind of housing association

* Housing Act 1961 section 7; see definition of 'special arrangements' in section 11 (1) *ibid*

6 Special premises

6.01 If an architect is designing any kind of building, he must take into account the controls exercised under town and country planning legislation (LEGAL STUDY 12) and under the Building Regulations (LEGAL STUDY 13); and he must consider the question of sewerage and mains services and the other matters discussed in this article. But if his building is of a specialised kind, or is to be used for some specialised purpose, additional controls may have to be considered; the more usual types of special control are outlined below.

Factories

6.02 The Factories Act 1961 imposes an *a posteriori* control over certain constructional matters in a factory (Factories Act 1961 section 175); there is no special control over plans (other than normal controls of the planning legislation and the Building Regulations), but if the requirements of the Act are not met in a particular factory, the occupier or (in a tenement factory) the owner will be liable to be prosecuted for an offence*. Many of these requirements relate to the use and fencing of machinery, keeping walls and floors clean and so on, and as such they are not of direct concern to the architect.

6.03 A fire certificate† will have to be obtained if more than 20 persons are employed or more than 10 persons are employed above (or below) the ground floor (Fire Precautions (Factories, Offices, Shops and Railway Premises) Order 1976, S.I. 1976 No. 2009). If a certificate is not required certain less stringent fire precautions must be observed (Fire Precautions (Non-Certificated Factories, Offices, Shops and Railway Premises) Regulations 1976, S.I. 1976 No. 2010).

6.04 The effluent from a factory's sewers or drains may well be 'trade effluent' and will then be subject to the special control of the Public Health (Drainage of Trade Premises) Act 1937 (para 2.13).

6.05 Under the Clean Air Acts 1956 and 1968, factories are subject to several constructional controls operating quite independently of the Building Regulations, but administered by the same local authorities (district councils). Thus any furnace installed in a building which will be used to burn pulverised fuel, or to burn any other solid matter at a rate of 100lb (45.36 kg) per hour or more, or any liquid or gaseous matter at a rate of 1 250 000 Btu/h (366.38 kW) or more, must be provided with plant for arresting emission of grit and dust which has been approved by the local authority or has been installed with plans and specifications submitted to and approved by the local authority (Clean Air Act 1968 section 6). Limits are set by regulations for the rates of emission of grit and dust, and there are certain exemptions from the provisions of section 3 (see sections 2 and 4 of the 1968 Act and the Clean Air (Emission of Grit and Dust from Furnaces) Regulations 1971)‡. In addition a furnace of a type to which the section applies (see 1968 Act section 6 (10)) may not be used in a building unless the height of the chimney serving the furnace has been approved by the local authority (1868 Act section 6).

---

* Sometimes by the district council, but more frequently (according to the section under which the proceedings are brought) by HM Inspector of Factories who is now subject to the supervision of the Health and Safety Executive

† See further under 'Hotels', para 6.09 below

‡ S.I. 1971 No. 162

Public houses and restaurants

6.06 A public house or other premises used for sale of intoxicating liquor either on or off the premises must be licensed by the local magistrates under the Licensing Act 1953. A new 'on-licence' may not be granted unless the premises are in the opinion of the magistrates 'structurally' adapted to the class of licence required (Licensing Act 1964 section 4 (2)). The magistrates themselves are the final judges of what is or is not structurally adapted. In the case of a licence for a restaurant or guest house or the like, an application may be refused by the magistrates on the grounds that the premises are not 'suitable or convenient' for the use contemplated (*ibid* section 98). A restaurant licence may be granted only for premises structurally adapted and *bona fide* used, or intended to be used for the provision of 'the customary main meal for the accommodation of persons frequenting the premises' (*ibid* section 94). Other alterations to licensed premises, eg where there will be increased facilities for drinking, must be the subject of a formal consent obtained from the magistrates (*ibid* section 20).

6.07 These controls are operated at the discretion of the magistrates. In practice they will normally not approve an application until they have received a report on the premises (or the proposed premises) from suitably qualified persons, such as an officer of the local fire brigade, an environmental health officer and often a senior police officer, but such requirements are at their discretion and details vary among different benches.

6.08 Under section 20 of the Local Government (Miscellaneous Provisions) Act 1976 the local authority may by notice require the owner or occupier of any premises used for public entertainment or exhibitions or as a betting office to provide and maintain in suitable positions a specified reasonable number of sanitary appliances for the use of persons frequenting the premises. When complying with such a notice, provision must be made, as far as is practicable and reasonable in the circumstances, for needs of disabled people (Chronically Sick and Disabled Persons Act 1970 section 6). If a 'refreshment house' is to be kept open late at night, a special licence will be required from the district council under the Refreshment Houses Acts 1860 to 1967.

Music and dancing

6.09 Any 'house, room, garden or other place', whether or not licensed for the sale of intoxicating liquor, that is kept or used for public dancing, singing, music or other public entertainment must be licensed by the local magistrates (Public Health Acts (Amendment Act) 1890 section 50). This does not apply to the temporary use of a room, eg for a festival, and it has been held that a dancing school does not need a licence, under a similar earlier provision (*Bellis v Burghall* (1799) 2 Espinasse 722). Conditions may be imposed on granting such a licence, and these frequently relate to structural matters.

Hotels

6.10 A fire certificate under the Fire Precautions Act 1971 is required for hotels (see S.I. 1972 Nos. 236 and 238). An application for a certificate must be made to the fire authority in respect of any new or existing hotel, and this application must be made on the prescribed form (copies of which will be obtainable from the fire authority, ie the county council). The authority may ask for plans of the building in support of the application, and they will carry out an inspection. They may then require steps to be taken as to the provision and availability of means of escape in case of fire and as to the means for fighting fire and giving warning in case of fire. If and when they are satisfied as to these matters, a fire certificate will be issued, which may itself impose requirements as to these and related matters. A right of appeal to the local magistrates lies against requirements so imposed by the fire authority. It is a criminal offence under the Act to put premises to a 'designated use' (this now includes a hotel) unless there is a valid fire certificate in force or an application is pending, and it is similarly an offence to fail to comply with any requirement imposed by a certificate.

Hotels will of course also have to comply with the legal provisions about intoxicating liquor (para 6.05 above), and possibly in relation to music and dancing (para 6.08).

Petroleum

6.11 Any premises used for keeping petroleum spirit must be licensed by the county council; otherwise the occupier is guilty of an offence (Petroleum Consolidation Act 1928 section 1). The only exception is when the spirit is kept in separate vessels containing not more than 1 pint (0.57 litre), with the total quantity not exceeding 3 gals (13.64 litres). Detailed conditions are usually imposed when such a licence is granted, and these normally follow the model conditions recommended by the Home Office. Petroleum licences are usually renewable each year (*ibid* section 2).

Theatres and cinemas

6.12 Theatres are subject to control under the Theatres Act 1968. No premises may be used for the public performance of a play except in accordance with the terms of a licence granted by the local authority*, and in granting such a licence, conditions may be imposed as to structure, exits, safety curtains and so on, but not so as to impose any censorship on the plays given in the theatre.

6.13 Similarly, showing cinematograph films at an exhibition of moving pictures produced on a screen by means including projection of light (Cinematograph Act 1952 section 9) must be licensed by the local authority and structural matters will normally be provided for in the licence (Cinematograph Act 1909). Again the local authority is the county council.

Shops and offices

6.14 Shops, offices and railway premises where persons other than close relatives of the employer (1963 Act sections 1 and 2) are employed to work are subject to control by the district council, under the Offices, Shops and Railway Premises Act 1963, provided the time worked at the premises exceeds 21 hours a week (*ibid* section 3). This Act provides for such matters as cleanliness, temperature within rooms, ventilation, lighting and the provision of wcs (if necessary for both sexes), washing accommodation and so on. The standards specified are detailed and the Act and regulations made thereunder should be referred to by architects designing such a building. See, in particular, the Sanitary Conveniences Regulations 1964† and the Washing Facilities Regulations 1964.‡ A fire certificate or special fire precautions are required for shops, offices and railway premises, or for factories (para 6.03 above).

Food

6.15 In addition, if any part of the premises is used for a business involving food, the more stringent provisions of the Food Hygiene (General) Regulations 1970* made under the Food and Drugs Act 1955 must be observed. Premises used as a slaughterhouse or a knacker's yard for the slaughter of animals need to be licensed under the Slaughterhouses Act, 1974.

Miscellaneous

6.16 Licences from the district council are also required for the storage or manufacture of rag flock (Rag Flock and other Filling Materials Act 1951), for the use of premises as a shop for the sale of pet animals (Pet Animals Act 1951), for storage or sale of scrap metal (Scrap Metal Dealers Act 1964), for boarding cats and dogs (Animal Boarding Establishments Act 1963) and for keeping a riding establishment (Riding Establishment Acts 1964 and 1970). Nursing homes must now be registered by the Secretary of State (Nursing Homes Act 1975). In all these cases the suitability or otherwise of the premises for the particular purpose may be an issue in the grant or refusal of the licence. Caravan sites used for human habitation also need a licence in addition to planning permission (Caravan Sites and Control of Development Act 1960, part 1), and detailed conditions as to hygiene and sanitary requirements are customarily imposed.

References

CROSS, C. A. Principles of local government. 5th Edition, London, 1974, Sweet & Maxwell.

FOULKES, D. F. Introduction to administrative law. 4th Edition, London, 1976, Butterworth.

LEWIS, J. R. Administrative law for the construction industry. London, 1976, Macmillan.

PITT P. H. and DUFTON J. Building in Inner London, 1976, Architectural Press.

WHITTAKER, C. The handbook of environmental powers. London, 1976, Architectural Press.

* S.I. 1970 No. 1172

* Theatres Act 1968 section 12 and schedule 1. The local authorities responsible for administering these provisions are the county councils and the GLC (see section 18)

† S.I. 1964 No. 966

‡ S.I. 1964 No. 965

The DEVIL *and the* LAWYER.

Legal study 10

Scottish statutory authorities

This study covers for Scotland the topics dealt with in
LEGAL STUDY 9. *It explains all the important changes in local government in Scotland brought about by the Local Government (Scotland) Act* 1973

1 Introduction: Local government in Scotland

1.01 The structure of local government in Scotland has been entirely remodelled by the Local Government (Scotland) Act 1973. This Act swept away the hotchpotch of counties of cities, counties, large burghs, small burghs and districts. Mainland Scotland now has a two-tier administrative structure with 9 regions making up the top tier and 53 districts on the lower tier. The Western Isles, Orkney and Shetland each have allpurpose islands councils exercising all functions which, on the mainland, are allocated between regional and district councils. The Act also provides for the creation, within each district and islands area, of community councils. Their role is mainly representative and they have no statutory functions in the administration of local government.

1.02 All councils—regional, district and islands—are directly elected. After a transitional period, members of all councils will hold office for a four-year-term. Elections will be staggered so that district councillors are voted in mid-way through the regional term of office.

1.03 As in England local authorities are separate legal persons which perform certain functions laid down by statute, and the doctrine of *ultra vires* also applies in Scotland (LEGAL STUDY 9 para 1.08) so that no authority may act outwith its statutory powers.

Officials and committees
1.04 Again, as in England, local authorities appoint officials and staff to enable them to carry out their statutory functions. The 1973 Act requires a regional authority to appoint a director of education and a director of social work. Otherwise it allows authorities a wide discretion in the matter of their internal organisation. But in practice all authorities on the same level tend to be organised on broadly similar patterns of departmental responsibility. Each department comes under the jurisdiction of the appropriate committee of the authority. The top official, responsible for co-ordinating the various branches of an authority's activity, is generally styled 'Chief Executive'. 'Director of Finance' is the official in charge of overall financial management. There may be a Director of Administration or Director of Legal Services to supervise internal administration and act as legal adviser to the council in place of the old-style 'town clerk' or 'county clerk'. At district level, from the architect's point of view, the key official will be called something like 'Director of Planning and

Building Control', the exact designation of the official and his department being a matter of choice for individual authorities. Certain officials, such as the assessor and electoral registration officer, have specific statutory duties which they must perform regardless of any instructions from the authority.

Committees
1.05 Much of the work of the authority is, as in England, delegated to various committees. A novel feature introduced with reorganisation, though one which has not been universally approved, is the concept of a single party policy committee to advise the whole council in mapping out general policy and allocating resources among the various departments. The implementation of policy is left to the appropriate service committee, such as the planning committee, the highways committee and the education committee, which have delegated powers in the area of their responsibility. In addition to standing committees such as these, the authority may also set up special committees from time to time to deal with particular problems as they arise.

1.06 In general all committees are composed of council members only. Officials are present at committee meetings to give advice when required, but without the right to vote.

Functions of local authorities
1.07 All functions exercised by the old-style councils have been taken over by the new authorities. The new authorities have also taken over functions exercised before reorganisation by other bodies such as the water boards. The major functions are now allocated by statute between regional and district authorities as follows:

Regional	District
Structure plans	Local plans
Highways	Housing
Transport, harbours, etc	Planning permission
Water	Building control
Sewerage	Listed building consent and tree preservation
Valuation	Designation of conservation areas
Police	Improvement grants
Fire	Licensing
Social Work	Environmental health
Education	Libraries
Parks	Allotments

There are certain exceptions to this scheme. The Borders and Lothian regions combine to form joint fire and police authorities. In the Borders, Highland and Dumfries and Galloway areas, the regional council is responsible for planning and building control. The same regions are also responsible for all library services in their area. Certain water authorities have jurisdiction over areas which fall within the boundaries of adjoining regions. As has already been mentioned, islands councils exercise *all* local authority functions within their area.

2 Connection to services

2.01 The 1973 Act is primarily concerned with the structure of local government and does not re-enact or spell out in detail the powers and functions which have been transferred from the old to the new authorities. The details are to be found in a mass of legislation going back for over a century. Much of this, particularly in the case of the cities of Glasgow, Edinburgh, Dundee and Aberdeen which have become districts in the new scheme, is purely local legislation. However, the Burgh Police (Scotland) Acts 1892 to 1911 do provide a useful starting point for examining the basic sorts of powers which local authorities have in relation to such things as highways and streets, building control and sanitation.

Sewers
2.02 The 1973 Act makes sewerage the responsibility of the regional authorities. The Sewerage (Scotland) Act 1968 details the powers and functions of those authorities in this area. The Act consolidates and simplifies all previous legislation, and introduces a statutory definition of 'drains' and 'sewers' which is the same as that used in England (LEGAL STUDY 9 para 2.02).

2.03 The Act provides that all public sewers will continue to be vested in local authorities, as will various new sewers. Junctions to public sewers are also vested in local authorities. Thus if a private drain is joined to a sewer, it will be the local authority's responsibility to maintain the junction.

2.04 Sewerage authorities are obliged to provide public sewers as may be necessary for draining their area of domestic sewage, surface water and trade effluent. The authority has to take public sewers to such a point as will enable owners of premises to connect their drains at reasonable cost. This is subject to the proviso that the authority need itself do nothing which is not practicable at a reasonable cost. Nevertheless, the responsibility for providing sewers is clearly that of the local authority, while the responsibility for installing drains in individual premises is that of the proprietor.

2.05 Local authorities have powers to construct, close or alter sewers or sewage treatment works. Where they are not under an obligation to provide public sewers (ie where they cannot do so at reasonable cost), they may enter into an agreement on construction and taking over of sewers and treatment with any person they are satisfied is about to construct premises in their area. Where authorities are under an obligation to provide sewers, they may not enter into such agreements.

Drains
2.06 Any owner of premises is entitled to connect his drains or private sewer to a public sewer and to allow his drains to empty into a public sewer on giving the authority 28 days notice. However, the authority may refuse permission or grant it subject to conditions. A proprietor may connect his drains to a sewer in a different local authority area, but he must first serve notice on both authorities. The Secretary of State has powers to require the authority in whose area the premises are situated to pay for the service which the other authority is providing. Previously it was the proprietor who had to make any payment required.

2.07 Where a notice regarding connection of a drain or sewer to a public sewer is served on an authority, the authority has powers to direct the manner in which the junction is to be constructed and to supervise construction. The authority has the same powers in relation to any new drain or private sewer if it appears likely that the drain or sewer will be wanted by it to form part of the general system. Authorities are bound to meet the extra cost arising from implementation of their instructions. To allow supervision, 3 days' notice of the start of work must be given to the authority.

2.08 A local authority can also require defects in private drains and sewers to be remedied and may itself carry out the work if the proprietor fails to do so. Where the defect represents a health hazard, the authority is empowered to carry out emergency repairs on the basis of a 48 hour notice. The cost of repairs carried out by the authority can be recovered from proprietors.

2.09 Provisions relating to trade effluent, trade effluent notices and agreements and so on, broadly similar to those contained in English legislation (LEGAL STUDY 9 para 2.12), are also included in the Act.

2.10 Sewage discharged into a public sewer must not be of such a nature as to cause damage to the sewer or, through mixture with other sewage, to cause a nuisance.

2.11 Where a new development is proposed the responsibility for providing sewers rests with the sewerage authority, although this does not apply in the case of an individual house where all that is necessary is a drain or private sewer to connect with the public system. The situation may arise where a delay by the authority in fulfilling its duty holds up development. If a developer chooses to install sewers at his own expense, he will be able to recover from the authority only if, from the start, he adopts the correct procedure (*Varney (Scotland) Ltd v Burgh of Lanark* 1976 SLT 46).

2.12 Under the Burgh Police Acts a district authority has powers to require the proprietor of a house or other building which does not have an adequate drain, to form a drain so that it empties into a sewer within 100yd (91.440m) of the premises or, if there is no sewer, into a cesspool or other place as directed by the authority. The authority may do the work itself and charge the proprietor with the cost if he fails to comply.

Water supply
2.13 The Water (Scotland) Act 1967 set up regional water boards as water supply authorities in Scotland. The 1973 Act transferred the functions of the boards to the new regional authorities. In terms of the Water (Scotland) Act 1946 persons erecting new buildings of any type are obliged to make adequate provisions to the satisfaction of the district authority for a supply of clean water for the domestic purposes of persons occupying or using the building. Local authorities may also require house owners to provide water supplies in, or if that is impracticable, immediately outside their houses.

2.14 Regional authorities are under an obligation to provide supplies of wholesome water to every part of their regions where a supply is required for domestic purposes and can be provided at reasonable cost. They are obliged to lay main water pipes so that buildings where domestic supplies are required can be connected at a reasonable cost. When a question arises as to whether or not water can be supplied in this manner to any area at a reasonable cost, the Secretary of State for Scotland must decide, if requested to do so by 10 or more local electors.

2.15 The authorities are also obliged to supply water at reasonable terms for other than domestic purposes, provided that to do so would not prejudice their ability to supply water for domestic purposes.

2.16 The procedure for obtaining a water supply for domestic purposes in Scotland is regulated by the third schedule to the Water (Scotland) Act 1946, and is basically similar to that in England (LEGAL STUDY 9 para 2.17). A period of 14 days' notice must be given to the authority of the intention to lay a supply pipe. The supply pipe is laid by the proprietor and then attached to the communication pipe by the authority.

Gas, electricity and telephones

2.17 On these topics, reference should be made to LEGAL STUDY 9 para 2.20 et seq as what is said there applies also to Scotland. The Gas Act 1948 applies with minor modifications in Scotland as in England. Likewise the Electricity Act 1947 applies with small modifications.

Construction of mains

2.18 Again the remarks on this topic in LEGAL STUDY 9 (para 2.26) should be referred to. The term for a 'way-leave' in Scotland is 'servitude' (LEGAL STUDY 7 para 3.07.)

3 Private streets and footpaths

3.01 The Highways Act 1959 (LEGAL STUDY 9 para 3.02) does not apply in Scotland, and the law on private streets is based on the Burgh Police (Scotland) Acts 1892 and 1903.

3.02 Public streets are those streets vested by the 1973 Act in the regional council. They are entered in the 'register of streets' kept by every council. A private street is basically a *street* (not just a footpath) open to the public, but not vested in the council; a purely private road is not a private street. The council is not liable for its upkeep in any way, but it has powers to have a street and footpath made up at the expense of the frontagers. When the street has been properly made up, the council may take it over on the application of one or more of the frontagers. If more than half the frontagers in the street apply, the council is bound to take it over.

Footpaths

3.03 The authority has powers under the Burgh Police Acts to require frontagers on a public street to make a footpath along the front of their property, or as a preliminary to taking over existing footpaths, it may require the frontagers of a particular area to put them in repair. In either instance it is bound to maintain them.

4 Grants

4.01 As in England various grants are obtainable by a proprietor in Scotland to assist him in alterations or improvements to his property. Discretionary improvements grants and standard grants are payable in Scotland under the

Housing (Financial Provisions) Scotland Act 1968, the Housing (Scotland) Act 1969 and the Housing (Scotland) Act 1974. Although made under different legislation, these grants are payable on the same basis as in England, details of which are found in LEGAL STUDY 9 para 4.01 et seq.

4.02 Various grants are available for improvement or rebuilding of agricultural workers' cottages. It is not proposed to examine these in detail, but it should be noted that special grants are available for the Highlands, islands and crofting areas. Local authorities may, under the Housing (Financial Provisions) Scotland Act 1968, prepare schemes for giving grants for new homes for agricultural workers in their districts. Where a grant has been given under one of the schemes relating to agricultural cottages, improvement grants are not normally payable.

4.03 Many other grants are payable by various authorities, but it should be noted that the Public Health Act 1936 does not apply in Scotland. Grants for installation of wcs are available in the form of standard grants. The Local Authorities (Historic Buildings) Act does not apply in Scotland. The Clean Air Acts and the Airport Authority Act apply and grants may be obtained under them where appropriate (LEGAL STUDY 9 paras 4.16 and 4.18). A grant may be obtained as a standard grant for bringing a supply of piped water into a house for the first time.

5 Housing associations

5.01 As in England (LEGAL STUDY 9 para 5.01 et seq) housing associations in Scotland are entitled to various benefits under the Scottish Housing Acts. The Secretary of State for Scotland may make advances to them, and they may also borrow money from the Public Works Loan Commissioners. In addition there are special statutory provisions to provide for the Scottish Special Housing Association by giving it financial assistance.

6 Special considerations

6.01 In Scotland as well as in England (LEGAL STUDY 9 para 6.01 et seq) special considerations apply to certain types of building. The Factories Acts, the Offices, Shops and Railway Premises Act and the Clean Air Acts all apply. Liquor licensing is operated under a separate statutory code, and the structural suitability of any premises is a question which is considered by the Licensing Courts.

6.02 Scottish readers are advised to check with all new legislation for applications and/or amendments to Scots law, For example, the Health and Safety at Work Act 1974 applies to Scotland, amending the Building (Scotland) Act 1959. Similarly the Control of Pollution Act 1974 has general application to Scotland (see section 106) and amends much other Scottish legislation of this kind. (See LEGAL STUDIES 9, 13 and 14.)

AJ Legal Handbook

Section 7
Copyright

Legal study 11

Copyright

In this study copyright law is described for architects, defining the nature, ownership and term of copyright. Particularly important is the discussion of two recent cases which give guidance on clients' implied rights to use architects' drawings (para 4). The study ends with a brief discussion of design registration.
A short note on copyright in Scotland is appended

1 Copyright and architects

1.01 'Copyright is not the sickle which reaps an architect's profit.' Few architects think that action for infringement or licence fees for use of their copyrights would form a useful additional source of revenue, but this comment by the judge in the leading case of architect's copyright (*Meikle v Maufe* (1941) 3 All ER) should serve as a warning. Many architects seem to believe that copyright is a powerful safeguard; the purpose of this study is to remind them of the severe limitations of this form of protection, bearing in mind the two very recent and important Court of Appeal cases of *Blair v Osborne & Tompkins* (para 4.07) and *Stovin Bradford v Volpoint Properties Ltd* (para 4.08). As an increasing number of architects are being commissioned to design components for use by the building industry, this article also discusses the special form of protection in registered designs for manufacture.

History of architects' copyright
1.02 Copyright in architectural drawings and sketches was first given statutory force in the Fine Arts Copyright Act 1842, although artistic quality was the criterion. Following the Berne Convention of 1908, the Copyright Act 1911 confirmed the protection of plans and sketches under the definition of 'literary works' (*sic*) and drawings under the definition of 'artistic works'. Despite considerable parliamentary opposition, protection was also accorded for the first time to 'architectural works of art' defined as any building or structure having artistic character or design, or any model for such building or structure.

1.03 The emphasis was on the artistic element although the few reported cases between 1911 and 1956 do not indicate that anything particularly original needed to be proved and it was probably sufficient to say that the work was the architect's personal labour whether or not it contained anything which others would have considered artistic. Modern law is based upon the Copyright Act 1956 which by section 3 provides, somewhat paradoxically, that 'artistic work' means *inter alia:* paintings, sculptures, drawings, engravings, photographs 'irrespective of artistic quality'; works of architecture being either buildings or models for buildings.

The nature of copyright
1.04 It must be remembered that copyright cannot exist in ideas but only in some tangible or physical manifestation of an idea. As architects are by the nature of their occupation likely to express their ideas in the form of sketches or drawings, this distinction is not likely to trouble them as much as it does the authors of literary or dramatic works. Copyright in relation to artistic work means the exclusive right to do and to authorise other persons to do certain acts in relation to that work within the UK and other countries to which the provisions of the Copyright Act 1956 have been extended. The relevant 'acts' for architects' drawings are:
1 Reproducing of the work in any material form.
2 Publishing the work.
3 Including the work in a television broadcast.

'Drawings' and 'buildings'
1.05 Copyright attaches to drawings 'irrespective of artistic merit'. The 1956 Act defines drawings as including any diagram, map, chart or plan, which probably covers all an architect's work in two-dimensional forms.
Works of architecture are defined as being either buildings or models for buildings; building is further defined as including any structure. Although no definition of structure is provided, it is thought that concerning the nature of copyright and the basic intention of protecting original artistic design, the word will be probably sufficient to cover most forms of structure although the borderline between a structure and a sculpture (which is in any case similarly protected by copyright) may be difficult to define. In the writer's opinion, the Blackpool Tower and the Statue of Liberty would almost certainly be structures within the statutory definition. The wideness of definition of works of architecture would seem to cover all work by an architect in three-dimensional forms.

Originality and artistic content
1.06 Buildings and models require in theory to have an artistic character or design, but in the few reported cases, it would appear that no architect has failed to prove an infringement even though the original building was so ordinary that it might be thought inevitable that someone else would design something substantially similar. In the case of *University of London Press Ltd v University Tutorial Press Ltd*, which concerned the copying of examination papers, the judge stated that 'the word "original" does not in this connection mean that the work must be the expression of original or inventive thought . . . but that it should originate from the author'.

1.07 For architectural works, the inclusion of some distinctive design detail will make the architect's task of proving infringement much easier. In the case of *Stovin-Bradford v Volpoint Properties Ltd* (*The Times* 25.5.71) the courts were influenced by the fact that although many details of the architect's drawings were not reproduced in the constructed buildings, 'a distinctive diamond-shaped feature which gave a pleasing appearance to the whole' was reproduced. In *Meikle v Maufe* the judge referred to many details in the original building and dismissed them as not being of artistic merit.

1.08 Some distinctive design feature may also be important when it could otherwise be proved that the person sued without any knowledge of the plaintiff's prior design, and that they produced identical solutions because of a similarity in circumstances. In *Muller v Triborough Bridge Authority* the United States Supreme Court held that a copyright of the drawing showing a novel bridge approach designed to disentangle traffic congestion was not infringed by copying, because the system of traffic congestion shown embodied an idea which cannot be copyright and was the only obvious solution to the problem.

Duration of copyright
1.09 The protection of copyright in an artistic work that is not mass-produced industrially extends for the lifetime of the author and a further period of 50 years from the end of the calendar year in which he died. In the case of architectural works, this is unaffected by non-publication. Mass-produced objects are considered below in 5.01 *et seq*.

2 Ownership

Qualified persons
2.01 In the case of unpublished works, copyright will subsist only if the author was a 'qualified person' at the time when the work was made, or, if it was being made over a period, for a substantial part of that period. In the case of a published work, the author must have been qualified at the time when the work was published, or immediately before his death (if earlier).

2.02 For copyright purposes, a 'qualified person' means not a registered architect, but a British subject, a citizen of the Republic of Ireland, a person domiciled or resident in the UK or in another country to which the Act extends, or a body incorporated under the laws of the UK or such another country. The other countries are the signatories to the Berne Copyright Convention.
The provision relating to corporations is not important to architects because a corporation cannot be the author of an artistic work.
'Publication' in copyright law means 'the issue of reproductions of the work to the public', but this does not include the issue of photographs of architectural works. It seems, therefore, that a building cannot be 'published', and this means that an English architect has a remedy if a building he has erected overseas is copied in the UK. This would not be the case had the work been first published outside the UK.

Architect as owner
2.03 Ownership of copyright resides with the architect who actually drew the plan, drawing, sketch or diagram, and, being personal property in law, passes to its owner's personal representatives after his death, and thence as directed in his will or in the event of intestacy to his next of kin.

Partners
2.04 Unless the partnership deed (LEGAL STUDY 3 para 2.05) states anything to the contrary, the copyright in all work produced during the currency of a partnership is a partnership asset, and like other assets is owned and passes in accordance with general provisions of the partnership deed concerning assets. To avoid dissemination of shares in copyright, it is usually desirable to provide that upon the death or retirement of a partner, his share in the copyright should vest in the surviving partners. Alternatively, partners could, in their wills, leave their shares in the copyright to their surviving partners.

Employees
2.05 The copyright in architects' drawings, buildings or models produced by an employee during his employment automatically vests in his employer, whether the latter is an architect in partnership, a limited company or public authority. Section 44 of the 1956 Act does, however, refer to employment under a 'contract of service or apprenticeship'. Frequently architects employ independent architects, and artists who carry out parts of the drawing service, and increasingly who would appear to be employees are for a variety of reasons (not unconnected with tax and Social Security payments) engaged as self-employed subcontractors. Such persons are rarely employed under 'a contract of service' as distinct from 'a contract for services' which is not the same thing (LEGAL STUDY 1 para 5.04). Employer architects would be well advised to make it an express term of such a subcontractor's appointment that any copyright arising out of his work should vest in the employing architect.

Ownership of drawings
2.06 Ownership of copyright in drawings should be distinguished from ownership of the actual pieces of paper upon which they are drawn. It is settled law that upon payment of the architect's fees the client is entitled to physical possession of all the drawings prepared at his expense. In the absence of agreement to the contrary, copyright remains with the architect who also has a lien on (right to withhold) the drawings until his fees are paid. If all copyright *is* assigned to the client he may make such use of it as he wishes. Architects should note that even if they have assigned the copyright, they may reproduce in a subsequent work part of the original design provided that they do not repeat or imitate the main design. This provision should enable the architect to repeat standard details which in theory pass to the client upon prior assignment of copyright.

Statutory restrictions on architects' copyright
Photographs, paintings
2.07 Frequently photographs of buildings designed by architects appear as part of advertisements by the contractors who constructed the buildings. As a matter of courtesy, the contractor usually makes some acknowledgement of the design, but he is not required to do so. By section 9 of the 1956 Act, the copyright in a work of architecture is not infringed by a photograph, painting, drawing or engraving of a building. Making of a drawing in this sense refers to a perspective or even detailed survey of the building as built. It would remain an infringement to copy the drawing or plan from which the building was constructed. Similarly, still photographs or a film of a building used in a cinematograph or television broadcast, do not infringe an architect's copyright.

Reconstruction
2.08 Where copyright exists in a building it is not infringed by any reconstruction of the building or part thereof. Also, if the original architect had licensed the original building owner to use his plans or drawings for the original construction, there will be no infringement if subsequent reconstruction of the building or part thereof is carried out by reference

to such original drawings or plans. This point is of particular importance in connection with the now established 'implied licence' considered in para 4.04 *et seq*.

Fair dealing

2.09 A general defence to any alleged infringement of copyright in an artistic work is 'fair dealing' for the purpose of criticism or review, provided that there is sufficient acknowledgement. As reproduction by photograph is the most likely method of illustrating a review and as a photograph of a building is specifically exempt from infringement, this defence of 'fair dealing' would appear to be needed only in the case of drawings. A sufficient acknowledgement is an acknowledgement identifying the building by its name and location, which also identifies the name of the architect who designed it. The 1956 Act, however, provides that the name of the copyright owner need not be given if he has previously required that no acknowledgement of his name should be made. As certain self-appointed groups have now taken to awarding prizes for ugliness in design, some architects might find themselves in the unusual position of wishing to have no acknowledgement made of their connection with a design, although perhaps such publicity would hardly be 'fair dealing'.

The Crown

2.10 Under section 39 of the 1956 Act, the Crown is entitled to the copyright in all artistic work 'made by or under the direction or control of Her Majesty or a government department'. This is perfectly clear concerning ministries or departments of State; but recently concern has been expressed by architects who have been informed by regional hospital boards and hospital management committees that by virtue of this section, copyright in an architect's work for them vests in the Crown. In the writer's opinion, this is not valid. The regional hospital boards and hospital management committees have separate corporate legal existence. All their finance may come from the Department of Health and Social Security but they are not themselves government departments within the meaning of section 39. Since the RIBA made representations on this point it is understood that the approach has changed and architects are being requested expressly to agree prior assignment of future copyrights under section 37 of the Act (para 4.01). In all cases where express prior assignment is required by a client the architect should, in the writer's opinion, enquire into the reasons for such a request.

3 Infringement

3.01 To prove infringement, a plaintiff must show:
1 Copyright subsists in his work.
2 The copyright is vested in him.
3 The alleged infringement is identical to his work in material particulars.
4 The alleged infringement was copied from his work.

3.02 No action for infringement of copyright can succeed if the person who is claimed to have infringed had no knowledge of the existence of the work of the owner. In this respect it differs from patents which must be registered but which give an absolute protection even if the person infringing a patent had no knowledge of its existence. Copyright restricts the right to copy, which presupposes some knowledge of the original by the copier. Ignorance of the fact that the work copied was the copyright owner's is not however a defence. It is in the nature of architects' copyright that the person allegedly infringing must have had access directly or in-

directly to the drawings. Infringement can therefore take three forms as detailed below.

Copying in form of drawings

3.03 It is rare for drawings to be copied in every detail, and many would-be infringers of an architect's copyright believe that if details are altered, infringement is avoided. This is not so, and section 49 of the 1956 Act makes it clear that references to reproduction include reproduction of a 'substantial part'. Cases under the 1911 Act indicate that the word 'substantial' refers to quality rather than quantity. Reference has already been made to the distinctive diamond-shaped detail in the Stovin-Bradford case. It does not matter that the size of the copy may have been increased or reduced or that only a small detail of an original drawing has been copied.

Copying the drawing in the form of a building

3.04 The leading case on this form of infringement is *Chabot v Davies* (1936) 3 All ER. Mr Chabot, who was not an architect but 'a designer and fixer of shop fronts and the like' prepared a drawing for the defendant who 'was just about to open what is known as a fish and chip shop'. Mr Chabot was lucky enough to be able to prove that the contractor had actually been handed his drawing by the defendant and had made a tracing from it, but the defendant argued that a plan cannot be reproduced by a shop front but only by something in the nature of another plan. The judge held, however, that 'reproduce . . . in any material form whatsoever' must include reproduction of a drawing by an actual building. This case may, however, be qualified by the words of section 9 of the 1956 Act which (paraphrased) provides that the erection of a building (ie an object in three dimensions) shall not be taken to infringe the copyright in a drawing or plan (ie an object in two dimensions) unless the building would appear to a layman (and a judge is a layman in this respect) to be a reproduction of the drawing. Again 'substantial' reproduction is important and a distinctive detail assists proof.

Copying a building by another building

3.05 The leading case on this type of infringement and until recently on architects' copyright generally is *Meikle v Maufe*. Most architects have heard of this case but the facts and argument bear repetition. In 1912 Heal & Son Ltd employed Smith & Brewer as architects for the building of premises on the northern part of the present site of Heal's store in Tottenham Court Road. At that time there were vague discussions about a future extension on the southern part of the site, but because of difficulties over land acquisition nothing could be done. In 1935 Heal's employed Maufe as their architect for the extension of the building. Meikle was by this time the successor in title to Smith & Brewer's copyright and he claimed that both the extension as erected and the plans for its erection infringed the original copyright. Maufe admitted that he thought it necessary to reproduce in the southern section of the facade the features which appeared in the original northern section. His object was 'to make the new look like the old throughout nearly the whole of the Tottenham Court Road frontage'. The layout of the interiors was also substantially reproduced. The defendants put forward three arguments:
1 There could not be a separate copyright in a building as distinct from copyright in the plans on which it was based.
2 If there were a separate copyright in a building it would belong to the building contractor.
3 It was an implied term of Smith & Brewer's original engagement that Heal's should have the right to reproduce the design of the original in the extension.

3.06 The first argument failed following *Chabot v Davies*. The second argument failed because copyright protection in a building is limited to the artistic character or design and in making of such character or design the contractor plays no part. The third argument failed in this particular case as the Copyright Act 1911, under which this case was tried, provided that copyright remained with its original author, unless he had agreed to pass the right to another. Heal's contended that Smith & Brewer had impliedly consented to the reproduction of their design because they had known of the possibility of extension. The judge having heard the facts concerning the discussions about land acquisition held that he could not reasonably imply such a term in this case.

4 Licence

Express licence

4.01 Section 1.5 of the RIBA Conditions of Engagement states that copyright in all drawings and in the work executed from them remains the property of the architect unless otherwise agreed (except in work for the Crown—see para 2.10). Section 37 of the 1956 Act permits prior assignment of future copyright so that client and architect can agree at the beginning of an engagement that the copyright which will come into existence during the commission will vest in the client.

4.02 Copyright may also be expressly assigned to the client at some later stage, but it is usual to grant a licence authorising use of copyright subject to conditions rather than an outright assignment of all the architect's rights. An increasing number of public and commercial clients make it a condition of the architect's appointment that all copyright shall vest in the client, but the architect should not consent to this without careful thought. Following *Meikle v Maufe* it would seem reasonable that a client should not be prevented from extending a building and incorporating distinctive design features of the original building so that the two together should form one architectural unit. If the time between the original building and the extension were 23 years, as in that case, it would be restrictive to make use of copyright to force the client into employing the original architect of his successor in title. Less scrupulous clients could, however, make use of an architect's design for a small and inexpensive original building with the undisclosed intention of greatly extending the building using the same design but at no extra cost in terms of architect's fees.

4.03 So far as drawings are concerned, it must be remembered that they are the subject of copyright 'irrespective of artistic quality' so that a prior express assignment of copyright to the client could theoretically grant him copyright in respect of even the most simple standard detail contained in the drawings (but see para 2.06).

Implied licence

4.04 As long ago as 1938, the RIBA took counsel's opinion on the theory that an architect impliedly licenses his client to make use of the architect's drawings for the purposes of construction even when the client does not employ the architect to supervise the building contract. Such an implied consent can be understood when from the beginning of the engagement the client made it clear that all he required of the architect was drawings; for if the client received the drawings and paid for them, they would be valueless unless he could use them for the purpose of construction. The courts would not allow an architect to use his copyright to prevent construction in such circumstances. Counsel advised further that even if it had originally been assumed that the architect

would perform the full service and supervise construction but the client subsequently decided that he did not require supervision, an implied licence to use the copyright in the drawings would arise in the client's favour when working drawings had been completed. Counsel did not then believe that an implied licence could arise at an earlier stage, but since 1938 the extent of architects' work and its stages have increased greatly. Cumulatively detailed drawings required for outline planning consent, detailed planning consent, and Building Regulation consent all create different stages and implied licence can now arise earlier than was contemplated in 1938.

4.05 Before any term can be implied into a contract, the courts must consider what the parties would have decided if they had considered the question at the time they negotiated other terms of the engagement. The courts are reluctant to imply a term unless it is necessary to give efficacy to the intention of the parties. Application of these rules to an architect's engagement would suggest that it is reasonable to infer that the architect impliedly consents to the client making use of his drawings for the purpose for which they were intended. If, therefore, the nature of the engagement is not full RIBA service but, for example, obtaining outline planning permission and no more, the architect impliedly consents to the client making use of his copyright to apply for such permission. Again, if an architect is instructed to prepare drawings of a proposed alteration for submission to the client's landlord, the client may use the drawings to obtain a consent under the terms of his lease (LEGAL STUDY 6 para 6.05) but not for any other purpose, and certainly not for the purpose of instructing a contractor to carry out the alteration work.

4.06 The whole question of implied licence has recently been considered by the Court of Appeal in the cases of *Blair* and *Stovin-Bradford*, both of which have been fully reported. The facts in these cases were as follows.

Blair v Osborne & Tompkins

4.07 Blair was asked by his clients whether it would be possible to obtain planning consent for development at the end of his clients' garden. Having made inquiries, Blair advised that it should be possible to obtain consent for erection of two semi-detached houses. The clients instructed Blair to proceed to detailed planning consent stage and agreed to pay on the RIBA scale. The application was successful and Blair sent the planning consent to his clients, with his account for £70 for 'taking instructions, making survey, preparing scheme and obtaining full planning consent'. As was well known to the architect, the clients did not at that stage know whether they were going to develop the land or sell it.

They paid Blair's account which he acknowledged adding 'wishing you all the best on this project' but did not employ him to do any further work because they sold the plot to a contractor/developer. They also handed over Blair's drawings to the contractor, who used his own surveyors to add the detail necessary to obtain Building Regulation consent, and this consent having been obtained the contractor erected the houses. When the architect discovered that his plans were being used he claimed that this was an infringement of his copyright. The Master of the Rolls pointed out that although the RIBA Conditions of Engagement stated that copyright remained with the architect, it was open to him to give a licence for the drawings to be used for a particular site. His Lordship was influenced by the provision in the RIBA Conditions which entitled both architect and client to terminate the engagement 'upon reasonable notice'. To his Lordship it seemed inconceivable that upon the architect withdrawing he could stop any use of the plans on the ground of infringement of copyright. It seemed equally inconceivable that he could stop their use at an earlier stage when he had done his work up to a particular point and been paid according to the RIBA scale. Lord Justice Widgery approved the defendant's submission that the implied licence was 'to use whatever plans had been prepared at the appropriate stage for all purposes for which they would normally be used, namely, all purposes connected with the erection of the building to which they related'. If this was not right 'the architect could hold a client to ransom and that would be quite inconsistent with the term that the engagement could be put an end to at any time'. In the writer's opinion this was an unfortunate decision and went much further than was required. But it must be lived with.

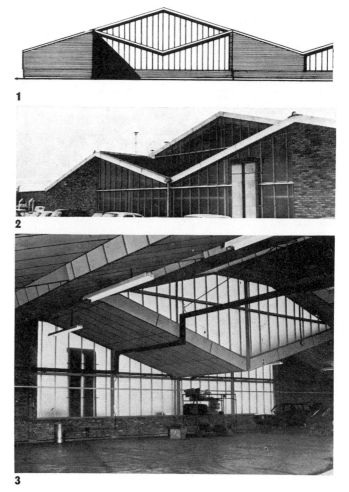

Stovin-Bradford v Volpoint Properties Ltd and Another

4.08 The defendant companies, which had their own drawing office, acquired an old factory which they considered had considerable development potential, and applied for planning consent for the erection of seven large warehouses. Permission was refused and the defendants approached Stovin-Bradford, whose work they had previously admired, explaining that they needed a plan and drawing that 'showed something which was more attractive looking than the existing building'. What they wanted was 'a pretty picture' but because they had their own drawing office, they did not need the full services of an architect. It was accepted by the court that although the then Conditions of Engagement were not incorporated in their contract, both architect and defendants were fully aware that they existed. It was also accepted that both parties were concerned only with obtaining planning permission. As the trial judge held, the agreement reached between the parties was very simple and amounted to this 'that Stovin-Bradford would suggest architectural improvements to the defendant's existing plan for the modification and extension of the existing building for the purpose of trying to obtain planning permission and that he would receive for this plan the sum of 100 guineas and his out-of-pocket expenses'. The drawing was produced showing an 'effect quite striking to the eye: a unification of two original structures into one with, in particular, a diamond feature in the left hand building caused by the arrangement of the roof line and the windows placed in the top part of the old portal frame building'. The plan was passed to the defendants, who made certain amendments and obtained planning permission. Stovin-Bradford had presented his account for the agreed 'nominal 100 guineas, headed it 'Statement no 1' and confirmed that the payment was 'for preparing sketch plans and design drawings in sufficient detail to obtain or apply for planning permission'. With commendable foresight, at the foot of the bill was typed a note saying: 'The copyright of the design remains with the architect and may not be reproduced in any form without his prior written consent.' The defendants proceeded to erect the buildings and although many details were changed, the result incorporated the particular features of the Stovin-Bradford design to which the trial judge drew notice **1, 2, 3.** At first instance, the trial judge held that there was an infringement and awarded £500 damages as the amount which would have been reasonably chargeable for a licence to make use of the copyright.

4.09 The Court of Appeal judgment in the Blair case having been published shortly afterwards, the defendants appealed on the ground that the Blair case was decisive authority for the view that whenever an architect prepared plans for

1 *Stovin-Bradford's original design, and warehouses as built* **2, 3**

obtaining planning permission, the client could use them for the building as he liked without further payment. This time Lord Denning, the Master of the Rolls, referred to the stages of normal service in the RIBA Conditions, which he defined as being: 1 plans up to an application for outline planning permission; 2 plans up to an application for detailed planning permission; 3 working drawings and specification for contractor to tender; 4 all an architect's work to completion of the building. (The author has often thought that this would be the most sensible division of the RIBA stages of normal service, but in fact the stages are not so defined in then existing Conditions—though the stages in the 1971 Conditions roughly correspond to this division.) Again the judges referred to the provision for termination upon reasonable notice and commented that the scale charges for 'partial services' seemed to be so fixed that they contained an in-built compensation for the use of designs and drawings right through to completion of the work. Lord Denning pointed out that in the Blair case charges had been in accordance with the RIBA scale ie $\frac{1}{6}$ of the full fee. But in this case the architect had charged on 'agreed nominal fee' basis and his fee was far less than the percentage fee (which would have been, at $\frac{1}{6}$, some £900). The Court of Appeal confirmed that there was an infringement, that an implied licence had not arisen and that damages of £500 were reasonable.

Conclusions

4.10 From these two decisions it would appear that charging by the RIBA scales for partial services (whether originally contemplated or brought about by a termination) will give rise to an implied licence while charging on some other basis, perhaps accompanied by warning notes and express reservations of copyright, will not. It is to be hoped that the RIBA will now change the Conditions of Engagement to provide that the client will have an express licence to use the drawings only for the specific purpose for which they were prepared, and in particular that the preparation of drawings for obtaining planning permission does not carry with it the right to use them for construction of the building without the architect's express consent (which ought not to be unreasonably withheld).

It would be wise to make it an express term of the Conditions of Engagement that even the licence to use the plans for the specific purpose comes into effect only when the architect has been paid the appropriate stage fees for the partial service he has undertaken or at least when the appropriate fee has been tendered. Certainly, as the Court of Appeal stressed in both cases, there should be something specific on clients' rights if the engagement is terminated in accordance with the Conditions. Although certain remarks of the court in the case of *Tingay v Harris* (1967) 1 All ER 855 suggested that implied licence can arise even if the architect's fees for partial service have not been paid, the writer is of the opinion that the further remarks in the Blair case confirm the view that implied licence can arise in the client's favour only when he paid or at least tendered the correct partial services fee.*

Remedies for infringement

Injunction
4.11 A common misconception among architects is that if they discover that their copyright in either drawings or buildings is being infringed they can obtain an injunction, or that by threatening an injunction they can obtain a substantial sum from the person erecting the building. Section 17 of the 1956 Act is, however, quite specific on this point and provides that no injunction can be granted after the construction of a building has started, nor can an injunction be granted to require the building (so far as it has been constructed) to be demolished.

Damages
4.12 In *Chabot v Davies* the court held that the measure of damages for infringement of the designer's copyright was the amount which he might reasonably have charged for granting a licence to make use of his copyright. In *Meikle v Maufe* the court rejected an argument that the architect might reasonably claim the profit which he would have made if he had been employed to carry out the work which infringed his copyright. 'Such profits do not provide either a mathematical measure for damages or a basis upon which to estimate damages. Copyright is not the sickle which reaps an architect's profit.'

Mr Justice Graham in the Stovin-Bradford case confirmed the licence fee basis of the two earlier cases and awarded £500 against the plaintiff's request for £1000 and the defendant's suggestion of between £10 and £20. Although this point has not been decided with reference to architect's copyright, it would appear that on general principles, exemplary damages could be awarded in addition to the licence fee where the breach was particularly flagrant.

5 Industrial designs

5.01 The law on this subject is complicated and extremely technical. It is not proposed to deal with this matter at length, but merely to warn architects, who may be commissioned to design components capable of mass reproduction, of the protections they should seek. Industrial design falls mid-way between copyright (not registrable in the UK) which is concerned with 'artistic quality' and patents which must be registered and are not concerned with artistic quality but function and method of manufacture. The law on industrial designs was considerably changed by the Copyright Act 1956 and further changes were contained in the Design Copyright Act 1968. The Copyright Act 1956 made new provisions in substitution of those of the Copyright Act 1911 and amended the Registered Designs Act 1949 with respect to design related to artistic works in which copyright subsists.

Design registration
5.02 Certain designs which are intended for industrial application may be registered at the Patent Office, under the provisions of the Registered Designs Act 1949. 'In this Act, the expression "design" means features of shape, configuration, pattern or ornament applied to an article by any industrial process or means, being features which in the finished article appeal to and are judged solely by the eye, but does not include a method or principle of construction, or features of shape or configuration which are dictated solely by the function which the article to be made in that shape or configuration has to perform' (Registered Designs Act 1949 section 1 (3)).

5.03 Unlike copyright, which is negative and entitles the owner to restrain infringements, registration of design is positive and grants to the registered owner exclusive right to make, sell, hire etc any article in respect of which the design is registered. This right is described in the Act as 'design copyright', but is much wider than the 'artistic copyright' conferred by the Copyright Acts, because it binds anyone who has independently evolved an identical design; for this reason design copyright can subsist, and a registration be valid, only if the design has not previously been used or published in the UK.

Copyright Act 1956
5.04 The Copyright Act 1956 established two different sets of rules in respect of artistic designs created before or after 1 June 1957. The basic principle concerning works created *before* this date is that copyright in the original artistic design may be lost if at the time it was created it was capable of being registered as a design under the Design Acts and the author had intended that his design should be used as a model for multiplication by industrial process. *Since* this date, artistic copyright was lost only in respect of designs actually used for industrial reproduction and only in so far as so used. Copyright protection continued for any other form of user, and as the date of actual use is what matters, previous publication of the artistic work does not prevent a subsequent registration of the design for industrial application. Perhaps an example will illustrate these differences.

If the proprietor of a stately home commissioned an architect to design a Greek temple for the island in the middle of his ornamental lake, the copyright in the drawings and the building would remain with the architect in accordance with the normal principles already discussed. If, however, the client were well known to be a commercially minded entrepreneur who maintained a flourishing business in the sale of souvenirs including models of his coach collection, gothic folly and classical mausoleum it may well be thought that the architect should have appreciated that within a season or two plaster models of the Greek temple would also appear for sale at the Tudor gatehouse. Under the pre-June 1957 rules, the architect would have no remedy against his client unless he had registered his designs at the time he created them. Under the

* See also editorial comment in the AJ (28:6:71) on the problems of the cases referred to above and the interpretation of the RIBA Conditions of Engagement

post-June 1957 rules the architect need not have registered his designs until their industrial application was first contemplated.

Design Copyright Act 1968

5.05 The policy behind the 1965 Act was simple: the Copyright Acts were concerned with articles of artistic craftsmanship, not mass-productions. The Registered Designs Act 1949 provided all the protection necessary for industrial designs, and those who did not avail themselves of it had only themselves to blame—there was no need for two hammers to hit one nail. Unhappily, design pirates often proved to be so much quicker than the Registrar that they frequently pinched the nail before the hammer fell. This led to the passing of the Design Copyright Act 1968, which amended the relevant section of the 1956 Act so that industrial designs which are also artistic works (and these include design and production drawings) can now enjoy artistic copyright for a period of 15 years.

Protection of registration

5.06 Unlike copyright, which is negative and entitles the owner to restrain infringements, registration of design is positive and grants to the registered owner exclusive right to make, sell, hire any article in respect of which the design is registered. The protection lasts for five years, on payment of fees, and is renewable up to 15 years. The owner of the registered design would normally be the original author, and therefore the copyright owner as well, but frequently manufacturers who commission a component insist upon the design being registered in their names. The 1956 Act provides protections for the copyright owner when without his know-ledge someone else registered a corresponding design.

Definition of industrial use

5.07 A copyright design is taken to have been used industrially if it is applied to more than 50 articles.

Conclusion

5.08 Any architect who designs something which he can foresee might have an industrial application is advised to consult a solicitor or a chartered patent agent before he publishes the design in any way. If he does reveal the design to a manufacturer before registration, his only remaining legal weapon is an action for misuse of confidential information.

© George Stringer 1971.

6 Law of Copyright in Scotland

6.01 Basically there is no difference between the law of copyright in Scotland or England. The Copyright Act 1956 applies equally to both countries and codifies all earlier statutes which applied to either country. There are relatively few reported cases dealing with copyright in Scotland, and the writer is not aware of any recent decisions of the importance of those decided recently in the English courts. For the architect practising in Scotland the chapter on copyright in M'Neil and Lillie's *The mercantile law of Scotland* (Edinburgh, 1965, W. Green) provides an adequate introduction and a fuller study is available in Copinger and Skone James' *Law of copyright* (London, 1965, Sweet & Maxwell).

AJ Legal Handbook

Section 8
Planning

Legal study 12

Planning Law

The following study describes the basis of planning law before discussing what an architect should do to determine whether his building is subject to planning controls and, if it is, what controls apply. Planning controls for special types of buildings, including offices and industrial development, and local authorities' power of enforcement are outlined

1 Introduction

1.01 Town and country planning control over the development of all land (including buildings) in England and Wales* is an administrative process deriving from the Town and Country Planning Act 1947. It has operated since 1 July 1948 and was brought about (to mention no other matter) for the simple reason that in England and Wales there is a limited amount of land for an increasing number of people who wish to live and work upon it, and who increasingly call for more space both for working and for leisure. Thus the pressure on land is great and is getting greater.

1.02 Today the principal Act on the subject is the Town and Country Planning Act 1971. It is nearly 400 pages long and contains 295 sections and 25 schedules. It came into operation on 1 April 1972. Its functioning has been modified by the Town and Country Planning (Amendment) Act 1972, the Local Government Act 1972 (see particularly sections 179 and 182 to 185 and schedule 16, part I) and the Town and Country Amenities Act 1974.

Planning control process
1.03 The planning control process is a bifurcated process involving, on the one hand, the making of development plans (that is to say, blueprints for the future) that seek to show what the state of affairs will be when all forseeable development (or non-development) in the area covered by the plan has been achieved. On the other prong of the bifurcated process there is the day-to-day control over the carrying out of development through the medium of grants or refusals of planning permission for development. All this is a highly simplified, not to say over-simplified, statement of the entire complicated and sophisticated process of town planning control.

1.04 In the ultimate analysis all this control is done by the minister for town and country planning by whatever name he may be known. At the moment he is known as the Secretary of State for the Environment, but this does not alter the fact that, under the Minister of Town and Country Planning Act 1943, one minister of the Crown is, by law, rendered responsible ultimately for the way in which all town planning control is carried out in England and Wales, and for his actions he is answerable to the Sovereign Parliament.

* There is similar but separate statutory provision for Scotland (see appendix)

1.05 In this article no attention is given to the first prong of this bifurcated process, namely, the making, approval and bringing into operation of development plans comprising 'structure plans' and 'local plans'. It is assumed for the purpose of this article that all the requisite development plans are in operation. Accordingly, attention in succeeding chapters is given to the day-to-day process of town planning control through the medium of grants or refusals of planning permission for development.

1.06 Moreover, it should be made clear at the start that this study is written primarily for the guidance of architects: it is deliberately slanted in the direction of architects. An effort has been made to pick out from the surging cauldron of town planning controls some of the more important controls, and particularly those that would affect an architect seeking to organise development on behalf of a client.

1.07 Accordingly, there will be found in succeeding paragraphs a brief statement on local planning authorities (para 2.01 *et seq*) and what they can do when faced with an application for planning permission for development (para 4.01 *et seq*). Development itself is treated in some detail (para 3.01 *et seq*) though, may be, not in all the detail into which the expression breaks up once it is investigated. The method of making planning applications is dealt with as are the consequences of a refusal or a grant of permission subject to conditions (para 4.01 *et seq*). Special reference is made to office development (para 5.01 *et seq*), to industrial development (para 6.01 *et seq*) and to buildings of special architectural or historic interest (para 7.01 *et seq*) because these are three matters which, although standing outside the main stream of town planning control, are nevertheless highly important matters to a developer and to any architect advising him.
There is brief reference to the enforcement of planning control over the development of land (para 8.01 *et seq*) or, in other words, there is a statement on what happens, or does not happen, if a person does indeed carry out development without getting the appropriate planning permission in advance. The Community Land Act 1975 is briefly mentioned in para 9.01 and, finally, a few personal thoughts of the writer appear in para 10.01 *et seq*.

1.08 The length of this article has been limited. This means that it has not been possible in every instance to put in all the qualifications, exceptions, reservations and so forth which, on a strict statement, would necessarily be appended to the general statements set out in the chapters which follow. Accordingly, it is emphasised that this article is in the nature of a guide—a guide for architects. It is hoped that it will be helpful to them, but in the limited space available it cannot be an exhaustive statement on everything on which the article touches. Further information can be obtained from *An outline of planning law*.

2 Local planning authorities; or who is to deal with planning applications?

2.01 The first thing an architect seeking to carry out development must do is to go out and inspect the site of the proposed development. It is most important nowadays to discover:
1 Whether it is a cleared site.
2 Whether it contains a building and, if it does, whether that building is a building of special architectural or historical interest (see para 7.01 *et seq*).

2.02 Second, the architect must consider carefully the definition of 'development' in the 1971 Act (section 22) with the Town and Country Planning (Use Classes) Order 1972. Many building operations and changes of use do not constitute development by virtue of the definitions and provisions of this section and the 1972 order. If they do not, then nothing in the town planning acts applies to them. 'Development' is defined in para 3.01 *et seq*.

2.03 Third, the architect must examine closely the type of development which is sought to be carried out. Is it development which can be dealt with in the normal run of planning control, or will it be subject to some additional control over and above the normal run? It certainly will be if it happens to be development
1 For office purposes (see para 5.01 *et seq*).
2 For industrial purposes (see para 6.01 *et seq*).

2.04 Fourth, the architect must satisfy himself whether the site for the development does or does not fall within a conservation area demarcated under section 277 of the 1971 Act (see para 4.18).

2.05 Fifth, the architect must investigate the Town and Country Planning General Development Order 1977 to ascertain whether the development is 'permitted' development under the Order because, if it is, it gets automatic planning permission and there is no need to make any application at all to a local planning authority (see para 4.02 and table IV).

2.06 All these are preliminary matters about which the architect should become fully informed at the outset. In this article it will be assumed, for the moment, that the architect is dealing with a cleared site (or, at least, a site *not* containing anything in the nature of a special building), and that the development he wishes to carry out is development that can be dealt with under the general run of town planning control and does *not* attract any additional, ie special, control. The special control over offices, industrial development and development which has to occupy the site of an existing building or architectural or historic interest is dealt with separately later. For the moment it is assumed that the development which the architect is considering is straightforward building development not subject to any special form of control, but only to general town planning control under the Town and Country Planning Act 1971.

Which authority?

2.07 This being the case, the next thing which the architect must consider is the local government authority to whom the application for planning permission is to be made. It must be made to the local planning authority.

2.08 The local government system in England and Wales was completely reorganised as from 1 April 1974 under the provisions of the Local Government Act 1972. (For further information on authorities, see LEGAL STUDY 9.)

2.09 The new system (which does not apply within the area of Greater London) provides for local government to be discharged at three separate tiers, namely:
1 By county councils—six metropolitan county councils (Greater Manchester, Merseyside, South Yorkshire, Tyne and Wear, West Midlands and West Yorkshire) and thirty-nine non-metropolitan county councils popularly called 'Shire' county councils.
2 By district councils (called metropolitan district councils if they happen to be in a metropolitan county), some of which have borough status.
3 By parish councils.

2.10 The county councils and the district councils are now all local planning authorities and thus the new nomenclature speaks of the 'county planning authority' and the 'district planning authority'. Broadly speaking, the county planning authority is responsible for 'structure plans' and the district planning authority for 'local plans'. However, both of these two different kinds of authority have a finger in the pie when it comes to the matter of the day-to-day control of development by the granting or refusal of planning permission—the county authority dealing with 'county matters' and the district authority with all other matters (see Local Government Act 1972 section 182 and schedule 16 paras 15 to 32). Parish councils are *entitled* to be consulted about planning applications affecting land in their areas.

2.11 In Greater London the GLC (for the whole of Greater London) and the London boroughs (each for its own borough) with the common council (for the City of London) are all local planning authorities.

2.12 Although the application for planning permission will be made to a local government authority of one kind or another, it will often be the case that a good deal of 'negotiation' relating to the application will take place between the applicant's architect and officers of the local planning authority. The power of a planning officer, acting within the scope of his duties as such to bind the planning authority in whose service he functions, is well illustrated in the highly important case of *Lever (Finance) Ltd v Westminster (City) London Borough Council* (1970) 3 All ER 496.

2.13 In this case certain developers, who proposed developing a piece of land by building 14 houses on it, applied for planning permission to the local planning authority, attaching to the application a detailed plan of the development showing one of the houses, house G, as sited 40ft away from all existing houses. Permission for the development in accordance with the detailed plan was given by the planning authority on 24 March 1969. A month later the developers' architect made some variations to the detailed plan submitted to the authority. The variations included altering the site of house G so that it was sited only 23ft away from existing houses. A further site plan showing this variation was sent to the planning authority.

2.14 The authority's planning officer had lost the file containing the original plan approved by the planning authority. Because of this he made a mistake and told the architect over the telephone that the variation was not material and that no further planning consent was required. The telephone conversation took place in May 1969 and the developers acted on this representation and went ahead with the development, including the erection of house G, which was started in September 1969.

2.15 The residents of the existing houses made representations to the planning authority about the variation of the site of house G. The planning authority suggested to the developers that they should apply for planning permission for the variation. On 17 March 1970 the developers did so apply, the application being supported by the authority's planning officer, but the planning authority refused the application. It also refused a further application, made in April 1970, to sanction a variation in the structure of house G, and resolved that an enforcement notice should be issued to take down the house. By this time house G had been erected but not glazed.

2.16 The developers brought an action against the planning authority, claiming a declaration that they were entitled to complete the house on the site where it was, and an injunction restraining the authority from serving an enforcement notice.

2.17 It was the practice of many planning authorities, after detailed planning permission had been given, to allow their planning officers to decide whether any proposed minor modifications to the detailed plan were material or not, and where the planning officer said that a variation was not material, for the developer to proceed with the work as varied without applying for any further permission.

2.18 On the foregoing facts the Court of Appeal held that there was a valid planning permission for the erection of house G on the site as varied and that an enforcement notice should not be served. The court came to that conclusion because (*per* Lord Denning, Master of the Rolls, and Lord Justice Megaw) a planning permission covered work specified in the detailed plans and any immaterial variation therein; and, having regard to the practice of planning authorities allowing their officers to decide on the materiality of minor alterations to an approved plan (a practice which should be affirmed), the planning officer's decision that the variation of the site of house G was not a material variation was a representation *within the officer's ostensible authority;* and, having been acted on by the developers, it was binding on the planning authority.

2.19 As already stated, this case is a highly important one. It warrants the closest reading and consideration because it illustrates how easily, in these days, a planning officer can bind the local planning authority in whose service he functions. It should be added that throughout the case mention is made of section 64 of the Town and Country Planning Act 1968 which later became section 4 of the Town and Country Planning Act 1971. That section 4 (relating to the delegation of functions to officers of local authorities) was repealed by the Local Government Act 1972 but this does not detract from the general principles enunciated in the *Lever* case. (See also section 101 of the Local Government Act 1972).

2.20 It is becoming more and more the custom for developers to engage, through their architects, in repeated interchanges with the planning staff of local planning authorities as to how, in detail, a piece of development shall be carried out. Do these interchanges bind the local planning authority? That is the question. There is no entirely clear answer. The position today, as a result of the case discussed above, is that such interchanges are *more prone* to bind the local authority than ever before. Even so, the ancient doctrine of *caveat emptor* may still be quoted as a warning to the developer and his architect. The purpose of negotiations with the planning staff of local planning authorities should be made clear; are negotiations intended to be binding or not? The architect (if he is the one doing the talking) owes to his client the duty of getting this important point made quite clear.

3 The meaning of development

3.01 The question as to whether that which the architect seeks to carry out is or is not development is a considerable one. The meaning of 'development' is amply defined in the Town and Country Planning Act 1971 section 22 and it is a question of taking the relevant provisions of this Act, working carefully through them and then applying the appropriate parts of these provisions to the matter in hand to ascertain if that which it is sought to do is, *in law* as well as in fact, development.

3.02 Putting the matter quite briefly, development consists of:
1 The carrying out of *operations* (that is to say, building or mining or engineering operations).
2 Or the making of any *material change in the use* of land (including buildings on land).
It will be seen that the big cleavage in the definition is between the carrying out of *operations* on the one hand and the making of a *material change of use* on the other.

What is an operation?
3.03 If the definition of what constitutes development is important, it may be said that the definition of what does *not* constitute development is equally important. Section 22 of the 1971 Act contains quite a list of operations (table I*) and uses which do *not* amount to development. If that which the architect seeks to do falls within this particular list, then he need worry no more about the 1971 Act or any part of it.

What is a change of use?
3.04 This list of exceptions in section 22 of the 1971 Act must be read with the Town and Country Planning (Use Classes) Order 1972 which contains 18 classes of use (table II). If that which the architect seeks to do is a material change of use, then if the existing use is any one of those specified in the 1972 Order, and if the change of use will still leave the use within the same use-class as specified in the order, then the proposed change of use will *not* constitute development. In short, a use may switch around without planning permission, provided its total manoeuvring does not take it out of its use-class as set out in the 1972 Order.

3.05 However, since the case of *City of London Corporation v Secretary of State for the Environment and Watling Street Properties Ltd* (1971) 21 December, QBD it is clear that, on granting planning permission, a local planning authority may impose such conditions as would prevent any future change of use, notwithstanding that any such change would *not* constitute development of land by virtue of the provisions of the Use Classes Order 1972 and section 22 (2) (f) of the 1971 Act.

* Tables follow at the end of this study

3.06 For the purpose of removing all doubt, section 22 of the 1971 Act specifically states that merely using a single dwelling-house as two or more separate dwelling-houses *does* involve making a material change of use and it is 'development' needing planning permission before it can take place. Thus the architect may carry out, at ground level or above, *internal* building operations (not affecting the exterior elevations) on a single house in order to adapt it for use as two houses. Such building operations will *not* need planning permission. However, when it comes to inaugurating the *use* of the former single house as two houses, this change of use *will* call for planning permission which may or may not be granted.

3.07 If the architect has any doubts as to whether that which he seeks to do is or is not 'development', he can apply (1971 Act section 53) to the local planning authority to determine the point for him. There is a right of appeal to the Secretary of State for the Environment (hereinafter referred to as 'the Secretary of State') against the decision of the authority. Alternatively, an application may be made to the High Court to determine the point. The jurisdiction of the court is not ousted by section 53 of the 1971 Act, as was shown in the case of *Pyx Granite Co Ltd v Ministry of Housing and Local Government* (1960) AC 260 (HL).

Compensation for refusal of permission

3.08 In addition, section 22 (5) of the 1971 Act gives a specialised definition of the expression 'new development' which means any development (as discussed in para 3.02) other than development of the kind specified in the eighth schedule to the 1971 Act (table III). This (sometimes called 'existing use development') is development which falls within the existing use of land. 'New development' is development which goes outside the bounds of existing use. While *all* development, new or otherwise, needs planning permission, certain classes of existing use development, ie those six classes set out in part II of the eighth schedule to the 1971 Act, have always carried a right to compensation for refusal of planning permission (see table III).

4 Control of development in general

4.01 Once the architect is satisfied that that which he seeks to do is indeed *development* he must next ascertain whether it falls within the privileged category of 'permitted development'. For this he will have to investigate the Town and Country Planning General Development Order 1977 (see table IV).

Permitted development

4.02 The 1977 Order carries no less than 23 separate classes of development which are categorised as *permitted* development, that is to say, they comprise development for which a standing planning permission is automatically given by virtue of the General Development Order 1977 itself. If development falls within any one of these 23 classes there is no need to make any application to any local planning authority for planning permission for the development. If the development is not permitted development, then a formal application must be made.

Other than permitted development

4.03 The requisite form on which the application is lodged can be obtained from the district planning authority and, in the making of the application, it is well worth paying attention to Part III of the memorandum to accompany ministry Circular 48/59, Town and Country Planning Act 1959 and

to the 'Notes for Applicants' set out in the Appendix to that Circular. These notes provide guidance not only to local authorities, but also to developers seeking to obtain planning permission for development.

4.04 If the application for planning permission is refused there is a right of appeal to the Secretary of State within six months of the authority's decision. Before deciding the appeal the Secretary of State will hear both parties and *may*, but is not obliged to, hold a public local inquiry. The decision of the Secretary of State is final (subject to appeal to the courts within six weeks on matters of law only), the procedure being regarded by the law as an administrative and not a justiciable procedure.

4.05 Even so, the increasing propensity of the judicature to interfere with an administrative decision if it is thought that the Secretary of State has come to a conclusion upon wrong evidence, or upon no evidence at all, is well illustrated in the case of *Coleen Properties Ltd v Minister of Housing and Local Government and Another* (1971) 1 All ER 1049.

4.06 Under section 36 (8) and schedule 9 of the 1971 Act, it is open to the Secretary of State to empower his inspector holding a local inquiry not only to hold the inquiry but to determine the appeal. This will save time but it is not a course which can be demanded by an appellant; it is at the discretion of the Secretary of State. The area in which an inspector can act in this fashion is limited by the Town and Country Planning (Determination of Appeals by Appointed Persons) (Prescribed Classes) Regulations 1977 to which reference should be made.

4.07 The statistics relating to planning applications make interesting reading. In 1973 in England and Wales there were 622 652 planning applications of which 491 174 were granted and 131 478 were refused, in other words 78.9 per cent of the applications were granted and 21.1 per cent were refused.

Outline permission

4.08 If the architect knows exactly what he wants to do by way of building operations he will be able to put in a complete detailed application for planning permission. But it may be that he wants in the first place to 'test the temperature of the water', that is to say, to see what are his chances of getting planning permission at all for, say, a block of offices 20 storeys high. If he wishes to do this, then he can save time, trouble and expense by putting in an application for *outline* planning permission so that the principle of having a block of offices 20 storeys high may be tested. If it is approved, then it will be necessary for the architect later on, within the period (if any) specified in the grant of outline planning permission *and before he begins any development*, to put in detailed plans and specifications for the approval of the local planning authority, these being what are called 'reserved matters', that is to say, matters reserved, at the stage when the local authority is granting the planning application in outline, for later and further consideration.

4.09 An outline application should make it clear that it *is* an application in outline and nothing more. Thus any plans and drawings which accompany it should be clearly marked as being by way of illustration only. At the stage of applying for outline permission, the architect, should not fetter himself as to the *styling* of the development. All he wants at the outline stage is to know whether or not he can, under any circumstances at all, have planning permission to do the *sort* of thing he wishes to do. If he gets that permission, then he must return, in due course, to the local planning authority with detailed plans and specifications so that the authority may consider these detailed matters.

4.10 If the outline application for planning permission is refused, there is a right of appeal (as explained in para 4.04) against that refusal to the Secretary of State within six months. Similarly, if the outline application is granted but, later on, the local authority refuses to approve reserved matters, that is to say, refuses approval of detailed plans and specifications, then again there is an appeal against such refusal to the Secretary of State (see para 4.04).

4.11 It will be seen that for an applicant who does not own land and who wonders how much he ought to pay for it, the making of an outline application to test the position *vis-à-vis* the local planning authority is a useful arrangement. It is not necessary for the applicant to go into details and incur the expense thereby involved. All he wants to know before he makes his bid for the land is whether, if he is able to buy the land, he will then be able to develop it in anything like the manner he has in mind. To get to know this, all that he need do is make an outline planning application.

Certificates
4.12 Any application for planning permission must now be accompanied by a certificate (in one or other of four different forms called A. B, C and D respectively) indicating the giving of notice to certain owners and agricultural tenants. If the appropriate certificate is not included with the planning application, then the local planning authority 'shall not entertain' the application. Which of the four forms of certificate is used depends on the circumstances of the case, but section 27 of the 1971 Act indicates which form is to be used, while article 9 and part I of schedule 4 to the General Development Order 1977 sets out each of the four forms of certificate from which the selection of one is to be made.

General publicity
4.13 In addition to the foregoing personal or private publicity deriving from the notices referred to in the previous paragraph, there must be what can be called *general* publicity by newspaper advertisement for certain planning applications. These relate to the nine classes of 'bad neighbour' development (as it is called) set out in article 8 of the General Development Order 1977. This bad neighbour development includes, among other things, *any* building over 20 metres in height, buildings for use as a public convenience, for the disposal of refuse and waste material, for sewage disposal, for use as a slaughterhouse or knacker's yard, for use as a theatre, cinema, music hall, dance hall, fun fair, bingo-hall, casino, skating rink, swimming bath or gymnasium (not forming part of a school, college or university), or for use as a turkish or other vapour or foam bath, or for indoor games. All these buildings are calculated to create noise or stench or to cause people to congregate in large numbers and hence are regarded as 'bad neighbour' development. Thus the owners and occupiers of neighbouring land must be informed of any application to carry out such development so that they may give their views and opinions to the local planning authority before a decision is arrived at.

Site notices
4.14 Moreover, in the case of 'bad neighbour' development a site notice, exhibited on the site where the development is to take place, must be given. The notice must be posted for not less than seven days during the month immediately preceeding the making of the application for planning per-

mission. It must be firmly fixed and displayed so as to be easily visible by the public, and it must state that the application is to be made and name a place *within the locality* where a copy of the application and of all plans and other documents related to it will be open to public inspection. It is the responsibility of *the applicant* and not the local planning authority to post the notice and make the plans and other documents open for public inspection at some place within the locality of the site.

4.15 If the development is within a conservation area a site notice must again be posted, but in this instance it is the responsibility of the local planning authority to post the notice.

4.16 Those instances in which a site notice must be posted are referred to (so far as concerns 'bad neighbour' development) in the 1971 Act section 26 and in article 8 and schedule 3 of the General Development Order 1977 and (so far as conservation areas are concerned) in the 1971 Act section 28.

Local authority procedure
4.17 On receipt of an application for planning permission, the local planning authority must consider the matter and, generally speaking, give a decision within eight weeks unless an extension of time is agreed. The authority may grant the application, may refuse it or may grant it subject to conditions. If the answer is a refusal or conditions are attached to the grant, the reasons for such action must be given. This is to enable the applicant to challenge the decision of the local planning authority if the applicant decides to appeal to the Secretary of State, as he may do within a period of six months. If no decision is given within the appropriate period, the applicant may appeal (again, within six months) to the Secretary of State *as if* he had been faced with a refusal.

Conservation areas
4.18 If the site of the development is within a conservation area designated under the 1971 Act section 277, then the local planning authority, in considering the application, will have to pay attention to sections 277A and 277B of the 1971 Act and to any directions given to them by the Secretary of State as to the manner in which they should consider applications for development within areas of special architectural or historic interest, the character or appearance of which ought to be preserved or enhanced. In other words, the local planning authority has less of a free hand in connection with development in a conservation area than it has elsewhere.

Conditions
4.19 The local planning authority in granting planning permission may attach such conditions as it thinks fit, but this does not mean that it can attach any conditions it likes; not at all. The conditions must be fit, that is to say, fit, meet and proper from a town planning point of view, because the legislation under which all this control functions is town planning legislation.

4.20 A local planning authority in attaching conditions must ensure that the conditions fairly and reasonably relate to the development. The authority is not at liberty to use its powers for an ulterior object, however desirable that object may seem to be in the public interest. If it mistakes or misuses its power, however *bona fide*, the court can interfere by declaration and injunction—*per* Lord Denning in *Pyx Granite Co Ltd v Ministry of Housing and Local Government* (1958) I QB 554 (CA).

4.21 Suppose one of the conditions attached to a grant is improper and thereby unlawful; does this invalidate the entire planning permission or can the unlawful condition be severed from the rest, leaving the planning permission intact but shorn of the improper condition? There have been several cases on this particularly difficult point and the last word was spoken in the decision in *Kent County Council v Kingsway Investments (Kent) Ltd* (1970) I All ER 70. It would appear from the decisions of the courts that the question of whether or not a planning permission is to be held wholly bad and of no effect, by reason of the invalidity of some condition attached to it, is a matter which could be decided on the basis of common sense and with particular inquiry as to whether the invalid condition is fundamental or trivial.

4.22 The views of the Secretary of State on attaching conditions to a grant of planning permission are set out at length in the interesting and instructive Circular 5/68, to which reference can be made with advantage (see References at end of Study).

4.23 It should be remembered that obtaining planning permission for development may not necessarily be the end of the matter. Certain specialised forms of development, eg development relating to the creation of caravan sites, development for offices and for industry, are subject to additional control over and above the general run of town planning control (see further paras 5.01 and 6.01 *et seq*).

4.24 Moreover, the architect must never forget that town planning control is a control which functions entirely without prejudice to the long-established control of building operations through the medium of building by-laws created under a code of law relating to public health and dating to the Public Health Act 1875 and even before. Irrespective of town planning control, such detailed matters as the thickness of walls, the opening of exit doors in public places in an outward and not an inward direction, the provision of means of escape in case of fire—all these are matters which are entirely separate from the sort of control over development which is discussed in this article. (For such matters see LEGAL STUDY 13.)

Duration of permission

4.25 Nowadays, any developer obtaining planning permission must remember that, unless the permission itself specifies otherwise, permission will last only for five years. This is to prevent, among other things, an accumulation in the records of local planning authorities of quantities of planning permissions granted from time to time over a long period of years and never acted upon. This sort of thing had been going on for a long time, but was brought to an end by provisions in the Town and Country Planning Act 1968, now sections 41 to 44 of the 1971 Act.

4.26 Anybody in possession of a planning permission granted before 1 April 1969 must remember that if he had not begun his development before the beginning of 1968, then he must begin it not later than five years from 1 April 1969, that is to say, not later than 1 April 1974.

4.27 In the case of a planning permission granted on or since 1 April 1969, or granted in the future, the limitation is again five years from the date of the grant unless the grant otherwise provides.

4.28 If that which is obtained is an outline planning permission (as discussed in para 4.08) granted on or since 1 April 1969, then it must be remembered that the submission of detailed plans and specifications under the aegis of that outline planning permission must be done not later than *three* years from the grant, while the development itself must be begun within five years of the grant or within two years of the final approval of any reserved matter, whichever of these two periods happens to be the longer. In the case of an outline planning permission granted before 1 April 1969, then the aforementioned periods of three and five years respectively run from 1 April 1969.

Starting development

4.29 When is a project of development to be regarded as having been begun? This an important question. The 1971 Act provides the complete answer in section 43 by providing that a project of development is begun on the earliest date on which a specified operation in connection with the development is started. A 'specified operation' will include, among other things, the digging of a trench which is to contain the foundations of a building. Thus, only a trivial amount of labour needs to be spent in order to ensure that development has been begun and that a town planning permission has been embarked upon.

Completion notices

4.30 Having begun his development, a developer must remember not to rest unduly upon his oars. If he is dilatory it is open to the local planning authority to serve him with 'a completion notice' requiring the completion of his development within a certain period. A completion notice will declare that the relevant planning permission will cease to have effect on such date as may be specified in the notice but this date may not be earlier than 12 months from the date of the notice. A completion notice will not take effect unless and until it is confirmed by the Secretary of State, who may substitute a longer period for completion. Any person served with a completion notice may demand to be given an opportunity of being heard by an inspector appointed by the Secretary of State. Of course, a local planning authority, having served a completion notice, may for good and sufficient reason be prevailed upon to withdraw it; the law authorises such withdrawal.

Revoking or modifying planning permission

4.31 It should be remembered that a planning permission once given ensures a right to develop for the benefit of all persons for the time being interested in the land, subject to any limitation of time contained in the grant of planning permission itself or imported into the matter by the 1971 Act, as mentioned in para 4.25. This, however, is subject to the right of a local planning authority to revoke or modify a planning permission by means of an order made by the authority and confirmed by the Secretary of State. Before confirming the order the Secretary of State must afford the owner and the occupier of the land affected by the order an opportunity of being heard by the Secretary of State's inspector. There are certain revoking or modifying orders which, being unopposed and unlikely to give rise to claims for compensation, can be made by the local planning authority without need for confirmation by the Secretary of State.

4.32 If the local planning authority wishes to make a revocation or modifying order it must remember to do so before buildings authorised by the planning permission in question have been started (in which case the revocation or modification may not affect so much of the building operations as have already been carried out) and also that compensation may become payable on the revocation or modification of a previously granted planning permission.

it is not solely the building which is to be considered but the entire background to the building.

7.08 When speaking of a building it must be remembered that the law is so framed as to give protection to any object or structure fixed to a building or forming part of the land on which the building stands and comprised within the curtilage of the building.

Listed building consent

7.09 There is no provision for the owner of a special building to appeal against the listing of his building. Once the building is listed the whole of the protective provisions of part IV of the 1971 Act automatically swing into operation. The consequence of this is that while (as already explained in para 3.08) it is necessary to get planning permission for any kind of development, if the site of the development happens to be occupied in whole or in part by a listed building, then the development simply cannot take place unless a new and additional form of consent, known as 'listed building consent', is first obtained.

7.10 Listed building consent must be obtained in order to demolish, alter or extend a listed building. It may be granted (like a planning permission) with or without conditions. The application for listed building consent is made to the district planning authority and the procedure is given in schedule 11 to the 1971 Act and in the Town and Country Planning (Listed Buildings and Buildings in Conservation Areas) Regulations 1972.

7.11 A grant of planning permission may sometimes act also as a grant of listed building consent. This is when the planning permission covers works for the *alteration* or *extension* (demolition is a totally separate matter) of a listed building and the permission itself is so framed as expressly to authorise such works of alteration or extension.

7.12 In deciding whether or not to grant planning permission or to grant listed building consent with respect to a special building, the district planning authority must pay special regard to the desirability of preserving the building and of preserving any features of special architectural or historic interest which the building possesses. Notwithstanding this, the writer takes the view that the grant of planning permission is one thing and the grant of listed building consent is another. Merely because planning permission is granted for development, it does not follow that listed building consent will be given to remove some obstructive listed building to allow development, pursuant to the planning permission, to go forward. The planning permission, once granted, will (as explained in para 4.25) last, generally speaking, for five years. During that time views and opinions about a listed building may change; views and opinions about architecture do tend to fluctuate. During the first years of the planning permission it may be impossible to get the requisite listed building consent to demolish some obstructive listed building. Later on different opinions about preservation may prevail or pressure to carry out development may become stronger. Thus, different considerations in the view of this writer apply when a local planning authority is considering whether or not it should grant planning permission for development and when it is considering whether or not it should grant listed building consent for the demolition of a listed building in order to allow planned development to go forward.

7.13 If listed building consent is refused, there is a right of appeal to the Secretary of State after the style of the appeal against refusal of planning permission.

7.14 It is an offence to demolish, alter or extend a listed building without first getting listed building consent. It is also an offence to fail to comply with any conditions attached to such consent. The penalty for each of these offences is (on summary conviction) a fine of £250 or imprisonment for three months or both, and on conviction on indictment, a fine or unlimited amount or imprisonment for 12 months or both.

7.15 If the owner is faced with a refusal of listed building consent and can demonstrate that in its present state his listed building has become incapable of reasonable beneficial use, then he may serve a listed building purchase notice on the district planning authority requiring the authority to purchase the building.

Listed building enforcement notice

7.16 If unauthorised works to a listed building are carried out, then the district planning authority, in addition to taking proceedings for the commission of a criminal offence, may serve a listed building enforcement notice upon the owner, requiring full reinstatement of the listed building. There is a right of appeal against the notice to the Secretary of State. Heavy penalties are provided in the case of non-compliance with the terms of the listed building enforcement notice. These penalties are recoverable from the person 'in default' and it should be remembered that this might include a subsequent owner. So the purchaser of a listed building must be careful to ascertain before he buys whether there are any listed building enforcement notices outstanding in respect of the building.

7.17 A local authority is authorised to acquire compulsorily any listed building which is not being properly preserved. This power may not be exercised until at least two months after the service on the owner of the building of a repairs notice specifying the work considered necessary for the proper preservation of the building. An owner faced with the possibility of having his listed building compulsorily acquired from him cannot appeal to the Secretary of State, but curiously enough, he can, within 28 days, go to a local magistrates' court to stay the proceedings under the compulsory purchase order. If the court is satisfied that reasonable steps have been taken for properly preserving the building, then the court may order accordingly. Against the order of the magistrates there is a further appeal to the Crown Court.

7.18 If a listed building is compulsorily acquired, then the compensation to be paid to the owner will, in general, disregard the depressive effect of the fact that the building has been listed. On the other hand, if it is established that the building has been allowed deliberately to fall into disrepair for the purposes of justifying the redevelopment of the site, then the 1971 Act provides for the payment of what is called 'minimum compensation'. This means that the compensation will be assessed at a price which disregards any profit which might have accrued to the owner from the redevelopment of the site. Against any direction in a compulsory purchase order providing for the payment of this minimum compensation there is a right of appeal and, again, this is to the local magistrates' court, with a further appeal to the Crown Court.

Building preservation notices

7.19 Are there any means today of protecting a building which is *not* a listed building, but which appears to the local planning authority to be of special architectural or historic interest? The answer is yes. Although the district planning authority can no longer make a building preservation order, it can serve on the owner of the building a building preservation notice which gives temporary protection for six months, during which time the building is protected just as if it were listed. The object of this is to give time for consideration by the district planning authority and the Secretary of State, or indeed by anybody else, as to whether the building should in fact be listed. If, at the end of six months, the Secretary of State will not make any such listing, then the building preservation notice automatically ceases and the district planning authority may not serve a further building preservation notice within the next 12 months. Moreover, compensation may become payable to the owner of the building for loss or damage caused by the service of the building preservation notice which failed to be followed by the listing of the building.

7.20 Certain buildings of undoubted architectural and historic interest do not come within the protection of listing at all. These are:
1 Ecclesiastical buildings in use for church purposes (but not the parsonage house, which *is* capable of being listed).
2 A building already the subject of a scheme or order under ancient monuments legislation.
3 A building included in a list of monuments published by the Secretary of State under ancient monuments legislation.

Buildings on conservation areas
7.21 In addition to the special protection given to listed buildings as described above, the Town and Country Amenities Act 1974 made important amendments to the Town and Country Planning Act 1971 (see sections 277, 277A and 277B of that Act) which give protection to *all* buildings if they happen to be in a conservation area designated under section 177 of the 1971 Act.

8 Enforcement of planning control

8.01 The Town and Country Planning Act 1968 (now sections 87 to 95 of the 1971 Act) made two important alterations to the law relating to enforcement of planning control wherever development is carried out without planning permission. One of these was the abolition of what is commonly called 'the four-year rule' in the case of development comprising a change of use of land (but not a building operation); and the other was the introduction of the 'stop notice' in the case of development comprising a building operation (but not a change of use of land).

8.02 Architects, being associated more with the sort of development that amounts to a building operation rather than a mere change of use, will be affected more by the new stop notice procedure than by the abolition of the four-year rule. Accordingly, the latter is mentioned only briefly in this article.

Four-year rule
8.03 The four-year rule derives from the fact that, under the form of town planning control introduced in 1948, if development is carried out without planning permission and if the authorities allow four years to elapse without doing anything about the matter (ie without taking action by serving an enforcement notice) then such development becomes validated automatically for town planning purposes and no enforcement action can be taken thereafter. It may be said at once that nothing in the 1971 Act interferes with this state of affairs so far as building development is concerned.

8.04 However, so far as development involving only a change of use of land is concerned the four-year rule is abolished, and nowadays it is open to a local planning authority to serve an enforcement notice in respect of a change of use of land which did not carry the appropriate planning permission even though the change of use took place more than four years previously. Indeed, in such circumstances there is now no period of limitation at all. There is one important exception to all this; ie the change of use of a building into use as a single dwelling-house, in which case the four-year rule still applies.

Certificate of established use
8.05 In the case of a use of land which was instituted before 1 January 1964 (ie four years before the Town and Country Planning Act 1968) provision is made in the 1971 Act section 94 for obtaining a new kind of certificate, namely a 'certificate of established use'. This is obtained from the local planning authority and there is a right of appeal to the Secretary of State if one is refused. The certificate makes it clear that the use in question, even though originally instituted without planning permission, is now immune from enforcement action.

Enforcement notices
8.06 Enforcement action is by way of enforcement notice served by the local planning authority upon the owner and occupier of the land to which it relates. Briefly, the notice requires the doing of all things necessary to amend the breach of planning control which, it is alleged in the notice, has occurred. There is an appeal to the Secretary of State against the notice, and the appeal must now state not only the grounds of the appeal but the facts on which the appeal is based.

8.07 Architects should note that a local planning authority is never *obliged* to serve an enforcement notice whenever there has been a breach of planning control. The authority always has a discretion which it must be expected to exercise reasonably, as must any public authority holding discretionary powers. What the authority has to consider is whether, notwithstanding the breach of planning control, it is *expedient* to take enforcement action, and on this the authority must have regard not only to the provisions of the relevant development plan but also to 'any other material considerations'.

8.08 Without doubt, enforcement notices are very tricky things indeed and the law reports are full of decisions of the courts, in which the validity of such notices has been challenged successfully on the ground of some legal flaw in the drafting or the service of the notice. However, all these things are problems for the local authority rather than for the developer and his architect.

Stop notices
8.09 The legal pitfalls associated with an enforcement notice have, in the past, sometimes led a developer to spin out the appeal procedure while getting on in the meantime with his building development. There is an appeal to the High Court on a point of law from the Secretary of State's decision in an enforcement notice appeal, and there are further appeals (on points of law) to the Court of Appeal and to the House of Lords. This is still the position but the 1971 Act now prevents a building developer from continuing his building operations while the protracted appeals procedure is working itself out. There is no longer the possibility of (quite lawfully) finishing the building before the appeal to, and in, the House

of Lords is concluded. The stop notice procedure prevents this from happening.

8.10 Once an enforcement notice relating to building operations (but not to changes of use) has been served, the local authority may follow it with a stop notice which brings all building operations to a halt under a penalty, for breach of the notice, of £400 on summary conviction or to a fine of unlimited amount on conviction or indictment. Further, daily penalties are recoverable for any continuing infringement of the stop notice.

8.11 There is no appeal against a stop notice. Such a notice is dependent entirely on the enforcement notice with which it is associated. If, on appeal, the enforcement notice fails, so does the stop notice. In this instance, compensation is payable in certain (but not all) cases for loss or damage arising from the stop notice. Thus a local authority will be inclined to think twice before serving a stop notice.

8.12 So when a stop notice is served, what is the position of a contractor carrying out building operations for a developer? Undoubtedly the contractor will be prevented from continuing to discharge his obligations under the building contract with the developer. In these circumstances the 1971 Act provides for the contractor a statutory right to compensation *from the developer*, provided the building contract was entered into on or before 31 December 1969. If the contract is made after that date, it will be for the contractor and the developer to settle between themselves what compensation (if any) is to be paid to the contractor by the developer in the event of the contractor being frustrated in the carrying out of the building contract by reason of the service upon the developer of a stop notice. These are matters calling for careful consideration before the building contract is signed.

9 Community Land Act 1975

9.01 The Community Land Act 1975 came into force on 6 April 1976 and calls for brief comment here.

9.02 The Act defines 'relevant development', 'designated relevant development', 'exempt development' and 'development land', and these expressions now need to be carefully noted as does the expression 'excepted development' which is found in the Community Land (Excepted Development) Regulations 1976. Since this Act came into operation one of the first things a developer must do is to ascertain if that which he proposes to do comes within any of the foregoing expressions. If it does then he must watch carefully the provisions of the Community Land Act 1975.

9.03 This Act does not detract from the planning control routines earlier dealt with in this study; but it does add to these routines. Thus today any 'development land' (another important expression defined in the Act) *may be* acquired compulsorily by the local planning authority and then leased for development by a lessee. If and when the Secretary of State makes a 'duty order' under the Act then, in this area where such an order functions, it will be the *duty* of the local planning authority to acquire all development land in that area if such land is to be used for 'designated relevant development'. Having bought the land the authority can then let it to a lessee for development. Thus, progressively, all development land will come to be owned by a public authority. Any lease of development land will usually be for 99 years but the Secretary of State can modify this. The development land will be purchased at market value less

development land tax at 80 per cent (66⅔ per cent until 31 March 1979 on the first £150 000 worth of realised development value)—as provided for in the Development Land Tax Act 1976—and will then be let by the public authority at market value. Thus, the public authority will acquire nearly all the rise of the development value of the land released by the grant of planning permission. When the second appointed day under the Community Land Act dawns—it will be fixed by order of the Secretary of State made at his discretion—all land acquired by a public authority will be purchased at current use value only.

9.04 In order to give time to a local authority to make up its mind whether to exercise the new power to acquire development land, any grant of planning permission will now be suspended for not more than 12 months. If the authority does not take a first step to acquire the land within 12 months then it loses the right so to do for five years. In any area where a 'duty order' is in operation, any grant of planning permission for designated relevant development is automatically suspended until the land becomes owned by, or has passed through the ownership of, the local authority.

10 L'envoi

10.01 The proof of the pudding is in its eating; the proof of planning control may be said to be in its administration. Heaven knows, there is enough planning *law* these days, as the size of the Town and Country Planning Act 1971 shows. After statutory pronouncement on the subject there come voluminous quantities of subordinate legislation in the form of rules and regulations. Then, all this legislation must be read in association with vast quantities of ministerial circulars, pronouncements and so forth.

10.02 Notwithstanding all these powers and legal authority it is said, from time to time, that planning control fails. If it does fail, the failure will have little to do with the powers but with the way they are used or (and this is often the case) *not* used.

10.03 Planning control is not a finite science but an artistic process in which there is, and always will be, room for more than one point of view. Architectural design comes prominently into the arena of planning control, and architectural design, like other types of design, is a matter of taste; eg one planning authority will like buildings built one way and another authority will like buildings built another way.

10.04 The important thing about buildings, one would have thought, is to get variety, that is to say, a state of affairs in which the buildings are different but not stridently in opposition to one another. Nobody wants bad manners in civic architecture. Thus, one would not regard it the responsibility of the local planning authority, as a matter of administration, always to turn down an application for planning permission purely because it does not entirely like the design of the building. The authority may not like it but, without doubt, somebody else will. It is not the job of the planning authority constantly to be redesigning buildings so that they conform with some overall corporate taste (established, no doubt, through the processes of a democratic vote) on the part of the authority. If this were to happen, it would lead to a progressive spread of something in the nature of a local government school of architecture. (If one wants to know what this could mean, one need look no further than the rash of metropolitan borough town halls which sprouted across London after the boroughs had been created in 1899.)

Table I Operations which do not constitute development—Town and Country Planning Act 1971 Section 22

GENERAL PLANNING CONTROL

Meaning of development and requirement of planning permission

Meaning of "development" and "new development".

22.—(1) In this Act, except where the context otherwise requires, "development", subject to the following provisions of this section, means the carrying out of building, engineering, mining or other operations in, on, over or under land, or the making of any material change in the use of any buildings or other land.

(2) The following operations or uses of land shall not be taken for the purposes of this Act to involve development of the land, that is to say—

(a) the carrying out of works for the maintenance, improvement or other alteration of any building, being works which affect only the interior of the building or which do not materially affect the external appearance of the building and (in either case) are not works for making good war damage or works begun after 5th December 1968 for the alteration of a building by providing additional space therein below ground ;

(b) the carrying out by a local highway authority of any works required for the maintenance or improvement of a road, being works carried out on land within the boundaries of the road ;

(c) the carrying out by a local authority or statutory undertakers of any works for the purpose of inspecting, repairing or renewing any sewers, mains, pipes, cables or other apparatus, including the breaking open of any street or other land for that purpose ;

(d) the use of any buildings or other land within the curtilage of a dwellinghouse for any purpose incidental to the enjoyment of the dwellinghouse as such ;

(e) the use of any land for the purposes of agriculture or forestry (including afforestation) and the use for any of those purposes of any building occupied together with land so used ;

(f) in the case of buildings or other land which are used for a purpose of any class specified in an order made by the Secretary of State under this section, the use thereof for any other purpose of the same class.

(3) For the avoidance of doubt it is hereby declared that for the purposes of this section—

(a) the use as two or more separate dwellinghouses of any building previously used as a single dwellinghouse involves a material change in the use of the building and of each part thereof which is so used ;

(b) the deposit of refuse or waste materials on land involves a material change in the use thereof, notwithstanding that the land is comprised in a site already used for that purpose, if either the superficial area of the deposit is thereby extended, or the height of the deposit is thereby extended and exceeds the level of the land adjoining the site.

(4) Without prejudice to any regulations made under the provisions of this Act relating to the control of advertisements, the use for the display of advertisements of any external part of a building which is not normally used for that purpose shall be treated for the purposes of this section as involving a material change in the use of that part of the building.

(5) In this Act "new development" means any development other than development of a class specified in Part I or Part II of Schedule 8 to this Act ; and the provisions of Part III of that Schedule shall have effect for the purposes of Parts I and II thereof.

Table II Use classes—Town and Country Planning (Use Classes) Order 1972 Schedule

Class I.—Use as a shop for any purpose except as :—
  (i) a shop for the sale of hot food;
  (ii) a tripe shop;
  (iii) a shop for the sale of pet animals or birds;
  (iv) a cats-meat shop;
  (v) a shop for the sale of motor vehicles.

Class II.—Use as an office for any purpose.

Class III.—Use as a light industrial building for any purpose.

Class IV.—Use as a general industrial building for any purpose.

Class V. (*Special Industrial Group A*)—Use for any work which is registrable under the Alkali &c Works Regulation Act 1906 , as extended by the Alkali &c Works Orders 1966 and 1971 and which is not included in any of Classes VI, VII, VIII or IX of this Schedule.

Class VI. (*Special Industrial Group B*)—Use for any of the following processes, except a process ancillary to the getting, dressing or treatment of minerals which is carried on in or adjacent to a quarry or mine :—
  (i) smelting, calcining, sintering or reduction of ores, minerals, concentrates or mattes;
  (ii) converting, refining, re-heating, annealing, hardening, melting, carburising, forging or casting of metals or alloys, other than pressure die-casting;
  (iii) recovery of metal from scrap or drosses or ashes;
  (iv) galvanizing;
  (v) pickling or treatment of metal in acid;
  (vi) chromium plating.

Class VII. (*Special Industrial Group C*)—Use for any of the following processes except a process ancillary to the getting, dressing or treatment of minerals which is carried on in or adjacent to a quarry or mine :—
  (i) burning of bricks or pipes;
  (ii) lime or dolomite burning;
  (iii) production of zinc oxide, cement or alumina;
  (iv) foaming, crushing, screening or heating of minerals or slag;
  (v) processing by heat of pulverized fuel ash;
  (vi) production of carbonate of lime and hydrated lime;
  (vii) production of inorganic pigments by calcining, roasting or grinding.

Class VIII. (*Special Industrial Group D*)—Use for any of the following purposes :—
  (i) distilling, refining or blending of oils (other than petroleum or petroleum products);
  (ii) production or employment of cellulose and employment of other pressure sprayed metal finishes (other than the employment of any such finishes in vehicle repair workshops in connection with minor repairs, and the application of plastic powder by the use of fluidised bed and electrostatic spray techniques);
  (iii) boiling of linseed oil and the running of gum;
  (iv) processes involving the use of hot pitch or bitumen (except the use of bitumen in the manufacture of roofing felt at temperatures not exceeding 220°C and also the manufacture of coated roadstone);
  (v) stoving of enamelled ware;
  (vi) production of aliphatic esters of the lower fatty acids, butyric acid, caramel, hexamine, iodoform, napthols, resin products (excluding plastic moulding or extrusion operations and production of plastic sheets, rods, tubes, filaments, fibres or optical components produced by casting, calendering, moulding, shaping or extrusion), salicylic acid or sulphonated organic compounds;
  (vii) production of rubber from scrap;
  (viii) chemical processes in which chlorphenols or chlorcresols are used as intermediates;
  (ix) manufacture of acetylene from calcium carbide;
  (x) manufacture, recovery or use of pyridine or picolines, any methyl or ethyl amine or acrylates.

Class IX. (*Special Industrial Group E*)—Use for carrying on any of the following industries, businesses or trades :—
  Animal charcoal manufacturer.
  Animal hair cleanser, adapter or treater.
  Blood albumen maker.
  Blood boiler.
  Bone boiler or steamer.
  Bone burner.
  Bone grinder.
  Breeder of maggots from putrescible animal matter.
  Candle maker.
  Catgut manufacturer.
  Chitterling or nettlings boiler.
  Dealer in rags or bones (including receiving, storing, sorting or manipulating rags in or likely to become in an offensive condition, or any bones, rabbit-skins, fat or putrescible animal products of a like nature).
  Fat melter or fat extractor.
  Fellmonger.
  Fish curer.
  Fish oil manufacturer.
  Fish skin dresser or scraper.
  Glue maker.
  Gut scraper or gut cleaner.
  Maker of feeding stuff for animals or poultry from any meat, fish, blood, bone, feathers, fat or animal offal, either in an offensive condition or subjected to any process causing noxious or injurious effluvia.
  Manufacture of manure from bones, fish, offal, blood, spent hops, beans or other putrescible animal or vegetable matter.
  Size maker.
  Skin drier.
  Soap boiler.
  Tallow melter or refiner.
  Tripe boiler or cleaner.

Class X.—Use as a wholesale warehouse or repository for any purpose.

Class XI.—Use as a boarding or guest house, or an hotel providing sleeping accommodation.

Class XII.—Use as a residential or boarding school or a residential college.

Class XIII.—Use as a building for public worship or religious instruction or for the social or recreational activities of the religious body using the building.

Class XIV.—Use as a home or institution providing for the boarding, care and maintenance of children, old people or persons under disability, a convalescent home, a nursing home, a sanatorium or a hospital.

Class XV.—Use (other than residentially) as a health centre, a school treatment centre, a clinic, a creche, a day nursery or a dispensary, or use as a consulting room or surgery unattached to the residence of the consultant or practitioner.

Class XVI.—Use as an art gallery (other than for business purposes), a museum, a public library or reading room, a public hall, or an exhibition hall.

Class XVII.—Use as a theatre, cinema, music hall or concert hall.

Class XVIII.—Use as a dance hall, skating rink, swimming bath, Turkish or other vapour or foam bath, or as a gymnasium or sports hall.

Table III Existing use development—Town and Country Planning Act 1971, Schedule 8

PART I

DEVELOPMENT NOT RANKING FOR COMPENSATION UNDER S. 169

1. The carrying out of any of the following works, that is to say—

(a) the rebuilding, as often as occasion may require, of any building which was in existence on the appointed day, or of any building which was in existence before that day but was destroyed or demolished after 7th January 1937, including the making good of war damage sustained by any such building ;

(b) the rebuilding, as often as occasion may require, of any building erected after the appointed day which was in existence at a material date ;

(c) the carrying out of works for the maintenance, improvement or other alteration of any building, being works which affect only the interior of the building, or which do not materially affect the external appearance of the building and (in either case) are works for making good war damage,

so long as (in the case of works falling within any of the preceding sub-paragraphs) the cubic content of the original building is not exceeded—

(i) in the case of a dwellinghouse, by more than one-tenth or 1,750 cubic feet, whichever is the greater ; and

(ii) in any other case, by more than one-tenth.

2. The use as two or more separate dwellinghouses of any building which at a material date was used as a single dwellinghouse.

PART II

DEVELOPMENT RANKING FOR COMPENSATION UNDER S. 169

3. The enlargement, improvement or other alteration, as often as occasion may require, of any such building as is mentioned in paragraph 1(a) or (b) of this Schedule, or any building substituted for such a building by the carrying out of any such operations as are mentioned in that paragraph, so long as the cubic content of the original building is not increased or exceeded—

(a) in the case of a dwellinghouse, by more than one-tenth or 1,750 cubic feet, whichever is the greater ; and

(b) in any other case, by more than one-tenth.

4. The carrying out, on land which was used for the purposes of agriculture or forestry at a material date, of any building or other operations required for the purposes of that use, other than operations for the erection, enlargement, improvement or alteration of dwellinghouses or of buildings used for the purposes of market gardens, nursery grounds or timber yards or for other purposes not connected with general farming operations or with the cultivation or felling of trees.

5. The winning and working, on land held or occupied with land used for the purposes of agriculture, of any minerals reasonably required for the purposes of that use, including the fertilisation of the land so used and the maintenance, improvement or alteration of buildings or works thereon which are occupied or used for those purposes.

6. In the case of a building or other land which, at a material date,, was used for a purpose falling within any general class specified in the Town and Country Planning (Use Classes for Third Schedule Purposes) Order 1948, or which having been unoccupied on and at all times since the appointed day, was last used (otherwise than before 7th January 1937) for any such purpose, the use of that building or land for any other purpose falling within the same general class.

7. In the case of any building or other land which, at a material date, was in the occupation of a person by whom it was used as to part only for a particular purpose, the use for that purpose of any additional part of the building or land not exceeding one-tenth of the cubic content of the part of the building used for that purpose on the appointed day, or on the day thereafter when the building began to be so used, or, as the case may be, one-tenth of the area of the land so used on that day.

8. The deposit of waste materials or refuse in connection with the working of minerals, on any land comprised in a site which at a material date was being used for that purpose, so far as may be reasonably required in connection with the working of those minerals.

PART III

SUPPLEMENTARY PROVISIONS

9. Any reference in this Schedule to the cubic content of a building shall be construed as a reference to that content as ascertained by external measurement.

10. Where, after the appointed day, any buildings or works have been erected or constructed, or any use of land has been instituted, and any condition imposed under Part III of this Act, limiting the period for which those buildings or works may be retained, or that use may be continued, has effect in relation thereto, this Schedule shall not operate except as respects the period specified in that condition.

11. For the purposes of paragraph 3 of this Schedule—

(a) the erection, on land within the curtilage of any such building as is mentioned in that paragraph, of an additional building to be used in connection with the original building shall be treated as the enlargement of the original building ; and

(b) where any two or more buildings comprised in the same curtilage are used as one unit for the purposes of any institution or undertaking, the reference in that paragraph to the cubic content of the original building shall be construed as a reference to the aggregate cubic content of those buildings.

12. In this Schedule "at a material date" means at either of the following dates, that is to say—

(a) the appointed day ; and

(b) the date by reference to which this Schedule falls to be applied in the particular case in question :

Provided that sub-paragraph (b) of this paragraph shall not apply in relation to any buildings, works or use of land in respect of which, whether before or after the date mentioned in that sub-paragraph, an enforcement notice served before that date has become or becomes effective.

13.—(1) In relation to a building erected after the appointed day, being a building resulting from the carrying out of any such works as are described in paragraph 1 of this Schedule, any reference in this Schedule to the original building is a reference to the building in relation to which those works were carried out and not to the building resulting from the carrying out of those works.

(2) This paragraph has effect subject to section 278(4) of this Act.

Table IV Town and Country Planning General Development Order 1977 Schedule 1, Permitted development

SCHEDULE 1

The following development is permitted under article 3 of this order subject to the limitations contained in the description of that development in column (1) and subject to the conditions set out opposite that description in column (2).

Column (1) Description of Development	Column (2) Conditions
Class I.—Development within the curtilage of a dwellinghouse 1. The enlargement improvement or other alteration of a dwellinghouse so long as: (a) the cubic content of the original dwellinghouse (as ascertained by external measurement) is not exceeded by more than 50 cubic metres or one-tenth whichever is the greater, subject to a maximum of 115 cubic metres: (b) the height of the building as so enlarged altered or improved does not exceed the height of the highest part of the roof of the original dwellinghouse; (c) no part of the building as so enlarged altered or improved projects beyond the forwardmost part of any wall of the original dwellinghouse which fronts on a highway: Provided that the erection of a garage, stable loose-box or coach-house within the curtilage of the dwellinghouse shall be treated as the enlargement of the dwellinghouse for all purposes of this permission including the calculation of cubic contents. 2. The erection or construction of a porch outside any external door of a dwellinghouse so long as: (a) the floor area does not exceed 2 square metres; (b) no part of the structure is more than 3 metres above the level of the ground; (c) no part of the structure is less than 2 metres from any boundary of the curtilage which fronts on a highway. 3. The erection, construction or placing, and the maintenance, improvement or other alteration, within the curtilage of a dwellinghouse, of any building or enclosure (other than a dwelling, garage, stable, loose-box or coach-house) required for a purpose incidental to the enjoyment of the dwellinghouse, as such including the keeping of poultry, bees, pet animals, birds or other livestock for the domestic needs or personal enjoyment of the occupants of the dwellinghouse, so long as: (a) no part of such building or enclosure projects beyond the forwardmost part of any wall of the original dwellinghouse which fronts on a highway; (b) the height does not exceed, in the case of a building with a ridged roof, 4 metres, or in any other case, 3 metres; (c) the area of ground covered by buildings within the curtilage (other than the original dwellinghouse) does not thereby exceed one half of the total area of the curtilage excluding the ground area of the original dwellinghouse. 4. The construction within the curtilage of a dwellinghouse of a hardstanding for vehicles for a purpose incidental to the enjoyment of the dwellinghouse as such. 5. The erection or placing within the curtilage of a dwellinghouse of a tank for the storage of oil for domestic heating so long as: (a) the capacity of the tank does not exceed 3500 litres; (b) no part of the tank is more than 3 metres above the level of the ground; (c) no part of the tank projects beyond the forwardmost part of any wall of the original dwellinghouse which fronts on a highway. *Class II.—Sundry minor operations* 1. The erection or construction of gates, fences, walls or other means of enclosure not exceeding 1 metre in height where abutting on a highway used by vehicular traffic or 2 metres in height in any other case, and the maintenance, improvement or other alteration of any gates, fences, walls or other means of enclosure: so long as such improvement or alteration does not increase the height above the height appropriate for a new means of enclosure. 2. The formation, laying out and construction of a means of access to a highway not being a trunk or classified road, where required in connection with development permitted by article 3 of and Schedule I to this order (other than under this class). 3. The painting of the exterior of any building or work otherwise than for the purpose of advertisement, announcement or direction. *Class III.—Changes of use* Development consisting of a change of use to:— (a) use as a light industrial building as defined by the Town and Country Planning (Use Classes) Order 1972 from use as a general industrial building as so defined; (b) use as a shop for any purpose included in Class I of the Schedule to the Town and Country Planning (Use Classes) Order 1972 from use as:— (i) a shop for the sale of hot food; (ii) a tripe shop; (iii) a shop for the sale of pet animals or birds; (iv) a cats meat shop; or (v) a shop for the sale of motor vehicles.	

Column (1) Description of Development	Column (2) Conditions

Class IV.—Temporary buildings and uses
1. The erection or construction on land in, on, over or under which operations other than mining operations are being or are about to be carried out (being operations for which planning permission has been granted or is deemed to have been granted under Part III of the Act, or for which planning permission is not required), or on land adjoining such land, of buildings, works, plant or machinery needed temporarily in connection with the said operations, for the period of such operations.
2. The use of land (other than a building or the curtilage of a building) for any purpose or purposes except as a caravan site on not more than 28 days in total in any calendar year (of which not more than 14 days in total may be used for the purpose of motor car or motor-cycle racing or for the purpose of the holding of markets), and the erection or placing of moveable structures on the land for the purposes of that use:
Provided that for the purpose of the limitation imposed on the number of days on which land may be used for motor car or motor-cycle racing, account shall be taken only of those days on which races are held or practising takes place.
 	
Class V.—Uses by members of recreational organisations
The use of land, other than buildings and not within the curtilage of a dwellinghouse, for the purposes of recreation or instruction by members of an organisation which holds a certificate of exemption granted under section 269 of the Public Health Act 1936, and the erection or placing of tents on the land for the purposes of that use.
 	
Class VI.—Agricultural buildings, works and uses
1. The carrying out on agricultural land having an area of more than one acre and comprised in an agricultural unit of building or engineering operations requisite for the use of that land for the purposes of agriculture (other than the placing on land of structures not designed for those purposes or the provision and alteration of dwellings), so long as:—
  (a) the ground area covered by a building erected pursuant to this permission does not, either by itself or after the addition thereto of the ground area covered by any existing building or buildings (other than a dwellinghouse) within the same unit erected or in course of erection within the preceding two years and wholly or partly within 90 metres of the nearest part of the said building, exceed 465 square metres;
  (b) the height of any buildings or works does not exceed 3 metres in the case of a building or works within 3 kilometres of the perimeter of an aerodrome, nor 12 metres in any other case;
  (c) no part of any buildings (other than moveable structures) or works is within 25 metres of the metalled portion of a trunk or classified road.
2. The erection or construction and the maintenance, improvement or other alteration of roadside stands for milk churns, except where they would abut on any trunk or classified road.
3. The winning and working, on land held or occupied with land used for the purposes of agriculture, of any minerals reasonably required for the purposes of that use, including—
  (i) the fertilisation of the land so used, and
  (ii) the maintenance, improvement or alteration of buildings or works thereon which are occupied or used for the purposes aforesaid,
so long as no excavation is made within 25 metres of the metalled portion of a trunk or classified road.
 	
Class VII.—Forestry buildings and works
The carrying out on land used for the purposes of forestry (including afforestation) of building and other operations (other than the provision or alteration of dwellings) requisite for the carrying on of those purposes, and the formation, alteration and maintenance of private ways on such land, so long as:—
  (a) the height of any buildings or works within 3 kilometres of the perimeter of an aerodrome does not exceed 3 metres;
  (b) no part of any buildings (other than moveable structures) or works is within 25 metres of the metalled portion of a trunk or classified road.
 	
Class VIII.—Development for industrial purposes
1. Development of the following descriptions, carried out by an industrial undertaker on land used (otherwise than (i) in contravention of previous planning control or (ii) without planning permission granted or deemed to be granted under Part III of the Act) for the carrying out of any industrial process, and for the purposes of such process, or on land used (otherwise than as aforesaid) as a dock, harbour or quay for the purposes of an industrial undertaking:—
  (i) the provision, rearrangement or replacement of private ways or private railways, sidings or conveyors;
  (ii) the provision or rearrangement of sewers, mains, pipes, cables or other apparatus;
  (iii) the installation or erection, by way of addition or replacement, of plant or machinery, or structures or erections of the nature of plant or machinery, not exceeding 15 metres in height or the height of the plant, machinery, structure or erection so replaced, whichever is the greater;
	Such buildings, works, plant or machinery shall be removed at the expiration of the period of such operations and where they were sited on any such adjoining land, that land shall be forthwith reinstated.

Column (1) Description of Development	Column (2) Conditions

(iv) the extension or alteration of buildings (whether erected before or after 1st July 1948) so long as the height of the original building is not exceeded and the cubic content of the original building (as ascertained by external measurement) is not exceeded by more than one tenth nor the aggregate floor space thereof by more than 500 square metres;
So long as:—
  (a) in the case of operations carried out under sub-paragraphs (iii) or (iv) the external appearance of the premises of the undertaking is not materially affected; and
  (b) in the case of operations carried out under sub-paragraph (iv) no certificate would be required under section 67 of the Act if an application for planning permission for the development in question were made:
Provided that the erection on land within the curtilage of any such building of an additional building to be used in connection with the original building shall be treated as an extension of the original building, and where any two or more original buildings comprised in the same curtilage are used as one unit for the purposes of the undertaking, the reference in this permission to the cubic content shall be construed as a reference to the aggregate cubic content of those buildings, and the reference to the aggregate floor space as a reference to the total floor space of those buildings.
2. The deposit by an industrial undertaker of waste material or refuse resulting from an industrial process on any land comprised in a site which was used for such deposit on 1st July 1948, whether or not the superficial area or the height of the deposit is thereby extended.
 	
Class IX.—Repairs to unadopted streets and private ways
The carrying out of works required for the maintenance or improvement of an unadopted street or private way, being works carried out on land within the boundaries of the street or way.
 	
Class X.—Repairs to services
The carrying out of any works for the purpose of inspecting, repairing or renewing sewers, mains, pipes, cables, or other apparatus, including the breaking open of any land for that purpose.
 	
Class XI.—War damaged buildings, works and plant
The rebuilding, restoration or replacement of buildings, works or plant which have sustained war damage, so long as:—
  (a) the cubic content of the building or of the works or plant immediately before the occurrence of such damage is not increased by more than such amount (if any) as is permitted under Class I or Class VIII;
  (b) there is no material alteration from the external appearance immediately before the occurrence of such damage except with the approval of the local planning authority.
 	
Class XII.—Development under local or private Acts, or orders
Development authorised (i) by any local or private Act of Parliament or (ii) by any order approved by both Houses of Parliament or (iii) by any order made under section 14 or section 16 of the Harbours Act 1964 being, in any such case, a local or private Act, or an order, which designates specifically both the nature of the development thereby authorised and the land upon which it may be carried out:
Provided that where the development consists of or includes the erection, construction, alteration or extension of any building (which expression shall include any bridge, aqueduct, pier or dam, but not any other structure or erection), or the formation laying out or alteration of a means of access to any highway used by vehicular traffic this permission shall be exercisable in respect of such building or access as the case may be only if the prior approval of (a) the district planning authority (except in Greater London or a National Park); (b) in Greater London, the local planning authority, or (c) in a National Park, the county planning authority is obtained for the detailed plans and specifications thereof; but that authority shall not refuse to grant approval, or impose conditions on the grant thereof, unless they are satisfied that it is expedient so to do on the ground that:—
  (a) the design, or external appearance of such building, bridge, aqueduct, pier or dam would injure the amenity of the neighbourhood and is reasonably capable of modification so as to conform with such amenity; or
  (b) in the case of a building, bridge, aqueduct, pier or means of access, the erection, construction, formation, laying out, alteration or extension, ought to be and could reasonably be carried out elsewhere on the land.
 	
Class XIII.—Development by local authorities
1. The erection or construction and the maintenance, improvement or other alteration by a local authority of:—
  (i) such small ancillary buildings, works and equipment as are required on land belonging to or maintained by them, for the purposes	

Column (1) Description of Development	Column (2) Conditions
of any functions exercised by them on that land otherwise than as statutory undertakers; (ii) lamp standards, information kiosks, passenger shelters, public shelters and seats, telephone boxes, fire alarms, public drinking fountains, horse-troughs, refuse bins or baskets, barriers for the control of persons waiting to enter public vehicles, and such similar structures or works as may be required in connection with the operation of any public service administered by them. 2. The deposit by a local authority of waste material or refuse on any land comprised in a site which was used for that purpose on 1st July 1948, whether or not the superficial area or the height of the deposit is thereby extended.	
Class XIV.—Development by local highway authorities or the Greater London Council The carrying out by a local highway authority or the Greater London Council of any works required for or incidental to the maintenance or improvement of existing highways being works carried out on land outside but abutting on the boundary of the highway.	
Class XV.—Development by drainage authorities Any development by a drainage authority within the meaning of the Land Drainage Act 1930 in, on or under any watercourse or drainage works, in connection with the improvement or maintenance of such watercourse or drainage works.	
Class XVI.— Development by water authorities Development of any of the following descriptions by a water authority established under the Water Act 1973 :— (a) the laying underground of mains, pipes or other apparatus; (b) the improvement, maintenance or repair of watercourses or land drainage works; (c) the erection, construction or placing of buildings, plants, or apparatus on land or the carrying out of engineering operations in, on, over or under land, for the purpose of surveys or investigations.	On completion of the survey or investigation, or at the end of 6 months from the commencement of the development permitted by this class, whichever is the sooner, all such operations shall cease and all such buildings, plant or apparatus shall be removed and the land restored to its former condition.
Class XVII.—Development for sewerage and sewage disposal Any development by or on behalf of a water authority (established under the Water Act 1973), or by a Development Corporation authorised under section 34 of the New Towns Act 1965 to exercise powers relating to sewerage or sewage disposal, being development not above ground level required in connection with the provision, improvement or maintenance of sewers.	
Class XVIII.—Development by statutory undertakers A. Railway or light railway undertakings. Development by the undertakers of operational land of the undertaking, being development which is required in connection with the movement of traffic by rail, other than: (i) the construction of railways; (ii) the construction or erection, or the reconstruction or alteration so as materially to affect the design or external appearance thereof, of— (a) any railway station or bridge; (b) any hotel; (c) any residential or educational building, office, or building to be used for manufacturing or repairing work which is not situate wholly within the interior of a railway station; (d) any car park, shop, restaurant, garage, petrol filling station or other building or structure provided in pursuance of the powers contained in section 14 (1) (d) of the Transport Act 1962 or section 10 (1) (x) of the Transport Act 1968 which is not situate wholly within the interior of a railway station. B. Dock, pier, harbour, water transport, canal or inland navigation undertakings. 1. Development by the undertakers or their lessees of operational land of the undertaking, being development which is required for the purpose of shipping, or in connection with the embarking, disembarking, loading, discharging or transport of passengers, livestock or goods at a dock, pier or harbour, or the movement of traffic by canal or inland navigation, or by any railway forming part of the undertaking, other than the construction or erection, or the reconstruction or alteration so as materially to affect the design or external appearance thereof, of:— (a) any bridge or other building not required in connection with the handling of traffic; (b) any hotel; (c) any educational building not situate wholly within the limits of a dock, pier or harbour; (d) any car park, shop, restaurant, garage, petrol filling station or other building not situate wholly within the limits of a dock, pier or harbour, provided in pursuance of the powers contained in any of the following enactments:— the Transport Act 1962 section 14 (1) (d);	

Column (1) Description of Development	Column (2) Conditions
the Transport Act 1968 section 10 (1) (x); the Transport Act 1968 section 50 (6). 2. The improvement, maintenance or repair of any inland waterway to which section 104 of the Transport Act 1968 applies which is not a commercial waterway or a cruising waterway, and the repair or maintenance of culverts, weirs, locks, aqueducts, sluices, reservoirs, let-off valves or other works used in connection with the control and operation of such waterways. 3. The use of any land for the spreading of dredgings.	
C. Water or hydraulic power undertakings. Development required for the purposes of the undertakings of any of the following descriptions, that is to say:— (i) the laying underground of mains, pipes, or other apparatus; (ii) the improvement, maintenance or repair of watercourses or land drainage works; (iii) the maintenance or repair of works for measuring the flow in any watercourse or channel or the improvement of any such works (otherwise than by the erection or installation, by way of addition or replacement, of any structures of the nature of buildings or of any plant or machinery); (iv) the installation in a water distribution system of booster stations, meter or switch gear houses, not exceeding (except where constructed underground elsewhere than under a highway) 29 cubic meters in capacity; (v) the erection, construction or placing of buildings, plant or apparatus on land, or the carrying out of engineering operations, in, on, over or under land, for the purpose of surveys or investigations.	On completion of the survey or investigation or at the expiration of six months from the commencement of the development the subject of this permission, whichever is the sooner, all such operations shall cease and all such buildings, plant or apparatus shall be removed and the land restored to its former condition.
(vi) any other development carried out in, on, over or under the operational land of the undertaking except:— (a) the erection, or the reconstruction or alteration so as materially to affect the design or external appearance thereof, of buildings; (b) the installation or erection, by way of addition or replacement, of any plant or machinery, or structure or erections of the nature of plant or machinery, exceeding 15 metres in height or the height of the plant, machinery, structure or erection so replaced, whichever is the greater.	
D. Gas undertakings. Development required for the purposes of the undertaking of any of the following descriptions, that is to say:— (i) the laying underground of mains, pipes, or other apparatus; (ii) the installation in a gas distribution system of apparatus for measuring, recording, controlling or varying the pressure flow or volume of gas, and structures for housing such apparatus not exceeding (except where constructed underground elsewhere than under a highway) 29 cubic metres in capacity; (iii) the construction, in any storage area or protective area specified in an order made under section 4 of the Gas Act 1965 of boreholes, other than those shown in the order as approved by the Secretary of State for Energy for the purpose of subsection (6) of the said section 4, and the erection or construction, in any such area, of any plant or machinery, or structure or erections in the nature of plant or machinery, not exceeding 6 metres in height which is required in connection with the construction of any such borehole; (iv) the placing and storage on land of pipe and other apparatus needed for inclusion in a main or pipe which is being or is about to be laid or constructed in pursuance of a planning permission granted or deemed to be granted under Part III of the Act;	On completion of the laying or construction of the main or pipe, or at the expiration of nine months from the commencement of the development, the subject of this permission, whichever is the sooner, such pipe and apparatus shall be removed and the land shall be restored to its condition before the development took place. Approval of the details of the design and external appearance of the buildings shall be obtained from (a) the district planning authority (except in Greater London or a National Park), (b) in Greater London, the local planning authority, or (c) in a National Park, the county planning authority before the erection of the building has begun.
(v) the erection on operational land of the undertaking, solely for the protection of plant or machinery, or structures or erections of the nature of plant or machinery, of buildings not exceeding 15 metres in height;	

Column (1) Description of Development	Column (2) Conditions

(vi) any other development carried out in, on, over or under operational land of the undertaking except:—
   (a) the erection, or the reconstruction or alteration so as materially to affect the design or external appearance thereof, of buildings;
   (b) the installation of any plant or machinery, or structures or erections of the nature of plant or machinery, exceeding 15 metres in height, or capable, without addition, of being extended to a height exceeding 15 metres;
   (c) the replacement of any plant or machinery, or structures or erections of the nature of plant or machinery, to a height exceeding 15 metres or the height of the plant, machinery, structure or erection so replaced, whichever is the greater.
 E. Electricity undertakings.
 Development required for the purpose of the undertaking of any of the following descriptions, that is to say:—
   (i) the laying underground of pipes, cables or any other apparatus, and the construction of such shafts and tunnels as may be necessary in connection therewith;
   (ii) the installation in an electric line of feeder or service pillars, or transforming or switching stations or chambers not exceeding (except when constructed underground elsewhere than under a highway) 29 cubic metres in capacity;
   (iii) the installation of service lines to individual consumers from an electric line;
   (iv) the extension or alteration of buildings on operational land as long as the height of the original building is not exceeded and the cubic content of the original building (as ascertained by external measurement) is not exceeded by more than one-tenth nor the aggregate floor space thereof by more than 500 square metres;
   (v) the sinking of any boreholes for the purpose of ascertaining the nature of the sub-soil, and the installation of any plant or machinery, or structures or erections of the nature of plant or machinery, as may be necessary in connection therewith;
 	
   (vi) the erection on operational land of the undertaking, solely for the protection of plant or machinery, or structures or erections, of the nature of plant or machinery, of buildings not exceeding 15 metres in height;
 	
   (vii) any other development carried out on, in or under the operational land of the undertaking except:—
     (a) the erection, or the reconstruction so as materially to affect the design or external appearance thereof, of buildings; or
     (b) the installation or erection, by way of addition or replacement, of any plant or machinery, or structures or erections of the nature of plant or machinery, exceeding 15 metres in height or the height of the plant, machinery, structure or erection so replaced, whichever is the greater.
 F. Tramway or road transport undertakings.
 Development required for the purposes of the undertaking of any of the following descriptions, that is to say:—
   (i) the installation of posts, overhead wires, underground cables, feeder pillars, or transformer boxes not exceeding 17 cubic metres in capacity in, on, over or adjacent to a highway for the purpose of supplying current to public vehicles;
   (ii) the installation of tramway tracks; conduits and drains and pipes in connection therewith for the working of tramways;
   (iii) the installation of telephone cables and apparatus, huts, step posts and signs required in connection with the operation of public vehicles;
   (iv) the erection or construction, and the maintenance, improvement or other alteration of passenger shelters and barriers for the control of persons waiting to enter public vehicles;
   (v) any other development of operational land of the undertaking, other than:—
     (a) the erection, or the reconstruction or alteration so as materially to affect the design or external appearance thereof, of buildings;
     (b) the installation or erection, by way of addition or replacement, of any plant or machinery, or structures or erections of the nature of plant or machinery,
	
	On completion of the development or at the expiration of six months from the commencement of the development the subject of this permission, whichever is the sooner, such plant or machinery or structures or erections shall be removed and the land shall be restored to its condition before the development took place.
	 Approval of the details of the design and external appearance of the buildings shall be obtained from (a) the district planning authority (except in Greater London or a National Park), (b) in Greater London, the local planning authority, or (c) in a National Park, the county planning authority, before the erection of the building has begun.

Column (1) Description of Development	Column (2) Conditions

exceeding 15 metres in height, or the height of the plant, machinery, structure or erection so replaced, whichever is the greater;
   (c) development, not wholly within the interior of an omnibus or tramway station, in pursuance of the powers contained in section 14 (1) (i) (d) of the Transport Act 1962 or section 10 (1) (x) of the Transport Act 1968.
 G. Lighthouse Undertakings.
 Development required for the purposes of the functions of a general or local lighthouse authority under the Merchant Shipping Act 1894 and any other statutory provisions made with respect to a local lighthouse authority, or in the exercise by a local lighthouse authority of rights, powers or duties acquired by usage prior to the Merchant Shipping Act 1894, except the erection, or the reconstruction or alteration so as materially to affect the design or external appearance thereof, of offices.
 H. The British Airports Authority.
 Development by the Authority of operational land of the undertaking, being development which is required in connection with the provision by the Authority of services and facilities necessary or desirable for the operation of an aerodrome, other than:—
   (i) the construction or erection, or the reconstruction or alteration so as materially to affect the design or external appearance thereof, of:—
     (a) any hotel;
     (b) any building (not being a building required in connection with the movement or maintenance of aircraft or with the embarking, disembarking, loading, discharge or transport of passengers, livestock or goods at an aerodrome); and
   (ii) the construction or extension of runways.
 I. Post Office.
 Development required for the purposes of the undertaking of any of the following descriptions, that is to say:—
   (i) the installation of public call offices (telephone kiosks), posting boxes or self-service postal machines;
   (ii) the placing of any telegraphic line as defined in the Telegraph Act 1878 in the exercise of an easement or other right compulsorily acquired under section 55 of the Post Office Act 1969 ;
   (iii) the use of land in case of emergency for the stationing and operation of movable apparatus required for the replacement of telephone exchanges, telephone repeater stations and radio stations and generators which have become unserviceable, for a period not exceeding six months;
   (iv) any other development carried out in, on, over or under the operational land of the undertaking except:—
     (a) the erection, or the reconstruction or alteration so as materially to affect the design or external appearance thereof, of buildings;
     (b) the installation or erection, by way of addition or replacement, of any plant or machinery, or structures or erections of the nature of plant or machinery, exceeding 15 metres in height or the height of the plant, machinery, structure or erection so replaced, whichever is the greater.
 	
 Class XIX.—Development by mineral undertakers
 1. Where mining operations have been carried out in any land at any time on or after 1st January 1946 and before 1st July 1948.
   (a) in conformity with the provisions of a planning scheme or of permission granted thereunder or in accordance with permission granted at any time before 22nd July 1943 by or under an interim development order and in force immediately before 1st July 1948, or
   (b) under article 4 of the Town and Country Planning (General Interim Development) Order 1946 ,
 and an application for permission to continue those mining operations in adjoining land was made during the period of six months from 1st July 1948 or was treated by virtue of paragraph 1 of Schedule 10 to the Town and Country Planning Act 1947 as having been made under that Act, the continuation of those operations until the application (or any appeal in respect thereof) has been dealt with.
 2. The erection, alteration or extension by mineral undertakers on land in or adjacent to and belonging to a quarry or mine comprised in their undertaking of any building, plant or machinery, or structure or erection of the nature of plant or machinery, which is required in connection with the winning or working of minerals, including coal won or worked by virtue of section 36 (1) of the Coal Industry Nationalisation Act 1946 , but not any other coal, in pursuance of permission granted or deemed to be granted under Part III of the Act, or which is required in connection with the treatment or disposal of such minerals:
 Provided that where the development consists of or includes the erection, alteration or extension of a building, this permission shall be exercisable in respect of such building only if the prior approval of the local planning authority, in Greater London, and elsewhere the county planning authority is obtained
	
	At the expiration of the period of use all such apparatus shall be removed and the land shall be restored to its condition before the development took place.

Column (1)	Column (2)
Description of Development	Conditions

for the detailed plans and specifications of the building; but that authority shall not refuse to grant approval, or impose conditions on the grant thereof, unless they are satisfied that it is expedient so to do on the ground that:— (*a*) the erection, alteration or extension of such building would injure the amenity of the neighbourhood and modifications can reasonably be made or conditions can reasonably be imposed in order to avoid or reduce the injury; or (*b*) the proposed building or extension ought to be, and can reasonably be, sited elsewhere. 3. The deposit of refuse or waste materials by, or by licence of, a mineral undertaker in excavations made by such undertaker and already lawfully used for that purpose so long as the height of such deposit does not exceed the level of the land adjoining any such excavation.	
Class XX.—Development by the National Coal Board Development of any of the following descriptions carried out by the National Coal Board, or their lessees or licensees, that is to say:— (i) the winning and working underground, in a mine commenced before 1st July 1948, of coal or other minerals mentioned in paragraph 1 of Schedule 1 to the Coal Industry Nationalisation Act 1946, and any underground development incidental thereto; (ii) any development required in connection with coal industry activities as defined in section 63 of the Coal Industry Nationalisation Act 1946 and carried out in the immediate vicinity of a pithead: Provided that where the development consists of or includes the erection, alteration or extension of a building this permission shall be exercisable in respect of such building only if the prior approval of the county planning authority is obtained for the detailed plans and specifications of the building, but the county planning authority shall not refuse to grant approval, or impose conditions on the grant thereof unless they are satisfied that it is expedient so to do on the ground that:— (*a*) the erection, alteration or extension of such building would injure the amenity of the neighbourhood and modifications can reasonably be made or conditions can reasonably be imposed in order to avoid or reduce the injury; or (*b*) the proposed building or extension ought to be, and can reasonably be, sited elsewhere; (iii) the deposit of waste materials or refuse resulting from colliery production activities as defined by paragraph 2 of Schedule 1 to the Coal Industry Nationalisation Act 1946 on land comprised in a site used for the deposit of waste materials or refuse on 1st July 1948, whether or not the superficial area or the height of the deposit is thereby extended;	1. If the County planning authority so require, the Board shall, within such period as the authority may specify (not being less than three months from the date when the requirement is made) submit to them for approval a scheme making provision for the manner in which the depositing of waste materials or refuse is to be carried out and for the carrying out of operations in relation thereto (including, where appropriate, the stripping and storage of surface soil and the after-treatment of the deposit) for the preservation of amenity, such scheme to relate only to the depositing and after-treatment of waste materials or refuse deposited after 1st April 1974. 2. Where a scheme submitted in accordance with condition 1 has been approved the depositing of waste materials or refuse and their after-treatment shall be carried out in accordance with the scheme, or in accordance with the scheme as modified by conditions imposed on the grant of approval, as the case may be.
(iv) development by the National Coal Board consisting of the temporary use of land for the purpose of prospecting for coal workable by opencast methods and the carrying out of any operations requisite for that purpose.	1. No development shall be begun until after the expiration of 42 days from the date of service of notice in writing on the county planning authority, indicating the nature, extent and probable duration of the prospecting. 2. At the expiration of the period of prospecting, any buildings, plant or machinery and any waste materials shall be removed and any boreholes shall be properly and sufficiently sealed and other excavations filled in and levelled, any topsoil removed being replaced as the uppermost layer.
Class XXI.—Uses of aerodrome buildings The use of buildings on an aerodrome which is vested in or under the control of the British Airports Authority for purposes connected with the air	

Column (1)	Column (2)
Description of Development	Conditions

transport services or other flying activities at such aerodrome.	
Class XXII.—Use as a caravan site The use of land, other than a building, as a caravan site in any of the circumstances specified in paragraphs 2 to 9 (inclusive) of Schedule 1 to the Caravan Sites and Control of Development Act 1960 or in the circumstances (other than those relating to winter quarters) specified in paragraph 10 of the said Schedule.	The use shall be discontinued when the said circumstances cease to exist, and all caravans on the site shall then be removed.
Class XXIII.—Development on licensed caravan sites Development required by the conditions of a site licence for the time being in force under Part I of the Caravan Sites and Control of Development Act 1960.	

Importance of preliminary discussion

10.05 Because town planning control is so much a matter of taste, it is felt that a highly useful purpose can always be served by the developer through the medium of his architect, discussing with the appropriate planning officer the design and styling of the development which is to be undertaken. There is always room for more than one point of view but if some form of agreement can be reached between the developer and the planning officer as a result of informal discussion and negotiation, all this is to the good. Later on it may lead to the developer getting a good deal of what he wants out of the planning authority. In addition he will be able to get all of this far more speedily than he would if he chose to stand on strict legal rights and formally appeal to the Secretary of State against a decision of the planning authority which did not entirely please him.

10.06 With today's rapidly rising costs there has never been an age when it could more truly be said that time is money. The planning control process can be a long one, but informal discussions with the planning authority (or its representative) can often achieve perfectly proper and entirely legal shortcuts to a decision which gives the developer a good deal of what he wants.

© Sir Desmond Heap 1977.

References

HEAP, DESMOND An outline of planning law. 7th Edition, London, 1977, Sweet & Maxwell

MINISTRY OF HOUSING AND LOCAL GOVERNMENT Circular 48/49, Town and Country Planning Act 1959. HMSO

—— Circular 5/68, The use of conditions in planning permissions. HMSO

BOISOT WATERS COHEN PARTNERSHIP The Community Land Act explained. London, 1976, Architectural Press

RIBA Client's Advisory Service Community Land Act 1975 1976

WHITTAKER, C. The handbook of environmental powers. London, 1976, Architectural Press

AJ Legal Handbook

Section 9
Construction regulations

COUNSELLOR. HUBBLE. BUBBLE.

Legal study 13

English construction regulations

This study explains the legal basis of the Building Regulations and administrative procedures for implementing building control as well as some important provisions of the Regulations. It covers other important national legislation which deals with building, before discussing local building law with emphasis on building control in inner London. Particularly interesting is the discussion of district surveyors and of party wall procedure. Readers practising in Scotland should read LEGAL STUDY 14

1 Building acts and regulations

1.01 Planning legislation is largely concerned with policy and, in relation to the external appearance of a building, with safeguarding of amenity (LEGAL STUDY 12). But obtaining planning permission is only the first legal hurdle. The architect is then faced with controls over the construction and design of buildings. In England and Wales (outside the 12 inner London boroughs) the basic framework of control is found in the Public Health Acts 1936 and 1961, and the Building Regulations made under them.
The Building Regulations 1972 came into force on 1 June 1972, and represent a consolidation and metrication of the Building Regulations 1965, as amended, which they superseded. There are currently, in 1977, three sets of amendments—July 1973, March 1974 and August 1976 (see also LEGAL STUDY 18 para 3.08).

The Building Regulations
1.02 The Building Regulations 1972 set out legal and constructional rules in greater detail. The Regulations govern:
1 Construction of buildings and the materials to be used.
2 Space about buildings, lighting, ventilation and dimensions of habitable rooms.
3 Height of buildings and chimneys.
4 Works and fittings, including drainage; sanitary conveniences; cesspools and septic tanks; private sewers; heating and cooking appliances; water supply (Public Health Act 1936 section 61 as amended; see schedule 5 of Health and Safety at Work etc Act 1974).
5 Conservation of fuel and power.
6 Prevention of waste.
7 Undue consumption.
8 Misuse or contamination of water.
9 Health and safety of occupants of buildings.

1.03 Part III* of the Health and Safety at Work etc Act 1974 provided for the extension of the scope and coverage of building regulations. The Act introduced various procedural improvements in the system of building control. The major changes so introduced are:
1 Scope of building regulation powers was widened to include more comprehensive control of building services and equipment.
2 The system has been rationalised by ensuring that structural requirements which were formerly in other legislation can now be included in building regulations.
3 Exemptions were removed and provision was made for the

* At the time of writing the provisions of part III have not yet been brought into force

regulations to apply to types of structure which were not formerly covered.
4 Provision has been made for fees to be charged in connection with building regulations applications and procedural changes were introduced in order to achieve greater flexibility.
5 Penalties for breach of building regulations requirements were increased to a maximum of £400, with a continuing penalty of £40 a day (Public Health Act 1961 section 4 (6) as amended).

1.04 Subject to a number of exemptions and partial exemptions which are dealt with later (see para 2.04 *et seq*), submission of drawings and approval under the Building Regulations is necessary before one can carry out any building operation, make any structural alterations or extensions to a building or make any material change in the use of a building or part of a building. This requirement is particularly important because the submission of plans brings into operation a number of other controls vested in the local authority.

1.05 Even a cursory reading of matters controlled by the Building Regulations shows the need to refer to other legislation, as the Regulations are not a self-sufficient code. Thus, sanitary conveniences are dealt with in part P of the Regulations. This leads back by inference to the Public Health Act 1936 section 43 which provides that drawings for new buildings or extensions deposited with the local authority shall be rejected unless they 'show that sufficient and satisfactory closet accommodation . . . will be provided, or the authority is satisfied that in the case of the particular building or extension it may properly dispense with' the requirement.

Nature of approval
1.06 Before considering in more detail the consequences of submitting drawings under the Regulations, and some of the particular requirements which they lay down, three important matters must be emphasised: discretion of local authorities, building without approval and dispensation.

Discretion of local authority
1.07 Local authorities have no discretion when considering plans submitted under the Regulations. The wording of section 64 of the Public Health Act 1936 is mandatory. It states that the local authority must pass the plans of any proposed work deposited with it under the Regulations unless the drawings are defective or show any contravention of the Regulations. In that case, 'they shall reject the plans'.

It follows that even a trivial defect or contravention suffices to bring about rejection.

Building without approval

1.08 If a building owner fails to make application and submit plans for approval under the Building Regulations, he is guilty of an offence, just as he is when work is done contrary to the Regulations (Public Health Act 1936 section 65; Public Health Act 1961 section 4). There has been one reported case dealing with this matter since the Regulations came into effect, *Sunley Homes Ltd v Borg* (1969) 3 All ER 332. One of the points at issue in that case was whether an offence against the Regulations could be complete even though work on the buildings concerned had not been finished, as the buildings were in the course of construction at the time the prosecution was brought. The builders argued that no offence was committed under section 4 of the Public Health Act 1961 until the building in question was complete or, alternatively, until the time when the builder could no longer say that he would have remedied the offending work before completion. Lord Parker (then Lord Chief Justice) summarised the problem in this way: 'No one has been able to satisfy me at what stage it might properly be said that a building is complete. If all the workmen have left but the Building Regulations have not been complied with, I should have thought one could say that the building is not complete. However it seems to me that this argument becomes untenable when one looks: (a) at the Regulations; and (b) at the powers given to local authorities to deal with contraventions. . . . (The) general tenor of the Regulations is clearly against (the developer's) contentions. They deal throughout with the erection of a building, and while erection might mean the completed building, it might also mean the operation of erecting the building. . . . (It) seems to me clear that the erection of a building refers to the operation of erecting and not the completed erection.'
No offence is committed by starting work before approval is given, but this is a dangerous practice, because should the proposals fail to secure the local authority's approval, the building owner would be liable for any removal or alteration work ordered by the local authority.

1.09 Under the enforcement provisions, the local authority may require the removal or alteration of offending work and/or it may initiate criminal proceedings (1936 Act section 65). Notice to remove, alter or pull down contravening work may not be given after the expiry of 12 months from the date of completion of the work in question. The wording of the statutory prohibition is important; time begins to run against the local authority from the moment when the particular contravention is complete, and not from the date when the building as a whole is completed. However, in a case where the 12 months' limitation period had run, the local authority could apply to the High Court for an injunction, but only with the consent and in the name of the Attorney-General.

Dispensations

1.10 An important dispensing power is conferred upon the local authorities by section 6 of the Public Health Act 1961, read in conjunction with Regulation A14. This enables the local authority to relax or dispense with any of the Regulations' requirements other than those in parts A (General), D (Structural Stability) and E (Structural Fire Precautions), with minor exceptions (see Regulation A14), where they consider 'that the operation of any requirement in Building Regulations would be unreasonable in relation to the particular case to which the application relates'. The local authority cannot relax the Regulations in relation to its own buildings, but must apply to the Secretary of State on the special form given in part A of schedule 3 to the Regulations.

1.11 A developer wishing for relaxation of any requirement in parts A, D or E must apply to the Secretary of State (through the local authority) on the special form given in part B of schedule 3. In practice, it is found that relaxations often have to be sought in relation to conversions of single dwelling-houses into flats, when it is thought that the requirements as to structural stability and fire precautions are unduly stringent: see further *The Building Regulations explained and illustrated* (chapter 5).

1.12 There is a right of appeal to the Secretary of State against a local authority's refusal to dispense or relax Regulation requirements (Public Health Act 1961 section 7). Valuable guidance to the Secretary of State's attitude is to be found in the HMSO series *The Building Regulations* 1965: *selected decisions* which indicate the factors the Secretary of State has found to be relevant in considering applications. Most of the common problems have now been resolved.

1.13 The Secretary of State can relax building regulation requirements where he considers that it 'would be unreasonable in relation to any type of building matter' (see Health and Safety at Work Act sections 66 and 67, which enable him to grant relaxations in respect of certain types of buildings and for approving these matters where they comply).

2 Applications and their consequences

2.01 The general rule is that anyone wishing to erect, extend or structurally alter buildings, to install works or fittings or to make material changes in the use of a building, must apply to the local authority for approval under the Building Regulations. The procedure on application is governed by Regulation A10 and the rules contained in schedule 2. There is no prescribed form of application, but by Circular 9/70 the Secretary of State for the Environment has recommended a standard form for use by all enforcing authorities.

Method of approval

2.02 The local authority must give notice of approval or rejection of drawings within five weeks from the date of the application, although this period may be extended by written agreement. If the local authority fails to reach a decision on the application within the time stated, it is deemed to have approved the drawings (Public Health Act 1936 section 64). If the drawings are rejected, the notice must specify the alleged defects or contraventions. The applicant then has a right of appeal to the Secretary of State (section 64 as amended). A local authority with whom plans of any proposed work are deposited in accordance with building regulations may in prescribed cases pass them by stages (Health and Safety at Work Act section 63).

Disputes

2.03 There is a further important power contained in section 67 of the 1936 Act. If there is dispute as to whether the Regulations apply in any particular case, or the drawings are in conformity with the Regulations or the work has been executed in accordance with the drawings as passed, it may be referred by joint application to the Secretary of State for determination. His decision is final although he may 'at any stage of the proceedings on the reference and shall, if so directed by the High Court, state in the form of a special case for the opinion of the High Court any question of law arising'.

Exemptions

2.04 There are five cases when work is *totally exempt* from the Regulations, and then there is no need to submit drawings or obtain approval. These are detailed in Regulation A5 and shown in checklist 1. For the most part, these total exemptions are of little practical importance, in contrast with the eight classes of building which are *partially exempt*. These are set out in part A of schedule 1 (see checklist 2). Submission of plans and the grant of approval under the Building Regulations is generally necessary in these cases. The partial exemptions relate to the substantive provisions of the Regulations, the effect of the exemptions being that buildings in these categories need comply only with the Regulations specified in columns 2, 3 and 4 of schedule 1.

2.05 There are three cases in which notice of intention to do building work does not have to be given to the local authority (see checklist 3).

2.06 It will be seen therefore that the net of control is spread very wide, and almost no works are too small or inoffensive to escape control under the Regulations.

3 Some provisions of the Building Regulations

3.01 Space does not permit a detailed analysis of the provisions of the Regulations, and readers should refer to *The Building Regulations explained and illustrated*, which is a narrative explanation of the provisions affecting residential buildings, and to the AJ *Metric guide to the Building Regulations*, a more general discussion of the provisions for all types of building.

Deemed-to-satisfy provisions

3.02 However, two particular aspects of the Regulations are worth emphasising. The first relates to the *deemed-to-satisfy* provisions (Regulation A3) printed in italics in the official text of the Regulations.

3.03 The deemed-to-satisfy provisions which follow certain Regulations are merely examples of constructions that will satisfy the preceding Regulation, usually by reference to a British Standard or Code of Practice. This is not exclusive; the Regulation itself specifies a standard of performance, and the deemed-to-satisfy provision which follows is an example of a construction or kind of material which will meet the standards set. It is not obligatory to use the method or materials suggested in the deemed-to-satisfy clause, but by doing so, there will be no room for dispute with the local authority. In many cases, there are equally effective (and sometimes better) methods of construction or materials, and useful reference may be made to the BRS publications and the certificates of the Agrément Board. In part G of the Regulations, there is an odd gap: deemed-to-satisfy constructions are given for walls and floors, but the Regulations contain no guidance as to what is meant by 'adequate resistance to the passage of sound'. It has been found that most local authorities have been able to accept as suitable the constructions classified in BRS digests 102 and 103 as party wall grade and Grade 1 for walls and floors respectively, and those set out in BRS national building studies—research paper 33.*

Structural fire precautions

3.04 Part E of the Regulations, which is concerned with structural fire precautions and is extremely complex, requires

* See References at end of this Study

some general comments. More relaxations have been granted in respect of part E requirements than of any other part of the Regulations. Part E divides buildings into purpose groups (eight in all), which are set out in the table to Regulation E2 (checklist 4). The Regulations do not attempt to achieve a non-combustible building, but rather to achieve three objectives as regards fire precautions:
1 To protect the occupants of the building from the effects of fire.
2 To keep the spread of fire within and between buildings to a minimum.
3 To insure the non-collapse of buildings within a specified period, which is sufficient to allow the occupants to escape.

3.05 To achieve these objectives, part E limits the openings in external walls, requires that structural elements be made of fire-resisting materials, and demands the provision of fire-resisting doors and a degree of fire resistance to internal walls and so on. Here the designer has a heavy responsibility, and it is found that these provisions are those most likely to cause difficulty.

4 Other controls under the Public Health Acts

4.01 When drawings are submitted for Building Regulation approval, other controls are brought into play. The most important are described below.

Building over sewers and drains

4.02 Section 32 of the 1936 Act states that local authorities must keep a map showing the location of all public sewers in their districts. The map distinguishes between public sewers, those with respect to which a vesting declaration has been made but which has not yet taken effect, and those subject to an agreement as to future declaration (see LEGAL STUDY 9 para 2.02 *et seq*). Where separate sewers are reserved for foul and surface water, this must be clearly shown. These four groups of sewers and drains are shown on the map.

4.03 Section 25 prohibits building over any sewer or drain shown on the map except with the local authority's consent. It provides, where the plans show that the building will be constructed over any sewer or drain, that the authority shall reject the plans unless they are satisfied that in the circumstances of the particular case they may properly consent to its erection.

4.04 The rejection of drawings showing an intended contravention of the Building Regulations, as described in para 1.06, is obligatory because of the wording of section 64. Section 25 is a provision which expressly authorises rejection. Any dispute between the applicant and the local authority as to whether the proposed building will be over a sewer and as to the granting of consent can be determined by the magistrates' court.

4.05 What is the position if a local authority simply passes the drawing and says nothing about the sewer or drain over which the building is erected? The point is undecided, but Lumley's *Public Health* suggests that in such circumstances the local authority must 'be taken to have been "satisfied" and to have consented unconditionally and cannot afterwards be heard to say that they had overlooked what was shown on the map'. The editors cite *A.-G. v Denby* (1925) CH 596, in support of this statement, and a reading of the case certainly gives strength to the contention.

New buildings and drains

4.06 Under section 37 of the 1936 Act new buildings must be provided with drains. This section states that unless the drawings show satisfactory provision for the drainage of the building, or the local authority is satisfied that it may dispense with any provisions for drainage in the particular case, the plans shall be rejected. 'Drainage' in this connection includes roof drainage. Where the local authority is not satisfied with the provision for drainage shown on the drawings, its decision can be challenged by reference to the magistrates' court.

4.07 This statutory provision is badly phrased, particularly in the wording of subsection (3) which does not make it clear whether the authority can pass the drawings subject to conditions instead of rejecting them. The best view is that it may impose any conditions or requirements that can be shown on a drawing, but not other conditions.

4.08 As a result of this provision, the local authority can insist on a separate drain being provided for each building, although in practice plans showing combined drainage are invariably approved. Moreover, under the next section (section 38) it may require buildings to be drained in combination into an existing public sewer 'where the drains of the building are first laid'. It cannot insist on drainage in combination where it has previously passed the plans, except with the agreement of the owners concerned.

Closet accommodation

4.09 Section 43 of the 1936 Act imposes a mandatory obligation to reject drawings of a building or extension unless they show that sufficient and satisfactory closet accommodation is provided, or the local authority is satisfied that it may properly dispense with the requirement in the particular case.

4.10 'Water closets and earth closets' are referred to in section 43 and it is for the local authority to decide which type is to be provided. It cannot reject the plans merely because an earth closet is shown 'unless a sufficient water supply and sewer are available'. This phraseology has an antiquated ring today, and is of little practical importance. Of more importance is the grant which can be claimed under section 47 of the Act when converting any kind of old-fashioned closet (including chemical closets) to a water closet (see LEGAL STUDY 9 para 4.15).

Water supply

4.11 The effect of section 137 of the 1936 Act is that drawings of a house deposited with the local authority are to be rejected, unless 'there is put before (the local authority) a proposal which appears to it to be satisfactory for providing the occupants with a supply of wholesome water sufficient for their domestic purposes', and if possible the water is to be from a piped supply.

Buildings constructed of materials unsuitable for permanent buildings

4.12 Section 64 of the Health and Safety at Work etc Act 1974 contains special provisions as to materials etc unsuitable for permanent buildings. It replaces section 53 of the 1936 Act and provides a wider power of control over the use in buildings of materials, components, fittings etc which are short-lived or for some other reason require special measures. Where plans show that it is proposed to construct a building of materials which are unsuitable for permanent buildings, the local authority may reject the plans, even though they are generally in accordance with the regulations. Alternatively, the local authority may set a period at the end of which the building must be removed, unless an extension is granted. The local authority may impose conditions which are relevant to the use of these materials (see Regulation B3 and Table thereto for the materials to which this provision applies). There is a right of appeal to the Secretary of State against the local authority's decision.

Continuing requirements

4.13 Section 65 of the same Act provides for imposing continuing requirements on owners and occupiers of buildings which were not subject to building regulations when erected. In the event of contravention of requirements so imposed, the local authority may execute the work and their charge for it.

Erection of buildings on ground filled with offensive matter

4.14 Section 54 confers on the local authority power to reject drawings where the site of the building is ground which has been filled up with any material impregnated with faecal or offensive animal or vegetable matter or upon which such material has been deposited. The rejection of plans is obligatory, for unless the council is satisfied that the offensive material has been removed or has become or been rendered innocuous, it has no discretion entitling it to pass the drawings.

4.15 Rejection of the drawings under section 54 does not give rise to any right of appeal, but the applicant may apply to the magistrates' court to determine 'whether the local authority ought to approve the erection of the building . . . on the site in question'. No time limit is imposed.

Removal of refuse

4.16 Section 55 of the 1936 Act requires the local authority to reject drawings for erection or extension of a house unless satisfactory means of access from the house to the street is provided for the removal of refuse. 'House' is defined section 343 of the Act as meaning a dwelling-house, whether a private dwelling-house or not. Thus, the power to reject drawings does not extend to other buildings such as commercial premises, albeit there is an equal need in such cases for the satisfactory removal of refuse. The provision is couched in imperative terms and there is a right of appeal to the magistrates' court.

Exits and entrances of public buildings

4.17 Section 59 of the 1936 Act allows local authorities to control entrances and exits of certain buildings, but it applies only to the kinds of buildings listed in subsection (5) (see checklist 5). The local authority must reject the plans for such a building unless they show that the building 'will be provided with such means of ingress and egress and passages or gangways as the authority deems satisfactory, regard being had . . . to the purpose for which the building is intended to be, or is, used, and the number of persons likely to resort thereto at any one time'.

In practice this may necessitate installation of fire-escapes, and is really a matter for liaison between the architect, the local authority and the local fire authority. (The provision of fire escapes in factories under section 40 of the Factories Act 1961 is different, and is dealt with in para 5.21 *et seq*.)

Other matters subject to control

4.18 The preceding eight cases are examples of the controls which come into play as the result of a deposit of plans under the Building Regulations. There are others, eg the height of chimneys controlled under section 10 of the Clean Air Act 1956 (dealt with in para 5.10), but the ones discussed serve to emphasise the importance of the Building Regulations procedure and the local authority's powers.

5 Other national legislation

5.01 More than 250 general statutes contain further provisions affecting the construction of buildings, although this is not apparent from the titles of the Acts concerned. There are also numerous Statutory Instruments made under powers conferred by many of these Acts. In this section some statutory rules which affect the bulk of building developments will be considered. This list does not claim to be exhaustive, nor does it cover all the relevant sections. (Some provisions of statutes not discussed here are covered in LEGAL STUDY 9.)

5.02 Certain requirements are dealt with automatically on the deposit of drawings under the Building Regulations or, in some cases, at the same time as the application for planning permission. The following are some of the more important provisions which are relevant at that stage.

The Fire Precautions Act 1971
5.03 The object of this Act is to meet the criticisms that the law relating to fire precautions in certain kinds of residential accommodation and places of public entertainment was inadequate. The method of control is similar to that provided by the Factories Act 1961 and the Offices, Shops and Railways Premises Act 1963 (see para 5.21).

5.04 In practice, the Act applies to four main categories of premises:
1 Places of amusement, recreation and public resort, theatres, cinemas, dance halls, and so on.
2 Residential establishments such as hotels, boarding houses, hospitals and institutions for the residential care of the young, elderly or handicapped.
3 Educational establishments.
4 Certain private dwellings, notably high-rise blocks of flats. Specifically excluded are factories, offices, shops and railway premises, mines and quarries, places of public religious worship and premises that consist of or are comprised in a house which is occupied as a single private dwelling.

5.05 Fire certificates issued by the local fire authority (ie the council of every county and county borough) are the main form of control under the Act. The occupier of affected premises must obtain a certificate to the effect that the premises are provided with such such means of escape in case of fire as may reasonably be required.

5.06 Under section 3 the fire authority (in consultation with the local authority) has power to serve a notice which makes a fire certificate compulsory for certain kinds of dwellings, mainly blocks of flats.

5.07 If premises fall within the Act, an application for a fire certificate must be made to the fire authority under section 5. The authority must then inspect the premises and, if they are satisfied as to the means of escape in case of fire and other relevant fire precautions, they must issue the certificate, or inform the applicant of what must be done to bring the premises up to standard.

5.08 It must be noted that the Secretary of State is empowered by section 11 to make Building Regulations regarding means of escape in new buildings. Once these Regulations have been made in relation to fire escapes in new buildings, the architect will know what requirements will satisfy the authority by way of fire escapes in any new building. There is a safeguard for the building owner: section 13 provides that except in specially defined circumstances, the fire authority cannot require alterations to a building or an extension, if it has already been subject to Building Regulations approval relating to means of escape. The various authorities concerned are also under a duty to consult each other in appropriate circumstances, eg under section 15, the local authority must consult the fire authority before passing plans under the Building Regulations if the premises are likely to require a certificate.

5.09 This new measure extends fire precautions to further categories of premises and aims to provide a comprehensive and flexible system of control. The greater part of the Act is now in force.

The Clean Air Acts 1956 to 1968
5.10 Among other things, these Acts control the height of chimneys on industrial premises, types of installation and the treatment of offensive fumes from appliances.

5.11 Section 6 of the 1968 Act requires the approval of the local authority for the height of a chimney serving a furnace, and approval may be granted subject to conditions as to the rate and/or quality of emissions from the chimney. There is a right of appeal to the minister.

5.12 Similarly section 10 of the 1956 Act provides that in other cases the local authority must reject plans of residences, shops or offices unless the height of the chimney as shown on the drawings will be sufficient to prevent fumes from being a nuisance or a health hazard. The factors to be considered are the purpose of the chimney, the position and description of nearby buildings, levels of neighbouring ground and other relevant matters. These provisions represent an important negative control. See further LEGAL STUDY 9 para 6.04.

Highways Act 1959
5.13 Sections 72 and 73 of the Highways Act 1959 deal with improvement and building lines respectively. An improvement line is designed to prevent the erection of buildings on land that may later be required for road widening. Where an improvement line has been prescribed, no new building may be erected nor may a permanent excavation be made nearer to the centre line of the street than the improvement line, except with the highway authority's consent. This may be granted subject to conditions. There is a right of appeal to the Crown Court against the refusal of consent or its grant subject to conditions.

5.14 A building line is a frontage line beyond which a building may not project, irrespective of road widening. A building line may be prescribed by the highway authority under section 73 and, where it is prescribed, no new building (other than the boundary wall) may be erected in front of the prescribed line except with the authority's consent. This may be granted subject to conditions, or for a limited time. In both cases, a new building includes an addition or extension to an existing building, and hence both provisions are always relevant at the design stage.

5.15 The Highways Act 1959, as amended, contains many other prohibitions and rules which affect the architect's work, including part VIII (sections 157 to 172) dealing with new streets. Where new street by-laws have been made, the proposed work must not contravene them, and plans showing any contravention will be rejected (section 161). Where a new street order has been made under section 159 and new street by-laws are in force, these will prescribe the centre line of the new street and lines defining its minimum width. Effectively, new buildings will have to be set back in order to leave sufficient land for a street of the necessary width to be formed at that point. Another relevant provision is section 206, which enables the authority to make a street designation order.

5.16 Even minor works of alteration and extension will not necessarily escape the net of the Highways Acts. For instance, if a building owner wishes to have a garage erected, it will be necessary in many cases for a carriage crossing to be constructed, thus bringing into play the provisions of section 40 of the Highways Act 1971. The building owner who wishes to provide new means of access to his premises to be constructed at his expense may initiate proposals for a carriage crossing. In addition, the local authority may, in certain circumstances, construct a crossing on their own initiative, again at the building owner's expense.

The Highways Act 1971
5.17 Section 2 of the 1971 Act gives power for a highway authority to be authorised by order of the Secretary of State for the Environment to stop up private access to highways from any premises, if it considers that the access is likely to cause danger to, or interfere unnecessarily with, traffic on the highway. Such an order can be made only where no access to the premises from the highway is reasonably required, or where other reasonably convenient means of access is available or will be provided. There is an objections procedure, and compensation may be payable (1971 Act, section 4 (2)).

5.18 Attention is also drawn to section 36 of the new Act which provides that if, in the course of carrying out building work in or near a street, an accident occurs which gives rise to the risk of serious bodily injury to a person in the street, the owner of the land or building where the work is being carried out is guilty of an offence punishable by a maximum fine of £500.

5.19 Again, section 38 places restrictions on construction (and subsequent alteration) of buildings over highways maintainable at the public expense, without the licence of the highway authority. Licences may be granted subject to conditions and are registrable as a local land charge (LEGAL STUDY 6 para 2.06).

5.20 Section 37 prescribes that precautions against accidents must be taken where a person is executing works in a street. These safety measures include, where appropriate, the shoring up of any building adjoining the street. Stringent safety precautions must be observed in relation to builders' skips, which may not be deposited on the highway without the highway authority's consent. This may be granted subject to conditions (1971 Act section 31).

The Factories Act 1961
5.21 The provisions of this complex measure and of the many Regulations made under it affect building construction in four ways: means of escape in case of fire; structural fire protection; provision of sanitary accommodation; health and welfare provisions generally.

5.22 No factory which employs more than 20 people may be used as such, unless it has a valid certificate granted by the local fire authority showing that it has proper means of escape in case of fire (sections 40 to 45). The fire authority is the county council or the county borough council.

5.23 The fire authority grants a certificate conditional upon specified alterations being made to the premises. If they do this they must fix a time within which the alterations must be carried out.

5.24 In three cases factories employing less than 20 people must also have a valid certificate.
1 Those built before 30 July 1937 where more than 10 people are employed above the first floor, or more than 20 above ground level.
2 Factories built subsequently and employing more than 10 people above the ground floor.
3 All factories containing explosive or highly flammable materials, irrespective of the number of people employed.

5.25 There is a right of appeal to the magistrates' court if a certificate is refused or cancelled, or if alterations are required; the length of time allowed for carrying out of any required alterations may also be the subject of appeal. Where an existing factory is to be extended, written notice must be given to the fire authority which will make a survey to see whether the means of escape need modifying. The obligation concerning fire escapes is a continuing one in that the employer must properly maintain the means of escape once installed.

Fire
5.26 There are special safety provisions relating to doors, exits and lifts (section 48). All doors must be capable of being easily opened from the inside. With the exception of sliding doors, two groups of doors must open outwards:
1 Doors leading from a room, containing more than 10 employees, to a staircase or corridor.
2 Exit doors from the factory.
This second provision does not apply to factories which were in use before July 1938.

5.27 Lifts and hoistways must be completely encased with fire-resisting materials and must be fitted with fire-resisting doors. The tops of lift shafts and hoistways must also be provided with a vent or be enclosed by a material which is easily broken by fire.
It is possible to obtain exemption from the requirements for lifts and doors, if it can be shown that they are inappropriate or undesirable in any particular case.

5.28 An adequate fire alarm system must be installed in all factories which are obliged to obtain a fire certificate. Fire alarms must be tested regularly. Appropriate fire-fighting equipment must also be provided (section 51).

Sanitary accommodation
5.29 Section 7, read in conjunction with the Sanitary Accommodation Regulations 1938, requires the provision of adequate sanitary accommodation for employees of both sexes. Where women are employed, there must be at least one sanitary convenience for every 25 females. There must be one suitable sanitary convenience (not simply a urinal) for every 25 men employed. However, where more than 100 men are employed and there is adequate urinal accommodation, one water closet for the first 25 employees and one for every 40 after that number are sufficient. Reference should be

made to the text of the Regulations for exemptions and for other contingencies. The preceding section (section 6) requires the provision of adequate floor drainage, eg by gulleys, where the factory process is likely to make the floor wet.

5.30 Other rules of the Factories Act concern architects. For example, sections 57 to 79 which, among other things, require the provision of cloakroom and clothes-drying accommodation, washing facilities and so on.

The Thermal Insulation (Industrial Buildings) Act 1957
5.31 This Act (and Regulations made under it) prescribes a standard of thermal insulation for industrial buildings. Section 2 empowers local authorities to reject drawings of proposed industrial buildings or of extensions to them where the drawings show that the building will not conform to the prescribed standard.

Notice of rejection or acceptance of the drawings for this purpose must normally be given within one month from the date of deposit, although this period is extended to five weeks in some cases. Disputes are determined by the minister and he may (and must, if so required) state a case for the opinion of the High Court.

The Offices, Shops and Railway Premises Act 1963
5.32 Similar rules to those in the Factories Act 1961 are applied by this Act to offices, shops, and railway premises (see further LEGAL STUDY 3 para 5.01 *et seq* and LEGAL STUDY 9 para 6.12).

Special classes of building
5.33 The legislation dealt with so far is, in one sense, of general application. The architect dealing with the design and construction of specialised types of buildings may find that special controls apply.

All these specialised provisions are extremely complex, and space does not permit any detailed examination of them. As examples, we may refer to the special controls applicable to cinemas and to the keeping and use of radioactive substances.

Cinemas
5.34 Regulations made by the Home Secretary under the Cinematograph Acts 1909 and 1952 lay down special requirements for this type of building. The regulations are the Cinematograph (Safety) Regulations 1955 (Statutory Instrument no 1129 of 1955), as amended by Statutory Instrument no 1530 of 1958.

The Regulations relate, among other things, to exits, seating, fire precautions, lighting and electrical installations and the structure and construction of projection and similar rooms.

Radioactive substances
5.35 The Radioactive Substances Act 1960 regulates the keeping and use of radioactive material, and its provisions must be kept in mind when dealing with hospital and educational buildings. Basically, those who use or keep radioactive substances require a licence granted by the Secretary of State for the Environment. An analogous measure is the Nuclear Installations (Licensing and Insurance) Act 1959 which controls, in the interests of safety, the building and operation of nuclear reactors and other nuclear installations as are prescribed. A 'nuclear site licence' (granted by the Government) is needed before building can begin.

5.36 Some further notes on special buildings are given in LEGAL STUDY 9 para 6.01 *et seq*.

6 Building in inner London

6.01 Inner London consists of the City of London and the 12 London Boroughs of Camden, Greenwich, Hackney, Hammersmith, Islington, Kensington and Chelsea, Lambeth, Lewisham, Southwark, Tower Hamlets, Wandsworth and Westminster (London Government Act 1963 section 43).

6.02 The design, construction and use of buildings in this area are regulated by the London Building Acts and By-laws, which form a code of control different from that which operates elsewhere. The code applies to new work, alterations, additions and conversions. Of course, construction in inner London is also affected by general legislation, such as the Town and Country Planning Act 1971 (LEGAL STUDY 12), but the local measures contain the basic system of control. The law is to be found in the London Building Acts 1930–1939, as amended, and in by-laws made under these Acts. The London By-laws cover similar ground to the Building Regulations 1972 (except that such things as sound and thermal insulation are not covered), but the London Building Acts give the GLC much greater control over, *inter alia*, certain large and high buildings (see para 6.19) and public buildings (see paragraph 6.26) and set out the procedure to be followed in party wall matters (see para 6.28 *et seq*). It should be noted that section 70 of the Health and Safety at Work etc Act 1974 enables building regulations to be applied to inner London, but this power is to be exercised only after consultation with the GLC and other local authorities concerned. It is the eventual intention to rationalise the system of building controls on a national basis, and hence section 70.

6.03 The provisions are administered and enforced by the GLC, although the London borough councils perform certain functions. The GLC acts through the Superintending Architect of Metropolitan Buildings and his staff. He is assisted by district surveyors in each of the 28 districts or geographical areas which were formerly the old metropolitan boroughs.

District surveyors
6.04 The district surveyor is a statutory officer peculiar to London and has wide power and responsibilities. He is appointed under section 75 (1) of the London Building Acts (Amendment) Act 1939. His duties are to be deduced from section 82 (1) of that Act which provides that: 'Every work to, in, or upon a building or structure and all matters relating to the width and direction of streets, the general line of buildings in streets, the provision of open spaces about buildings, the height of buildings, and all works in pursuance of the provision of means of escape shall be subject to the supervision of the district surveyor.'

6.05 It is the district surveyor's duty to ensure that the statutory provisions are complied with. He must survey any work placed under his supervision as and when necessary and see that the provisions are observed. If he learns of any actual or probable contravention with which he is not competent to deal, section 82 (3) enjoins him to give notice to the council 'forthwith'.

6.06 Fees for the district surveyor's services are payable by the builder or, in default, by the owner or occupier. Normally they fall due 14 days after the roof of the building is covered in, or the work is completed (section 92, 1939 Act). One-third of the fees may be payable earlier, even on an estimated basis (London County Council (General Powers) Act 1955 section 12).

Powers of entry

6.07 The district surveyor and other authorised officers have wide powers of entry, inspection and examination to enable them to carry out their functions (section 142, 1939 Act, for example). It is an offence to obstruct the district surveyor in the exercise of his functions. The maximum fine is £20, with a daily fine of £5 for continued contravention (section 148 (1) 1939 Act).

Appeals tribunal

6.08 There is a special Tribunal of Appeal which hears appeals referred to it under the London Building Acts and By-laws. It has power to award costs and wide powers to require the production of documents, plans, specifications and so on. A further appeal lies, by way of the 'case stated' procedure, to the Queen's Bench Divisional Court.

There is, however, no appeal against a district surveyor's decision where work is required to be carried out in a proper and workmanlike manner and such work has not been so carried out (section 86 (1) 1939 Act), and there is no appeal further than to the Council, against a district surveyor's decision on a matter which, in the Council's opinion, is likely to affect the stability or protection in case of fire of a building or structure (section 86 (2) 1939 Act).

Building notices

6.09 The district surveyor usually learns of proposed works when he receives a building notice. The procedure is governed by section 83 of the 1939 Act. This imposes a duty on the builder to give 48 hours' notice before beginning any work to which the Acts and by-laws apply. Similar notice must be served when work is resumed after it has been suspended for any period exceeding three months.

6.10 It must be noted that the notice is to be served by the builder. He is defined by section 4 (1) of the 1939 Act as the person who is employed to build or to execute work to, in or upon a building or structure. If no builder is employed, the owner of the building must serve the notice.

6.11 Considerable detail is required. The notice must state the situation, area, height, number of storeys and proposed use of the building or structure. It must also give particulars of the proposed work, the estimated cost, the name and address of the builder and the names of the owner in possession and the occupier. Normally, the cubical extent of the works must also be given, although the district surveyor may waive this requirement (section 84 *ibid*).

6.12 Within 14 days of completion of the works, the builder must give a written statement of its cost to the district surveyor who may require further information on this point. In many cases, the statutory fees payable are dependent on the cost of the work.

Notice of Objection

6.13 If the building notice discloses a contravention of the provisions, the district surveyor must serve Notice of Objection on the builder or owner or other person causing or directing the work. In effect, this provides a *locus poenitentiae* (an opportunity for repentance).

However, there is a right of appeal to the magistrates' court, exercisable within 14 days after service of the notice (section 87 *ibid*).

Notice of Irregularity

6.14 The district surveyor also has power to serve Notice of Irregularity under section 88 of the 1939 Act. This is appro-

priate where work has begun, and it was decided in *Coggin v Duff* (1907) 96 LT 670, that failure to give notice of objection is not a bar to proceedings under Notice of Irregularity. This notice will be served where the builder has failed to give the required notice or where a contravention comes to light as the works proceed. Its effect is to require the builder to amend any contravention within 48 hours. The notice cannot be served upon the builder when he has completed the building, but there is power to serve notice on the owner, occupier or other person directing the work.

6.15 The sanction behind a Notice of Irregularity is a fine not exceeding £5. However, the district surveyor may apply to the magistrates' court for an order requiring the builder to comply with the notice within the stated time. Failure to obey an order of the court renders the builder liable to a daily fine of £20 (section 148 1939 Act).

Relaxation of requirements

6.16 Section 9 (1) of the London Building Acts (Amendment) Act 1935 confers upon the GLC power to waive or modify any of the by-law requirements in any particular case. This can only be done upon application, and consent may be given subject to conditions. The application must be in writing, signed by the building owner or his agent and state the nature and extent of the proposed modification, with reasons for seeking the dispensation.

Exemptions

6.17 The provisions of the London Building Acts and By-laws do not apply to certain specified categories of building, eg Crown property, certain markets, railway premises and so on. These are not of general importance.

There are, however, some partial exemptions which are of interest, since the statutory provisions relating to the construction of buildings do not apply. The main classes are certain public buildings, including local authority educational buildings over 250 000 cu ft (7079 210 m³) in extent, and the following:

1 Low buildings, eg buildings other than public buildings or buildings for human habitation or trade, not exceeding 200 sq ft (18 581 m²) in superficial area, at least 10ft (3 048 m) distant from other buildings and the land of adjoining owners or not exceeding 800 sq ft (74 322 m²) and at least 15ft (4 572 m) away (1939 Act section 149 (1)).

2 Boundary walls not more than 6ft (1 829 m) in height above ground level.

3 Greenhouses.

There are also exemptions from provisions about means of escape in case of fire, for instance in the case of building subject to the Factories Act 1961, there being no need for duality of control.

Additionally, the large local authority educational buildings mentioned above are not exempt from the means of escape provisions.

However, a building notice (see para 6.09) must still be served in respect of these exempt buildings, subject to certain exceptions.

Specific provisions

6.18 There is no up-to-date commentary on the London Building Acts and by-laws, and the only available source of reference is Halsbury's *Laws of England*. Space does not permit a detailed examination of all the provisions, but consideration will be given to several points of practical importance.

Large and high buildings

6.19 Section 20 of the London Building Acts (Amendment) Act 1939 is important, and gives the Greater London Council wide control over the following buildings, so far as relates to precautions against fire:

(a) Buildings of excess height ('high' buildings) over 100ft (30 480 m) high, or over 80ft (24 380 m) high if the area of the building (at any level) exceeds 10 000 sq ft (929 020 m²).

(b) Certain buildings of additional cubical extent ('cube' buildings), ie buildings over 250 000 cu ft (7079 210 m³) used for trade (including warehouses and departmental stores) or manufacture.

Except where a trade building is properly subdivided into fire divisions each less than 250 000 cu ft (7079 210 m³), all buildings coming within the scope of section 20 require the specific consent of the Council and should be designed generally in accordance with the Greater London Council's Code of Practice. This is a recently revised document (publication 7168 0316) covering structural fire precautions in a very comprehensive way, including the provision of access for fire fighters up to the building, fire fighting 'lobby approach' staircases, smoke outlets from basements, fire dampers in ventilation ducts and other requirements affecting the heating, lighting, electrical and ventilating arrangements, the isolation of and special precautions within special risks and so on.

Special or temporary buildings

6.20 There is a set procedure for the approval of special and temporary buildings not intended to conform to the general provisions. Consent is required for the erection of special and temporary building under sections 29 and 30 of the 1939 Act. There is an exception in favour of builder's site offices and certain hoardings. Conditions may be attached.

6.21 Of practical importance is the fact that in most cases the consenting authority is the London borough council, as opposed to the GLC. This is so in the case of temporary buildings or structures not exceeding 7ft 6in (2 286 m) in height or 200 sq ft (18 581 m²) in area, temporary stands and allied structures and other temporary structures wholly or partly made of wood. Additionally, the GLC has now delegated to the borough councils the function of consenting to most temporary buildings and structures not exceeding 500 sq ft in area and 10ft in height.

Means of escape in case of fire

6.22 Part V of the London Building Acts (Amendment) Act 1939 deals with means of escape in case of fire. An application, accompanied by drawings, must be made to the GLC for approval as to the proposed means of escape for every new building (broadly, those built after 1939) to which section 34 of the 1939 Act applies. The notice and drawings must be deposited before or at the same time as building notice is given. The new buildings concerned are:

1 All public buildings.

2 Places of worship or of assembly.

3 Every other new building which:

(a) if of one storey, exceeds six squares* in area

(b) if of more than one storey, exceeds 10 squares* in aggregate floor area, exclusive of any basement used for storage

(c) has a storey at a greater height than 20ft (6 096 m)

(d) in which more than 10 people are employed above the ground storey.

The Greater London Council also has the power to require proper and sufficient means of escape to be provided from

* A square is the space of 100 sq ft (9.290 m²) section 5 1930 Act

most old buildings (broadly those built prior to 1940). For exemptions and exceptions, see provisos to sections 34 and 35 of the 1930 Act, and also section 149 of the 1939 Act. If, in the case of a new building, the GLC does not reach a decision on the application within two months of the date when the notice and plans are deposited, consent is deemed to be granted. There is the usual power to extend this period by agreement.

The approved means of escape arrangements from buildings to which part V of the 1939 Act applies are required by section 133 to be maintained, and fines for contravention of this are laid down in section 148.

Public buildings

6.23 A public building is one used wholly or partly as a place of public worship (other than a dwelling-house so used), a public library, place for public entertainment or assembly, or a building with a cubic extent exceeding 250 000 cu ft (7079 200 m³) which is used wholly or partly as a hotel, hospital, school or other place of instruction (section 4 (1) 1939 Act).

6.24 Construction of public buildings must be to the approval of the district surveyor or, where there is a dispute, as determined by the Tribunal of Appeal (section 26 (3), 1939 Act). This is a provision peculiar to the inner London system, emphasising the importance of the district surveyor's function. His certificate (or that of the tribunal) is necessary to show that requirements have been met. Normal rules governing construction do not apply to public buildings, and a higher standard may be required by the district surveyor than with other buildings, notably as regards stability and fire protection (1939 Act section 26 (2) (b)).

Party structures

6.25 Part VI of the 1939 Act contains a special statutory code governing party structures and rights of adjoining owners. Common law rules (LEGAL STUDY 6 para 4.14) are excluded to the extent of these statutory provisions which do not affect the legal title to the structure or any easements or rights in connection with them (section 54).

Party wall

6.26 Section 44 gives a special definition of 'party wall':
1 A wall which forms part of a building and stands on lands of different owners. Projection of any artificially formed support on which the wall rests on to land of any adjoining owner does not make the wall a party wall.
2 Any part of any other wall as separates buildings belonging to different owners.

Party structure

6.27 Party structure is a party wall, floor, partition or other structure separating buildings or parts of buildings approached only by separate staircases or entrances from outside the building (section 4). Tenancy separations in blocks of flats and maisonettes are therefore normally excluded.

Party fence wall

6.28 The legislation also refers to a 'party fence wall'. This is a wall that is not part of a building, but which stands on the lands of different owners and is used or constructed for separating such lands. It does not include a wall constructed on one owner's land, of which only artificially formed supports project on to the adjoining land. Thus rights of adjoining owners do not arise where only the foundations project on to the adjoining land if the wall concerned is a boundary wall, not being part of a building, but they do arise if such wall separates buildings belonging to different owners.

Procedure

6.29 A special procedure has to be followed if the building owner wishes to invoke his rights under the Act. These are more extensive than the limited rights he has at common law, and as regards existing structures, may be summarised:

1 Where a structure is defective, he may repair, make good, thicken or underpin it, or demolish and rebuild it.

2 If he wishes to build against it and it is of insufficient height or strength, he may rebuild it subject to making good all damage to adjoining property, and raising the height as necessary of chimney and flues.

3 He may carry out all necessary incidental works to connect with the adjoining premises.

A full list of the authorised works is given in section 46 (checklist 6); see also W. A. Leach, *Party structure rights in London.*

Section 50 deals with the underpinning of independent buildings and confers valuable rights on both adjoining owners.

6.30 The first step in the process is for the building owner to serve a *party structure notice* upon adjoining owners, except where their prior written consent has been given or the work is necessary as a result of a dangerous structure notice. The RIBA publish precedent notices (forms A to G). The notice contains particulars of the proposed works and is normally accompanied by a party-wall drawing, although drawing need only be served where it is proposed to use 'special foundations', ie foundations in which steel beams or rods are used to spread the load. The notice must be served at least two months before the work is to be commenced in the case of a party structure or one month in the case of special foundations or a party fence wall (section 47 (2)). The adjoining owner has the right to serve counter notice requiring carrying-out of additional works for his protection.

6.31 The adjoining owner may, in fact, consent to the proposed works under section 49. If an owner does not so express his consent in writing to a counter notice or a notice within 14 days of service, a 'difference' is deemed to have arisen between the parties section (49). The special procedure for settlement of differences is in effect an arbitration (LEGAL STUDY 8) and is contained in section 55. This enables the parties to agree to the appointment of an agreed surveyor who will make an award upon the difference. This is not usual. In practice, each party appoints his own surveyor, and normally the difference is settled by negotiation between them and they make a joint award. There is provision for the two nominated surveyors to call in a third surveyor who acts as intermediary, but this is very rare.

6.32 When the party wall award has been agreed, it is engrossed (expressed in legal form) and executed in duplicate, each copy being signed and witnessed by the two surveyors. The award will deal with the supervision of the works and the costs. Normally, costs will be borne by the building owner, but this is not necessarily the case. The award can be challenged by an appeal to the County Court within 14 days of issue, or, in certain circumstances by appeal to the High Court.

6.33 Expenses in respect of party structures are dealt with by section 56. Where works are for the benefit of both owners (normally when a party structure is in disrepair) the costs are to be shared proportionally. The adjoining owner

may also be liable to contribute towards the costs when he makes any use of the works as compared with the use when the works were begun. Such a right of contribution does not exist at common law. Section 56 is not clear as to what can be included in the 'expenses incurred', for which the building and adjoining owners may be severally or jointly liable, and these have been held to include district surveyors', surveyors' and architects' fees in connection with design (see *Fifoot v Apperley* (1905) reported only in 'Building News', 18 September 1905). The costs of the party wall itself are not included, as these will be dealt with specifically in the award itself.

6.34 Any works which are carried out by a building owner under the provisions of the Act are subject to four general conditions under section 51:

1 The work is not to be carried out in such a way or at such a time as to cause unnecessary inconvenience to the adjoining owner or occupier. It is submitted that building work carried out at normal times and in a normal manner and taking reasonable precautions to reduce noise and dust to a minimum cannot be said to cause 'unnecessary inconvenience', just as it would not constitute a nuisance at common law (*Andreae v Selfridge & Co* (1938) 1 CH 9).

2 Where any part of the adjoining land or building is laid open, the building owner must erect and maintain at his own expense proper protective hoardings and so on for protection and security of the adjoining occupier.

3 The works must comply with the London Building Acts and By-laws.

4 The works must be in accordance with any plans, sections and particulars agreed between the owners or approved by their surveyors in the party-wall award.

6.35 The works which are authorised by the Act are set out in section 46 (checklist 6). However it must be remembered that special foundations (see para 6.30) cannot be placed under adjoining land without the adjoining owner's written consent.

6.36 Section 53 confers on the building owner, his servants, agents and workmen a power of entry upon premises, and if the building is closed, he may break open doors to enter, provided he is accompanied by a police officer. Notice of 14 days must be given, except in emergency.

Space at rear and internal courts

6.37 Sections 42–46 and 48–49 of the London Building Act 1930 are still in force and control respectively the provision of open space at the rear of buildings and courts within buildings; the function of administering such sections of the Act has been delegated by the Greater London Council to the Inner London Borough Councils.

Dwelling-houses on low-lying land

6.38 Part XII of the London Building Act 1930 prohibits the erection or rebuilding of dwelling-houses on low-lying land without the consent of the Greater London Council. In *Gyle-Thompson v Wall Street Properties Ltd* (1974) 1 All ER 295, the High Court considered what Mr Justice Brightman described as 'important points of law' arising out of the operation of the 1939 Act. His lordship held that, in the absence of any express right to lower a party fence wall, sections 46 (a) and (k) of the Act (which give a building owner the right to demolish and rebuild) require reconstruction of the wall to its original height. The defendants also contended that under section 55 (para 6.31 above) the award was conclusive against the plaintiff and could be challenged only by an appeal to the county court. The judge rejected this submission, saying that it is not correct 'in relation to an award which is *ultra vires* and therefore not a valid award'. This case also emphasises that the steps laid down by the Act as to procedure 'should be scrupulously followed throughout, and short cuts are not desirable'.

7 Local legislation outside London

7.01 Although the Building Regulations 1972 were intended to provide a national code, there are many provisions in local Acts which impose a measure of control on the construction of buildings. These local requirements supplement the Building Regulations. In 1965 (Ministry of Public Buildings and Works Circular 3) it was recommended that all local enactments be repealed in so far as they dealt with matters covered by the Building Regulations. The Building Regulations (Local Enactments) Order 1966 repealed many local provisions, but others were left untouched.

The following is not an exhaustive list, but indicates the sort of local provisions which may be encountered.

Approval void after stated interval
7.02 A great many local Acts contain a provision to the effect that if the work specified in drawings deposited with the local authority is not begun within a specified period (usually two or three years), the deposit of the drawings and the council's approval will be null and void.

This provision is found in many parts of the country, but notably in the North.

Minimum area of habitable rooms
7.03 Some local Acts provide for minimum areas for habitable rooms in dwelling-houses.

By-laws about stables
7.04 An antiquated provision inherited from the horse-drawn era empowers local councils to make by-laws governing lighting and ventilation of stables and the prevention of insanitary conditions in them. Oddly, this is a very widespread provision and is to be found in many local Acts of recent vintage.

Underground parking places
7.05 Local Acts in many large urban areas (eg the Southampton Corporation Act 1960 section 66) contain a provision which empowers the local authority to reject plans for the erection, alteration or extension of underground parking places where it is not satisfied as to the arrangements proposed for preventing or reducing danger from fire.

Party walls
7.06 In certain provincial cities, there is party wall legislation similar to that which applies in inner London. The City and County of Bristol is, perhaps, the best-known example, and indeed, its special system of control is in many respects analogous to that in London, so far as application procedures are concerned.

The party wall position in Bristol is governed by sections 24 to 32 of the Bristol Improvement Act 1847, as amended by the Bristol Corporation Act 1926 sections 91 to 93, which provide for party wall awards, thicknesses of party walls and arches, and joint contributions.

7.07 The awards procedure (section 26 of the 1847 Act) provides that if a party wall is defective or insufficient in thickness, one owner may give notice to the other requiring him to appoint a surveyor and the two surveyors can make a joint survey and award. In case of default, the person serving

the notice may appoint a surveyor to act on behalf of the adjoining owner. The surveyors are required to certify what works, if any, are necessary. If they fail to make an award within a month of their appointment, the building owner may apply to a magistrate to appoint another surveyor to act as umpire. There is a right of appeal against the certificate or award within 30 days of issue.

Party walls must be of a specified thickness. Separate side walls (other than external walls) must be of a minimum thickness of 13½in (342·9 mm). The corporation has power to make by-laws regulating the thickness of party walls, arches and so on.

Section 92 of the 1926 Act provides for the reimbursement of the expense of building and maintaining party walls or arches in certain cases of joint benefit.

Section 93 contains provisions enabling a building owner to raise the height of external and party walls, subject to his raising any adjoining flues or chimneys.

Other provisions
7.08 This is not an exhaustive catalogue of local legislation. Many other provisions are encountered in different local authority areas. The authorities concerned are of the opinion that they form an essential part of the machinery of control, although their continued existence militates against uniformity of building control.

Checklist 1: Five classes of building work exempt from Building Regulations under Regulation A5

1 Buildings specified in section 71 of the Public Health Act 1936. These are:
(a) buildings required for the purposes of any educational establishment erected or to be erected according to plans which have been approved by the Secretary of State for Education and Science
(b) buildings constructed by a local authority in accordance with plans approved by the minister under the Smallholdings and Allotments Acts
(c) buildings of statutory undertakers held and used in them for the purpose of their undertaking.
2 Buildings used in connection with any mine or quarry, other than houses, offices or showrooms.
3 Movable dwellings to which section 269 of the Public Health Act 1936 applies.
4 Buildings used exclusively for accommodation of hoppickers and others who are engaged temporarily in agricultural or horticultural activities.
5 Buildings subject to the Explosives Acts 1875 to 1923.

Checklist 2: Buildings partially exempt from Building Regulation control (part A of schedule 1)

Class 1 Small buildings used as, eg summer-houses, poultry-houses, greenhouses, conservatories, orchard-houses, boat-houses, coal-sheds, garden tool-sheds, potting or garden sheds of not more than 30 m³ in capacity, and sited not less than 6ft (2 m) from any other residential or institutional building within the same boundaries.
Class 2 Buildings such as site offices used only in connection with and during the construction, alteration or repair of any building or other work.
Class 3 Monuments specified in the Ancient Monuments Acts.
Class 4 Wholly-detached buildings used, for a limited period,

in connection with the sale or letting of plots in the course of an estate development, and erected on or in close proximity to the estate.

Class 5 Small detached garages of not more than 30 m² in floor area.

Class 6 Single-storey storage buildings used exclusively for storage, plant or machinery, or the housing of livestock.

Class 7 Single-storey agricultural glasshouses, subject to limitations.

Class 8 Other wholly-detached storage buildings within the curtilage of a works, and subject to conditions.

Checklist 3: Cases in which notice of intention to build does not have to be given to local authority

1 For the *replacement* of existing fittings covered by parts N, P or Q (drainage, sanitary conveniences and so on).

2 For the installation or replacement of a Class II gas appliance, or a Class I or II gas-fired incinerator, provided that it is installed by or under the supervision of the Gas Board, and no structural work apart from the construction of a flue-pipe is required by part M (heat-producing appliances and incinerators).

3 For the replacement of an appliance covered by part M, except a high-rating appliance, a Class II gas appliance, or a Class I or II gas-fired incinerator, and where the only structural work involved is the provision of fire-guard anchorages.

Checklist 4: Purpose groups under Regulation E2

Number	Description	Intended use of building or compartment
I	Small residential	Private dwelling-house (not including a flat or maisonette). By Regulation E20 certain small garages and open carports are treated as being of purpose group I
II	Institutional	Hospital, home, school or other similar establishment used as living accommodation for, or for treatment. care or maintenance of, persons suffering from disabilities due to illness or old age or other physical or mental disability or under the age of five years, where such persons sleep in the premises
III	Other residential	Accommodation for residential purposes other than any premises comprised in groups I and II
IV	Office	Office, or premises used for office purposes, ie for administration, clerical work (including writing, book-keeping, sorting papers, filing, typing, duplicating, machine calculating, drawing and the editorial preparation of matter for publication), handling money and telephone and telegraph operating; or as premises occupied with an office for the purposes of the activities there carried on
V	Shop	Shop or shop premises, ie premises not being a shop but used for carrying on retail trade or business (including sale to members of the public of food or drink for immediate consumption, retail sales by auction, the business of lending books or periodicals for the purpose of gain, and the business of a barber or hairdresser) and premises to which members of the public are

invited to resort for the purpose of delivery of their goods for repair or other treatment or of themselves carrying out repairs to, or other treatment of, goods

VI	Factory	Factory within the meaning ascribed to that word by section 175 of the Factories Act 1961 (but not including slaughterhouses and other premises referred to in paragraphs (*d*) and (*e*) of subsection (1) of that section)
VII	Other assembly place	Place, whether public or private, used for the attendance of persons for or in connection with their social, recreational, educational, business or other activities, and not comprised within groups I to VI
VIII	Storage and general	Place for storage, deposit or parking of goods and materials (including vehicles), and any other premises not comprised in groups I to VII

Checklist 5: Types of building subject to special control over entrances and exits (Public Health Act 1936 section 59(5))

This section applies to the following:

1 Any theatre, and any hall or other building which is used as a place of public resort.

2 Any restaurant, shop, store or warehouse to which members of the public are admitted and in which more than 20 persons are employed.

3 Any licensed club required to be registered.

4 Any school not exempted from the operation of Building Regulations.

5 Subject as hereinafter provided, any church, chapel or other place of public worship:

Provided that this section does not apply to a private house to which members of the public are admitted occasionally or exceptionally, or to a building which was used as a church, chapel or other place of public worship immediately before the date when section 36 of the Public Health Acts Amendment Act 1890, or a corresponding provision in a local Act, came into operation in the district or contributory place, or which in a district or contributory place where neither that section, nor any such corresponding provision, ever came into operation was so used immediately before the commencement of this Act.

Checklist 6: Authorised works to party structures (London Building Acts (Amendment) Act 1939 section 46)

Where lands of different owners adjoin and at the line of junction the said lands are built on, or a boundary wall being a party fence wall or the external wall of a building has been erected, the building owner shall have the following rights:

1 To make good, underpin, thicken or repair or demolish and rebuild a party structure or party fence wall in any case where such work is necessary on account of defect or want of repair of the party structure or party fence wall.

2 To demolish a timber or other partition which separates buildings belonging to different owners but is not in conformity with the London Building Acts or any by-laws made in pursuance of those Acts and to build instead a party wall in conformity therewith.

3 In relation to a building having rooms or storeys belonging to different owners intermixed to demolish such of those rooms or storeys or any part thereof as are not in conformity

with the London Building Acts or any by-laws made in pursuance of those Acts and to rebuild them in conformity therewith.

4 Where buildings are connected by arches or structures over public ways or over passages belonging to other persons to demolish such of those buildings arches or structures or such parts thereof as are not in conformity with the London Building Acts or any by-laws made in pursuance of those Acts and to rebuild them in conformity therewith.

5 To underpin, thicken or raise any party structure or party fence wall permitted by this Act to be underpinned thickened or raised or any external wall built against such a party structure or party fence wall subject to:

(a) making good all damage occasioned thereby to the adjoining premises or to the internal finishings and decorations thereof

(b) carrying up to such height and in such materials as may be agreed between the building owner and the adjoining owner or in the event of difference determined in the manner provided in this part of this Act all flues and chimney stacks belonging to the adjoining owner on or against the party structure or external wall.

6 To demolish a party structure which is of insufficient strength or height for the purposes of any intended building of the building owner and to rebuild it of sufficient strength or height for the said purposes subject to:

(a) making good all damage occasioned thereby to the adjoining premises or to the internal finishings and decorations thereof

(b) carrying up to such height and in such materials as may be agreed between the building owner and the adjoining owner or in the event of difference determined in the manner provided in this part of this Act all flues and chimney stacks belonging to the adjoining owner on or against the party structure or external wall.

7 To cut into a party structure subject to making good all damage occasioned thereby to the adjoining premises or to the internal finishings and decorations thereof.

8 To cut away any footing or any projecting chimney breast jamb or flue or other projection on or over the land of the building owner from a party wall, party fence wall, external wall or boundary wall in order to erect raise or underpin an external wall against such party wall, party fence wall, external wall, or boundary wall or for any other purpose subject to making good all damage occasioned thereby to the adjoining premises or to the internal finishings and decorations thereof.

9 To cut away or demolish such parts of any wall or building of an adjoining owner overhanging the land of the building owner as may be necessary to enable a vertical wall to be erected against that wall or building subject to making good any damage occasioned thereby to the wall or building or to the internal finishings and decorations of the adjoining premises.

10 To execute any other necessary works incidental to the connection of a party structure with the premises adjoining it.

11 To raise a party fence wall to raise and use as a party wall, a party fence wall, or to demolish a party fence wall and rebuild it as a party fence wall or as a party wall.

For the purposes of this section a building or structure which was erected before the commencement of this Act shall be deemed to be in conformity with the London Building Acts and any by-laws made in pursuance of those Acts if it is in conformity with the Acts and any by-laws made in pursuance of the Acts which regulated buildings or structures in London at the date at which it was erected.

Nothing in this section shall authorise the building owner to place special foundations on land of the adjoining owner without his previous consent in writing.

References

WHYTE, W. S. and POWELL-SMITH, V. The Building Regulations explained and illustrated. 4th Edition with 1976 Supplement, London, 1976, Crosby Lockwood Staples

JOINT COMMITTEE ON BUILDING LEGISLATION Relaxations of Building Regulations: parts 1 to 3. London, 1968, RIBA

DEPARTMENT OF THE ENVIRONMENT The Building Regulations, 1970

LUMLEY, W. G. Public Health, 12th Edition, London, 1959, Shaw & Sons & Butterworth

ELDER, A. J. AJ Metric guide to the Building Regulations. 2nd Edition, London, 1971, Architectural Press

BUILDING RESEARCH STATION Digest 102 Sound insulation of traditional dwellings. 1969, HMSO

BUILDING RESEARCH STATION Digest 103 Sound insulation of traditional dwellings. 1969, HMSO

BUILDING RESEARCH STATION Research Paper 33 Field measurement of sound insulation between dwellings. 1961, HMSO

EVERTON, A. Fire and the law. London, 1972, Butterworth.

HALSBURY. Laws of England volume 31. 3rd Edition, London, 1960, Butterworth

LEACH, W. A. Party structure rights in London. London, 1961, Estates Gazette

MINISTRY OF PUBLIC BUILDING AND WORKS Circular 3 Public Health Act 1961 Building Control. 1965, HMSO

PITT, P. H. and DUFTON, J. Building in Inner London—a practical guide to building law. London, 1976, Architectural Press

O'KEEFE, P. Building Regulations checklists and index, 3rd Edition, 1976, London. Home Information Services

Legal study 14

Scottish construction regulations

This study explains the legal basis of the Scottish Building Regulations before discussing important aspects of the Regulations themselves. It also covers general building legislation as it applies to Scotland. Particularly useful are the notes for people practising in Scotland for the first time (para 5.01)

1 Introduction

1.01 Building control in Scotland is based on Building Acts. To understand Scottish practice, a knowledge of the Acts is required as well as the Regulations made under them. The Building Standards (Scotland) Regulations 1971–1975 are only one part of the whole scene, although admittedly a very important part. Anyone trying to compare Scottish and English building control must bear the above in mind, so that there is a comparison of like with like wherever possible.

1.02 This study is intended to describe the main provisions of the Act and procedures laid down under it, as well as the various Statutory Instruments associated with it. The whole subject of building control is now an endorsement subject to the Higher National Certificate in Building. The course takes some 180 hours of lectures so it will be appreciated that only the main issues are being discussed here.

Historical background
1.03 Building control is not new and records of building law go back to the pre-Christian era. Fire precautions which have always formed a major part of building codes were an accepted factor of Roman law and of English law from the 12th century.

Dean of Guild Courts
1.04 In Scotland building control in royal burghs was exercised by Dean of Guild Courts where these existed. Originally, the Dean of Guild was the president of the merchants' guild which was composed of traders who had acquired the freedom of a royal burgh. The post is an ancient one, eg in 1403 one Simon de Schele was appointed Dean of Guild and Keeper of the Kirk Work by Edinburgh Town Council. The Dean of Guild Court's original mercantile jurisdiction fell gradually into disuse to be replaced by a jurisdiction over such areas as markets, streets and buildings. 'Questions of neighbourhood' were dealt with by Edinburgh Dean of Guild as early as 1584. Gradually the scope and nature of the powers of the Dean of Guild Courts became more precise until in the last 130 years they have been subjected to a process of statutory modification.

1.05 Not all burghs had Dean of Guild Courts and it was not until 1947 that the Local Government (Scotland) Act required burghs without Dean of Guild Courts to appoint one. In other burghs, the functions of the Dean of Guild Courts were either carried out by magistrates or the town council itself. In counties, plans were usually approved by a sub-committee of the public health committee. There was no warrant procedure as in burghs.

By-laws
1.06 During the last 150 years, statutory requirements laid the foundation of specific and more widely applicable standards. The Burgh Police Act of 1833 empowered burghs to adopt powers of paving, lighting, cleansing, watching and supplying water. However, the building legislation content of the 19th century Acts was not large and was related mainly to ruinous property and drainage, attention to the latter being attracted by the large scale outbreaks of cholera at that time.
In 1892 the Burgh Police Act introduced a detailed set of building rules which were repealed by the 1903 Burgh Police Act. This Act gave powers to make by-laws. Meanwhile in the counties, the Public Health (Scotland) Act 1897 had already given them the power to make by-laws.

1.07 By-laws made under these Acts, although limited in scope, remained the main form of building control until 1932 when the Department of Health for Scotland published model building by-laws for both burghs and counties. Local authorities could, if they wished, adopt these by-laws for application in their own area. However, many did not. The model by-laws were revised in 1934 and 1937 but, apart from a widening of scope, later editions did not differ much from the original 1932 version. A much more comprehensive review was carried out in 1954. Although many local authorities adopted the 1954 model by-laws, adoption was at the discretion of the local authority and many did not. (By 1957, 26 of the 33 counties, 127 of the 173 small burghs, 13 of the 20 large burghs and none of the cities had adopted the model by-laws.) However, Edinburgh, Aberdeen and Glasgow had local Acts which combined many of the requirements of old statutes and by-laws with local features.

1.08 The then existing legislation fell short of the requirements of a modern building code able to cope with the rapidly expanding building of post-war Scotland where new techniques and materials were rapidly being introduced. It was decided that the whole concept of building control should be reviewed, and to this end a committee under the chairmanship of Lord Guest was appointed by the Secretary of State.

1.09 The Committee's terms of reference required that it examine the existing law pertaining to building and jurisdiction of the Dean of Guild Courts and make recommendations on the future form of a building control system for counties and burghs, which was to be flexible enough to take account of new techniques and materials.

1.10 The committee published its report in October 1957. Its main recommendation was that legislation was essential to enable a comprehensive building code to be set up in the form of national regulations to achieve uniformity throughout the country. The basic purpose of building control should be the protection of the public interest as regards health and safety. The law must ensure that occupants, neighbours and passers-by are protected by preventing the erection of buildings that are liable to collapse or lead to unhealthy or insanitary conditions. It must also prevent individual and collective fire hazards.

1.11 The recommendations were accepted and led to the existing form of control now established in Scotland.

2 Building (Scotland) Acts 1959 and 1970 (as amended by the Health and Safety at Work etc Act 1974 and the Local Government (Scotland) Act 1973)

2.01 As a direct result of the deliberations of the Guest Committee, the Building (Scotland) Act 1959 was passed. The aim of the Act was to introduce a system which while utilising some of the then current practice in a more modern form, produced new procedures and standards which were flexible enough to meet rapidly changing building processes. The Act itself was unique in UK legislation and gave Scotland the lead in the field of national building control.

2.02 Certain sections of the Act came into effect on the day the Act was passed, 30 April 1959, but the main provisions did not come into effect until 15 June 1964, a day appointed by the Secretary of State.

2.03 In common with much of our legislation, the Building Acts have in their short history been subject to amendment because of changes in other spheres of Government and in particular the effect of the Local Government (Scotland) Act 1973 and the Health and Safety at Work etc Act 1974. While the basic philosophy of the original Building Act and that of 1970 has not changed, details in the enforcement of the requirements and indeed the scope of the Act have been altered. These have been incorporated in the text.
The Act is laid out in four parts and a brief summary of the content of each is given below.

Local authorities
2.04 The requirement in the 1959 Act for local authorities to appoint building authorities was amended by the Local Government (Scotland) Act 1973, which vested building control in authorities as follows: in the Highland, Borders and Dumfries and Galloway regions, the regional councils and in other cases, the district councils or island authorities. The Act gave the authorities power to set up their own means of building control and this has varied from large independent building control departments with directors in charge to combined departments under either planning, environmental health, architectural services or technical services. It means also that powers to deal directly with warrant applications vary with the amount of delegation given to officials. In some instances the chief building control officer deals with and signs warrants for all unopposed applications, in others all applications are put before the appropriate committee and in others delegation to officials is based on whether or not the application is for work valued above or below a certain financial limit. While the principle of the Local Government Act was to give autonomy to authorities this in its turn has given rise to anomalies which were not there under the previous specific legislation of the 1959 Act.

Building Standards
2.05 Part II as amended by section 75 and schedule 7 of the Health and Safety at Work Act 1974*. deals with building standards and building operations. Section 3 of the Act gives the Secretary of State power to prescribe Building Standards Regulations and details the necessary procedure to be carried out before making Regulations (described below in para 2.15). The basis of the Building Standards Regulations is stated as follows: 'they shall be such as in the opinion of the Secretary of State can reasonably be expected to be attained in buildings of the classes to which they relate, having regard to the need for securing the health, safety, *welfare* and convenience of the persons who inhabit or frequent such buildings and the safety of the public generally' *and for furthering the conservation of fuel and power. The standards may make reference to any document published by the Secretary of State or other persons. This means in practice that the Secretary of State can deem-to-satisfy any document he thinks fit. Certain buildings are exempted from regulations eg some Atomic Energy Authority Buildings. The Secretary of State has also been given the power to repeal or modify any enactment in force before or passed in the same session as the Health and Safety at Work Act 1974 if he considers it inconsistent with or unnecessary or requires alteration in consequence of any provision of the building standards regulations.*

2.06 The Secretary of State may also make regulations for the conduct of building operations as he thinks necessary to secure the safety of the general public.

2.07 Only the Secretary of State is given power to relax Building Standards Regulations. However, section 2 of the 1970 Act gives the Secretary of State power to make regulations delegating the ability to give relaxation to the local authority. Section 6 is one of the most important sections of the Act. It requires that no person shall construct or demolish a building to which the Building Standards apply or change the use of any building without first obtaining a warrant from the local authority. Warrants will be granted if the local authority is satisfied that the operations will be carried out in accordance with the Building Operations Regulations and that the building when erected will meet the Building Standards Regulations. In addition, in the case of a change of use, the building must conform to as many of the Building Standards Regulations as will become applicable or will apply more onerously to the building by reason of the change of use.

Type approvals
2.08 *The Secretary of State has powers to issue type approvals.†* *The purpose of this is for the Secretary of State to issue a document stating that a particular type of building meets the Building Regulations specified. The purpose of this would mean that where a building is so approved, building control officers would automatically have to accept compliance with the specified regulations. The end result would it is hoped save considerable time and work particularly in complicated or unusual cases compared to the present system where inspectors in different authorities would each have to check every aspect of the building in the regulation context.*

Warrants for construction
2.09 A warrant for construction is issued subject to the conditions that the building is built in accordance with the

---

* In the following paras the amendments of the Health and Safety at Work etc Act 1974 are italicised

† Not yet activated

description in the warrant, drawings and specification. The building must also conform to the Building Standards Regulations and any direction from the Secretary of State relaxing any of the Regulations.

Local authorities have the power, however, to grant warrant for work to be carried out in stages. This is a discretionary power. Warrant for the demolition of a building must state the length of time the works will take.

2.10 Section 6 (8) as amended by the 1970 Act gives provisions where it would be competent for a building authority to refuse warrant. This important section is worthy of careful study as incorrect interpretation could cause inconvenience and delay. Local authorities can refuse warrant if:
1 The application has not been made in the prescribed manner.
2 The authority considers that application for alterations or extensions to a building would result in either of the following:
(a) where a building conforms to the Regulations at the time of application, but would fail to conform as a direct result of the proposed works or;
(b) where a building fails to conform to the Regulations at the time of application and would fail to conform to even greater degree as a direct result of the proposed works.

2.11 The phrase 'as a direct result' is the important point. The following examples may help to elucidate it:
1 A complete unit containing a new kitchen and bathroom was added to the rear of an existing house with low ceiling heights. The extension did not make the situation regarding existing ceiling heights any worse, so only the extension is dealt with in consideration of warrant.
2 An extension to a factory resulted in the travel distance* within the building as a whole being made worse; therefore the travel distance of the whole building, new and existing, was subject to the building standards for a new building.

2.12 After consulting the highways authority, the local authority is given authority to make an order allowing the occupation of parts of roads for deposit of materials and so on during building operations. The 1970 Act makes it an offence to deposit materials without permission from the buildings authority.

Certificates of completion
2.13 Section 9 relates to the issue of completion certificates by the buildings authority. Where electrical installations are concerned, another certificate is required from the installer certifying that the installations meet the necessary requirements of the Building Standards Regulations. No person may occupy a building erected under warrant unless a certificate of completion has been issued. However, temporary certificates may be issued at the discretion of the buildings authority. 'The Secretary of State has powers to extend the provision for certification to other than electrical installations eg gas installations.'

2.14 Powers are given in section 9 to deal with buildings erected without warrant or in contravention of warrant, and procedures are described. Power is given to the *local* authority to enforce certain provisions of the Building Standard Regulations on existing buildings.

* Though not specifically interpreted in part 1 section A2 of the Building Standards, this expression is frequently employed to denote distance from point to point   Editor

New Regulations
2.15 Section 12 requires the Secretary of State to appoint a Building Standards Advisory Committee, the main purposes of which are to advise him on the making of Building Standards Regulations and keeping the operation of the Regulations under review. The members of the committee are selected as individuals and not as representatives of particular interests. The committee is usually reconstituted at three-year intervals. The 1976–79 Committee consists of a chairman who is a chartered engineer and architect, two other architects, two building control officers, a director of environmental health and a director of technical services whose departments deal with building control, a trade union official, a chartered engineer (mech and vent), a structural engineer, a firemaster, a chartered surveyor, a builder, an electrical engineer and a fire insurer.

2.16 The procedure for making regulations is as follows: the Secretary of State consults the Building Standards Advisory Committee and other such bodies which are representative of the interests concerned. In practice, over 200 bodies are asked for their comments or proposed amendments to the Building Regulations. 'This is usually done by issuing a document which details the proposals and invites comments and representations.'

Dangerous buildings
2.17 Part III deals with dangerous buildings and goes into detail regarding action to be taken to make them safe, the powers of local authorities with regard to purchasing buildings where owners cannot be found and the selling of materials from buildings demolished by the local authority.

Civil liability
2.18 *New section* 19A *lays down breaches of regulations which may be actionable so far as damage is concerned. Damage includes death or injury of persons.*

Crown rights
2.19 It is now made clear that Crown buildings must conform to the Standards Regulations regarding new buildings and extensions and alterations to other buildings. While Crown buildings do not have to follow the warrant application procedure other 'rules' apply and relaxation applications have to be submitted to the Secretary of State.

Enforcement officers
2.20 Section 21 of the 1959 Act which laid down a requirement for the appointment of masters of works was repealed and the enforcement of building control left in the hands of local authorities. There are at present, therefore, no specific qualifications laid down for building control officers.

Schedules
2.21 These relate to matters in regard of which regulations may be made, recovery of expenses, evacuation of dangerous buildings, minor and consequential amendments of enactments.

Commencement orders
2.22 It should be noted that the extra powers contained in the Health and Safety at Work Act have to be activated by Commencement Order and the first of these was issued as Commencement No. 2 Order 1975 and came into force on 27 March 1975.

Other provisions
2.23 Part IV is concerned with supplementary provisions and

deals with appeals, references to other enactments such as Ancient Monuments acts, building preservation orders and so on, inspection and tests, penalties, fees, transitional provisions and general interpretation.

Building (Scotland) Act 1970

2.24 The main purpose of the Building (Scotland) Act 1970 was to amend the 1959 Act as regards making Building Standards Regulations, depositing building materials on roads and application for warrants. These points have already been mentioned.

2.25 The following additional powers were granted under the Act:

Section 2 gives the Secretary of State powers to delegate to local authorities the power of relaxation, and allows him to relax regulations for certain types of building. This power, which might be described as an 'omnibus relaxation', permits him to direct that a building which may not meet the exact requirements of the regulations can nevertheless be accepted by local authorities when warrant applications are made. Class relaxations have been issued, eg the non-combustibility requirement for party walls has been relaxed in one- and two-storey housing on certain conditions, as well as certain components in the chimney and drainage fields. These are situations where individual relaxations would be required in each case.

Section 4 permits the Secretary of State to call in any application for warrant received by a local authority and enables him to determine whether the building concerned will conform to the Building Standards Regulations, to give relaxations and to impose, after consulting the Building Standards Advisory Committee, requirements additional to or more onerous than those in the Building Standards Regulations. This power is most useful in very large and complex developments where for instance the traditional means of protection from fire to have be supplemented by automatic detection systems and sophisticated ventilation schemes.

Building (Procedure) (Scotland) Regulations 1975

2.26 The Procedure Regulations were laid before Parliament on 15 April 1975 and came into force on 15 May 1975; they replaced the previous Procedure Regulations which had been in force since 1971. The Regulations prescribe in detail the procedures to be followed by local authorities and changes from the previous regulations were necessitated by the change in local government brought about by the 1973 Local Government Act.

Interpretation

2.27 Part I of the Regulations deals with interpretation, definitions, powers of authorities to charge fees, to issue warrant for the construction of a building in specified stages and time within which a local authority shall grant or refuse a certificate of completion. Attention is drawn specifically to the definition of 'local authority' which can include a committee, sub-committee, officer of the local authority or other local authority to which powers may be delegated. Note also the definition of 'affected proprietor' which is vital when notification has to be given in respect of a warrant application.

Applications for warrant

2.28 Part II of the Regulations deals with applications for warrant. The following is a précis of the main requirements. The application should be lodged with the local authority, in writing in the prescribed form and accompanied by the principal plan and a duly certified copy. The buildings

authority can require up to two additional copies. Every block or location plan must show a north point.

2.29 Warrants are valid for three years or such extended period as may be granted by the buildings authority. Before lodging his application, the applicant must serve a copy on every other affected proprietor (as defined in regulation 5). Provision is made for this requirement to be dispensed with, if the applicant gets an affected proprietor to sign the form of application dispensing with formal service. Objections to the grant of warrant must be made within 14 days of the application for warrant. Objections must be in writing to the local authority and may be made by any affected proprietor or any other person claiming an interest in the application. If objections are lodged the local authority must give at least 7 days' notice (to the objector and applicant) of the local authority meeting where the application will be heard. The objector is given the opportunity of stating his case as well as the applicant. If applications are unopposed or objections are resolved, the buildings authority can grant warrant at any meeting after the expiry of the 14 days' objection period.

Calling in warrants

2.30 Part III deals with the procedure to be followed where the Secretary of State 'calls in' an application for warrant to deal with it wholly or partly himself. The Secretary of State must if, for instance, he intends to impose requirements additional to, or more onerous than, those in the Building Regulations at present, consult the applicant, the local authority, the Building Standards Advisory Committee and other persons he considers to have an interest.

Appeals

2.31 Part IV gives the procedures for dealing with relaxations by local authorities and provides for appeals against decisions to be made to the authority by interested parties.

Part V gives the procedure for appealing to the Secretary of State against the refusal of a local authority to grant relaxation or against any condition of relaxation.

Part VI takes the place of schedule 5 of the 1959 Act and prescribes the procedures for applying to the Secretary of State for relaxation. A requirement is that a copy of the application for relaxation should be lodged with the local authority at the same time as application is made to the Secretary of State. The Secretary of State may, if he thinks fit, give an objector the opportunity to state his case to a person appointed by the Secretary of State.

Part VII deals with the new powers of the Secretary of State of granting a class relaxation (para 2.25).

Temporary occupation of roads

2.32 Part VIII lays down procedure for methods of dealing with notices under section 8 of the principal Act which allows temporary occupation of portions of the road adjoining building operations, and the highways authority must now be consulted before such operations are started.

Buildings constructed without warrant

2.33 Part IX lays down procedures for orders relating to buildings constructed without warrants or in contravention of conditions of warrant. Orders relating to dangerous buildings are also covered in this part.

General

2.34 Part X is a general section and deals with meetings of local authorities (which must be in public), appointing of assessors (if considered necessary), maintenance of records and inspection by the public of records. Decisions of building authorities must follow well-defined rules.

2.35 Persons carrying out operations under the warrant must give notice to the clerk of the buildings authority of the following:
1 The date the work is commenced.
2 When a drain has been laid and is ready for inspection or test.
3 When a drain has been infilled and is ready for a second inspection or test as required by the Building Standards Regulations.
4 The date operations are completed.
Items 1 and 4 should be notified in writing.

Drawings required: fees
2.36 Schedule 1 goes into detail of particulars of plans required when applications for warrant are made for erection, alteration, extension, change of use and demolition of a building.
Schedule 2 lays out the fees which may be charged. These are on a sliding scale based on the estimated cost of the works.

Building Operations (Scotland) Regulations 1975
2.37 The Secretary of State had powers conferred on him by section 5 of the Building (Scotland) Act 1959 to make regulations for the conduct of operations for the construction, repair, maintenance or demolition of buildings, as he thinks expedient for securing the safety of the public while building operations are in progress.

2.38 The Building Operations (Scotland) Regulations 1975 which came into operation on 16 May 1975 revoke the previous regulations made in 1963. They lay down requirements for the safety of passers-by and deal with such matters as the erection of hoardings, barricades and fences, footpaths with safe platforms, handrails, steps or ramps, overhead coverings and so on. In addition, protective works are to be properly lit to the satisfaction of the master of works.

2.39 There are also provisions for clearing footpaths and the securing of partly constructed or demolished buildings. A special Regulation deals with additional requirements for demolition operations.
These Regulations are administered by the local authority.

Building (Forms) (Scotland) Regulations 1975
2.40 Section 24 of the Building (Scotland) Act 1959 gave the Secretary of State power to make Regulations prescribing the type of form to be used in the various procedures under the Act. The Building (Forms) (Scotland) Regulations 1975 prescribed the forms in which applications, warrants, notices, orders and other documents should be made under the Act. As a result of the 1970 Act and the Local Government Act 1973 the Forms Regulations have been revised to incorporate requirements due to new procedures and powers, and the chance was taken to simplify and improve the existing ones.

Building Standards (Relaxation by Local Authorities) (Scotland) Regulations 1975
2.41 These Regulations are made under section 4 (2) of the Building (Scotland) Act 1959 as read with the Building (Scotland) Act 1970. The main provisions of these Regulations are to delegate certain powers of relaxation to local authorities for existing buildings, which are defined as those built before the present Regulations came into force on 14 June 1964, and to revoke previous delegation Regulations.

2.42 The following parts of the Building Standards Regulations are relaxable by a buildings authority in relation to alterations, extensions and change of use of a particular existing building namely: Parts D, E, F, G, H, J, K, L, M, P, Q, R, S. This leaves Parts A, B, C and N outwith the buildings authorities' delegation powers, and these parts which relate to interpretation, materials and durability, structural strength and stability and electrical installations can only be relaxed by the Secretary of State, in the few and rare circumstances when relaxation can be justified.
The powers of delegation are limited in the Regulations to applications regarding alterations and extensions.

2.43 Delegation powers are disapplied:
(a) in the case of a building in Occupancy Sub-Group A1 or A2 (houses or flats), where the extension or alteration results in an increase of more than 50 cubic metres or 10 per cent of the cubic capacity of the building, whichever is the *greater;*
(b) in all other buildings, where there is an increase of more than 2 800 cubic metres or 20 per cent of the cubic capacity of the building, whichever is the *less.*

In calculating (a) and (b) above, the mode of measurement in schedule 1 of the Building Standards Regulations applies. The Regulations contain one significant change from their predecessor, namely that building authorities may relax in respect of certain buildings built after 1964 in certain circumstances. These are those buildings ancillary to existing A1 and A2 occupancy sub-groups. The object is to bring within the delegation all applications for relaxations affecting structures within the curtilage of *pre*-1964 dwelling-houses. Ancillary buildings in this context include garages, sheds, greenhouses and other outhouses.

2.44 The Regulations do not apply to applications from local authorities nor to a case where the application for warrant has been referred to the Secretary of State under the powers contained in the Building Acts.
The procedure to be followed both in applying for relaxation and in appealing against a decision of a local authority should this be sought is detailed under the Building (Procedure) (Scotland) Regulations 1975 and the Building (Forms) (Scotland) Regulations 1975.
The Regulations under this heading came into force on 16 May 1975. It should be noted that the 1971 Regulations were followed by the publication of a list of selected decisions dealing with the building types covered by the delegated powers.

3 Building Standards (Scotland) Regulations 1971 to 1975

3.01 The Building Standards (Scotland) Regulations were laid before Parliament on 11 December 1963 and came into force on 15 June 1964. They had been issued for public comment in 1961 and the final document took into respect the many hundreds of representations made to the department. Subsequent amendments were made in 1964, 1967, 1970 and 1971 and the Regulations themselves were consolidated in 1970 and 1971. The latter consolidation introduced the Regulations in a fully metricated form and came into force on 9 February 1972. Subsequent amendments to the consolidated amendments were issued in 1973 and 1975.

3.02 The Regulations are laid out in the form of 17 parts and 11 schedules. Originally they were numbered consecutively throughout, but after consolidation in 1970 a system of lettered parts and numbered Regulations in each part, similar to that of England and Wales, was introduced. Where an asterisk appears beside a Regulation number this denotes a deemed to satisfy provision. The deemed to satisfy specifications are included in schedule 10 and are not part of the main body of the Regulations.

3.03 The interpretation of the meaning of individual regulations is the province of the enforcing authority and if dispute is with the enforcing body, then final interpretation is for the Sheriff Court to decide.

Part A: General interpretation

3.04 The first four Regulations deal with definitions. Note the definition of 'building', 'element of structure' and 'storey' in Regulation A3; the definition of storey is different from that in England and Wales. Regulation A4 deals with 'land in different occupation' and is important particularly with regard to fire precautions and daylighting requirements. Regulation A6 deals with buildings by classification of occupancy as detailed in schedule 2. It is important to establish the correct classification at the beginning, as a mistake here could affect the whole application of the Regulations to a building. Regulation A7 deals with the occupant capacity of a building ie the number of persons a room or storey is capable of holding for the purposes of the Regulations. The occupant capacity controls ventilation, means of escape and sanitary accommodation requirements. Care should be taken to establish the correct occupant factor at the earliest stage of the planning of a building.

3.05 Regulation A9 refers to the application of the Regulations and to exempted classes schedule 3. Regulation A12 is important in its references to deemed to satisfy specifications. These are accepted as meeting the requirements of the specific Regulations involved, and most important, Regulation A12 (2) is most specific in stating that because a specification does not meet a deemed to satisfy one, nothing shall prevent the use of any other material, component, design, method of construction or operation or combination of these provided that the alternative satisfies the functional requirement of the Regulations.

Part B: Materials and durability

3.06 This part is in broad functional terms along the lines previously used in the model by-laws. However a proviso allows the use of relatively short-lived but otherwise suitable materials in circumstances where protection can be given or periodic maintenance readily and easily carried out. The proviso does not seem to appear in the English and Welsh Regulations.

Part C: Structural strength and stability

3.07 This part differs from that in the model by-laws, in that the performance standard is based on stress and deflection instead of deflection and deformation. The whole of the part was revised in the amendments which came into force on 1 January 1972 and was reprinted *in toto*. Regulation C2 deals with foundation and structure above foundation, and is entirely functional in nature. It requires, however, that calculations of dead and imposed loads shall be in accordance with the recommendations of BS Code of Practice CP3: Chapter V Part 2 1967 as amended and wind loads in accordance with BS Code of Practice CP3; Chapter V Part 2 1972 as amended. There are two important exceptions to this rule:
1 Proven types of timber floors and ceiling joists construction (detailed in the Regulation) do not require special calculation.

2 Where a buildings authority is satisfied that dead or imposed or wind loads will be different from those in the Codes, then the actual loads may be substituted.
Regulation C3 is new and is a result of the Ronan Point aftermath and applies to buildings of five storeys and over: in addition to the requirements of Regulation C2 its requirements are designed to guard against progressive collapse. They require either strengthening of critical members, or the use of 'the alternative path' method.
Regulation C4 requires loading notices to be exhibited at each doorway or stairway giving access to a floor supporting an imposed floor load of 2·5 kilonewtons per square metre or more. The notice must state the maximum load on the floor which must not be exceeded. Similarly where a roof of a building cannot support a concentrated load of 0·9 kilonewtons per 130 millimetres square there must also be a clear and visible warning drawing attention to that danger.

Part D: Structural fire precaution

3.08 The theory of fire resistance embodied in the by-laws was intended to ensure that each individual building would contain its own fire as far as possible and would be protected against fire from outside. This applied as much to buildings on a plot of land in one occupation as to buildings on separate plots. Two changes were made by the Regulations:
1 It is considered unnecessary that buildings should resist fire from outside if they are capable of containing any fire starting within them.
2 Control has been restricted to safeguarding public interest by preventing general conflagration.

3.09 This has been achieved first by laying down requirements for fire resistance of the structure and of the type of materials ie whether non-combustible or combustible materials can be used in certain situations. Roofs have been classified by their resistance to penetration and resistance to spread of flame, but note that a roof is not an element of structure under Regulation A3 and does not as such require a fire resistance. Regulation D10 as amended lays down detailed requirements for pipes and ducts passing through compartment, separating and fire division walls and floors. Second, the principle has been accepted that as long as a building is far enough away from its boundary, it will not spread fire to adjoining buildings on land in different occupation. Regulation D17 as read with the schedules 6 and 9 carries out this principle. The nearer a building is to the boundary, the less area of radiating opening is allowed until on the boundary the wall must be imperforate. It is essential when applying this part to check carefully with schedule 9, tables 6 and 7. These detail the fire resistance requirements for different components and occupancy groups. It should also be noted that Regulation D6 requires *all* separating walls to be non-combustible. This differs from England and Wales. A Class Relaxation has, however, been issued for separating walls in up to two-storey timber framed housing to have fire resistance only instead of both fire resistance and non-combustibility. On 1 January 1972 all requirements dealing with small garages, greenhouses, huts etc were completely revised. These buildings are treated as a complete unit and as such most requirements of Part D are disapplied. The requirements for detached domestic garages are laid out in tabular form and separated from the other small buildings such as huts and greenhouses which are grouped into a separate table. The new requirements are less onerous than those they replace and are much easier to follow in the revised form. In addition the range of exemptions relating to ancillary buildings is extended and the conditions under which these are granted can be found under Class 11 in Schedule 3.

3.10 This part also contains a Regulation dealing with fuel oil storage tanks. The fire resistance requirements, which are based on capacity and siting, are found in a table to the Regulation. In addition a proper catchpit is required under certain circumstances as well as a lockable drainage outlet valve or cock. The latter is also an anti-vandal and anti-pollution device. England and Wales do not have an equivalent regulation, but may well soon have.

Part E: Means of escape and assistance to fire service
3.11 This part applies to all buildings except subgroup A1 which is included in Regulation E16 (internal linings). Regulation E2 as amended goes into considerable detail defining exits, places of safety, protected zones and so on. Regulations E3 and E4 deal with provisions of exits. These Regulations should be read with schedule 9 table 10, which details the number of exits required as a minimum for certain occupancy groups. Regulation E4 also specifies the number of exits required from a room or storey based on the occupant capacity. However, Regulation E5 could affect the number decided on by Regulation E4, because it lays down a maximum travel distance. This travel distance is based on the speed a person can travel in $2\frac{1}{2}$ min at 12.5 m per min (except in a specific ground-storey situation when the speed is reckoned to be 18.00 m/min); these figures apply when two exits are available from any point in a storey. Where only one exit is available, travel distance is reduced to 2/5 of that described above. Provided half the exits from a room are by way of a protected doorway, escape may be made through a fire division wall into an adjoining room, rather than every exit leading directly to the outside at ground level. Attention is drawn particularly to the 1975 amendments which lay out a simple rule for determining if two or more exits are available from a point. This basically says that from any point escape can be made in two directions which are at an angle of 45° to each other or in the case of an odd shape or dead-end, travel may be in one direction to the limit permitted for one exit situations, but if along that one direction it becomes possible for the direction of travel to another exit to diverge at a specified angle, then the rules for two exits apply. The angle is calculated by a simple formula of $45° + 2\frac{1}{2}°$ for every metre travelled.
Regulation E6 lays down requirements for exits. It states that every exit shall lead to a place of safety, thereby restating a basic principle of means of escape. Requirements for exits across flat roofs including conditions regarding fire resistance of the roof, distance from skylights and protection of the route. Minimum heights of exit routes are also stated as 2 metres.

3.12 Widths of exits and exit stairways are covered in Regulations E7 and E8, exit width being based on the number of persons for which the exit is provided. A unit width of 530 mm is used in calculations. Regulation E9 gives detailed requirements for the enclosure of stairways forming part of an exit.

3.13 Part E* also contains requirements on the provision of access lobbies for buildings over 24 m in height, control of smoke spread, resistance to spread of flames across internal doors in exits, lighting of exits and minimum height of exits. Access for firefighters and provision of escape windows and hard surfaces capable of taking the weight of fire appliances are detailed in Regulations E16, E17 and E19, while Regulation E18 requires the provision of fire mains in certain buildings

and the provision of hydrants in or within a specified distance of other buildings.

Part F: Chimneys, flues, hearths and installation of heat-producing appliances
3.14 This part is divided into two main sections:
1 Requirements dealing with solid fuel and oil burning appliances up to 45 kW output rating.
2 Requirements dealing with gas appliances having an input rating not exceeding 45 kW.
In addition there is a general functional requirement for all appliances over the ratings above (Regulation F31), and requirements regarding access to roofs and special conditions for appliances for heating and cooking.

3.15 The object of this part is to prevent the risk of ignition of any part of a building or danger to persons using the building from appliances requiring chimneys and flues. The part therefore goes into detail regarding the construction of chimneys, flue pipes, lining of flues, thickness of material around fireplace openings, hearths and also requires fireguard fittings to be installed where there are open fires in buildings of group A. Requirements for factory insulated chimneys were formerly covered by class relaxations have been included in the Regulations by the 1973 amendments.

3.16 Gas requirements differ from those of the solid fuel and oil section because of the much lower temperatures involved (up to 1000°C for the solid fuel and up to 120°C for gas).

Part G: Resistance of sites and resistance to passage of moisture
3.17 Generally, the part is written in functional terms to allow the most flexible possible requirements to safeguard the users of a building and its fabric. It contains requirements regarding the protection of a site and the ground in its vicinity, which must be drained or treated to prevent harmful effects of ground and flood water in the building. Certain requirements of this part do not apply to temporary buildings of any occupancy group other than A1 and A2.

3.18 Safeguarding existing drains and removal of harmful matter from a site as well as removal of surface soil and vegetable matter are dealt with in this part. It is required that the solum* be treated to prevent any harmful effects in the building or to the health of its occupants, and suitable damp proof coursing is necessary. Every building must be constructed in such a way as to resist moisture from rain or snow.

Part H: Resistance to transmission of sound
3.19 This part refers to houses only and lays down functional requirements and the method of testing. Table 12 lays down the levels of sound insulation in houses for airborne sound and impact sound. It gives the frequency in Hertz, relating these to the minimum sound reduction for the various components of separating walls and floors in both flats and houses. A deemed to satisfy clause relating to heavily deafened timber floors has been included as it might be onerous to have no alternative to concrete.

Part J: Resistance to transmission of heat
3.20 This part covers all residential buildings ie hotels, hostels and so on, with the exception of hospitals, ancillary buildings and temporary buildings in A3 and A4. This regulation underwent a major revision in the 1975 amendments

---

* At the time of writing, the whole of part E has been the subject of a comprehensive technical reappraisal and has completed the major part of the consultative process

* The area within the containing walls of a building after removal of surface soil and vegetable matter

and the requirements and method of calculation to be employed were considerably altered. Guidance is given in a memorandum issued with the SI and it is recommended as a valuable aid. Roofs are required to have a thermal transmittance coefficient of not more than 0.60 W/m² deg C, external walls 1.00 and certain internal walls 1.7. The Regulation is backed up by a considerable number of specifications in schedule 10, including tables relating to the effect of double glazing.

Values for floors apply only where the floor is open to the external air eg where a floor spans over a pend.*

Part K: Ventilation

3.21 This part is quite comprehensive in its requirements, but does not apply to buildings subject to the Factories Act 1961 or to schools as defined in the School Premises (Scotland) Regulations 1967 or theatres or cinemas. The amendments of January 1972 recognised that the former requirement of permanent ventilations as an alternative to mechanical ventilation in houses, hotels, offices etc was unsatisfactory in use. There was a tendency to block these up because of draughts due to bad siting, excess size or exposure to wind. The amendments substituted the term 'controllable ventilators' which allow fine adjustment to suit the individual comforts of the inhabitants. The part is divided into several sections which deal with:
1 Specific types of buildings eg houses, garages, other buildings.
2 General requirements on ventilation.

3.22 The provisions of Part K recognise that ventilation in houses can be achieved in two ways, natural ventilation ie windows, roof lights and so on which may be supplemented by controllable ventilators or mechanical ventilation. Estimating natural ventilation is still based on empirical formulae, but calculating mechanical ventilation is more precise, and air changes required for different rooms or users are detailed in schedule 9 table 13.

3.23 Small garages must have a certain amount of permanent ventilation, the amount increasing with size of the floor area. Basement garages have to be mechanically ventilated with duplicate systems and detailed warning devices which function even if the mains power supply fails.

3.24 Ventilation of buildings other than houses and garages is based on a sliding scale of either natural or mechanical ventilation. This scale is based on the number of occupants a room is calculated to hold (Regulation A7 occupant capacity) and the amount of cubic space per person.

3.25 There are also requirements for sleeping rooms other than in houses eg in hotels, hostels to provide either mechanical or natural ventilation and lift walls and machine rooms as well as rooms with flueless gas heaters are also covered. General requirements on positioning of ventilators and their relationship to courts and passages are covered in some detail.

Part L: Daylighting and space about houses

3.26 This part states that every room shall have a standard of daylight as laid down in table 14. Calculation of daylight factors is discussed in detail in Regulation L5 and the effect of balconies and projections on the calculations given in Regulation L7. This regulation gives a dispensation to permit

* The part of a building which spans a wynd or open passage

sunporches, as defined, to be erected over existing daylighting windows.

3.27 Regulation L8 deals with the relationship of a building to its boundary for daylighting purposes. Schedule 7 goes into details for meeting the requirements of Regulations L4 and L8, by using permissible height indicators, or, where buildings containing houses are under 12·5 m high, an alternative method. The schedule also gives a diagram of a permissible height indicator.

3.28 Table 16 gives minimum widths of window openings (rooms with one window situated in the middle of the external wall) which will meet the requirements of the main Regulation. It must be stressed, however, that the table is not the only way of meeting the requirements, and careful calculation by other methods might result in smaller width of windows being acceptable. Circumstances vary from building to building between country and town and several methods should be tried if table 16 is too onerous.

3.29 This part also contains two other interesting Regulations. Regulation 9 relates to an application for warrant for more than one building, when a layout which contains a number of houses is designed as a single unit. As the exact position and height is known, the exact spacing and window sizes can be calculated beforehand and for the purposes of this part, the boundary between them is disregarded, each house being regarded as an existing obstruction.

Privacy

3.30 Regulation 10 deals with the distance between windows and has been termed loosely 'the privacy Regulation'. Where windows are not directly opposite, the distance between them can decrease in accordance with table 15, which is based on angle and distance. The erection of a suitable screen between windows would make the requirement non-applicable.

Part M: Drainage and sanitary appliances

3.31 The whole of this part is based mainly on functional requirements backed up by deemed to satisfy requirements and British Standard Codes and specifications. Every building must have a drainage system for foul water either connected to a public sewer or a sewage treatment works (usually a septic tank in rural areas). No cesspools are allowed. Drainage requirements are very flexible so as to permit use of new materials which may prove satisfactory eg rigid pipes with flexible joints and flexible pipes themselves as well as the traditional fireclay and concrete pipes. This approach is extended to soil pipes, water pipes, ventilating pipes, rainwater pipes, gutters and channels. Ducts in houses of two storeys or more must be situated inside the building with suitable access panels. Provision is also made for suitable and sufficient sanitary accommodation in subgroups A3 and A4 and groups B and C. Houses are dealt with in part Q (para 3.34). Attention is drawn to the requirements of the Sewerage (Scotland) Act 1968, whose requirements may overlap those of Building Regulations. Examples of excessive demands of materials and design have been reported under that Act and designers should note circulars sent out to local authorities in 1975 and Building Note 2/76 issued by the Scottish Development Department.

Part N: Electrical installations

3.32 This part gives detailed definitions regarding electrical apparatus, appliances and services with requirements for conductors, apparatus, fuses, circuit breakers, switches, isolation of systems, precautions against metal becoming live, connections, voltages over 200 v and so on. All these have the regulations of the Institute of Electrical Engineers as deemed to satisfy specifications. In addition there is a Regulation dealing with electric lighting fittings or appliances in baths or showers. All buildings to which the part applies, other than houses, must display a schematic diagram, at either the main switch or other suitable place.

Part P: Prevention of danger and obstruction

3.33 This refers to projections or fixtures which might be dangerous, requiring them to be secured so as not to cause danger or obstruction. There is a Regulation dealing with pipes discharging steam, smoke, hot water and so on. The Regulations contain requirements for the safe cleaning of windows any part of which is more than 4 metres above ground level. There are differing conditions for housing and for other classifications of buildings. A new Regulation introduced in 1973 covers safety requirements in escalators and passenger conveyors, including emergency stop switches and notices to be displayed.

Part Q: Housing standards

3.34 Housing standards were covered previously in various enactments eg Housing Acts, Burgh Police, Public Health Acts. The Guest Committee recommended that the requirements should all be brought together under the Building Regulations. It should be stressed that all the new requirements are minimum requirements. In this part are detailed regulations dealing with access to houses, and within a house a requirement that a house should have a stairway. Lift requirements and details of the scale of lifts are given.

3.35 The internal components of a house are dealt with, details being given of bathroom and wc requirements, areas of rooms, heights of ceilings, details of kitchens, larders, storage, fuel stores, laundry facilities, heating, water supply to baths, sinks and so on, artificial lighting, scale of power points and refuse disposal arrangements.

In order to keep abreast of developments in housing since the Regulations were introduced, an alternative set of space standards are now permitted. The Regulation is couched in functional terms, but the real effect is to permit houses built to the standards laid down in the Scottish Development Department's Housing Handbook No. 1 *Metric space standards* to be deemed to satisfy the Building Regulations. It should be stressed that the two sets of standards are alternatives and one must use either one or another and not select a mixture of the two standards.

Part R: Ashpits and dungsteads

3.36 This part allows for the siting and construction of ashpits provided for occupancy groups A1, A2 and A3 and for all dungsteads.

Part S: Construction of stairways, landings and balconies

3.37 This new part to the Regulations came into force on 1 January 1972 and brought together all the requirements for stairways, landings and balconies previously located in various other parts of the Regulations. The new part takes account of metric changes and dimensional co-ordination and by the use of tables wherever possible simplifies the interpretation of the specific requirements.

3.38 Regulation s2 defines the four different types of stairway to be found in the Regulations and lays down a mode of measurement of the minimum required widths. These are different for different types of stairs and are based on the use of the stairs; eg an exit stair should be as unobstructed as possible and its width is a calculated one depending on the number of persons likely to use it for escape purposes, whereas a stair in a house will have very intermittent use and is unlikely to be heavily loaded with persons. *Note* that where a stair falls into more than one category, the most onerous requirements apply.

Regulation s2 also gives definitions used throughout the part and attention is drawn to those of 'balustrade' and 'handrail' particularly. Those two components are often taken in error to be synonymous. The definition of balustrade is couched in such terms as to allow the Master of Works flexibility in interpretation depending on the case in question. For example a balustrade of horizontal railings, which are an open invitation to children to climb them, would not be permitted say in a school!

Regulation s3 gives general requirements for all stairs. A point to note is that it now only requires one value, that of vertical headroom instead of the traditional method of measurements vertically from and at right angles to the pitch line. Requirements are also stated for open riser stairways, provision of handrails and balustrades, protection of external stair wells where a stair descends below ground level, and protection of glazed areas in stairways.

Regulation s4 is in tabular form and allows ready reference and comparisons to be made between the four different types of stair.

Regulation s5 deals with landings. Particular note should be made of the minimum balustrade heights required where a landing is open to the external air and is part of a house or building primarily used by children.

Regulation s6 deals with balconies and is similar in its requirements to those for landings, but does include balconies which are not necessarily part of a stairway.

Schedules

3.39 Throughout these comments reference has been made to various schedules and tables. These are wide in scope and content. Attention is drawn to schedule 1 which lays down the mode of measurement to be used throughout the Regulations. Others of particular interest are schedule 10 which contains the deemed to satisfy requirements, and schedule 11 which gives specifications for preparation of sites and resistance to moisture of many different building materials.

Conclusion

3.40 The Regulations are subject to regular scrutiny and subsequent alteration by amendment in order to take cognisance of new building processes and materials and to bring references to British Standards Codes of Practice and Specifications up to date. The form and presentation of the Regulations are also under review, in order to improve their interpretation by both designer and enforcement officer alike. It must, however, be remembered that the Regulations are a legal document and revision is subject to that discipline.

It may be useful to mention here the main areas of difference between the Scottish and English and Welsh Regulations. Scottish Regulations include the following parts not included in those other Regulations:

1 Means of escape from fire. The requirements in the English Regulations are at present couched in functional terms and limited in application to certain categories of buildings using Codes of Practice as deemed to satisfy conditions.

2 Assistance to fire fighters.

3 Daylighting and space about buildings.

4 Electrical installations.
5 Housing standards.
6 Obstruction and prevention of danger.

3.41 In addition the Scottish Regulations are more detailed in their requirements for ventilation, fire precautions for small buildings such as garages, huts etc and give a wide range of total exemptions (in schedule 3) from the Regulations. There are considerable differences in the contents of schedules.

3.42 The Scottish Development Department issues a detailed set of explanatory memoranda with the Regulations. These are related to the specific parts of the Regulations, and contain sketches and diagrams to help in interpretation. It must, however, be understood, when using the memoranda, that they are an aid to interpretation and carry no statutory value whatsoever. Another point to bear in mind is that a check should always be made to ensure that a Regulation has not been amended, the date of publication of the memoranda, and the date of reference. Revised metricated editions of Explanatory Memoranda have been published since 1972 and deal with individual parts or groups of parts of the Regulations. In addition a supplementary publication covering the 1973 and 1975 amendments to procedure, relaxation, forms etc Regulations has also been published.

3.43 The Regulations in metric form came into force on 7 February 1972 and use the SI system of measurement.

4 Other national legislation affecting building

4.01 The following list of legislation (although not completely exhaustive) applies in Scotland, and the comments under each heading may give guidance regarding the Scottish scene.

Offices, Shops and Railway Premises Act 1963
4.02 Precise standards for ventilation, means of escape from fire and occupant load factors are laid down in the Building Standards Regulations. The requirements in the Offices, Shops and Railway Premises Act 1963 are in general framed so that standards of the Building Regulations are *usually* taken by the enforcing authority to meet the requirements of the Act. However, the Building Standards Regulations accept the Sanitary Convenience Regulations 1964 made under the Act (Regulation D24 (2) proviso (1)—provision of sanitary accommodation).
Section 29 of the Offices, Shops and Railway Premises Act previously covered fire and certification, but has been repealed and responsibility passed to the Fire Precautions Act from 1 January 1977. Check also the amendments contained in the Health and Safety at Work etc Act 1974.

Clean Air Acts 1956 to 1968
4.03 Section 6 of the 1968 Act provides a new control for the heights of chimneys serving furnaces. The situation, therefore, is that special application must be made to the local authority for chimney height approval for furnace chimneys. The height of non-furnace chimneys is dealt with under the Building Regulations without need for special application. Constructional details of all chimneys are of course subject to local authority approval. See further LEGAL STUDY 9 para 6.04 and LEGAL STUDY 13 para 5.10.

Thermal Insulation Act 1957
Thermal Insulation (Industrial Buildings) Regulations 1972
4.04 The purpose of this Act is to secure greater economy in the use of fuel by preventing unnecessary loss of heat through lack of adequate insulation in industrial buildings. It also recognises, however, that certain insulating materials might be a fire risk if not properly used and restrictions are placed on the use of certain of these materials.
The Thermal Insulation Regulations lay down the standards of both insulation and surface spread of flame.
The Thermal Insulation Act 1957 was amended to take account of the procedures of the Building (Scotland) Acts 1959 and 1970. The local authority examines plans for industrial buildings to see that compliance with the Thermal Insulation Act is met as well as the Building Regulations. The local authority can refuse warrant if plans do not meet the requirements of the Thermal Insulation Act.
The appeals procedure in the Act does not apply in Scotland, but there is of course appeal to the Sheriff against refusal to grant warrant. The application for exemption of individual buildings should be made directly to the Secretary of State for Trade and Industry and *not* the *local* authority. The latter, however, do have the power to require the removal or alteration of a building not conforming to the prescribed standard.

Factories Act 1961
4.05 Provisions of part K (ventilation) do not apply to premises subject to the Factories Act 1961 and it is advised that particular ventilation requirements should be discussed with the factory inspectorate at an early stage. However, means of escape for fire requirements are subject to part E of the Building Standards Regulations. Fire certification previously under this Act is now the responsibility of the Fire Precautions Act as from 1 January 1977—see the Fire Precautions (Factories, Offices, Shops and Railway Premises) Order 1976. In Scotland, fire authorities are area authorities, eight in number, with their boundaries roughly equivalent to the local authority regional boundaries, but with one brigade covering the Lothian and Borders area. See further LEGAL STUDY 9 para 6.02 *et seq* and LEGAL STUDY 13 para 5.21. Check carefully the implications of amendment contained in Health and Safety at Work etc Act 1974.

Fire Precautions Act 1971
4.06 Under this Act, certain premises must obtain a fire certificate from the fire authority as to the suitability of their means of escape. The premises are designated by order and on 31 January 1972 the Secretary of State designated hotels and boarding houses above a certain size as the first class of premises requiring certificates. The order came into force on 1 June 1972. As the Building Standards Regulations contain requirements for the provision of means of escape, certain sections of the Fire Precautions Act are disapplied to Scotland and certain others apply only to Scotland. Section 14 contains a statutory bar in that where the means of escape meet the Building Regulation requirements, then they must be accepted for fire certificate purposes. This does not mean that all *existing* premises necessarily have to meet Building Regulations standards for new buildings and many will have reasonable means of escape at present (although not quite up to new building standards). The fire officer has scope to use his judgement in existing premises as far as the statutory bar allows. Attention is also drawn to the definition of 'owner' which differs from that in England. See LEGAL STUDY 13 paras 5.03 *et seq*.

Fire Certificates (Special Premises) Regulations 1976

4.07 These provide that a certificate issued by the Health and Safety Executive shall be required for premises of a kind specified in schedule 1 of these regulations and lay down the conditions which may be imposed. The statutory bar for building regulations does not apply to these buildings, but they are of such a specialised nature that close consultation would take place with the relevant authorities at an early stage of design. The regulations came into force on the 1 January 1977.

Sewerage (Scotland) Act 1968

4.08 This Act, which came into force on 1 May 1973, has a bearing on the requirements of the drainage section Part M of the Building Standards Regulations. The main effect is to limit the range of the Building Standards Regulations, as many parts of what are now termed common drainage will in future become 'public sewer' and will be vested in a local authority. The term 'drain' is defined as that within the curtilage of a building and for its sole use. Attention is drawn to the definitions in section 59.

The Act under section 12 and subject to the conditions of that section gives an owner a right to connect to a local authority sewer or sewage treatment works. The owner of any premises who proposes to connect his drains or sewers to a public sewer or works of a local authority, or who is altering his drain or sewer in such a way as to interfere with those of a local authority, must, however, give 28 days' notice to the *local* authority, who may or may not give permission for the work to proceed. The authority can give conditional approval and the owner has right of appeal against any decision.

Powers are given in the Act to require defects in drains or sewage treatment works to be remedied. Local authorities have the powers to take over private sewage treatment works, including septic tanks. Other powers include rights to discharge trade effluents into public sewers, emptying of septic tanks, provision of temporary sanitary conveniences etc.

Health and Safety at Work etc Act 1974

4.09 The most important effect of this Act is contained in section 75 as read with schedule 10. These clauses introduce amendments to the principal Building Acts and extend and alter the powers contained in them. It should be noted that part III of the Act on section 75 is applicable to Scotland.

The Act also includes important changes in transferring fire certification carried out under other legislation eg Offices, Shops and Railway Premises Act and Factories Act to the Fire Precautions Act. See LEGAL STUDY 13 para 1.03.

Local acts

4.10 A few local Acts exist, for instance in Edinburgh and Glasgow. While the Building Standards (Scotland) Regulations must be complied with, there may be fringe areas outside that control where slight differences may arise.

NB Advice should be sought from the authority concerned. Local legislation is repealed from 1979 by the Local Government Act 1973.

5 General

5.01 The following points may be useful to persons wishing to design and build in Scotland for the first time:
1 Scots law differs from that of the rest of the UK (see Scottish articles in this handbook).
2 Building control is exercised by local authorities.
3 Warrant must be obtained from the local authority before any building (including alterations and extensions) can begin and it is separate from planning permission. A small fee related to the total cost of the job is usually payable in accord-

Table I Classification of buildings by occupancy (schedule 2 of Regulations)

CLASSIFICATION OF BUILDINGS BY OCCUPANCY			
Occupancy group (1)	Occupancy sub-group (2)	Description of occupancy use (3)	Standard Industrial Classification (4)
A (Residential)	1	Houses of not more than 2 storeys—other than flats—including any surgeries, consulting rooms, offices and other accommodation not exceeding an aggregate of 46 square metres, forming part of the house of any person providing professional or scientific services and used in his professional or scientific capacity	871†, 872†, 873†, 874†, 875†, 876†, 879†
	2	Houses of more than 2 storeys and flats—including any surgeries, consulting rooms, offices and other accommodation not exceeding an aggregate of 46 square metres, forming part of the house of any person providing professional or scientific services and used in his professional or scientific capacity	871†, 872†, 873†, 874†, 875†, 876†, 879†
	3	Residential clubs	887†
		Residential colleges and schools	872†
		Residential ecclesiastical buildings	875†
		Hotels	884, 899(3)†
		Motels	
		Hostels	
		Lodging houses	
		Boarding houses	
		Bothies and chaumers	—
		Chalets	—
		Fire stations with sleeping or residential accommodation attached	906(2)†
		Police stations with sleeping or residential accommodation attached	906(1)†
	4	Children's homes	899(3)†
		Old people's homes	
		Special schools for handicapped children	
		Hospitals	874†
		Private nursing homes	
		Sanatoria	
B (Commercial)	1	Office premises (including Post Office sorting offices and telephone exchanges)	708†, 709†, 860–866, 871†, 873†, 874†, 875†, 876†, 879†, 881†, 899†, 906(3)†

†*Note:* Throughout this Schedule the presence of a dagger against a numbered head in column (4) denotes that the numbered head is common to more than one occupancy group or sub-group.

B (Commercial)—cont.	2	Shop premises (including sub-post offices attached thereto but excluding shop premises to which other occupancy sub-groups apply)	810–812†, 820, 821, 831†, 895†
		Licensed betting offices	883†
		Beauty parlours	889
		Hairdressers	
		Television, radio, recording and film studios	881†
		Laboratories	874†, 876†, 879†
		Launderettes (self-service)	892†
		Dry cleaning (self-service)	893†
C (Assembly)	1	Bus passenger roadside shelters	702(1)†
		Passenger stations	701, 702(1)†
		Public conveniences	906(3)†
		Grandstands	
		Stadia	
		Sports pavilions	
		Gymnasia	
		Indoor bowling alleys	
		Indoor games courts	
		Riding schools	882†
		Skating rinks	
		Swimming baths (including any swimming pool, changing rooms, slipper baths, turkish baths or similar facilities pertaining thereto)	
		Funfairs	
		Menageries and zoos	
		Amusement arcades	883†
	2	Non-residential clubs	887†
		Non-residential colleges and schools	872†
		Clinics, surgeries, consulting rooms and related accommodation (other than those covered in occupancy sub-groups A1 and A2)	874†, 876†, 879†
		Ecclesiastical buildings, meeting houses	875†
		Court rooms	906(3)†
		Museums, art galleries	899(4)†
		Libraries to which persons other than employees have access	899(4)†, 906(3)†
		Public houses	886
		Fire stations (other than those covered in occupancy sub-group A3)	906(2)†
		Police stations (other than those covered in occupancy sub-group A3)	906(1)†
	3	Theatres, cinemas, radio and television studios to which the public are admitted	881†
		Casinos and bingo halls	883†
		Concert halls	881†
		Restaurants, cafes, canteens	885, 887†, 888
		Exhibition halls	899(4)†
		Dance halls, dancing schools	882†

Table I continued

Occupancy group (1)	Occupancy sub-group (2)	Description of occupancy use (3)	Standard Industrial Classification (4)
D (Industrial)	1	Mining and quarrying other than coal and shale mining	102, 103, 109
		Manufacture, process or repair of any of the following—	
		tobacco;	240
		steel tubes;	312
		aluminium and aluminium alloys;...	321
		mechanical handling equipment; ...	337
		mechanical equipment or parts not elsewhere specified; ...	349
		photographic and document copying equipment;...	351
		watches and clocks;	352
		surgical instruments and appliances;	353
		scientific and industrial instruments and systems;	354
		electrical machinery;...	361
		insulated wires and cables; ...	362
		telegraph and telephone apparatus and equipment;	363, 708†
		radio and electronic components; ...	364
		broadcast receiving and sound re-producing equipment; ...	365
		electronic computers;	366
		radio, radar and electronic capital goods;	367
		electric appliances primarily for domestic use;	368
		other electrical goods;	369
		aerospace equipment;	383
		locomotives and railway track equipment;	384
		railway carriages, wagons and trams;	385
		cutlery;	392
		bolts, nuts, screws, rivets etc;	393
		wire and wire products; ...	394
		cans and metal boxes; ...	395
		metal goods not elsewhere specified;	399
		hosiery and other knitted goods; ...	417
		glass;	463
		cement;...	464
		abrasives and building materials not elsewhere specified; ...	469
		plaster cast, image and models ...	499(2)
D (Industrial)— cont.	2	Agriculture and horticulture	001
		Coal mining	101
		Exploration (including boring) for and extracting petroleum; mining oil shale	104
		Shipbuilding and marine engineering...	370†
		Paper, printing and publishing ...	481–486, 489
		Laundries and dry cleaners ...	892†, 893†
		Slaughterhouses and abattoirs ...	810(2)†
		Motor repairers, distributors, garages and filling stations	894
		Manufacture, process or repair of any of the following—	
		food and drink;	211–218, 229, 231, 232, 239
		chemicals and allied industries; ...	261–263, 271–274, 276–279
		metal;	311, 313, 322, 323
		engineering and electrical goods; ...	331–336, 338, 339, 341, 342
		vehicles;	380–382, 494(2), 708†
		tools and implements;	390, 391
		jewellery and precious metals; ...	396
		textiles;	411–415, 418, 419, 423, 429
		fur;	433
		clothing and footwear;	441–445, 449, 450, 895†
		bricks, fire clay and refractory goods;	461
		pottery;	462
		rubber;	491†
		brushes and brooms;	493†
		stationers' goods;	495
		gas, electricity and water	601–603
		Any other industry not separately classified in occupancy sub-groups D1 or D3	
D (Industrial)— cont.	3	Manufacture, process or repair of any of the following—	
		animal and poultry foods;	219
		vegetable and animal oils and fats;	221
		soap and detergents;...	275
		rope, twine and net;...	416
		narrow fabrics;	421
		made-up textiles;	422
		leather (tanning and dressing); ...	}431
		sheepskin wool (fellmongery); ...	
		leather goods;	432
		hats, caps and millinery;	446
		timber;	471
		furniture and upholstery;	472
		bedding and similar goods;... ...	473
		shop and office fittings;	474
		wooden containers and baskets; ...	475
		miscellaneous wood and cork goods;	479
		linoleum, plastic floor covering; ...	}492
		leather cloth and similar material;...	
		toys, games and sports equipment;	494(1) and (3)
		plastic products not elsewhere specified;...	370†, 491†, 493†, 496
		musical instruments	499(1)
E (Storage)	1	(a) Storage of goods and materials not specified as hazardous in occupancy sub-group E2	708†, 810†, 812†, 831†, 832†
		(b) Garages used solely for the storage or parking of motor vehicles, multi-storey car parks, transit sheds and transport services other than any used for the storage of vehicles loaded with hazardous materials or for the storage of hazardous materials in transit	702†, 703–707, 708† 709(1) and (3)

Table I continued

Occupancy group (1)	Occupancy sub-group (2)	Description of occupancy use (3)	Standard Industrial Classification (4)
E (Storage)— cont.	(1) cont.	(c) Libraries (other than those covered in occupancy sub-group C2) ...	872†, 899(4)†, 906(3)†
	2	(a) Storage of hazardous materials including—	
		(i) any compressed, liquified or dissolved gas;	
		(ii) any substance which becomes dangerous by interaction with either water or air;	
		(iii) any liquid substance with a flash point below 65° Celsius including whisky or other spirituous liquor;	709(2), 811†, 831†, 832†
		(iv) any corrosive substance;	
		(v) any substance that emits poisonous fumes when heated;	
		(vi) any oxidising agent;	
		(vii) any substance liable to spontaneous combustion;	
		(viii) any substance that changes or decomposes readily giving out heat when doing so;	
		(ix) any combustible solid substance with a flash point less than 121° Celsius;	709(2), 811†, 831†, 832†
		(x) any substance likely to spread fire by flowing from one part of a building to another	
		(b) Transit sheds and transport services used for the storage of hazardous materials or vehicles loaded with hazardous materials	

ance with the scale laid down in the table of fees (schedule 2 of the Procedure Regulations).

4 Ensure that the latest amendments to the Building Standards Regulations are available as well as a copy of the Regulations themselves, the Procedure Regulations and the correct forms (paras 2.26 and 2.41).

Table II Classes of buildings exempt from Building Regulations (schedule 3 of Regulations)

Description	Limitations
Class 1. A building erected on agricultural land having an area of more than 0·4 hectare and comprised in an agricultural unit, being a building required for the use of that land for the purposes of agriculture and of which every part falls within one or more of the following descriptions— (a) building for housing cattle (other than milking dairy cattle), horses, sheep or dogs; (b) barn, shed or other building for storage purposes in which no feeding stuffs for livestock are prepared; (c) gate, fence, wall or other means of enclosure not exceeding 2·1 metres in height.	(i) In the case of a building falling under head (a) or (b)— (A) the cubic capacity does not exceed 1130 cubic metres; (B) no part thereof is nearer to the boundary of the agricultural unit than 13 metres. (ii) In the case of a wall falling under head (c), no part of the wall which is over 1·2 metres in height adjoins any road or other place to which the public have access as of right.
Class 2. A building erected on land used for the purposes of forestry (including afforestation), being a building required for the use of the land for such purposes and of which every part falls within one or more of the following descriptions— (a) building for housing animals; (b) shed or other building for storage purposes; (c) gate, fence, wall or other means of enclosure not exceeding 2·1 metres in height.	(i) In the case of a building falling under head (a) or (b)— (A) the cubic capacity does not exceed 1130 cubic metres; (B) no part thereof is nearer to the boundary than 13 metres. (ii) In the case of a wall falling under head (c), no part of the wall which is over 1·2 metres in height adjoins any road or other place to which the public have access as of right.
Class 3. A building consisting only of plant or machinery or of a structure or erection of the nature of plant or machinery.	No part of the building is nearer to any point on the boundary than— (A) 13 metres, or (B) the height of the building, whichever is the less, unless at that point the boundary is a boundary with agricultural land on which there is no building nearer to the point than 13 metres.

Table II continued

Description	Limitations
Class 4. An electricity transformer not exceeding 1000 kVA capacity and switchgear and control pillars associated therewith.	No part of the apparatus is nearer to the boundary of the site than 1 metre.
Class 5. A building used only to house fixed plant or machinery in which there is no human occupation or no human occupation other than intermittent occupation for the purposes of maintenance.	As for Class 3.
Class 6. A building essential for the operation of a railway and comprising or erected within— (*a*) a locomotive depot; (*b*) a carriage depot; (*c*) a goods yard; (*d*) a marshalling yard; (*e*) a signal box: Provided that a building shall not be excluded from this class by reason only that a part thereof of a cubic capacity not exceeding one-tenth of the total cubic capacity of the building does not conform to this description.	There shall not be included in this Class any building of occupancy sub-group D1.
Class 7. A bus passenger roadside shelter providing no facilities other than a waiting room.	(i) The building does not exceed 9 square metres in area. (ii) The building is constructed of non-combustible materials, or if constructed of combustible materials, is sited not less than 6 metres from any other building.
Class 8. A building essential for the operation of a dock, harbour or pier and erected within the area of the dock, harbour or pier undertaking.	There shall not be included in this Class any building in respect of the construction of which the approval or consent of the local authority would have been required under a local act in force immediately before the coming into operation of these regulations.
Class 9. A work of civil engineering construction including dock, wharf, harbour, pier, quay, sea defence work, lighthouse, embankment, river work, dam, bridge, tunnel, filter station (including filter bed), inland navigation, water works, viaduct, aqueduct, reservoir, pipe line, sewerage work, sewage treatment works, gas holder, gas main, electric supply line and supports.	

Description	Limitations
Class 10. A building in respect of which there is constructional control by virtue of the powers under the Explosives Acts 1875 and 1923(a).	
Class 11. A garden hut, greenhouse or other building ancillary to a house including one used or intended to be used for the keeping of poultry, bees, birds or other animals for the domestic needs or personal enjoyment of the occupants of the house.	(i) There shall not be included in this Class any garage, carport, sun porch or sun lounge. (ii) The building is erected on land in the same occupation as a building in occupancy sub-group A1 or A2. (iii) The height of the building does not exceed 2·3 metres. (iv) The floor area of the building does not exceed 4·5 square metres or 9 square metres in the case of a greenhouse of which not less than three-quarters of the total external area is of glass (including glazing bars). (v) The building is at a distance of not less than 500 millimetres from the boundary:
	Provided that in the case of a building an external wall of which is situated on the boundary— (*a*) such external wall shall have no opening in terms of regulation D2(1); and (*b*) the building shall be of non-combustible material (other than the internal framing which may be of timber).
Class 12. A building constructed to be used only in connection with and during the construction, alteration, demolition or repair of any building or other work.	The building is neither used nor intended to be used for human habitation.
Class 13. A moveable dwelling including a tent, caravan, shed or similar structure used for human habitation.	
Class 14. A building erected on a site during a period of not more than 28 days in any period of 12 months.	
Class 15. (*a*) A gate or fence not exceeding 2·1 metres in height; (*b*) a wall or other means of enclosure not exceeding 1·2 metres in height.	In the case of a building falling under head (*a*)—the gate or fence does not adjoin any road or other place to which the public have access as of right.
Class 16. A pipe, cable or other apparatus laid underground.	There shall not be included in this Class— (*a*) a drain provided so as to comply with Part M; (*b*) a conductor or apparatus provided so as to comply with Part N.

(a) S.I. 1961/195 (1961 I, p. 308).

5 Relaxation of the Regulations (except for certain extensions and alterations to existing buildings) is the responsibility of the Secretary of State for Scotland.

6 If problems occur, consult the building control officer of the appropriate authority, but remember that although he will normally give advice, he is not there to design or redesign, draw or redraw plans.

7 Check carefully the requirements of the sewerage authority where appropriate.

Building Notes
5.02 The Scottish Development Department has issued Building Notes to local authorities giving guidance on Building Regulation matters and drawing attention to Agreement Certificates, ANTS tests and other related matters.

References

List of enactments and publications
Building (Scotland) Act 1959
Building (Scotland) Act 1970
Local Government Act 1973
Health and Safety at Work etc Act 1974
Sewerage (Scotland) Act 1968
Building Standards (Scotland) Regulations 1971 to 1975
Building Operations (Scotland) Regulations 1975
Building (Procedure) (Scotland) Regulations 1975
Building (Forms) (Scotland) Regulations 1975
Building Standards (Relaxation by Local Authorities) (Scotland) Regulations 1975
Report of the Committee on Building Legislation in Scotland (Guest Report)
Memorandum on Draft Building Standards (Scotland) Regulations 1961
Explanatory Memorandum issued by the Scottish Development Department
Selected Decisions Affecting Existing Dwelling-Houses
Selected Decisions Affecting Existing Buildings Other than Dwelling-Houses
Fire Precautions Act 1971
Fire Certificates (Special Premises) Regulations 1976
Fire Precautions (Factories, Offices, Shops and Railway Premises) Order 1976
Thermal Insulation Act 1957
Thermal Insulation (Industrial Buildings) Regulations 1972
Clean Air Acts 1956–68
Offices, Shops and Railway Premises Act 1963
Institute of Electrical Engineers Regulations
Health and Safety at Work etc Act 1974 Commencement Order No 2 1975
See also FRANKLIN, P. K. Building Regulations Scotland checklists and index, 1975, Home Information Services Ltd

AJ Legal
Handbook

Section 10
Professional conduct

Legal study 15

Professional conduct in England

This study discusses reasons for having professional codes of conduct and covers architects' responsibilities generally, the principles of impartiality, conflicts of interest and remuneration. The discussion of directorships and permitted occupations is interesting. The latter part deals with loyalty to professional colleagues, advertising and public relations. The study as formerly published has been extensively amended to take account of the revised versions of both the ARCUK and RIBA Codes—published simultaneously and having effect as from 1 January 1976

1 Professionalism

1.01 A professional person is an expert who advises and acts on behalf of others who lack the necessary knowledge and skill. In this relationship he brings to his client's affairs wider values than an individual might consider relevant. The result is a relationship of mutual trust, which is unique in the world of business and which requires considerable dedication on the part of practitioners and protection from society if it is to survive.

1.02 The professional relationship becomes most meaningful when contrasted with commercial relationships. Traditionally the latter are involved with growing, manufacturing, or buying goods, and selling at a profit. Only recently has the concept of service developed in commercial relationships, and an essential characteristic of trade has been that buyer and seller are free to drive a hard bargain, each at his own risk (*caveat emptor*). Apart from fair dealing, neither party is expected to look to the other's interests. In contrast, professionalism has evolved to reduce the risks which would otherwise be much greater for individuals seeking personal services on a commercial basis. The client must have faith in those from whom he seeks advice (*credat emptor*).

1.03 A common misconception about professionalism is that it is concerned mainly with technical skill. Hence the resentment of some architects that they should be deprived of the professional title for which they have qualified by examination, merely because they choose to practise in a particular way. Professional people are experts; where no specialist knowledge and skill is required there is no need for professional advice. But they have no monopoly of expertise. Traditionally it has been available only from those whose lives have been devoted to a particular calling; from this stems the common use of the word to distinguish the man who earns his living at some activity from the amateur. But suitably qualified amateurs may in fact offer their services professionally and be judged accordingly, while the necessity of earning a living may create interests that conflict with the disinterested nature of professional service. Therefore professional institutions developed with two-fold objectives. On the one hand they provide additional protection to the public by reinforcing the law of contract with an assurance of special competence and a code of ethics. On the other, they have sought to protect the professional man by creating a climate in which relationships of mutual trust with clients may flourish, free from the need to advertise, to drive hard bargains over fees, and the fear of unfair competition during a job.

1.04 By definition a code of professional conduct is concerned not with competence or performance, but with a professional's relationships with others, including his fellow professionals. The law governing professional relationships is based on the law of agency (LEGAL STUDY 1 para 4.01 *et seq*), but may be reinforced specifically by a code of professional conduct. As well as a duty in contract to his client or employer, a professional (in common with all citizens) owes a duty of care to others who may be affected by his act or omission. Higher standards will be expected from him than from others, and these may also be reinforced by codes.

1.05 Ideally a professional code should consist of precept and exhortation, for there may be much to be said for encouraging members of a group to subscribe to standards of behaviour which it may not be possible to enforce upon all. But wherever a code seeks to lay down specific rules of behaviour, it is important to see that these are both enforceable and enforced, otherwise the whole code will fall in disrepute.

The Codes of Professional Conduct
ARCUK *Code*

1.06 Architects in the United Kingdom must by definition be registered in accordance with the Architects' (Registration) Acts 1931 to 1938. The intention of the principal Act of 1931 was to provide, because it was considered in the public interest to do so, for the registration of architects and for the establishment of an Architects Registration Council (ARCUK), the Council's first duty being to set up a register of all with prescribed qualifications who were entitled to be registered under the Act. The Architects' Registration Act 1938 went a stage further by restricting the use of the title 'architect' (with some exceptions)* to Registered Architects. So that under s.1 (1) 'a person shall not practice or carry on business under any name, style, or title containing the word 'architect', . . . unless he or she is a person registered under the principal Act'. Parliament was not necessarily concerned with the way in which architectural services were provided and did not go so far as to protect architectural practice or exclude therefrom persons capable of performing such services. It was concerned only to see that those who called themselves architects were suitably qualified; and the minimum necessary provisions were set out so as to enable the Council to make its own regulations, and for prescribing the qualifications appropriate for admission to the Register, including the recognition of examinations in architecture. With a view to the maintenance

---

* Section 1 (1) of the 1938 Act excludes the use of designations 'naval architect', 'landscape architect' or 'golf-course architect'

and control of correct standards of professional conduct* the Council is required, *inter alia*, to appoint annually a Discipline Committee for the purpose of inquiring into and reporting to the Council on 'any case of which it is alleged that a registered person has been guilty of conduct disgraceful to him or her in the capacity as an architect' (s.7 (1) (2) of the 1931 Act), including that of a registered person convicted of a criminal offence. Powers and procedures are also provided for admission of persons to and removal from the Register and for prosecuting those who abuse the title protected by the Acts.

1.07 Though it may be held to have no direct statutory validity (indeed, there is no obligation imposed by the Acts to promulgate any official code) the ARCUK Code has much to commend it as a means of assisting the Disciplinary Committee, architects and the public in determining what constitutes professional misconduct. It does so by enjoining general standards of conduct upon architects in the form of 'principles', the interpretation of which it recognises may be changed 'from time to time to meet the impact of modern custom and prevailing conditions in architectural practice'. These principles are illustrated by examples, in turn supplemented by reports of the Disciplinary Committee, published in the ARCUK Annual Report.

ARCUK Code—Introduction

The object of the Code is to promote the standard of professional conduct or self-discipline required of an architect in the interest of the public.

In considering its application architects must bear this object in mind as well as their obligations towards clients, employers, brother architects and the building industry.

Architects must also appreciate they may be held responsible not only for their own actions but also for the conduct of their practices, of whatever nature. They are advised therefore to bring this Code to the notice of all those associated with them in practice.

The three Principles of the Code are of universal application; the Rules are specific injunctions indicating the proper standard of behaviour. Principles have one digit (eg. 1), rules have two digits (eg. 1.1), and notes to the principles and rules have three digits (eg. 1.1.1).

The RIBA Notes that have been printed as an Appendix to the Code are for the guidance of architects and explain the particular application of a Principle or Rule, in some cases indicating the conditions under which certain activities are permitted. But they do not form part of the ARCUK Code.

The attention of architects is drawn more particularly to the provisions of Sections 7, 8 and 9 of the Architects (Registration) Act 1931, relating to the possibility of removal of a person's name from the Register for conduct disgraceful to him in his capacity as an architect and to the powers and functions in relation thereto of the Discipline Committee and the Council.

Architects desiring guidance are advised to consult the Registrar.

RIBA Code
1.08 In addition to the ARCUK Code, members of the RIBA are required when applying for membership, whether as student or fully qualified members, to pledge their loyalty to the Institute's own Code of Professional Conduct, which is specifically referred to in by-law 5.1 of the Charter and by-laws, and which provides for reprimand, suspension and expulsion of members. From the Institute's point of view the inadequacy of the text and format of the RIBA Code is compensated for by the generality of this by-law which affords disciplinary powers over any member 'conducting himself in a manner which is derogatory to his professional character or engaging in any occupation which (in the opinion of the Council) is inconsistent with his membership of the Royal Institute'. In practice most charges of professional misconduct preferred by the RIBA are based on this by-law, coupled with reference to any appropriate clause in the Code.

* See Appendix 2 to ARCUK Code at the end of this Study

RIBA Code—Preface

Code of professional conduct

Applicable from 1 January 1976

Preface

The objects of the Royal Institute of British Architects, as described in the Charter, are 'the advancement of Architecture and the promotion of the acquirement of the knowledge of the Arts and Sciences connected therewith'.

Members of the Royal Institute are governed by its Charter, Bye laws, Regulations and Code of Professional Conduct under and in addition to the general law.

The object of this Code of Professional Conduct is to promote the standard of professional conduct, or self-discipline, required of members of the Royal Institute in the interest of the public.

The Code comprises Principles and Rules, and Notes to the Principles and Rules. The three Principles are of universal application; under the Principles are Rules which are specific injunctions. The Notes explain particular applications of a Principle or Rule, in some cases laying down conditions under which certain activities are permitted. Printed with the Notes are advisory Notes (marked with an asterisk) indicating good practice and how best to observe a Principle or Rule.

Further Rules or Notes may be published by the Council from time to time in the *RIBA Journal*, before their incorporation into a revised edition of the Code. Members are expected to be familiar with new provisions from the date of their publication.

A member may be required to answer inquiries concerning his professional conduct in accordance with the Regulations made under Bye law 5.2. A member is liable to reprimand, suspension or expulsion under Bye law 5.1 and the Regulations if his conduct is found by the Professional Conduct Committee to be in contravention of the Code or otherwise inconsistent with his status as a member or derogatory to his professional character. Contravention of the Code includes conduct of a member which dishonours any of its Principles, whether or not the member has contravened any Rule.

The two Codes
1.09 As the majority of architects practising in the UK are subject to both the ARCUK and RIBA Codes and since the revised versions of each introduced in January 1976 are for all intents and purposes identical, the following commentary deals with them together. The ARCUK version is printed out in full, and attention is drawn to all instances where there is a difference between it and the RIBA Code. For example, the Principles and Rules in the ARCUK Code are addressed as to 'an architect', whereas the RIBA Code refers to 'member'. This is because the former is concerned only with persons enrolled on the statutory Register of Architects—limited to those permitted the use of the title 'architect'. The RIBA, operating under a Royal Charter, includes two general categories of membership, corporate and non-corporate. The class of corporate members consists of those who may use the affix 'RIBA' and—provided they are on the ARCUK Register—the title 'chartered architect'. The non-corporate membership includes honorary members, student members and subscribers. The subscriber class is not currently active except at RIBA branch level (see RIBA Handbook, pp 18 and 29–30.). In this Study the following abbreviations are used:
1 The marginal notation of each code is identical. Principles have one digit (eg 1); Rules have two sets of digits (eg 1.1); Notes have three sets of digits (eg 1.1.1).
2 Where reference to previous editions of the ARCUK Code is desirable, a roman numeral refers to one of the Principles (eg ARCUK V (1973) refers to Principle V of the 1973 Edition). When this is followed by an arabic number, an 'example'

that illustrates the Principle is indicated (eg ARCUK V (3) means Principle V, example 3). Note: The selected examples quoted under Appendix 1 which were a feature of earlier editions of the ARCUK Code have now been abandoned. However, as they are considered useful in explaining the application of the policy behind the code in terms of practice, a number of them have been retained in this Study.

3 ARCUK followed by a date and page number refers to an ARCUK Annual Report (eg ARCUK 1966 p 7 means page 7 of the 1966 Report).

4 The RIBA Notes, attached to the ARCUK Code as Appendix 1, explain particular applications of a Principle or Rule and what it is or is not intended to prohibit, in some cases laying down conditions under which certain activities are permitted. Advisory Notes indicating good practice or how best to uphold a Principle or Rule are marked with an asterisk and are printed in this LEGAL STUDY in italics in order to distinguish them from the main Notes.

The new Codes
1.10 Comparing the old codes with the 1976 revisions reveals that the 1973 version of the ARCUK Code consisted of nine principles and two appendices. Appendix 1 provided information in the form of selected examples of the standards of conduct expected. These examples have now been omitted (but see para 1.09 above). Appendix 2 is retained. The RIBA Code consisted of seventeen clauses unencumbered by any appendices or notes. In the new Codes of 1976 the number of Principles is reduced to three (set in bold type) with a number of Rules applicable to each Principle. The form of both ARCUK and RIBA Codes is similar and each reproduces as Appendix 1 the 'RIBA Notes to the Principles and Rules' referred to above (para 1.09, 4).

1.11 With the revised versions of both Codes published simultaneously and with effect as from 1 January 1976, it has become clear that there is no difference of opinion between the two bodies as to what constitutes proper standards of conduct required of architects. The main 'principles' laid down in each of the two Codes are identical. Accordingly objections to two disciplinary bodies and two Codes are less significant in practice than in theory. ARCUK as the statutory body is more powerful in the conduct of its affairs, but restricted in its scope of action. Procedures are formal, and its decisions must withstand the scrutiny of the High Court in the event of appeal. The RIBA is less powerful, less formal, but relatively free to make its own membership rules, provided they do not conflict with the restrictions imposed by ARCUK. At the same time the RIBA can in some ways go further than ARCUK in discussing and advising on the implications of its principles of conduct in practice; and as long as the RIBA does not contravene the laws of natural justice in the conduct of its affairs, the courts will not interfere with its decisions. There is also now less significance in the objections that with the existence of two disciplinary bodies offenders may be tried twice for the same offence. In practice ARCUK delegates preliminary investigation and jurisdiction to the RIBA in respect of its own members; and where a hearing by ARCUK is necessary it can only be held in the interests of the architect concerned. Similarly, while it is often suggested that justice might be better served if proceedings against architects accused of unprofessional conduct took place in public, both the ARCUK Disciplinary Committee and the RIBA Professional Conduct Committee hold their proceedings in private. ARCUK has reaffirmed this policy in the interests of individuals but, nevertheless, has expressed a willingness to relax it in any case where open justice 'can be fairly served' and is in the public interest.

2 Responsibilities

ARCUK Code—Principle 1

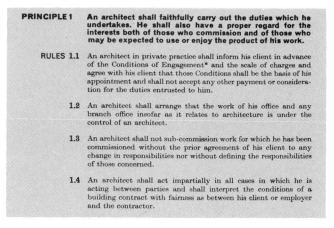

PRINCIPLE 1	An architect shall faithfully carry out the duties which he undertakes. He shall also have a proper regard for the interests both of those who commission and of those who may be expected to use or enjoy the product of his work.
RULES 1.1	An architect in private practice shall inform his client in advance of the Conditions of Engagement* and the scale of charges and agree with his client that those Conditions shall be the basis of his appointment and shall not accept any other payment or consideration for the duties entrusted to him.
1.2	An architect shall arrange that the work of his office and any branch office insofar as it relates to architecture is under the control of an architect.
1.3	An architect shall not sub-commission work for which he has been commissioned without the prior agreement of his client to any change in responsibilities nor without defining the responsibilities of those concerned.
1.4	An architect shall act impartially in all cases in which he is acting between parties and shall interpret the conditions of a building contract with fairness as between his client or employer and the contractor.

* The only recognised Conditions of Engagement are those published by one or other of the constituent bodies of the Council referred to in the First Schedule to the Architects (Registration) Act 1931, paragraph 1, sub-paragraphs (i) to (vi)

RIBA Notes—Principle 1

The following Advisory Notes are applicable only to the RIBA Code; they are not reproduced in the ARCUK Code.
Rule 1.1 Note 1.0.1 A member is advised before undertaking or continuing with any work to arrange that his resources are adequate and properly directed to carry it out.
1.0.2 A student member who undertakes a commission is advised to seek guidance from an architect.
1.1.1 A member is advised always to explain the application of the RIBA Conditions of Engagement to his client's requirements and define his own responsibilities in relation to the commission at the outset and where there is any change in circumstances. He is also advised to confirm fee agreements in writing.

2.01 In marked contrast to the brevity of Principle I (1973) of the earlier Codes, which simply stated that 'An architect must faithfully discharge his responsibilities to his client', the 1976 revisions expand the range and not only are more specific about an architect's responsibilities to his client but also stress the regard he must have for architecture in general and for all those who may be expected to use or enjoy the product of his work. Formerly there obviously may have been grounds for thinking that ARCUK did not see the wider responsibilities as part of their concern and that also, perhaps, the RIBA had considered discharge of duties to a client more a matter of professional competence and contract law than of professional conduct. Nevertheless, as the public frequently looks in vain to ARCUK or the RIBA to remedy an architect's shortcomings, it is worthwhile recalling Gurth Higgin's definition of guarantees essential to a professional relationship (RIBA *Journal* April 1964 p 139): 'First, that the professional is sufficiently competent in his desired field of practice, and second that there is some guarantee to the client that in allowing the professional to share in decisions on his behalf the professional will be guided by his (the client's) best interests. The second guarantee is what we are concerned with here. It is essentially an assurance that the interests of other parties, including those of the professional himself, will be subordinated to those of the client.'

2.02 In case 109 (ARCUK 1966 p 7), an architect was acquitted of a charge of disgraceful conduct under Principle I (1966) for want of conclusive evidence, but the substance of the complaint illustrates the kind of behaviour considered deplorable in a professional man. 'It was alleged against him (the architect) that well knowing he had failed to carry out his client's instructions to lodge an application for an improvement grant (to which he had obtained the client's signature) with the local authority, he assured her (the client) on several occasions that he had lodged the application; and that he had untruthfully advised her that the local authority required further works to be carried out before the grant could be granted.'

2.03 In January 1967 the RIBA Professional Conduct Committee warned that members who fail persistently to reply promptly to letters from clients or from the RIBA render themselves liable to a charge under the provisions of by-law 23 (now 5.1). This refers not to the common failing to answer letters in which most of us share, but in effect to persistent neglect of responsibilities to clients or evasion of charges of professional misconduct simply by ignoring letters.

2.04 More recently in a comment on indemnity insurance premiums (RIBA *Journal* February 1970), some of the reasons given for increases in cost were described as being evident in 'four clearly recognisable stages at which architects have tended to be negligent', namely at:
1 Pre-design stage. In regard to (a) land levels, drains, soil conditions etc and particularly through failure to check records in the case of made-up ground, and (b) buildings, resulting in enormous overexpenditure in comparison with the original estimate of cost given to the client.
2 Design stage. Negligent design by the architect or his staff. This would appear to be the most frequent type of claim, where architects have not paid sufficient regard to BSI standards and codes of practice. Negligence in design, calculations etc by consultants or specialist sub-contractors or suppliers for whom the architect is primarily responsible to the client. Also negligence in the choice of untested materials and methods of construction.
3 Negligence in service. (a) By failure to advise client on any consents necessary from superior or adjoining landlords, (b) by failure to obtain necessary statutory eg planning, building regulations, fire authorities', and justices', and (c) failure to supply information to the contractor giving rise to a claim by the contractor against the architect's client.
4 Negligence in supervision. Inadequate attendance, allowing the contractor to conceal much defective work between visits; and failure to detect defective work both during construction and before issue of the final certificate.

Engagement
2.05 Rule 1.1 of Principle 1 introduces into the Codes for the first time the specific requirement (touched upon only briefly by Principle II (1974)) for an architect to inform his client in advance of his Conditions of Engagement and scale of charges as the basis of his appointment. Principle 3, Rules 3.2 and 3.3 (qv) furthermore requires the architect to uphold and apply the recognised Conditions of Engagement.

Delegation
2.06 Rule 1.2 and Rule 1.3. As a result of complaints from clients who found their affairs were being neglected, the RIBA in 1969 issued a warning against delegation of work to unqualified assistants, particularly in branch offices (RIBA *Journal* July 1969 p 302). At that time architects were instructed to observe the principles that (a) firms with more

than one office should ensure that each office was always under the control of an architect, and (b) that all jobs should be controlled by an architect. Architects who are sole principals should make provisions for another architect to take charge in the event of their absence, serious illness or death. Both of these matters have now been incorporated in the Codes of Conduct.

Impartiality
2.07 Rule 1.4 does little more than replace Principle III (1974) in respect of an architect's responsibility for acting in an impartial manner and with entire fairness between employer and contractor. It contributes nothing by way of a professional interpretation of the architect's quasi-arbitral role which in recent years has attracted so much attention and comment, mainly as a result of the case of *Sutcliffe v Thakrah* (1974), a case which overruled the widely held presumption based on the decision of *Chambers v Goldthorpe* (1901) that an architect was immune from liability for negligence in such circumstances. The pronouncement by Lord Reid in *Sutcliffe v Thakrah* is appropriate to quote in the present context as a reminder of the standards which both the ARCUK and the RIBA Codes of Conduct expect of architects. Lord Reid said: 'The building owner and the contractor make their contract on the understanding that in all such matters the architect will act in a fair and unbiased manner, and it must therefore be implicit in the owner's contract with the architect that he shall not only exercise due care and skill, but also reach such decisions fairly, holding the balance between his client and the contractor.' Lord Reid pointed out that the architect is not jointly engaged by the parties to the building contract, nor do they submit contentious evidence to him; and he said: 'The architect makes his own investigations, and comes to a decision. It would be taking a very low view to suppose that, without his being put in a special position, his employer would wish him to act unfairly, or that a professional man would be willing to depart from the ordinary honourable standards of professional conduct'. (See also LEGAL STUDY 1 para 5.08 *et seq* and LEGAL STUDY 3 para 4.02.)

2.08 The judicial role of the architect was summed up by Lord Shaw in the case of *Hickman and Co v Roberts* (1913) AC 229: 'The position of an architect in a building contract is one of great delicacy. He is placed in that position to act judicially when, to the knowledge of both parties, the person who is his master and his paymaster is one of the parties to the contract. It has been affirmed by courts of law, however, that being the case, his judicial position must be accepted, and it follows from that, in the peculiarly delicate situation in which such a man stands the courts of law must be particular to see that his judicial attitude is maintained.'

2.09 Lord Shaw's dictum makes it clear that the architect occupies a remarkable position in the administration of a building contract, and that the courts accept it. The role of an instructed and paid agent (LEGAL STUDY 1 para 4.01) is subordinated to a judicial one when supervision of the building process starts (LEGAL STUDY 4 para 5.02). But while this role is generally understood, it is increasingly questioned, not only because of the potential conflict with the architect's own interests in determining matters, eg responsibility for delay, but because of the unreasonable inference that an architect's professional integrity may be guaranteed in any occupational position. Is general recognition of the architect's impartiality in contract administration undermining the profession by encouraging people to assume a similar impartiality from architects employed by package dealers?

Package deals

2.10 There is a distinct difference in the position of an architect when he is employed by a seller, as in a package deal, rather than by the buyer, as in the standard form of building contract. The nature of building services puts the seller in the stronger position. The buyer, even with the help of expert inspection and supervision must take the majority of the work on trust; therefore it is not unreasonable that his agent should act as arbitrator in a form of contract which does not neglect the contractor's interests. But there is an increasing tendency for architects to be named as arbitrators in a lot of other contracts, eg between a speculative builder and his customers. Here an architect employed by the builder should not act in any contract with the customer, irrespective of the agreement of the parties. But there has been no pronouncement on this issue by ARCUK or the RIBA.

2.11 Official and salaried architects have the same obligations to the contractor as architects in private practice; and ARCUK has advised that the chief architect of a public authority should not sign building contracts on behalf of his employing authority in which he is also named as 'the architect'. This advice is clearly meant to avoid unnecessary confusion between the position of a salaried architect as an employee, and his professional role. There are others who can sign on behalf of the employer. This raises the question of the architect building his own house. May he properly act as architect in a contract for which he is the employer? There is no doubt that it is done, but the prudent architect, if not entrusting supervision of the works to a professional colleague, might be well-advised to agree with the contractor the name of an architect to act as arbitrator, before any conflict arises.

Arbitrators

2.12 Where an architect is formally appointed as arbitrator by the president of the RIBA (LEGAL STUDY 8 para 2.03), conflicts of interest should not arise, but the RIBA have advised members not to allow an appointment for a fact-finding exercise to be extended into that of arbitrator. In the case which the Professional Services Board considered, there was no question of the architect, who was called in to advise, acting in bad faith. But his professional colleagues involved in the case naturally felt aggrieved at finding themselves drawn step-by-step into accepting the adverse findings of an arbitration which might have been avoided had they looked in the first place to their own interests rather than those of their clients.

2.13 In all questions of contract administration, and wherever he is acting between parties, an architect must act impartially, and he should beware of accepting positions in which his ability to do so is prejudiced, or might appear to be.

Limited companies

2.14 Both ARCUK and the RIBA Codes in Principle 2, Rule 2.4 are now agreed that an architect (or member) shall not carry on practice in the form of a limited liability company. Principle V (1973) provided for this prohibition though it was then not paralleled in the RIBA Code. It is a prohibition which has hitherto never been challenged, although a recent counsel's opinion suggests that it would not stand up against section 17 of the 1931 Act. This opinion is reinforced by recent court decisions in Australia (where practice in the form of a limited liability company is permitted), which suggest that the courts would not allow such companies to limit the personal liability of a professional director for his acts or omissions, although unlike partners, his fellow directors might escape (see further LEGAL STUDY 3 para 2.09 *et seq*).

2.15 In practice the question of whether architects may take steps to define limits to their liability when entering into agreements with clients may be more important than the controversy over limited companies. RIBA Council has approved such a proposal in principle and will be considering the question of limited liability companies. Meanwhile ARCUK has permitted office premises and furniture to be purchased by limited liability companies owned by architects, subject to various professional safeguards (LEGAL STUDY 3 para 3.06) (ARCUK 1959 p 9), but a proposal by a firm of architects to form a limited liability company where shares would be held by a merchant bank as a sleeping partner, was rejected as 'wholly repugnant to a professional practice of architects' (ARCUK 1966 p 11).

Overseas work

2.16 Of rather special significance at the present time, when more and more architects are seeking to practice outside the UK, is the publication by the RIBA of a Practice Note (RIBA *Journal* September 1976) with reference to overseas work, entitled 'Overseas Work: Limited Liability Companies and the Application of the Code of Professional Conduct'. The Practice Note begins by referring to the express prohibition under Rule 2.4 of practice in the form of a limited liability company as one that remains in the UK because of professional traditions and customs peculiar to this country and the public expectation which flows from them, but recognises that a different position exists in many countries overseas. It was because of this difference that in December 1971 the RIBA Council decided to grant a dispensation from the Rule in respect of practice overseas and to permit members to incorporate their practices with limited liability outside the UK where such incorporation was permitted by law and the local codes of conduct.* The Practice Note indicates that experience since has not revealed any reason for rescinding that decision, but notes that, because there could be substantial tax advantage if a company formed for the purpose of carrying out work overseas were to be incorporated in the UK or in a country or place other than that in which the work was to be done, the Council in July 1976 decided that the dispensation should remain and further agreed that a member would not be held in breach of Rule 2.4 if, should he wish, he formed such a limited liability company registered in the UK, with the important proviso that the memorandum and articles of association of the company contains a clause expressly prohibiting the company from carrying out any of its objects within the UK and further prohibiting the company from ever accepting a commission for part or all of the normal services in respect of work which is intended to be constructed within the United Kingdom. (See LEGAL STUDY 17.)

2.17 The RIBA Practice Note goes on to refer in detail to the activities and composition of the company, consortium or group, noting that in all other respects than the specific nature of the dispensation, members remain governed by the RIBA Charter and By-laws and emphasising the responsibility of all members, partners or directors for ensuring that the business of the company is conducted in conformity with the Code of Professional Conduct. The Practice Note deals also with agents in those countries where the law requires such companies to be represented by a resident national agent. Those agents must be bound by Rule 3.1 of the Code and may not give inducements in any form for the introduction of clients or work; and by Rule 3.6, which prohibits soliciting commissions (para 4.11). Rule 3.6 is also to apply to the company's agents in respect of the public relations policy of the company, consortium or group. Members are referred in particular to Guidance Note 3.6.2 and the need to furnish a declaration in so far as the work of any local office relates to the architect. Rule 1.2 requires a member to arrange for such work to be under the control of an architect. The final paragraphs of the Practice Note deal with questions of taxation and the availability of additional information on overseas practice obtainable from RIBA sources.

Undesirable partners

2.18 Rule 2.7 replaces Principle IX (introduced in January 1969) in wider and more positive terms, to the effect that an architect shall not have, take or continue in practice with any person who has been disqualified from the ARCUK Register under s.7 of the 1931 Act or with a person who engages in any of the occupations specified under Rule 2.1. Provisions are also made under RIBA Note 2.1.1 (*infra*) for a 'member' who wishes to act as director, principal, partner or manager in certain circumstances to give a written declaration to the RIBA stating particulars and reasons why he would not be in breach of the Rule.

ARCUK Code—Principle 2

PRINCIPLE 2 An architect shall avoid actions and situations inconsistent with his professional obligations or likely to raise doubts about his integrity.

RULES 2.1 An architect shall not have such an interest in or connection with any business as would or might breach this principle. In particular he shall not be, nor act as, proprietor, director, principal, partner or (subject to 2.6) manager of any body corporate or unincorporate engaging in any of the following occupations: carrying on the business of trading in land or buildings, property developers, auctioneers, house agents or estate agents†; or contractors, subcontractors, manufacturers or suppliers in or to the building industry.

2.2 An architect shall not take discounts, commissions or gifts as an inducement to show favour to any person or body; nor shall he recommend or allow his name to be used in recommending any service or product in advertisements.

2.3 An architect shall not improperly influence the granting of planning consents or statutory approvals.

2.4 An architect shall not carry on his practice in the form of a limited liability company.

2.5 An architect shall not act in disregard of the professional obligations or qualifications of those from whom he receives or to whom he gives authority, responsibility or employment, nor of those with whom he is professionally associated.

2.6 An architect who is appointed to superintend or control the architectural business of any body corporate or unincorporate (including a central government department, a local authority, public board or corporation or commercial firm or company) shall arrange with his employer that the business of that body so far as it relates to architecture is conducted in conformity with this Code. An architect who is unable to ensure that the business of his employer is so conducted shall furnish the ARCUK with a written declaration of the facts.

2.7 An architect shall not have or take as partner or co-director in his firm any person who is disqualified for registration by reason of the fact that his name has been removed from the register under Section 7 of the Architects (Registration) Act 1931, or any person who engages in any of the occupations proscribed under Rule 2.1 even though that person engages in any such occupation in a firm or company separate from the architectural firm.

2.8 An architect who in circumstances not specifically covered in these Rules finds that his interests whether professional or personal conflict so as to risk a breach of this Principle shall, as the circumstances may require, either withdraw from the situation or remove the source of conflict or declare it and obtain the agreement of the parties concerned to the continuance of his engagement.

RIBA Notes—Principle 2
ARCUK Code—Appendix 1

Note 2.1.1 A member who wishes to act as director, principal, partner or manager of any body corporate or unincorporate which under its Memorandum of Association or the like is *empowered to carry on any proscribed occupation but which does not in fact exercise such power, is required to furnish the* RIBA *with a written declaration. The declaration shall state full particulars of the body and the reason why the member concerned would not be in breach of this Rule were he to act as proposed.*

Note 2.1.2 A member may, subject to Rule 2.1, invest on his own or his firm's account in any body corporate or unincorporate carrying on such a business as is specified in the Rule.

Note 2.4.1 A member may by prior written agreement with his client exclude liability for loss of use, loss of profits or other consequential loss.

Rule 2.5† In upholding this Rule a member is advised to have regard to the following Notes, which with the Rule form the Code of Employment authorized by the RIBA *Council.*

Note 2.5.1* An employing architect should define the terms of employment, authority, responsibility and liability of the architects he employs having regard to the particular responsibilities of project architects.

Note 2.5.2* An employing architect should ensure that the architects he employs are enabled to exercise their professional skills, and should provide them with opportunities to accept progressively greater delegated responsibility in accordance with their ability and experience.

Note 2.5.3* The participation and responsibility of project architects should be appropriately recognised by the employing architect and credit given (for example, in any literature, description of illustration).

Note 2.5.4* To benefit the competence of the whole profession an employing architect should enable the architects he employs to maintain and advance their competence by participating in continuing education.

Note 2.5.5* An employing architect should permit the architects he employs to engage in sparetime practice, but an architect should not do so without the knowledge of his employer and should ensure that there can be no conflict of interest between his employer and his responsibilities to his client.

Note 2.5.6* An employing architect should permit the architects he employs to enter architectural competitions but they should not do so without the knowledge of their employer.

Note 2.5.7* Whenever possible, an employing architect should enable the architects he employs to have reasonable time off to participate in the affairs of the profession.

Note 2.5.8* An architect who employs students should cooperate with the RIBA *and schools of architecture in the practical training scheme: should provide as varied experience as possible compatible with his professional responsibilities; and should allow student employees to take reasonable time off for academic purposes leading to the qualifying examinations.*

Note 2.8.1 An example of the application of this Rule is that a member who has been appointed assessor for any competition shall not subsequently act in any other capacity for the work except that he may act as arbitrator in any dispute between the promoters and the selected architect or as consultant where that appointment was arranged before his appointment as assessor.

† 'Auctioneers', 'house agents' and 'estate agents' are deemed to be only those persons or businesses who hold themselves out to the public as prepared to undertake the buying and selling or letting of property. 'Land agents' (ie those who act as agent for the management of an estate) are not affected

* Note: In the RIBA Code insert the following here: '*any person disqualified for membership of the* RIBA *by reason of expulsion under by-law 5.1.: any person disqualified for membership of another professional institution by reason of expulsion under the relevant disciplinary regulations (unless the* RIBA *otherwise allows); any person who is an undischarged bankrupt*'

3 Conflicts of Interest

3.01 A discerning client wishes to be assured that the professional person he has commissioned is not only competent to advise him, and that he appreciates the nature of his

† This Rule and Advisory Notes do not appear in the ARCUK Code
* RIBA *Journal* February 1972 pp 52, 88, 90

responsibilities, but that he is also free from conflicting interests and responsibilities which may prejudice his advice. Needless to say few clients are sufficiently discerning, the majority being concerned to receive technical advice, and it would probably be insufficient for the professional bodies to rely on a simple declaration of interest by architects. Architects themselves are drawn easily into impossible situations through a desire both to practise and to please. Clauses in the codes dealing with conflicts of interest may therefore be said to protect both clients and architects against themselves and each other.

Occupations

3.02 Certain groups of trade or business are held to be inconsistent or out of keeping with the fitting and proper discharge of an architect's professional duties. Rule 2.1 thus forbids an interest in or connection with any business as might breach the Principle, particularly an architect must not be, or act as, proprietor, principal or partner in a number of businesses; these fall into two main groups:
1 Carrying on the business of trading in land or buildings, property developers, auctioneers, house agents and estate agents.
2 Contractors, sub-contractors, manufacturers or suppliers in or to the building industry.
They are prohibited for various reasons: fundamental incompatibility with an architect's impartial role when advising on building; the likelihood that an architect's advice would frequently be prejudiced; and rising out of the interconnections of building and development companies, the unfair advantage that such businesses would give an architect over his colleagues.

3.03 In 1961 ARCUK noted the 'appreciably increasing number of architects who wish to become directors of companies whose main business is trading in land or buildings'. They were advised to resign rather than 'attempt by ingenuous devices to have a foot in both camps' (ARCUK 1961 p 11). In 1963 the head of a firm of architects was advised that it would be improper to join a consortium of which an estate agent was a member, of if there were any likelihood of any other member of the consortium soliciting business (ARCUK 1963 p 14).

3.04 Those who complain that architects' professional codes exclude them from occupations where technical knowledge and skill might most usefully be employed are missing the point that professionalism is concerned with relationships, and that it is precisely in those areas where their skill is in demand that the interests of director, principal, partner or manager may be incompatible with an architect's professional responsibilities.

Salaried employment and directorships

3.05 The question of directorship is separate from, though related to, the question of prohibited occupations. Salaried employment is usually taken for granted because for some time now only a minority of architects have practised in the traditional role of principal in private practice, but it is worth considering in the context of directorships, as architects are permitted to be salaried employees in businesses in which they may not become principals.

3.06 The traditional professional view is that all employees have their freedom of action compromised by their employers' powers of dismissal, that government employees are subjected inevitably to bureaucratic aims and methods and that

principals in private practice are the only true professionals. But it may be easier for a salaried employee to withdraw from an unprofessional situation than his principal who may have considerably more at stake, not least the livelihood of those who depend on his practice.

3.07 All salaried employees are entitled to the protection of a contract of employment which can safeguard their professional obligations (LEGAL STUDY 3 para 4.05 *et seq*). The salaried employee in a commercial organisation, who has no corporate responsibility, may therefore be in no less a professional relationship to his employer than his colleague in private practice commissioned by the same organisation. But boardroom responsibilities are different, and a company director has corporate responsibilities and constraints from which he cannot dissociate himself easily. The real danger in architect directorships lies not in the architect's lack of professionalism, but in the acts of his fellow directors who unlike partners in professional practice would not necessarily be bound by his professional code.

Specific conflicts of interest

3.08 Specific conflicts of interest are most likely to arise from prior obligations, particularly where salaried architects are concerned. The codes do not prohibit spare time practice, although architects are always advised to obtain their employer's consent, and this may be a matter for their contracts of employment.

3.09 It is generally accepted that the position of official architects is a particularly vulnerable one. Principle VIII (1973) (5) was important and has now been replaced by an injunction in Rule 2.6 to apply to architects with senior appointments in central and local government departments, public boards, corporations, commercial firms or companies, to arrange that, so far as it relates to architecture, the business of that body is conducted in conformity with the Code. If unable to do so the architect is required to furnish ARCUK with a written declaration of the facts.

Planning

3.10 Town-planning consultancy combined with architectural practice also creates potential conflicts of interest, which are covered by an extensive guidance note issued by the RIBA Professional Practice Committee (RIBA *Journal* June 1967 p 255). This committee has advised that an architect should not accept private commissions for sites, eg in central areas, on which he is giving simultaneously planning advice to a public authority. A planning consultant must also beware of advising or appearing to advise a planning authority on applications from his own office. An architect combining planning consultancy with private practice must not attract work into his office on the assumption that he can facilitate granting planning approvals. This would be unfair to professional colleagues and the public, and it may therefore be desirable that a member retained by a small local authority should restrict his private practice in that area.

3.11 The golden rule where any potential conflict of interest is concerned is to declare it. But declaration in itself does not necessarily eliminate the conflict. The counsel given by Rule 2.8 to architects who in circumstances not specifically covered by the Rules find their interests whether professional or personal conflict so as to risk a breach of the Code shall, as the circumstances require, either withdraw from the situation or remove the source of conflict or declare it and obtain the agreement of the parties concerned to the continuance of the engagement.

Remuneration

3.12 In its evidence to the Monopolies Commission the RIBA quoted the following description of a professional organisation from R. H. Tawney's *The acquisitive society:* 'It is a body of men who carry on their work in accordance with rules designed to enforce certain standards both for the better protection of its members and for the better service of the public. The rules themselves sometimes appear to the layman arbitrary and ill-conceived. But their object is clear. It is to impose on the profession itself the obligation of maintaining the quality of the service, and to prevent its common purpose being frustrated through the undue influence of pecuniary gain upon the necessities or cupidity of the individual.'

3.13 The Codes recognise that architects may be paid by salary, and ideally all professional remuneration would be on a time basis, but clients would be uncertain of their financial commitment, while architects, being fallible, would lack the necessary spur to efficiency that pre-determined remuneration brings. The RIBA scale of fees may be arbitrary, but the principle is well-tried and effective. It is a scale that depends for its fairness on the principle of swings and roundabouts rather than any precise calculation of the amount of work incurred on a particular job. Some jobs may yield a considerable profit, but this goes to subsidise others, and no client need fear that the architect has any justification for a lesser standard of care, merely because the fees on a particular project are beginning to run into the red. Moreover, the idea that a fixed scale of fees encourages architects to design extravagantly is erroneous, for the architect who exceeds cost limits agreed with his client may run the risk of losing his fee.

3.14 Principle 1 of the Code deals with the Conditions of Engagement and the agreement with the client of the scale of charges, which the architect is charged to uphold and apply by Rule 3.2 of Principle 3. Each of these provisions is reinforced by RIBA Notes 1.1.1 and 3.2.1 respectively. Rule 3.3 forbids work without payment or at a reduced fee, except as permitted by the Conditions of Engagement. Nor may he or she prepare designs in competition with other architects, save in an architectural 'competition' organised in accordance with RIBA Regulations (para 4.11). (See LEGAL STUDY 17.)

3.15 Professional services are different in kind from branded goods for which a consumer may shop around to get the best price. Not only would the mutual trust on which professional relationships depend be eroded by hard bargaining (which for many public servants would become an official obligation), but standards of service would inevitably be adjusted to meet the price. In this context it is interesting to note an RIBA Council ruling that an official architect who is privy to fee agreements with a private architect which is not in accordance with the RIBA scale is liable to be charged with contravening the code (RIBA *Journal* 1966 p 330). In practice few, if any, official architects are likely to be privy to such agreements, but a sympathetic official architect can do a lot to assist his professional colleagues in their agreements with treasurers or town clerks.

3.16 In 1960, in a report arising out of case 96, ARCUK advised 'that an architect should undertake a commission only on the instructions of a client on a contractual basis' (ARCUK 1960 p 6). This kind of agreement is likely to safeguard an architect's remuneration. In case 98, an architect was accused of disgraceful conduct for *inter alia* 'offering his services as an architect at half the scale fees, in infringement of principle II of the code', but he resigned from the register before the case was heard (ARCUK 1962 p 6).

Discounts and gifts

3.17 Besides laying down how architects shall be paid, the Codes also ensure that their duties to clients shall not be compromised by improper payments. An architect must not take discounts, commissions or gifts as an inducement to show favour to any person or body (Rule 2.2). Likewise by Rule 3.1 an architect shall not give discounts, commissions, gifts or other inducements for the introduction of clients or of work. However, an exception is made in respect of commissions within a practice to qualified architectural staff for introducing clients (ARCUK 1960 p 9). This ruling was designed to avoid payment to staff not subject to the Codes, but does not deal adequately with the question of such commissions in a multi-professional practice.

3.18 These provisions would preclude even the practice of the architect in *The Honeywood File* who always accepted gifts while regretting that he would no longer be able to employ the donor on future work. This clause is clearly aimed at payments arising out of works for a client and is meant to eliminate the receipt of bribes from unsuccessful as well as successful tenderers. This raises the question of trade discounts widely received by architects in a private capacity, which might be held to prejudice their professional judgment. It is usually impossible to establish prejudice of this kind, although individual architects should be well aware when it exists. In this context, it is interesting to note that the RIBA Professional Conduct Committee deprecates the practice of manufacturers inviting architects on free trips abroad (RIBA *Journal* July 1966 p 330).

ARCUK Code—Principle 3

PRINCIPLE 3 An architect shall rely only on ability and achievement as the basis for his advancement.

RULES 3.1 An architect shall not give discounts, commissions, gifts or other inducements for the introduction of clients or of work.

3.2 An architect shall uphold and apply the recognized Conditions of Engagement.*

3.3 An architect shall not work without payment or at a reduced fee except as permitted in the Conditions of Engagement; nor shall he prepare designs in competition with other architects for a client without payment or for a reduced fee except in a competition conducted in accordance with the RIBA Regulations for the promotion and conduct of competitions or a competition otherwise approved by the RIBA and the International Union of Architects.

3.4 An architect shall not attempt to supplant another architect.

3.5 An architect on being approached or instructed to proceed with work upon which he knows, or can ascertain by reasonable inquiry, that another architect is or has been engaged by the same client shall notify the fact to such architect.

3.6 An architect shall not solicit either a commission or engagement for himself or business for a client or employer, but he may make his or his practice's availability or experience known by giving information which in substance and in presentation is factual, relevant and neither misleading* nor unfair to others nor discreditable to the profession, in response to a direct request.†

* See footnote to para 2, Rule 1.1

† It would be a breach of this Rule if an architect permitted his name to be used by unqualified persons in such a way as to suggest to the public that they, or their firms, are entitled to style themselves 'architects'

‡ It would not be considered a breach of this Rule for an architect to give information under this Rule in accordance with RIBA note 3.6.1

§ Note: In the RIBA Code this final sentence continues with '*or in accordance with the Notes to this Rule*'

RIBA Notes—Principle 3 (ARCUK Code—Appendix 1)

PRINCIPLE 3

3.0.1 Members are encouraged to participate by means of RIBA regional and branch activities, amenity societies and other bodies concerned with the quality of the environment, in local and national affairs concerning the environment and to criticise what they believe to be harmful, shoddy or inappropriate provided that criticism is not malicious or contrary to any Rule under this Principle.

Rule 3.2

3.2.1 This Rule applies not only directly between a member and his client but also indirectly where a member is concerned with the appointment of another. The Rule requires him to ensure that the conditions of the commissioned architect's appointment are in accordance with the RIBA Conditions of Engagement. A member who is unable so to ensure is required to furnish the RIBA with a written declaration of the facts.

3.2.2 It would be contrary to this Rule for a member to submit estimates of fees and expenses knowing that they would be used for the purpose of competition with other members.

Rule 3.3

3.3.1 Rule 3.3 does not prevent a member from donating his services to a charitable cause in appropriate circumstances, provided that in doing so he intends to gain no advantage over another member.

Rule 3.5

3.5.1 A member who is asked to give an opinion on the work of another architect shall observe this Rule except where it can be shown to be prejudicial to prospective litigation to do so. A member appointed to give expert advice shall not subsequently allow his terms of reference to be extended into those of an arbitrator.

Rule 3.6

3.6.1 A member is permitted to:

(a) send to the media articles and scripts about his own work or about architectural topics of general interest, and to allow his work to be displayed in exhibitions, provided that he gives no monetary consideration for publication or exhibition of his work;

(b) exhibit his name outside his office and on buildings in the course of construction, alteration or extension, provided that such exhibition of his name is done unostentatiously.

(c) and is encouraged to sign buildings where he has been commissioned for and is completing the Normal Services as described in the Conditions of Engagement, provided that the signing is done unostentatiously.

(d) allow his name and professional affix to appear on the letterheads and literature of his client or employer as consultant or staff architect but only for the purposes of his appointment and consistently with this Rule;

(e) send Practice Information Forms to the persons and in the manner approved by the RIBA Council;

(f) respond to an advertisement addressed to architects by a prospective client, overseas or at home, who wishes to hear from architects willing and able to undertake a particular project;

(g) apply or advertise for salaried employment;

(h) advertise in any form for staff and the advertisement may include details of salaries and other rewards offered, qualifications and experience required and indications of the type of work available provided that:
—the advertisement is not such, or advertising of such frequency, as to give the appearance that an attempt is being made solely or partly to bring the activities of the member or firm concerned to the notice of the public;
—no illustrations are used;
—the advertisement contains no comparatives or superlatives;

(i) notify a new or changed address, formation of or change in firms or partnerships by post once to his correspondents, and by advertisement in classified run-on form simultaneously and on one occasion only in any publication.

(j) pay for his name, address and telephone number only to be printed in standard form in a classified directory and for an expanded entry in any directory approved by the Council of the RIBA.

3.6.2 A member may commission an external public relations consultant or similarly designated person to carry out all or any aspect of his public relations policy provided that he furnishes the RIBA with a written declaration signed by the appointed person that he has received and read Bye-law 5, this Code and the Practice Note entitled "Members and public relations". In the declaration the appointed person must acknowledge that he will be in breach of contract with his client if any action of his brings the latter into breach of the Bye-laws or any Rule of this Code at any time.

4 Loyalty to professional colleagues

4.01 Professionalism has become institutionalised and professional institutes become confused easily with privileged bands of brothers affecting superior virtues. Those who would defend such institutions are often their own worst enemies, excusing lack of enterprise by professional dignity, and accepting brotherhood as the primary reason for rules which should be judged solely by whether they are in the public interest. Nevertheless, to question the place of a loyalty clause in a professional code is to question the need for a profession.

4.02 Contrary to what governments might admit, the architectural profession is highly competitive. Protection of a mandatory fee scale encourages architects to compete in terms of standards of service. Moreover, because of the nature of their pursuit, architects seem more critical of each other than members of most professions. Lawyers enjoy the fellowship which thrives on conflicts, while architects suffer the frustration of inadequate client relations and work loads which appear to depend more on luck than on merit.

4.03 In these circumstances it is important that a sense of professional loyalty should strengthen common acceptance of professional rules which both clients and architects may be tempted to break. Lord Devlin summed up the case for professional loyalty in *Hughes v* ARCUK, when he said: 'If a man joins a profession in which the use of trade weapons is barred and then proceeds to employ them, he is taking an unfair advantage over his fellows. They restrain themselves, believing rightly or wrongly that such restraint is essential to the good health of the profession as a whole; he gets the benefit of their restraint and fills his purse at their expense.'

4.04 The merit of particular rules is a separate issue. Lord Devlin makes it clear, particularly in the case of the RIBA, that there are strong ethical reasons for honouring undertakings entered into voluntarily.

Supplanting

4.05 Collective loyalty to professional colleagues is implicit in several clauses of the codes, covering instructions on occupations, fees, advertising and so on. By Rule 3.4, it is prohibited for an architect to 'attempt to supplant another architect'. Unlike those in previous issues the new codes quote no specific examples of unfair competition between architects or firms, as, for instance, by emphasising the importance of restraint on a natural tendency for one architect to feel he could do a job better than another. Before an architect's worth could be evaluated, competition of this sort would quickly inhibit or destroy proper architect-client relationships on which the professional service depends.

An architect's engagement is easily terminated, and it is often difficult to establish whether or not supplanting has taken place. ARCUK has pointed out that 'it is not sufficient to prove the mere fact that architect B is carrying on or has been instructed to carry on work in respect of which the client has formerly instructed architect A. A requisite of the offence is that architect B for personal gain, has ousted A from his appointment to the client and superseded him by some improper means or inducement' (ARCUK 1961 p 11).

4.06 Rule 3.5 simplifies the provisions of the previous ARCUK VI (1973) sub-clause (3) and RIBA (1974) (11) in regard to the requirement that an architect (or student) on being approached or instructed by a client to carry on architectural work that he knew or ought to have known another architect had been engaged upon, was obliged to notify the first architect accordingly. It is surprising that no reference is made in the revised RIBA Code or in the Notes thereto imposing a similar prohibition upon student members who might well find themselves in this situation.

4.07 There is further the undesirable probability that architects might inadvertently find themselves competing on a fee basis has increased in recent years for two reasons: an increasing amount of work is done on time basis; and public authorities are increasingly demanding precise estimates of fees at the outset of a job.

4.08 An architect reducing a previous estimate, particularly in terms of a quoted percentage, as a result of information about a competitor's estimate would be in breach of the codes. While clients are entitled to know the extent of their commitment, architects are frequently uncertain about the nature of the works, the appropriate percentages, the time required, or whether they are in competition for a job. The danger is that they may allow themselves to quote fees competitively, that they will be selected on the basis of price not merit, and that a tentative estimate will be regarded as a firm commitment. Clients are not above exploiting this situation, particularly for town planning work. Architects should read 'Note on estimates and fees' (RIBA *Journal* September 1968 p 346), and remember the concluding advice: 'Like so many of the architect's tasks this calls for tact, anticipation, but above all firmness.'

4.09 Rule 3.5 requires an architect, on being approached or instructed to proceed with work upon which he knows, or can ascertain by reasonable inquiry, that another architect is or has been engaged by the same client, to notify the other architect. This obligation is easily discharged, often to the second architect's advantage. Failure to comply can cause needless hardship or distress to architects who may otherwise be unaware that their services have been dispensed with. ARCUK has ruled that this obligation cannot be delegated to a client who should always be asked whether he has previously employed or is employing another architect. Architects employed by non-architectural organisations, eg package dealers who may take over work, are not exempt from the rule (ARCUK 1964 p 12).

4.10 There is no obligation to hold up work until the first architect's fees have been paid, although it may be useful to know what the situation is; nor is it disloyal to report on a colleague's work, otherwise clients might be denied the opportunity to remedy inadequate advice (ARCUK 1959 p 9). Many architects prefer not to accept such a commission, or wish to do so only on the basis that the first architect is informed. Should an architect accept such a brief unconditionally, his first duty to his client may prevent him from informing his professional colleague, and it might be difficult for him to accept any further commission in respect of the works, without arousing suspicions of supplanting. An architect asked to pass judgment on another's work should clearly not appear to gain at the other's expense.

Soliciting

4.11 Architects must not solicit work In case 98 an architect was found guilty of disgraceful conduct for *inter alia* 'approaching developers for the purpose of interesting them in the purchase of land for development' (ARCUK 1962 p 7). In case 101 an architect, retired from local government, was found guilty of disgraceful conduct for advertising his services and soliciting business as an adviser on town and country planning (ARCUK 1963 p 11). Because of the rule against soliciting, architects acting for developers who wish to submit uncommissioned schemes to local authorities are advised not to make the first approach. If the local authority wishes to consider a developer's proposal, an architect may then submit schemes and take part in negotiations, but only when acting on his client's express instructions (ARCUK 1963 p 13).

Speculative work

4.12 Architects must not work on a speculative basis, whether on their own initiative or for clients. An architect, x, knowing that a certain local site belonging to a city corporation was to be developed, prepared a scheme for its development. Another architect, Y, then hawked the scheme to estate agents who in turn approached a firm of developers. The architects did a great deal of work, as the site was enlarged and scheme developed, but all without remuneration and on the understanding that if the scheme were to go ahead, Y would get the job (ARCUK 1960 p 8).

Giving services free

4.13 ARCUK has advised that architects may act in an honorary capacity provided they do not give their services to advance their own interests or to gain an unfair advantage over professional colleagues, but has suggested that services to Citizens Advice Bureaux would best be organised through a local professional society (ARCUK 1968 p 11). But see also Rule 3.3 and Note 3.3.1. The latter comments that the Rule does not prevent a member from donating his services to a charitable cause in appropriate circumstances.

Competitions

4.14 In the revised codes there are two references to competitions. Principle 3, Rule 3.3 prohibits the preparation of designs in competition (*sic*) with other architects for a client without payment or for a reduced fee *except in a competition* conducted in accordance with RIBA Regulations or a competition otherwise approved by the RIBA and the International Union of Architects (UIA).* While RIBA, secondly, Note 2.8.1 forbids a 'member' who has been appointed assessor for any competition from subsequently acting in any capacity for the work except that he may act as arbitrator in any dispute between the promoters and the selected architect or as consultant where that appointment was arranged before his appointment as assessor. The RIBA Rules are a model of their kind, but even in the UK it is sometimes difficult to dissuade architects from taking part in loosely defined limited competitions, in which a client may get six designs on the cheap, while competing architects have no assurance that their entries will be judged properly.

Copyright

4.15 No reference is made in the revised codes to copyright. This is quite a reasonable omission to expect, since copyright is a matter of law and not of professional conduct. LEGAL STUDY 11 deals with the law, in breach of which architects are threatened more by their clients than their fellows. Nevertheless, although imitation in architecture can be a sincere form of flattery, architects would be well-advised to consult their colleagues before copying their designs.

Employer and employee

4.16 The codes at present have nothing to say about loyalty between architect employers and employees as professional colleagues. So it is interesting to see a practice note (RIBA *Journal* July 1966 p 330) advocating more acknowledgement to members of the design and building team when projects are described in the technical press.†

5 Advertising and public relations

RIBA members and public relations

5.01 The Practice Note issued with the above title by the RIBA (RIBA *Journal* May 1973 p 250) clearly defines the Institute's policy and the architect's responsibility in all matters of advertising and public relations in conforming with the requirements of the Code of Professional Conduct. The rules which govern the conduct of members in their public relations are based on Principle 3: that '*An architect shall only rely on ability and achievement as the basis of his advancement*'. With particular reference to the employment of external public relations consultants and to help members avoid the risk of breaching the rules the Council has approved the following measure (para 9 of the Practice Note):

Any member or firm who commissions an external public relations consultant or similarly designated person to carry out all or any aspect of that member's public relations policy must furnish the RIBA with a written declaration signed by the appointed person that he has received and read bylaw 5, the code of professional conduct, and this practice note. In the declaration, the appointed person must acknowledge that he will be in breach of contract with his client if any action of his brings the latter into breach of the bylaws or any clause of the code of professional conduct at any time.

Failure to fulfill this requirement would be prima facie evidence of professional misconduct on the part of the member or the firm concerned.

The requirement will not operate retrospectively, but any member with an existing contract with a PR consultant is expected to bring this practice note to his attention, and to obtain the consultant's confirmation that he will comply with the note in all respects. If the consultant refuses to give such confirmation, then the member is expected to terminate the contract.

Conduct not prohibited

5.02 Para 5 of the Practice Note:

Conduct not prohibited either specifically under the code of professional conduct or otherwise under the RIBA's disciplinary bylaws includes:

being named in or writing for the press, radio, or television

submitting unsolicited details and photographs of a member's own work to the architectural professional and technical press

taking part by invitation in radio or television programmes, films, or other public appearances featuring an architect's work

being featured in articles relating to a member's work

submitting unsolicited articles and scripts to the press, radio, or television on architectural topics of general interest

Examples of activities allowed

5.03 Para 6:

Examples of activities which are allowed, and may therefore form part of the duties undertaken by the person responsible for implementing a member's public relations policy, subject to the prohibitions set out in paragraph 7 and the warning in paragraph 8, are these:

instructing and advising on a public relations or communications plan

sending out practice information forms

entering the practice for awards and prizes (eg, Civic Trust, DOE housing, RIBA architecture, Concrete Society, British Steel, Reynolds)

entering allowed exhibitions (eg, Royal Academy)

organising photographs, slides, plans, and other records of buildings as they are designed and completed

ensuring that the practice holds a record of plans, drawings, slides, photographs, written material, lectures, and publications about a selection of its buildings, its reports, and its work in general

advising on the best selection of such work and maintaining the record

telling the architectural professional and technical press (home or abroad) about the practice's work, and placing research articles

keeping press lists and recording interests of particular publications

preparing material for efficient responses to any inquiries about work from the press, radio and television, publishers, students, potential clients visitors, and exhibitions

preparing brochures, subject to the following guidelines: they should be strictly factual and unostentatiously designed (photographs of buildings may be used, but no photographs of the architects concerned should appear), and they may be sent, in strictly limited quantities, only to existing clients or in response to a bona fide direct request

organising a practice's corporate image: the general house style of its name, stationery, reports, brochures, and offices

---

* RIBA Regulations for the Promotion and Conduct of Competitions and for Two-Stage Competitions (Model Form of Conditions). The International Union of Architects was founded in 1948

† It is AJ policy to name job architects and other members of the design team whenever a building is described in their pages. But some principals and senior architects in public offices are remarkably secretive about the contributions of their assistants THE EDITORS

keeping press cuttings and advising on replies

advising on writing for the press, on speaking on television, and on dealing with the media in general

advising clients on dealing with the publicity attached to buildings (eg, their opening)

obtaining feedback from clients on buildings in use

advising and dealing with internal public relations, the firm's relationship to its staff, an internal magazine

examining and analysing a practice's strengths and weaknesses, and the potential national and local workload, to advise how the practice can and should respond in the proper way to existing and future fields of work (eg, by locating existing and future fields of work by types of client groups, distinct market sectors, changes in professional structures, building types, and technical trends, using national, economic, industrial, and commercial trends, public and private sector expenditure, credit and interest rates, statistical forecasting and restraints, changes in political structure, and size and growth rate of client groups and building types)

Conduct prohibited
5.04 Para 7:

Conduct prohibited either specifically under the code of professional conduct or otherwise under the RIBA's disciplinary bylaws includes:

advertising or offering professional services by means of circulars or otherwise, and making paid announcements in the press (with certain exceptions, eg advertisements for staff)

distributing literature to potential clients without their request

soliciting personal features in the press, or personal appearances on radio or television

submitting unsolicited details and photographs of a member's own work to the lay press, radio, or television *

recommending the work or product of an advertiser

unfair competition, supplanting, inducements

Paragraph 8 warns that

Members should beware of the fact that some journalists write not only for the architectural professional and technical press, but also for the lay press. Therefore, a member should ensure that details and photographs of his own work are addressed to the editor of the architectural professional journal or technical magazine, and not to any journalist by name, or he will run the risk of contravening the ban on sending unsolicited material about his own work to the lay press.

ARCUK Code—Appendix 2
Architects (Registration) Act 1931 Sections 7, 8 and 9

Removal of name from Register for criminal offence or professional misconduct

7
(1) If any registered person is convicted of a criminal offence, or if the committee appointed for the purposes of this section, after an inquiry held thereunder in respect of any registered person, report to the Council that that person has been guilty of conduct disgraceful to him in his capacity as an architect, the Council may, subject to the provisions of this section, cause the name of that person to be removed from the Register, and where the name of any person is duly removed from the Register under this subsection, he shall, during such period thereafter as the Council may determine on the occasion of the removal, be disqualified for registration under this Act:

* But they may be submitted to the Architectural Press THE EDITORS

Provided that the Council may at any time, either of their own motion or on the application of the person concerned, cause his name to be restored to the Register, either without payment of a fee or on payment of such fee not exceeding the fee payable for registration under this Act as the Council may determine.

(2) For the purposes of this section there shall, subject as hereinafter provided, be appointed annually by the Council a committee (in this Act referred to as 'the Discipline Committee') consisting of eight persons, of whom four shall be registered persons nominated by the Council (including one person who is practising as an architect in Scotland), one shall be nominated by the Commissioners of Works, one shall be nominated by the Minister of Health, and two shall be nominated by the President of the Law Society, and it shall be the duty of the said Committee, if so directed by the Council to inquire into, and report to the Council on, any case in which it is alleged that a registered person has been guilty of conduct disgraceful to him in his capacity as an architect:

Provided that, in the case of any inquiry under this section in respect of a registered person who is a member of any of the bodies referred to in the First Schedule to this Act, the council or other governing body of each such body of which the registered person is a member shall (except where the Discipline Committee already includes a member of that body) be entitled to nominate one person for membership of that Committee, and upon the name of any person duly nominated as aforesaid being submitted to them in the prescribed manner, the Council shall appoint that person to be an additional member of the Discipline Committee for the purposes of the inquiry and of the report of the Committee in connection therewith.

(3) It shall be the duty of the Council to direct the Discipline Committee to hold an inquiry under this section in any case in which it appears to the Council that such an inquiry is necessary.

(4) Where the Council direct the Discipline Committee to hold any inquiry under this section in respect of a registered person, the Council shall forthwith cause to be served on that person a written notice of the proposed inquiry, specifying the time and place at which it is to be held and the subject matter thereof, and that person shall, on application made in the prescribed manner and within the prescribed period from the date of the service of the said notice, be entitled to be heard by the Discipline Committee at the inquiry, either in person or by counsel or a solicitor.

(5) Where the Council intend to remove the name of any person from the Register in pursuance of this section, then, before so doing, the Council shall cause a written notice of their intention to be served on that person and shall, on application made by that person in the prescribed manner within three months from the date of the service of the said notice, consider any representations with regard to the matter which may be made by him to the Council, either in person or by counsel or solicitor.

Notice of removal of name from Register

8
Where the Council cause the name of any person to be removed from the Register, they shall forthwith cause written notice of the removal to be served on that person, and where, in connection with the removal, the Council have determined that the person in question shall, during any period, be disqualified for registration, the determination of the Council shall be specified in the said notice:

Provided that nothing in the foregoing provisions of this section shall apply in a case where the Council cause the name of any person to be removed from the Register in consequence of the death of that person.

Right of appeal against removal of name from Register

9
Any person aggrieved by the removal of his name from the Register, or by a determination of the Council that he be disqualified for registration during any period, may, within three months from the date on which notice of the removal or determination was served on him, appeal to the High Court or Court of Session against the removal or determination, and on any such appeal the Court may give such directions in the matter as they think proper, and the order of the Court shall be final.

Acknowledgements

The print at the beginning of this section is reproduced by courtesy of the Trustees of the British Museum. The print on page 174 is from an original drawing in Lincoln's Inn Library, by courtesy of the librarian.

References

Architects (Registration) Act 1931

Architects (Registration) Act 1938

Architects (Registration) (Amendment) Act 1969

ARCUK Code of Professional Conduct. January 1976 revision

RIBA Code of Professional Conduct. January 1976 revision

RIBA Charter (1937), Supplemental Charter 1971 and By-laws

RIBA Practice Note 'Members and public relations', RIBA Journal, May 1973

ARCUK Annual Reports

ARCUK Booklet (General information) March 1976

HIGGINS, GARTH 'The architect as professional', RIBA Journal, April 1964

Legal study 16

Professional conduct in Scotland

This study describes reasons for having a separate Code of Professional Conduct for Scottish architects before discussing the RIAS Code clause by clause and comparing it with the RIBA Code.
The Royal Incorporation of Architects in Scotland has yet to consider revision of the Scottish Code of Conduct. In the meantime, readers are referred to LEGAL STUDY 15, which covers the revised ARCUK and RIBA Codes, both of which may also be binding on architects practising in Scotland

1 Introduction

The Codes of Professional Conduct published by ARCUK and the RIBA are obviously binding on their members wherever they practise, but members of the RIBA who practise in Scotland and are also members of the RIAS have a third Code with which to contend, namely the Code of Professional Conduct published by the RIAS. This Code is also obviously binding upon RIAS members who do not belong to the RIBA. Architects practising in Scotland may therefore be subject to either three or two Codes of Professional Conduct depending upon whether they belong to the RIBA and the RIAS or only the RIAS.

To the general public it must seem strange that architects are subject to so many Codes of Conduct and one would think it would not be beyond the bounds of human capabilities to produce one 'super' Code acceptable to all three organisations. The grounds for confusion have increased recently since the RIBA completely rewrote its own Code in 1975; prior to this the RIAS and the RIBA Codes were identical in many respects, but they now approach the problem of professional conduct from completely different angles. The fact of the matter is that the RIAS Code is outmoded and out of date, and it is to be hoped that the RIAS Council will take an early opportunity of revising it.

To appreciate reasons for the existence of the RIAS Code it is necessary to remember that when established in 1916 the RIAS became the headquarters of the architectural profession in Scotland. The RIBA had at that time little influence in that country, and many architects practising there belonged only to the RIAS and as a body with its own Royal Charter it was right that the RIAS should publish its own Code. Times have changed and the RIBA's presence is felt to a greater or lesser degree throughout Scotland today although in practice it has delegated nearly all its functions in that country to the RIAS which fulfils entirely the duties of an English RIBA Regional Office as well as carrying out many national functions. Furthermore there are still in Scotland a number of architects who do not belong to the RIBA and who would therefore have no Code of Conduct at all (apart from that published by the ARCUK) if the RIAS did not publish its own.

2 RIAS disciplinary procedure

The existence of these two codes raises some interesting points on occasions when an architect has to be disciplined by his professional organisation. On the maxim that a man cannot be punished twice for the same offence, it is, one assumes, unthinkable that an architect dealt with under the RIAS Code should be punished for the same offence under the RIBA one, or vice versa. On the other hand if an architect is struck off the RIBA roll for some offence, he would also be unacceptable to the RIAS. In practice a *modus vivendi* has

been worked out between the RIAS and the RIBA, which has been given official recognition in the latest revision of the RIBA Supplemental Charter and By-laws, and empowers the RIBA council to take account *inter alia* of a report of the Disciplinary Committee of the RIAS and of the decision of the council of the RIAS

If the RIAS takes disciplinary action against one of its members, it can do so only under the RIAS Code, and it would be incompetent for the RIAS to take proceedings under the RIBA Code. It follows that the RIAS is not able to discipline a member of the RIBA practising in Scotland unless the latter also belongs to the RIAS, but as the great majority of architects practising in this country have dual membership, this difficulty has not, so far as is known, arisen.

3 Study of the RIAS Code

An Architect in practice, if a Member of the Royal Incorporation or a Member of the RIBA practising in Scotland, is governed by established customs accepted and observed by the Architectural profession, and more particularly by the Charter and Bye-laws of the Royal Institute and Royal Incorporation which render him liable in the case of unprofessional conduct to reprimand, suspension, or expulsion at the discretion of these Councils.

The following may be considered to record in a general way the practice of Architects and also to indicate a standard of conduct in any special cases not specifically referred to therein.

Clause 1 The RIAS Code starts by recognising the fact that architects practising in Scotland may be subject to two Codes of Conduct. Clause 1, which follows closely the wording of clauses 2 and 3 of the 1964 RIBA Code, is in the following terms:

1 An Architect is remunerated solely by his professional fees and is debarred from any other source of remuneration in connection with the works and duties entrusted to him. It is the duty of an Architect to uphold in every way possible the Scale of Professional Charges adopted by the Royal Incorporation. An Architect must not accept any work which involves the giving or receiving of discounts or commissions, nor must he accept any discount, gift or commission from contractors or tradesmen, whether employed upon his works or not.

2 If an Architect own, or have a commercial interest in, any material, device, or invention used in building he must inform his client thereof, and must obtain his sanction before permitting it to be used in works executed under his direction.

Clause 2 has no exact counterpart in either the revised or previous RIBA Codes; it makes quite clear that if an architect owns or has a commercial interest in any material he must first obtain his client's sanction before permitting it to be used in works executed under his direction. A member of the RIAS should conform with the requirements of this clause at all times.

Clause 3 is in the following terms:

> 3 An Architect may be a director of any company, including a building society registered under the Building Societies Acts, the Building Centre, London, and the Building Centre, Scotland, except a company trading in materials used in or whose activities are otherwise connected with the building industry or engaged in the financing or erection of buildings.
>
> His name and affix may appear on the notepaper of the company.

This clause, which no longer reflects current architectural opinion on whether architects should be directors of limited companies involved in the building industry in any way, is an example showing why there is an urgent need to revise the RIAS Code. Theoretically a member of the RIAS is bound by this clause although modern thinking on the subject is contained in the current RIBA Code (see LEGAL STUDY 15 para 3.01 *et seq*).

> 4 An Architect must not publicly advertise nor offer his services by means of circulars. He may, however, publish illustrations or descriptions of his work, and exhibit his name on buildings in course of execution (providing it is done in an unostentatious manner) and may sign them when completed.

Clause 4 is a fair summary of what was contained in clauses 6, 7, 8 and 9 of the former RIBA Code and still reflects current opinion on this topic.

> 5 An Architect must not attempt to supplant another Architect nor must he compete with another Architect by means of a reduction of fees or by other inducement.

Clause 5 is identical to Clause 10 of the former RIBA Code and while still obligatory it is interesting to note that though even 5 years ago it was considered unthinkable that an architect should seek to undercut a fellow architect by reducing his fees, reports and comments published by the Monopolies Commission and others suggest the day may not be far off when a fee scale is no longer mandatory.

> 6 In all cases of dispute between employer and contractor the Architect must act in an impartial manner. He must interpret the conditions of a contract with entire fairness as between the employer and the contractor.

Clause 6 is self-explanatory and is identical with clause 13 of the former RIBA Code.

> 7 An Architect must not permit the insertion of any clause in tenders, bills of quantities, or other contract documents which provides for payment to be made to him by the contractor (except for duplicate copies of drawings or documents) whatever may be the consideration, unless with the full knowledge and approval of his client.

Clause 7 is identical with clause 14 of the former RIBA Code.

> 8 An Architect should not take part in any competition as to which the preliminary warning of the Royal Institute or Royal Incorporation has been issued, and must not take part in any competition as to which the Council of the Royal Institute shall have declared by a Resolution published in the Journal of the Royal Institute that Members or Licentiates must not take part, because the Conditions are not in accordance with the published Regulations of the Royal Institute or Royal Incorporation for Architectural Competitions.

Clause 8 contains similar prohibitions to those found in the former RIBA Code.

> 9 An Architect must not act as Architect or joint Architect for a work which is or has been the subject of a competition in which he is or has been engaged as Assessor.

Clause 9 repeats the first paragraph of clause 17 of the former RIBA Code.

> 10 An Architect having any matter for complaint or protest against another member of the profession or against the conduct of an architectural competition in which he agrees to take part, or an Assessor's award therein, should bring the matter before the Council of the Incorporation through his own Chapter and must on no account make any other protest.

Clause 10 This important clause has no counterpart in either the present or the former RIBA Code. Its value should not be underestimated as it provides a dignified way of dealing with differences of opinion between professional colleagues which otherwise might have to be argued out in public with consequent detrimental effect to the profession as a whole. It is to be hoped that when the RIAS revises its Code this clause is retained and that it will find a place in any 'super' Code which might eventually be published.

> 11 It is desirable that in cases where the Architect takes out the quantities for his buildings he should be paid directly by the client and not through the Contractor except with the previous consent of the client.

Clause 11 is identical with clause 15 of the former RIBA Code.

> 12 The business of Auctioneering and House Agency are inconsistent with the profession of an Architect.

Clause 12. The provisions of this clause are found in clause 5 (b) of the former RIBA Code although one should notice that the latter included a firm prohibition against a directorship in the type of Company concerned, whereas the RIAS Code merely states it is 'inconsistent with the profession of an Architect'.

> 13 An Architect must not accept an appointment in any commercial firm in which the extent of his remuneration is affected by the profits of the firm.

Clause 13 is identical with clause 4 of the former RIBA Code.

AJ Legal Handbook

Section 11
Conditions of engagement

Legal study 17

Conditions of engagement

This study introduces important practical legal aspects of the architect's appointment by his client before giving a detailed commentary on the latest edition of the RIBA Conditions of Engagement with an explanation of the fee scales.
The RIBA Conditions apply to Scotland as well as England

1 The appointment

1.01 An architect has many factors to consider when considering a commission and it is important that he should fully appreciate their implications before entering into a legal commitment to undertake the work.

He must be satisfied that the client has the authority and resources to commission the work; he must appreciate the background to the proposal and understand its scope at least in outline; and he must be aware of any other consultants who have been or are likely to be associated with the project.

The architect must be satisfied that he has the experience or competence to undertake the work; that the office has the necessary finance, staff and resources; and that the proposal will not be in conflict with the Code of Professional Conduct, other commissions in the practice or the policy of the practice.

The preliminary negotiations between the parties may involve the exchange of business references and where the architect and employer are previously unknown to each other more detailed inquiries may be necessary.

Some aspects of the architect/client relationship are discussed in the RIBA *Handbook of architectural practice and management*.

1.02 The employer, particularly in the commercial field, is often unaware of the Code of Professional Conduct or its significance, and the architect in accepting a commission must ensure that he is not in breach of the Code (see LEGAL STUDIES 15 and 16). In addition to being responsible for upholding the Code, the architect has a duty to explain its significance and to satisfy himself that the commission is being offered within the conditions of the Code. He has a duty to check whether another architect has been previously engaged upon the project and if so must inform him, provided of course that he can be contacted (LEGAL STUDY 15 para 4.06 and 4.09). However, unless there has been improper conduct, the former architect has no power to prevent the new architect undertaking the work, although questions of outstanding fees, the ownership of drawings and copyright (see LEGAL STUDY 11) may arise.

2 Memorandum of Agreement

2.01 Although in law a verbal agreement may be accepted as the basis of a contract of engagement between architect and employer, the risks inherent in such an arrangement are obvious and a formal procedure of appointment should always be adopted (LEGAL STUDY 1 para 4.07 *et seq*). Such a procedure creates a clearly identifiable legal basis for the commission and establishes a sound business approach to the relationship between architect and employer. The appointment may be made by either an informal exchange of letters or exchange of a formal memorandum of agreement, in each case accompanied by copies of the Conditions of Engagement. The exchange of letters is frequently used but it is not recommended. Informal letters of appointment are liable to misinterpretation and misunderstanding and are often the source of difficulties and subsequent disagreements between the parties (LEGAL STUDY 1 para 3.02 and 4.07).

FORM OF AGREEMENT FOR GENERAL USE BETWEEN A BUILDING OWNER AND AN ARCHITECT OR FIRM OF ARCHITECTS

Memorandum of Agreement

made this _____ day of _____ 19__

BETWEEN _____

of _____

(hereinafter called 'the Employer') of the one part and _____

practising under the style and title of _____

at _____

(hereinafter called 'the Architect') of the other part.

WHEREAS the Employer is proposing to _____

at _____

(hereinafter called 'the building project').

AND WHEREAS the Employer wishes to appoint an Architect in connection with the building project.

NOW THIS AGREEMENT WITNESSETH AND IT IS HEREBY AGREED between the parties as follows:

1 THE Employer hereby appoints the Architect, and the Architect hereby agrees to act as Architect in connection with the building project upon the terms of the RIBA Conditions of Engagement, current at the date hereof, a copy whereof is annexed hereto.

2 [A] THE Employer hereby agrees to pay the Architect for the services specified in Part 2·11 of the said RIBA Conditions of Engagement fees at the rate set out in Table 1/2* of the said RIBA Conditions of Engagement and for any other services performed by the Architect in connection with the building project, such additional fees as may be prescribed in regard thereto in the said RIBA Conditions of Engagement.

2 [B] THE Employer hereby agrees to pay the Architect for the normal service specified in Part 2·11 of the said RIBA Conditions of Engagement fees at the rate of __% of the total construction cost. Where for any reason partial services only are performed, the fees for such services shall be as follows, that is to say: for the services listed in work stages A and/or B of the said RIBA Conditions of Engagement fees upon the basis of a time charge; for the services listed in work stage C fees equivalent to 15% of the aforementioned percentage; for the services listed in work stage D fees equivalent to 20% of the said percentage; and for the services listed in work stages EFG fees equivalent to 40% of the said percentage. If the Architect carries out in connection with the building project services other than those falling within the said Part 2, the Employer agrees to pay such additional fees as may be prescribed in regard thereto in the said RIBA Conditions of Engagement.

Delete reference to Table 1 or Table 2 as appropriate; in the case of New Works, Table 1 will apply; in the case of Works to Existing Buildings, Table 2 will apply.

Note: *If a higher percentage than the basic percentage for normal services mentioned in Tables 1 or 2 is to be charged paragraph 2 [A] must be deleted and paragraph 2 [B] must be completed by inserting the percentage which is to be charged.*

2.02 The Memorandum of Agreement form prepared by the RIBA 'for general use between a building owner and an architect or firm of architects' or its equivalent drawn up by a solicitor should be used. Its title may be clumsy and misleading but its contents are precise.

Some large industrial and commercial companies and some public authorities require the use of their own forms of agreement to appointments. These forms are occasionally adaptations of forms prepared for other purposes such as

3* In so far as fees for any of the services referred to in the preceding paragraph fall to be assessed upon the basis of a time charge under Part 5 of the said RIBA Conditions of Engagement, the Employer agrees to pay the Architect fees for principal's time at the rate of .... pounds per hour.

4 The Employer hereby agrees to pay the Architect's fees in accordance with paragraphs 2 and 3 hereof on demand by instalments as provided in the said RIBA Conditions of Engagement.

5 The Employer hereby agrees to employ and pay a Quantity Surveyor in accordance with Section 1.2 of the said RIBA Conditions of Engagement to prepare bills of quantities, measure and value authorised variations on the building contract and make valuations for certificates, and to assist in the preparation of details of the final account as mentioned in paragraph 8 hereunder.

6 The employment and payment of Consultants shall be in accordance with Section 1.2 of the said RIBA Conditions of Engagement.

7 The employment and payment of a Clerk of Works shall be in accordance with Section 1.6 of the said RIBA Conditions of Engagement.

**8 The Architect hereby agrees that as soon as he has issued his Final Certificate he will supply to the Employer such details of the final account as will enable Standing Orders or other Financial Regulations to be complied with.

9 If the Architect shall die or become incapacitated from acting as such Architect as aforesaid, the Employer may make full use of all or any drawings, estimates or other documents prepared by the Architect pursuant to and for use under this Agreement without prejudice to the lien on such drawings or documents against unpaid fees. The Employer shall make no use of such drawings or documents except for the purpose of the building works the subject of this Agreement.

10 If any question, difference or dispute shall at any time arise between the parties in respect of the construction of this Agreement or concerning anything herein contained or arising out of this Agreement or as to rights, liabilities or duties of the parties hereunder the same shall be resolved in accordance with the provisions of Sections 7.3, 7.4 and 7.5 of the said RIBA Conditions of Engagement.

*Note: An appropriate hourly remuneration should be inserted in this paragraph if principal's time is to be charged at a higher rate than the 5 pounds per hour mentioned in Section 5.1 of the RIBA Conditions of Engagement.

**Note: Paragraph 8 is applicable only where the Employer is a Public Authority, or where the Employer is a body corporate other than a Public Authority whose own internal audit arrangements require such information to be available In other cases the paragraph should be deleted.

As witness the hands of the parties the day and year first above written

Witness to the Signature of the Employer

Name

Address

Description

Witness to the Signature of the Architect

Name

Address

Description

OR

In witness whereof the Common Seal of the Employer has been hereunto affixed and the Architect has hereunto set his hand and seal the day and year first above written

The common seal of

was hereunto affixed in the presence of

Signed, Sealed and Delivered by the said

in the presence of

Name

Address

Description

* Memorandum of Agreement. Copyright RIBA 1971. Amended April 1973

engineering services and may not be immediately applicable without modification. They are often more complicated than the RIBA form and not necessarily more precise or comprehensive.

If an employer insists upon the use of his own form of memorandum of appointment, the conditions should be carefully compared with those of the RIBA form, and where there are material differences the advice of the RIBA or a solicitor should be sought.

2.03 The authority of the architect is strictly limited to the terms of his appointment, ie as shown in the form of Memorandum of Agreement and in the Conditions of Engagement. It is in the interest of the employer, the architect, the quantity surveyor and other independent consultants that these terms should be fully and clearly understood (LEGAL STUDY 1 para 4.07 et seq).

2.04 Where a commission arises out of a recognised competition, the competition conditions usually form the conditions of appointment. Difficulties develop occasionally when the subsequent building is substantially different from that originally envisaged and where there has been a material change in the conditions.

2.05 Difficulties arise when the form or scope of the service required changes during an engagement. It is important that the client should be immediately informed of the implications of changes, particularly in relation to responsibilities and fees.

2.06 Forms of memoranda of appointment should be signed by both parties, each keeping a copy, before the beginning of work and the signatures should be formally witnessed. The forms may be sealed if either party should so desire. The normal formalities would be involved and of course the architect would have to consider his extended responsibilities carefully (LEGAL STUDY 1 para 3.02).

2.07 The architect's contract of engagement is usually personal to himself or the partnership. He cannot delegate his duties completely but he is under no obligation to carry out all the work personally nor to go into every detail himself. The extent to which he may be prepared to delegate his duties to an assistant is a matter of competence, confidence, reliability and experience of the assistant and the principal. The architect has become increasingly dependent upon the skill and labour of others within his office and elsewhere, but he remains responsible to his client within the terms of his appointment and continues to be responsible for the acts and defaults of his subordinates. The subordinates in turn are responsible to their principal and could be held liable to their employer for the results of their acts (see LEGAL STUDY 2 para 4.02 and LEGAL STUDY 15 para 2.04).

3 Termination

3.01 The contract of engagement between the architect and his employer may be terminated by either party on reasonable notice. Reasons for the termination need not be stated, but in the event of dispute over outstanding fees or payments, the cause of the termination would be of importance to an arbitrator or court in determining an award.

In the event of the termination of the contract, any outstanding fees for work properly carried out become due to the architect, but it is unlikely that the employer could be held responsible for any loss of anticipated profits on work not yet carried out.

3.02 Difficulties sometimes arise in connection with the use of material prepared before termination of engagement*. It is generally assumed that if the work was substantially advanced at the time of termination it would be unreasonable for the employer not to be entitled to complete the project, and it is usually accepted that the employer is entitled to a licence to use the drawings to complete the work effectively. The copyright remains with the architect (see LEGAL STUDY 7 para 7.09 and 11 para 4.01 *et seq*).

3.03 In the event of the death or incapacity of the architect, it is usually held that the employer is entitled to the use of the drawings and other documents to complete the work. Provision for the procedure to be adopted in such circumstances is included in the standard forms of agreement. The death of either party to a personal contract generally dissolves the contract (LEGAL STUDY 1 para 3.05), but it is usually possible (with agreement) for a third party to assume responsibility for completion of the contract. Agreements of appointment should be between companies and partnerships wherever possible, rather than between individuals so as to avoid the occasional embarrassing technical difficulties and delays that occur in the transfer of responsibility to the company or partnership in the event of death.

3.04 In the event of the bankruptcy of either party, the contract can usually be continued, subject to assurances about fees and monies which may be due or become due.

4 Ownership

4.01 Ownership of drawings and other documents is often a source of debate. Correspondence and other documents exchanged between the architect and others in connection with the approval of plans, the running of the project or the administration of the contract by the architect (in his role as agent) technically belong to the employer, although it is unusual for all these documents to be transferred to the employer (LEGAL STUDY 11 para 2.06). Other material prepared in the architect's professional capacity belongs to the architect. This accounts for the greater part of the documentation prepared in the course of a project.

5 Conditions of Engagement

5.01 'An Architect in private practice shall inform his client in advance of the Conditions of Engagement and the scale of charges. . . .' (LEGAL STUDY 15 para 2.05). The scales recognised are those of the constituent bodies of ARCUK. In practice the RIBA scale is most commonly used.
Members of the RIBA are required to uphold and apply the scale of professional charges adopted by the council of the RIBA. This scale of charges has varied from time to time but the principle of remuneration based upon a percentage of the total building cost with a time charge where a percentage fee is not applicable has remained throughout.

5.02 In May 1976 the RIBA issued revised Conditions of Engagement, the latest in a long sequence which began with *Professional practice and charges of the architects* in 1862 (see Frank Jenkins, *Architect and patron*).
This edition of the conditions, like its predecessors, attempts to define the services of the architect and the charges applicable to an ever-widening range of activities. It attempts to define the services comprehensively and concisely. Inevitably

* Two recent cases (*Stovin-Bradford v Volpoint Properties Ltd* and *Blair v Osborne & Tomkins*) have resulted in amendments to the conditions to try to clarify the position

it is criticised on both counts. Some architects dislike the precise definitions of service, especially in connection with the work stage definitions of normal service, and would have preferred a more generalised statement which might have allowed more flexibility in interpretation of particular cases. Other architects, including some who represent clients, would have liked an even more detailed statement.

5.03 The Monopolies and Mergers Commission is currently engaged in a study of the application of the Scale of Charges by architects. This study is the latest of a series of similar exercises which have taken place over the last twelve years. These enquiries have mainly concerned the mandatory application of the fee scale. The RIBA attitude has been expressed in *The Case for mandatory minimum fees*.

Scale of charges
5.04 A number of detail changes in the Scale of Charges have been made since the new form of Conditions of Engagement was introduced in 1971. Further changes are likely to be made from time to time and although changes are usually concerned with minor matters it is important that a copy of the current Conditions should be kept with the Memorandum of Agreement for each commission.

5.05 Critics have rightly complained that the Conditions of Engagement are not understood readily by lay clients, particularly in such matters as interpretation of additional services and reduction of fees for repetitive work. The architect has a clear responsibility to explain the scale to his client at the outset; it may not be assumed that the architect has discharged his responsibility simply by issuing a copy of the conditions to his client.

5.06 Members of the RIBA who have been engaged may provide provisional cost forecasts of their professional services quoting the appropriate percentage fees on any constructional cost limits supplied by the client and estimated time charges on other work. But as in all cases of financial forecasts, it is important that the service to be provided should be clearly defined and that care should be taken in drawing up estimates of time charges (LEGAL STUDY 15 para 3.1 *2et seq*).

5.07 Estimates of fees for competitive purposes may not be submitted and architects may not compete in respect of fees or charges.

5.08 The fees and charges laid down are a minimum scale only and special circumstances might justify higher fees and charges, but if these are to be levied they must be agreed at the outset between employer and architect.

5.09 Any Value Added Tax (VAT) chargeable on the services of the architect is chargeable to the client at the appropriate rate current at the time. Clients who are taxable persons under the Finance Act 1972 are able to recover such input tax from the Customs and Excise department.

5.10 Where the RIBA Conditions of Engagement are not recognised, members are required to uphold any local scales which are applicable. If there are no locally-recognised scales, the architect may adopt his own, provided that in so doing he does not come into conflict with a fellow member.

5.11 It should be noted that the Scale of Charges applies to all commissions including those for Government bodies.

6 Content of the Conditions

6.01 The RIBA Conditions of Engagement are in seven parts with three tables.

Part 1 General: this deals with the general Conditions of Engagement and applies irrespective of the nature or extent of service provided.

Part 2 Normal service: this describes the services normally provided by the architect. The fees for work stages c to H, ie outline proposals to completion, are generally charged on a percentage basis as described in part 3. Other fees are charged additionally on a time basis as described in part 5. Initial consultations may be given free of charge.

Part 3 Fees for normal services: this defines how the percentage fees for the normal services are calculated and may be varied, and when they and other charges become due. The percentage fees are based upon the actual total construction cost.

Part 4 Other services: this describes other services which may be provided by the architect, usually on a time basis.

Part 5 Time charges: this defines the method of calculating charges on the basis of a minimum hourly rate for principals and other staff, taking into account the complexity of the work, the qualifications, experience and responsibility of the architect and the character of any negotiations.

Part 6 Out-of-pocket expenses: this outlines the range of reasonable out-of-pocket expenses to which the architect is entitled.

Part 7 Termination, abandoned works and interpretation: this describes the basis of remuneration for abandoned work and the procedures to be adopted in connection with resumed commissions, interpretation of the Conditions of Engagement, disputes, and arbitration.

RIBA Conditions of Engagement*

7 Part 1: General

1.00 This part deals with general conditions of engagement and will apply irrespective of the nature or extent of services to be provided.

1.1 Remuneration

1.10 The services normally provided by an architect in studying his client's needs, advising him, preparing, directing and co-ordinating design and inspecting work executed under a building contract are described in Part 2: Normal Services. Other services that an architect may provide are described in Part 4: Other Services.

1.11 The Normal Services for a building project are divided into a sequence of Work Stages A to H through which the architect's work progresses, augmented by services which vary widely in nature and extent with the circumstances of the project.

1.12 Fees for Work Stages C to H are generally calculated as a percentage of the total construction cost of the works, as described in Part 3 of these Conditions.

1.13 Fees for Work Stages A and B and for those other services which are likely to vary widely in nature and extent are charged additionally on a time basis, as described in Part 5 of these Conditions.

1.14 In exceptional circumstances, any service normally charged on a percentage fee may, by prior written agreement between architect and client, be charged on a time basis, in which case the architect shall notify the RIBA.

1.15 The minimum fees and charges described in these Conditions may not be sufficient in all circumstances, in which case higher fees and charges may be agreed between the client and architect when the architect is commissioned.

1.16 The amount of any value added tax on the services of the architect arising under the Finance Act 1972 (or any statutory modification or re-enactment thereof) shall be chargeable to the client in addition to the amount of the architect's fees and charges calculated in accordance with Part 3, Part 5 and Part 6 of these Conditions.

Remuneration

7.01 Clauses 1.10 to 1.13 are references to comments upon the principles of remuneration which appear elsewhere.

Clause 1.14 provides the authority for changing from a percentage basis to a time basis in exceptional circumstances

* As amended May 1976

subject to prior agreement between architect and employer (and notification of the RIBA). Notification of the RIBA, which is the important feature of this clause, protects both architect and employer.

Clause 1.15 provides the architect with authority to charge higher fees in exceptional circumstances subject to prior agreement between architect and employer.

Clause 1.16 clearly states that the fees do not include VAT or other taxes and that separate charges must be made for any statutory taxes.

1.2 Consultants

1.20 Normal Services do not include quantity surveying, town planning, civil, structural, mechanical, electrical or heating and ventilating engineering or similar consultants' services. Where the provision of such services is within the competence of the architect's own office or where they are provided by consultants in association with the architect, fees shall be in accordance with the scales of fees of the appropriate professional bodies, but all time charges shall be in accordance with Part 5 of these Conditions.

1.21 Where the services of more than one profession are provided by a single firm or consortium, fees shall be the sum of the appropriate fees for the individual professional services rendered.

1.22 The architect will advise on the need for independent consultants and will be responsible for the direction and integration of their work but not for the detailed design, inspection and performance of the work entrusted to them.

1.23 Independent consultants and quantity surveyors should be nominated or approved by the architect in agreement with the client. They should be appointed and paid by the client.

Consultants

7.02 Clause 1.20 identifies the more obvious services that are outside the normal services of the architect and makes provision for additional fees for them at the scales of the appropriate bodies.

Clause 1.21 covers the case of fees in the multi-professional office or consortium and presumably allays suspicions that the multi-professional situation offers the opportunity of fee-cutting in an all-in service.

Clause 1.22 somewhat ambiguously charges the architect with direction and integration of the work of independent consultants but not responsibility for detailed design and performance. The principle is clear but the practical interpretation is a source of misunderstanding, friction and dispute.

Clause 1.23 implies that the architect has the right to refuse the employer's proposals for an independent consultant or quantity surveyor. The architect must have sound reasonable grounds for the refusal and vexatious refusal could result in the termination of the architect's own appointment. Responsibility for the appointment and payment of consultants is stated clearly.

1.3 Responsibilities

1.30 The architect must have the authority of his client before initiating any service or Work Stage.

1.31 The architect shall not make any material alteration, addition to or omission from the approved design without the knowledge and consent of the client, except if found necessary during construction for constructional reasons in which case he shall inform the client without delay.

1.32 The architect shall inform the client if he has reason to believe the total authorised expenditure or contract period are likely to be materially varied.

1.33 The architect shall advise on the selection and appointment of the contractor and shall make such periodic visits to the site as he considers necessary to inspect generally the progress and quality of the work and to determine in general if the work is proceeding in accordance with the contract documents.

1.34 The architect shall not be responsible for the contractor's operational methods, techniques, sequences or procedures, nor for safety precautions in connection with the work, nor shall he be responsible for any failure by the contractor to carry out and complete the work in accordance with the terms of the building contract between the client and the contractor.

Responsibilities

7.03 It is important that the architect should recognise the significance of clause 1.30. Failure to obtain approval before initiating any service or work stage could result in the architect not only losing his claim to the professional fees involved in the particular stage, but also possibly being held responsible for the costs incurred in the work.

Similarly clause 1.31 requires the architect to obtain the approval of the employer before proceeding with any material alteration, addition or omission, except where such changes are found necessary for constructional reasons, in which case the employer has to be informed as soon as possible. The significance of the clause lies mainly in the interpretation of the meaning of 'material change'. In practice it relates to the professional understanding between architect and employer and it is a matter of trust and confidence between the parties. Nevertheless it is a source of potential difficulty and the architect should not assume an authority which he has not been given, to make material changes.

Clause 1.32 is a useful reminder to architects. Disputes between architects and employers largely centre around problems of time and cost, and this clause reminds architects that it is their duty to inform their clients of progress in terms of both time and cost throughout projects.

Clause 1.33 limits the architect's responsibility for inspection to such periodic visits as he may consider necessary to ensure that the work is proceeding in accordance with the contract. It is not the architect's responsibility to provide constant supervision but if he believes that constant supervision is necessary, he has an obligation to inform his employer of what is required and to invite him to sanction arrangements for the appointment of suitable site staff (see clause 1.6. Inspection—para 7.06 of this study).

Clause 1.34 states the areas of work for which the architect cannot be held responsible and, in particular, emphasises that he cannot be held responsible for the failure of the contractor to carry out or complete the works. It is an important safeguard and it protects the architect, but it does not remove the onus from the architect in reporting to his client upon the progress of the contractor (para 7.03).

1.4	**Specialist sub-contractors and suppliers**
1.40	The architect may recommend that specialist sub-contractors and suppliers should design and execute any part of the work. He will be responsible for the direction and integration of their work, and for general inspection of their work in accordance with Stage H of the Normal Services, but not for the detailed design or performance of the work entrusted to them.

Specialist sub-contractors and suppliers

7.04 Clause 1.40 establishes the relationship between the architect and specialist subcontractors and suppliers and in particular emphasises that the architect cannot be held responsible for detailed design or the performance of work entrusted to specialist subcontractors and suppliers.

1.5	**Copyright**
1.50	The provisions of this Section shall apply without prejudice to the architect's lien on drawings against unpaid fees.
1.51	In accordance with the provisions of the Copyright Act 1956, copyright in all drawings and in the work executed from them, except drawings and works for the Crown, will remain the property of the architect unless otherwise agreed.
1.52	Where an architect has completed Stage D or where an architect provides detail design in Stage EFG the client unless otherwise agreed shall, on payment or tender of any fees due to the architect, be entitled to reproduce the design by proceeding to execute the project, but only on the site to which the design relates.
1.53	Where an architect has not completed Stage D or where he and his client have agreed that Clause 1.52 shall not apply, the client may not reproduce the design by proceeding to execute the project without the consent of the architect and payment of any additional fee that may be agreed in exchange for the architect's consent.
1.54	The architect shall not unreasonably withhold his consent under Clause 1.53 but where his services are limited to making and negotiating town planning consents he may withhold his consent unless otherwise determined by an arbitrator appointed in accordance with Clause 7.50.

Copyright

7.05 Section 1.5 has arisen out of recent cases concerning the disputed use of drawings. It emphasises that copyright in all drawings and work executed from them remains with the architect except in special agreed circumstances. It describes the client's rights concerning the use of drawings and to some extent alleviates the difficulties discussed in para 3.02 above.

1.6	**Inspection**
1.60	During his on-site inspections made in accordance with Clause 1.33 the architect shall endeavour to guard the client against defects and deficiencies in the work of the contractor, but shall not be required to make exhaustive or continuous inspections to check the quality or quantity of the work.
1.61	Where frequent or constant inspection is required a clerk or clerks of works should be employed. He shall be nominated or approved by the architect and be under the architect's direction and control. He may be appointed and paid by the client or employed by the architect.
1.62	Where the need for frequent or constant on-site inspection by the architect is agreed to be necessary, a resident architect shall be appointed by the architect.
1.63	Where the architect employs a resident architect or a clerk or clerks of works he shall be reimbursed by the client in accordance with Part 5 and Part 6 of these Conditions.

Inspection

7.06 Clause 1.60 may be well-intentioned but it is difficult to imagine how it might be interpreted legally. In view of clause 1.33 (para 7.03) it appears somewhat superfluous. Clauses 1.61 to 1.63, concerning the employment of site supervisory staff, are self-evident and should be read in conjunction with clause 1.33.

1.7	**Delay and changes in instructions**
1.70	Extra work and expense caused in any Stage resulting from delay in receiving instructions, delays in building operations, changes in the client's instructions, phased contracts, bankruptcy or liquidation of the contractor or any other cause beyond the control of the architect, shall be additionally charged on a time basis.

Delays and changes in instructions

7.07 Clause 1.70 provides authority for the architect's claim to additional payment for extra work and expense caused by matters beyond his control (the additional payments being calculated upon a time basis). Although it is not always possible to recognise the occurrence of extra costs in advance and claims may be made retrospectively, clients should be warned when additional costs are foreseen.

1.8	**Fees for hospital works**
1.80	The Health Ministers have asked Hospital Boards to apply these scales to their commissions and have advised the Boards that claims from architects to renegotiate terms for long-running commissions, from some suitable future breakpoint and where a substantial amount of work remains to be done, should be considered.
1.81	For certain hospitals, defined as 'hospital projects let as a single commission by a client representing a University and a Hospital Board' with a total construction cost of £7,000,000 or more, the minimum fee shall be 6%. Such projects are to be assessed as a whole, irrespective of any phases into which they might be divided for building.

Fees for hospital work

7.08 These clauses arise from the long discussions that have been held concerning inappropriate fees for work in this complicated area. Clause 1.80 concerns the renegotiation of unsatisfactory fee arrangements for existing long-running commissions for hospital work.

Clause 1.81 introduces an exemption to the minimum fee rule of Table 1 and authorises a minimum fee of 6 per cent (instead of 5.5 per cent) for projects of £7,000,000 or more.

1.9	**Signing buildings**
1.90	Where the architect has been commissioned for and is completing the Normal Services he shall be entitled at his own expense, or may be required by the client at the client's expense, to sign the building by inscription or otherwise on a suitable and reasonably visible part of the permanent fabric of the building.

Signing buildings

7.09 Clause 1.90 provides the right for an architect to sign his work and gives alternative methods for meeting the cost of a sign.

8 Part 2: Normal services

2.00 This part describes the services normally provided by an architect for a building project. The fees for Work Stages C to H are generally charged on a percentage basis as described in Part 3 of these Conditions. Stage C begins where the architect's brief has been determined in sufficient detail. Fees otherwise, including work in Stages A and B to determine the architect's brief, are charged additionally on a time basis as described in Part 5 of these Conditions. Initial consultations may be given free of charge.

2.1 Work Stages

2.10 Work Stages charged on a **time** basis:

A Inception
Receiving an initial statement of requirements, outlining possible courses of action, and advising on the need for a quantity surveyor and consultants. Determining the brief in sufficient detail for subsequent Stages to begin.

B Feasibility studies
Undertaking a preliminary technical appraisal of a project sufficient to enable the client to decide whether and in what form to proceed, and making town planning inquiries or application for outline town planning approval. Such an appraisal may include an approximation of the cost of meeting the client's requirements, a statement on the need for consultants, an outline timetable and a suggested contract procedure.

2.11 Work Stages normally charged on a **percentage** basis:

C Outline proposals
Analysing the client's requirements and where necessary instructing the quantity surveyor and consultants. Preparing, describing and illustrating outline proposals, including an approximation of the cost of meeting them. Informing the client of any major decisions which are needed and receiving any amended instructions.

D Scheme design
Preparing in collaboration with the quantity surveyor, and consultants if appropriate, a scheme design consisting of drawings, and outline specification sufficient to indicate spatial arrangements, materials and appearance. Presenting a report on the scheme, the estimated cost and timetable for the project, for the client's approval.

E F G Detailed design, production drawings, specifications and bills of quantities
Completing a detailed design, incorporating any design work done by consultants, nominated sub-contractors and suppliers. Carrying out cost checks as necessary. Obtaining quotations and other information from nominated sub-contractors and suppliers. Preparing production drawings and specification of materials and workmanship required. Supplying information necessary for the preparation of bills and quantities, if any.

H Tender action to completion
Obtaining and advising on tenders and preparing and advising on the contract and the appointment of the contractor. Supplying information to the contractor, arranging for him to take possession of the site and examining his programme. Making periodic visits to the site as described in Clause 1.33; issuing certificates and other administrative duties under the contract. Accepting the building on behalf of the client, providing scale drawings showing the main lines of drainage and obtaining drawings of other services as executed, and giving initial guidance on maintenance.

Work stages

8.01 This section is a valuable basis of explanation of the range and content of the architect's normal service.

Clause 2.10 recognises the increasing importance of the inception and feasibility study stages and makes provision for their payment on a time basis. It is desirable that architects should bring these stages of work to the attention of employers and ensure that, where this work is necessary, it is properly carried out as a separate service and not compounded into the percentage fee of stages C to H.

Clause 2.11 describes the normal basic service of the architect in six stages which relate to the plan of work (RIBA *Handbook of architectural practice and management*). Unless other arrangements have been made (section 3.6), a proportion of the total cumulative fee becomes payable at the completion of stages C to H in accordance with Table 3. Division of the normal service into these stages caused considerable discussion, but it is generally recognised that not only does this offer a sound basis of remuneration but it also provides a useful starting point for the programming of work.

Sections 2.2 to 2.5 cover work and special studies beyond the scope of those outlined in clauses 2.10 and 2.11. It is the architect's duty to advise his employer upon the need for these services. An employer might not be held responsible for the cost of these services unless he had given prior approval to the work. Some of these services might be carried out in conjunction with other independent consultants, and questions of responsibility and remuneration should be discussed at the outset with the parties involved.

Section 2.6 makes provision for a wide range of legal and quasi-legal matters beyond those normally included in the basic service. Again it is the architect's duty to inform his employer of any special matters which will entail additional costs.

Section 2.7 concerns material that may be required for special purposes and it should be noted that 'special drawings' may embrace a whole range of presentation techniques.

Section 2.8 is a source of potential difficulty and it is necessary to carefully identify the items and areas of work concerned at an early stage.

Section 2.9 is a formality extending the comments of clause 2.11 and section 2.6 in relation to approvals and licences. It should be noted that it is not the architect's responsibility to make the application for approvals in Scotland.

2.2 Development studies
To be charged on a time basis

2.20 Services where a client's initial statement of requirements in Stage A requires a special service (such as operational research) before consideration of the brief and development of outline proposals as described in Stage C can begin.

2.3 Development plans
To be charged on a time basis

2.30 Preparing development plans for any large building or complex of buildings which will be carried out in phases over a number of years.

2.31 Preparing a layout only, or preparing a layout for a greater area than that which is to be developed immediately.

2.4 Sites and buildings
To be charged on a time basis

2.40 Advising on the selection and suitability of sites, conducting negotiations concerned with sites or buildings, making measured surveys, taking levels and preparing plans of sites and buildings or existing buildings.

2.41 Making inspections, preparing reports or giving general advice on the condition of premises.

2.42 Work in connection with soil investigations.

2.5 Constructional research
To be charged on a time basis

2.50 Research where the development of a scheme design in Stage D involves special constructional research, including the design, construction or testing of prototype buildings or models.

2.6 Negotiations
To be charged on a time basis

2.60 Exceptional negotiations such as those arising from applications for Town Planning, Building Byelaw, Building Act or Building Regulations approvals.

2.61 Providing information, making all applications other than those covered by the Normal Services, such as those including applications for licences, negotiations in connection with party walls and grant aids.

2.62 Submission to the Royal Fine Art Commission and town planning appeals.

2.7 Special drawings
To be charged on a time basis

2.70 Preparing any special drawings, models or technical information specially for the use of the client, or for Town Planning, Byelaw and Building Regulations approvals; for negotiations with ground landlords, adjoining owners, public authorities, licensing authorities, mortgagors and others.

2.8 Furnishings and works of art
To be charged on a time basis

2.80 Advising on the selection and suitability of loose furniture, fittings and soft furnishings, on the commissioning or selection of works of art, obtaining tenders and supervising their installation.

2.9 Approvals in the Normal Services

2.90 Except in Scotland, Stages C to E F G of the Normal Services include the duty of making and negotiating applications for Town Planning consents, Building Byelaw, Building Act and Building Regulations approvals, as appropriate. All work in connection with these applications will not necessarily be included in any particular Stage.

2.91 In Scotland, the normal Services cover the duty of preparing drawings and technical information necessary for submission of applications for licences, Town Planning and Building (Scotland) Act approvals as appropriate. The actual completion of the application and its presentation to the appropriate Court is not part of the architect's responsibility.

9 Part 3: Fees for normal services

3.00 This part describes how the percentage fees for the Normal Services are calculated and may be varied, and when they and other charges are due. Percentage fees are based on the total construction cost of the works and on the issue of the final certificate shall be re-calculated on the actual total construction cost.

3.1 Total construction cost

3.10 The total construction cost shall be the cost, as certified by the architect, of all works (including site works) executed under his direction, subject to the following conditions:

3.101 The total construction cost shall include the cost of all work designed or supervised by consultants which the architect is responsible for directing and co-ordinating in accordance with Clause 1.22, irrespective of whether such work is carried out under separate building contracts for which the architect may not be responsible. The architect shall be informed of the cost of any such separate contracts.

3.102 The total construction cost shall not include nominated sub-contractors' design fees for work on which consultants would otherwise have been employed. Where such fees are not known, the architect shall estimate a reduction from the total construction cost.

3.103 For the purpose of calculating the appropriate fees, the total construction cost shall include the actual or estimated cost of any work executed which is excluded from the contract but otherwise designed by the architect.

3.104 The total construction cost shall include the cost of built-in furniture and equipment. Where the cost of any special equipment is excluded from the total construction cost, the architect shall charge for work in connection with such items on a time basis.

3.105 Where appropriate the cost of old materials used in the work shall be calculated as if they were new.

3.106 Where any material, labour or carriage are supplied by a client who is not the builder, the cost shall be estimated by the architect as if they were supplied by the builder and included in the total cost.

3.107 Where the client is the builder, a statement of the ascertained gross cost of the works may be used in calculating the total construction cost of the works. In the absence of such a statement, the architect's own estimate shall be used. In both a statement of the ascertained gross cost and an architect's estimate there shall be included an allowance for the builder's profit and overheads.

3.11 The fee for any part of the work omitted on the client's instruction shall be calculated in accordance with Section 3.5 of these Conditions.

9.01 Section 3.1 gives the rules for the determination of the total construction cost used in the calculation of the fee on a percentage basis. Matters covered include design or supervision of work by consultants; nominated sub-contractors' design fees; estimates for design work which is excluded from the contract; built-in furniture and fittings; the use of old materials; work carried out by clients, and omitted work.

3.2 New works

3.20 Fees for new works generally are shown in Table 1

3.3 Works to existing buildings

3.30 Higher percentages are chargeable for works to existing buildings and are shown in Table 2

3.31 The percentage in Table 2 will not necessarily be sufficient for alterations to all buildings, especially those of historic importance, and higher fees may be appropriate.

3.32 Where extensions to existing buildings are substantially independent, fees may be as for new works, but the fee for those sections of works which marry existing buildings to the new shall be charged separately at the fee in Table 2 applicable to an independent commission of similar value.

Fees for new works

9.02 Fees on new works are calculated on a limited tapering scale with minimum charges for each stage (see Table 1). The special conditions applying to certain hospital buildings should be noted.

Fees for existing buildings

9.03 Fees for works to existing buildings are on a similar but higher limited tapering scale (Table 2). The fees indicated are again minimum fees and higher charges may be made in special circumstances subject to 'prior agreement between architect and employer'.

Clause 3.32 provides guidance to charges to be made for extensions to existing buildings, a source of occasional dispute between architect and employer.

3.4 Repetition

3.40 Where a building is repeated for the same client fees for the superstructures excluding all work below the top of ground floor slabs may be reduced as follows:

3.401 On all except the first three of any houses of the same design.

3.402 On all except the first, i.e. the prototype, of all other building types to the same design.

3.41 Where a single building incorporates a number of identical compartments such as floors in multi-storey or complete structural bays in single-storey buildings, fees may be reduced on all identical compartments in excess of 10 provided that the building does not otherwise attract fee reductions and that it is completed in a single contract.

3.42 Reductions shall not be made for repeated individual dwelling units in multi-storey housing schemes but such schemes may qualify for fee reductions under Sub-clause 3.402 or Clause 3.41.

3.43 Reductions in accordance with Clauses 3.40 and 3.41 shall be made by waiving the fee for either Stages D and E F G of the Normal Services where a complete design can be re-used without modification other than the handing of plans, or Stage E F G where a complete design can be re-used with only minor modification.

3.44 The handing of a plan shall not constitute a modification.

3.45 The total construction cost of the works shall be taken first and the fee for normal or partial services calculated thereon. The appropriate reduction shall then be applied to the cost of the repeated superstructures or sections and the result deducted from the full fee.

3.46 Screen walls and outbuildings and garages shall be excluded from the construction cost of works on which fees are waived unless they are included in the type drawings and specifications.

3.47 The fees for work in Stage H of the Normal Services shall not be reduced for repetitive works or repeated buildings, and any additional work arising out of repetition shall be charged on a time basis.

Repetition

9.04 Section 3.4 gives the rules for calculating the reductions in fees which may be made for repetitive work. The basis for reductions may not be readily appreciated by an employer who may, by a cursory reading of this section, assume that the reductions are greater than they are in fact. Reductions may be made only in the cases of the repeat of more than three houses of the same design; the repeat of an identical building other than a house; or the repeat of more than ten identical compartments in a single building.

The reduction may be made by waiving the fee for stages D and EFG, or stages EFG only, on the repeated work.

The procedure of calculating the fee reduction should be noted.

3.5 Partial services

3.50 Where for any reason the architect provides only part of the Normal Services described in Part 2 of these Conditions he shall be entitled to commensurate remuneration, and his fees and charges shall be calculated as follows:

3.501 Where an architect completes the work described in any of Stages C to E F G he shall be entitled to the appropriate proportion of the full percentage fee for the service in accordance with Table 3.

3.502 Where an architect is commissioned to undertake only the work described in Stage H, whether in whole or part, fees shall be on a time basis.

3.503 Where an architect originally engaged to provide the Normal Services does part only of the work described in Stage H, he shall be entitled to not less than the percentage fee otherwise due to him under Clause 3.61.

3.504 Where an architect provides part only of the services described in Stages C to E F G, fees for service in any Stage which is incomplete shall be on a time basis, except by prior written agreement in accordance with Clause 3.51.

3.505 Where an architect has previously completed the work described in Stages C to EFG on a commission which has been abandoned under the terms of Part 7 of these Conditions and the commission is resumed within two years, fees for the work in Stage H shall be on a percentage basis. Where the commission is resumed after two years Sub-Clause 3.502 will apply.

3.51 Where work done by a client results in the omission of part of Stages C to H described in Part 2 of these Conditions or a sponsored constructional method is used, a commensurate reduction in fees may be made by prior written agreement, provided each such agreement specifies in sufficient detail the work to be done by the client which would otherwise have formed part of the Stages provided by the architect, and is either made in accordance with the RIBA Memorandum on the application of this Clause or is approved by the RIBA.

Partial services

9.05 Charges for work which is less than the full normal service are frequently a source of dispute, largely because this partial service often arises out of the failure of the project to be completed as originally envisaged by the parties. However, the rules for calculating fees for partial services are quite clear, and provided that the architect's terms of appointment are clearly agreed disputes from this area should be reduced.

Subclause 3.501 provides for the normal apportioned percentage fee for the completion of any of the stages C to G, ie outline proposals, scheme design, detail design, production information or bills of quantities (see table 3).

Sub-clauses 3.502 and 3.503 concern stage H, ie tender action to completion. Where this is the only stage for which the architect is commissioned the fee is determined on a time basis for the work done. In the case of an architect commissioned to carry out the full Normal Services but unable to complete all of stage H, the fee is determined in relation to the value of work certified or work completed.

Where the architect is not required to complete the work of stages C to EFG the due fee is determined on a time basis unless there is a prior written agreement where the client carried out part of the service himself (sub-clause 3.504). Sub-clause 3.505 was introduced to meet the case of work delayed at the tender stage. When the work is resumed within two years the usual percentage fee applies but if the resumption takes place after two years the fee is measured on a time basis (sub-clauses 3.505 and 3.502).

Clause 3.51 has resulted in a special memorandum* which provides precise rules for determining partial services fees in the case of a commission from a public authority or other client represented by a chief architect, or a commission where a sponsored constructional method is used. The first case is straightforward and although there may well be organisational problems the rules under clause 1.1 and 1.2 of the memorandum are clear.

The second case is more complicated and it provides detailed rules for fee reductions in connection with three types of sponsored constructional methods. Type A, the completed factory-made and fitted building, may attract a reduction of up to five-eighths. Type B, comprising a specialised system where the sponsor prepares detailed design and production drawings from the architect's scheme design, may entail a reduction of up to two-fifths. Type C, comprising programmed constructional elements and components, may entail a reduction of one-fifth.

The reductions apply to the superstructures only, of course. These rules should be carefully studied, especially in the case of repetitive works using sponsored constructional methods. Tables 1 and 2 demonstrate the application of appropriate fee reductions.

Clauses 3.52 and 3.53 provide guidance on assessment of construction costs for determining fees for partial services.

* See Appendix at end of this Study

Mode and time of payment

9.06 Section 3.6 authorises payment of the architect during the course of the work. It safeguards architect's rights to payment but allows architect and employer to negotiate a mutually convenient arrangement. This may take place at the formal completion of each stage, by instalments proportionate to the work completed or by interim payments on a regular basis throughout the project.

Percentage fees for the Normal Services

Minimum charges are laid down in Tables 1 and 2 so that a fee shall not be less than the fee for works having a lower construction cost.

Table 1: New works

Total construction cost	Minimum % rate	Minimum charges for work stages completed up to and including:			
		H	EFG	D	C
Up to £2,500	10·0	—	—	—	—
£2,500–£8,000	8·5	£250	£187·50	£87·50	£37·50
£8,000–£14,000	7·5	£680	£510·00	£238·00	£102·00
£14,000–£25,000	6·5	£1,050	£787·50	£367·50	£157·50
£25,000–£750,000	6·0	£1,625	£1,218·75	£568·75	£243·75
*£750,000–£1,750,000	5·75	£45,000	£33,750·00	£15,750·00	£6,750·00
*£1,750,000 and over	5·5	£100,025	£75,468·75	£35,218·75	£15,093·75

* Does not apply to certain hospitals (see Clause 1.81) or to works for which the fee is reduced for repetition as provided in Section 3.4. In those cases the minimum fee for works having a total construction cost of £25,000 and over shall be 6·0%.

Table 2: Works to existing buildings

Total construction cost	Minimum % rate	Minimum charges for work stages completed up to and including:			
		H	EFG	D	C
Up to £2,500	13·0	—	—	—	—
£2,500–£8,000	12·5	£325	£243·75	£113·75	£48·75
£8,000–£14,000	12·0	£1,000	£750·00	£350·00	£150·00
£14,000–£25,000	11·0	£1,680	£1,260·00	£588·00	£252·00
£25,000 and over	10·0	£2,750	£2,062·50	£962·50	£412·50

Table 3: Apportionment of fees between stages of service

On completion of each Stage of the Normal Services described in Part 2 of these Conditions, the following proportions of the cumulative fee shown in Tables 1 and 2 are payable:

Work stage	Proportion of fee	Cumulative total
C	15%	15%
D	20%	35%
E F G	40%	75%
H	25%	100%

10 Part 4: Other services

4.3 Garden and landscape design

4.30 Fees for garden and landscape design executed under separate landscape contracts shall be in accordance with the Scale of Professional Charges of the Institute of Landscape Architects.

4.4 Building surveys and structural investigations

4.40 Preparing schedules of dilapidations and negotiating them on behalf of landlords or tenants; taking particulars on site, preparing specifications for repairs or restoration work, inspecting their execution.

4.41 Making structural investigations, the limits of which shall be clearly defined and agreed in writing, such as are necessary to ascertain whether or not there are defects in the walls, roof, floors and drains of a building which may materially affect its life and value.

4.5 Separate trades contracts

4.50 Where there are separate contracts for each trade the fees shall be determined by prior written agreement and shall not be less than 20 per cent higher than the fee for Stages C to H of the Normal Services.

4.6 Interior design, shopfitting and furniture design

4.60 Fees may be charged on a percentage or time basis for the following work. Where percentage fees are charged, rates up to double those shown in Table 1 will normally be appropriate:

4.601 Special services, including the provision of special sketch studies, detailed advice on the selection of furniture, fittings and soft furnishings and inspection of making up such furnishings for interior design work executed under a special building contract or subcontract or a contract separate from that for other works on which the architect may be employed.

4.602 Works of a special quality, such as special shopfitting, fronts and interiors, exhibition design and similar works, including both the remodelling of existing shops and the design of new units, both independently and within the shell of an existing building, irrespective of whether the architect is employed for shopfitting design only or the work forms part of a general building contract.

4.61 Where all shopfitting drawings are provided by specialist subcontractors the fee shall be as for the Normal Services described in Part 2 of these Conditions.

4.62 For the design of special items of furniture and fittings for limited production only, i.e. not more than 49 off, the percentage fee shall be either 15 per cent of the total production cost or calculated on a time basis.

4.63 Payment for the design of mass-produced items of furniture may be by royalty, or by time charges and sale of copyright. Fees for the design of prototypes shall be either on a time basis or an advance on royalties.

4.7 Building systems and components

4.70 For the development of building systems, percentage fees on the total production cost may be agreed specially. Otherwise, fees shall be either on a time basis or an advance on royalties.

4.71 Payment for the design of mass-produced building components may be by royalty or by time charges and sale of copyright. Fees for development work in connection with the design of prototypes shall be either on a time basis or an advance on royalties.

4.72 Where an architect recommends to an independent client the use of a building system or components on which he is receiving royalties, the client shall be so informed. The total construction cost shall not be reduced but the architect may reduce his fees to the extent of the royalties received.

4.8 Litigation and arbitration

4.80 For qualifying to give evidence, settling proofs, conferences with solicitors and counsel, attendance in court or at arbitrations or town planning inquiries, or before other tribunals, for services in connection with litigation, and for arbitration, fees shall be on a time basis.

4.81 Time charges shall be in accordance with Part 5 except that the time rate for arbitrators shall be not less than £6 per hour with a minimum fee of £30.

4.9 Consultancy

4.90 For acting as consultant architect, fees shall be on a time basis.

4.91 Where an architect is retained to provide consultancy or other services on a regular or intermittent basis, annual retention fees may be charged, and where appropriate may be merged with subsequent percentage fees or time charges.

10.01 Sections 4.1 to 4.3 cover the cases of architects operating in the fields of town planning, quantity surveying, valuing and surveying, garden and landscape design, and are directed towards uniformity of professional remuneration.

Services described in section 4.4 are in addition to the normal services and the architect engaged in works to existing buildings must advise his client when special surveys and investigations are necessary.

The extra fee due for work in connection with separate trades contacts has varied over the last few years, and it is apparent that all architects are not agreed upon the principle or appli-

cation of clause 4.50. Nevertheless it is mandatory.

Section 4.6 covers the specialised field of interior design in which it is notoriously difficult to make a forecast of likely fees and charges. In the absence of experience on previously identical projects the architects should not commit themselves to any forecast.

Section 4.7 concerns an area of work of increasing importance. The conditions have found a formula which does not inhibit the architect's position and at the same time safeguards the interests of the client and the professional status of the architect.

Sections 4.8 and 4.9 are self-evident and should not cause any difficulties, but architects should very carefully consider their competence and experience in these specialised areas before undertaking such work.

11 Part 5: Time charges

5.00 Time charges are based on a minimum hourly rate for principals and other operational staff. In assessing the rate at which time should be charged, all relevant factors should be considered, including the complexity of the work, the qualifications, experience and responsibility of the architect, and the character of any negotiations.

5.1 Hourly rates

5.10 The minimum hourly rate for principals shall be £5 per hour.

5.11 The minimum hourly rate for architectural and other operational staff, including resident architects and clerks of works not appointed and paid direct by the client, shall be 15 pence per hour for each £100 of gross annual salary, which shall include bonus payments and the employer's share of other overheads such as national insurance and occupational pension schemes.

5.2 Travelling time

5.20 Where work is being charged on a time basis, travelling time shall be charged in accordance with Section 5.1 of these Conditions.

5.21 Where work charged on a percentage fee is at such a distance that an exceptional amount of time is spent in travelling, additional charges may be made by prior written agreement.

11.01 Section 5.1 is clear in principle but the rate of £5 per hour for principals is regarded by many as inadequate and charges considerably in excess of £5 are being made. It is obviously important that the employer be informed of the rate to be charged.

Section 5.2 is the cause of occasional difficulties. When time charges are in use it is mandatory to charge all travelling time, but where work is being charged on a percentage basis exceptional travelling time may be charged only by prior agreement.

12 Part 6: Out-of-pocket expenses

6.00 In addition to the fees under any other part of these Conditions, the architect shall be reimbursed for all reasonable out of pocket expenses actually and properly incurred in connection with the commission. Such expenses include the following:

6.1 Drawings and documents

6.10 Printing, reproduction or purchase costs of all documents, drawings, maps, models, photographs, and other records, including all those used in communication between architect, client, quantity surveyor, consultants and contractors, and for enquiries to contractors, sub-contractors and suppliers, notwithstanding any obligation on the part of the architect to supply such documents to those concerned, except that contractors and suppliers will pay for any prints additional to those to which they are entitled under the contract.

6.2 Hotel and travelling expenses

6.20 Hotel and travelling expenses, including mileage allowances for cars at recognised rates, and other similar disbursements.

6.3 Disbursements

6.30 All payments made on behalf of the client, including expenses incurred in advertising for tenders, clerks of works, and other resident site staff, including the time and expenses of interviewers and reasonable expenses for interviewees.

6.31 Fees and other charges for specialist professional advice, including legal advice, which have been incurred by the architect with the specific authority of the client.

6.32 Postage and telephone charges incurred by the architect may be charged by prior written agreement.

6.4 Compounding of expenses

6.40 By prior written agreement, expenses may be estimated or standardised in whole or part, or compounded for an increase in the percentage fee.

12.01 Sections 6.1, 6.2 and 6.3 list the items for which the architect is normally entitled to reimbursement. The architect is entitled only to the reimbursement of fees and other charges for specialist advice, including legal advice, where these expenses have been incurred on the specific authority of the client. Similarly postage and telephone charges may be charged only by prior agreement.

Section 6.4 authorises the payment of expenses in a mutually convenient manner by agreement between architect and employer.

13 Part 7: Termination, abandoned works and interpretation

7.00 An engagement entered into between the architect and the client may be terminated at any time by either party on the expiry of reasonable notice, when the architect shall be entitled to remuneration in accordance with Section 3.5.

7.1 Abandoned commissions

7.10 Where the construction of works is cancelled or postponed on the client's instructions, or the architect is instructed to stop work indefinitely at any time, the commission may be deemed to be abandoned and fees for partial service shall be due.

7.11 Notwithstanding Clause 7.10, if instructions necessary for the architect to continue work are not received from the client six months after such instructions were requested, the commission shall be deemed to have been abandoned.

7.12 Where a commission is abandoned or any part of the works is omitted at any time before completion, fees for partial service in respect of the whole or part of the works shall be charged for all service provided with due authority.

7.2 Resumed commissions

7.20 If a commission which has been abandoned is resumed without substantial alteration within six months, any fees paid under Section 7.1 shall rank solely as payments on account toward the total fees payable on the execution of the works and calculated on their total construction cost.

7.21 Where a commission which has been abandoned is resumed at any time with substantial alteration or is resumed after six months, any fees paid under Section 7.1 above shall be regarded as final payment for the service originally rendered. The resumed commission shall then be deemed separate, and fees charged in accordance with Section 3.5 of these Conditions.

7.22 All additional work arising out of a commission which is resumed in accordance with Clause 7.20 shall be charged on a time basis.

7.3 Interpretation

7.30 Any question arising out of these Conditions may be referred in writing by architect or client to the RIBA for advice provided always that any difference or dispute between them is determined in accordance with either Clause 7.40 or 7.50.

7.4 Disputes

7.40 Any difference or dispute on the application of these Conditions to fees charged by a member of the RIBA may by agreement between the parties be referred to the RIBA for an opinion, provided always that such opinion is sought on a joint statement of undisputed facts and the parties undertake to accept it as final.

7.5 Arbitration

7.50 Where any difference or dispute arising out of these Conditions cannot be resolved in accordance with Clause 7.40, it shall be referred to the arbitration of a person to be agreed between the parties or, failing agreement within 14 days after either party has given to the other a written request to concur in the appointment of an arbitrator, a person to be nominated at the request of either party by the President of the Institute of Arbitrators, provided that in a difference or dispute arising out of the provisions of Section 1.5 the arbitrator shall, unless otherwise agreed, be a chartered architect.

13.01 Section 7.1 defines situations in which the works are deemed to be abandoned and in which fees for partially completed work become due. Clause 7.11 is designed to

protect the interest of the architect if an employer who does not wish to continue with the project but hopes to avoid liability for fees on abandoned work.

Section 7.2 provides for the resumption of abandoned work and gives the procedure for fee adjustment. It may be helpful for the architect to explain the significance of the six-month rule if it is likely that work will be resumed at any time in the future.

Sections 7.3, 7.4 and 7.5 offer a three-tier system for the resolution of difficulties between the architect and the employer; first by means of requests to the RIBA for interpretation of the conditions; second by means of an agreed presentation of a dispute to the RIBA; and finally by recourse to arbitration (LEGAL STUDY 8). Arbitration is also referred to in the standard form of memorandum of agreement.

APPENDIX: Memorandum on Clause 3.51 of the Conditions of Engagement RIBA March 1972

Part 1:
Commissions from a public authority or other client represented by a chief architect

1.00 The subdivision of a commission or of Work Stages within Normal Services is not recommended because of difficulty in defining the division of responsibility between client and commissioned architect and because it could lead to an increase in the total cost of the architect's services.

1.1 Work Stages

1.10 **A Inception**
Where information supplied by a client determines the brief in sufficient detail for subsequent Work Stages to begin, time charges for Work Stage A will not arise.

1.11 **B Feasibility studies**
Where information supplied by a client determines building requirements at the outset of the commission, time charges for Work Stage B will not be made.

1.12 **C Outline proposals**
The provision of rough sketches, reports, detailed user requirements and assistance in interpreting and meeting the client's needs will not reduce significantly the commissioned architect's work in assimilating the brief. Provision of such information and assistance will not of itself, therefore, justify any reduction of the fee for Work Stage C but may avoid a charge under Section 2.2 *Development Studies* of the Conditions of Engagement.

1.13 **D Scheme design**
Where the client's architect prepares both outline proposals and scheme design, the fee for Work Stage D may be reduced by up to half and the fee for Work Stage C omitted.

1.14 **EFG Detail design, production information, bills of quantities**
Provision by the client of standard specification clauses, typical room layouts and similar information does not reduce the commissioned architect's duties sufficiently to justify any reduction of the fee for Work Stage EFG.

1.15 **H Tender action to completion**
Where the commissioned architect is named in the building contract the fee for Work Stage H will not be reduced.
Otherwise, the commissioned architect's responsibility for work in Work Stage H must be defined in the memorandum of agreement between client and commissioned architect and the basis of remuneration for Work Stage H will be the time spent on work in that Work Stage by the commissioned architect, subject to Sub-clause 3.503 and Clause 3.61 of the Conditions of Engagement.

1.2 **Approvals in the Normal Services**
Whilst a client may avoid time charges under Section 2.6 *Negotiations* of the Conditions of Engagement by assisting the commissioned architect in carrying out his duties under Section 2.9 *Approvals in the Normal Services* of those Conditions, the fee for the Normal Services will not be reduced.

Part 2:
Commissions where a Sponsored Constructional Method is used

2.00 Where an architect is commissioned or agrees with his client to use one of the three categories of Sponsored Constructional Method of building described in this memorandum, fees for Normal Services may be reduced as follows.

2.1 The use of other types of Sponsored Constructional Method may also reduce the Normal Services duties of the commissioned architect. But, except for types described in this memorandum, any reduction of fees for the Normal Services must be approved by the RIBA in accordance with Clause 3.51 of the Conditions of Engagement.

2.10 Where an architect is for the first time commissioned to use a Sponsored Constructional Method of any particular type described in this memorandum, or a new mark of such a method, he will need to assimilate information on the constructional method and procedures and any reduction in fee shall not be more than half the difference between the full Normal Services percentage fee and the reduced fee provided for in Clause 2.3 of this memorandum.

2.2 Types

2.20 A
Sponsored Constructional Method A comprises a complete building type, factory built and fitted, to be incorporated in the outline proposals and scheme design and requiring no additional design details or production drawings.

2.21 B1
Sponsored Constructional Method B1 comprises a specialised system for which the sponsor carried out detailed design and production drawings from the commissioned architect's scheme design, the architect being responsible for collaboration, co-ordination and integration of the sponsor's work.

2.22 B2
Sponsored Constructional Method B2 comprises programmed constructional elements and components including:
(a) specification details;
(b) component details;
(c) assembly details;
(d) component prices;
(e) general, detailed and technical design information for their application.

2.3 Maximum permitted reductions

2.31 Type B2
One-fifth of fee on the value of the Sponsored Constructional Method work apportioned between Work Stages as shown in Table 1.

2.32 Type B1
Two-fifths of fee on the value of the Sponsored Constructional Method work apportioned between Work Stages as shown in Table 1.

2.33 Type A
Five-eighths of fee on the value of the Sponsored Constructional Method work apportioned between Work Stages as shown in Table 1.

2.4 Application of reductions

2.40 Reductions are calculated only on those buildings or parts of the commission to which the Sponsored Constructional Method relates. The reductions apply to all building types, including dwelling units, and to works of any value.

2.41 Reductions in accordance with Clauses 2.31, 2.32 and 2.33 above shall be applied as follows to the fees for the superstructures only, excluding all work below the top of ground floor slabs or joists:

2.42 to the combined fee for Work Stages D and EFG

2.43 to the prototypes in a repetitive scheme, i.e.
first three of any houses of the same design
first of any other building of the same design
first 10 compartments of the same design
after which Clause 3.43 of the Conditions of Engagement will apply (Table 2)

2.44 The use of a Sponsored Constructional Method will not reduce the commissioned architect's duties, responsibilities or fees under Section 2.9 *Approvals in the Normal Services* of the Conditions of Engagement.

2.5 Work Stages

2.51 A Inception, B Feasibility studies and C Outline proposals
Fees for these Work Stages will not be reduced.

2.52 D Scheme design and EFG Detail design, production information, bills of quantities
The combined fees for Work Stages D and EFG may be reduced as shown in Section 2.3 and in Part 3.

2.53 H Tender action to completion
The fee for Work Stage H may be reduced only for Sponsored Constructional Method A, and the reduction may not exceed half the normal fee for that stage as shown in Part 3.

Part 3:
Fee entitlement applying the maximum permitted reductions in Part 2

Table 1
Non-repetitive contracts

	C	D	EFG	H	Total	
1. Normal Services	15	20	40	25	100%	Fees on cost of normal work
2. SCM A	15	10		12·5	37·5%	Fees on cost
B1	15	20		25	60%	of SCM
B2	15	40		25	80%	superstructure

Fees for SCM expressed as a percentage of the total percentage fee for Normal Services.

There are no reductions for work in Stage C.

Total construction cost should be divided into two parts—the SCM superstructure and the remainder of the work.

Table 2
Contracts combining use of Sponsored Constructional Method with repetitive works

	C	D	EFG	H	Total	
Fee for normal services on substructure &c.	15	20	40	25	100%	Fee for normal services
A Prototypes	15	10		12·5	37·5%	Prototypes A
Full repeats	15	—		12·5	27·5%	Repeats
B1 Prototypes	15	20		25	60%	Prototypes B1
Full repeats	15	—		25	40%	Repeats
B2 Prototypes	15	40		25	80%	Prototypes B2
Full repeats	15	—		25	40%	Repeats

Fees for SCM used in a repetitive scheme, expressed as a percentage of the total percentage fee for Normal Services.

There are no reductions for work in Stage C.

Total construction cost should be divided into 3 parts as follows:
The SCM prototype superstructure, the repeated superstructures and the remainder of the work.

References

RIBA Handbook of architectural practice and management, 1973

RIBA Agreement for the appointment of an architect, 1973

RIBA Conditions of Engagement, 1976

JENKINS, F. Architect and patron. London, 1961, Oxford University Press, o.p.

RIBA The case for mandatory minimum fees: a statement by the Royal Institute of British Architects to the Monopolies and Mergers Commission, March 1976

AJ Legal Handbook

Section 12
Professional examinations

Legal study 18

The RIBA part 3 examination

This study discusses the syllabus of the RIBA part 3 examination. Although it is not the only way of entering the profession, it ought to set the standard for the others. But there are good grounds for believing that many professional practice exams set by the schools are not as demanding as the RIBA exam—which, as the author points out, is itself defective in modern conditions. But it is at least reasonably rigorous and it is not entirely inappropriate as a means of deciding who should enter the profession for without a working knowledge of relevant law, no one should feel safe, or be allowed to, practice architecture.
Both candidates and examiners should find this study a useful guide to what is expected of them

1 Introduction

1.01 This Study is concerned solely with part 3* (Subject G —Professional Practice and Practical Experience) of the RIBA's Examination in Architecture, and is based upon the Guidance Notes and Regulations issued by the Institute. It is the Institute's declared aim that the part 3 examination be related in scope and standard to current practice and its requirements; and its anticipated development in the near future. The new syllabus, which has introduced three special sections (G1, G2 and G3), puts a strong emphasis upon the need and importance for greater study of law; it came into operation in May 1976.

1.02 Every profession has its own duty and problems to present an appropriate public image, to establish codes of professional conduct and to offer guarantee of standards from its members. This is best achieved by careful selection of membership and an examination system to assess new entrants in terms of knowledge, skill in application, experience and attitude of mind. In the case of architects, legislation (the Architects' Registration Acts of 1931, 1938 and 1969 (Amendment Act)), safeguards both professional and public interest by reserving the title 'architect' to those suitably qualified to practise architecture and at the same time delegates statutory authority to architects themselves to formulate codes and regulate education and conduct of their fellow members.

ARCUK and Architects' Registration Acts

1.03 The body vested with the responsibility for the registration of architects and the general administration of the other provisions in the Acts is the Architects' Registration Council of the UK (ARCUK). To summarise the Acts very briefly: the principal one of 1931 authorised: setting up and maintenance by the Council of a voluntary register of persons entitled under the Act to use the style of 'registered architect'; setting up a Board of Architectural Education (section 5 (1) (a)), and an Admission Committee (section 5 (1) (b)). The former recommends to the Council suitable examinations qualifying for registration. Section 7 (1) makes provision for removal from the register of the name of any person convicted

of a criminal offence or who has been guilty of conduct disgraceful to him in his capacity as an architect (see LEGAL STUDY 3 para 2.11).

1.04 The Act of 1938 extended the principal Act by restricting the 'use of the name architect to registered architects'. Therefore the voluntary character of the first registration Act was replaced by obligatory registration (under section 1 (1)), with the wording 'a person shall not practise or carry on business under any name, style or title containing the word "architect" unless he is a person registered under the principal Act'.

1.05 In each of these relatively short pieces of legislation Parliament lays down principles and leaves the details to be worked out by a non-parliamentary body (in this case ARCUK) (see LEGAL STUDY 1 para 2.07). An example of how this policy is furthered in the courts arose in a King's Bench case in 1945 when Judge Lewis pointed out that there was nothing in the Architects' Registration Acts to give guidance on the meaning of the word 'architect' and that it must be left to the Council of Architects to decide what was the proper degree of skill and the proper qualification for a man who was entitled to be called a 'registered architect'.

Professional examinations

1.06 Whatever the shortcomings of the traditional form of examination (to date, no one has come up with any really positive and constructive alternative for testing professional ability to apply knowledge and skill), it does provide an incentive to work for high standards of efficiency and it gives an indication of the individual's chance of future success. The RIBA as agent for ARCUK has stated frequently that its examinations have been aimed consistently at raising standards and never at restricting membership. It takes the view that the interests of the general public are the primary consideration. In approving the performance of the candidates the RIBA gives guarantee that successful candidates are 'safe to practice'.

RIBA examination in professional practice and practical training

1.07 The RIBA part 3 examination is one (but by no means the only one) of the examinations that are recognised as a qualification for registration under section 6 (1) (c) of the

---

* Part 3 of the RIBA Examination in Architecture consists of one subject identified as subject G with three sections G1, G2 and G3.

1931 Act. Others similarly recognised are those of architecture faculties or departments within universities and other schools.

Section 6 (1) (d) of the principal Act also affords other means of recognition under ARCUK regulations 26 and 27. The new system for the RIBA examination in professional practice proposes two categories of candidate only:

1 Students engaged in study at a School of Architecture and taking the RIBA Examination in Architecture (part 1 and part 2) at the appropriate times, and

2 Those who are given entry to the part 3 through one of the following systems of admission—Special Entry, By-law 2.5 (RIBA), or the ARCUK Regulation 27.

The Examination in Architecture

1.08 The RIBA examination in professional practice and practical training, which is held only in London and provincial centres when the number of candidates creates the need, is the third main part of what should now be regarded as one examination, which approximates as closely as possible to a continuous and progressive assessment of a candidate's ability.

1.09 Part 1, equivalent to the former intermediate exam, is concerned broadly with principles and foundations of knowledge of the whole building field and the understanding and appreciation of architecture in its historic and social context. Additionally it must include the first introduction to management and building law.

1.10 Part 2 of the examination, equivalent to the former Finals I and II, is usually taken at the end of a five-year, full-time course. It tests the prospective architect's overall competence in architectural design, building technology, including advanced management techniques and the effects of general building legislation upon design and practice, particularly in the application of building regulations and by-laws.

1.11 The general principle underlying the proposed new system for the part 3 examination is that the candidate would take each of the three sections when taking the appropriate parts of the examination in architecture; eg section G1 of the part 3 syllabus with part 1 of the main examination.

Use of references

1.12 The regulations of the RIBA part 3 examination permit candidates to take into the examination room certain reference works, ie the RIBA and ARCUK codes; the standard form of building contract; the RIBA *Handbook of architectural practice and management;* and the RIBA Conditions of Engagement. Naturally the majority of candidates are eager to take advantage of the concession. Just how advantageous this dispensation actually is depends upon the ability to find a way quickly through the mass of information available; a good deal of it, particularly in the RIBA *Management handbook* is unrelated to the immediate task.

Oral examination

1.13 It has long been accepted by the RIBA that written examinations are an inadequate means of assessment, and they have been combined with a close study of portfolio work, records of practical experience and oral examination. The prime purpose of the oral is to make personal contact with the candidate. It takes the form of a reasonably relaxed interview with examiners who discuss the written papers and problems which may arise in general practice. The aim

is to test a candidate's application of theoretical knowledge and to appraise his personal qualities.

Practical training

1.14 Academic work or specialisation in a particular field does not create an able architect so much as ability to apply a breadth of knowledge in practice and in relation to actual problems with which he is likely to be faced; many of these are related to the general law. Therefore, architectural education now follows the principle that acquisition of knowledge and understanding and development of design and technical skills should be co-ordinated with application. The RIBA scheme for practical training is designed to contribute its share to the guarantee that the young architect on qualification will not fail in his professional responsibilities.

1.15 How and where the candidate decides to gain his practical experience must in the long run depend upon his own circumstances and preferences. Variety has much to commend itself but short spells in several offices are not generally favoured by employers for obvious reasons and tend to restrict the student's own chance to establish himself with his colleagues for long enough to derive the fullest benefit. On the other hand the disadvantage of experience with one employer or firm is that it is impossible to see all aspects of architecture even in the busiest and most extensive practices. Experience that is too restricted may be assessed as inadequate and the candidate may be advised to extend it before it is acceptable to the examiners.

Aims of the part 3 examination

1.16 This examination is the last in the series for professional reasons, and the most difficult in assessment. It leads directly to corporate membership of the RIBA and to registration as an 'architect'. The examination has three main aims: 'to test knowledge of professional practice and ability to apply it; to review practical experience already gained; and to reveal understanding of the ethics and responsibilities of the professional man'. As this examination is the gateway to the profession, the candidate is examined as a complete person to ensure that he has attained a reasonable standard of professional competence and a sense of responsibility.

2 Examination syllabus

2.01 The Guidance Notes and Regulations clearly indicate that the scope of the new part 3 examination has been widely extended from what it was formerly. The syllabus is not defined in any detail. Indeed it would be impracticable to cover the entire range and variety of possible problems and fields for study and interrogation. Tough though this would appear to be at so early a stage in the young architect's career, there are obvious long-term educational and professional advantages to be gained by compelling him to forage for his own material and in so doing extend his professional horizons. The intelligent candidate will soon discover for himself the necessary breadth and depth of knowledge expected of him and at the same time accustom himself to keep abreast of current problems and with all changes in law and in government policy as it affects the building industry and his future profession.

Scope of examination

2.02 The RIBA Guidance Notes divide the scope of the examination into four main 'areas of study', as follows:

Legislation and architecture

General principles of English/Scottish law; its sources,

systems and divisions. Planning and building legislation and procedures. Law of property. Law of contract. Disputes. Principles of Arbitration. Standard forms of contract. Building Regulations and Acts. Codes of Practice and Standards.

The professions and the industry
Current concepts of professionalism. Structure of the architectural profession and relationships with allied professions. Structure of the building industry. Registration. Professional responsibilities and codes. Architect/client relationships; conditions of engagement.

Management in principle and in practice
Management processes and their application to the professional office: organisation and structure, communication and human relations, office services, programming, budgetary control and accounting.

Project control
Design management and team working; briefing methods and data handling; resource allocation and control. Formal communications; consents; sub-contractors and suppliers; tendering, contract documents; pre-contract planning; instructions and certificates; supervision, quality control; completion and post-control procedures.

2.03 Examination of the candidate's knowledge in these areas is undertaken by two written papers—sections G1 and G2— each accompanied by an essay of between 3 000 and 5 000 words, submitted in advance with titles and topics which will have been published by the RIBA six weeks in advance of the examination date. A third section, G3 is concerned with the candidate's general competence and experience assessed by examination based jointly upon written and oral evidence.

2.04 Section G1 will comprise the Essay and a written paper in three divisions:
1 English/Scottish law; Building Regulations and Acts; planning legislation; Codes of Practice and Standards.
2 Law of property; rights of owners; party wall procedures. Administration of building law; duties and roles of official administrators.
4 The professions and the industry; roles and responsibilities in practice; codes of conduct.

2.05 Section G2 will comprise the Essay and a written paper in four divisions:
1 Law of contract; forms of contract, contract administration; disputes and arbitration.
2 Management of the office, organisation and structure, development of briefing methods.
3 Project administration and control, formal communications, team working; quality control.
4 Conditions of engagement, fees; job costing and programming.

2.06 The syllabus for the two written papers, quoted above, can only be regarded as an 'outline' and must be understood to include a wide variety of matters not specifically mentioned, such as—easements; rights of light; all forms of liability in tort including negligence; partnerships; copyright, patents and registered designs; insurances, etc, etc.

2.07 Section G3 requires the submission of written evidence by candidates and their employers, including a completed Log-book supplemented by the candidate's own written evaluation of the experience he has gained and an assessment

of his capability by his principal employers. With this he must also submit a comprehensive case-study, in order to demonstrate an ability to investigate a project and report on its background and progress from inception to its present state. For this Study—of between 6 000 and 10 000 words— the candidate is at liberty to choose his own subject from (to quote the Regulations) 'a project on which he is actively engaged or one which is currently in progress but on which he is not working or a project which has already been completed by himself or others. The choice of subject should, however, be made with the knowledge and agreement of his employers'.

3 Building law, regulations and by-laws

3.01 The paragraphs which follow are included with the special interests of students in mind in order to provide brief notes on general aspects of building law and administration and to facilitate retrieval of more comprehensive information from other reference sources; in particular, other sections of the AJ *Legal handbook*. In consequence it will be found that there may be some repetition of the information given here.

London
3.02 The law relating to all building within the City of London (with some special exceptions) and the inner London boroughs will be found almost entirely in the London Building Acts 1930–1939 and in the London Building (Constructional) By-laws 1972. This new issue of the by-laws came into force on 1 May 1973, followed by additional amending by-laws in 1974. The London Building Acts and the by-laws are essential references. The construction by-laws are published in detail by the GLC; for an excellent summary see Pitt and Dufton's *Building in Inner London*.

By-laws
3.03 By-laws may be defined as rules (laws) that operate within the area of some authority under powers conferred by statute and are regulations by which local authorities exercise their regular functions (see LEGAL STUDY 1 para 2.08 and LEGAL STUDY 13).

London by-laws
3.04 In London the statute which confers authority to make by-laws for regulation and control of construction is the London Building (Amendment) Act 1935. Important are: section 8 which gives the procedure for making by-laws, defining what this is and how it is done; and section 9 (5) which requires registration of all decisions made modifying or waiving requirements of by-laws made under the Acts. The register, which is open for inspection, shows the terms and conditions, if any, on which modifications or waivers have been granted (see LEGAL STUDY 13 para 6.16). This process is, in part, comparable with powers conferred on local authorities enabling them to relax or dispense with certain requirements of the Building Regulations 1972 (see LEGAL STUDY 13 para 1.10). There is no register of decisions made in respect of deviations from the Building Regulations, but selections of particular cases are sometimes published by HMSO. Unlike the Register of Waivers under the London Building Acts, they should not be taken as precedents for the assumption that a relaxation may be granted.

Codes of practice
3.05 London-based students must be aware of the various other by-laws relevant to buildings, usually made under the Public Health Acts. For instance:
1 Drainage.

2 Sanitation, water closets, urinals, cesspools and so on.
3 Removal of refuse.

3.06 Useful guides to architects who practice in London and elsewhere where specific regulations on similar matters do not exist are the codes of practice which the GLC publishes on the council's Regulations for guidance of anyone preparing schemes for submission when approvals have to be obtained. The best known of these codes are:
1 For buildings of excess height and/or additional cubical extent requiring approval under section 20 of the London Building Acts (Amendment) Act 1939.
2 Means of escape in case of fire.
3 Means of escape in case of fire at houses in multiple occupation. Application of Housing Act 1961 section 16.
4 Places of public entertainment—technical regulations.

By-laws outside London
3.07 Outside London there are no statutes for control of building construction comparable with the London Building Acts. Local authorities derived their powers to make by-laws within their own areas under section 61 of the Public Health Act 1936; and local authority by-laws on constructional matters used to vary throughout the country, as did the measures taken to enforce them. In 1965 existing Model By-laws were replaced by new Building Regulations introducing a new system of building construction control on a national basis which distinctly separated what applied in the City of London and the 12 London boroughs (formerly the London County Council administrative area) from what applied elsewhere in England and Wales (see LEGAL STUDY 13).

3.08 The current Building Regulations are those made in 1976, and are based on those of February 1972, as amended in July 1973, March 1974 and August 1975 respectively. These have now not only superseded existing by-laws but, as from 1 February 1966, the powers of local authorities to make by-laws also lapsed. Thereafter, under section 4 (3) of the Public Health Act 1961, it became the function of all local authorities to enforce the national by-laws in their own districts. However, the new regulations did not replace *all* local by-laws or restrict the powers of local councils to introduce new ones not concerned directly with building construction; subject always to the approval of the appropriate minister—a requirement of all by-law legislation.

British Standards and Codes of Practice
3.09 As well as the codes published by the GLC (para 3.05), British Standards and the Codes of Practice issued by the British Standards Institution have an important place in modern building legislation. Such standards are referred to in relation to numerous deemed-to-satisfy clauses not only in the Building Regulations themselves, but in other statutory legislation, for example the Health and Safety at Work etc Act 1974 (see LEGAL STUDY 13 para 4.12).

Rights of owners
1 Rights of building and adjoining owners in London and outside London (see LEGAL STUDY 13).
2 Easements of light (LEGAL STUDY 6 para 4.12) and support (LEGAL STUDY 6 para 4.11); party wall procedure (LEGAL STUDY 13 para 6.26).

3.10 These two sections of the syllabus have much in common with the first, for they depend mainly upon the London Building Acts. In London, adjoining owners have only the rights given by the Acts. These are currently laid down in the London Building Act (Amendment) Act 1939.

Part VI is most important. (See also part I for definitions, and refer to part I of the 1930 Act for other definitions not subsequently amended.) Part VI of the 1939 Act deals in detail with party wall structures and owners' rights. Sections 45 and 46 define 'rights'; and sections 47 to 49 procedures for service of notices. Section 50 deals with underpinning, and section 55 settlement of differences (see LEGAL STUDY 13 para 6.28 *et seq*).

3.11 Outside London, with certain exceptions, adjoining owners' rights are subject to rights at Common Law. The exceptions are provincial cities with their own legislation for dealing with such matters (see LEGAL STUDY 6 para 4.14 *et seq* and LEGAL STUDY 13 para 7.01 *et seq*).

Special problems
3.12 The kinds of problems likely to arise and therefore meriting special study include:
1 Works involving an adjoining owner's foundations (LEGAL STUDY 6 para 4.15).
2 Effects and liabilities resulting from exposure of part of an old party wall such as might occur where a building is set back when the site is redeveloped to new building lines (LEGAL STUDY 6 para 4.14.)
3 Where the whole of the adjoining owner's face of a party wall is exposed to weather (LEGAL STUDY 6 para 4.14).
4 Where there is any disturbance to a party wall, however slight, such as would be occasioned by fixing thereto any element of the new or reconstructed building. Apart from the necessity of observing statutory obligations in respect of party structures any unlawful interference constitutes an actionable trespass under the law of torts (see LEGAL STUDY 1 para 5.14 *et seq* and LEGAL STUDY 6 para 3.01 *et seq*).

3.13 Although the RIBA syllabus does not specifically extend beyond easements of light and support and party wall procedures, there have been questions set in the examination on rights of way. In practice, architects find themselves involved with a much wider range of easements and similar matters affecting adjoining owners and public interests—especially when concerned with large scale development projects in urban areas or on extensive sites. Accordingly a much more comprehensive study is desirable than the syllabus implies, to include rights of way, highways, watercourses, drainage, and boundaries and fences (LEGAL STUDY 6 para 3.05 *et seq* and LEGAL STUDY 9 para 2.01 *et seq*).

3.14 At the earliest possible stage of any job the architect *must* discover (generally with the help of the building owner's solicitor) whether the adjoining owner has any rights of water, light, way or other easement (including particular easements in respect of any party wall) and whether there are any reservations, covenants or other obligations whatsoever relating to the building owner's or adjoining owner's property.

Dilapidations
3.15 The term 'dilapidation' is used to describe the legal liability which arises from the defective or dangerous conditions of buildings and land. The law concerning it is closely associated with that of waste (see LEGAL STUDY 6 para 6.02). (NB: The RIBA syllabus does not include specifically 'dangerous structures', but these notes do.)

3.16 Many young architects have started in practice with a dilapidation survey on their hands but with little knowledge of what was required of them. This type of work, often unattractive and time-consuming, usually arises from the requirement in repairing leases that the lessee keeps and in due course relinquishes the premises in good and substantial repair. On the expiry of the lease it becomes expedient to survey and where necessary settle claims.

3.17 Dilapidation has been defined as '. . . the result of the failure of a tenant in temporary occupation to keep premises let to him in repair, and the word expresses this state of disrepair. . .'. In practice it refers to defects arising from neglect or misuse and *not* arising from age—ie accepting fair wear and tear. A dilapidation schedule sets out in detail the various parts of building which are out of repair and the way and extent to which they are out of repair. It is not its purpose to specify the manner of carrying out the repair: that is a matter for further work after negotiations between landlord and tenant, and upon receipt of client's instructions. However experienced an architect may be in preparation of surveys and reports, unless he has an above-average knowledge of the law relating to landlord and tenants' covenants, fixtures and so on, he will need the services of a solicitor to interpret the terms of his client's lease; and possibly those of a quantity surveyor for preparation of cost estimates. The architect's functions as surveyor of dilapidations may be best understood by reference to the RIBA Conditions of Engagement (part 4, other services, section 4.40): 'Preparing schedules of dilapidations and negotiating them on behalf of landlords or tenants; taking particulars on site, preparing specifications for repairs or restoration work, inspecting their execution'. Preparation of schedules of dilapidations and negotiating them on behalf of landlords and tenants taking particulars on site and preparing specifications of repairs requires experience and a degree of specialised knowledge of law which few architects are trained for or possess. Nevertheless if they hold themselves out as being competent to undertake this kind of work and, in the event, fail because they lack the necessary skill and experience, they lay themselves open to claims for negligence (see LEGAL STUDY 1 para 5.08).

Dangerous structures in London
3.18 In the London area dangerous and neglected structures are fully covered by part VII (section 61 *et seq*) of the 1939 London Building Act, in particular in respect of representations made through district surveyors by means of which the GLC may require a survey to be made, and from this they may give directions 'to take down repair or otherwise secure' the structure. Powers for removal of dilapidated and neglected structures are made under section 69 of the Act. Dangerous structures notices are served by the GLC, except in the City area where notices are served by the City Common Council—commonly known as the City Corporation (see section 83 and 84 of part IX, London Building Act 1939: service of building notices and their contents).

Dilapidated and dangerous structures outside London
3.19 Local authorities generally have powers to deal with dangerous structures upon application for an order from the magistrates' courts requiring the owner to repair, demolish or restrict the use of dangerous or dilapidated buildings (Public Health Act 1936 (section 50) as amended by the Public Health Act 1961). Failure to comply with a magistrate's order and to remove rubbish from resulting demolition may incur a fine. The local authority may also carry out the work and recover the cost. Similarly they may shore up or fence dangerous property at the owner's expense. If immediate action is required in the public interests, the local authority may take emergency measures without application to the magistrates' courts.

Administration of building law
1 The duties of district surveyors, building surveyors, health inspectors, inspectors of factories, and other administrators of building law.
2 The administration of building law in London and outside London.

Administration of building law in London
3.20 In London, matters relating to building and planning control are the responsibility of the GLC under general direction of the superintending architect, aided by the small but competent body of district surveyors who carry the very heavy responsibility of supervising all building works in their respective districts to ensure that they comply with all provisions of the London Building Acts (see LEGAL STUDY 13 para 6.04 *et seq*).

Administration of building law outside London
3.21 Local authorities are required under the Local Government Act 1933 to appoint a surveyor; this office is frequently filled by an engineer and the holder sometimes enjoys the title of *engineer and surveyor* with responsibility for all construction and maintenance work, including building, highways, sewage and refuse disposal, and almost invariably except in the larger authorities, all the duties associated with building control and planning. In practice he is normally assisted by a building surveyor or building inspector who are chiefly concerned with administration of the Building Regulations. In rural districts a building surveyor performs many of these functions though usually on a smaller scale, as planning, highways and so on come under the direction of the county authority (see LEGAL STUDY 9, particularly para 1.11 and table I).

Health inspectors
3.22 As their title implies, health inspectors have duties under public health legislation, the Factories Act and so on.

Factory inspectors
3.23 Factory inspectors are appointed by the Secretary of State for Trade and Industry and share the responsibility for enforcing provisions of the Factories Act 1961 with local authority officers. Their duties are varied: they include welfare, health and safety of workers, sanitation, fire precautions and means of escape, protection of dangerous machinery and disposal of injurious waste matter. This involves co-operation with many departments of the local authority, eg the engineer, surveyor, building inspector and the medical officer. Factory inspectors have powers to enter factories and warehouses at all times of night or day. Architects can avail themselves of inspectors' experience for consultation on all matters related to the many requirements of the Factories Acts and of the orders issued in pursuance thereof.

Fire authorities
3.24 In England and Wales, the GLC, the county councils and county boroughs are the fire authorities responsible for overall supervision of means of escape and fire precautions, for advising on such matters and for the issue of certificates where required under provisions of the Fire Services Acts 1947–1959, and for certificates of means of escape under the Factories Act 1961 (section 40). The fire authorities have special responsibilities for advising, inspection and control under the Fire Precautions Act 1971 and similar powers under the Offices, Shops and Railway Premises Act 1963 (much amended by the Health and Safety at Work etc Act 1974). Part E, Structural Fire Precautions, of the Building Regula-

tions is the special concern of the fire services. The Building Regulations deal with new buildings, whereas the Fire Precautions Act 1971 is also concerned with the upgrading of existing buildings; at present, however, only limited types are affected, eg hotels and boarding houses. In due course designation orders in respect of other types will follow; offices, places of public entertainment, hospitals and so on will then be brought within the provisions of the Act.*

Health and Safety at Work etc Act 1974
3.25 The Health and Safety at Work etc Act 1974 is possibly the most important and far-reaching piece of legislation affecting the construction industry and public welfare alike of recent years, for it penetrates into every imaginable kind of activity and place. The act must be carefully read and studied by every architect, in particular part III, on which the Department of the Environment have issued a special circular.† This part of the Act 'provides for the extension of the scope, purposes and coverage of building regulations and introduces various procedural improvements in the system of building control. It will enable building regulations to be made about a much larger range of matters, including electrical and other building services, water fittings and access for firemen and the disabled. It extends the purposes for which building regulations may be made to include not only health and safety, but also the welfare and convenience of persons in or about buildings and the conservation of fuel and power, and prevention of waste and contamination of water. . . '.

Responsibility for the Environment
3.26 The Control of Pollution Act 1974 is yet another piece of recent legislation which adds to the responsibility and powers of the local authorities. It is important not only because of the wide scope of its provisions but particularly for the effect by way of extension and/or amendment the Act has had on much comparatively recent law. It provides a good illustration of how necessary it is for architects and students to keep constantly abreast of all changes; the final pages of almost every statute draw attention to consequential amendments to other Acts. It is not uncommon, for example, to hear amenity societies still quoting from the Civic Amenities Act 1967 as if it were the beginning and end of the law on conservation when, in fact, very little of the original Act is intact today! The Control of Pollution Act 1974 deals with four principal issues: waste on land, pollution of water, noise and the pollution of the atmosphere. On *waste* it is concerned with the disposal on land of any substance which constitutes scrap material, effluent or other unwanted surplus arising from the application of any process, and any substance or article which requires to be disposed of as being broken, worn out, contaminated or otherwise spoiled (s.30). *Pollution of water* includes practically all English waters—coastal, tidal, rivers and streams. It is an offence to discharge poisonous, noxious or polluting matter. At the same time the Act authorises regulations restricting any activities likely to give rise to pollution. Part III of the Act deals with *noise*, including vibration, and give authorities wide powers of inspection in detecting any noise which might amount to a nuisance; and part IV covers similar matters in relation to pollution of the atmosphere.

Town Planning Acts and procedure in respect of applications
3.27 To keep pace with and understand the complex and ever-changing pattern of planning legislation and the politics which inspire it, in all its ramifications, requires considerable agility of mind and constant vigilance. It would only seem fair, therefore, not to stretch demands on candidates beyond what has direct application at present. It should be enough if they concentrate on the Town and Country Planning Act of 1971, and upon subsidiary legislation of the kind dealing with civic amenities, historic buildings and conservation, and with planning controls affecting special building types, for instance offices and industrial works (see LEGAL STUDY 12). The examination has in the recent past introduced questions on the history of town planning and on the work of civic and preservation societies; too much history can be irrelevant. Candidates must have a good working and up-to-date knowledge of planning applications and procedures. The 1968 Act is more concerned with procedure and should be consulted.

The Town and Country Planning Act 1971 is the most important recent legislation affecting, in particular, development and general planning control. It should be carefully studied by candidates, for whom there are really no short cuts when preparing for the planning aspects of the part 3 examination. Experience and day-to-day reading of everything going on are essential in order to keep up with this complex and seemingly very confused activity. The best advice is to read carefully through one of the many good general textbooks, such as Heap's *Outline of planning law*, and Hamilton's *Development and planning* (with supplement) and the same author's *Planning procedure tables* (this is a very helpful 'working tool').

4 Contracts, Conditions of Engagement, and Code of Conduct

4.01 The outstanding aspects of the written papers of section G1 in the part 3 examination are mainly those which call for a good working knowledge of statutory requirements affecting planning and design and construction, as reflected in the London Building Acts, Building Regulations, and the numerous controls and procedures, including the whole field of town and country planning. Section G2, on the other hand, depends on a thorough understanding of the operation of the standard forms of building contracts and their legal implications (LEGAL STUDIES 4 and 5); of the professional ethics as formulated in the codes (LEGAL STUDIES 15 and 16); and of the architect's general and legal responsibilities (LEGAL STUDIES 1, 15, 16 and 17). But, indeed, it goes far beyond this to include those 'areas of study' referred to in para 2.02 involving management and project control in principle and practice—matters only partly concerned with law and for which the candidate is referred to the RIBA *Management handbook* (Revised (single volume) Edition 1973).

4.02 The method of giving fairly comprehensive notes and references to each syllabus item adopted for paper I is not appropriate to paper II for two reasons. First, with the possible exception of arbitration (LEGAL STUDY 8), each item may be studied directly from documents published by RIBA or ARCUK; codes, conditions of engagement, standard contracts and so on, to which candidates are permitted to refer during the examination. Second, most items are dealt with in detail throughout the AJ *Legal Handbook*. For paper II, there can be no effective substitute for concentrated reading of the published documents and of the handbook. Therefore

---

* See 'The Fire Precautions Act in Practice', published by The Architectural Press; also the AJ Technical Study (14:6:72) on 'How the Fire Precautions Act affects the Architect'.

† The Act is summarised in DoE Circular 127/74 (194/74 Welsh Office), 10 September 1974.

comments on the syllabus for this part of the written paper have been replaced by mention of selected references.

JCT forms of contract with and without quantities
4.03 See LEGAL STUDY 4 and the JCT Standard Form of Contract (with RIBA practice notes in the RIBA *Journal*). For Scottish practice see LEGAL STUDY 5 and the Scottish Supplement to JCT schedule of conditions of building contract (with notes for guidance).

Conditions of Engagement and scale of professional charges
4.04 See LEGAL STUDY 17 and the new RIBA Conditions of Engagement; The RIBA Memorandum of Agreement; The RIBA Form of Agreement for general use between a building owner and an architect or a firm of architects.

Codes of professional conduct of RIBA and ARCUK
4.05 With the revised versions of both codes, published simultaneously and with effect as from 1 January 1976, the two codes are now, except in minor details, identical (LEGAL STUDY 15).

Duties, liabilities and relationship of employer, architect, and clerk of works, both in official and private practice
4.06 See LEGAL STUDIES 1, 4, 17 and the RIBA *Management handbook:* eg Responsibility pp 11–12; allied professions p 54 *et seq;* Planning Control p 409.

Finance for buildings, how money is raised; time factor in construction and its relationship to cost; first cost and its relationship to maintenance and running costs
4.07 See RIBA *Management handbook.*

General structure of the building industry and of the professions and specialised trades concerned with buildings
4.08 See RIBA *Management handbook, Placing and management of contracts for building and civil engineering work, Organisation and practices for building and civil engineering* and *Research and development management handbook.*

Arbitration procedure
4.09 See LEGAL STUDY 8 and *The architect as arbitrator.*

Types of contract for works of alteration or addition where a lump sum is not suitable
4.10 See JCT Agreement for minor building works, and supplement to LEGAL STUDY 4.

Tendering and contractual procedures
4.11 RIBA *Management handbook*, pp 77 and 419–22. See Supplement to LEGAL STUDY 4 and special references thereto.

5 Examination technique

5.01 The purpose of part 3 (professional practice) is to assess whether candidates have reached an appropriate standard of competence to be allowed to enter the profession. Examinees must know the facts and be able to interpret them.

5.02 Verbatim knowledge of facts is perhaps less important than formerly, as most examining boards permit texts, eg the Codes of Professional Conduct and the RIBA *Management handbook*, to be taken in to the exam. Interpretation of facts ultimately depends on office experience which can be sup-plemented by study. Study should progress from general reading to understanding principles and to intensive study of detail where necessary. For the architect there are few better general books on practice then *Architectural practice and procedure* and *The architect in practice*. Inevitably some facts must be memorised but understanding of principles is far more important than encyclopaedic knowledge of details. A candidate will usually be given credit if, though unable to recall details, he knows general principles and can retrieve details later.

5.03 Statutes are usually very difficult to read, but they are important to architects who must keep up with the increasing burden of building and planning legislation. But most legal principles can be expressed as general rules in simple terms. An interesting and useful guide to those who may find legal interpretation difficult is *Legal interpretation for surveyors*.

5.04 Examinees may be helped by the following:
1 Sketch out a rough outline of facts and opinions arranged in order.
2 Use clear, correct, economical language, in legible hand-writing with orderly presentation.
3 Comply with all printed instructions.
4 Where applicable start with a good definition and come straight to the point. Length of an answer is not necessarily important—nor is there virtue in a long-winded statement if it ignores the question. Tabulation is a useful time-saver but can be as revealing of ignorance as it is useful, but it should never be used as a substitute or escape route where detailed information would be more appropriate.

5.05 In an examination there is little time to spare for florid language—apt phrases must result directly from clear thinking and good habits of communication. Questions which require drafting a letter are very popular with examiners, and are alarmingly revealing in their results. *The architect in practice* (p 211) offers sound suggestions for people incapable of letter-writing without secretarial support.

Oral examination
5.06 Points omitted in the written examination due to lack of time can be elaborated at the oral examination. The oral can also afford a further opportunity to expand ideas or express opinions. But ideas are seldom clearly understood if they are not clearly explained and communicated to others.

References

London Building Acts 1930–1939, HMSO
London Building (Constructional) By-laws 1972, HMSO
PITT, P. H. and DUFTON, J. Building in inner London—a practical guide to building law. London, 1976, Architectural Press
DEPARTMENT OF THE ENVIRONMENT Guide to statutory provisions. 1973, HMSO
WHITTAKER, C. The handbook of environmental powers. London, 1976, Architectural Press
Building Regulations 1976, superseding Regulations of 1972 and Amendments 1973, 1974, 1975. HMSO
LEWIS, R. J. Administrative law for the construction industry. London, 1976, Macmillan
JONES, B. Advanced level law. London, 1971, Hammick, Sweet & Maxwell (Concise College Texts)
TURNER, H. Architectural practice and procedure. 6th Edition, London, 1974, Batsford

WILLIS, A. J. & GEORGE, W. N. The architect in practice. London, 1970, Crosby Lockwood

LEACH, W. A. Legal interpretation for surveyors. London, 1966, Estates Gazette

—— Party structure rights in London. London, 1961, Estates Gazette

POWELL-SMITH, V. The law of boundaries and fences. London, 1967, Butterworth

WOOD, R. D. Building and civil engineering claims (Supplement 1974), London, 1971, Estates Gazette

PARRIS, J. Building law reports. London, 1976 (three volumes per annum), George Godwin

BOISOT WATERS COHEN PARTNERSHIP The Community Land Act explained. London, 1976, Architectural Press

'Community Land Act—an architect's guide', Architects' Journal, 31 March 1976

HEAP, D. An outline of planning law. 7th Edition, London, Hammicks, Sweet & Maxwell

HAMILTON, R. N. D. A guide to development and planning. 6th Edition, London, 1975, Oyez Publishing. Supplement and Noter-up published separately 1976

—— Planning procedure tables. 3rd Edition, London, 1976, Oyez Publishing

Which builder? Tendering and contractual procedures. London, 1975, Aqua Group, Crosby Lockwood. A companion volume to the Aqua Group's Pre-contract practice and contract administration

RIBA Handbook of architectural practice and management. Revised single volume Edition, 1973

RIBA Building contract manual, R. J. M. JOHNSTONE, editor. 2 vols, London, 1977. Deals with every aspect of contract procedures and includes commentaries on standard and other published forms of contract, with model letters and forms

The attention of readers is drawn to the lists of selected references published annually in the AJ Technical review.

Appendix 1 Selected references

A selection of works of special interest for architects chosen from those quoted by individual contributors in their reference lists at the end of each of the foregoing Legal Studies.
The Architects' Journal publishes in January each year, as part of The Annual Technical Review, comprehensive and fully updated lists on all subjects dealt with in the Review.
References are listed below under handbook section headings. Acts, Statutory Instruments and regulations are not included; for these see Table of Statutes.

1 Introduction to the law
1 OSBORNE, P. G. A. A concise law dictionary. London, 1964, Sweet & Maxwell
2 WALKER, R. J. and WALKER, M. G. The English legal system, 3rd edition. London, 1972, Butterworths
3 SIMS, R. S. and SCOTT, R. M. M. 'A' Level English law, 4th edition. London, 1974, Butterworths
4 Baker, J. H. An introduction to English legal history. London, 1971, Butterworths
5 WILLIAMS, G. Learning the law, 9th edition. London, 1973, Stevens & Sons
6 MARSHALL, ENID A. General Principles of Scots Law, 2nd edition. Edinburgh, 1975, W. Green & Son
7 BUILDING LAW REPORTS. Three volumes a year reporting and commenting on judgements in cases relevant to the construction industry. London, 1976/1977, George Godwin

2 The office and the law
1 RIBA Handbook—Architectural practice and management, Revised single volume edition, 1973
2 STEWART-PEARSON, N. (ed.) Legal problems of employment. London, 1976, The Industrial Society
3 RIBA Guide to group practice and consortia
4 Offices, Shops and Railway Premises Act. A general guide, 1964. H.M.S.O.
5 PORTER, R. Guide to employment conditions. London, 1976, George Godwin

3 Building Contracts
1 KEATING, D. Building contracts and practice. London, 1977 (fully revised edition), Sweet & Maxwell
2 McCANLIS, E. W. Tendering procedures and contractual arrangements. Survey for Research and Information Group. London, 1967, RICS
3 RIBA Building contract manual, Johnston, R. J. M. (editor): to deal with every aspect of contract procedures, with commentaries on published standard forms etc. 2 Vols, in preparation, London, 1978
4 BOWYER, J. T. Small works contract documentation. London, 1976, The Architectural Press
5 WOOD, R. D. Building and civil engineering claims. London, 1971 (Supplement 1974, ICE 5th Ed. Conditions)

4 The law of property and land
1 HARWOOD, D. M. English land law. London, 1975, Sweet & Maxwell
2 POWELL-SMITH, V. The law of boundaries and fences. London, 1967, Butterworths
3 ANSTEY, B. and CHAVASSE, M. The right to light. London, Estates Gazette

5 Arbitration
1 GILL, WILLIAM H. Evidence and procedure in arbitration, 2nd Ed. London, 1973, Sweet & Maxwell
2 —The law of arbitration. London, 1975, Sweet & Maxwell
3 PARRIS, J. The law and practice of arbitration. London, 1974, George Godwin
4 —A casebook of arbitration. London, 1976, George Godwin
5 RIBA Architect as arbitrator:
Revised edition in preparation, 1977

6 Statutory authorities and consents
1 CROSS, C. R. Principles of local government law, 5th Ed. London, 1974, Sweet & Maxwell
2 FOULKES, D. Introduction to administrative law, 4th Ed. London, 1976, Butterworths
3 LEWIS, J. R. Administrative law for the construction industry. London, 1976, Macmillan
4 PITT, P. H. and DUFTON, J. Building in inner London—a practical guide to building law. London, 1976, The Architectural Press
5 TAYLOR, J. and COOKE, G. (Eds.) The Fire Precautions Act in practice. London, 1977, The Architectural Press
6 WHITTAKER, C. The handbook of environmental powers. London, 1976, The Architectural Press

7 Copyright
1 McNEIL, A. and LILLIE, J. The mercantile law of Scotland. Edinburgh, 1965, W. Green
2 COPINGER, W. A. and SKONE JAMES, F. E. Law of Copyright. London, 1965, Sweet & Maxwell

8 Planning
1 HEAP, D. An outline of planning law, 7th Ed. London, 1977, Sweet & Maxwell
2 WHITTAKER, C. The handbook of environmental powers. London, 1976, The Architectural Press
3 BIGHAM, D. A. The law and administration relating to the protection of the environment. London, 1973, Oyez Publishing
4 BOISOT WATERS COHEN PARTNERSHIP. The Community Land Act explained. London, 1976, The Architectural Press
5 'Community Land Act—an architect's guide'. *The Architects' Journal* 31st March 1976
6 BOYNTON, J. N. Compulsory purchase and compensation, 4th Ed. London, 1977, Oyez Publishing

9 Construction regulations
1 WHYTE, W. S. and POWELL-SMITH, V. The Building Regulations explained and illustrated, 5th edition. London, 1976, Crosby Lockwood Staples
2 ELDER, A. J. Guide to the Building Regulations 1976. London, 1977, The Architectural Press
3 PITT, P. H. and DUFTON, J. Building in Inner London. London, 1976, The Architectural Press
6 LEACH, W. A. Party structure rights in London. London, 1961, Estates Gazette

10 Professional conduct
ARCUK Code of Professional Conduct, January 1976 revision

11 Conditions of engagement
1 RIBA Handbook of architectural practice and management
2 RIBA Agreement for the appointment of an architect 1973
3 RIBA Conditions of Engagement, 1976

12 Professional examinations
1 TURNER, H. Architectural practice and procedure, 6th Ed. London, 1974, Batsford
2 WILLIS, A. J. and GEORGE, W. N. The architect in practice. London, 1970, Crosby Lockwood Staples
3 RIBA Handbook of architectural practice and management, revised, single volume, edition 1973
4 LEWIS, R. J. Administrative law for the construction industry. London, 1976, Macmillan
5 HEAP, D. An outline of planning law, 7th Ed. London, Hammicks Sweet & Maxwell
6 HAMILTON, R. N. D. A guide to development and planning, 6th Ed. London, 1975, Oyez Publishing
7 BOWYER, J. T. Guide to domestic building surveys. London, 1971, The Architectural Press

Appendix 2 Table of cases

Appendix 3 Table of Statutes and Statutory Instruments

Appendix 4   General Index